Monarchs
Rulers
Dynasties
and
Kingdoms
of the
World

COMPILED BY R. F. TAPSELL

Monarchs
Rulers
Dynasties
and
Kingdoms
of the
World

THAMES AND HUDSON

© Copyright 1983 Thames and Hudson Ltd, London
First paperback edition 1984

Printed and bound in Great Britain
by R. J. Acford Limited, Chichester, Sussex

Contents

FOREWORD

6

INTRODUCTION

8

BIBLIOGRAPHY

13

SECTION I

Alphabetical guide to dynasties and states

17

SECTION II

Dynastic lists

151

TABLE OF LISTS

152

ABBREVIATIONS IN THE LISTS

158

LISTS BY REGION AND PERIOD

159

IN THE LATE twentieth century the captains and the kings have largely departed from the seats of power. Parliamentary democracies are run by politicians and bureaucrats who of necessity must be seen as fallible creatures amenable to the discipline of the ballot-box. Other societies tend to favour the party chairman or the ruling junta. But a fascination with monarchy persists among many. Within the three months before the writing of this foreword the people of Britain have welcomed the birth of an heir to the throne, the United States and Europe have witnessed the untimely end of the actress who became Princess of Monaco, and the people of Swaziland have been plunged into mourning and uncertainty for their future with the death of their king, the longest-reigning of all the world's monarchs. Decidedly there is still life in the institution of monarchy.

Some years ago, Mr Tapsell set himself the formidable task of compiling as complete as possible a checklist of the world's dynastic monarchies. He has succeeded amply in his endeavours. This is a useful work of reference. Practising historians, particularly those whose interests take them beyond the major powers, should appreciate the convenience of a book containing chronologies, dynastic relationships, and dates in this easily accessible form. The coverage is awe-inspiring. Take the United Kingdom. Many works of reference have given us the mainstream descent of the present royal family from Cedric or Egbert to Elizabeth II, but where else may we find such convenient access to the Picts and Dalriadans who initiated Scotland or the Lords of the Isles, the earls of Orkney and the rulers of the Isle of Man? The international scope is equally thorough. How can one fail to be impressed by a work that brings together such a disparate collection as the prince-bishops of Montenegro, the Merina rulers of Madagascar and the Khans of the Kazakh Horde?

From this it should be evident that for the reader who is not a professional historian there is much pleasant dipping and browsing to be found in this book. Edward Lear inquired:

> Who, or why, or which, or what
> Is the Akond of Swat?

Tapsell could have informed him that the Swati dynasty began with a Muslim adventurer from Swat who seized Kashmir from the Hindus in the mid-fourteenth century, establishing a regime which lasted for two hundred years – and incidentally beginning a political rivalry which has persisted to this day. The dipper and browser through this volume will pick up a good deal of out-of-the-way lore. The rise and fall of the Hudid dynasty, the provenance of Ptolemy Auletes the flute-player and Eric Bloodaxe, the complex vicissitudes of Transoxania are all set forth clearly and informatively. And one of the great merits of this book is its lack of Europeo-centricity. Asia, Africa and the Pacific are all represented here in full force.

Towards the end the reader may experience a growing sense of the vanity of human wishes. A dynasty seizes power; the family prevails for two centuries, three or four; but in the end they die without heirs, go into exile, suffer conquest, succumb to treachery, or are required by the inexorable dialectic of history to make way for a new emerging ruling class. Another reigns in their stead. It is an old but salutary reminder for those who seek lasting political authority.

Preaching is not the purpose of this book. It is meant to be used and enjoyed. With so much unostentatious learning, with its cast of thousands, and with its pioneering scope and range, Tapsell on Monarchs could well become a classic reference work.

G. C. BOLTON
University of London

SINCE THE BEGINNINGS of recorded history more than 5,000 years ago, the great majority of civilized peoples have lived under the rule of monarchs. Yet to define the office of monarch is not easy – the powers and duties of kings have varied enormously from one time and place to another, and there have been exceptions to even the most basic characteristics of kingship, such as life tenure and hereditary succession. The distinction between monarchs and other kinds of heads of state has never been absolutely clear. To us, Augustus Caesar was the first of a long line of Roman Emperors, the later ones unquestionably royal autocrats with an aura of divinity, but during his lifetime it was not clear whether Augustus was a king, a dictator, the president of a republic or simply the most prominent of Roman citizens. History is full of rulers who were kings in reality but not by title – puppet-masters and men with purely nominal overlords, sovereign dukes and princes, Shoguns and Popes, Atabegs and Nizams. If such rulers were members of established lines or dynasties, they have been included in this book, and for general convenience one nonmonarchical list has also been provided, that of the Presidents of the United States.

The work is in two sections:

SECTION I is an alphabetical dictionary of dynasties and states, containing about 1,200 entries with cross-references and a number of charts showing family links within the major multi-national royal families. Each main entry indicates the corresponding dynastic list(s) in Section II.

SECTION II contains about 1,000 dynastic lists arranged in geographical and chronological order, giving names, reign dates and concise genealogical information for some 13,000 rulers.

The lists in Section II are not arranged strictly under the names of today's national states, but in broad geographical groupings within the various continents. Most users will find this arrangement more convenient and logical – for example, the rulers of Algeria, Tunisia and Morocco are grouped together rather than scattered through an alphabetic sequence, as are certain other natural groups such as Norway, Sweden and Denmark, Rome and Byzantium, and so on. It would be quite artificial to force some dynasties and kingdoms of the past into headings under the names of modern states, whose frontiers happen to contain all or part of their territory but whose history has nothing to do with them or only a vague and distant connection. Where under current national headings, for example, could one properly put the Caliphs, the Roman Emperors, the Timurids? However, any dynastic list not found immediately in Section II can be located via the alphabetical Section I, where the list number is given.

For most rulers listed in Section II, only the date of accession to the throne is given, and it may be taken that in such cases the reign lasted until the accession of the next ruler. Where the reigns of joint or rival rulers overlapped, dates for both beginning and end of each reign are given. Occasionally a date in this work will differ from the corresponding one in other sources (though rarely by more than a year or two) and there are various explanations, the most usual being a difference of opinion among historians as to the correct date. There is some doubt, for example, whether King Edward the Martyr of England was assassinated in 978 or 979. Only the Muslim year of an event may be known for a Muslim ruler, leaving a choice of AD date (1000 AH ran from October 1591 to October 1592). In China, a new emperor allowed his predecessor's reign-title to run on to the end of the calendar year, so that Sheng Tsu, most commonly known as the K'ang Hsi emperor, died in late 1722, but the K'ang Hsi period did not officially finish until early 1723. Even the AD calendar has its well-known change from Julian to Gregorian reckoning, involving the loss of ten to thirteen days and adopted by some European states in 1582 and by others later, including Great Britain (1752) and Russia (1918). Empress Elizabeth of Russia died on 25 December 1761 (Julian) but on 5th January 1762 (Gregorian). More substantial complications occur where local dating has been based on some era with an uncertain AD starting-point, the best-known instance being the Saka Era associated with the Kushan ruler Kanishka, for whom accession dates more than a century apart have been proposed.

A short horizontal line between the dates of one ruler and the next in a list in Section II indicates a break in the series for some reason – a brief republican interlude, temporary foreign conquest, rule of a short-lived usurping dynasty listed elsewhere, lengthy delay in finding a successor, and so on. A dotted line (very rare) in mid-dynasty means a gap in the historical record and uncertainty as to whom the rulers were in the interval – at the end of a list, it indicates either that no more is known about the dynasty or that it faded into insignificance.

Where an individual accession date is followed by a full stop, this means that the ruler in question occupied the throne during only part of his accession year and then died or lost his crown. Thus Harold Godwinson, last Saxon ruler of England, became king in January 1066 and was killed at Hastings in October – '1066.' indicates the fact that his reign began and ended in that same year.

Traditional names for dynasties come from various sources and are sometimes simply invented by historians – William the Conqueror and his sons did not describe themselves as the 'Norman Dynasty'. Certain very old ruling houses have no generally accepted dynastic name at all, including the imperial line of Japan and the royal lines of early medieval Spain.

Generally speaking, dynastic names derive either from geographical locations or from ancestral family names, with plenty of exceptions – Habsburg and Wittelsbach were ancient castles, Valois and Angevin come from feudal territories, Tudor and Romanov from personal names become surnames, and Stuart, rather exceptionally, comes from the office of High Steward of Scotland. The Greeks named dynasties after their founders

(Seleucidae, Seleucids) or after the founder's father or some important ancestor, and the Arabs have mostly followed the latter practice – thus the ruling house founded by the famous Saladin (Yusuf ibn Ayyub) is called the Ayyubid dynasty. Further east, Islamic houses are sometimes called by founders' titles, as with the dynasty founded by Ahmad Nizam Shah, the Nizam Shahis. Hindu ruling lines are often known by clan or tribal names – Rathor, Bhonsla, Pandya, etc.

Chinese dynasties usually chose their own names, mostly from some territorial connection. The first emperor of the great T'ang family had been duke of T'ang under the Sui emperors. The names of the ancient feudal states of the Chou period – Han, Sung, Wei and others – were often used, in some cases more than once, so that distinguishing titles have to be added by historians – Earlier Sung, Later Liang, Western Yen and so on. Occasionally, non-territorial names were adopted, such as Chin (Golden) by the Juchen, whose emperor was therefore known to his Mongol enemies as Altan Khan, the Golden King, and Ming (Bright) by the last native Chinese dynasty.

Indeed, the only thing that can be said with confidence about dynastic titles is that there is no rule without exceptions.

Royal titles

Many and various words have been used which signify 'king', from the literal 'Shah' and 'Khan' of Iran and the steppelands to the Aztec 'Tlatoani' (Speaker) and the Islamic 'Caliph' (Successor). The imperial masters of Rome shunned the detested title of Rex in their so-called republic, yet the alternatives which came into use developed into royal titles more impressive – Imperator, Caesar, Augustus. In later Europe, only formally independent rulers were usually styled kings, lesser terms such as duke, margrave, prince and count implying subordination to king or emperor, but the passing of time often changed the reality to produce quite autonomous potentates with less than kingly titles. Conversely, all titles of rank tend to suffer devaluation with time, including those of royalty. As a result of the Napoleonic Wars, several tiny kingdoms and sovereign grand duchies appeared in Germany, and by the end of the 19th century, there were three emperors in Europe instead of the single Holy Roman Emperor of tradition. The Indian title of Raja, in ancient times the prerogative of major monarchs, was used by the most insignificant princes in modern times, and the Islamic 'Sultan' suffered equally from inflationary usage.

Classifications and definitions

Various dynasties and states of the past do not fall very easily into neat geographical or chronological slots, as a few examples will show. The 'Abbasids, the famed Caliphs of Baghdad, ruled a vast empire in 800 AD but were powerless puppets in 1000 AD and independent rulers of much of 'Iraq by 1250. The Duke of Burgundy controlled a large and virtually sovereign state in the 15th century, but bore an empty title in the 17th century. The Fatimids ruled the Maghrib but not Egypt in 950 AD, and Egypt but not the Maghrib in 1150. In Central Asia, Babur the Timurid was the last prince of a collapsing dynasty, in Afghanistan the ruler of a small principality, in India the first of the mighty Moghul Emperors, yet he never ceased being a monarch somewhere or other. Within settled kingdoms there can be problems of *de facto* versus *de jure* rule – regents have often thrust aside young heirs after uncertain intervals, ageing kings have crowned their heirs but monopolized real power, rivals have temporarily divided realms. Such matters have been handled as clearly as possible in the dynastic lists, and important points are mentioned in the alphabetical entries in Section I.

Personal names

These constitute a special problem – does one anglicize consistently all names that have English equivalents, render them invariably in the form used in the country or state over which a monarch ruled, or compromise with customary usage? History does not treat royal names consistently, and they have not been so treated in this work. The present king of Spain appears as Juan Carlos, since it would be ridiculous to use John Charles, whereas it would be equally pendantic to use Felipe for his predecessor of Armada fame, who appears as Philip II. Comparable choices occur with names of Arabic origin – there are a dozen ways of transliterating Muhammad (Mohammed, Mehmet, Mohamman and others), to mention but one instance. In general, accents and other diacritic marks have been omitted, in the belief that most users will not need them enough to justify the very considerable typesetting complications and expense which their inclusion would involve.

Monarchy today

Despite its long history, as long as that of civilization itself, monarchy has collapsed in the present century with a speed surely unequalled by any other vanishing human institution. In 1900, the world was full of monarchs, mostly absolute, and nearly nine-tenths of humanity lived under monarchical government, whereas today less than one-tenth live in states with hereditary rulers and less than one per cent under kings with real power. The major change in fact took place very rapidly, in just over a decade (1912–22), when half humanity overthrew its monarchs, in China, Russia, Germany, Austria-Hungary and Turkey. Since then, more than a score of independent monarchies have fallen, violently or peacefully (see list below) and many formerly independent kingdoms in Asia and Africa, later colonial protectorates, have been abolished by post-colonial regimes in India, Uganda, South Yemen and elsewhere.

Monarchies recently abolished:

1945	Albania and Yugoslavia	1964	Zanzibar
1946	Italy and Bulgaria	1966	Burundi
1947	Indian Empire and Rumania	1967	Greece (formally from 1973)
1953	Egypt	1969	Libya
1955	Annam (Viet-Nam)	1970	Cambodia (throne vacant from 1960)
1957	Tunisia		
1958	'Iraq	1973	Afghanistan
1959	Tibet (flight of Dalai Lama)	1974	Ethiopia
1961	Rwanda	1975	Laos and Sikkim
1962	Yemen (North)	1979	Iran and Central African Empire

Sovereign monarchies still surviving also number rather more than a score (see list below), and certain once-independent kingdoms continue to exist within larger states, some of their rulers retaining a degree of political power (as in the United Arab Emirates) and others performing very limited, largely ceremonial roles. The Papacy is in some respects a monarchy too, since the Pope is the sovereign of the Vatican City State.

Monarchies extant in 1983:

Bahrain	Jordan	Morocco	Swaziland
Belgium	Kuwait	Nepal	Sweden
Bhutan	Lesotho	Netherlands	Thailand
Brunei	Liechtenstein	Norway	Tonga
Denmark	Luxemburg	Qatar	'Uman
Japan	Malaysia	Sa'udi Arabia	United Kingdom*
	Monaco	Spain	

*The United Kingdom of Great Britain and Northern Ireland shares its monarch with a number of Commonwealth countries which are also constitutionally monarchies, the main such countries being Australia, Canada and New Zealand.

By far the oldest dynasty still occupying a throne today is the imperial house of Japan, whose current emperor can trace an unbroken male ancestry back for some 2,000 years and 70 generations. Another contender for the status of oldest surviving monarchy, however, is Nepal, ruled by ill-chronicled but probably quite authentic dynasties since before the time of Christ, though its reliable king lists do not commence until the 9th century AD and its present royal dynasty came to power only in the 18th century. Prior to its abolition in 1974, the Solomonic monarchy of Ethiopia would have been a third contender, with a plausible claim for 2,000 years of history, even if one discounts much remoter descent from Solomon and the Queen of Sheba.

Sources

The number of books and periodical articles relevant in some way to this book is obviously astronomical, and the number actually consulted in detail or to check particular points runs to several hundreds. The list given in the bibliography is very basic, and includes only books and articles which provide substantial amounts of information on specific dynasties and states, or which are themselves chronological or genealogical surveys of wider regions. Most of these works have been published within the last twenty years, which explains why it has become possible now to compile a comprehensive world survey from more specialized published sources. Even so, a number of important earlier works have also been listed, not least the remarkable massive tomes of Stokvis, published nearly a century ago and in many details outdated, but still unrivalled in their coverage of European rulers, both lay and ecclesiastical, hereditary and elected.

In reducing to some degree of consistency the vast amount of material accumulated for this present work, I have inevitably been obliged to make decisions in fields where I cannot claim any special expertise, and the results are therefore open to criticism from all manner of specialists. All I ask of potential critics is that they should bear in mind the similar limitations they would themselves encounter in compiling a comparable broad survey. At the same time, I have of course done my utmost to avoid errors of fact and to provide the latest available authoritative information.

This book was assembled largely during a period of residence in Western Australia, where access to nearly all the material needed was provided by the libraries of Murdoch University and the University of Western Australia, without which facilities the task would have been virtually impossible in Perth, a very beautiful city with nearly a million inhabitants, but located well over a thousand miles from other major centres of population. I am very grateful to those two institutions, and also to the British Library, the Bodleian Library and the School of Oriental and African Studies, London University, all of which supplied particularly elusive publications.

Abbreviations

BASOR Bulletin of the American Schools of Oriental Research
BSOAS Bulletin of the School of Oriental and African Studies, London
JAH Journal of African History
JRASMB Journal of the Royal Asiatic Society, Malay Branch

Abdullah, M. M. *The United Arab Emirates* (1978)
Akinjogbin, I. A. *Dahomey and its neighbours 1708–1818* (1967)
Albright, W. F. *The Biblical Period from Abraham to Erza* (1963)
—*The Chronology of Ancient South Arabia* (BASOR No. 119, 1950)
Alpers, E. A. *Dynasties of the Mutapa-Rozwi Complex* (JAH No. 11, 1970)
Anderson, M. O. *Kings and Kingship in Early Scotland* (1973)
Barth, H. *Travels and Discoveries in North and Central Africa*, 5 vols. (1857–58)

Barthold, V. V. *Four Studies in the history of Central Asia* (1956–62)

Basham, A. L. (ed.) *Papers on the date of Kanishka* (1968)

Baumgarten, N. *Généalogies et mariages occidentaux des Rurikides Russes du Xe au XIIIe siècle* (Orientalia Christiana No. 35, 1927)

—*Généalogies des branches régnantes des Rurikides du XIIIe au XVIe siècle* (Orientalia Christiana No. 94, 1934)

Beach, D. N. *The Mutapa Dynasty* (History in Africa No. 3, 1976)

Bell, H. C. P. *The Maldive Islands* (1940)

Bhatia, P. *The Paramaras* (1967)

Bickerman, E. J. *The Chronology of the Ancient World* (1968)

Bosworth, C. E. *The Islamic Dynasties* (1967)

Brown, D. E. *Brunei: the structure and history of a Bornean Malay Sultanate* (1970)

Budge, E. A. W. *A History of Ethiopia, Nubia and Abyssinia* (1928)

Burke's Guide to the Royal Family (1973)

Burke's Royal Families of the World, Vols. I and II (1977, 1980)

Bustin, E. *Lunda under Belgian rule* (1975)

Byrne, F. J. *Irish Kings and High Kings* (1973)

Cambridge Ancient History 1st ed. (1923–39) 12 vols.; 3rd ed. (1970–) Vols. I-II

Cambridge History of Africa (1975–) Vols. 1–5

Cambridge History of China (1978–) Vols. 3, 10–11

Cambridge History of India (1922–32) Vols. I, III-VI

Cambridge History of Iran (1968–) Vols. 1, 4–5

Cambridge History of Poland, 2 vols. (1941)

Cambridge Medieval History, 8 vols. (1913–1936; 2nd ed. Vol. IV Pt 1 1966)

Cambridge Modern History, Vol. XIII (1911)

Cappeli, A. *Cronologia, cronografia e calendario perpetuo* (1930)

Caulk, R. A. *Harar Town and its neighbours in the 19th century* (JAH No. 18, 1977)

Chavannes, E. *Mémoires historiques de Se-Ma Ts'ien* (1967)

Chaytor, H. J. *A History of Aragon and Catalonia* (1969)

Chittick, N. *The 'Shirazi' colonisation of East Africa* (JAH No. 6, 1965)

Choudhury, P. C. *History of the Civilization of the people of Assam* (1959)

Cieza de Leon, P. *The Incas* (1969)

Claridge, W. W. *History of the Gold Coast and Ashanti*, 2nd ed. (1964)

Coe, M. D. *Mexico* (1966)

Coèdes, G. *The Indianised States of South-East Asia* (1968)

Coquelle, P. *Histoire du Montenegro et de la Bosnie* (1895)

Coupez, A. and Kamanzi, T. *Récits historiques Rwanda* (1962)

Crowder, M. *The Story of Nigeria*, 3rd ed. (1973)

Davies, N. *The Aztecs* (1973)

Debevoise, N. C. *Political History of Parthia* (1938)

Dickinson, W. C. *Scotland from the earliest times to 1603*, 3rd ed. (1977)

Doubleday, H. A. et al. *Complete Peerage*, Vol. X (1945)

Dozy, R. P. A. *Spanish Islam* (1913)

Duran, D. *The Aztecs* (1964)

Egharevba, J. U. *Short History of Benin*, 4th ed. (1968)

Encyclopedia of Islam (1st ed. 1913–48; 2nd ed. 1954–)

Encyclopedia Judaica (1971–72)

Francke, A. H. *The Antiquities of Indian Tibet* (1972)

Freeman-Grenville, G. S. P. *The Medieval History of the Coast of Tanganyika* (1962)

Frye, R. N. *The Heritage of Persia* (1963)

Gardiner, A. H. *Egypt of the Pharoahs* (1961)

Gaury, G. de *The Rulers of Mecca* (1954)

Giurescu, C. C. et al. *Chronological History of Rumania* (1972)

Glélé, M. A. *Le Danxome* (1974)

Grover, B. S. K. *Sikkim and India* (1974)

Gugushvili, A. *The Chronological and Genealogical Table of the Kings of Georgia* (Georgica I, Nos. 2 and 3, 1936)

Guldescu, S. *A History of Medieval Croatia* (1964)

Gupta, P. L. *The Imperial Guptas* (1974)

Haarh, E. *The Yar-Lun Dynasty* (1969)

Hall, D. G. E. *History of South-East Asia*, 3rd ed. (1970)

Hamilton, J. R. *Les Ouighours à l'époque des Cinq Dynasties d'après les documents chinois* (1955)

Hammond, N. G. L. *Epirus* (1967)

Hammond, N. G. L. and Griffith, G. T. *A History of Macedonia*, 2 vols. (1979)

Han Woo-Keun *History of Korea* (1970)

Hasan, M. *Kashmir under the Sultans* (1959)
Hassan, A. and Na'ibi, M. S. *A Chronicle of Abuja* (1962)
Hawley, D. *The Trucial States* (1970)
Hayavadana Rao, C. *History of Mysore* (1943)
Hill, G. *History of Cyprus*, 3 vols. (1940–48)
Hinz, W. *The Lost World of Elam* (1972)
Hiskett, M. *The 'Song of Bagauda'* III (BSOAS No. 28, 1965)
Hitti P. K. *History of the Arabs*, 10th ed. (1970)
—*Lebanon in History*, 2nd ed. (1962)
—*History of Syria*, 2nd ed. (1957)
Hodgkin, A. S. *History of the Anglo-Saxons*, 3rd ed. (1952)
Hogben, S. J. and Kirk-Greene, A. H. M. *The Emirates of Northern Nigeria* (1966)
Howorth, H. H. *History of the Mongols*, 4 vols. (1876–1927)
Hulbert, H. B. *History of Korea* (1905)
Huntingford, G. W. B. *'The Wealth of Kings' and the end of the Zague Dynasty* (BSOAS No. 28, 1965)
Indian States Gazetteer Series Volumes for various districts
Isenburg, W. K. *Stammtafeln zur Geschichte der Europäischen Staaten*, Vols. I–II (1960)
Johnston, H. A. S. *The Fulani Empire of Sokoto* (1967)
Jones, A. H. M. *Sparta* (1968)
Jones, F. *The Princes and Principality of Wales* (1969)
Justi, F. *Iranisches Namenbuch* (1895)
Kagwa, A. *The Kings of Buganda* (1971)
Karugire, S. R. *History of the Kingdom of Nkore* (1971)
Katoke, I. K. *The Karagwe Kingdom* (1975)
Keightley, D. N. *Sources of Shang History* (1978)
Khaketla, B. M. *Lesotho 1970* (1971)
Khan, Mir Ahmad Yar *Inside Baluchistan* (1975)
Kurup, K. K. N. *The Ali Rajas of Cannanore* (1975)
Lalanne, L. *Dictionnaire historique de la France*, 2 vols. 2nd ed. (1877)
Lane-Poole, S. *The Mohammedan Dynasties* (1894)
Lang, D. M. *Armenia* (1970)
—*The Last Years of the Georgian Monarchy* (1957)
Langer, W. L. *Encyclopedia of World History*, 5th ed. (1968)
Law, R. *The Oyo Empire* (1977)

Lemarchand, R. *Rwanda and Burundi* (1970)
Levtzion, N. *The 13th and 14th century kings of Mali* (JAH No. 4, 1963)
Linehan, W. *Coins of Kelantan* (JRASMB No. 12, 1934)
—*History of Pahang* (JRASMB No. 14, 1936)
Livermore, H. *The Origins of Spain and Portugal* (1971)
Lloyd, J. E. *History of Wales to the Edwardian Conquest*, 2 vols. 3rd ed. (1939)
Macmichael, H. A. *History of the Arabs in the Sudan*, 2 vols. (1922)
Mackerras, C. *The Uighur Empire* (1972)
MacNiocall, G. *Ireland before the Vikings* (1972)
Mahalingam, T. V. *Kanchipuram in early South Indian History* (1969)
Majul, C. A. *Muslims in the Philippines* (1973)
Majumdar, A. K. *The Chaulukyas of Gujerat* (1956)
Majumdar, R. C. et al. *An Advanced History of India*, 3rd ed. (1967)
Majumdar, R. C. (ed.) *History and Culture of the Indian People*, Vols. I–VI (Bombay 1951–60)
Majumdar, R. C. and Altekar, A. S. *The Gupta-Vakataka Age* (1967)
Maring, J. M. and E. G. *Historical and Cultural Dictionary of Burma* (1973)
Maspero, G. *Le Royaume de Champa* (1928)
Menon, A. S. *A Survey of Kerala History* (1968)
Miller, W. *The Latins in the Levant* (1908)
—*Trebizond, the last Greek Empire* (1926)
Minns, E. H. *Scythians and Greeks* (1913)
Mitra, S. *The Early Rulers of Khajuraho* (1958)
Moule, A. C. *The Rulers of China* (1957)
Nachtigal, G. *Sahara und Sudan*, 3 vols. (1879–89)
Nadel, S. F. *A Black Byzantium* (1942)
Narain, A. K. *The Indo-Greeks* (1956)
Navaratnam, C. S. *Tamils and Ceylon* (1958)
Nicholas, C. W. and Paranavitana, S. *Concise History of Ceylon* (1961)
Nicholls, C. S. *The Swahili Coast* (1971)
Nilakanta Sastri, K. A. *History of Southern India*, 4th ed. (1976)
Notton, C. (ed.) *Annales du Siam*, Vol. III (1932)
Nyakatura, J. W. *Anatomy of an African Kingdom* (1973)

O'Corrain, D. *Ireland before the Normans* (1972)

O'Callaghan, J. F. *History of Medieval Spain* (1975)

Oxford Classical Dictionary, 2nd ed. (1970)

Palmer, H. R. (trans.) *History of the first twelve years of the reign of Mai Idris Alooma of Bornu by Ahmad ibn Fartua* (1926)

Papinot, E. *Historical and Geographical Dictionary of Japan* (1972)

Pelenski, J. *Russia and Kazan* (1974)

Petech, L. *The Kingdom of Ladakh* (1977)

Philby, H. St. J. *The Background of Islam* (1947)

Philips, C. H. (ed.) *Handbook of Oriental History* (1963)

Piotrovsky, B. B. *Urartu* (1969)

Pokotilov, D. *History of the Eastern Mongols during the Ming Dynasty* (1976)

Powicke, M. and Fryde, E. B. (ed.) *Handbook of British Chronology* (1963)

Previté-Orton, C. W. *Shorter Cambridge Medieval History*, 2 vols. (1952)

Ray, H. C. *Dynastic History of Northern India*, 2 vols. (1931–36)

—*History of Ceylon*, Vol. I, Pt. 2 (1960)

Regmi, D. R. *Medieval Nepal*, 3 vols. (1965–66)

Richardson, H. E. *Tibet and its history* (1962)

Roberts, A. *Tippu Tip, Livingstone and the chronology of Kazembe* (Azania No. 2, 1967)

Rogers, M. C. *The Chronicle of Fu Chien* (1968)

Rostovtzeff, M. I. *Social and Economic History of the Roman Empire* (1957)

Roux, G. *Ancient Iraq* (1964)

Runciman, S. *History of the Crusades*, 3 vols. (1951–54)

Segal, J. B. *Edessa* (1970)

Sheppard, M. *Short History of Negri Sembilan* (1965)

Sherwani, H. K. and Joshi, P. M. *History of the Medieval Deccan*, 2 vols. (1973–74)

Shinnie, P. L. *Meroe* (1967)

Smith, H. E. *Historical and Cultural Dictionary of Thailand* (1976)

Smith, S. *Events in Arabia in the 6th century AD* (BSOAS No. 16, 1954)

Smyth, A. P. *Scandinavian York and Dublin*, Vol. I (1975)

Snellgrove, D. L. and Richardson, H. E. *Cultural History of Tibet* (1968)

Somani, R. V. *History of Mewar* (1976)

Spuler, B. *Die Goldene Horde* (1965)

Spuler, B. and Ross, M. *Rulers and Governments of the World*, 3 vols. (1977–78)

Staniland, M. *The Lions of Dagbon* (1975)

Stokvis, A. M. H. J. *Manuel d'histoire, de généalogie et de chronologie de tous les états du globe*, 3 vols. (1888–93)

Sufi, G. M. D. *Kashir (History of Kashmir)* (1974)

Tate, M. *The Making of Modern South-East Asia*, Vol. I (1971)

Tchang, P. M. *Synchronismes chinois* (1905)

Teeuw, A. and Wyatt, D. K. *The Story of Patani*, 2 vols. (1970)

Thapar, R. *Asoka and the decline of the Mauryas*, 2nd ed. (1973)

Thompson, E. A. *The Goths in Spain* (1969)

Tod, J. *Annals and Antiquities of Rajastan*, 2 vols. (1829–32)

Toumanoff, C. *Manuel de généalogie et de chronologie pour l'histoire de la Caucasie chrétienne* (1976)

Vansina, J. *Kingdoms of the Savanna* (1966)

Vernadsky, G. *Political and Diplomatic History of Russia* (1937)

Ward, W. E. F. *History of Ghana*, 4th ed. (1966)

Weinstein, W. *Historical Dictionary of Burundi* (1976)

Whitelock, D. (ed.) *English Historical Documents c.500–1042*, 2nd ed. (1979)

Whitfield, D. J. *Historical and Cultural Dictionary of Vietnam* (1976)

Wilkinson, R. J. *The Early Sultans of Pahang* (JRASMB No. 10, 1932)

Winstedt, R. O. *History of Kedah* (JRASMB No. 14, 1936)

—*History of Selangor* (JRASMB No. 12, 1934)

—*A Malay History of Riau and Johore* (JRASMB No. 10, 1932)

Winstedt, R. O. and Wilkinson, R. J. *History of Perak* (JRASMB No. 12, 1934)

Yazdani, G. *Early History of the Deccan* (1960)

Zambaur, E. K. M. de *Manuel de généalogie et de chronologie pour l'histoire de l'Islam* (1927)

SECTION I

Alphabetical guide to dynasties and states

Words capitalized in an entry will themselves be
found as main entries. The numbers
at the end of entries give the relevant list
or lists of rulers in Section II.
In the dynastic charts, an arrow linking
two individuals indicates that one or more
generations separate them.

'**Abbadids** Muslim dynasty of SEVILLE, Spain in 11th century, most important of the REYES DE TAIFAS. They annexed several of the neighbouring Muslim kingdoms and took a leading role in inviting the ALMORAVIDS to Spain to resist the Christian advance. Al-Mu'tadid, the last of the dynasty and a famous poet, was deposed by the Almoravids, who annexed his domains. (48a)

'**Abbasids** The second Caliphal dynasty of Islam, the 'CALIPHS of Baghdad', descended from an uncle of Muhammad the Prophet (see QURAISHI dynasties). In the mid-8th century, they launched a long-prepared revolt in KHURASAN against the UMAYYAD rulers of the Islamic world, and in 750 overthrew that dynasty, shifting the centre of Caliphal power from Syria to 'Iraq. Their capital and court long remained the political and cultural metropolis of Islam, but the great empire they had acquired gradually broke up. SPAIN became independent almost immediately under a refugee Umayyad prince and other outlying provinces in IRAN and North Africa soon became autonomous – the Caliphs themselves fell under the control of powerful ministers. In the 10th–12th centuries, they were puppets of the BUYIDS and then of the SELJUK Sultans, and had barely recovered their independence and effective control of 'Iraq when the MONGOLS captured Baghdad and extinguished their state in 1258. Members of the family were maintained as puppet-Caliphs in Cairo by the MAMLUKS until the final suppression of the dynasty by the OSMANLI Turks in the 16th century. (103c, 135c)

'**Abdalis 1** Founding dynasty of modern AFGHANISTAN, see DURRANIS
2 Ruling family of the sultanate of LAHEJ in the ADEN PROTECTORATE from the early 18th century until the abolition of their state in 1967 by the newly independent government of South YEMEN. (172m)

'**Abdul-Wadids** See ZAYYANIDS.

Abgarids Ancient Arab dynasty of OSRHOENE, their capital being EDESSA (modern Urfa in south-eastern Turkey). They rose to power in the 2nd century BC on the decline of the SELEUCIDS and became a client-kingdom of ROME, which suppressed the state in the mid-3rd century AD. (164)

Abkhazia Region of north-western GEORGIA (Caucasus), a virtually independent principality under the SHARVASHIDZE family from the 15th century until its annexation by Russia in 1864. The name was used in medieval times for a larger kingdom extending over all western Georgia (ancient Colchis, later LAZICA and still later IMERETI), ruled from the 8th century by the ANCHABADS and then by the BAGRATIDS, who combined it with IBERIA in 1008 to form the Georgian kingdom. (151a)

Abu Dhabi Largest of the UNITED ARAB EMIRATES, ruled by the AL-BU-FALAH family since the late 18th century. (178d)

Abuja See ZARIA.

Abyssinia See ETHIOPIA.

Acciajuoli Florentine family which ruled the Duchy of ATHENS in the 14th–15th centuries. They captured the city from the GRAND CATALAN COMPANY and held it until the OSMANLI Turkish conquest of Greece. (85g)

Achaea Region of the Peloponnese, Greece and formal name of a CRUSADER STATE bettern known as the Principality of MOREA (which see).

Achaemenids Early imperial dynasty of IRAN, founded by Hakhamanish (Achaemenes) and originally rulers of the minor kingdom of Parsa (FARS). In 550 BC, Cyrus the Great overthrew the ruler of the MEDES, and he and his successors (particularly Darius the Great) rapidly built up a vast empire extending from Egypt and Asia Minor to the Indus. Achaemenid power declined under later members of the dynasty, but their state held together until conquered in its entirety by Alexander the Great during the period 334–328 BC. (187b)

Achin (Atjeh), northern region of SUMATRA and former sultanate founded at the end of the 15th century. It was a powerful and militantly Islamic state in the 16th and 17th centuries, sometimes contesting control of the Malacca Straits with the Portuguese and Dutch. The sultanate was annexed by the Dutch in 1874, though local resistance continued until 1904. (245a)

Adal See AWFAT.

Aden/Aden Protectorate The city, an important commercial port since ancient times, has for much of its history been controlled by the rulers of YEMEN. It was the centre of power of the ZURAY'ID dynasty in the 11th–12th centuries and a British Colony 1839–1967, since when it has been capital of South Yemen. The Protectorate was an extensive region of Southern Arabia ruled for about a century by Britain as protecting power of numerous small sultanates and amirates abolished by the new independent government of South Yemen in 1967. The most important of the states were LAHEJ under the 'ABDALIS and SHIHR AND MUKALLA under the QU'AITIS. (172m-n)

'Adil Shahis Ruling dynasty of BIJAPUR, one of the DECCAN SULTANATES, founded by Yusuf 'Adil Shah in 1490. After a siege of more than a year, the capital fell to the MOGHULS in 1686 and the state was annexed to the Moghul empire – by which time, however, much of its territory was already in the hands of the rebel MARATHA kingdom. (217l)

Aeacids Kings of EPIRUS in north-western Greece in the 4th/3rd centuries BC, originally chiefs of the Molossi – they claimed descent from the legendary hero Achilles. Olympias, mother of Alexander the Great, was an Aeacid, as was Pyrrhus of 'Pyrrhic' victory fame. The dynasty was eventually replaced in Epirus by a republican regime. (84)

Afghanistan Though a well-defined national state today, this region has for most of its history been ruled by neighbouring power, and often divided among them. The stronger rulers of IRAN usually controlled the area or most of it, but it formed the core of the Greek kingdom of BACTRIA, of the KUSHAN empire and the GHAZNAVID and GHURID states. The KART family ruled HERAT between the collapse of the ILKAN regime and the TIMURID conquest, and the last Timurid prince

Babur established his headquarters at Kabul after the loss of his lands in TRANSOXANIA, going on to found the MOGHUL empire, whose rulers held much of Afghanistan until the early 18th century. Nadir Shah AFSHAR conquered the region, which was seized after his death by one of his Afghan generals, Ahmad Shah DURRANI, founder of the present state. After a long struggle involving the British in the early 19th century, the Durranis were supplanted by the related BARAKZAIS, whose last monarch was deposed in 1973, the monarchy being abolished. (195–197)

Afrighids Semi-legendary Iranian dynasty which ruled KHWARIZM from about the 4th century AD. The later rulers were certainly historical, and the last was overthrown by the MA'MUNIDS in 995.

Afsharids Family which briefly ruled IRAN in the 18th century, founded by Nadir Shah, who restored order after the collapse of SAFAVID rule. He conducted victorious campaigns in both west and east, his best-known exploit being the sack of Delhi in 1739, but his empire fell apart on his assassination, though his grandson ruled in KHURASAN to 1796. (187k)

Aftasids Muslim kings of BADAJOZ, Spain, in the 11th century, a dynasty of the REYES DE TAIFAS. Their kingdom was annexed by the ALMORAVIDS. (48b)

Aghlabids Rulers of the eastern MAGHRIB in the 9th century AD, their centre of power being modern Tunisia. The founder was appointed governor of the region by the 'ABBASIDS, and the dynasty ruled nominally on behalf of the CALIPHS but in fact independently, later conquering SICILY from BYZANTIUM. The last of the family was overthrown by the founders of the FATIMID state. (109a)

Agiads One of the two simultaneous ruling dynasties of SPARTA (the other being the EURYPONTIDS), traditionally from 1102 BC, though the dates of the kings are very uncertain until much later. Leonidas, killed at Thermopylae in 480 BC, was a member of this family, which provided kings for Sparta until almost the end of the 3rd century BC. (82)

Agilulfings Early tribal dukes in BAVARIA in the 6th–8th centuries. The dynasty was extinguished and its lands annexed by Charlemagne (see CAROLINGIANS) in 788. (38a)

Ahmadnagar City in India, capital of a state of the same name, one of the DECCAN SULTANATES, ruled by the NIZAM SHAHI dynasty 1490–1633 (Founder Ahmad Nizam Shah, also founder of the city). The state was annexed by the MOGHULS in 1633. (217i)

Ahoms SHAN/THAI people and ruling dynasty of ASSAM, 13th century invaders of the region who gradually extended their control over most of it. The Ahom state was overrun by the Burmese in 1819 and eventually annexed by the British in 1838. (215b)

Aidin Town in western Turkey, capital of one of the ANATOLIAN AMIRATES of the same name ruled by the Aidin-oghlu family from the early 14th century until the second conquest of their territory by the OSMANLI Turks in 1425. (142g)

Ailech Early kingdom in western ULSTER, ruled from the 5th century AD by the northern branch of the O'NEILL dynasty, many of its kings being also HIGH KINGS of Ireland. The state survived the Anglo-Norman conquest as a minor chieftain-ship, its dynasty becoming in due course Earls of Tyrone. (14f)

'Ajman One of the UNITED ARAB EMIRATES, ruled by the AL-BU-KHURAIBAN (Al-Nu'aimi) family since the early 19th century. (178f)

Akkad Ancient name for Central 'Iraq, and one of the earliest firmly historical kingdoms (*c.*2371–2191 BC), founded by the first major empire-builder in Western Asia, Sharrukin (Sargon). The state collapsed under barbarian attacks. (180a)

Al-, Al-Bu-, Banu Arabic terms meaning sons, family, descendants, dynasty. See examples which follow, Beware of confusion between 'Al-' and the definite article 'al-'.

Al-'Ali (Al-Mu'alla) Ruling family of UMM-AL-QAWAIN, one of the UNITED ARAB EMIRATES, since the late 18th century. (178g)

Al-Bu-Falah (Al-Nihayyan) Ruling family of ABU DHABI, largest of the UNITED ARAB EMIRATES, since the mid-18th century. (178d)

Al-Bu-Falasah (Al-Maktum) Ruling family of DUBAI, one of the UNITED ARAB EMIRATES, since the early 19th century. (178e)

Al-Bu-Khuraiban (Al-Nu'aimi) Ruling family of 'AJMAN, one of the UNITED ARAB EMIRATES, since the early 19th century. (178f)

Al-Bu-Sa'id Sultans of 'UMAN and ZANZIBAR, successors of YA'RUBIDS. The dynasty reached the zenith of its power under Sa'id ibn Sultan, on whose death in 1856 its dominions were divided between separate branches of the family in Arabia and East Africa. The Zanzibar sultanate was abolished in 1964 and replaced by a republican regime. (125c, 179b)

Al-Khalifah Ruling dynasty of BAHRAIN since 1783, when Ahmad ibn Khalifah conquered the island from the Persians (177b)

Al-Maktum See AL-BU-FALASAH.

Al-Mu'alla See AL-'ALI.

Al-Nihayyan See AL-BU-FALAH.

Al-Nu'aimi See AL-BU-KHURAIBAN.

Al-Rashid Amirs of Ha'il in Central Arabia, rulers of the Jabal Shammar region and for a period in the later 19th century the dominant power in NAJD. Their rise followed the crushing of the AL-SA'UD state by the Egyptians in 1818, and they prevented a major revival of Sa'udi power until the early 20th century, when their lands were conquered by 'Abdul-'Aziz ibn Sa'ud. (175)

Al-Sabah Ruling family of KUWAIT since the mid-18th century. (177a)

Al-Sa'ud Ruling family of SA'UDI ARABIA, Amirs of NAJD and leaders of the Wahhabi sect of Islam from the mid-18th century. Their very considerable power at the beginning of the 19th century was broken by MUHAMMAD 'ALI in 1818, and the Al-Sa'ud were overshadowed by the AL-RASHID until early in the present century, when 'Abdul-'Aziz ibn Sa'ud conquered most of Arabia, including the Al-Rashid lands and the HIJAZ to establish the present Sa'udi kingdom. (176)

Al-Thani Ruling family of QATAR since the mid-19th century, at first under OSMANLI Turkish and later under British protection but now as independent Amirs. (177c)

Aladahonu dynasty Kings of DAHOMEY in West Africa *c*.1625–1894, for long as vassals of OYO but as important independent rulers in the 18th and 19th centuries. The last king was deposed and his state annexed by France – it now forms (approximately) the independent state of Benin. (121c)

Alamut Fortress in MAZANDARAN, northern Iran, headquarters of the Grand Masters of the ASSASSINS from 1090 until the destruction of their state by the Mongol ILKHAN Hulegu in 1256. (180f)

Alaungpaya dynasty Last ruling family of BURMA, founded in 1752 on the fall of the TOUNGOO dynasty. The early rulers of the new dynasty were powerful and aggressive, their armies overrunning THAILAND and capturing AYUTHIA in 1767. However, the later kings came into collision with the British, who annexed Lower Burma in 1852 and the remainder of the kingdom in 1885. (237f)

'Alawids (Filalis), present royal house of Morocco, a SHARIF dynasty, originally rulers of the TAFILALT area beyond the Atlas range. They seized power in Morocco on the collapse of the regime of their distant relatives the SA'DIDS in the early 17th century. In the first half of the present century, their kingdom was a French protectorate, but has been independent since 1956. (112i)

Albania (Balkans) Modern state partly overlapping the region of ancient EPIRUS. It became independent of OSMANLI Turkish rule in 1912 but was not firmly established as a state until some years later. In 1928 it became a kingdom under Ahmad Zog, previously president, who was expelled by Italy in 1939. Since 1945 it has been a republic. (81)

Albania (Caucasus) Classical name for what is now Soviet AZERBAIJAN, a kingdom

in ancient times, usually under the overlordship of IRAN, though its history is very obscure. For later period see ARRAN and SHIRVAN.

Aleppo (Haleb), very ancient city in northern SYRIA, centre of a kingdom in the 2nd millennium BC and capital of various Muslim dynasties. (159, 167)

Aleramids Medieval dynasty of northern Italy, descendants of Aleram, Margrave of MONTFERRAT, where his family ruled 967–1305. Another branch of the dynasty ruled SALUZZO until the mid-16th century. (67a–b, 85c)

Algeciras City in southern SPAIN, one of the REYES DE TAIFAS states of the 11th century under the HAMMUDIDS, conquered by the 'ABBADIDS. (48i)

Algeria/Algiers This modern state and its capital are historically part of the MAGHRIB, and the region has usually been either part of larger states or divided between neighbouring powers, though several minor Muslim dynasties have ruled kingdoms based in the area – see RUSTAMIDS, HAMMADIDS, ZAYYANIDS. Algeria fell under OSMANLI Turkish rule in the 16th century, but the Pashas and Deys of Algiers soon became virtually independent. Their dominions were annexed by France in 1830. (110, 111c)

'Ali Raja dynasty The only Muslim ruling family of KERALA, Rajas of CANNANORE from medieval times, though firm dates are only available from the 16th century. Their mainland territory was very limited, but they also controlled the Laccadive Islands until these were taken over by the British in the late 19th century. The dynasty survived as minor princes until Indian independence. (220e)

'Alids General name for the dynasties and individuals descended from Muhammad the Prophet's son-in-law and cousin, 'Ali ibn Abi Talib, the fourth CALIPH. See QURAISHI dynasties, also SAYYID and SHARIF.

Almeria City in SPAIN, centre of the BANU SUMADIH kingdom, one of the 11th century REYES DE TAIFAS states. (48e)

Almohads (Muwahhids) Berber Muslim dynasty of 12th/13th centuries, leaders of a puritan religious movement in the MAGHRIB. They overthrew the ALMOR-AVIDS, and at the height of their power ruled the entire Maghrib region plus Muslim SPAIN. After their crushing defeat at Las Navas de Tolosa in 1212 by the Christian Spanish kings, they lost their European provinces and were eventually extinguished in Morocco by the MARINDS, their more easterly dominions falling to HAFSIDS and ZAYYANIDS. (112e)

Almoravids (Murabitids) Berber Muslim dynasty of 11th/12th centuries, originally Saharan nomad leaders of a religious movement who broke the power of the GHANA empire and conquered much of the MAGHRIB. Invited to SPAIN to assist the REYES DE TAIFAS against Christian attacks, they annexed most of these small Muslim states and halted the Christian advance – their main opponent was Rodrigo de Bivar (El Cid) of Valencia. Within a century, they were overthrown by the ALMOHADS, though their relatives the BANU GHANIYA of MAJORCA led re-sistance in the eastern Maghrib for several decades more. (112d)

Alpuente City in SPAIN, centre of the BANU QASIM kingdom, one of the 11th century REYES DE TAIFAS states. (48d)

Amber RAJPUT state better known by the name of its modern capital, Jaipur, founded in the 12th century and ruled by the KACHWAHA dynasty. It was overshadowed by the older and more powerful state of MEWAR until the MOGHUL period, when the rulers of Amber served the Moghul emperors and rose to great importance in RAJASTAN. Their state later came under MARATHA and then British overlordship, and is now part of the Republic of India. (206d)

Amirids Kings of VALENCIA, one of the 11th century REYES DE TAIFAS states, descended from al-Mansur Muhammad ibn Abi Amir, the all-powerful Grand Vizier of the UMAYYAD Caliph at the end of the previous century. Their lands were later acquired by the famous Rodrigo de Bivar (El Cid), whose heirs were obliged to surrender the city to the ALMORAVIDS. (48c)

Anatolia Modern name for ASIA MINOR,

the western (peninsular) part of Turkey-in-Asia. See OSMANLIS.

Anatolian Amirates On the disinte-gration of the SELJUK Sultanate of RUM and the weakening of Byzantine control in western Asia Minor under the PALAE-OLOGI, numerous small Turkish amirates arose in Anatolia, among them the OSMANLI state, which increased rapidly in importance, largely by conquests in the Balkans, and then annexed most of the other Turkish principalities. However, after his great defeat of the Osmanli Sultan in 1402, Timur (see TIMURIDS) re-established some of the amirates, which fell to the revived Osmanli power during the early 15th century. Initially the most important of these states and the last to resist conquest was QARAMAN. Two minor amirates in the south-east survived under Osmanli suzerainty into the 16th century – see DHU'L-QADR and RAMADAN-OGHLU. (142)

Anchabads Georgian dynasty, rulers of greater ABKHAZIA from the 8th century AD until their kingdom was inherited by the BAGRATIDS and soon combined with IBERIA to form the medieval kingdom of GEORGIA. (151a)

Andhra Pradesh Province of modern India in the eastern DECCAN, centre of various Hindu and Muslim kingdoms since early times. See also VENGI. The SATAVAHANA dynasty are sometimes, though incorrectly, called the Andhras. (218)

Angeli Imperial family of BYZANTIUM, related to the COMNENI, whom they succeeded in the late 12th century. (1c)

Angevins Name of two dynasties de-scending from counts of ANJOU, France. The first of these dynasties, whose later members are more usually known as the Plantagenets, ruled Anjou and later Touraine from the 9th century. Count Fulk V abdicated and went to Palestine, where he and his heirs became kings of JERUSALEM 1131–1186. His eldest son Geoffrey Plantagenet married Empress Matilda, grand-daughter of William the Conqueror, and later seized NORMANDY on behalf of his son Henry (II of England), a claimant to the English throne, who also became ruler of AQUITAINE by right of his wife, and king of England in 1154. Later in his reign, he acquired the overlordship of IRELAND. Anjou and Normandy were lost to the French crown in 1204, together with much of Aquitaine, but the later Plantagenets held various parts of France in the succeeding centuries, and did not lose the last remnant of Aquitaine until 1453. They ruled England, in the main line and then in the branches of Lancaster and York, until 1485. (6b, 24a, c, 24s)

The second Angevin dynasty was founded by Charles, brother of Louis IX of France, count of Anjou and PROVENCE and later king of NAPLES (1266). His descendants ruled Naples until 1435, being succeeded by the ARAGONESE dynasty. Other branches of the CAPET family, to which the later Angevins belonged, succeeded in Anjou and Provence in 1290 and 1382 respectively. Several members of the dynasty ruled in HUNGARY. (24c, 24t, 62c, 71b)

Angola See KONGO kingdom.

Angouleme Feudal county in France from the 9th century, ruled by the LUSIGNANS during most of the 13th century. It was annexed to the French crown in 1308. (24q)

Anhalt Principality in northern GERMANY under the ASCANIAN dynasty from the 11th century, much subdivided among various branches of the family into smaller states (Dessau, Zerbst, Bernburg, etc.) but finally re-united as the Duchy of Anhalt 1863–1918. (31)

Anjou Feudal county in France, ruled by the successive ANGEVIN dynasties from the 9th century and then by a branch of the VALOIS. It was annexed to the French crown in 1480. (24c)

Ankole See NKORE.

Annam See VIET-NAM.

Antalya Ancient Attalia, city in Turkey. Centre of TEKE, one of the ANATOLIAN AMIRATES, ruled by the HAMID dynasty in the 14th/15th centuries, finally conquered by the OSMANLIS in 1423. (142h)

Antigonids Macedonian dynasty founded by a general of Alexander the Great, who ruled a large state based on Asia Minor from c.319 BC. After his defeat and death in 301, the dynasty went through varying fortunes, at times controlling only a few ports and islands, until firmly established in MACEDONIA in 272. The Antigonids ruled that kingdom until the Roman conquest in 168 BC. See also DIADOCHI. (83c)

Antioch Syrian city (now in Turkey), capital of the SELEUCID empire and later the eastern metropolis of the Roman empire. In the 12th–13th centuries it was the centre of a principality under the HAUTEVILLES (see CRUSADER STATES) until conquered by the MAMLUKS in 1268. (167b)

Antipatrids Antipater was regent in in MACEDONIA during Alexander the Great's campaigns in Asia. After the death of both men, the Macedonian throne was seized by Antipater's son Cassander (310 BC), whose own sons proved quarrelsome and lost the kingdom to the ANTIGONIDS. (82b)

Antonines Group of Roman emperors who ruled 138–192 AD, a period generally accepted as the zenith of power and prosperity for the empire. (1a)

Anushtiginids Ruling dynasty of KHWARIZM in the 11th–13th centuries, at first as governors for the SELJUKS and later as vassals of the QARA KHITAI, but finally as independent rulers of TRANSOXANIA and most of IRAN. Khwarizm itself was conquered by the MONGOLS in 1220, but the last ruler of the dynasty, Jalal-ud-Din, put up a determined resistance to the Mongol advance into Iran, at the same time extending his power into AZERBAIJAN and GEORGIA, until his death in 1231. (199b)

Apafi Family of which two members ruled as princes of TRANSYLVANIA in the later 17th century. (76)

Apulia Region of southern Italy. Until the mid-11th century it formed part of the Byzantine empire, but was then seized by the HAUTEVILLES, under whom it became an independent county and then (with Calabria) a duchy, being absorbed into their kingdom of SICILY in 1127. (68e)

Aq-Qoyunli ('White Sheep'), a Turkoman tribe and its ruling family based in KURDISTAN in 14th/15th centuries. After overcoming their rivals the QARA-QOYUNLI in 1467, they extended their rule over 'IRAQ and much of IRAN. Their western territories were conquered by the OSMANLIS and they were extinguished in AZERBAIJAN by the SAFAVIDS. (188f)

Aquitaine Ancient and medieval name for a large area of south-western France, ruled as a kingdom by members of the CAROLINGIAN dynasty. It became a feudal duchy, usually combined with the county of POITIERS, in the 9th century, and the ANGEVIN Henry II of England acquired it by marriage with the daughter of its last independent duke. Most of the duchy was lost to the French crown at the beginning of the 13th century, but its southern part, Gascony, remained under English control until its last remnants fell to the French kings in the mid-15th century. A branch of the ducal house of Aquitaine became rulers of ANTIOCH and TRIPOLI by marriage in the mid-12th century, and a branch of that line in turn became kings of CYPRUS in the same way in 1267, though taking the name of LUSIGNAN. (24s, 144, 167b–c)

Arabia The peninsula has never been under the control of a single power except very briefly under the early CALIPHS, though most of it now forms the kingdom of SA'UDI-ARABIA. For the history of its various regions, see YEMEN, HIJAZ, NAJD, 'UMAN and the smaller Gulf States.

Arab-Shahids Rulers of KHWARIZM/KHIVA, 16th/18th centuries, one of the CHINGIS-KHANID dynasties, their history being rather obscure. They were succeeded by the INAKIDS. (199c)

Aragon/Aragonese dynasty Aragon was originally a small county in north-eastern Spain, absorbed into the kingdom of NAVARRE in the 10th century, but was re-established as a larger state under a son of Sancho the Great in 1035. The counts of BARCELONA obtained the kingdom by marriage and united it with their wealthy domains in the 12th century, after the state had been much strengthened by the conquest of ZARAGOZA. James the Conqueror added VALENCIA and MAJORCA, though an independent junior branch of the family ruled Majorca until 1343. Other branches of the dynasty ruled SICILY 1282–1516 and NAPLES 1435–1516, and also in PROVENCE and ATHENS. All the Spanish and Italian lands, combined under Ferdinand the Catholic, fell to the HABSBURG Charles V in 1516. (47b, 49, 50c, 62d)

Arakan Former independent kingdom ruled by various dynasties over more than a thousand years prior to its conquest by the ALAUNGPAYA kings of BURMA, of which it now forms part, in 1785. (238)

Aravidu dynasty Last ruling family of the VIJAYANAGAR empire of southern India. The founder was the real ruler under the later TULUVA kings but died at the battle of Talikota (1565) which destroyed the military power of the state. His relatives seized the throne of the disintegrating empire, which vanished in the late 17th century. The site of modern Madras was granted to the British in 1645 by the last effective king of the dynasty. (222d)

Archaeanactids Earliest kings of BOSPHORUS in the Crimea in the 5th century BC. They were succeeded by the SPARTOCIDS. (90a)

Arcot Town near Madras, India, capital of the Nawabs of Arcot, rulers of the CARNATIC from the late 17th century as MOGHUL viceroys. They soon became virtually independent, and added the NAYYAK kingdom of MADURAI to their dominions in 1736, but fell under the control of Britain, which annexed their territory in 1825. (223g)

Argeads Founding dynasty of the kingdom of MACEDONIA in the 7th century BC. Their state was for long unimportant but from the mid-4th century came to dominate Greece under Philip II and Alexander (III) the Great, briefly becoming the centre of a vast empire under the latter ruler. In the struggles between the DIADOCHI for control of the Macedonian dominions after the death of Alexander, his son was murdered (310 BC) and the dynasty extinguished. (83a)

Arghuns Afghan family claiming descent from the ILKHANS, pushed south by the MOGHUL conquests into SIND, where they overthrew the SAMMA dynasty and ruled the region for most of the 16th century. Their kingdom was annexed by the Moghul empire in 1591. (205d)

Argungu See KEBBI.

Ariarathids Dynasty of Persian origin, rulers of CAPPADOCIA c.350–95 BC at first as satraps under the later ACHAEMENIDS. Crushed by the DIADOCHI, they recovered power as independent kings in the early 3rd century, but the family was extinguished during the struggle between the Romans and Mithridates the Great of PONTUS, who temporarily controlled Cappadocia. (137c)

Armenia Historically a much larger area than the present Soviet Republic of Armenia, the region extended across much of eastern Turkey to the upper Euphrates. In the 9th–7th centuries BC this area formed the kingdom of URARTU, and was later part of the ACHAEMENID empire, becoming independent under its Persian ORONTID rulers on the fall of the Achaemenids. After a brief flourishing under the ARTAXIADS, the Armenian kingdom became a bone of contention between ROME and PARTHIA, ruled by a branch of the ARSACID dynasty until the abolition of the monarchy in 428 AD. From the 5th to the 9th century, the region was controlled by Byzantine or Persian viceroys, usually members of one or other of the many Armenian princely families. Gradually the BAGRATID dynasty became dominant, and revived the kingdom in 885 as a major power. However, junior branches of the family became independent in KARS and LORI in the late 10th century, and most of the region was annexed by BYZANTIUM in the following century, just before the whole area was overrun by the SELJUKS. There were other minor states in southern and eastern Armenia during medieval times (see SIUNIA and VASPURAKAN), and the Muslim SHAH-ARMANIDS and SALTUQIDS also ruled in the region. From the 13th century, Armenia has been controlled by neighbouring major powers, most recently Turkey and Russia. (146–148)

Armenia, Lesser A medieval kingdom consisting of Cilicia and the Taurus region (now part of south-eastern Turkey), founded in the 11th century by Armenian settlers. Ruled by the RUBENID and then the HETHUMID families, its last kings being members of the LUSIGNAN dynasty of Cyprus. The kingdom was annexed by the MAMLUKS of Egypt in 1375. (140)

Arpad dynasty Founding dynasty of HUNGARY, descendants of Arpad, chief of the Magyars at the time of their conquest of the Hungarian Plain at the end of the 9th century AD. Stephen I was recognized as the first king of Hungary in 1000 AD and the Arpad state was an important European power, surviving temporary MONGOL conquest in 1241–2. The dynasty died out in 1301, being succeeded after some disorder by a branch of the ANGEVINS of Naples. (71a)

Arran Medieval name for the western section of ancient ALBANIA (Caucasus), the modern Soviet AZERBAIJAN, in the early Middle Ages ruled by Armenian princes and later by Muslim dynasties until its conquest by the ILKHANS (see SHADDADIDS). The minor Khanates of GANJA, SHEKA and QARABAGH established in this region on the decline of Iranian power in the later 18th century were annexed by Russia, together with many other states of the Caucasus area, in the early 19th century. (155–158)

Arsacids (Arshakuni), Iranian dynasty, rulers of the PARTHIAN empire, originally chiefs of the nomadic Parni, who established themselves in the former ACHAEMENID satrapy of Parthia (modern KHURASAN) in the 3rd century BC and gradually conquered IRAN and 'IRAQ from the SELEUCIDS. They blocked the expansion of ROME in the east and ruled as overlords of various vassal states, including IBERIA and (intermittently) ARMENIA, in both of which kingdoms branches of the Arsacid family were put on the thrones. Early in the 3rd century AD, the dynasty was overthrown and replaced in Iran by its vassals in FARS, the SASANIDS, though the Armenian and Iberian lines survived until 428 and 284 respectively. (146d, 149b, 187c)

Artaxiads Successors of the ORONTIDS as kings of ARMENIA c.200 BC. The best-known ruler of the dynasty was Tigranes the Great, who temporarily conquered Syria from the SELEUCIDS and supported Mithridates the Great of PONTUS against ROME, but was subdued by the Romans in 69 BC. On the extinction of the dynasty *c*.1 BC, Rome and PARTHIA fought for control of the kingdom, placing various rulers on the throne, until a branch of the ARSACIDS was installed under Roman overlordship. (146b)

Artois Feudal county in France in the 13th century under a son and grandson of Louis VIII (Robert I 1237–1250 and Robert II 1250–1302) of the CAPET dynasty, thereafter passing by marriage to the rulers of FRANCHE COMTÉ.

Artsrunids Armenian dynasty, rulers of VASPURAKAN in southern Armenia from ancient times, though their history is sketchy until the 8th century AD. Their state became a kingdom in 908. Its last ruler ceded his lands to BYZANTIUM in 1021. (147b)

Artuqids Muslim dynasty of Turkish origins in KURDISTAN, established *c*.1100 AD, one branch ruling at HISN KAIFA until dispossessed by the AYYUBIDS in the 13th century, and another at MARDIN until their lands were conquered in the 15th century by the QARA-QOYUNLI. (185e–f)

Ascanian dynasty North German ruling family (named after an ancestral castle, Aschersleben) from the 11th century. Its most powerful early member was Albert the Bear (d.1170), who ruled ANHALT, SAXONY and BRANDENBURG. His descendants formed three branches in these territories, those in Saxony and Branden-

burg dying out in the later Middle Ages. The Anhalt line much subdivided its lands, but these were combined to form the Duchy of Anhalt 1863–1918. Catherine (II) the Great of Russia was a member of this dynasty, from the Anhalt-Zerbst branch. (27a, 31, 33a–b)

Asen dynasty The Asen brothers rose in revolt against BYZANTIUM in the late 12th century and founded the Second Bulgarian empire, at first a major Balkan power, though it fell under MONGOL overlordship in the mid-12th century. The Asen dynasty was succeeded by the TERTERS in 1280. (80d)

Ashanti West African kingdom founded in the early 17th century. It controlled much of what is now Ghana, but was conquered by the British in 1896. Its ruling family were later restored as chiefs. (120a)

Ashikaga A SHOGUN dynasty of JAPAN in the 14th–16th centuries, distantly descended from the 9th century Emperor Seiwa. Its last ruler was deposed by the dictator Oda Nobunaga in 1573. (236e)

Asia Minor The peninsular part of Turkey-in-Asia, later called ANATOLIA. It was the centre of HITTITE power in the 2nd millennium BC and later dominated by LYDIA. After the destruction of the ACHAE-MENID empire by Alexander, various small kingdoms flourished in the area, all being annexed by ROME in the 2nd/1st centuries BC. Asia Minor remained part of the Roman and then the Byzantine empire until the 11th century AD, when much of it fell under the rule of the SELJUK Sultans of RUM (see also NICAEA

THE ASCANIAN DYNASTY

Albert the Bear, Duke of Saxony, Margrave of
Brandenburg, Count of Anhalt, d.1170

Dukes of Saxony 1180–1260	Margraves of Brandenburg to 1320	Princes of Anhalt from 1212
Dukes and Electors of Saxe-Wittenberg 1260–1422	Dukes of Saxe-Lauenburg 1260–1689	Princely lines of Dessau, Bernburg, Zerbst, Kothen, etc.

Anhalt-Dessau line

Dukes of Anhalt 1863–1918

and ANATOLIAN AMIRATES). It was conquered by the OSMANLI Turks during the 14th/15th centuries. (136–143)

Askiyas Rulers of the SONGHAI empire in the western SUDAN in succession to the SUNNI dynasty. The major part of the state was conquered by the SA'DIDS of Morocco in 1591, after a century of Askiya rule, but members of the dynasty maintained some power in the Dendi area of the south until the mid-17th century. (119c)

Aspurgids Kings of the BOSPHORUS in the 1st/4th centuries AD, client-rulers under the overlordship of ROME. Their state vanished in the great tribal upheavals north of the Black Sea in the 4th century. (90d)

Assam Region of north-eastern India. In ancient times its most important state was KAMARUPA, succeeded in the 13th century by the AHOM kingdom. It was largely conquered by the rulers of BURMA in the early 19th century, and later annexed by the British. (215)

Assassins A militant SHI'A sect which used assassination as a systematic policy against its enemies. It was founded in the late 11th century AD by Hassan-i Sabbah, who established a small state in MAZANDARAN, Iran, with his capital at ALAMUT. He was succeeded by a series of Grand Masters of the sect, which also set up a semi-autonomous branch in Syria. The Assassin state in Iran was destroyed by the ILKHAN Hulegu in 1256 and the Syrian branch extinguished in 1273 by the MAMLUKS. (189f)

Assyria (Asshur), an ancient kingdom in what is now northern 'Iraq. It became important after the fall of the MITANNI state in the 13th century BC and expanded into a very powerful empire in the 8th/7th centuries, controlling much of Western Asia and, at times, Egypt. The Assyrians were notoriously militaristic, their rule harsh and brutal, and their empire was finally destroyed by an alliance of BABYLON with the MEDES. The central region of the kingdom was overrun in 612 BC and the last Assyrian army crushed on the Middle Euphrates in 609. (183)

Astrakhan City on the Lower Volga, capital of a khanate of the same name in the 15th/16th centuries, one of the successor-states of the GOLDEN HORDE and ruled by a CHINGIS-KHANID dynasty to whom the JANIDS of BUKHARA were closely related. Astrakhan was annexed by Ivan (IV) the Terrible in 1556, thus giving the Russians control of the entire length of the Volga. (96d)

Asturias Province of north-western Spain, earliest centre of Christian resistance after the Muslim conquest in the 8th century, where originated the kingdom later known as LEON. The title 'Prince of Asturias' has been borne by the heir to the throne of Spain for some centuries. (45)

Atabeg Turkish title given to an officer appointed as guardian to a SELJUK prince sent to govern a province. Some of these officers usurped the power themselves as the Seljuk empire weakened, and founded virtually independent states. Thus 'Atabeg' came to mean a ruling prince in the 12th–13th centuries in the Middle East.

Athens The leading Greek city-state in ancient times and capital of modern Greece. On the Latin conquest of Constantinople in 1204, Athens and the surrounding region became a duchy under the De La ROCHE family until its occupation by the GRAND CATALAN COMPANY, who placed members of the ARAGONESE dynasty on its throne. The Florentine ACCIAJUOLI family acquired the duchy in the late 14th century and held it until the whole of Greece was absorbed into the OSMANLI empire. (85g)

Atropatene (Media Atropatene, modern Persian AZERBAIJAN), a kingdom in ancient times, founded in the late 4th century BC by Atropates, a Persian satrap who went over to Alexander the Great on the fall of the ACHAEMENID empire and secured his independence during the wars of the DIADOCHI. Very little is known about the history of the state, which was usually subject to the ARSACIDS of Iran and was eventually annexed by them. The name Azerbaijan is in fact a much-altered version of Atropatene.

Attalids Ruling dynasty of western Asia Minor, probably Greek by origin, their capital being PERGAMUM. At first they recognized the overlordship of the SELEUCIDS, but became independent kings from the mid-3rd century BC. The last monarch of the family bequeathed his lands to ROME in 133 BC. (137f)

Austria (Oesterreich, the 'eastern state'), originally the eastern march (Ostmark) of Bavaria, a margravate from the 10th century and duchy from 1156 under the BABENBERG family, after whose extinction it was acquired by Rudolf of HABSBURG in 1276. To the original mark his successors added STYRIA, CARINTHIA, CARNIOLA and TYROL, and this enlarged Austria formed the core of the later Habsburg empire. At the beginning of the 19th century, the HOLY ROMAN EMPIRE was abolished and the Habsburg ruler adopted the title Emperor of Austria (later of AUSTRIA–HUNGARY). (40, 41)

Austria-Hungary Dual monarchy under the HABSBURGS established in 1867 and consisting of the Empire of AUSTRIA and the Kingdom of HUNGARY. All the territories of the realm had in fact been under Habsburg rule for several centuries, the new constitutional arrangement being adopted to placate the Hungarians. After the First World War, the empire was broken up to form modern Austria, Hungary and Czechoslovakia, other provinces going to Yugoslavia, Poland, Rumania and Italy. (41)

Auvergne Region of southern France, medieval feudal county from the 9th century but split in 1155 into the County and the Dauphinate, under separate branches of the same dynasty. Both areas were annexed to the French crown in the 17th century. (24l–m)

Ava City in BURMA, capital of the SHAN kingdom established in 1364 by the union of the smaller states of MYINSAING–PINYA and SAGAING. The new state dominated Upper Burma until its conquest by the TOUNGOO kings in 1555. (237d)

Avars Nomadic Turkish or Mongol people, usually linked by historians with the JUAN-JUAN rulers of Mongolia. In the late 6th century AD, they invaded the plain of Hungary and set up a powerful kingdom. Their most able ruler, Bayan,

led his army to besiege Constantinople, but after his death in 602, the Avar power began to decline and the later history of their state is obscure. At the end of the 8th century, the CAROLINGIAN Charlemagne destroyed the Avar kingdom.

Avadh (Oudh), region of northern India, in modern Uttar Pradesh, a province of the MOGHUL empire whose Nawab (governor) established his independence as the empire broke up in the early 18th century. Avadh was annexed by the British in 1856 (and proved a main centre of the Indian Mutiny of the following year). (204d)

Aviz dynasty Kings of PORTUGAL 1385–1580, the first of the dynasty being an illegitimate brother of the last ruler of the Burgundian CAPET line. They were succeeded by the Spanish HABSBURGS, who were expelled in the mid-17th century by an illegitimate branch of the Aviz family, the BRAGANZAS. (54b)

Awfat (Ifat, later called Adal), a Muslim state in eastern ETHIOPIA and SOMALIA, ruled by the WALASMA' dynasty from the late 13th century until its overthrow by the Imam Ahmad Gran, founder of the Amirate of HARAR in the same region. (124)

Awlad Muhammad Ruling family of the FEZZAN region of Libya from the late 16th century in succession to the obscure earlier dynasties of Banu Khattab and Banu Nasur. Their state was conquered by the OSMANLI Turks in 1842. (106c)

Axum City in northern ETHIOPIA, centre of the earliest Ethiopian kingdom from about the 1st century AD, having close connections with the South Arabian HIMYAR kingdom, which came under Axumite control more than once. Very little is known of the history of this state, from whose rulers the later SOLOMONIC dynasty of Ethiopia claimed descent.

Aydin See AIDIN.

Ayuthia Historic city near modern Bangkok, centre of a kingdom usually called by the same name, direct predecessor of the present state of THAILAND and founded in 1350. The city was captured and largely destroyed by the

Burmese in 1767 after a long siege, and Bangkok then became the Thai capital. (239c)

Ayyubids Ayyub was a Kurdish general of the ZANGIDS – his son Salah-ud-Din Yusuf (Saladin) became independent ruler of EGYPT in 1169 and later supplanted the Syrian Zangids, also conquering most of the CRUSADER STATE kingdom of JERUSALEM. Various branches of his family ruled in Egypt, SYRIA, KURDISTAN and YEMEN, being succeeded in the first two regions in the mid-13th century by the MAMLUKS. A minor line of the dynasty survived at HISN KAIFA until almost the end of the 15th century. (102, 166f–j, 172i, 185l–m)

Azerbaijan Region of north-western Iran, now divided into the areas of Persian and Soviet Azerbaijan:

1 Persian Azerbaijan was the ancient Media ATROPATENE, a kingdom founded by a former satrap of the ACHAEMENIDS during the struggles of the DIADOCHI in the late 4th century BC – the early and present name of the area both derive from his name, Atropates. Various later dynasties have ruled in the region. (188)

2 Soviet Azerbaijan was the ancient ALBANIA (Caucasus), in later times divided into ARRAN and SHIRVAN. (155–158)

Aztecs Ruling people in MEXICO in the 15th and early 16th centuries. The Aztec kingdom, based on Tenochtitlan (modern Mexico City) was founded in the late 14th century after the disintegration of the TOLTEC empire and was at first a minor state. The rulers formed a confederation with the neighbouring kingdoms of TEXCOCO and Tlacopan, which league they soon came to dominate. Their extensive empire was conquered by Hernando Cortes for SPAIN in 1521. (250a)

B

Baalbek Ancient Heliopolis, city in Lebanon, centre of a small principality under a branch of the AYYUBID dynasty in the 12th/13th centuries, later absorbed by the DAMASCUS branch. (166j)

Babenbergs Margraves of AUSTRIA from the 10th century, dukes 1156, also dukes of STYRIA from 1192, the last of the dynasty being killed in battle in 1246. Their extensive lands were then seized by the ruler of BOHEMIA, from whom they were conquered by Rudolf of HABSBURG. (40d)

Babito dynasty Kings of BUNYORO from the 15th century and for long the most powerful rulers in UGANDA, until overshadowed by the BUGANDA kings in the 19th century. Bunyoro became a British protectorate in 1896 and the kingdom was abolished by independent Uganda in 1967. (126)

Babylon/Babylonia Ancient city and kingdom (modern southern 'Iraq), sometime called CHALDAEA. The kingdom was established in the 19th century BC, its first important ruler being the law-maker Hammurabi. Various dynasties, including the KASSITES, ruled the kingdom in later centuries, and its independence was repeatedly suppressed by ASSYRIA in the 8th/7th centuries BC. After the fall of Assyria, the Neo-Babylonian empire controlled 'Iraq and Syria for nearly a hundred years, the most powerful of its kings being Nebuchadrezzar (Nabu-kudurri-usur II). The state was annexed to the ACHAEMENID realm by Cyrus the Great in 539 BC. The city remained the largest and most important in Western Asia for a further three centuries. (182)

Bactria Modern northern AFGHANISTAN, perhaps an early Iranian kingdom and then a satrapy of the ACHAEMENID empire. It broke away from the SELEUCID domains as an independent Hellenistic kingdom in the mid-3rd century BC and was at first a powerful state, its rulers conquering large areas of northern India. In the later 2nd and early 1st centuries BC, it was fragmented by dynastic rivalries (see EUTHYDEMIDS and EUCRATIDIDS) and overrun by nomadic invaders. (195)

Badajoz Spanish city, ancient Pax Augusta, centre of the 11th century AFTASID kingdom, one of the REYES DE TAIFAS states. (48b)

Baden City and region in south-western Germany, ruled by the ZAHRINGEN dynasty as margraves from the early 12th century, split into the two states of Baden-Baden and Baden-Durlach in 1527, reunited in 1771 and made a Grand Duchy in 1806. The state was abolished with the other German kingdoms and principalities in 1918. (36)

Baduspanids Minor Iranian dynasty in MAZANDARAN, claiming descent from officials of the SASANID empire. It survived with varying fortunes until extinguished under the SAFAVIDS. (189b)

Baghdad Now the capital of modern 'Iraq. Founded by the second 'ABBASID Caliph in 762 AD as the intended capital of the Muslim world and for centuries its political and cultural centre. It was largely destroyed by the Mongols in 1258 and never recovered its former importance, though it remained the administrative centre of 'Iraq.

Bagirmi A sultanate in what is now southern Chad, SUDAN, established in the early 16th century under the KENGA dynasty, sometimes subject to BORNU. It became a French protectorate in 1912. (114d)

Bagratids Dynasty of ARMENIA and GEORGIA, minor princes in Armenia from at least the 4th century AD and frequently viceroys of that country under BYZANTIUM or the CALIPHS prior to their establishment of the medieval Armenian kingdom in 885. Their state declined in the 11th

century, the separate kingdoms of KARS and LORI breaking away under branches of the family, and late in that century all their lands fell to Byzantium and then to the SELJUKS. A Georgian branch inherited the GUARAMID lands and ruled IBERIA as viceroys before combining that region with ABKHAZIA and KAKHETI to form the kingdom of Georgia in the early 11th century. As a result of the MONGOL invasion and dynastic strife, the kingdom declined and at the end of the 15th century split into the three states of KARTLI (Iberia), KAKHETI and IMERETI (Abkhazia) under branches of the dynasty. All these kingdoms were annexed by Russia in the early 19th century after a long period of overlordship by the rival rulers of IRAN and the OSMANLI Turkish empire. (146e–f, 147c–d, 151d, 152–153)

Bahawalpur Successor-state of the MOGHUL empire in the lower Sutlej area of the PUNJAB, under Nawabs of the DAUDPUTRA family, founded in the mid-18th century, abolished by independent Pakistan in 1955. (203e)

Bahinda dynasty Descendants of Ruhinda, king of KARAGWE (in Tanzania) and NKORE (in Uganda) in the 15th century, rulers of both kingdoms in separate branches until both were abolished, by Tanzania in 1963 and Uganda in 1967 respectively. (127)

THE BAGRATID DYNASTY

Bagrat, Hereditary Coronant of the Armenian kings 4th century AD

Chosroid Kings of Iberia 284–580 AD

Bagratid Viceroys of Armenia 7th/9th centuries

Guaramids

Bagratid Kings of Armenia 885–1045

Bagratid Viceroys and Kings of Iberia, 9th/10th centuries

Kings of Kars 962–1064

Kings of Lori 982–1081

Bagratid Kings of Georgia 1008–1490

Kings of Kakheti 1039–1105

Kings of Imereti 1258–1810

Kings of Kartli 1490–1800

Kings of Kakheti 1466–1800

Bahmanids Sultans of the DECCAN, India. Their state was founded on the collapse of the TUGHLUQ empire in the mid-14th century and was for over a hundred years a major power. At the end of the 15th century, it broke up into the five DECCAN SULTANATES. (217h)

Bahrain Independent island state in the Persian Gulf. From the 9th century AD it was a power-base of the Qarmatian sect of Islam, though its later history is somewhat obscure until its conquest from Iran by the Arab AL-KHALIFAH family in 1783 – that dynasty still rule as Amirs. (177b)

Bahri Mamluks See MAMLUKS.

Balliol family Anglo-Norman family, originally from Bailleul in Picardy, provided two kings of SCOTLAND, father and son, installed with English support, who reigned briefly in the late 13th and early 14th centuries respectively. Balliol College, Oxford, was founded by another member of the family. (11b)

Balshichi Family which gained control of Zeta (modern MONTENEGRO) after the break up of the NEMANJICH Serbian empire in the mid-14th century. At the height of their power they also ruled much of northern Albania, but lost most of their lands to the Venetians and the OSMANLI Turks, to be succeeded in Zeta by the CRNOJEVICHI in the early 15th century. (75a)

Baluchistan Region of Pakistan, very little being known about its ancient and medieval history. From the mid-17th century, the most important state in the area was KALAT. (205e)

Bamiyan (Bamian), town and region in northern Afghanistan, centre of a kingdom under a branch of the GHURID dynasty in the 12th/13th centuries, conquered by the ANUSHTIGINIDS of KHWARIZM. (197c)

Bangladesh See BENGAL.

Bantam Muslim sultanate in western Java, founded in the early 16th century after the break-up of the MAJAPAHIT empire and at first a powerful state controlling parts of Sumatra and Borneo, though later overshadowed by MATARAM. It was brought under Dutch suzerainty in the late 17th century and annexed to the Netherlands East Indies in 1832. (246c)

Banu (Beni-), Arabic plural of Ibn (son), often used as dynastic prefix, as in the examples which follow – see also AL-, AL–BU-, BANU.

Banu 'Ammar Name of two Muslim dynasties:
1 Rulers of TRIPOLI in Lebanon – they established a small state based on the city in the mid-11th century AD, but came under attack by the forces of the First Crusade at the beginning of the following century – their capital fell after a long blockade in 1109 and became the centre of a CRUSADER STATE. (168a)
2 Rulers of TRIPOLI in Libya (unrelated to the Lebanese dynasty) during most of the 14th century. Their principality was annexed by the HAFSIDS of Tunis in 1401. (106a)

Banu Ghaniya Amirs of MAJORCA in the 12th century, originally as viceroys of the ALMORAVIDS. After the fall of the latter dynasty, the Banu Ghaniya continued the struggle against the victorious ALMOHADS, at times controlling large areas of the eastern MAGHRIB until finally defeated early in the next century. (50b)

Banu Qasim Rulers of ALPUENTE, one of the 11th century REYES de TAIFAS states in Spain. (48d)

Banu Qitada A branch of the Hashimid dynasty of MECCA, rulers in the HIJAZ from the beginning of the 13th century until the SA'UDI conquest in 1924. See HASHIMIDS/HASHEMITES.

Banu Sumadih Rulers of ALMERIA, Spain, one of the 11th century REYES DE TAIFAS states. (48e)

Banu Yahya Rulers of NIEBLA, Spain, one of the 11th century REYES DE TAIFAS states. Their kingdom was annexed by the 'ABBADIDS. (48f)

Bar (-le-Duc) Town in north-eastern France, centre of a feudal county of the same name from the 10th century, a duchy from 1355, inherited by the house of LORRAINE in the early 15th century and united with the latter duchy. (24g)

Barakzai dynasty Afghan family which contested the throne of AFGHANISTAN with their relatives the DURRANIS during the early 19th century and ultimately prevailed, ruling that state until the abolition of the monarchy in 1973. (197f)

Barcelona Spanish city, capital of Catalonia and of a powerful independent county in the 9th/12th centuries. Its ruling family acquired the throne of ARAGON by marriage and the two states were united in 1162. (47c)

Barid Shahis Sultans of BIDAR, one of the five DECCAN SULTANATES which partitioned the BAHMANID state. Bidar represented what was left of the Bahmanid territory after the secession of the other four sultanates, and the Barid Shahis ruled at first in the name of puppets of the old dynasty, but later dispensed with them. The state was annexed by BIJAPUR in 1619. (217k)

Baroda MARATHA state in GUJARAT, India, founded by Pilaji GAEKWAR in the early 18th century and ruled by his dynasty until its absorption into the Republic of India in 1949. (208g)

Barotse/Barotseland See LOZI.

Basutos/Basutoland See LESOTHO.

Bathory family Princes of TRANSYLVANIA 1571–1613 with interruptions. The greatest of the dynasty was Stephen Bathory, also king of POLAND. (76)

Battiads Greek kings of CYRENE in Libya, descended from the founder of the city in the 7th century BC. Their kingdom was taken over by a republican regime in 439 BC. (105)

Bauchi Amirate in northern Nigeria, one of the FULANI states, founded in the early 19th century by a lieutenant of the first of the SOKOTO rulers. (118c)

Bavandids Iranian dynasty of MAZANDARAN, founded on the fall of the SASANID empire and at first hostile to Islam, but soon converted. They survived with varying fortunes for some six centuries. In the mid-14th century, most of their territory fell into the hands of the SAYYIDS. (189a)

Bavaria Large region of southern Germany and for most of its history an independent or semi-independent duchy or kingdom. Ruled by the AGILULFINGS from the 6th century until conquered by the CAROLINGIAN Charlemagne, later under dukes of various families, including the WELFS. In 1180 it came under the rule of the WITTELSBACHS, becoming an ELECTORATE in 1623 and a kingdom in 1806. It was part of the German Empire in the later 19th century, and the kingdom was abolished with the other German states in 1918. (38)

Begtiginids ATABEG dynasty of IRBIL (ancient Arbela) in northern 'Iraq in the 12th/13th centuries. The last of the family bequeathed his lands to the 'ABBASID Caliph. (185k)

Belgium Modern kingdom deriving its name from ancient Belgic Gaul but known during most of its history as the southern Netherlands. Its various provinces, BRABANT, FLANDERS, HAINAULT, LIMBURG, etc., were counties and duchies in medieval times, mostly under the suzerainty of the German emperors, and were united by the VALOIS duke of BURGUNDY, whose HABSBURG heirs ruled the entire Netherlands until the 16th century Dutch revolt and the southern region (the 'Austrian' Netherlands of the 18th century) until Napoleonic times. In 1814, north and south were united as a kingdom under the ORANGE dynasty, but the south revolted in 1830 and became an independent state under kings of the COBURG family, a branch of the WETTINS. (20)

Benevento Ancient Maleventum, a Samnite city of southern Italy, renamed Beneventum by the Romans. Capital of a powerful LOMBARD duchy from the late 6th century, soon virtually independent of the Lombard kings. In the mid-9th century it split into three states, a smaller duchy and the principalities of CAPUA and SALERNO. The duchy, much reduced in size and importance, was annexed to the PAPAL STATES in 1077. (68b)

Bengal Large region of north-eastern India, the eastern area now constituting the independent state of Bangladesh. Bengal formed part of the early MAURYA and GUPTA empires, and was then ruled by various independent dynasties, particularly the PALAS and SENAS. It was conquered by the first sultans of DELHI, but formed a separate state from the late 13th century under various families, the most durable line being the ILYAS SHAHIS. Conquered by the MOGHULS in 1576, Bengal became virtually independent again in the early 18th century under its Moghul viceroys (Nawabs) until effective British control was established after the battle of Plassey in 1757. It was annexed by Britain in 1770 and partitioned between India and Pakistan in 1947. (214)

Benin Name of a former kingdom now part of Nigeria, and also the name recently adopted by the modern state previously called DAHOMEY. The historic kingdom was founded at about the end of the 12th century AD and became a powerful, well-organized state. It was conquered by the British in 1897, but is still nominally in existence, though its kings have only a ceremonial role. (121a)

Berar City and province in India, one of the DECCAN SULTANATES founded at the end of the 15th century, ruled by the 'IMAD SHAHIS, conquered by AHMADNAGAR in 1572. (217j)

Berg Feudal county in north-western Germany from the early 12th century, duchy 1380. Its ruler inherited JULICH in the early 15th century, and Berg was thereafter united with Julich, and later with CLEVES and MARK. In the time of Napoleon, his brother-in-law Joachim Murat, later king of NAPLES, reigned briefly as Grand Duke of Berg and Cleves. (39c)

Bernadotte dynasty Present royal house of SWEDEN, descended from Napoleon's marshal Jean Bernadotte, a Frenchman elected Crown Prince of Sweden in 1810 – he succeeded as King Karl XIV in 1818. (18g)

Bernicia Early Anglo-Saxon kingdom in Northumberland and south-eastern Scotland, traditionally founded in 547 AD but soon united with DEIRA to form the kingdom of NORTHUMBRIA. (5f)

Bethlen family One of the several families which provided princes of

TRANSYLVANIA during the 17th century. (76)

Bharatpur State in RAJASTAN, India, founded by Jat rebels against the MOGHUL empire in the early 18th century, absorbed into the Republic of India in 1948. (206h)

Bhati dynasty RAJPUT rulers of JAISALMER state in RAJASTAN. The state was founded in the late 12th century AD. It is now part of the Republic of India. (206g)

Bhonsla MARATHA clan to which belonged Shivaji, founder of the Maratha empire and rebel against Muslim rule in the DECCAN in the late 17th century. His descendants, known as the Rajas of SATARA, soon lost real power to their ministers, the PESHWAS, but remained nominal heads of the Maratha federation. When the lands of the Peshwa were annexed by the British, the Satara Rajas were allowed to retain possession of a small territory, which was also annexed in 1848. Another branch of the family ruled KOLHAPUR until 1949 and a third branch, established at TANJORE by a brother of Shivaji, survived until 1855. The Maratha state of NAGPUR was also ruled by a Bhonsla dynasty, not related to Shivaji's line. (217m–o, 223f)

Bhopal State in MALWA region of India, established on the collapse of the MOGHUL empire in the early 18th century by a Muslim adventurer who took the title of Nawab. It came under British protection in the early 19th century, and was ruled by several successive females (Begums) over most of the hundred years up to 1926. It was absorbed into the Republic of India in 1948. (207g)

Bhutan Himalayan state which was jointly controlled by a spiritual and a temporal ruler until 1907 – since that date it has been ruled by kings of the WANGCHUK dynasty. (213)

Bidar City and kingdom in India, one of the DECCAN SULTANATES, ruled by the BARID SHAHIS from 1492, annexed by BIJAPUR in 1619. (217k)

Bijapur City and kingdom in India, one of the DECCAN SULTANATES founded on the fall of the BAHMANIDS, ruled by the 'ADIL SHAHIS from 1490 until MOGHUL conquest of their state in 1686 – by which time the rebel MARATHAS controlled much of their territory. (217l)

Bikanir State in northern RAJASTAN, founded in 1465 by a prince of the RATHOR dynasty of MARWAR (Jodhpur), absorbed into the Republic of India with the other princely states in 1949. (206c)

Bithynia Ancient kingdom in north-western Asia Minor. The Bithynians were migrants from THRACE, a warlike people who established their autonomy under the later ACHAEMENIDS in the 4th century BC and contrived to gain complete inde-pendence during the wars of the DIADOCHI, their chief taking the royal title *c*.297. The state became a client-kingdom of ROME in the 2nd century and was annexed by the Romans in 75 BC. (137b)

Blois Feudal county in France from the 10th century, its early history and ruling family being closely connected with those of CHAMPAGNE. United by purchase with the duchy of ORLEANS in 1391. (24e)

Bohemia Region of Central Europe, now the main component part of CZECHOSLO-VAKIA, established as a duchy under the PREMYSLID dynasty in the 9th century and soon combined with MORAVIA to form a strong Slav state under the suzerainty of the HOLY ROMAN EMPIRE. Bohemia became a kingdom in 1198, and on the extinction of the Premyslids in 1306 passed to other families, including the LUXEMBURGS and the JAGIELLONS. The kingdom was in-herited by the HABSBURGS in 1526 and remained part of their domains until the break-up of their empire in 1918. (69)

Bonaparte family Napoleon I, Emperor of the French, and his relatives, Corsicans by origin. During his domination of most of Europe at the beginning of the 19th century, Napoleon placed various members of his family on existing or created thrones, though they rarely ex-ercised any real power and fell with Napoleon himself, who ruled France as Emperor 1804–1814 and briefly in 1815. His nephew later ruled as Napoleon III until 1870. Other relatives reigned in HOLLAND 1806–1810, WESTPHALIA 1807–1813, SPAIN 1808–1814, NAPLES 1806–1815, and TUSCANY 1808–1814. Napoleon's

HABSBURG wife ruled PARMA 1814–1847. (19c, 22b, 33g, 53b, 62f, 64b, 65c)

Borneo See BRUNEI and SARAWAK.

Bornu See KANEM-BORNU.

Bosnia Region of YUGOSLAVIA, ruled by Slav Bans from the 12th century, usually under the overlordship of HUNGARY. Bosnia broke away from the control of Hungary to become an independent kingdom in the 14th century, but was conquered by the OSMANLI Turks in 1463. (73)

Bosphorus Kingdom of (Cimmerian) Bosphorus, an ancient state centred on the Straits of Kerch and the eastern CRIMEA, ruled by successive dynasties from the 5th century BC. After the fall of the MITHRIDA-TIDS, it became a client-state of ROME under the ASPURGIDS, and vanished during the troubles of the 4th century AD. (90)

Bourbon duchy Feudal state in France, ruled by branch of the CAPETS from 1327, forfeited to crown 1523. A junior Bourbon line inherited the French throne in 1589 – see Bourbon dynasty below. (24k)

Bourbon dynasty A branch of the CAPET family, descended from a brother of St Louis IX of FRANCE, dukes of Bourbon 1327–1523. A junior line acquired NAVARRE by marriage and in 1589 the king of Navarre, the nearest heir of the VALOIS in the male line, succeeded to the French throne as Henry IV – his descendants ruled France until the revolution of 1789 and again during 1814–1848 (see also ORLEANS). A branch of the family has ruled SPAIN with interruptions since 1700, the Spanish line providing kings of NAPLES and SICILY and dukes of PARMA (see also ETRURIA) in the 18th/19th centuries. (22b, 24k, 53, 62f, 64b, 65d)

Brabant Province of BELGIUM, medieval duchy originally called Lower Lorraine, separated from (Upper) LORRAINE in the 10th century. It was acquired by the VALOIS dukes of BURGUNDY in 1430 and inherited later by the HABSBURGS. A branch of the early Brabant dynasty ruled HESSE from the 13th century to 1918. (20a)

Braganza dynasty In 1640, PORTUGAL revolted against the rule of the Spanish

HABSBURGS under John, Duke of Braganza, illegitimately descended from the AVIZ kings. The new dynasty ruled in Portugal until the abolition of the monarchy in 1910, its last members being in fact WETTINS in the male line. During most of the 19th century, a branch of the family ruled independently in BRAZIL. (54d, 253)

Brandenburg Region of north-eastern Germany conquered from the Slavs in the 11th century and established as a margravate in the German empire. It was ruled by the ASCANIANS and then by the WITTELSBACHS and LUXEMBURGS before its acquisition as an ELECTORATE by Frederick of HOHENZOLLERN, Burgrave of Nuremberg, in 1415. It remained the core of the Hohenzollern domains when they became kings of PRUSSIA and finally German Emperors. (27)

Brankovichi Family which ruled briefly as princes of SERBIA in the 15th century, just prior to the OSMANLI Turkish annexation of the state. (72b)

Brazil Discovered by the Portuguese in 1500 and gradually settled as a possession of the kings of PORTUGAL. In 1807 the BRAGANZA family took refuge there from Napoleon, and the Crown Prince remained in Brazil as regent after their return to Europe. In 1822 he was installed as independent emperor of Brazil – his successor was deposed in 1889 and the country became a republic. (253)

Brienne family Counts of Brienne in north-eastern France, who provided a king of JERUSALEM and LATIN EMPEROR (John of Brienne, d.1237) and a duke of ATHENS (Walter of Brienne, killed in battle by the GRAND CATALAN COMPANY in 1311).

Britain See GREAT BRITAIN and UNITED KINGDOM.

Brittany Ancient Armorica, settled in the 5th/6th centuries AD by Celtic migrants from Britain and virtually independent of the rulers of France in early medieval times under Breton counts. The province was ruled briefly by the ANGEVINS in the late 12th century, and then by the DREUX branch of the CAPETS (Dukes from 1297) until united with the French crown by marriage at the end of the 15th century. (24b)

Brooke English family which ruled as Rajas of Sarawak in Borneo 1841–1946. See SARAWAK. (247b)

Bruce family Anglo-Norman family with branches in Yorkshire and SCOTLAND which acquired a claim to the Scottish throne by marriage. At the beginning of the 14th century, Robert Bruce established himself as king of Scotland after a long struggle with the English, his son being succeeded in 1371 by the related STUARTS. (11b)

Brunei (i.e. Borneo), name of a city and a sultanate in northern Borneo. The state was established in the early 15th century and at the height of its power controlled much of the island, but had considerably weakened by the mid-19th century, when SARAWAK broke away, and later became a British protectorate, which it still is. (247a)

Brunswick (Braunschweig), city and region of north-western Germany. It was part of the early duchy of SAXONY, but was created a separate duchy in 1235 for the WELFS, dispossessed of Saxony in 1180. In later centuries it was much subdivided among various branches of the dynasty, until most of the Welf lands were united in the 17th century to form the ELECTORATE of HANOVER. The remainder became the duchy of Brunswick (-Wolfenbuttel) in 1735, abolished in 1918. (33e–f)

Buganda Kingdom in Uganda, Africa, founded in the 15th century, at first a minor power. It became the dominant state in the region in the 19th century, and a British protectorate in 1893, its monarchy being abolished by independent Uganda in 1967. (128)

Bugis A sea-going people from Celebes who gained control over several of the sultanates of MALAYA in the 18th century, under the leadership of five brothers, contesting the Dutch control of MALACCA. Their most permanent achievement was the establishment of a Bugis sultanate in SELANGOR.

Bukhara Ancient city of TRANSOXANIA (now in the Uzbekistan republic of the U.S.S.R.). Capital of the western QARA-

KHANIDS and later important under the SHAIBANIDS and JANIDS. Khanate under the HAIDARIDS from the late 18th century, reduced to vassal status in 1868 by the Russians, who abolished the state in 1920. (198b, i–j)

Bulgaria The Bulgars after whom the modern state is named were originally a Turko-Mongol nomadic people, perhaps connected with the earlier HUNS, who ruled a khanate in the Ukrainian steppe-lands in the 7th century AD (see GREAT BULGARIA). On the break-up of that state, a section of the Bulgar horde moved to the region of the Lower Danube and established a new khanate which became a powerful and extensive empire controlling much of what are now Bulgaria and Rumania, reaching the zenith of its importance under the KRUM dynasty in the 9th/10th centuries. The lands north of the Danube were lost to other nomads while the Bulgars were gradually absorbed by their Slav subjects. Late in the 10th century, Bulgaria was overrun by Sviatoslav of KIEV and then annexed by BYZANTIUM, though a Bulgarian kingdom survived in Macedonia until 1018. Some two hundred years later, independence was regained under the ASEN family, who once again raised Bulgaria to major power in the Balkans. However, the kingdom was reduced to vassalage by the GOLDEN HORDE in the 13th century and conquered by the OSMANLI Turks at the end of the following century. In 1879, under the pressure of the European Powers, a Bulgarian principality was established, later an independent kingdom ruled by the COBURG dynasty (from 1887). Its monarchy was abolished in 1946. (80)

Bundelkhand An area in Madhya Pradesh, India, centre of a powerful Hindu kingdom in the 11th century AD under the CHANDELLA dynasty. Their power was broken by the early sultans of DELHI in the 13th century. (204b)

Bundi State in RAJASTAN, India, founded in the 14th century and ruled by the CHAUHAN dynasty – its dominions were much reduced in the early 17th century by the break-away of KOTAH under a branch of the family. It was absorbed into the Republic of India in 1949. (206e)

Bunyoro Kingdom in Uganda under the BABITO dynasty, who succeeded the legendary Chwezi kings of Kitara in the 15th century. Bunyoro was for long the dominant state in the region, until over-shadowed by BUGANDA in the 19th century. It became a British protectorate in 1896 and was abolished by independent Uganda in 1967. (126)

Burgundy A region of eastern France settled in the 5th century AD by the Burgundians, a Germanic people who established a kingdom which was conquered by the Franks in the 6th century. In the late 9th century, on the disintegration of the CAROLINGIAN empire, the region east of the Saone became the centre of a new kingdom of Burgundy extending southwards to include PROVENCE, the later 'Kingdom of Arles', which was acquired by the HOLY ROMAN EMPERORS in 1032. Eastern Burgundy then became the Free County of Burgundy (Franche Comté). Western Burgundy remained part of the French kingdom as a duchy under a branch of the CAPETS, succeeded in the mid-14th century by a branch of the VALOIS. The Franche Comté was ruled by various families, including members of the HOHENSTAUFFEN, until it too was acquired by the Valois dukes in 1405. Under these latter rulers, Burgundy became an important power in Western Europe, their state incorporating most of the NETHERLANDS. On the extinction of their male line in 1477, Franche Comté was obtained by the HABSBURGS and the Burgundian duchy by France. (23, 24i–j)

Burids ATABEG dynasty of DAMASCUS during the first half of the 12th century in succession to the Syrian SELJUKS. Its lands were annexed by the ZANGIDS of Aleppo in 1154. (166d)

Burji Mamluks See MAMLUKS.

Burma A strong kingdom based at PAGAN appeared in upper Burma in the mid-11th century AD and soon conquered the MON region of the south. This state was destroyed by MONGOL invasion and the Mons of PEGU became independent, while upper Burma was overrun by the SHANS – two short-lived Shan kingdoms were combined under the AVA rulers, who controlled the north until the mid-16th century. The country was re-united by the TOUNGOO dynasty and that family was succeeded in the mid-18th century by the dynasty of ALAUNGPAYA, both lines of rulers being powerful monarchs who made repeated efforts to subdue the states of THAILAND. The last Burmese kings came into conflict with the British, who annexed ARAKAN in 1826, southern Burma in 1852 and the remainder of the kingdom in 1885. (237)

Burundi Central African state, formerly a kingdom from the late 17th century. In the late 19th century it came under the control of Germany and later that of Belgium. Following independence in 1962, its TUTSI monarchy was abolished in 1966. (129b)

Buyids (Buwayhids), family from DAYLAM, originally military adventurers, who rose to power in Iran and 'Iraq in the mid-10th century, reducing the 'ABBASID Caliphs at Baghdad to puppets. The three brothers who founded the dynasty were succeeded by various descendants who ruled jointly in the different provinces of the state, usually recognizing the supremacy of one of their number. In the mid-11th century, their lands were conquered and their position as puppet-masters of the Caliphs taken over by the SELJUKS. (187e)

Byzantium Original name of Constantinople, modern Istanbul, a Greek colonial city founded in the 7th century BC, but also the most usual name for the later Eastern Roman Empire, which survived the western section by more than a thousand years after the final division at the end of the 4th century AD (see ROME). The Byzantine emperors temporarily recovered Italy and North Africa in the 6th century but soon lost most of Italy to the LOMBARDS and all the North African provinces plus Syria to the Muslim Arabs. From the 7th to the 11th century, Byzantium was the strongest and most civilized European power, controlling the Balkan region and Asia Minor until the disastrous battle of Manzikert in 1071, as a result of which large parts of the interior of Asia Minor were lost to the SELJUKS. A century later, BULGARIA rose in revolt,

and in 1204 Constantinople itself fell to the Fourth Crusade, together with much of Greece (see CRUSADER STATES (2)). The Byzantines resisted in a number of areas – see TREBIZOND, EPIRUS, THESSALONICA, NICAEA – and in 1261 the short-lived LATIN EMPIRE was suppressed by the Nicaean emperors, who recovered Constantinople. However, the last dynasty of Byzantium, the PALAEOLOGI, ruled a small and ever-shrinking remnant of the empire, finally reduced to the capital alone, being surrounded by the sultanate of the OSMANLI Turks, who took the city in 1453. For other Byzantine dynasties, see MACEDONIANS, COMNENI, DUCAS, ANGELI. (1c–f)

C

Calicut (Kozhikode), port in northern KERALA, India, capital of an important state from about the 12th century AD under rulers with the title of Zamorin. Many of their names and some of their dates are unknown. At the zenith of their power, the Zamorins ruled much of northern Kerala, beating off Portuguese and Dutch attacks, but their state was virtually destroyed by Tipu Sultan of MYSORE in 1788, though nominal Zamorins continued to reign in Calicut until the present century.

Caliphate/Caliphs From Arabic 'Khalifah' (successor, i.e. of Muhammad the Prophet), originally the head of the whole Muslim world. From the death of Muhammad in 632 AD there was disagreement concerning the succession to this office, though unity was maintained under the ORTHODOX Caliphs and the UMAYYAD dynasty of Damascus (see SUNNI and SHI'A). The 'ABBASIDS, successful rebels against the Umayyads, took over the Muslim dominions more or less intact but could not hold the remoter provinces, losing SPAIN at once to an Umayyad counter-rebellion and other regions within a few decades. The early independent Muslim rulers hesitated to claim the Caliphal title, but the FATIMIDS, whose movement was an open campaign to supplant the 'Abbasids entirely, called themselves Caliphs from their first successes in 909, and the Spanish Umayyads followed their example in 929. The continuing collapse of 'Abbasid power encouraged other rulers to adopt Caliphal functions and sometimes the title too, though the 'Abbasids at Baghdad were generally recognized until the MONGOLS extinguished their Caliphate in 1258. The MAMLUKS maintained puppet 'Abbasids at Cairo, and the OSMANLI Turkish Sultans claimed the title, little recognized outside their own domains. (135, 101, 103C, 44)

Cambodia (Kampuchea), state in Indo-China. A kingdom called Fu-Nan by the Chinese existed in this area from at least the 1st century AD, and was succeeded in the 6th century by the Cambodian monarchy, a Hindu state which reached its zenith under the Angkor kings between *c.*800 and the 13th century, controlling much of what is now THAILAND and southern VIET-NAM. In later centuries, the kingdom came under heavy attack by its Thai and Vietnamese neighbours and was saved from extinction only by the establishment of a French protectorate in

1864. Formal independence was recovered in 1955, and the monarchy lapsed in 1960, to be abolished in 1970. (241)

Canmore dynasty Kings of Scotland 1058–1290, Malcolm III Canmore and his descendants. Malcolm III was the son of Duncan I of Dunkeld, and Duncan plus his successors to 1290 are alternatively (and more tidily) known as the House of Dunkeld. By Canmore's marriage to St Margaret of Wessex, the later Scottish kings were also descended from the Saxon kings of England. They were ultimately succeeded by the Bruce family after a determined English effort to conquer the country. (11a)

Cannanore Port in northern KERALA, ruled from medieval times by the 'ALI RAJA dynasty, Rajas of a small principality on the coast and overlords of the Laccadive Islands until the late 19th century. (220e)

Capet dynasty Family which ruled FRANCE in the main line and then in its VALOIS and BOURBON branches from the 10th to the 19th century. King Hugh,

THE CAPET DYNASTY OF FRANCE
AND ITS DESCENDANTS IN THE MALE LINE

Robert the Strong, Margrave of Neustria, d.866

Hugh Capet, King of France, d.996

Capet Kings of France 987–1328

Latin Emperors of Constantinople 1216–1261	Counts and Dukes of Brittany 1213–1488	Capet Dukes of Burgundy 1032–1361	Dukes of Bourbon
Valois Kings of France 1328–1589	Angevin Kings of Naples and Hungary Counts of Anjou and Provence 13th/14th centuries	Kings of Portugal 1139–1580	Bourbon Kings of France 1589–1848
		Dukes of Braganza	
Valois Dukes of Burgundy 1363–1477	Dukes of Orleans 1344–1498	Dukes of Anjou and Counts of Provence 1360–1481	Bourbon Kings of Spain since 1700

Braganza Kings of Portugal 1640–1826

Braganza Emperors of Brazil 1822–1889

Bourbon Kings of Naples and Sicily 1734–1860

Bourbon Dukes of Parma 1731–1859 and Kings of Etruria 1801–1807

surnamed Capet, who succeeded the last CAROLINGIAN in 987, was in fact the third of his family to occupy the throne. The Dukes of BURGUNDY 1032–1361, the ANGEVINS (2), the rulers of BRITTANY from 1213 (see DREUX family) and the early kings of PORTUGAL to 1580 were also branches of the main Capet line, and various other ruling families descend in the male line via Valois and Bourbon, including the present king of Spain. (22)

Cappadocia Ancient name for the eastern part of the central plateau of ASIA MINOR, originally including the northern coastal region called Pontic Cappadocia and later simply PONTUS. The area became autonomous under the ARIARATHID family within the later ACHAEMENID empire, and inland Cappadocia established its independence as a kingdom under the same dynasty during the struggles of the DIADOCHI. It became a client state of ROME and was annexed by the empire in 17 AD. (137c)

Capua Ancient city of southern Italy, capital of a medieval LOMBARD principality which broke away from the Duchy of BENEVENTO in 840, though its princes also ruled the duchy 900–982. Capua was acquired by the Norman counts of Aversa in 1058, and annexed to the HAUTEVILLE domains in 1156. (67d)

Carinthia Region of Austria, medieval margravate and later duchy, acquired by the HABSBURGS in 1335 and thereafter united with the Austrian lands of that dynasty. (40b)

Carnatic The eastern coastal region of southern India, in ancient times divided between the kingdoms of the CHOLAS (in the north) and the PANDYAS (in the south). It was controlled by the PALLAVA rulers in the 7th/9th centuries AD and then formed the centre of the great Chola empire until the mid-13th century, though a revived Pandya state emerged in the south c.1190. The Carnatic was briefly overrun by the ruler of DELHI at the beginning of the 14th century, but his viceroys at MADURAI soon became independent rulers. The whole region was absorbed into the VIJAYANAGAR empire later in the same century, and on the break-up of that state in the late 16th century was divided among various rulers, including the sultans of GOLKUNDA and the NAYYAK dynasties of Madurai and TANJORE. On the MOGHUL conquest of Golkunda, Nawabs of the Carnatic were established with their capital at ARCOT. The region came under British control in the late 18th century. (223)

Carolingians Family so named from Charlemagne (Carolus Magnus), whose ancestors ruled the kingdom of the FRANKS in fact from the late 7th century AD as Mayors of the Palace to the later MEROVINGIANS and formally as kings from 751. Under Charlemagne, Frankish rule was extended over much of Western Europe, his empire including France, western Germany, the Netherlands and much of Italy and Austria. The long-defunct Western Roman Empire was revived on his behalf in 800, developing into the HOLY ROMAN EMPIRE of later centuries, but after his death the Carolingian dominions were repeatedly divided between his descendants. Gradually the French, Italian and German components became separate states, other families replacing the dynasty, which was supplanted in France, its last domain (in 987) by the CAPET family. (3b)

Carraresi (Da Carrara), a family which ruled as lords of PADUA, Italy, during most of the 14th century. The city fell to VENICE in 1405. (67f)

Carthage (Kart Hadasht, 'new city'), ancient colonial city founded by the Phoenicians of TYRE and located near modern Tunis. Established about 800 BC, it became the centre of an extensive maritime empire in North Africa and the Western Mediterranean islands. Ruled by kings in its early days, it was a republic in later centuries. Having lost Sicily to ROME in the First Punic War, the Carthaginians then conquered much of Spain through the efforts of the semi-royal family of the Barcids, to which Hannibal belonged. These domains too were lost to Rome after the long and hard-fought Second Punic War, and the remaining territory was annexed by the Romans on the destruction of Carthage in 146 BC.

Cashel Town in Ireland, one of the main strongholds of the EOGANACHT and O'BRIEN kings of MUNSTER, often called kings of 'Cashel and Munster'. (14a)

Cassel (Kassel), town in north-western Germany. On the division of the Landgravate of HESSE into two states in 1567, it became the centre of Hesse-Cassel (from 1803 the ELECTORATE of Hesse), annexed by PRUSSIA in 1866. (See also DARMSTADT) (34c)

Castile Large region of SPAIN, formerly a kingdom. In the early 10th century, Castile was established as a border-county of LEON, around Burgos, and passed by inheritance to Sancho (III) the Great of NAVARRE, under whose son Ferdinand it became a kingdom which soon absorbed Leon (1037). Thereafter, Castile-Leon became the most extensive of the Christian kingdoms in Spain, taking a leading part in the conquest of the Muslim south. In 1479 Castile and ARAGON were brought under combined control by the marriage of Isabella of Castile to Ferdinand II of Aragon, and both kingdoms, constituting modern Spain, were inherited in 1516 by the HABSBURG heir, later Emperor Charles V. (51)

Catalonia Region of north-eastern Spain, virtually an independent state under the Counts of BARCELONA from the 9th century until its union with ARAGON in the mid-12th century. (47c)

Central African Empire Previously the French colonial territory of Ubangi-Shari, independent as a republic in 1960 but in 1976 proclaimed an empire under Emperor (Jean) Bokassa, who was overthrown in 1979, since when the state has again been a republic.

Cephalonia (Kefallinia), Ionian island conquered by the Normans of SICILY from BYZANTIUM in the late 12th century and ruled as a county (with Zante and Ithaca) by the ORSINI and later the TOCCO families until it came under the control of VENICE in the late 15th century. (85b)

Ceylon (Sri Lanka) The origins of the early kingdom in Ceylon are legendary, but an important state was established in the island from at least the 3rd century BC, ruled by various successive families, though the extent of their territory varied and rarely included the entire island. The kingdom was repeatedly attacked by invaders from southern India, and particularly by the CHOLAS in the 10th/11th centuries. An independent TAMIL state existed at JAFFNA in the north in medieval times, and when the Portuguese arrived in the early 16th century, the island was divided among several rulers – see KOTTE, SITAWAKE, KANDY. By the end of that century, most of Ceylon was under the control of the Portuguese, later passing to the Dutch and then the British – only the mountain kingdom of Kandy remained independent, until annexed by the British in 1815. (224)

Chach dynasty Hindu kings of Sind in the 7th/8th centuries AD, successors of an earlier and obscure Buddhist dynasty. The last Chach ruler was overthrown by Muslim invaders and his lands annexed to the UMAYYAD empire. (205a)

Chaghatai dynasty Descendants of Chaghatai (Jaghatai), a son of Chingis Khan, rulers of TRANSOXANIA and TURKESTAN from the early 13th centuries. They were reduced to puppets and then supplanted by the TIMURIDS in their western lands at the end of the following century, but a branch of the dynasty survived in ZUNGARIA into the 16th century. See also CHINGIS-KHANIDS. (198 d–e)

Chak family Sultans of KASHMIR in the 16th century. The dynasty was established by Ghazi Khan Chak, who dethroned the last SWATI ruler. Kashmir was conquered by the MOGHULS in 1589. (209e)

Chakri dynasty Present ruling family of THAILAND. In 1767 the country was overrun by the Burmese, who took and destroyed its historic capital AYUTHIA. The invaders were expelled and order restored by P'ya Taksin, a general who proclaimed himself king but became insane and was deposed in 1782 by Rama I, founder of the Chakri line. In the 19th century, the family produced several very able monarchs, who contrived to maintain Thai independence and to consolidate their control of the northern part of the

Malay Peninsula, though their efforts to gain overlordship of CAMBODIA were thwarted by the French. Thailand was occupied by the Japanese during the Second World War but resumed independence in 1945. (239d)

Chaldaea Originally the coastal area at the head of the Persian Gulf, a centre of Babylonian resistance to ASSYRIA, but the name was later used to signify the entire realm of the rulers of BABYLON.

Chalukyas Three related dynasties of the DECCAN:

1 Chalukyas of Badami (Early Chalukyas), rulers of an extensive kingdom in the western Deccan in the 6th to 8th centuries. They were supplanted by the RASHTRAKUTAS. (217c)

2 Chalukyas of Kalyana (Later Chalukyas), descended from the Early Chalukyas, who overthrew the Rashtrakutas in the late 10th century and re-established Chalukya rule in the western Deccan. They were temporarily dethroned by the KALACHURIS, and their kingdom finally collapsed at the end of the 12th century, giving way to the YADAVAS in the north and the HOYSALAS in the south. (217e)

3 Chalukyas of VENGI (Eastern Chalukyas), branch of the Early Chalukyas who became independent in the ANDHRA region, ruling a small kingdom eventually combined through marriage with the CHOLA crown in the 11th century. (218d)

Champa Strongly Indianized kingdom in what is now central VIET-NAM from at least the 2nd century AD, an important maritime power often at war with the Vietnamese state, to the southern expansion of which it formed an impassable barrier until conquered by the Later LE rulers in the mid-15th century. Vijaya, the Cham capital, is now Binh-Dinh. (242)

Champagne Region of northern France, a feudal county from the 10th century. Its counts were closely related to the rulers of BLOIS. In 1234 they inherited the crown of NAVARRE. Their county passed to the French crown by marriage at the end of the 13th century. (24d)

Chandellas RAJPUT dynasty of BUNDEL-KHAND, in central India, in the 9th/12th centuries an important power after the fall of the PRATIHARAS in the north. They sank into obscurity on the establishment of the DELHI sultanate. (204b)

Chandra dynasty An early ruling family of ARAKAN in the 8th/11th centuries AD. (238a)

Chao Name of an ancient state and several later dynasties in China:

1 One of the three states into which the earlier realm of CHIN, one of the CHOU STATES, was divided at the end of the 5th century BC. Chao was conquered by the founder of the imperial CH'IN dynasty in 228 BC. It was located in what is now northern Honan. (228l)

2 Chao dynasty of NAN-YUEH, based on Canton, founded by a rebel governor on the collapse of the CH'IN empire in 207 BC. Annexed by the Western HAN empire in 111 BC. Chao rule extended into TONKIN and it is also regarded as an early dynasty of VIET-NAM under the Vietnamese version of the name, TRIEU. (228q)

3 Earlier Chao (or Northern Han), one of the SIXTEEN KINGDOMS of the 4th century AD, founded by the last ruler of the southern HSIUNG-NU in Shansi province. Their state was conquered by the Later Chao. (230a)

4 Later Chao, another of the SIXTEEN KINGDOMS dynasties, also based in Shansi province and of HSIUNG-NU origin. Overthrown by the Earlier YEN in 352 AD. (230d)

Chauhans (Chahamanas), RAJPUT clan which ruled several small states in Rajastan in medieval times and led resistance to the Muslim GHURID invaders under Prithviraja of Ajmer, killed in battle in 1192. In the 14th century, a branch of the clan established the state of BUNDI, from which KOTAH broke away in 1625. Both these states are now part of the Republic of India. (206e–f)

Chaulukyas (Solankis), rulers of GUJARAT from the mid-10th century until the mid-13th century, when they were succeeded by the VAGHELAS. (208b)

Ch'en Name of an ancient state and a later dynasty in CHINA:

1 One of the CHOU STATES, founded in the 9th century BC in Honan. It was conquered by CH'U in 479 BC. (228d)

2 Southern Ch'en dynasty, short-lived imperial dynasty of southern China in the later 6th century AD, overthrown by the founder of the SUI dynasty, who thus reunited China after centuries of division. (227m)

Cheng One of the CHOU STATES in China, 8th/4th centuries BC, in Honan. It was conquered by HAN state in 375 BC. (228f)

Ch'eng-Han One of the SIXTEEN KINGDOMS of the 4th century AD in China, centred in Szechuan. It broke away from the Western CHIN empire but was reconquered by the Eastern Chin in 347. Its ruling dynasty was Tibetan in origin. (230b)

Cheras Ancient people of southern India, see KERALA.

Chernigov Russian city, centre of one of the RIURIKID principalities from the division of the KIEV state in 1054, at first important until the rise of GALICIA and SUZDAL-VLADIMIR. The state was destroyed by the MONGOL invasion of the mid-13th century. (92f)

Ch'i Name of an ancient state and two later dynasties in CHINA:
1 One of the CHOU STATES, in northern Shantung region, conquered by the founder of the imperial CH'IN dynasty in 226 BC. (228h)
2 Southern Ch'i dynasty, imperial family in southern China at the end of the 5th century AD, successors of Earlier SUNG, supplanted by the Southern Liang II. (227k)
3 Northern Ch'i dynasty, successors of the Eastern WEI in north-east China in the 6th century AD, suppressed by Northern CHOU. (232b)

Chiang Mai City in northern THAILAND and capital of a Thai kingdom of the same name founded in the late 13th century. Control of this state was long disputed between BURMA and AYUTHIA, the latter power ultimately absorbing Chiang Mai in the 16th century. (239b)

Chin Name of an ancient state and of several later dynasties in CHINA:
1 One of the CHOU STATES, in Shansi and Hopei provinces, eventually divided into three smaller kingdoms at the end of

the 4th century BC – WEI, HAN and CHAO ('The Three Chin'). (228i)
2 Western Chin, imperial dynasty of the 3rd/4th centuries AD which unified China after the THREE KINGDOMS period but soon lost the north to the SIXTEEN KINGDOMS. (227h)
3 Eastern Chin, virtually a direct continuation of the related Western Chin in southern China, overthrown by the Earlier SUNG. (227i)
4 Later Chin, one of the short-lived imperial dynasties of the 10th century AD between T'ANG and SUNG. (227r)
5 Later Chin (Manchu), original title adopted by the Manchu conquerors of China for their dynasty, soon changed to CH'ING.
6 Chin dynasty of the Juchen, 12th/13th centuries, ruling family of the powerful empire in northern China founded by the Juchen, a people closely related to the later Manchus. Originally subjects of the LIAO (Khitan) state, they supplanted their overlords. Their empire was one of the first victims of MONGOL attack, to which the Juchen put up a prolonged and determined resistance – the last Chin cities fell in 1234. (232f)

Ch'in Name of an ancient state and of several later dynasties in CHINA:
1 One of the CHOU STATES, established in the 9th century BC in north-western China. It developed into a strong military power in the 4th century and completed the conquest of the other surviving Chou States under its last ruler in 221 BC (see CHINA.) (228b)
2 Ch'in dynasty 221–206 BC, the first true imperial dynasty of China, founded by the king of Ch'in state on his conquest of all the other Chinese states – thus it is probable that the European name for his country comes from his dynasty. Shih Huang-Ti, the 'First Emperor' was overbearing and ruthless, and his empire collapsed on his death, to be replaced by the HAN regime. (227d)
3 Earlier Ch'in dynasty of the 4th century AD, one of the SIXTEEN KINGDOMS, founded by a family of Tibetan origin in Shensi province. One ruler of this dynasty, Fu Chien, conquered a large part of northern China, but his brief supremacy

was ended in 383, when the imperial Eastern CHIN defeated him on the Fei River. His family was supplanted by the Later Ch'in. (230g)

4 Later Ch'in, another of the SIXTEEN KINGDOM dynasties, also of Tibetan origin, which replaced the Earlier Ch'in in the late 4th century AD. Their state was re-annexed to the Chinese empire by the Eastern CHIN in 417. (230h)

5 Western Ch'in, a dynasty and state founded by the Hsien-Pi nomads in Kansu province, one of the SIXTEEN KINGDOMS, conquered by the Northern WEI in 431 AD. (230k)

China The earliest Chinese state for which there is historical evidence, that of the SHANG, arose in the plain of the Yellow River, amidst surrounding barbarian tribes which slowly absorbed Shang culture. Under their successors, the CHOU, many other states developed in northern and central China, some established as vassal states by the Chou rulers themselves and others recognizing Chou supremacy (see CHOU STATES). Over several centuries, Chou power declined to insignificance and warfare between the various states reduced their number until, in the 3rd century BC, the north-western realm of CH'IN conquered the other survivors, its ruler founding the Chinese empire as 'First Emperor' of the Ch'in dynasty in 221 BC. After a brief interval of confusion following his death, the HAN established a stable imperial regime which lasted four centuries (with the short interval of the HSIN dynasty). In the early 3rd century AD, their state broke into the THREE KINGDOMS, temporarily reunited by the Western CHIN, which soon lost the northern provinces to the various barbarian invaders who set up the SIXTEEN KINGDOMS, later consolidated into the Northern WEI empire. After nearly three centuries of north-south division, China was again united in 589 by the SUI founder, whose family was shortly afterwards succeeded by the most famous of all the Chinese dynasties, the T'ANG, who ruled from the early 7th century to the end of the 9th, their empire at the height of their power extending into large areas of Central Asia. On the collapse of the

T'ang, several short-lived dynasties ruled in the north in succession, while the TEN KINGDOMS arose in the south and elsewhere. Reunification was yet again achieved by the SUNG in the later 10th century, though the extreme north was lost to the LIAO state set up by the Khitan nomads, and the whole north to the CHIN empire of the Juchen, founded in the early 12th century. At the beginning of the next century, Chingis Khan began the long MONGOL struggle to conquer China – he and his successors had crushed the Chin state by 1234 and overcome the last Sung resistance by 1279, founding a new imperial dynasty, the YUAN and making China the centre of the great Mongol empire. However, widespread rebellion resulted in the expulsion of the Mongols by the MING founder in 1368, and this last native Chinese dynasty ruled for nearly three centuries before it too collapsed amid rebellion, opening the way to invasion from MANCHURIA. Under the CH'ING dynasty, rulers of the Manchus and conquerors of China in the mid-17th century, the Chinese empire reached the zenith of power and prosperity, absorbing TIBET and MONGOLIA plus large areas of Central Asia whilst exercising suzerainty over KOREA and VIET-NAM. In the later 19th century, internal disorder and European intervention weakened the Ch'ing, who were dethroned in 1912, the empire being replaced by a republic. Chinese emperors prior to the Ming are in most cases known to historians by the title posthumously given to them, their personal names being dropped on accession – the great second emperor of the T'ang, Li Shih-min before his accession, became (T'ang) T'ai Tsung. From HAN times it was customary for an emperor to take a reign-title – some rulers kept the same title for their whole reign and others changed it up to a dozen times. However, the Ming and Ch'ing emperors kept a single title and it became usual to refer to each ruler by his reign-name (given in brackets in the lists for these two dynasties only) – thus the founder of the Ming is 'The Hung Wu Emperor'. (227–234)

Ch'ing Last imperial dynasty of China 1616–1912, founded by rulers of the

THE DYNASTIES OF CHINA

Hsia (legendary/mythical)			
Shang (Yin) *c.*1766–1122 BC			
Western Chou *c.*1122–771 BC. Overlords of the Chou States			
Eastern Chou 770–249 BC. Nominal overlords of the Chou States, the stronger of which gradually annex the weaker until the final victory of Ch'in.			
Ch'in Dynasty 221–206 BC			

Western Han 206 BC–8 AD Hsin 9–23 AD Eastern Han 25–220 AD	Chao Dynasty 207–111 BC

The Three Kingdoms:	Wei 220–266	Wu 222–280	Shu-Han 221–263

Western Chin 266–316

The Sixteen Kingdoms in the north 302–439			Imperial Dynasties in the south: Eastern Chin 317–420 Earlier Sung 420–479 Southern Ch'i 479–502 Southern Liang 502–557 Southern Ch'en 557–589
Northern Wei 386–534 Western and Eastern Wei 534–557			
Northern Ch'i 550–577	Northern Chou 557–581	Later Liang 555–587	

Sui Dynasty 581–618

T'ang Dynasty 618–907

Western Hsia (Tanguts) 1032–1227	Liao (Khitan) 907–1125	THE FIVE DYNASTIES: Later Liang 907–923 Later T'ang 923–936 Later Chin 936–947 Later Han 947–951 Later Chou 951–960	The Ten Kingdoms 901–979
		Northern Sung 960–1127	
	Chin (Juchen) 1115–1234	Southern Sung 1127–1279	

Yuan (Mongol) Dynasty 1206–1368

Ming Dynasty 1368–1644

Ch'ing Dynasty (Manchus) 1644–1912

Note: Neither time nor territory are represented to scale in this chart, which is simply to clarify the dynastic sequence

MANCHU people in what is now MANCHURIA. On the collapse of the MING regime in 1644, the Manchus invaded China and soon conquered the entire country. The Ch'ing reached a peak of power in the 18th century, but faced increasing internal opposition and European intervention in the later 19th century, culminating in the fall of the dynasty and the establishment of a republic in China in 1912. The last Ch'ing emperor was set up as puppet ruler of MANCHUKUO (1934–45) by the Japanese. (227y, 233b)

Chingis Khanid dynasties Various ruling houses descended from Chingis Khan (d.1227), founder of the MONGOL empire. His immediate successors were his sons and grandsons, whose appanages soon became virtually independent kingdoms, though the formal superiority of a line of Great Khans was acknowledged for a century or so. These latter rulers at first controlled both MONGOLIA and CHINA, assuming the dynastic title of YUAN as Chinese emperors, but were expelled from China in 1368, continuing to rule in Mongolia (as the Northern Yuan) until the break-up of their Khanate in the 17th century. In Iran, a grandson of the founder established the ILKHAN dynasty (1256–

1353), and TRANSOXANIA and TURKESTAN constituted the CHAGHATAI realm until that branch of the family was suppressed by the TIMURIDS at the end of the 14th century – a Chaghatai line survived in ZUNGARIA until the 16th century. In Russia and the western steppelands, the JUCHIDS, descended from the founder's eldest son, ruled as Khans of the GOLDEN HORDE and the WHITE HORDE, and later in a number of successor-states of these khanates – KAZAN, ASTRAKHAN, KASIMOV, Krim (CRIMEA) and the KAZAKH Khanate. Other Juchid lines ruled in Central Asia – SHAIBANIDS, SHAH-RUKHIDS, ARAB-SHAHIDS, JANIDS – and the chiefs of many other minor states and tribal groups in Northern Asia were descended or claimed to be descended from Chingis Khan or his close relatives.

Cholas A TAMIL people who inhabited the CARNATIC region of Southern India (the Coromandel area, Chola-mandal) from early historical times. The names of some Chola kings of the first centuries AD are known, but their state later fell under the rule of the PALLAVAS until the emergence of a new Chola dynasty at the end of the 9th century. In the 10th/12th centuries, the Chola empire became the leading state

THE CHINGIS-KHANID DYNASTIES

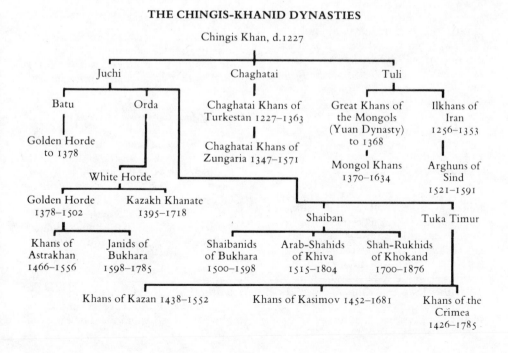

in Peninsular India, conquering the PANDYA kingdom, KERALA and part of CEYLON, and also absorbing the Eastern CHALUKYA kingdom. The Cholas possessed a powerful navy, which plundered as far afield as Sumatra, dealing a ruinous blow to the SRIVIJAYA state in that island. However, they were severely weakened by the revival of the PANDYA kingdom and their state declined to insignificance in the late 13th century. (221b)

Chosroids Iranian family, perhaps a branch of the SASANIDS, who ruled IBERIA in the Caucasus from the late 3rd century AD until the abolition of their monarchy in 580 – the line continued in KAKHETI until the beginning of the 9th century, and a junior branch, the GUARAMIDS, were minor princes in south-western Georgia, sometimes serving as Viceroys of Iberia, their lands being inherited by the BAGRATIDS. (149c, 150, 151b)

Chou Name of several dynasties in CHINA:
  1 Second historical dynasty of China, who overthrew the SHANG at the end of the 2nd millennium BC, usually divided into Western Chou (to 771 BC), a strong ruling line, and Eastern Chou, who lost power to their vassal states (see CHOU STATES) but remained nominal overlords and ruled a small central territory until suppressed by the CH'IN founders of the true Chinese empire in 249 BC. (227b–c)
  2 Northern Chou dynasty of the 6th century AD, which seized power from the Western WEI in north-western China and unified the north by conquest of the Northern CH'I before being supplanted by the SUI. (232c)
  3 Later Chou dynasty, last of the ephemeral regimes which ruled China in the 10th century between T'ANG and SUNG. (227t)

Chou States Various states were established in north and central CHINA as vassals of the CHOU rulers in the early part of the 1st millennium BC or otherwise entered the Chinese world by recognizing Chou supremacy, some of the ruling families claiming to be junior Chou lines. With the decline of Chou power, these states became virtually independent and involved in serious, continuous warfare,

the stronger annexing the weaker, until by the 3rd century BC a few survivors were fighting for all China. The winner was CH'IN, which conquered its last rivals in the later part of that century. (228)

Ch'u name of two states in China:
  1 One of the CHOU STATES, in Hupeh/Honan provinces. Though its early history is very obscure, it conquered several of its neighbours during the last centuries of the Chou period, and emerged as the main rival of CH'IN for mastery of all China – the conquest of Ch'u in 223 BC was decisive for the ultimate Ch'in victory. (228g)
  2 One of the TEN KINGDOMS of the 10th century AD, in Hunan. It was annexed by the imperial SUNG in 963. (231d)

Chudsama dynasty A RAJPUT family which ruled SAURASHTRA, sometimes subject to the CHAULUKYAS of Gujarat, from the 9th century AD until their state was conquered by the Sultans of GUJARAT in 1472. (208d)

Cilicia Coastal region south of the Taurus mountains in Turkey, centre of the Lesser ARMENIA kingdom in the 11th/14th centuries and ruled by the RAMADAN-OGHLU dynasty thereafter until absorbed into the OSMANLI Turkish empire at the beginning of the 17th century. (140, 142k)

Cleves (Kleve), city in north-western Germany, centre of a medieval county from the 11th century, duchy 1417, united with JULICH in the 16th century. (39e)

Coburg German town in SAXONY, ruled by various members of the WETTIN dynasty (Ernestine branch) in combination with other towns from the 16th century. The duchy of Saxe-Coburg-Gotha was established in 1826, Albert the Prince-Consort of Queen Victoria being a son of its first duke. Other members of this Wettin branch founded the dynasty which ruled BULGARIA until 1946 and that which ruled BELGIUM since 1831, both known as Coburgs. (20f, 80g)

Cochin Port and former kingdom in KERALA, India. Its rulers became important in the 16th century and the state survived until its absorption into the Republic of India in 1949. (220c)

Cochin China Former name for the region around the delta of the Mekong river, the most southerly part of VIET-NAM, capital Saigon. This area was for many centuries part of the kingdom of CAMBODIA, being conquered by the Vietnamese in the early 18th century under the NGUYEN family.

Commagene Ancient kingdom in eastern Turkey, west of the upper Euphrates. It became independent of the SELEUCIDS in the early 2nd century BC but was soon a client-state of ROME, annexed to the empire late in the 1st century AD. (137g)

Comneni Imperial family of BYZANTIUM in 11th/12th centuries. The ablest of the dynasty, Alexius I, restored order and reorganized the empire after the loss of most of Asia Minor to the SELJUKS. They were succeeded by the related ANGELI, but after the fall of Constantinople to the Fourth Crusade in 1204, some members of the family fled to TREBIZOND and set up an independent state which survived until it was conquered by the OSMANLI Turks in 1461. (1c, 141)

Congo Major African river, also name of a state (formerly a French colonial territory) and former name of Zaire (the Belgian Congo). A kingdom in northern Angola bore the name too – see KONGO.

Connachta dynasty Irish family, descendants of the legendary Conn of the Hundred Battles, ruling house of CONNAUGHT. The O'NEILLS, HIGH KINGS and rulers of MEATH and AILECH were a branch of the Connachta. (13, 14d–f)

Connaught Province of Ireland, the land of the CONNACHTA dynasty, which ruled it from ancient times, several of its kings being also HIGH KINGS of Ireland. The region was taken over by Anglo-Norman nobles early in the 13th century. (14d)

Constantinople See BYZANTIUM.

Coorg (Kodagu), district of the south-western DECCAN, India, a former state founded by the HALERI dynasty in the early 17th century on the decline of the VIJAYANAGAR empire. In 1834, the British

deposed the last Raja and annexed his territory. (219g)

Cordoba Ancient Spanish city in Andalusia, capital of the UMAYYAD rulers of Spain from the 8th century. On the fall of the Umayyads it became a small independent state under the JAHWARIDS, one of the 11th century REYES DE TAIFAS dynasties, until annexed by the 'ABBADIDS. (48j)

Crete A very early centre of civilization under the Minoans in the 2nd millennium BC, but thereafter its history is very obscure. It became a Roman and then a Byzantine province, until conquered in the early 9th century AD by Muslim refugees from Spain, who set up an amirate under the HAFSID family. Crete was reconquered by the Byzantines in 961, passing to VENICE after the Fourth Crusade and then to the OSMANLI Turks before becoming part of Greece. (85a)

Crimea (Krim), peninsula in the Black Sea, its southern coast being a sheltered region of mild climate where several early Greek colonies were established. Much of the region was included in the kingdom of the Cimmerian BOSPHORUS from the 5th century BC until the state was destroyed in the 4th century AD. On the break-up of the empire of the GOLDEN HORDE in the 15th century, the CHINGIS-KHANID dynasty of the GIRAI set up a powerful khanate in the Crimea and the Ukrainian steppes. The Krim khans soon became vassals of the OSMANLI sultans and for long the northern bastion of the Turkish empire against the Russians, who finally annexed the Crimea in 1785. (90, 97)

Crispi Italian family who usurped power from the SANUDI dukes of NAXOS in the late 14th century – their duchy was annexed by the OSMANLI Turks some two centuries later. (85i)

Crnagora See MONTENEGRO.

Crnojevichi Dynasty which ruled in MONTENEGRO from the early 15th to the early 16th century in succession to the BALSHICHI. The last of the family handed over power to elected bishops, from whom derived the later ruling dynasty of the PETROVICHI. (75b)

Croatia (Hrvatska), region of Yugoslavia, an early Slav state under Bans and later kings from the 9th century AD. At the end of the 11th century its crown was united with that of HUNGARY, of which it became an important province until the break-up of the Austro-Hungarian state in 1918. (74)

Crusader States As a result of the Crusades, two groups of states under dynasties of French, German or Italian origin were founded in the Eastern Mediterranean lands in medieval times:

1 In Syria-Palestine the First Crusade overran most of the coast and some inland areas, its leaders founding the kingdom of JERUSALEM, the principality of ANTIOCH and the counties of EDESSA and TRIPOLI in 1098–1099. These states were gradually reconquered for Islam by various Muslim rulers, notably Saladin the AYYUBID, and the last coastal fortresses fell to the MAMLUKS in the late 13th century. Numerous further crusades were organized during this period to defend or recover Christian territory, and as a result of the Third Crusade at the end of the 12th century, CYPRUS was conquered from the Byzantines, becoming a kingdom under the LUSIGNANS until its acquisition by VENICE in 1489. (144, 167)

2 The Fourth Crusade captured Constantinople in 1204 and set up a LATIN EMPIRE, much of the territory of BYZANTIUM being divided among crusading leaders as feudal vassals while many ports and islands were allotted to VENICE. Though large parts of the lost territory were recovered by the Byzantines, who seized Constantinople in 1261, several crusader states survived until the 15th/16th centuries – see ATHENS, ACHAEA (Morea), NAXOS. (85)

Courland See KURLAND.

Cutch See KACHH.

Cyprus In ancient times the island was divided among various city-kingdoms under Greek and Phoenician rulers, subject in turn to ASSYRIA and the ACHAEMENIDS. The kings were suppressed by the PTOLEMIES, from whom the island passed to ROME and BYZANTIUM. In 1191 Cyprus was conquered from a Byzantine rebel by Richard Coeur-de-Lion during his crusade and sold to the former king of JERUSALEM, Guy of LUSIGNAN, whose family ruled it as a kingdom until its annexation by VENICE in 1489. A century later it fell to the OSMANLI Turks. (144)

Cyrene Ancient city in LIBYA, founded in the 7th century BC by Greek colonists whose leaders, the BATTIADS, ruled it as kings for two hundred years. It was later acquired by the PTOLEMIES and occasionally independent under certain members of that dynasty. (99, 105)

Czechoslovakia Modern state established on the break-up of AUSTRIA-HUNGARY in 1918, consisting of BOHEMIA, MORAVIA and Slovakia.

D

Da Carrara See CARRARESI.

Da Polenta See POLENTANI.

Dabuyids Family of Iranian rulers which became independent in GILAN and Tabaristan (see MAZANDARAN) on the fall of the SASANID empire in the mid-7th century, and resisted UMAYYAD conquest, though they were extinguished by the 'ABBASIDS in 761 AD. (189c)

Dacia Modern TRANSYLVANIA, a strong kingdom under Burebista in the 1st century BC, revived by Decebalus in the following century, conquered by ROME in 106 AD. In the mid-3rd century it was abandoned by the Romans as indefensible.

Dadiani dynasty Princes of MINGRELIA, a small state in western GEORGIA which became independent of IMERETI in the late 15th century. A branch of the family ruled neighbouring GURIA. Mingrelia was annexed by Russia in 1866. (154a)

Dagomba West African kingdom in what is now Ghana, founded in the 15th century. Its rulers became Muslims in the early 18th century and the state fell under the influence of ASHANTI later in that century. (120b)

Dahomey West African kingdom under the ALADAHONU dynasty, established in the 17th century and for long subject to OYO. It became a major power in the

18th/19th centuries, and was annexed by France in 1894. It is now the republic of BENIN. (121c)

Dalai Lamas Series of spiritual leaders and often temporal rulers in TIBET, each believed to be a further incarnation of the first of the line, who was born in 1391. The Chinese intermittently controlled Tibet under the CH'ING emperors, and finally occupied the country in 1950 – the 14th Dalai Lama fled into exile in 1959. (226d)

Dal Cais See O'BRIEN.

Dallazawa Amirs of KATSINA in northern Nigeria in the 19th century, established by FULANI conquest. Succeeded in 1906 by the SULIBAWA. (118d)

Dalriada Originally a kingdom in ULSTER which acquired extensive lands in western SCOTLAND in the 6th century AD. The Irish territory was later lost and the kingdom of Dalriada confined to Scotland. By his conquest of the PICT kingdom in the mid-9th century, Kenneth mac Alpin of Dalriada became ruler of all Scotland – see MACALPIN. (10)

Damascus Capital of modern SYRIA, one of the oldest still-inhabited towns in the world. Centre of a kingdom under Aramaean rulers from the 10th century BC until conquest by ASSYRIA in 732 BC. In the 7th/8th centuries AD the city was the centre of the vast empire of the UMAYYAD Caliphs, and later the capital of several Muslim dynasties or branches of dynasties – see SELJUKS, BURIDS, ZANGIDS, AYYUBIDS. (160, 166c–f)

Danishmendids Turkish dynasty of Asia Minor in 11th/12th centuries in two branches at SIVAS and MALATYA, nominally vassals of the SELJUK rulers of RUM, who eventually annexed their domains. (139)

Darfur Region of the eastern SUDAN, former sultanate. Its history is largely unknown before the KAYRA dynasty which ruled from the mid-17th century. Darfur was annexed by EGYPT in 1874 and conquered by the forces of the MAHDI Muhammad Ahmad a decade later. It was re-established by a member of the Kayra family in 1898 on the fall of the Mahdist state but annexed in 1916 to the Anglo-Egyptian Sudan. (114b)

Darmstadt Town in north-western Germany. After the division of the Landgrave of Hesse in 1567, it became the centre of the state of Hesse-Darmstadt, later the Grand Duchy of Hesse and the Rhine, abolished in 1918. See also CASSEL. (34b)

Daudputra dynasty Nawabs of BAHAWALPUR, a state in the western PUNJAB, founded by local chiefs on the break-up of the MOGHUL empire in the early 18th century. Their state was absorbed by Pakistan in 1955. (203e)

David, House of Descendants of David, king of Israel-Judah *c*.1000 BC. Rulers of Judah only, after the division of the Hebrew state, until its annexation by BABYLON in the 6th century BC. See also JUDAEA. (161a, c)

Daylam Medieval name for a region of western MAZANDARAN. Its warlike people were among the last Iranians to be converted to Islam, though as mercenaries in the 10th century they founded several Muslim dynasties in western IRAN, particularly the BUYIDS.

Deccan (Dakshina), name used in its widest sense to mean all peninsular India, but more specifically the plateau region south to Mysore. Ruled in whole or in part by numerous dynasties from very early times. Part of the MAURYA empire, later conquered by the sultans of DELHI and by the MOGHULS. (217–219)

Deccan Sultanates Five independent states set up on the disintegration of the BAHMANID sultanate at the end of the 15th century, mostly by provincial governors – AHMADNAGAR, BERAR, BIDAR, BIJAPUR and GOLKUNDA. They were frequently at war with each other, though in a rare moment of co-operation, four allied to resist a VIJAYANAGAR invasion in 1565 and destroyed the military power of that empire. Berar and Bidar fell victim to the others, which were conquered by the MOGHULS during the 17th century. (217i–l, 218g)

Deheubarth South WALES, a principality from early post-Roman times, acquired in 872 by Rhodri Mawr of GWYNEDD who thus united all Wales. A branch of his descendants ruled the region until the

Norman invasion of the 11th century, and thereafter remained local lords in some areas. (8b)

Deira Early Anglo-Saxon kingdom in Yorkshire region, traditionally founded *c.*560 AD but soon united with BERNICIA to form the kingdom of NORTHUMBRIA. (5f)

Delhi Series of cities in the same locality, of which the latest is New Delhi, capital of the Republic of India. At the beginning of the 13th century, Delhi became the centre of the sultanate usually known by its name, which rapidly came to control most of India for more than a century under the successive SLAVE, KHALJI and TUGHLUQ dynasties. After the disintegration of the Delhi sultanate, the city remained the capital of the SAYYID and LODI rulers, falling to the MOGHUL Babur in 1526. It was usually the capital of the Moghuls, whose last emperors ruled it nominally until 1858. (201)

Della Rovere See ROVERESCHI.

Della Scala See SCALIGERI.

Demak Town in central JAVA and centre of a sultanate which briefly dominated the island in the early 16th century after the fall of MAJAPAHIT, but which soon lost its supremacy to BANTAM and MATARAM. (246b)

Denia Town on the east coast of Spain, capital of the MUJAHIDS, one of the 11th century REYES DE TAIFAS dynasties, which also ruled MAJORCA. The town was annexed by the HUDIDS. (48k)

Denmark The first firmly historical dynasty to rule in Denmark was that founded by GORM the Old in the early 10th century. His descendants ruled in various lines until 1448, when the present OLDENBURG family, also distantly related to the Gorm dynasty, acquired the throne. (16)

Derbend Ancient city on the western coast of the Caspian Sea in the Dagestan region of the U.S.S.R., controlling the route between the areas north and south of the eastern Caucasus range. It was known to the Arabs as Bab-al-Abwab (Gate of Gates) and was ruled in the 9th/11th centuries by the HASHIMID dynasty, suppressed by the SELJUKS. (156)

Dhu'l-Nunid dynasty Kings of TOLEDO, Spain, one of the 11th century REYES DE TAIFAS families. The city fell to CASTILE in 1085, and it was this disaster which prompted the other Muslim kings in Spain to call in the ALMORAVIDS. (48g)

Dhu'l-Qadr dynasty Turkoman family which founded an amirate centred on MALATYA in the area west of the upper Euphrates (ancient COMMAGENE). It was at first tributary to the MAMLUKS, and then to the OSMANLI Turks, who suppressed the principality in the early 17th century. (142j)

Diadochi The 'Successors' of Alexander the Great, various Macedonian generals who fought for all or part of his empire during the half-century following his death in 323 BC. From these wars, three major states emerged, those of the ANTIGONIDS, SELEUCIDS and PTOLEMIES. See also THRACE.

Dinh dynasty Family which briefly ruled VIET-NAM in the 10th century AD, in succession to the NGO, supplanted by the Earlier LE. (243c)

Diyar Bakr City (ancient Amida) and surrounding region in Turkish KURDISTAN, in classical times called SOPHENE. Various Muslim dynasties have ruled small states in this area. (185d)

Doghras People of Jammu, from whose ruling family came the last KASHMIR dynasty. The founder was governor of Jammu for the Sikh ruler of LAHORE but went over to the British and acquired Kashmir by arrangement with them in 1846. A century later, the last of the line declared for union with India, but his mainly Muslim state is now partitioned between India and Pakistan, the major part under Indian control. (209f)

Dreux family Branch of the CAPETS, descended from Louis VI of France, counts of Dreux and later rulers of BRITTANY, from the early 13th century until their heiress brought the duchy to the French crown by marriage at the end of the 15th century. (24b)

Dubai One of the UNITED ARAB EMIRATES, ruled by the AL-BU-FALASAH family since they secured independence from ABU DHABI in 1833. (178e)

Dublin Capital of Ireland under the English kings and now capital of the Irish Republic (Eire). Centre of VIKING power in the 9th/12th centuries AD and ruled by Scandinavian kings. The city was captured by the Anglo-Normans in 1170. (15)

Ducas Byzantine family which provided several emperors of BYZANTIUM in the 11th century and later. On the fall of Constantinople to the Fourth Crusade in 1204, members of the family established themselves as rulers in EPIRUS and later in THESSALONICA and NEOPATRAS (Thessaly). (1c, 85d–f)

Dughlats Mongolian tribe, members of which established a state at KASHGAR in the mid-14th century, seizing territory from the CHAGHATAI rulers of ZUNGARIA – who suppressed their rivals, however, early in the 16th century. A member of the dynasty, the historian Haidar Mirza Dughlat, conquered KASHMIR in 1540, but was killed in a revolt in 1551. (198f)

Dulafids Dynasty which ruled a small principality in the JIBAL region of Iran in the 9th century AD, nominally under 'ABBASID suzerainty. On the death of the last of the family, his lands reverted to the CALIPH. (190a)

Dunkeld, House of See CANMORE.

Durrani dynasty (Abdalis), rulers of AFGHANISTAN. On the assassination of Nadir Shah AFSHAR of Iran in 1747, one of his generals, the Afghan Ahmad Shah Durrani, founded a kingdom which also included much of the PUNJAB, later lost to Ranjit Singh of LAHORE. The Durrani feud with the BARAKZAI family cost them the Afghan throne, despite a British invasion to restore them in 1839–1842. (197e)

E

Early/Earlier Various dynasties are so called (Early Pandya, Earlier Sung, etc.) to distinguish them from later ruling families of the same name – see under the dynastic name (PANDYA, SUNG, etc.)

East Anglia Region of England and early Anglo-Saxon kingdom of which the history is rather obscure. The names of its rulers are known from the beginning of the 7th century AD. In the late 9th century it was conquered by the VIKINGS and ruled for the remainder of that century by Scandinavian kings. (5e)

Eastern For dynasties thus named, see the main dynastic name – Eastern YEN, Eastern HAN, etc.

Eastern Roman Empire See BYZANTIUM.

Edessa Modern Urfa, in south-eastern Turkey, capital of the kingdom of OSRHOENE under the Arab ABGARID dynasty from the late 2nd century BC until the mid-3rd century AD. It was the centre of a short-lived county, a CRUSADER STATE founded by Baldwin of Boulogne, later king of JERUSALEM, in 1098, but conquered by the ZANGIDS in the middle of the following century. (164, 167d)

Egmont family Dukes of Gelders in the 15th/16th century. They acquired the duchy by inheritance but had to resist persistent efforts by the VALOIS dukes of BURGUNDY and their HABSBURG heirs to seize it. Only in 1543, after the extinction of the Egmonts, did Gelders fall to the Emperor Charles V. (39g)

Egridir Town in southern Turkey, centre of HAMID, one of the ANATOLIAN AMIRATES, during most of the 14th century. (142i)

Egypt A land matched only by 'IRAQ in the antiquity of its historical record as revealed by archaeology. From the first union of the country under one ruler at the end of the 4th millennium BC, it was ruled by a long series of dynasties traditionally numbered I to XXXIII (see PHARAOH), the first six forming the period of the Old Empire and the XI-XII dynasties, after a brief interval of confusion, constituting the Middle Empire. Asiatic invaders, the HYKSOS, conquered the north in the 17th century BC, but after their expulsion, ancient Egypt reached the zenith of its power under the New Empire (XVIII-XX dynasties), controlling much of Syria-Palestine and NUBIA. Then began a long period of decline, the country being partly conquered by ASSYRIA in the 7th century and incorporated into the ACHAE-MENID empire in the 6th century BC. After its occupation by Alexander the Great, it was again the centre of an important realm under the PTOLEMIES (Dynasty XXXIII), but was annexed to ROME in 30 BC, remaining part of the Roman/ Byzantine empire until the Arab conquest in the 7th century AD. Having been a province of the UMAYYAD and early 'ABBASID Caliphs and then virtually independent under TULUNIDS and IKHSHIDIDS, Egypt became in the mid-10th century the power-base of the FATIMIDS, and then of the AYYUBIDS (12th–13th centuries), after which it was ruled by the MAMLUK sultans until the OSMANLI Turkish conquest in 1517. In the 19th century, the country achieved independence under the family of MUHAMMAD 'ALI, becoming a kingdom in 1922. The monarchy was abolished in 1953. (98–104)

Eire See IRELAND.

Elam The region of modern Khuzistan in south-western Iran, in ancient times a kingdom closely associated with the states of early 'Iraq, though its history is somewhat patchy. From the 19th century BC it was ruled by the EPARTI family, and later raised to major power by the IGEHALKIDS and SHUTRUKIDS. The kingdom was finally destroyed in the mid-7th century BC by the rulers of ASSYRIA. (186)

Eldiguzids See ILDEGUZIDS.

Electorate Name given to several of the states within the HOLY ROMAN EMPIRE whose rulers were entitled to cast a vote in the election of the emperor under a system formally established in 1356. At first the electors numbered seven, the Archbishops of Mainz, Cologne and Trier plus the king of BOHEMIA, the Count Palatine of the Rhine (see PALATINATE) and the 'Electors' of SAXONY and BRANDENBURG. In later centuries, BAVARIA, HANOVER and HESSE (-Cassel) also became electorates.

England There were Celtic tribal kingdoms in England before the Roman conquest, and also Romano-British states after the collapse of Roman rule in the 5th century AD, but only with the establishment of the various Anglo-Saxon kingdoms in the late 5th and the 6th centuries does the historical record become clear enough to provide king-lists. The strong states of NORTHUMBRIA and MERCIA were destroyed by VIKING invaders in the late 9th centuries, but WESSEX survived in the south-west, its rulers gradually reconquering England, including the Scandinavian kingdom of YORK, in the next century. Thereafter, apart from brief periods of disorder, England has remained united under successive dynasties – the NORMAN family of William the Conqueror from 1066, then the ANGEVINS (Plantagenets) and TUDORS. In 1603, England and SCOTLAND were dynastically combined under the STUARTS – see GREAT BRITAIN. From the late 12th century until the independence of Eire in the present century, the lordship, later the kingdom, of IRELAND was also combined with the English crown. (5–6)

Eoganacht Irish dynasty, rulers of MUNSTER from ancient times. The kingship moved between several branches of the family and finally to the O'BRIENS, descendants of Brian Boru (d.1014), HIGH KING of Ireland, who were a non-Eoganacht dynasty. The kingdom came to an end in the late 12th century, split between various minor rulers. (14a)

Eparti dynasty Kings of ELAM in the 19th/16th centuries BC. Their state was a major power dominating southern 'Iraq, but the circumstances surrounding both the rise and the disappearance of the family are unknown. After an obscure period of more than a century, they were succeeded by the IGEHALKIDS. (186a)

Epirus Region of Greece in the northwest, extending into what is now Albania. In the 4th/3rd centuries BC it was a kingdom under the AEACID dynasty. After the fall of Constantinople to the Fourth Crusade in 1204, members of the DUCAS family established an independent Byzantine state in Epirus, being supplanted by the ORSINIS of CEPHALONIA a century later. The state was eventually absorbed into the Serbian empire of the NEMANJICHI. (84, 85e)

Eretnids Family which ruled in eastern Asia Minor, their capital at SIVAS. The founder was a viceroy for the ILKHANS and declared his independence on the break-up of the Ilkhan state in the mid-14th century. The regent for the fourth of the dynasty seized power himself under the title of Sultan Ahmad Burhan-ud-Din and began to build a strong state but was eventually defeated and killed by the AQ-QOYUNLI (in 1398). His territory, however, soon fell into the hands of the OSMANLI Turks. See also ANATOLIAN AMIRATES. (142c)

Erzerum Byzantine Theodosiopolis, in eastern Turkey, centre of a small state ruled by the SALTUQID family in the 12th century, after the Turkish conquest of the region. It was captured by the SELJUKS of RUM in 1201 and ruled by a branch of that dynasty until annexed to the main sultanate in 1230. (148b-c)

Essex Early Anglo-Saxon kingdom, considerably larger than the modern county, in the 7th/9th centuries AD. Both its beginnings and its end are very obscure, as indeed is most of its history. (5d)

Este dynasty (Estensi), ruling house of FERRARA and MODENA from the 13th century, lords of Este (near Padua) from the 11th century. The family acquired the WELF lands in Bavaria in 1055, and from its Bavarian branch descends the later Welf dynasty of BRUNSWICK and HANOVER. The Italian branch became dukes in the 15th century but lost Ferrara to the PAPACY in 1597. They were expelled from Modena during the Napoleonic Wars, but the duchy was restored to their heirs, the HABSBURGS, after the fall of Napoleon. (66a)

Ethiopia From about the 1st century AD a kingdom existed in northern Ethiopia, based on AXUM, but not much is known about its history, though it was the direct predecessor of the later Ethiopian state. In the 12th century the ZAGWE dynasty rose to power, to be overthrown in the middle of the following century by a ruler of SHOA who claimed descent from earlier kings and indeed from Solomon and the Queen of Sheba. This 'SOLOMONIC' dynasty ruled a strong and extensive state in late medieval times, but was brought to the edge of ruin by Muslim invaders under the Imam Ahmad Gran of HARAR in the early 16th century. After a period of recovery, the country fell into disorder and division in the later 18th century, to be reunited in the mid-19th century by successive strong rulers from various families, the third of whom was Menyelek of Shoa, a descendant of the Solomonic kings, founder of the modern state. The reign of his last successor, Haile Selassie, was interrupted by Italian conquest in 1936. He was restored by the British in 1941 and eventually deposed by republican revolutionaries in 1974, the monarchy being abolished. (122–123)

Etruria Ancient name for TUSCANY, revived as the title of a kingdom set up in 1801 by Napoleon for the BOURBONS of PARMA. It was abolished in 1807, its second monarch eventually recovering his Parmesan duchy in 1847. (65d)

Eucratidids One of the ruling families of BACTRIA, who disputed rule with the EUTHYDEMIDS in the 2nd/1st centuries BC. (195)

Eurypontids One of the two simultaneous ruling dynasties of SPARTA (the other being the AGIADS), traditionally from 1102 BC (though the dates of the kings are very uncertain until much later) until the end of the monarchy in the early 2nd century BC. (82)

Euthydemids A ruling family of BACTRIA. Euthydemus I became king c.235 BC and his successors extended Greek rule into large areas of northern India, but had to face the rivalry of the EUCRATIDIDS from the mid-2nd century and possibly that of a third family of which the most important member was Menander. There is much uncertainty about the dates and relationships of the Bactrian rulers, and about the territories controlled by the various kings, the last of whom vanishes from historical view in about 55 BC amid barbarian invasions. (195)

F

Farghana The valley of the upper Jaxartes (Syr Darya) in Soviet Central Asia, very little being known of its early history, though it formed part of the empires of the QARA-KHANIDS and the CHAGHATAIS. Under the TIMURIDS it became a small state inherited by the MOGHUL founder Babur, who lost it to the SHAIBANIDS. From the early 18th century until the Russian conquest in 1876 it was ruled by the SHAH-RUKHIDS of KHOKAND. (198k)

Farnese Dukes of PARMA in the 16th/18th centuries, installed in the duchy by Pope Paul III (Alessandro Farnese). The Spanish BOURBONS acquired Parma by marriage in 1731. (64a)

Fars Province of south-western Iran, ancient Parsa from which derives 'Persia'. It was the base from which the ACHAE-MENIDS built their great empire in the 6th century BC and from which the SASANIDS conquered Iran in the 3rd century AD, being ruled between these two regimes by an obscure line of kings subject to SELEUCID and then to ARSACID Great Kings. During the Muslim period, Fars was at various times an independent state, and was the power-base of the ZAND Shahs in the mid-18th century. (191)

Faruqids Sultans of Khandesh, a small state in central India founded on the collapse of the TUGHLUQ sultanate at Delhi in the mid-14th century, and annexed by the MOGHULS in 1601. (207e)

Fatimid dynasty A SHI'A dynasty of QURAISHI descent, rulers of a state founded in the MAGHRIB at the beginning of the 10th century AD. The founders planned to seize control of the Muslim world from the 'ABBASIDS of Baghdad, and took the title of CALIPH – having overthrown the AGHLABIDS and RUSTAMIDS, they moved east to conquer EGYPT in 969 and much of SYRIA, briefly controlling Baghdad itself in 1059. Their power declined rapidly there-after, however, and they lost the Maghrib to their viceroys the ZIRIDS and HAMMADIDS, and Syria-Palestine to the SELJUKS and the Crusaders. In Egypt they survived until 1171, when their Caliphate was abolished by Saladin the AYYUBID. (101)

Ferrara Italian city acquired as a lordship by the ESTE family in the early 13th century. It became a duchy in the 15th century but was annexed by the PAPACY in 1597, though the Este dukes retained MODENA. (66a)

Fezzan Region of southern Libya, ruled by several little-known Muslim dynasties before the AWLAD MUHAMMAD in the late 16th century. These latter rulers resisted the attacks of the QARAMANIDS of Tripoli but were suppressed by the OSMANLI Turks in the mid-19th century. (106c)

Filalids See 'ALAWIDS.

Finland The country was gradually conquered and Christianized by SWEDEN in the 12th/13th centuries, and remained Swedish territory under viceroys (some-times royal dukes) until seized by RUSSIA in 1809. It then became a grand duchy under the ROMANOV Tsars until the fall of the Russian monarchy in 1917 – then, after an attempt to establish a kingdom of Finland under a member of the HESSE family, the country became an in-dependent republic.

Flanders A medieval county from the mid-9th century, inherited by the VALOIS dukes of BURGUNDY at the beginning of the 15th century and thereafter part of the southern NETHERLANDS. Most of the old county is now in BELGIUM, the remainder being French territory. (20b)

Flavians Family of Roman emperors who came to power under Vespasian in 69 AD and fell with Domitian in 96 AD. (1a)

Florence (Firenze), ancient city in TUSCANY which has dominated that region since medieval times. It became a lordship under the MEDICI in the 15th century and later served as the capital of their Grand Duchy of Tuscany. (65b)

Folkungs Scandinavian family which ruled SWEDEN in the 13th/14th and NORWAY in the 14th centuries, acquiring both kingdoms by marriage. Their successor in both states was Margaret I of DENMARK, who thus united all three Scandinavian crowns. (17b, 18b)

Former See EARLIER and under dynastic title for Chinese and Vietnamese dynasties sometimes called 'Former' HAN, LI, etc.

France For history prior to 10th century AD see FRANKS. The kingdom of France emerged as a result of the break-up of the CAROLINGIAN empire, at first ruled by a branch of that dynasty. In 987 the last Carolingian was succeeded by Hugh CAPET, whose descendants in the male line ruled France until 1789 and again in 1814–1848. The main Capet line was succeeded by the VALOIS branch in 1328 and the BOURBON branch in 1589. After the revolution of 1789, the country was ruled by Napoleon BONAPARTE and then by the restored Bourbons, then by the ORLEANS branch of the Bourbons and finally by Napoleon III Bonaparte, becoming a republic for the third time in 1870.

From the collapse of the Carolingian empire until late in the Middle Ages, the authority of the French kings over many parts of their kingdom was incomplete or negligible, various feudal duchies and counties maintaining virtual independence, though royal control gradually increased until it became effective throughout the lands in the late 15th century. Only the rulers of the more important of the numerous French feudal territories are listed in Section II. (3, 22–24)

Franche Comté The 'Free County' of Burgundy, in contrast to the duchy – see BURGUNDY.

Franconia (Franken), region of central Germany deriving its name, like France, from the FRANKS. Important duchy from the 10th to the late 12th century, after which it became only a geographical expression, divided among many minor rulers. (39a)

Franconian Emperors Family which ruled GERMANY in the 11th/12th centuries, the first of the line being a duke of FRANCONIA. (4)

Franks Originally a Germanic people of the Rhineland region, invaders of the Roman empire but disunited until the time of the MEROVINGIAN king Clovis (d.511), who led them to the conquest of most of Gaul from Romans and VISIGOTHS, establishing a state which included also the Netherlands and Rhineland. In the late 8th century the Frankish realm was expanded into an empire under the CAROLINGIAN Charlemagne. (3)

Fujairah One of the UNITED ARAB EMIRATES, which established its independence from SHARJAH in 1952 under the SHARQI family. (178h)

Fujiwara An important ministerial family in medieval JAPAN which provided two SHOGUNS in the 13th century, and which traditionally supplied the brides of the imperial family until modern times. (236c)

Fulani A people of the western SUDAN who established a number of states in the area, notably the sultanate of SOKOTO and its vassal amirates in Northern Nigeria. A Fulani religious leader, 'Uthman dan Fodio, began a holy war in the region at the beginning of the 19th century, as a result of which the HAUSA kingdoms were conquered and Fulani rulers installed in them under the suzerainty of 'Uthman's successors at Sokoto. All these states came under British rule later and are now part of the Republic of Nigeria. (117–118)

Fung (Funj), name of the people and ruling dynasty of the sultanate of SENNAR in the eastern SUDAN, founded at the beginning of the 16th century, largely at the expense of the ancient Christian kingdoms of NUBIA. It was a strong power in the 16th/17th centuries, but had declined to minor importance before its conquest by Egypt in 1821. (114a)

Gaekwars Maharajas of BARODA, India, from the early 18th century. The dynasty was founded by a MARATHA general, whose state extended over much of GUJARAT. Baroda was absorbed into the Republic of India in 1949. (208g)

Gahadavalas (Gaharwars), a RAJPUT dynasty belonging to the RATHOR clan, successors of the PRATIHARAS in the Ganges valley, their capital being Varanasi (Benares). They rose to power in the late 11th century but their state was conquered by the GHURIDS at the end of the next century and became part of the DELHI sultanate. (204a)

Gajapati dynasty Kings of ORISSA, India, in the 15th/16th centuries, successors of the GANGAS. (216c)

Galicia Name of two quite separate regions of Europe:

1 The north-western corner of Spain. It was part of the kingdom of the SUEBI until conquered by the VISIGOTHS, and was never effectively controlled by the UMAYYAD rulers of Spain, becoming part successively of the Christian kingdoms of ASTURIAS-LEON and CASTILE.

2 The basin of the upper Dniestr in western Russia, around the city of Galich. It formed one of the RIURIKID principalities after the division of the early KIEV state, and was briefly a kingdom in the 13th/14th centuries, then being absorbed into the Polish state. The name was later used to include the more westerly region of southern Poland when the whole area was occupied by the Austrians on the partition of Poland. (92a)

Gangas Ancient Indian dynasty which ruled in both ORISSA and MYSORE. Minor rulers in Kalinga from c.500 AD, they supplanted the SOMAVAMSIS in Orissa in the early 12th century, being succeeded by the GAJAPATIS in the mid-15th century, while the Western Gangas were kings in Mysore even earlier, though they were suppressed by the CHOLAS at the beginning of the 11th century AD. (216b, 219a)

Ganja (now Kirovabad, in Soviet AZERBAIJAN), one of the main towns of ARRAN and capital of the SHADDADIDS in the 10th/11th centuries. Also centre of a khanate in the 18th century, annexed by Russia in 1806. (155, 158a)

Gelders (Geldern), town in western Germany and feudal county from the 11th century, a duchy from 1339. Early in the 15th century, it was inherited by the EGMONT family, whose claim was disputed by the VALOIS dukes of BURGUNDY. The Egmonts held it with interruptions until their extinction, and it eventually fell to the HABSBURGS in 1543. (39g)

Georgia Region of Caucasia, now one of the republics of the U.S.S.R. From the 3rd century BC a kingdom existed in eastern Georgia, known in classical times as IBERIA, its original native dynasty being replaced by a branch of the Iranian ARSACIDS in the 2nd century AD and by the CHOSROIDS in the 3rd century. The monarchy was abolished in 580 and the country divided among various princely dynasties – branches of the Chosroids continued to rule in the eastern region of KAKHETI and in the south-west (see GUARAMIDS), both lines intermittently acting as Viceroys of Iberia for Byzantines or Persians. In western Georgia, a kingdom was formed in the 5th/6th centuries AD (LAZICA) but annexed by BYZANTIUM, and later the ANCHABADS of ABKHAZIA extended their control over the west. A branch of the Armenian BAGRATID dynasty gradually acquired all the Georgian lands in the 10th/11th centuries, creating a powerful kingdom which flourished until the MONGOL invasions of the 13th century. Western Georgia broke away temporarily at that time, and the kingdom broke up between branches of the Bagratids at the end of the 15th century, three kingdoms being formed – IMERETI in the west, Kakheti in the east and KARTLI, the central region of the Georgian state. After three centuries of chequered history under the domination by turns of Persians, OSMANLI Turks and Russians, these states were finally annexed by Russia in the early 19th century, together with several smaller principalities which had broken away from Imereti – MINGRELIA, GURIA and Abkhazia (see SHARVASHIDZE). (149–154)

Germany The southern and western borderlands of Germany were ruled by ROME at the height of the Roman empire, the remainder of the country being controlled by Germanic tribes, who formed various kingdoms in Western Europe on the fall of the empire. The FRANKS of the Rhineland formed the MEROVINGIAN kingdom, which included most of France, and the AGILULFINGS set up a duchy in BAVARIA. The CAROLINGIAN successors of the Merovingians extended the Frankish state to include virtually all of what is now West Germany and Austria, and converted the realm to an empire in 800 AD (see HOLY ROMAN EMPIRE). Under the later rulers of the dynasty, their dominions gradually split up and a German kingdom emerged, becoming associated with the imperial title. From the 10th to the mid-13th century, the German kingdom/empire was an important European power, though the rulers of the great duchies became increasingly independent of royal control – see SAXONY, FRANCONIA, SWABIA, Bavaria, and AUSTRIA. On the fall of the HOHENSTAUFFEN dynasty, the rule of the emperors became little more than nominal outside their own hereditary dominions, and the imperial office, previously semi-hereditary, passed from one princely house to another with great frequency. In the north-east, the German lands were much extended at the expense of Slav peoples in the 12th/13th centuries – see BRANDENBURG and PRUSSIA. In the 16th and 17th centuries, the HABSBURG emperors, having established a practical monopoly of the imperial crown, made great efforts to gain real control of the feudal states of Germany, but after 1648 the numerous states of the north and west became entirely independent, and in the early 19th century the Habsburgs abandoned their nominal claims to authority outside their own hereditary lands, which they converted to a new empire of Austria. In 1871, the HOHEN-ZOLLERNS, already rulers of much of the north, brought the remaining German states into a new German empire, which fell in 1918, when all the various kingdoms, duchies and principalities within the empire were abolished. (3–4, 26–39)

Germiyan One of the ANATOLIAN AMIRATES of the 14th/15th centuries, based on Kutahya in western Turkey, initially a strong state from which the principalities of AIDIN and SARUKHAN soon broke away. It was annexed by the OSMANLIS in 1429. (142e)

Ghana Name of an ancient empire in the western SUDAN and of a modern African state (the former Gold Coast) named after the historic kingdom. The empire flourished from about the 6th century AD until supplanted by MALI, though seriously weakened by ALMORAVID attacks in the 11th century. No list of the kings of Ghana is available.

Ghassanids Pre-Islamic Arab dynasty which ruled in northern Arabia and inland Syria in the 6th/7th century under Byzantine suzerainty and as rivals of the LAKHMIDS. Their kingdom was suppressed

by the Byzantines shortly before the Muslim conquest of Syria. (165)

Ghazna/Ghaznavid dynasty Ancient city in Afghanistan and line of rulers whose capital it was. The Ghaznavid state was founded by a rebel SAMANID governor in the 10th century AD, and its most famous ruler was Sultan Mahmud (d. 1030), who controlled much of eastern Iran and made a series of raids far into India, acquiring enormous plunder and demonstrating the inability of the Hindu kings to resist Muslim attacks. His successors soon lost their Iranian territories to the SELJUKS and were driven from Ghazna by the GHURIDS, who annexed their remaining lands in the PUNJAB in 1186. (197a)

Ghilzais Afghan tribe, the earlier KHALJIS, who provided two rulers of IRAN in the early 18th century, supplanting the SAFAVIDS. Their regime was overthrown by Nadir Shah AFSHAR. (187j)

Ghur/Ghurids (Ghor/Ghorids), region of Afghanistan and name of two Muslim dynasties:
    1 Family of the tribal chiefs of Ghur, who became involved in a feud with the GHAZNAVIDS in the 11th century and eventually supplanted them, establishing a short-lived realm in Afghanistan and northern India, various members of the dynasty ruling in partnership at Ghur, Ghazna and BAMIYAN. Early in the 13th century, their Afghan lands were conquered by the KHWARIZM–Shahs, while their viceroy in India founded the DELHI sultanate (see SLAVE dynasty). (197b–c)
    2 Sultans of MALWA in the late 14th/early 15th centuries, founded by a governor under the TUGHLUQS who declared his independence. They were succeeded by the KHALJI family. (207c)

Gilan Caspian coastal province of northern Iran, one of the last Iranian regions to fall to Islam. In the 10th/11th centuries it was ruled by a branch of the MUSAFIRIDS, a local dynasty of DAYLAM. (189d)

Girai dynasty Khans of Krim (CRIMEA and southern Ukraine), a branch of the CHINGIS-KHANIDS, who founded their state in the early 15th century as the khanate of the GOLDEN HORDE broke up. They became vassals of the OSMANLI sultans and for long held the northern frontier of the Turkish empire against Poles and Russians. Their state was finally annexed by the Russians in the late 18th century. (97)

Gobir One of the HAUSA kingdoms in Northern Nigeria from medieval times, though the dates and relationships of its kings are obscure before the later 18th century. The FULANI uprising at the beginning of the 19th century was centred in Gobir territory, though its king held out a little longer than some of his neighbours – his capital, Alkalawa, fell to the Fulani in 1808 and his lands were annexed to the sultanate of SOKOTO.

Golden Horde Name of the MONGOL khanate in Russia established in the mid-13th century by the senior CHINGIS-KHANID line, the JUCHIDS, at first a great power dominating Eastern Europe and controlling the surviving RIURIKID princi-palities, until the successful challenge to the 'Tartar Yoke' by MOSCOW in the late 14th/early 15th century. In Western Siberia, another Juchid line ruled the WHITE HORDE until it was temporarily combined with the Golden Horde under Tokhtamysh Khan, who embarked upon a long and ruinous struggle with the founder of the TIMURID dynasty. During the 15th century, the Golden Horde broke up into several khanates, all of which were eventually conquered by the Russians – see KAZAN, ASTRAKHAN, KASIMOV, CRIMEA and KAZAKHS. (95)

Golkunda (Golconda), town near modern HYDERABAD, India, early capital of one of the DECCAN SULTANATES of the same name, established by the first of the QUTB SHAHI dynasty on the break-up of the BAHMANID state at the end of the 15th century. In 1687 the MOGHUL ruler Aurangzib took the later capital, Hyderabad, after a desperate defence, and annexed the sultanate. (218g)

Gonzaga family Rulers of MANTUA, Italy, as Captains-General from the early 14th century, margraves 1433 and dukes 1530. Their state was annexed by the HABSBURGS in 1708. (67d)

Gorm dynasty Earliest firmly historical ruling house of DENMARK, founded by Gorm the Old at the beginning of the 10th century AD. His direct descendants occupied the throne until the mid-15th century, when they were succeeded by the OLDENBURGS. (16a)

Goths Ancient Germanic tribe which probably originated in Scandinavia. They first appear in history in Poland and later in the Ukraine, where they became divided into OSTROGOTHS and VISIGOTHS, being driven westwards in the 4th century AD by the HUNS – see under the names of the two sections of this people.

Granada Spanish city which became important after the Muslim conquest in the 8th century AD. On the break-up of the UMAYYAD state in Spain, Granada became the capital of one of the REYES DE TAIFAS states in the 11th century under a branch of the ZIRID dynasty, later annexed by the ALMORAVIDS. Amid the disorders and Christian advance which followed the great defeat of the ALMOHADS by the Christian kings in 1212, Muhammad ibn al-Ahmar established himself at Granada and founded the NASRID dynasty, rulers of the last Muslim state in Spain, who held on to their small kingdom until its conquest in 1492 by Ferdinand and Isabella, the organizers of the final union of Spain. (48l, 52)

Grand Catalan Company Mercenary army from CATALONIA which entered the service of the government of BYZANTIUM at the beginning of the 14th century, but soon quarrelled with their employers. Marching away into Greece, they killed in battle Walter of Brienne, Duke of ATHENS, with most of the nobility of his duchy (1311), and occupied the conquered land. The Catalans installed members of a branch of the ruling dynasty of their homeland, the ARAGONESE dynasty of SICILY, as nominal dukes. (85g)

Great Britain Main island of the British Isles, brought under one ruler by the STUART succession to the English throne in 1603 and ruled by the HANOVER/WINDSOR dynasty since 1714. The kingdom of Great Britain was formally established in 1707, and the UNITED KINGDOM of Great

Britain and Ireland in 1801. For earlier history see ENGLAND, SCOTLAND, WALES, IRELAND. (6d–e)

Great Bulgaria For a short period in the 7th century AD, a powerful khanate dominated the European steppelands under the Bulgars, a Turco-Mongol confederation which perhaps included remnants of the HUNS, from whose rulers the Bulgars khans claimed descent. When this realm broke up, one section of the horde moved into the region of the lower Danube to establish the early state of BULGARIA, while another section migrated to the area around the junction of the Volga and Kama rivers to found a khanate usually known as Great Bulgaria. These Volga Bulgars settled down to prosper for centuries as a trading state, their ruler taking the title of Amir when his people were converted to Islam. In 1237 the kingdom was overrun and destroyed by the MONGOLS, the consequent loss of historical records making it impossible to reconstruct any list of the rulers. The surviving Bulgars became subjects of the GOLDEN HORDE and then of the khanate of KAZAN, a state controlling much the same territory as Great Bulgaria.

Great Poland (Wielkopolska), region of western Poland around Poznan and Gniezno, the earliest capitals of the original PIAST state. On the division of Poland in the 12th century, it became a principality and briefly a kingdom before its absorption into the re-united kingdom of Poland in the early 14th century. (87b)

Greater Moravia See MORAVIA.

Greece In the Heroic Age of ancient Greece there were, according to legend, various territorial and city kingdoms, but by the 7th century BC, when firmly historical details begin to emerge, nearly all the Greek cities were republics, though often in practice ruled by semi-monarchical tyrants. SPARTA retained its double kingship until the end of the 3rd century BC and royal lines continued to rule in the semi-Greek lands of the north – the ARGEADS in MACEDONIA and the AEACIDS in EPIRUS. From the mid-4th century the Macedonian kings dominated Greece until the Roman conquest in the

2nd century, after which the whole area became part of the empires of ROME and BYZANTIUM for more than a thousand years, to the beginning of the 13th century AD, when the leaders of the Fourth Crusade seized various parts of Greece – see CRUSADER STATES. The resultant patch-work of feudal principalities, Byzantine territories and Venetian colonies was gradually overrun by the OSMANLI Turks, VENICE in particular offering a lengthy resistance which was finally overcome in 1715. A century later, revolt broke out in Greece, and a national state was established under members of the WITTELSBACH and then the OLDENBURG dynasties. The Greek monarchy survived with a brief republican interval until 1967, when the king went into exile, and was formally abolished by referendum in 1973. (82–86)

Grimaldi dynasty Family of Genoese origin, rulers of MONACO since the early 14th century. Their small lordship became a principality in 1612 and has maintained its formal independence, apart from a brief annexation to France by Napoleon BONAPARTE, to the present day. (25)

Guaramids A junior branch of the CHOSROIDS of IBERIA (GEORGIA), rulers of a principality in south-western Georgia from the abolition of the Iberian monarchy in the 6th century AD until their own extinction in the mid-8th century, also serving intermittently as viceroys of Iberia. Some of their lands passed by marriage to the BAGRATIDS, who thus became established in Georgia. (150)

Guelf/Guelph See Welf.

Guhilas RAJPUT clan to which belonged the ruling family of MEWAR (Udaipur), also known as Sisodias. Their state was the oldest of the principalities of RAJASTAN to survive into modern times and its ruler the most respected, though not the most powerful in recent centuries, bearing the superior title of Rana or Maharana. The Guhilas became established in Mewar in the 8th century AD and had become the dominant power in Rajastan by the 15th century, but their power was broken in a long struggle against the MOGHUL emperors, under whom the Ranas became at times virtually fugitives. The dynasty recovered some of its former territory and influence as the Moghul empire declined, abandoning its ancient capital, Chitor, for the new city of Udaipur, by which name the state is often known. Mewar was incorporated into the Republic of India in 1949. (206a)

Gujarat Region of western India, often under independent rulers over the centuries. Having been conquered by the imperial GUPTAS from the KSHATRAPAS, Gujarat was ruled by successive Hindu dynasties until annexed by the Muslim sultans of DELHI at the beginning of the 14th century, becoming an independent sultanate under the MUZAFFARIDS in the same century until its conquest by the MOGHULS. On the decline of the Moghul empire in the 18th century, the area came under the control of the MARATHA general Pilaji GAEKWAR, who founded the state of BARODA in part of Gujarat, while other sections soon came under direct British rule. (208)

Gupta dynasty Imperial ruling family in northern India in the 4th/6th centuries AD. Their empire included most of the north and parts of the DECCAN, but disintegrated in the 6th century under pressure of major invasions from the north-west by peoples from Central Asia. Minor kings probably connected with the dynasty continued to rule in the north-east for several centuries. (200d)

Gurgan Ancient Hyrcania, province of Iran around the south-eastern corner of the Caspian Sea, part of modern MAZANDARAN.

Guria/Gurieli dynasty A small principality in western Georgia and its ruling family. Guria became virtually independent of the kings of IMERETI in the 15th century under the Gurielis (or Dadian-Gurielis), a branch of the DADIANI family. Their state was annexed by the Russians in 1829. (154b)

Gurkhas Ruling people and dynasty of NEPAL. The founder of the modern state was ruler of a small hill kingdom who conquered the three MALLA kingdoms of central Nepal in the mid-18th century to establish a strong and extensive realm which has contrived to maintain its independence. From the mid-19th century until 1951, the Nepalese kings were puppets of a ministerial family, the Ranas, but have been constitutional rulers since that date. (211h)

Gwalior City in central India, an important fortress which changed hands between Hindu and Muslim rulers several times over the centuries. In the mid-18th century it was taken from the MOGHULS by the MARATHAS and soon became the capital of a state of the same name under the SINDHIA dynasty, incorporated into the Republic of India in 1948. (204e)

Gwandu Amirate in north-western Nigeria, established by the FULANI after the conquest of the HAUSA kingdoms in the early 19th century. The first ruler of Gwandu was a brother of the founder of the SOKOTO sultanate, and his territory was based on the former KEBBI kingdom. (118f)

Gwynedd Modern county in WALES and name of the northern Welsh kingdom or principality which existed between about 500 AD and the English conquest of the late 13th century. According to tradition, the kingdom was founded by a British chief from the Lothian area of Scotland. The later rulers of Gwynedd were descended from Rhodri the Great, who united all Wales in the 9th century, but whose lands were divided on his death in 878. (8a)

H

Habe dynasties Ruling families of KANO and other HAUSA states in Northern Nigeria prior to the FULANI conquest in the early 19th century. The origins of most of these dynasties are obscure and legendary, and long lists of kings exist in tradition for which no chronology or historical evidence is available. Some of the Habe kings put up strong resistance to the Fulani and maintained control of parts of their kingdoms – see ARGUNGU and ABUJA (116)

Habsburgs Major European dynasty descended from the counts of Habsburg, a castle now in Switzerland. The founder of their great power was Rudolf I, elected as German King after the fall of the HOHENSTAUFFEN and the Great Interregnum, in 1273. Though he failed to establish an immediate hereditary claim for his descendants to the imperial crown of the HOLY ROMAN EMPIRE, he acquired the duchies of AUSTRIA and STYRIA, to which later Habsburgs added CARINTHIA, Carniola and TYROL, thus forming an important territorial block in the southeastern German lands. In 1440, a Habsburg obtained the crown permanently (as it turned out) for the family, and by his son's marriage to the heiress of the VALOIS dukes of Burgundy, the dynasty acquired most of the NETHERLANDS. By a further lucky marriage, the Spanish realms of CASTILE and ARAGON, with their dependencies in Italy and the Americas, fell to a Habsburg heir, Emperor Charles V, and his brother Ferdinand succeeded the JAGIELLONS in BOHEMIA and in what was left of the Hungarian kingdom, most of which fell into OSMANLI Turkish hands after 1526. In the mid-16th century, the extensive Habsburg lands were split between a Spanish and an Austrian branch, the former line ruling the Spanish empire, NAPLES and SICILY, such of the Netherlands as were not lost in the Dutch revolt under William of ORANGE, and (for a while) Portugal and its overseas empire – on their extinction in 1700, they were succeeded in most of their possessions by a branch of the BOURBONS. The Austrian line ruled the German family lands and Bohemia, holding the imperial title, and at the end of the 17th century recovered HUNGARY from the Turks. During the Napoleonic period, the Habsburg emperor abandoned his Holy Roman title and established the Empire of Austria (from 1867 AUSTRIA-HUNGARY), a vast multi-national state which broke up in 1918, when the Habsburg monarchy was abolished. Branches of the dynasty also ruled in TUSCANY and MODENA. (4, 40e, 41, 53a, 54c, 65c, 66b)

Hafsids Two Muslim dynasties:

1 Amirs of CRETE in the 9th/10th centuries AD, founded by refugees from a failed rebellion in Spain who conquered the island from the Byzantines – who recovered it, however, in 961. (85a)

2 Rulers of TUNIS from the early 13th to the late 16th century, the founder being originally a governor for the ALMOHADS who established his independence. At times the dynasty controlled all the eastern MAGHRIB, but in the mid-16th century Tunis changed hands several times between Hafsids, Spaniards and OSMANLI-backed corsairs before falling finally to the latter contenders. (109c)

Haidar 'Ali and Tipu Sultan Rulers of MYSORE, India, in the later 18th century, the former gaining power though puppet Maharajas of the Hindu WADIYAR dynasty and extending his rule over large areas of southern India. His son Tipu proved a major opponent of the British and was killed when they stormed Srirangapatnam, his capital, in 1799. The Wadiyars were then restored to power. (219d)

Haidarids Khans of BUKHARA from the late 18th century in succession to the JANIDS, reduced to vassalage by the Russians in 1868. The last of the dynasty was deposed by Soviet revolutionaries in 1920, and was eventually defeated in an effort to recover his throne in 1922 with the aid of the exiled Turkish leader Enver Pasha (who was killed in the fighting). (198j)

Ha'il Town in northern Arabia, capital of the AL-RASHID Amirs, rivals of the Al-Sa'ud, from the mid-19th century until their overthrow by 'Abdul-'Aziz ibn Sa'ud in 1921. (175)

Hainault Province of Belgium, a medieval county ruled at times in combination with HOLLAND or FLANDERS, and eventually inherited by the VALOIS dukes of Burgundy. (20c)

Haiti Caribbean republic, western part of the island of Hispaniola, settled by the Spaniards in the 16th century and acquired by France in 1697. A revolt of the negro plantation slaves broke out during the French Revolution and the region became independent, resisting the efforts of Napoleon BONAPARTE to reconquer it. During the 19th century, several of the numerous dictators of Haiti declared themselves king or emperor, but none of their regimes survived for more than a few years. (251)

Haleri dynasty Rajas of Coorg (Kodagu), a district of the south-western DECCAN, who established their rule in the mid-16th century, originally as vassals of the NAYYAKS of IKKERI. In 1834, the last Raja was deposed and his state annexed by the British. (219g)

Hamadan Ancient Ecbatana, in the JIBAL region of western Iran, capital of the kings of the MEDES in the 7th/6th centuries BC and a city of major importance in later times. (190b)

Hama Syrian city of considerable antiquity, centre of an AYYUBID principality of the 12th/14th centuries, one of its last rulers being the historian Abu'l-Fida. The city was annexed by the MAMLUKS in 1341. (166i)

Hamdanids Two Muslim dynasties:
1 Arab family of northern 'Iraq and Syria which ruled in two branches at MOSUL and ALEPPO in the 10th century, the Syrian branch bearing the brunt of a Byzantine military revival. The FATIMIDS annexed Aleppo at the beginning of the 11th century, while Mosul fell to the 'UQAILIDS. (166a, 185a)
2 Rulers of SAN'A in the Yemen in the 12th century, successors of the SULAYHIDS. In common with other Yemeni dynasties of the period, they were supplanted by the AYYUBID conqueror Turan Shah. (172h)

Hamid One of the ANATOLIAN AMIRATES of the 14th/early 15th centuries, ruled by a dynasty of the same name whose capital was at EGRIDIR. A branch of the family ruled the neighbouring Amirate of TEKE, centred on ANTALYA. (142h–i)

Hammadids A branch of the ZIRID dynasty of the eastern MAGHRIB which ruled much of the central (Algerian) part of that region, formally as viceroys of the FATIMIDS, from the early 11th to the mid-12th century, when their lands were conquered by the ALMOHADS. (110b)

Hammudids Muslim dynasty in Spain, descendants of the IDRISIDS of Morocco and therefore a QURAISHI dynasty. Early in the 11th century, the founder seized the Caliphal throne of the Spanish UMAYYADS at Cordoba, which changed hands between the two families several times over a decade before the final collapse of the Spanish Caliphate. The Hammudids maintained their rule in MALAGA until it fell to the ZIRIDS of Granada in 1057, while another branch of the family ruled in ALGECIRAS until a year later, when their lands were annexed by the 'ABBADIDS of Seville. (see also REYES DE TAIFAS). (44b, 48h–i)

Han Name of an ancient state and of several dynasties in CHINA:
1 One of the CHOU STATES, formed at the end of the 5th century BC on the break-up of CHIN, located in northern Honan. It was conquered by CH'IN in 230 BC. (228k)
2 Second imperial dynasty of China, founded in the struggle for power which followed the collapse of the CH'IN in 206 BC. At its zenith, the Han empire extended far into Central Asia and northern VIET-NAM. The dynasty is divided into two lines, Western and then Eastern Han, separated by the brief reign of Wang Mang (see HSIN) in 9–23 AD. In the early 3rd century AD, the Han state broke up into the THREE KINGDOMS. (227e, g)
3 Shu-Han. Ruling house of one of the THREE KINGDOMS of the 3rd century AD, in Shu (modern Szechuan). Its founder claimed descent from an emperor of the Western Han. The kingdom was conquered by WEI in 263 AD. (229c)
4 Northern Han (4th century AD). See Earlier CHAO.
5 Northern Han (10th century AD). One of the TEN KINGDOMS, in Shansi. Its founder was a brother of the first emperor of the imperial Later Han. It was conquered by the SUNG in 979. (231j)
6 Southern Han. One of the TEN KINGDOMS of the 10th century AD, in Kwangtung, conquered by the SUNG in 971. (231e)
7 Later Han. Sha-t'o Turkish family, one of the five dynasties which briefly ruled China between T'ANG and SUNG in the 10th century AD. (227s)

Hanover Town in north-western Germany and name of an ELECTORATE from 1692 and kingdom from 1814 created from the duchy of BRUNSWICK-Luneburg under the WELF dynasty. Between 1714 and 1837, the rulers of Hanover were also

BRITISH DYNASTIES AND THEIR CONNECTIONS

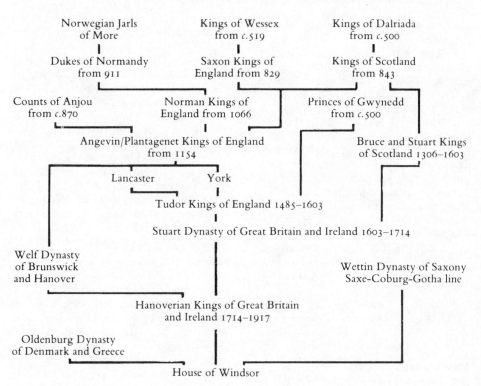

kings of Great Britain – see HANOVER/ WINDSOR. The kingdom was annexed by PRUSSIA in 1866. (33e)

Hanover/Windsor Ruling house of GREAT BRITAIN since 1714, succeeding the STUARTS. The first of the line was Elector of HANOVER and a member of the WELF dynasty of BRUNSWICK, and Hanover remained dynastically united with Britain until 1837, when Victoria inherited the British throne and her uncle the throne of Hanover (a kingdom since 1814). Since Albert the Prince-Consort of Victoria was a WETTIN, his descendants in the male line may be regarded as members of that dynasty, and for similar reasons, the present Prince of Wales is an OLDENBURG by male descent, though the British Royal Family adopted the title House of Windsor in 1917. (6e)

Harar Town in eastern Ethiopia, formerly the centre of a Muslim amirate. It became the capital of the state of Adal (see AWFAT) under the last of the WALASMA' dynasty, who was overthrown in 1526 by the Imam Ahmad Gran, founder of a new line of rulers. After a period of obscurity at the end of the 16th century, the amirate or sultanate at Harar was revived in the middle of the next century. The city was occupied by Egyptian forces in 1875–1885 and annexed by Ethiopia in 1887. (123b)

Harsha (Harshavardhana), the only important ruler of the Pushpabhuti dynasty, king of Thanesar and KANAUJ (in modern Uttar Pradesh), who built up an empire extending over much of northern India during the first half of the 7th century AD. On his death, however, the state disintegrated. (200e)

Hasanuyids (Hasanwayhids), Kurdish family which established a small principality in the JIBAL region of Iran, controlling HAMADAN and near-by areas in the mid-10th century AD. Their territory was annexed by the BUYIDS early in the following century. (190b)

Hashemites Alternative spelling for HASHIMIDS.

Hashimids Name of various Muslim dynasties:

1 A general term for the various families descended from Hashim, great-grandfather of Muhammad the Prophet, and thus including both the 'ABBASIDS and the 'ALIDS – see also QURAISHI dynasties.

2 Rulers of MECCA from the 10th century AD, of 'ALID descent (BANU QITADA branch from the 13th century). They were usually subject to stronger powers, the MAMLUKS and then the OSMANLI Sultans, until the First World War, when Sharif Husain proclaimed his independence as king of the HIJAZ. The family was soon expelled from Mecca by the AL-SA'UD, but branches had meanwhile established themselves in 'IRAQ (until 1958) and Transjordan (later JORDAN) (to date). (170, 183, 1850)

3 Amirs of DERBEND in the Caucasus in the 9th/11th centuries, nominal vassals of the 'ABBASID Caliphs. Their lands were absorbed by the SELJUKS. (156)

Hasmoneans (Maccabees), rulers of JUDAEA, family which led the Jewish revolt of the mid-2nd century BC against SELEUCID rule and established an independent kingdom in Palestine. Dynastic feuds led to Roman overlordship a century later, and the last king of the dynasty, installed with ARSACID Parthian aid in 40–37 BC, was overthrown by ROME and replaced by the HERODIANS. (163a)

Hausa Most numerous linguistic group in northern Nigeria, who established various kingdoms in the region under HABE dynasties in medieval times, though the origins and early history of these states are lost in legend. Most were destroyed in the early 19th century by the great FULANI religious wars under 'Uthman dan Fodio, founder of the SOKOTO sultanate, who set up his own lieutenants as rulers of KANO, KATSINA, ZARIA and other former Hausa kingdoms. However, certain Hausa dynasties resisted vigorously enough to retain control of parts of their former territory as minor amirates, as in ABUJA and ARGUNGU. (116)

Hauteville dynasty Descendants of Tancred of Hauteville, a knight of Normandy, whose numerous sons entered the service of the various powers of southern Italy as mercenaries, and there acquired territory as independent rulers. The ablest of these sons, Robert Guiscard, became duke of APULIA and Calabria in 1059 and his brother Roger conquered SICILY a few years later. All the Hauteville lands were united by Roger II, with the title of King of Sicily from 1130. This state, the later kingdom of 'Naples and Sicily', was seized by the HOHENSTAUFFEN emperors at the end of the 12th century. A crusading son of Guiscard founded the principality of ANTIOCH in Syria (see CRUSADER STATES) and his descendants ruled there until the MAMLUK conquest in the later 13th century. (62a, 68e, 167b)

Hawaii Polynesian tradition gives long lists of the chiefs of the various Hawaiian islands, but they were combined into a single kingdom only at the beginning of the 19th century by Kamehameha I. The last monarch of Hawaii was deposed in 1893 by republicans proposing union with the U.S.A., which annexed the islands in 1898. (249a)

Haykids Armenian dynasty which ruled SIUNIA in south-eastern Armenia from ancient times. Their state split into eastern and western sections in the 9th century AD but was re-united as a kingdom in the following century. Much reduced in importance as a result of the SELJUK conquest of Armenia, the Haykid state disappeared in the 12th century, its kings succeeded by local princes. (147a)

Hazaraspids An ATABEG dynasty, rulers of LURISTAN in western Iran in the 12th/15th centuries, founded by a general of the SALGHURIDS. The Hazaraspids survived the Mongol conquest to become ILKHAN vassals, but were suppressed by the TIMURIDS. (190d)

Hejaz See HIJAZ.

Heraclids Semi-legendary dynasty of LYDIA in Asia Minor, its last king being overthrown by the more firmly historical MERMNAD dynasty at the end of the 8th century BC.

Herat City in western Afghanistan, capital

of the ancient province of Ariana under the ACHAEMENIDS and one of the many 'Alexandrias' established by Alexander the Great. In the 13th/14th centuries, it was the centre of a small kingdom under the KART dynasty, initially as ILKHAN vassals and then independent, until their state was annexed by Timur (see TIMURIDS) in 1389. (197d)

Herodians Family of Idumaean Arab origin which ruled JUDAEA and neighbouring regions as client-kings of ROME, the best-known of the dynasty being Herod the Great, who supplanted the HASMONEANS in 37 BC. The various lands ruled by his descendants were annexed by Rome during the later 1st century AD. (163b)

Hesse (Hessen), region of western Germany which became a Landgravate in the 13th century under a branch of the house of BRABANT. In 1567 the state was permanently split into two parts – Hesse-CASSEL, which became an ELECTORATE in 1803 and was annexed by PRUSSIA in 1866, and Hesse-DARMSTADT, the Grand Duchy of Hesse and the Rhine from 1806, abolished in 1918. The family of Battenberg (Mountbatten) is a branch of the Hesse-Darmstadt line. (34)

Hethumids Armenian noble family which established itself in CILICIA in the 11th century AD and supplanted the Rubenids as kings of Lesser Armenia in 1226. Their state was conquered by the MAMLUKS in 1375. See ARMENIA, LESSER. (140b)

High Kings of Ireland Also called High Kings of TARA from their traditional capital, a series of rulers who claimed with varying success to be overlords of the provincial kingdoms of Ireland. The first of them was Niall of the Nine Hostages, in the early 5th century AD, and most of the later High Kings were his descendants (see O'NEILL), though the O'BRIENS and O'CONNORS contested the office in the 11th/12th centuries, and it vanished on the Anglo-Norman invasion. (13)

Hijaz Region along the western coast of Arabia, containing the holiest of Muslim cities, MECCA and Medina and controlled

by the early CALIPHS. The HASHIMID rulers of Mecca exercised a varying degree of overlordship in the region from the 10th century, usually as vassals of stronger powers, until the last of them repudiated OSMANLI Turkish suzerainty in 1916, establishing the 'Kingdom of the Hijaz', only to lose their lands to the AL-SA'UD in 1924–25. (173)

Hillah Town in central 'Iraq, near ancient Babylon, centre of an Arab principality established in the mid-10th century AD by the MAZYADID family. The SELJUKS annexed their state in the mid-12th century. (185c)

Hims (Homs, ancient Emesa), very old town in Syria, centre of a sun-worship cult with hereditary chief-priests, one of whom became Roman Emperor (Heliogabalus, 218–222 AD). In the 12th/13th centuries, Hims formed a small principality under a branch of the AYYUBIDS, annexed by the MAMLUKS in 1262. (166h)

Himyar Ancient kingdom in what is now called YEMEN, successor of the SABA kingdom, its rulers initially calling themselves kings of 'Saba and Dhu Raidan'. At first a powerful state exercising influence over much of Arabia and the Ethiopian lands across the Red Sea, Himyar became a battle-ground in the 6th century AD between the Ethiopian kings at AXUM and the SASANID rulers of Iran. In 628, the Persian viceroy of Himyar surrendered to Muhammad the Prophet. (171c)

Hindu Shahi dynasty Family which ruled on the north-western frontier of India, around Peshawar and Kabul. They supplanted an earlier line known as Turki Shahis, about whom little is known, in the mid-9th century AD, and for some time blocked Muslim penetration into India. By breaking their power, Mahmud of GHAZNA opened the way for his great raids and the later GHURID conquests – the last of the dynasty perished in 1026. (203a)

Hira Ancient town near modern Kufah, 'Iraq, capital of the Arab LAKHMID dynasty in the 4th/6th centuries AD. They controlled north-eastern Arabia as vassals of the SASANIDS of Iran and were rivals of the GHASSANIDS of Syria. Their kingdom was suppressed by the Persians in the early 7th century, perhaps making easier the Muslim onslaught into 'Iraq a few years later. (184)

Hisn Kaifa (Hasankeyf), town now in Turkish KURDISTAN, centre of a small state ruled in the 12th/13th centuries by a branch of the ARTUQID dynasty and from 1232 by a branch of the AYYUBIDS, who retained power there long after the fall of the main lines of their dynasty. The principality was eventually annexed by the AQ QOYUNLI late in the 15th century. (185e, m)

Hittites (Khatti), ruling people of an ancient empire centred in Asia Minor and at times extending into northern Syria. It emerged *c.*1800 BC, and an early ruler put an end to the First Dynasty of BABYLON – the Hittite empire reached its zenith in the 14th/early 13th centuries, contesting supremacy in Western Asia with EGYPT. In about 1200 BC, the Hittites were overwhelmed in the invasion from the west by the Sea-Peoples, an alliance of marauding tribes, but a number of cities in Syria remained under the rule of Hittite princes for several centuries longer, falling eventually to conquest by ASSYRIA. (136)

Hkrit dynasty A family which ruled briefly in ARAKAN in the later 12th century AD. (238d)

Ho dynasty Briefly rulers of VIET-NAM in the early 15th century, the founder deposing the TRAN family – who were restored with the aid of MING troops from China a few years later. (243g)

Hohenstauffen Imperial dynasty of GERMANY in the 12th/13th centuries. They became dukes of SWABIA in 1079 and FRANCONIA in 1115, and rulers of Germany in 1138. The premature death of Henry VI in 1197, just after he had added the kingdom of SICILY to his possessions, led to temporary eclipse for the family, and the last effective Hohenstauffen, Emperor Frederick II, concentrated his efforts on building up a great Mediterranean power based in Italy, which involved him in a ruinous struggle with the PAPACY and the loss of real control in Germany. After his death in 1250, the dynasty was soon extinguished, its last ruling member, Manfred of Sicily, being killed in battle in 1266. (4, 39a–b, 62b)

Hohenzollern Major German dynasty, originally Counts of Zollern in Swabia, Burgraves of Nuremberg from the late 12th century and rulers of the ELECTORATE of BRANDENBURG from 1415. The last Grand Master of the Teutonic Knights of PRUSSIA, also a Hohenzollern, converted his lands into a hereditary duchy in 1525, and this region came into the hands of the Brandenburg line in 1618, greatly increasing the power of their state – they assumed the title of King in Prussia in 1701, and acquired further lands in northern Germany in the 18th century, emerging as the dominant power in that region. Making more gains as a result of the Napoleonic wars, Prussia brought about the unity of Germany in 1871 under a Hohenzollern emperor. Minor branches of the dynasty ruled small territories in southern Germany, and a member of the Sigmaringen line became king of RUMANIA in the mid-19th century, his descendants

THE HOHENZOLLERN DYNASTY

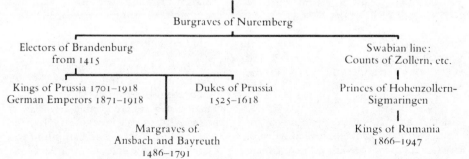

Burchard, Count of Zollern, d. 1061

Burgraves of Nuremberg

Electors of Brandenburg from 1415 — Swabian line: Counts of Zollern, etc.

Kings of Prussia 1701–1918 German Emperors 1871–1918 — Dukes of Prussia 1525–1618 — Princes of Hohenzollern-Sigmaringen

Margraves of Ansbach and Bayreuth 1486–1791 — Kings of Rumania 1866–1947 ruling that country until the abolition of its monarchy in 1947. The German Empire and all its constituent kingdoms, grand duchies and other states were abolished at the end of the First World War, in 1918. (26, 27b–d, 79)

Holkar dynasty Maharajas of INDORE, a major state of central India, established by the MARATHA general Malhar Rao Holkar in the early 18th century. In 1948 their territory was incorporated into the Republic of India. (207f)

Holland Alternative name for the NETHERLANDS but more accurately the name of its largest province, which formed a county within the German empire from the 10th century. It became united with HAINAULT under the same counts in 1300, and passed to the VALOIS dukes of BURGUNDY and to their HABSBURG heirs. In the later 16th century, the province of Holland took the lead in the Dutch revolt against the Spanish Habsburgs and became the main component of the United Netherlands under the House of ORANGE. At the beginning of the 19th century, Napoleon BONAPARTE set up a kingdom of Holland for his brother Louis, who abdicated in 1810. (19)

Holstein Region of north-western Germany, a county from the 12th century. It was acquired together with SCHLESWIG in the 15th century by the OLDENBURGS of Denmark and soon divided among junior branches of that family, the main such branch being that of Holstein-Gottorp which controlled large areas of both Schleswig and Holstein. In 1721, Denmark obtained full control of Schleswig, and in 1773 obtained the remaining lands of the Gottorp branch in exchange for Oldenburg. In 1866, Denmark was forced to cede Schleswig and Holstein to Germany, re-acquiring part of Schleswig in 1920. (29)

Holy Roman Empire Name formally adopted in the 10th century for the empire founded in Western Europe in 800 by Charlemagne the CAROLINGIAN as a conscious revival of the long-vanished Western Roman Empire. From about 900, the empire more or less coincided with the German kingdom which had emerged

as one of the fragments of the Carolingian state, though the emperors intermittently controlled northern Italy until the fall of the HOHENSTAUFFEN in the mid-13th century. The office of Holy Roman Emperor and German King was never hereditary, though strong rulers often managed to keep the title in their family for several generations, and a formal election system was introduced in 1356 (see ELECTORATE). In medieval times, only those rulers crowned in Rome were regarded as entitled to be styled emperors, but when the HABSBURGS obtained permanent possession of the office in the 15th century, they abandoned the custom and took the imperial title automatically on accession. After the Hohenstauffen, the imperial power amounted to very little, and the Habsburg attempts to revive it in the 16th/17th centuries ultimately failed – see GERMANY. The title of Holy Roman Emperor was abandoned by the Habsburgs in 1806. (4)

Hoysala dynasty Rulers of a kingdom in the MYSORE region, India, which became an important power on the decline of the CHALUKYAS in the 12th century. Their strength was broken by the rulers of DELHI in the mid-14th century, though the last rulers of the dynasty may have laid the foundations for the VIJAYANAGAR empire which took over their territory. (219b)

Hrebeljanovichi Family which ruled SERBIA in the late 14th and early 15th centuries. Lazar Hrebeljanovich led the Serbs in the disastrous battle at Kossovo in 1389 against the OSMANLI Turks and perished on the field – his son was a loyal vassal of Sultan Bayazid I and fought on the Osmanli side against the TIMURID army at Ankara in 1402. The family was succeeded by the BRANKOVICHI. (72b)

Hsia Name of several dynasties in CHINA:
   1 Legendary, probably mythical first dynasty of China, predecessors of the SHANG in the early 2nd millennium BC.
   2 Ruling family of HSIUNG-NU origin in one of the SIXTEEN KINGDOMS of the 4th/5th centuries AD. Their state was based in Shensi and conquered by the Northern WEI in 431. (230q)
   3 Western Hsia, ruling dynasty of the Tangut kingdom in north-western China.

The Tanguts were a people related to the Tibetans, and established a powerful realm in Kansu and the Ordos region after the fall of the T'ANG, taking the imperial title in 1032. Their state was one of the first victims of the MONGOLS, resisting the initial attacks – Chingis Khan spent the last year of his life crushing Tangut opposition, and the dynasty was extinguished in 1227 AD. (232g)

Hsin One-emperor dynasty founded by Wang Mang, a relative of the last Western HAN rulers, who seized the throne of CHINA in 9 AD. He was an able and energetic but unrealistic reformer, and was killed in widespread disorder and rebellion from which emerged the Eastern Han regime. (227f)

Hsiung-Nu Nomadic people of MONGOLIA, usually identified or connected with the HUNS of European history, the first of the great tribal confederations which ruled the eastern steppelands. They were persistent and dangerous enemies of early imperial CHINA, establishing their empire around 200 BC under rulers entitled Shan-Yu. In the mid-1st century AD, the Chinese succeeded in splitting them into two hordes, a northern group whose kingdom was conquered by other nomads in the second century, and a southern state under Chinese overlordship. The leader of this latter horde founded the short-lived Earlier CHAO state of the early 4th century, one of the SIXTEEN KINGDOMS, in Shansi. (225a–c)

Hudid dynasty (Banu Hud), one of the REYES DE TAIFAS families, kings of ZARAGOZA in north-eastern Spain in succession to the TUJIBIDS. Most of their territory, including their capital, fell to the ALMORAVIDS early in the 12th century, but they maintained a small state based on Rueda de Jalon until 1142. The last of the dynasty took advantage of the collapse of Almoravid power to head a Muslim revolt against that regime, and briefly established his rule over a wide area of southern Spain, but was killed in battle in 1146. (48n)

Hue Coastal city of central VIET-NAM, capital of the NGUYEN family from the 16th century as rulers of the southern Vietnamese territory under the nominal suzerainty of the Later LE emperors. When the Nguyen themselves became emperors in the early 19th century, Hue became the imperial capital. (243l–m)

Hungary The modern Hungarian state is only a part of the historical kingdom of Hungary, which included all the territory within the arc of the Carpathian mountains, incorporating Slovakia, TRANSYLVANIA and part of what is now northern Yugoslavia. The Hungarian plain south of the Danube formed the Roman province of Pannonia, and after the collapse of frontier defence in the 5th century AD barbarian tribes overran the area, which was the centre of the HUN empire under Attila, and later of the AVAR realm. The short-lived kingdom of Greater MORAVIA controlled the western section of the plain in the later 9th century, but around 900 AD the whole region was conquered by the Magyars, nomadic invaders from the western steppes, under the ARPAD dynasty, who founded a strong kingdom formally Christianized a century later. In 1095, the kingdom of Croatia was united with that of Hungary and remained so until 1918, extending Hungarian territory to a large section of the Adriatic coast. After the extinction of the Arpads in 1301, various families, mostly of foreign origin, ruled the state, which remained a major power until its conquest by the OSMANLI Turks in the early 16th century. Transylvania then became a separate principality, while a small western remnant of the kingdom was held by the HABSBURGS, who reconquered all the region at the end of the 17th century. Thereafter, the Hungarian kingdom was part of the Habsburg empire until the Austro-Hungarian monarchy was broken up in 1918. (71)

Huns Nomadic people of the steppelands, usually identified with the HSIUNG-NU opponents of the Chinese in MONGOLIA in the 1st/2nd centuries BC and AD. In the late 4th century AD, the Huns appeared in the western steppes, crossed the Volga and destroyed the kingdoms of the GOTHS in the Ukraine, later moving on to overrun the plain of HUNGARY. This latter region formed the centre of a great Hun empire in Central Europe under Attila in the mid-5th century, which collapsed, however, on his death in 453 AD. The early khans of BULGARIA claimed descent from one of his sons.

Husainids Rulers of TUNIS from the beginning of the 18th century in succession to the MURADID Beys. The family claimed descent from the HAMMUDIDS of Spain, and were nominally vassals of the OSMANLI sultans but virtually independent until the establishment of a French protectorate in Tunisia in 1881. The Husainid monarchy was abolished in 1957 by newly independent Tunisia. (111b)

Hyderabad (Haidarabad), city in the eastern DECCAN, India, capital of the last rulers of GOLKUNDA sultanate before the MOGHUL conquest in 1687. In the early 18th century, the Moghul viceroy of the Deccan, Nizam-ul-Mulk Asaf Jah, established himself as virtually independent ruler at Hyderabad, which became the capital of a large and important state, its ruler the premier Indian prince under British overlordship. On the British withdrawal from India, the Nizam of Hyderabad attempted to establish his independence, but his state was absorbed into the Republic of India in 1948. (218h)

Hyksos (Hiqa-khasut), a people from Western Asia who conquered much of EGYPT in the 17th century BC and whose kings form Dynasty XV of the PHARAOHS. It has long been suspected that the Hyksos regime was in some way connected with the sojourn of the Hebrews in Egypt prior to the Exodus. The invaders were expelled by the founder of Dynasty XVIII in the mid-16th century BC. (98)

I

Iberia Ancient name for two different regions:

1 The Spanish peninsula, a name derived from one of its early peoples, the Iberi.

2 Eastern GEORGIA in the Caucasus, later known as KARTLI. An Iberian kingdom existed from the 3rd century BC until the abolition of its monarchy in the late 6th century AD. Thereafter it was ruled by viceroys for BYZANTIUM or the CALIPHS until the BAGRATIDS re-established the monarchy in the 9th century, soon combining Iberia with ABKHAZIA to form the medieval Georgian kingdom. (149–150)

Iclings Ruling dynasty of MERCIA, the Anglo-Saxon kingdom of central England, from its emergence at the beginning of the 7th century AD until at least the early 9th century, the ancestry of the last kings before the VIKING conquest being unknown. The Iclings claimed descent from the earlier kings of the Angles in Schleswig. (5d)

Idrisids One of the first Muslim dynasties to seize independence from the ʿABBASID Caliphs, descended from Hasan ibn ʿAli, grandson of Muhammad the Prophet (see QURAISHI dynasties). The founder established a kingdom in MOROCCO in the late 8th century which survived precariously under threat from stronger neighbours and was eventually extinguished in the late 10th century by the Spanish UMAYYADS. The later HAMMUDID family in Spain were of Idrisid descent. (112b)

Ifat See AWFAT.

Ifranids (Banu Ifran), a Zenata Berber clan which established a number of small and short-lived principalities in the MAGHRIB in the 8th/11th centuries AD.

Igehalkids Dynasty which ruled the kingdom of ELAM in Iran in the 14th and 13th centuries BC, its origins being obscure. The family was succeeded by the SHUTRUKIDS. (186b)

Ikhshidids 'Ikhshid' was a royal title of Central Asian origin, and the founder of the dynasty of this name evidently claimed descent from some Transoxanian ruling family, though he established his independence in EGYPT, being at first a governor for the ʿABBASIDS. His kingdom, set up in the mid-10th century, was of brief duration, since his last successor was dispossessed in 969 by FATIMID conquest. (100b)

Ikkeri Kingdom in northern MYSORE, India, founded by a NAYYAK family on the collapse of the VIJAYANAGAR empire in the 16th century. It was annexed by HAIDAR ʿALI in 1763. (219f)

Ikshvaku dynasty Early rulers of the ANDHRA region of the Deccan, India, successors in that area of the SATAVAHANAS in the 3rd century AD. (218a)

Ilak Khans (Ilek, Ilig Khans, etc.) See QARA-KHANIDS.

Ildegizids (Eldiguzids), an ATABEG dynasty, originally governors of western Iran for the SELJUKS, whose last rulers they controlled for some years in the later 12th century. The last Ildegizids held only AZERBAIJAN, where they were suppressed by the KHWARIZM-Shah Jalal-ud-Din in 1225. (188c)

Ilkhans One of the CHINGIS-KHANID dynasties, rulers of the empire in Western Asia established by Hulegu Khan, grandson of Chingis Khan, who conquered Iran, 'Iraq and Transcaucasia in the mid-13th century. The Ilkhan empire was a major power for nearly a hundred years, after which it collapsed abruptly, its territory falling to various minor dynasties including the JALAYIRIDS, MUZAFFARIDS, ERETNIDS, SARBADARIDS and KARTS. (187h)

Ilorin FULANI Amirate in Nigeria, formerly a province of the OYO empire which broke away in the early 19th century under a governor who was soon supplanted by a Fulani ruler owing allegiance to the sultan of SOKOTO. (118h)

Ilyas Shahis Family which ruled as sultans of BENGAL in the 14th/15th centuries. (214c)

'Imad Shahis Ruling dynasty of BERAR, one of the DECCAN SULTANATES, established in 1490 by Fath-Allah 'Imad-ul-Mulk. Berar was annexed in the late 16th century by AHMADNAGER. (217j)

Imereti Western GEORGIA, the region variously known in earlier times as Colchis, LAZICA and (greater) ABKHAZIA. It broke away in the 13th century and again in the 15th century from the Georgian kingdom to form a separate kingdom under BAGRATID branches, the smaller states of MINGRELIA, BURIA and Abkhazia (see SHARVASHIDZE) breaking away from Imereti in turn. The kingdom was annexed by Russia in 1810. (153c)

Inakids Khans of Khiva (see KHWARIZM/ KHIVA) from the beginning of the 19th century and the real rulers for some time previously under the last ARABSHAHIDS. They were compelled to become Russian vassals in 1872, and the khanate was abolished by the Soviet government in 1919. (199d)

Incas People who ruled an empire centred in PERU in the 15th and early 16th centuries, their monarch being entitled 'Sapa-Inca' but usually called the 'Inca' by historians. Founded in about the 12th century AD, their kingdom was a minor highland state at first, gradually expanding over a vast area of South America along the Andes from Ecuador to northern Chile. Their dominions were mostly conquered by the Spaniards under Pizarro in 1533 and the following years, but the dynasty held out in Andean strongholds until 1572. (252)

India The Indian sub-continent, currently divided into the three states of Pakistan, Bangladesh and the Republic of India, is best treated as a single historical region, since present international boundaries have little relevance to dynastic history in particular. A number of kingdoms and other states existed in India prior to Alexander the Great's invasion in the late 4th century BC, but not much is known of their history – the first great Indian dynasty was the MAURYAS, whose founder rose to power directly after the Macedonian incursion and perhaps as a result of it. Maurya rule extended over most of India except the extreme south for about a century, after which the empire broke up, power falling to various provincial rulers. The realm of the GUPTAS in the 4th/5th centuries AD was less extensive, but included most of the north and part of the DECCAN, while the south remained divided among other rulers. Another period of fragmentation and foreign invasion in the north followed the fall of the Guptas, and from the confusion emerged the many RAJPUT clans who almost monopolized political power in northern India and the Deccan until the Muslim invasions, warring among themselves and unable to create stable kingdoms, though the PRATIHARAS ruled a large dominion in the north-east in the 9th/10th centuries. The

GHAZNAVID raids of the early 11th century paved the way for the more permanent GHURID conquests and the foundation of the DELHI sultanate in 1206, and this latter state rapidly extended Muslim rule over nearly the whole sub-continent within the next century, but then broke up into a number of independent sultanates, while a strong Hindu empire, VIJAYANAGAR, arose in the south. In 1526, the remnants of the Delhi sultanate were conquered by the MOGHULS, who re-united most of India under their rule until the early 18th century, when their empire too disintegrated. In the resultant warfare and confusion, the main contenders for power were MARATHAS, Afghans and British, and by the early 19th century, the British were predominant, gaining control of the entire sub-continent within a few decades. In 1947, India was divided between the two independent states of Pakistan and the Indian Republic, the eastern region of Pakistan becoming a separate state as Bangladesh in 1971.

The above is the barest broad summary of Indian history – the various provinces and regions have often been ruled by independent dynasties, and some further detail will be found under the names of individual areas – see Section II (203–223) for the more important regions. Under British rule, many formerly independent states continued to exist, only a score or so of which, the largest or historically most important, are listed in this book. All these states have now been abolished. See 200–202 for the main imperial dynasties of India.

Indonesia Before the Dutch conquest of the various islands which constitute this modern state, its history was simply that of the separate islands, though some of the Javanese empires extended their authority to parts of neighbouring regions. See JAVA, SUMATRA, SULU, RIAU and also BRUNEI.

Indo-Parthians/Indo-Scythians The history of eastern IRAN, AFGHANISTAN and the PUNJAB during the period between the collapse of the kingdom of BACTRIA and the emergence of the KUSHAN empire (1st centuries BC and AD) is obscure and much debated. A number of so-called 'Indo-Parthian' and 'Indo-Scythian' rulers in the area are known mostly from their coins, but their dates and territories are very uncertain, as are their connections, if any, with the ARSACID kings of Iran. Some of the viceroys (satraps) of these rulers founded kingdoms of their own in India, mostly short-lived except for the KSHATRAPA state in MALWA. (196a–b)

Indore City in central India, capital of the state of the same name founded by the MARATHA general Malhar Rao HOLKAR in the early 18th century, now part of the Republic of India. (207f)

Inju'ids Muslim family who acquired control of FARS as vassals of the ILKHANS at the beginning of the 14th century. After the collapse of Ilkhan power, they became involved in a long struggle with the MUZAFFARIDS, who eventually annexed their territory. (191b)

Iran Modern and historic name for the country often called Persia, though in its widest sense including other Iranian-speaking or once Iranian-speaking lands in Afghanistan and Transoxania. The earliest kingdom on Iranian soil was that of ELAM, centred in modern Khuzistan, but the first Iranian empire was founded by the MEDES in the 7th century BC, soon supplanted by and incorporated into the ACHAEMENID empire, the state which ruled Western Asia in the 6th/4th centuries until its overthrow by Alexander the Great. In the struggles following Alexander's death, Iran fell to the SELEUCIDS, from whom it was gradually conquered by the ARSACID (Parthian) kings in the 3rd/2nd centuries BC. The Parthian empire generally included 'Iraq and parts of Transcaucasia, though to what extent the Arsacids controlled eastern Iran is uncertain (see INDO-PARTHIANS). In a great resurgence of Persian national feeling, the Parthians were overthrown by the local ruler of FARS, who founded the SASANID dynasty in the early 3rd century AD. Under his successors, Iran became a great power exercising authority over all the lands from the Oxus to the Euphrates, and on occasion further afield, as in the early 7th century, when the whole Roman east was temporarily overrun by the Persians. However, in the middle of that century, the Muslims conquered the whole of Iran, which became part of the empire of the UMAYYAD and 'ABBASID Caliphs. As the latter dynasty declined, various independent dynasties arose, most of which were swept away by the BUYIDS or their SELJUK successors in the 10th and 11th centuries. On the disintegration of the Seljuk empire, Iran again became divided, and fell to MONGOL conquest in the mid-13th century, forming the heart of the great ILKHAN state until that too broke up a hundred years later. The brief and destructive regime of the TIMURIDS in the decades around 1400 did little to re-unite the county, which was finally restored to unity only at the beginning of the 16th century by Shah Isma'il, founder of the SAFAVID dynasty and of a regime which has had a recognizable continuity to the present, despite several changes of dynasty and the abolition of the monarchy in 1979. See also under the various regions of Iran. (186–194)

'Iraq Arab name for the region which includes ancient BABYLONIA and MESOPOTAMIA, together with part of KURDISTAN now within the borders of the modern state. Civilization arose in the plain of the lower Tigris and Euphrates rivers perhaps even earlier than in EGYPT, and city-kingdoms existed in this area (SUMER and AKKAD) from the early 3rd millennium BC. The first substantial territorial state was that of Akkad in the 24th/23rd centuries, and in the 19th century BC the kings of Babylon came to dominate the region, maintaining a varying degree of supremacy until the rise of the northern power, ASSYRIA. The Assyrian state, having grown into a vast empire controlling much of Western Asia in the 8th and 7th centuries, was destroyed shortly before 600 BC, and the Neo-Babylonian kings ruled 'Iraq until the whole of Western Asia came under ACHAEMENID Persian rule in the late 6th century. Thereafter, 'Iraq remained for many centuries part of the successive empires of SELEUCIDS, ARSACIDS, SASANIDS, UMAYYADS and 'ABBASIDS, always a wealthy and populous province – under the early 'Abbasid Caliphs, it was the central region of a realm stretching from the MAGHRIB to

SIND and TRANSOXANIA. Various minor Muslim dynasties ruled in the region in later medieval times, but ruinous devastation was caused during the Mongol conquest of the 13th century and the struggles following the breakdown of the ILKHAN empire. From the early 16th century, with a brief period of Persian rule, 'Iraq formed a province under the OSMANLI sultans, often semi-independent under the Pashas at Baghdad, until the First World War. Then it was made a kingdom for a branch of the HASHIMIDS of Mecca, becoming a republic in 1958. (180–185)

Irbil Ancient Arbela, city in northern 'Iraq, centre of a small state ruled in the 12th/13th centuries by an ATABEG family, the BEGTIGINIDS, the last of whom bequeathed his realm to the 'ABBASID Caliph. (185k)

Ireland Myth and legend provide long lists of early Irish kings, but firmly historical provincial kingdoms emerge only in the 5th century AD, dominated intermittently by the HIGH KINGS at Tara, most of these belonging to the dynasty founded by Niall of the Nine Hostages (see O'NEILL), which also ruled in MEATH and AILECH and was itself a branch of the CONNACHTA dynasty of CONNAUGHT. In the 9th century, Ireland suffered heavily from invasion by the VIKINGS, who founded city-kingdoms at DUBLIN and elsewhere. Viking power was broken at Clontarf in 1014 by Brian Boru of MUNSTER, and thereafter the O'BRIENS contested the High Kingship with the O'Neills and the O'CONNORS of Connaught until the Anglo-Norman invasion in the late 12th century destroyed the Irish kingdoms (though in many cases the former ruling families retained part of their authority and in due course acquired Irish peerages). From 1171 Ireland was a lordship, and from 1541 a kingdom, attached to the English crown, until Eire became independent in the present century. (13–15)

Isaurian dynasty Imperial family of BYZANTIUM in the 8th century, founded by Leo III the Isaurian, who held Constantinople against the Arabs in the great UMAYYAD siege of 717–718. Isauria was a district of southern Asia Minor famous in antiquity for the warlike spirit and banditry of its inhabitants. (1c)

Isfahan Ancient Aspadana, city in Iran, capital of certain princes of the BUYID, KAKUYID and MUZAFFARID dynasties and one of the major cities of Asia in the 16th/17th centuries as capital of the SAFAVID Shahs.

Isfandiyarids See JANDARIDS.

Isin Ancient city in 'Iraq, centre of an important kingdom in the 19th/18th centuries BC after the decline of UR. It was conquered by ELAM. (180d)

Isles, kingdom and lordship of In the mid-12th century AD, a ruler of probably Scandinavian origin established a kingdom in the Western Isles of SCOTLAND, briefly ruling also in MAN. His successors continued to rule as more or less independent lords, their family named after his grandson (see MACDONALDS) until the Scottish kings managed to assert their suzerainty and finally to confiscate the lordship in the late 15th century. (12b)

Israel See JUDAEA.

Italy For early history, see ROME. On the fall of the Western Empire, Italy became a kingdom under the OSTROGOTHS until its reconquest by the Eastern Emperor Justinian in the mid-6th century AD. Almost at once, however, much of the country was overrun by the LOMBARDS, who established a kingdom in the north and the large duchies of SPOLETO and BENEVENTO, soon to become virtually independent, in the south. For several centuries, the Byzantines held various towns and territories around the southern coasts, while the north was conquered by the CAROLINGIANS in the late 8th century and controlled by the stronger of the German kings until the fall of the HOHENSTAUFFEN dynasty in the mid-13th century. The Lombard duchies and Byzantine lands were combined to form the kingdom of SICILY (later 'Naples and Sicily'), formally established in 1130, and the PAPACY gradually built up a territorial state in central Italy during medieval times. The Emperor Frederick II, also king of Sicily, made a great effort to bring

all Italy under his control, but after his death in 1250, the country became divided between many minor states. It was dominated by Spain in the 16th/17th centuries, and in the 18th/19th centuries by the Austrian HABSBURGS in the north, the Papacy in the central regions and the BOURBONS of Naples in the south (apart from the brief control by Napoleon BONAPARTE) until the unification of Italy under the SAVOY dynasty in 1861. The monarchy was abolished in 1946. See also under the names of the various states and dynasties. (55–68)

J

Jadejas RAJPUT dynasty which ruled KACHH in western India from the mid-16th century until the state was absorbed into the Republic of India in 1948. The family is said to have originated in SIND. (208f)

Jaffna City in CEYLON, centre of a kingdom under Tamil rulers from medieval times until the Portuguese conquest of the early 17th century. (224b)

Jaghatai See CHAGHATAI.

Jagiellon dynasty Descandants of Vladislav V Jagiellon of POLAND, otherwise Grand Duke Jogaila of Lithuania, who acquired the Polish throne through marriage to its ANGEVIN heiress, famous for his great victory over the Teutonic Knights of PRUSSIA in 1410 at Grunwald (Tannenberg). The Jagiellons ruled Poland until 1572 and arranged the permanent union of that state with their Lithuanian dominions in 1569. Members of the dynasty also ruled in HUNGARY and BOHEMIA in the 15th and early 16th centuries. (69b, 71b, 87h, 89)

Jahwarids Rulers of CORDOBA, Spain, immediate successors of the last UMAYYAD Caliph in his capital city. One of the 11th century REYES DE TAIFAS dynasties, whose little state was conquered by the 'ABBADIDS of Seville. (48j)

Jaipur See AMBER.

Jaisalmer City in northern RAJASTAN and capital of a state founded in the 12th

JAPANESE DYNASTIES

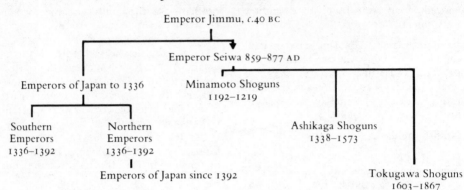

Emperor Jimmu, c.40 BC

Emperor Seiwa 859–877 AD

Emperors of Japan to 1336

Minamoto Shoguns
1192–1219

Southern
Emperors
1336–1392

Northern
Emperors
1336–1392

Ashikaga Shoguns
1338–1573

Emperors of Japan since 1392

Tokugawa Shoguns
1603–1867

century by the BHATI Rajput clan, which ruled until the incorporation of their kingdom into the Republic of India in 1949. (206g)

Jalayirids A MONGOL dynasty of the Jalayir tribe which seized control of 'Iraq and part of western Iran on the disintegration of the ILKHAN empire in the mid-14th century, with their capital at BAGHDAD. They were deprived of much of their territory by the TIMURIDS, and finally extinguished by the AQ-QOYUNLI in the mid-15th century. (185n)

Jandarids (Isfandiyarids), rulers of a state centred on Kastamuni, one of the ANATOLIAN AMIRATES of the 14th/15th centuries, whose lands were eventually annexed to the OSMANLI empire. (142b)

Janids Family closely related to the rulers of ASTRAKHAN and of CHINGIS-KHANID descent, who succeeded the SHAIBANIDS in TRANSOXANIA. Their realm had shrunk to constitute only the khanate of BUKHARA by the time they were succeeded by the HAIDARIDS in the late 18th century. (198i)

Japan A state ruled by the same dynasty from ancient times to the present, its first emperor traditionally dated at 660 BC. In reality he probably ruled a small region in southern Honshu in the 1st century BC and his successors gradually extended their control over the various islands of Japan, though Hokkaido was not brought under Japanese rule until modern times. In the 9th century AD, the FUJIWARA gained effective control of the govern-

ment, reducing the emperors to a largely ceremonial role, and in the 12th century the MINAMOTO family seized power with the title of SHOGUN. Various families later held this office, particularly the ASHIKAGA in the 14th/16th centuries – it was suppressed by the dictator of Japan, Hideyoshi, in 1573, but revived by the TOKUGAWAS at the beginning of the next century, and they remained effective rulers until a rather complicated revolution brought about the abdication of the last Shogun and the establishment of constitutional government under the emperor in 1868. The present emperor is directly descended from his first predecessor through some 70 generations. (236)

Jaunpur Town in Uttar Pradesh, India, capital of a sultanate of the same name which broke away from the DELHI sultanate under the SHARQI dynasty at the end of the 14th century and became an important state. It was reconquered by the LODIS of Delhi a hundred years later. (204c)

Java From ancient times the most heavily populated island of Indonesia and usually divided into two or more kingdoms, though its history before the 13th century AD is little known. The SAILENDRA dynasty, rulers of the SRIVIJAYA empire in SUMATRA, were probably of Javanese origin. Early in the 13th century, the SINGOSARI kingdom arose in eastern Java, to be succeeded at the end of the century by MAJAPAHIT, a powerful empire which extended its influence and perhaps control over nearby islands. With the spread of Islam into

Java and the collapse of the Majapahit state in the later 15th century, the island became divided among several sultanates, notably DEMAK, BANTAM and MATARAM, the latter state coming to dominate the eastern and central regions until the establishment of the Dutch power in Indonesia in the 17th/18th centuries. Mataram split into the two states of JOGJAKARTA and SURAKARTA in 1755, both surviving until Indonesian independence in 1949, though under the overlordship of the Dutch, who annexed Bantam in 1832. (246)

Jazirah Ibn 'Umar (modern Cizre), a town in south-eastern Turkey which formed a minor principality under a branch of the ZANGIDS in the 12th/13th centuries. (185i)

Jenghiz-Khanids See CHINGIS-KHANIDS.

Jerusalem From its capture by King David about 1000 BC, the city served as capital of the Hebrew state, and then of the kingdom of Judah until its capture by BABYLON in the early 6th century BC. When JUDAEA again became independent under the HASMONEANS, Jerusalem was their capital also, and that of the HERODIANS until Roman annexation of Judaea in the 1st century AD, being captured by the Muslims from BYZANTIUM in the 7th century. In 1099, the army of the First Crusade took the city by assault, and it became the centre of a CRUSADER STATE, the Kingdom of Jerusalem. While the city fell to the AYYUBIDS in 1187, the kingdom survived along the coast of Palestine until the MAMLUK conquest a century later. (161, 163, 167a)

Jibal Region of Iran, the central part of ancient MEDIA, containing the important cities of HAMADAN, ISFAHAN and Tehran. (190)

Jodhpur City in RAJASTAN, modern capital of MARWAR state. (206b)

Jogjakarta City and former state in JAVA, one of the two kingdoms into which the sultanate of MATARAM split in 1755. The state survived under the suzerainty of the Dutch and is now part of Indonesia. (246e)

Johore Sultanate in southern MALAYA, now one of the states of MALAYSIA. It was established by the last sultan of MALACCA after the fall of that city to the Portuguese in 1511, and was ruled by his dynasty until its Johore line became extinct at the end of the 17th century. In the next century, the state came under BUGIS control, and early in the 19th century, real power was acquired by the chief ministers, descended from an earlier sultan, while the nominal rulers retained only the RIAU-LINGGA islands. In 1885, the chief minister (Temenggong) took the title of sultan himself, the state having by that date come under British suzerainty. (244e)

Jordan Modern Arab kingdom known as Transjordan until 1949, established as an amirate in 1921, under a son of the HASHIMID ruler of Mecca, in the region east of the Jordan. (170)

Juan-Juan Nomadic tribal confederation which dominated MONGOLIA in the 4th/6th centuries AD. Their power was broken by the T'U-CHUEH (Turks) but some historians identify the AVARS of European history with a section of this people. (225d)

Juchen People of Manchuria, founders of an empire in northern CHINA, see CHIN 6.

Juchids Descendants of Juchi, eldest son of Chingis Khan, who was allocated western Siberia as an appanage and died shortly before his father. His sons established their rule in Russia – see GOLDEN HORDE and CHINGIS KHANID dynasties.

Judaea Modern Palestine, the inland area of which was overrun by the Hebrews in the late 2nd millennium BC and formed a kingdom from about 1020 BC, though within a century it became divided into the northern state of Israel and the small southern state of Judah. Israel was ruled by successive short-lived dynasties until its conquest by ASSYRIA in the late 8th century BC, while Judah remained under the original Hebrew royal dynasty of DAVID until it fell to the Neo-Babylonian empire (see BABYLON) in 587 BC. During this period the coast of Palestine was controlled by other peoples, notably the Philistines. The whole region formed part of the ACHAEMENID empire, and then was disputed between PTOLEMIES and SELEUCIDS, until in the mid-2nd century BC a Jewish revolt against Seleucid rule resulted in the establishment of an independent state under the HASMONEAN dynasty (Maccabees), whom the Romans replaced by the HERODIANS as client kings before annexing the land to their empire in the first century AD. Since that time, the region has remained under the control of various kingdoms and empires until the present century, except for the period in the 12th/13th centuries when it formed the CRUSADER STATE kingdom of JERUSALEM. (161, 163, 167a)

Judah See JUDAEA.

Julich Town in north-western Germany, a county from the 11th century and duchy from 1356, united with CLEVES in 1524. On the extinction of its ruling family in 1609, various claimants contended for succession, and eventually the dominions of the Julich line were divided, Cleves and MARK going to BRANDENBURG while Julich and BERG went to a branch of the WITTELSBACHS of the PALATINATE, passing later to BAVARIA. (39f)

Julio-Claudians First ruling family of the Roman empire, Augustus Caesar and his descendants plus those of his wife by her first husband, a member of the Claudian family. A very high proportion of the Julio-Claudians and their close relatives died violently or in suspicious circumstances amid family feuds, and they became extinct with the suicide of Nero in 68 AD. (1a)

Kachh (Cutch), district of Gujarat province, India, formerly a princely state ruled by a RAJPUT dynasty, the JADEJAS, migrants from Sind, who acquired control in the mid-16th century. The area is now part of the Republic of India. (208f)

Kachwahas RAJPUT clan to which belong the former ruling dynasty of AMBER (Jaipur) in Rajastan, established in the 12th century AD and at first a minor state. However, its maharajas greatly increased their importance under the MOGHULS, whom they served as generals and administrators. The state was absorbed into the Republic of India in 1949. (206d)

Kadamba dynasty Rulers of the Kanara region of the western DECCAN, who headed a revolt in the area against the PALLAVAS in the mid-4th century AD. Their state was conquered by the CHALUKYAS early in the 7th century. (219e)

Kajars See QAJARS.

Kakatiya dynasty Rulers of the WARANGAL kingdom in the eastern DECCAN, where they succeeded the CHALUKYAS of Kalyana, asserting their independence in the 12th century. Their state was conquered by the DELHI sultans in the early 14th century. (218e)

Kakheti Region of eastern GEORGIA, a principality after the abolition of the Iberian monarchy in the 6th century AD, initially under a branch of the former royal dynasty, the CHOSROIDS. It was then ruled by other families and acquired by a branch of the BAGRATIDS in the early 11th century, being absorbed into the Georgian kingdom in 1105. When that state broke up in the late 15th century, it again became independent as a kingdom under Bagratid rulers, and was annexed by the Russians in 1801. (151b–d, 153b)

Kakuyids (Kakwayhids), a family from DAYLAM which rose to power in the JIBAL region of Iran on the decline of the BUYIDS in the 11th century, ruling ISFAHAN and HAMADAN. Later they governed Yazd under the SELJUKS. (190c)

Kalachuris Family which temporarily supplanted the CHALUKYAS of Kalyana in the 12th century as rulers in the western DECCAN. (217f)

Kalat Town in BALUCHISTAN, centre of a state of the same name which became the most important power in the region in the mid-17th century. It came under British control in the later 19th century and is now part of Pakistan. (205e)

Kalba Former Shaikhdom, now part of SHARJAH in the UNITED ARAB EMIRATES. It was briefly a separate dominion 1936–1951 under a branch of the QASIMIDS of Sharjah. (178c)

Kalbids Dynasty of Kalbite (Syrian Arab) origin who ruled SICILY from the mid-10th century AD, initially as governors for the FATIMIDS but soon independently. Their state broke up among various amirs in the mid-11th century, opening the way for the conquest of the island by Roger of HAUTEVILLE. (61)

Kalmak (Calmuck), see ZUNGAR KALMAKS.

Kampuchea See CAMBODIA.

Kamarupa Ancient kingdom in ASSAM from the 2nd century AD, supplanted by the AHOM state in the 13th century. (215a)

Kanauj Ancient city on the Ganges in Uttar Pradesh, India. Under HARSHA it became the capital of a short-lived but extensive empire in the 7th century AD, gaining a prestige which made it a prize for later would-be empire-builders. In the 9th century it became the capital of the powerful PRATIHARA dynasty, rulers of much of northern India in their heyday, until 1018, when it fell to the famous Muslim invader Mahmud of GHAZNA. (200e–f)

Kandy Highland city in CEYLON, capital of the kingdom of the same name which remained independent in the late 16th century, when the rest of the island passed under Portuguese rule. It was annexed by the British in 1815. (224d)

Kanem-Bornu Kingdom of the central SUDAN, originally based in the region of Kanem, north-east of Lake Chad, ruled by the SAIFAWA dynasty from the 8th century AD. In the late 14th century, the Saifawa lost control of Kanem and moved their power-base to Bornu, south-west of the lake, where their state rose to great importance in the 16th century, re-incorporating Kanem. At the beginning of the 19th century, Bornu was attacked by the FULANI conquerors of the HAUSA kingdoms and preserved only by the efforts of a new dynasty, the SHEHUS, who at first ruled in the name of Saifawa puppets, but later deposed the ancient dynasty. In 1893 the Shehus were expelled by the empire-builder RABEH Zubair, but restored in 1902 – their state is now part of Nigeria. (115)

Kano Ancient city in northern Nigeria, centre of a HAUSA kingdom under a HABE dynasty from around 1000 AD until the FULANI conquest of 1807, when the region became an amirate subject to the SOKOTO sultanate. (116a, 118a)

Kanva dynasty Successors of the SUNGAS as rulers of the remnants of the MAURYA empire in the 1st century B.C in the Ganges plain. Their state was suppressed by the SATAVAHANAS. (200c)

Kara- For Turkish names beginning thus, see under QARA-.

Karageorgevichi and **Obrenovichi** Two families which disputed the rule of SERBIA in the 19th century. In 1804, Kara George led a revolt against the OSMANLI Turkish government which was eventually suppressed, while shortly afterwards Milosh Obrenovich led a second, more successful revolt and established himself as ruler. The throne of the principality (a kingdom from 1882), changed hands several times between their respective heirs, until the last Obrenovich king was murdered in 1903. The Karageorgevichi then ruled Serbia, and later the much enlarged kingdom of Yugoslavia, until the abolition of their monarchy in 1945. (72c)

Karagwe Kingdom west of Lake Victoria, ruled by a branch of the BAHINDA dynasty from the 15th century AD until the abolition of their state by the independent government of Tanzania in 1963. (127b)

Karkota dynasty The first ruling family of Kashmir, in the 7th/9th centuries AD, for which there is reliable historical detail. They were succeeded by the UTPALAS. (209a)

Karnataka dynasty A RAJPUT family from the Tirhut region of northern Bihar, India, who temporarily established themselves as overlords of NEPAL in the 14th century AD. The local MALLA rulers recovered their independence about a hundred years later. (211g)

Kars Ancient Armenian town now in eastern Turkey, centre of a BAGRATID kingdom which separated from the kingdom of ARMENIA in the 10th century AD. The state was annexed by BYZANTIUM in 1064. (147c)

Kart dynasty Rulers of HERAT and the region around it, now part of Afghanistan.

They were originally vassals of the ILKHANS from the mid-13th century, but later became independent. Their kingdom was conquered by the founder of the TIMURID empire at the end of the 14th century. (197d)

Kartli Later name for ancient IBERIA, the central region of the kingdom of GEORGIA, which became itself a kingdom under the main BAGRATID line when the Georgian state broke up in the late 15th century. It was annexed by Russia in 1801. (153a)

Kashgar (Su-Fu), a very old city in Chinese TURKESTAN (Sinkiang). It was the capital of a branch of the QARA-KHANIDS in the 10th/13th centuries and the centre of the DUGHLAT state in the 14th/16th centuries, later falling under the rule of the CH'ING emperors of China. In the late 19th century, a local chief, Ya'kub Beg, established an independent khanate in the area, but was eventually conquered by the Chinese in 1878. (198a, f)

Kashmir Himalayan region now partitioned, the major portion under the control of the Republic of India and the rest under Pakistan. It was part of the MAURYA empire, one member of that dynasty being credited in tradition with the founding of an independent kingdom in the area. However, Kashmiri history is very obscure until the end of the 6th century AD, when the KARKOTA kings acquired power, to be succeeded by various Hindu dynasties until the Muslim SWATI family established a sultanate in 1339. In the mid-16th century, Kashmir was conquered by Haidar Mirza DUGHLAT, though the Swatis were soon restored and then succeeded by the CHAK family, whose kingdom was annexed by the MOGHULS in 1589. On the break-up of the Moghul empire in the 18th century, the region was occupied by the DURRANI rulers of Afghanistan, and then by the SIKH maharaja Ranjit Singh. In 1846, Gulab Singh DOGHRA of Jammu became ruler of Kashmir by arrangement with the British, and the last of his successors opted to take his mainly Muslim state into the Indian Republic in 1947, a decision which was contested by Pakistan and resulted in the present partition. (209)

Kasimids See QASIMIDS.

Kasimov A state set up under Russian protection in the mid-15th century in opposition to KAZAN and ruled by a branch of the Kazan dynasty, CHINGISKHANIDS of the GOLDEN HORDE. After the fall of Kazan, Kasimov remained a vassal khanate of the Muscovite rulers until they annexed it in the late 17th century. (96c)

Kassites Ancient people of the Zagros mountains, who gained control of BABYLON in the 16th century BC. A Kassite dynasty ruled the Babylonian kingdom until the 12th century BC. (182b)

Kathiawar See SAURASHTRA.

Katsina Ancient city in northern Nigeria, centre of a HAUSA kingdom under a HABE dynasty from the 12th century AD, the first Muslim ruler coming to power at the end of the 15th century. The state was conquered by the FULANI in 1806 and has been ruled by the DALLAZAWA and then by the SULIBAWA families since that date as vassals of SOKOTO. (116b, 118d–e)

Kayra dynasty Sultans of DARFUR in the eastern SUDAN from the mid-17th century, successors of an earlier and very obscure line of rulers. Most of their state was conquered by EGYPT in the mid-19th century, later falling under the control of the MAHDI Muhammad Ahmad. On the destruction of the Mahdist state in 1898, a member of the Kayra family re-established the sultanate, but in 1916 this ruler, 'Ali Dinar, rose in revolt against the British and was killed by them in battle, his state being annexed to the Anglo-Egyptian Sudan. (114b)

Kazakh khanate On the break-up of the GOLDEN HORDE at the beginning of the 15th century, members of the WHITE HORDE branch of the JUCHIDS established a state in the region of western Siberia now called Kazakhstan – in 1718 it split into the Great, Middle and Little Hordes, which were gradually brought under Russia in the 18th and early 19th centuries. (96e)

Kazan City in Russia, formerly capital of a khanate of the same name, one of the successor-states of the GOLDEN HORDE under a JUCHID dynasty, founded in the mid-15th century. So long as this powerful state held the middle Volga region, Russian expansion into Siberia was blocked, despite the establishment of a rival khanate at KASIMOV by the Russians. In 1552, however, Ivan IV the Terrible took the city by storm and annexed the Kazan state. (96b)

Kazembe Title of the rulers of a kingdom in what is now the most northerly area of Zambia, central Africa, on the Luapula river. It was founded in the early 18th century by LUNDA colonists, and annexed by the British in 1899. (132c)

Kebbi Town and former kingdom in northern Nigeria. The state was founded in the 16th century by a revolt from the SONGHAI empire, and was an important power in the 16th/17th centuries, but was one of the first victims of FULANI conquest at the beginning of the 19th century. Most of its territory was incorporated into the new amirate of GWANDU, but the Kebbi dynasty maintained their independence in the smaller amirate of Argungu. (117d)

Kedah Sultanate in northern MALAYA, in early times a Hindu state of which the ruler became a Muslim in the 12th century. In the early 19th century, it was temporarily annexed by THAILAND, and on the Thai withdrawal in 1843, the new state of PERLIS was separated from Kedah territory. The sultanate is now one of the constituent states of MALAYSIA. (244c)

Kelantan Sultanate in northern MALAYA, very little being known about its history before the establishment of the present ruling dynasty in the late 18th century. It is now one of the states of MALAYSIA. (244j)

Kenga dynasty Ruling family of the sultanate of BAGIRMI from the foundation of the state in the 16th century. Their lands came under French control in the late 19th century and are now part of the Chad Republic. (114d)

Kent English county and traditionally the earliest Anglo-Saxon kingdom, founded in the mid-5th century AD by the mercenary leader Hengest after a revolt against his Romano-British employers. The dynasty allegedly descended from him were called OISCINGS. Their state was incorporated into the WESSEX kingdom in the early 9th century. (5a)

Kerala Province of southern India, the ancient kingdom of the Cheras, one of the TAMIL states. The names of various Chera kings are known, but their dates and relationships are uncertain. In the 9th/11th centuries, the KULASEKHARAS ruled the region, which then became divided among several states, particularly CALICUT and COCHIN, and the small kingdom of VENAD. In the early 18th century, the ruler of this latter state expanded his dominions to establish the kingdom of TRAVANCORE, controlling much of southern Kerala. (220)

Kerman See KIRMAN.

Kettler family Dukes of KURLAND, modern southern Latvia. The founder of the duchy was the last Master of the Teutonic Order in Livonia, and converted part of his territory into a hereditary state under the suzerainty of Poland. The family became extinct in 1711. (89b)

Khalifah See 1 CALIPH and 2 AL-KHALIFAH dynasty (of Bahrain).

Khaljis Afghan tribe, now called GHILZAIS which provided two dynasties in India:

1 Sultans of DELHI in the late 13th/early 14th centuries, the only important ruler being 'Ala-ud-Din Muhammad Shah, who extended his control over almost the whole of the sub-continent. The dynasty and much of the empire vanished soon after his death, and the throne fell to the TUGHLUQS. (201b)

2 Sultans of MALWA in the 15th/16th centuries, the first of the line being a minister of the GHURID sultan who seized the throne. Malwa was conquered by GUJARAT in 1531, though it fell to the MOGHULS shortly afterwards. (207d)

Khandesh ('Land of the Khans'), a Muslim kingdom in central India established by the FARUQID dynasty, who broke away from the DELHI sultanate in the late 14th century. Their state was annexed by the MOGHULS in 1601. (207e)

Khatti See HITTITES.

Khazars A nomadic Turkish people who set up an extensive state in the steppelands east and west of the lower Volga in the 6th century AD. They were converted to Judaism around 800, and resisted all efforts by the early Muslims to penetrate beyond the Caucasus range. Very little is known of their internal history. In the later 10th century, a series of attacks by the rulers of KIEV broke their power.

Khedives of Egypt See MUHAMMAD ʿALI dynasty.

Khitan See LIAO and QARA-KHITAI.

Khiva See KHWARIZM/KHIVA.

Khokand City in FARGHANA, now in modern Uzbekistan, capital of a khanate of the same name founded at the beginning of the 18th century by the first of the SHAH-RUKHID family, who seceded from JANID control. After considerable resistance, the state was annexed by Russia in 1876. (198k)

Khurasan Province of north-eastern Iran, corresponding to the Parthian satrapy of the ACHAEMENIDS, the original power-base of the ARSACID dynasty. The ʿABBASID Caliphs handed over Khurasan to the semi-independent TAHIRIDS in the 9th century AD, and after brief rule by the SAFFARIDS, it passed to the SAMANIDS in the next century. The region suffered immense devastation and depopulation during the MONGOL conquest of the early 13th century and has been of considerably less importance since that time. On the break-up of the ILKHAN state, Khurasan became independent under local rulers, the SARBADARIDS, in the mid-14th century, until their suppression by the founder of the TIMURID dynasty. It was incorporated into modern Iran by the SAFAVIDS in the 16th century. (194)

Khwarizm/Khiva Region of the lower Oxus (Amu Darya), now in Uzbekistan. In ancient times this area was a kingdom sometimes subject to the overlordship of the rulers of Iran, and from *c.*300 AD was ruled by the semi-legendary AFRIGHID dynasty, overthrown by the MAʾMUNIDS in the late 10th century. The ANUSHTIGINIDS, at first governors under the SELJUKS, later became independent rulers controlling TRANSOXANIA and much of IRAN until the MONGOL conquest of their empire in the 13th century. All these dynasties bore the title of Khwarizm-Shah, from the ancient name of the region. After the fall of the

ILKHANS, the area fell under the control of the SHAIBANIDS until their relatives, the ARAB-SHAHIDS, established an independent khanate known from their capital as Khiva. In 1804, they were supplanted by the INAKID family, for long the real rulers of their state, who were obliged to submit to Russian overlordship in the mid-19th century. The last khan of Khiva was deposed by the Soviet government in 1919. (199)

Kiev Russian city on the Dniepr river, capital of the earliest Russian state, a principality which emerged in the 9th century under a dynasty known as the RIURIKIDS from a semi-legendary ancestor, a prince of NOVGOROD. The state grew rapidly to extend over much of European Russia north of the Ukrainian steppelands, but on the death of Yaroslav the Wise in 1054, the Riurikid lands were divided among various members of his family, and the number of principalities steadily multiplied under a hierarchical system of increasing complexity. The prince of Kiev was for a while recognized as the senior ruler, but the princes of GALICIA in the south-west and of SUZDAL-VLADIMIR in the north-east gradually became more important. Kiev was taken and destroyed by the MONGOLS in 1240, and never recovered its old importance – it later fell under the rule of LITHUANIA and was eventually recovered by the Riurikids of the MOSCOW line. (91)

Kilwa Ancient port on the coast of Tanzania, centre of an important Muslim state in medieval times, though its power was based mainly on trade and its authority did not extend beyond the Arab coastal towns. The sultanate fell under Portuguese control in the early 16th century. (125a)

Kindah Short-lived pre-Islamic kingdom of the 5th/6th century AD in central Arabia, probably established with the aid of the rulers of HIMYAR. The state was destroyed by the LAKHMIDS of Hirah. (174)

Kirman Town and region of south-eastern Iran. In the 11th/12th centuries, it formed a separate principality under a branch of the SELJUK dynasty. The area then came under the rule of the ANUSH-

TIGINIDS of Khwarizm, during whose struggle with the MONGOLS it was seized by a former officer of the QARA-KHITAI, founder of the QUTLUGH-KHANID dynasty, vassals of the ILKHANS. In 1303, Kirman was brought under direct Ilkhan rule. (192)

Kitara See BUNYORO.

Koguryo See KOREA.

Kolhapur A town in the south-western DECCAN, India, capital of a state of the same name ruled by a branch of the BHONSLA dynasty, descendants of the MARATHA king Shivaji, from the beginning of the 18th century. It was absorbed into the Republic of India in 1949. (217n)

Kondavidu Town in Andhra Pradesh, India, capital of a kingdom ruled by the REDDI dynasty in the 14th/15th centuries. The state was annexed by the BAHMANID sultans of the DECCAN in 1424. (218f)

Kongo African kingdom in what is now northern Angola, though it gave its name to the Congo river. It was discovered by the Portuguese in the late 15th century and brought under strong European influence, at least as regards its rulers and leading families, who adopted Christianity, Portuguese names and other features of European life. In the mid-17th century, the state was disrupted by invasion and civil war, and after a recovery in the next century, it disintegrated largely as a result of wars arising from the slave-trade. (131)

Korea The northern part of Korea came under Chinese influence in the 1st millennium BC and was conquered by the early HAN emperors, but in the late 1st century BC a local kingdom, Koguryo, established its independence in the north, and two more states appeared in the 4th century AD, PAEKCHE in the west and SILLA in the south-east. After repeated efforts to conquer Koguryo in the 7th century, the Chinese finally achieved success by means of a naval expedition which first overran Paekche, thus outflanking the northern state. However, Silla, initially a Chinese ally, then drove the invaders out and unified most of the country, whilst another state, largely Korean and called P'O-HAI, was founded in southern Manchuria and the northern areas of Korea. In the early 10th century, P'o-Hai was conquered by the Khitan founders of the LIAO empire in northern China, and Silla collapsed, to be succeeded in the peninsula by the WANG dynasty, founders of the national Korean kingdom. After a long struggle during the 13th century, the Wang were obliged to submit to MONGOL overlordship and to support the disastrous efforts of Kubilai Khan to invade Japan, but they survived for a further century, until their overthrow by the YI family in 1392. The Yi in turn survived a major Japanese invasion in the late 16th century, with Chinese help, and thereafter remained nominal vassals of China until renewed Japanese attacks led to annexation by Japan and the suppression of the Korean monarchy in 1910. Since the end of the Second World War, Korea has been independent but divided into two states, northern and southern. (235)

Kotah State in RAJASTAN which broke away from BUNDI under a separate branch of the CHAUHAN dynasty in the early 17th century. It was absorbed into the Republic of India in 1949. (206f)

Kotte Town in CEYLON, near Colombo, capital of the last kings of the main ruling line in the island, who controlled only a limited part of the ancient kingdom in the 15th/16th centuries. In 1521 the state of SITAWAKE broke away under a branch of the royal family, whose remaining territory was annexed by the Portuguese in 1598. (224a)

Krim khanate See CRIMEA.

Krum dynasty Family which ruled BULGARIA in the 9th/10th centuries. The founder was leader of the Pannonian Bulgars, who seized the throne of the main Bulgarian khanate in 803, revitalizing the declining monarchy. His successors reached the zenith of their power in the early 10th century, becoming the dominant rulers in the Balkans and a serious threat to BYZANTIUM. In 925 the Bulgarian king took the title of emperor, but decline was rapid after his death and an invasion of the kingdom by the RIURIKID Sviatoslav of Kiev broke Bulgarian strength. Having expelled the Russian invaders, the Byzantines annexed the state in 972. (80b)

Kshatrapa dynasty Rulers of MALWA and GUJARAT in western India in the 2nd/4th centuries AD, initially viceroys (satraps) of the INDO-PARTHIAN kings, later as independent monarchs, until their state was conquered by the GUPTAS *c.*395 AD. (207a)

Kujavia Region of central POLAND which formed a principality under various PIAST rulers in the 12th/13th centuries, until its ruler Vladislav (IV) the Short reunified the Polish kingdom early in the 14th century. (87d)

Kulasekhara dynasty A family of Chera kings who ruled KERALA in the 9th/11th centuries. Their state broke up around 1100 AD, though the Rajas of VENAD, later rulers of TRAVANCORE, claimed to be their heirs. (220a)

Kurdistan Extensive region of which parts are now under the control of Turkey, 'Iraq and Iran, inhabited by Kurdish tribes whose ancestors have occupied the area for many centuries, probably from 2000 BC or earlier. Various minor dynasties have ruled in this region, some of Kurdish origin, when it has not been controlled by stronger neighbouring powers. (185)

Kurland (and Semigallia) Latvia south of the Dvina river, now part of the U.S.S.R. This region was part of the Baltic lands conquered by the Order of Teutonic Knights in medieval times. In 1562, the last Master of the Order in Livonia, Gotthard KETTLER, surrendered his province to POLAND and was granted part of it as the hereditary duchy of Kurland and Semigallia under Polish overlordship. In the following century, the dukes made a determined effort to establish their own overseas colonies in West Africa and the Caribbean, but were unable to hold their initial settlements. On the extinction of the Kettlers in 1711, the duchy fell under Russian control and was eventually annexed to Russia at the end of the century. (89b)

Kushans A nomadic people of much-debated racial origins known to the Chinese as the Yueh-Chi, who invaded TRANSOXANIA from the eastern steppe-lands and established an extensive empire in AFGHANISTAN and northern India in the

1st century AD, suppressing the INDO-PARTHIANS. The dating of the ruling dynasty of the empire is a subject of continuing debate, and the chronology of many events of this period in the region hinges on the accession-date of Kanishka, the greatest of the Kushan rulers, variously placed in the 1st and 2nd centuries AD. The state was weakened and perhaps overthrown by the SASANIDS, who conquered much of its territory in the 3rd century. (196c)

Kutb Shahis See QUTB SHAHI.

Kutlugh-Khanids See QUTLUGH-KHANIDS.

Kuwait Port and state in the Persian Gulf, ruled by the AL-SABAH family since their establishment of the principality in 1756. It was a British Protectorate from 1899, but became an independent amirate in 1961. (177a)

L

La Marche Region of central France which formed a feudal county from the mid-10th century AD. It was acquired by the Montgomery family at the end of the 11th century, and by the LUSIGNANS in 1199. In the 14th and 15th centuries, it formed part of the BOURBON lands, being confiscated by the French crown with the Bourbon duchy in 1523. (24p)

Laccadive Islands See 'ALI RAJAS and CANNANORE.

Ladakh Himalayan region, now part of KASHMIR, established as a kingdom in the 10th century AD by a branch of the YAR-LUN family, former kings of Tibet. The succession and dates of the rulers are uncertain until the 16th century. In the mid-19th century, Ladakh was conquered by the DOGHRAS and annexed to the Kashmir state. (210)

Lagid dynasty See PTOLEMIES.

Lahej Former sultanate in South YEMEN (see ADEN PROTECTORATE), which became independent of the Yemen in the early 18th century under the 'ABDALI family. The state was a British protectorate in the 19th century and was abolished by the newly independent government of South Yemen in 1967. (172m)

Lahore City in Pakistan, for long a major administrative centre in the PUNJAB under the GHAZNAVIDS, the sultans of DELHI and the MOGHULS. In 1799 it was acquired by the SIKH leader Ranjit Singh and became the capital of his extensive and powerful state, until the annexation of the Punjab by Britain in 1849. (203c)

Laigin See LEINSTER.

Lakhmids Pre-Islamic Arab dynasty which ruled a kingdom centred on HIRAH, near modern Kufah in 'Iraq, as vassals of the SASANIDS of Iran. They were rivals of the Byzantine-backed GHASSANIDS. The dynasty was suppressed by the Persians at the beginning of the 7th century AD. (184)

Lancaster, House of See ANGEVINS.

Lan Chang Kingdom in Indo-China which included much of modern LAOS, founded by THAI settlers in the 14th century. It was formed by the union of several small states, its capital being at first Lan Chang (modern LUANG PRABANG) and later VIEN CHANG. In 1707 it split into two states based on those two cities. (240a)

Langah dynasty Rulers of MULTAN in the Punjab in the 15th/16th centuries, after the break-up of the DELHI sultanate. Their state was conquered by the ARGHUNS OF Sind, who took the capital in 1528. (203b)

Laos In early medieval times, Laos was under the domination of the kings of CAMBODIA, though settled by THAI-speaking tribes who set up various small states. In the mid-14th century, the ruler of one of these states united them into a kingdom with its capital at LAN CHANG (modern LUANG PRABANG) – that state split into two separate kingdoms in 1707, based on Luang Prabang and VIEN CHANG, and both came under attack by their neighbours of Thailand and VIET-NAM. Vien Chang was annexed by Thailand in 1828, and Luang Prabang became a French protectorate later in the 19th century, its ruler taking the title King of Laos in 1947. The country became formally independent in 1949 and the monarchy was abolished in 1975. (240)

Larsa Very ancient city in SUMER (modern southern 'Iraq), centre of a kingdom which arose after the fall of UR at the end of the 21st century BC. Its rulers long contested supremacy in the region with ISIN, conquering the latter city early in the 18th century BC, just before their own state was annexed by BABYLON. (180c)

Later- For dynasties thus names (Later Yen, Later Pandya, etc.), see under main dynastic name (YEN, PANDYA, etc.).

Latin Empire at Constantinople Name generally used for the state set up by the leaders of the Fourth Crusade after their capture of the city in 1204. The Latin Emperors were the nominal overlords of the other CRUSADER STATES established on Byzantine territory, but in fact lacked the power to do more than hold their capital and very limited areas around it, until Constantinople itself was recaptured by the Greeks of NICAEA in 1261. (1d)

Latin States in the eastern Mediterranean lands See CRUSADER STATES.

Launggyet dynasty Family which ruled the kingdom of ARAKAN in the 13th/14th centuries. (238f)

Lazica Region of western Georgia, ancient Colchis, see also Greater ABKHAZIA and IMERETI. It formed a kingdom in the 5th/6th centuries AD, the rulers being generally under the suzerainty of BYZANTIUM.

Le name of two dynasties of VIET-NAM:

1 Earlier Le, rulers in the late 10th century, the first of them being Le Hoan, who supplanted the DINH dynasty. However, his successor was soon deposed by the founder of the Later LI. (243d)

2 Later Le, longest-reigning dynasty of Viet-Nam, though in fact the later rulers of the family were mostly puppets. The founder expelled MING Chinese occupying forces, and his early successors reached the zenith of Le power in the late 15th century, but were temporarily overthrown by the MAC family, who ruled at Hanoi during most of the 16th century. The Le were restored in the south in 1533 with the aid of the NGUYEN, and later returned to Hanoi as puppets of the TRINH rulers of the north. The dynasty was finally deposed by the TAY-SON rebels at the end of the 18th century. (243h)

Lebanon The modern state approximately corresponds to ancient Phoenicia, in which there were various coastal city-kingdoms from the mid-2nd millennium BC, notably TYRE and SIDON, which maintained a large degree of independence under the successive masters of Western Asia until time of Alexander the Great and the DIADOCHI. Thereafter, the region formed part of the PTOLEMAIC and SELEUCID kingdoms and the Roman empire until the Muslim conquests of the 7th century AD. In the late 11th century, the BANU 'AMMAR established a small and short-lived principality based on TRIPOLI, which fell after a long siege to the Crusaders, to become the capital of a county including much of Lebanaon (see CRUSADER STATES) until its conquest by the MAMLUK sultans in 1289. Under the OSMANLI Turkish sultans, the region was ruled with some degree of independence by the MA'NID and then by the SHIHABID Amirs, until they were suppressed by their overlords in the mid-19th century. (168)

Leinster Province of Ireland, formerly a kingdom (ancient Laigin) from about the 5th century AD under various related families, the last king being Dermot McMurrough, who brought in the Anglo-Norman Richard de Clare of Pembroke to support and succeed him in the late 12th century. (14c)

Leon Ancient city of north-western Spain, which owes its name to its service as a legionary headquarters in Roman times. In the 10th century AD, the king of ASTURIAS made Leon his capital and the kingdom was thereafter known as Leon, until that state was united with CASTILE in 1037. (45)

Lesotho Modern kingdom in southern Africa (formerly Basutoland), a state founded around 1823 during the upheavals arising from the ZULU conquests. It is now independent, though it was for some time a British protectorate. (133e)

Lesser Armenia See ARMENIA, LESSER.

Li Name of two dynasties of VIET-NAM:
  1 Earlier Li, family which led a revolt against Chinese rule in the late 6th century AD and maintained a precarious hold on the throne of Viet-Nam until Chinese reconquest of the country. (243a)
  2 Later Li, rulers in the 11th/13th centuries, the first dynasty to establish its power firmly in Viet-Nam after the country's final breakaway from a thousand years of Chinese rule. They were succeeded by the TRAN in 1225. (243e)

Liang Name of several dynasties in CHINA:
  1 Earlier Liang, one of the SIXTEEN KINGDOMS of the 4th century AD, located in Shansi, conquered by the Earlier CH'IN. (230c)
  2 Later Liang I, another of the SIXTEEN KINGDOMS, founded in Kansu by a Tibetan general of the Earlier CH'IN, conquered by the imperial Eastern CHIN in 403 AD. (230l)
  3 Later Liang II, continuation in Hupeh of the imperial Southern Liang after their overthrow at Nanking by the Southern CH'EN. Their state fell to the SUI in 587 AD. (232d)
  4 Later Liang III, first of the five brief regimes which ruled China between the fall of the T'ANG and the rise of the SUNG. (227p)
  5 Northern Liang, one of the SIXTEEN KINGDOMS, established in Kansu by a rebel HSIUNG-NU general of the Later Liang I at the end of the 4th century AD. The state was conquered by the Northern WEI. (230n)
  6 Southern Liang I, another of the SIXTEEN KINGDOMS and also founded in Kansu as a result of rebellion against the Later Liang I, by a Hsien-Pi general. This state fell to the imperial Eastern CHIN. (230m)
  7 Southern Liang II, imperial dynasty in southern China in the early 6th century AD, supplanted the Southern CH'I. They were overthrown at Nanking by the Southern CH'EN, but held out in Hupeh as the Later Liang II (see above). (227l)
  8 Western Liang, yet another of the SIXTEEN KINGDOMS, in Kansu in the early 5th century, conquered by the Northern Liang in 421 AD. The founder of the imperial T'ANG dynasty claimed descent from this family. (230p)

Liao Name of two related dynasties in CHINA and Central Asia:

1 Rulers of the Khitan people, relatives of the later MONGOLS, who established a powerful empire in Manchuria, Mongolia and part of northern China in the 10th/12th centuries AD. They were overthrown by their vassals the JUCHEN, founders of the CHIN empire. (232e)

2 Western Liao dynasty, founded by a member of the Liao family who led a section of the Khitan into Central Asia after the Juchen victory, and founded the QARA-KHITAI empire (which see). (198c)

Libya Classical name for North Africa, though now a state in part of that region. CYRENE formed an ancient kingdom under the Greek BATTIADS, and Libyan TRIPOLI was capital of a principality under the BANU ʿAMMAR in the 14th century AD. In the early 18th century, the QARAMANIDS broke away from the OSMANLI empire to establish a state also based on Tripoli, reconquered by the Osmanlis in 1835. See also FEZZAN. The leaders of the SANUSI religious movement acquired great influence in Libya in the 19th century under Osmanli and later Italian rule, and the Sanusi leader became king of Libya in 1951, but was deposed by republicans in 1969. (106)

Licchavis A people of ancient India who provided a ruling dynasty for NEPAL between the 4th and 9th centuries AD, though its history is extremely obscure.

Liechtenstein Small principality in Central Europe, ruled by a family which has possessed lands in the area since medieval times – it was created as a state within the HOLY ROMAN EMPIRE in 1719, and has been independent since 1866. (42)

Limburg Feudal county of the medieval Netherlands from the 11th century, a duchy from 1155, absorbed by BRABANT in the late 13th century. (20e)

Lithuania Baltic region now part of U.S.S.R. It was one of the last areas of Europe to convert to Christianity, in the 13th/14th centuries, when it became a state of great size and power, controlling much of western Russia and absorbing a number of RIURIKID principalities. It was dynastically united with POLAND in the late 14th century under the JAGIELLON

family, and the two states were constitutionally linked by the Union of Lublin in 1569. The eastern parts of Poland-Lithuania were gradually annexed by Russia during the 17th/18th centuries, and the small republic of Lithuania, independent from 1918, was annexed by the U.S.S.R. in 1940. (89)

Little Poland (Malopolska), region of southern POLAND, around Krakow, which formed a PIAST principality during the division of Poland in the 12th/13th centuries. (87c)

Lodi dynasty Sultans of DELHI in the 15th and early 16th centuries, members of the Afghan Lodi tribe, who supplanted the SAYYIDS and began to rebuild the power of the almost defunct sultanate. However, the last of the dynasty was killed in battle in 1526 by the TIMURID Babur, who conquered his territory and thus founded the MOGHUL empire. (201e)

Lombards (Langobardi), Germanic people who invaded ITALY from the Hungarian plain in the mid-6th century AD, shortly after the fall of the OSTROGOTH kingdom to Byzantine reconquest. They overran most of Italy and founded a kingdom which exercised effective control only in the north, the south being partly retained by the Byzantines and partly ruled by the autonomous Lombard dukes of SPOLETO and BENEVENTO. The CAROLINGIAN Charlemagne annexed the Lombard kingdom to his empire in 774, but the southern duchies survived, two principalities breaking away from Benevento in the 9th century (CAPUA and SALERNO). The Lombard lands in the south were eventually incorporated into the HAUTEVILLE domains in the 11th century. Many of the later ruling families in northern Italy were or claimed to be of Lombard descent. (58, 68a–d)

Lori Medieval town in ARMENIA, centre of a state which became independent of the main Armenian kingdom under a branch of the BAGRATID dynasty in the late 10th century AD, but was conquered by the SELJUKS a hundred years later. (147d)

Lorraine Originally Lotharingia, a kingdom formed for the CAROLINGIAN Lothair

II in the mid-9th century and consisting of a broad band of territory from the Alps to the North Sea. Somewhat reduced in area, it remained one of the great duchies of the German kingdom, soon split into Lower Lorraine (the later BRABANT), and (Upper) Lorraine, the historic province now part of France. In the mid-18th century, the last duke of the ancient ruling family, Francis III, exchanged his duchy for TUSCANY and later became Holy Roman Emperor, Lorraine passing to the ex-king of Poland, Stanislav Leszczynski, on whose death in 1766 it was annexed by France. (24f)

Lozi (Barotse), people of Central Africa who established a kingdom around the beginning of the 17th century in what is now south-western Zambia. The state became a British protectorate in the late 19th century, and now forms part of independent Zambia. (133a)

Lu One of the CHOU STATES of ancient China, in southern Shantung, the native state of Confucius, its ruling family claiming to be a branch of the imperial CHOU dynasty. Lu was conquered by CH'U in 255 BC. (228a)

Luang Prabang City in LAOS, earlier called LAN CHANG and capital of the kingdom of that name until supplanted by VIEN CHANG. At the beginning of the 18th century, the Laotian state split into two realms and Luang Prabang became capital of one (and Vien Chang of the other). In the late 19th century, the kingdom of Luang Prabang came under French protection – its rulers became constitutional monarchs of Laos in 1947. The Laotian monarchy was abolished in 1975. (240c)

Luba (Baluba), a people of southern Zaire, who established a number of kingdoms in Central Africa in the 15th century and a powerful empire in the late 18th century, which disintegrated a hundred years later. (132a)

Lu'lu dynasty Family which seized power from the ZANGIDS in MOSUL in the early 13th century. It was extinguished by the ILKHANS in 1262. (185j)

Lunda (Balunda), a people of southern Zaire who founded an extensive empire

in the 17th century, their ruler being called the Mwata Yamvo and related, according to tradition, to the LUBA kings. Lunda colonists also set up the KAZEMBE kingdom. The Lunda empire broke up in the late 19th century, though its royal dynasty survived as minor chiefs into the post-colonial period and the Katanga secessionist leader Moise Tchombe, active in the 1960s, was a member of the family. (132b)

Luneburg City in north-western Germany, ruled by various branches of the WELF dynasty of BRUNSWICK. In 1692 the duchy of Brunswick-Luneburg was made an ELECTORATE, thereafter usually called HANOVER. (33e)

Luristan Region of the Zagros mountains in western Iran, ruled in the 12th/15th centuries by ATABEGS of the HAZARASPID dynasty. Their state survived under the ILKHANS but was annexed by the TIMURIDS. (190d)

Lusignans Originally lords of Lusignan in Poitou, the family acquired the county of LA MARCHE in 1199 and that of ANGOULEME in 1218. One of its members ruled as king of JERUSALEM in the late 12th century, and then obtained CYPRUS from Richard Coeur-de-Lion. The Cypriot branch ruled the island as kings until its acquisition by VENICE in 1489, and several of its members occupied the throne of Lesser Armenia in the 14th century. (24p–q, 140b, 144, 167a)

Luxemburg City and modern state, originally a county of the German empire. At the beginning of the 14th century, its ruler was elected emperor as Henry VII, and his family rose to major importance, at various times ruling BOHEMIA, HUNGARY and BRANDENBURG as well as the empire. Luxemburg was made a duchy in 1354, and on the extinction of its dynasty in the mid-15th century passed to the VALOIS dukes of Burgundy, and then to the HABSBURGS. After the Napoleonic Wars it was granted to the king of the NETHERLANDS as a Grand Duchy, but was partitioned on the establishment of the new state of Belgium, a large section going to the Belgian kingdom. On the failure of male heirs in the Orange-Nassau dynasty of the Netherlands in 1890, the reduced Grand Duchy was inherited by their distant cousins, the dispossessed family of NASSAU, who have ruled Luxemburg since that date. (21)

Lydia Ancient kingdom in western Asia Minor. Its early history is obscure until the HERACLIDS were supplanted by the MERMNAD kings in the early 7th century BC. The last ruler of Lydia, Croesus of proverbial wealth, was overthrown by Cyrus the ACHAEMENID in 547 BC and his lands incorporated into the Persian empire. (137a)

Mac Dynasty of VIET-NAM, whose founder deposed the Later LE ruler in 1527 but was opposed in the southern and central regions of the country by the NGUYEN and TRINH families, who established puppet Le emperors. The Mac lost Hanoi to the Trinh in 1592, but held out with Chinese support on the northern frontier until the late 17th century. (243i)

Macalpin dynasty Descendants of Kenneth mac Alpin of DALRIADA, who conquered the PICT kingdom in the mid-9th century AD and thus created the kingdom of SCOTLAND. The family ruled for nearly two hundred years, until succeeded by the CANMORE/DUNKELD family. (11a)

Maccabees See HASMONEANS.

Macdonalds of the Isles Family whose power was founded by Somerled, King of the Isles, a 12th-century ruler of probably Scandinavian origin, though the dynasty took its name from a grandson. Initially their lands were under Norwegian suzerainty, but passed under nominal Scottish overlordship in the mid-13th century. The Lordship of the Isles remained largely autonomous, however, until abolished in 1493 by the crown. (12b)

Macedonia Ancient semi-Greek kingdom in northern Greece, formed under the ARGEAD dynasty in the mid-7th century BC and for long a minor power, until the mid-4th century BC, when Philip II and Alexander the Great dominated all Greece. During the wars of the DIADOCHI, the Argeads were extinguished and the throne was occupied by the ANTIPATRIDS and other rulers until finally secured by the ANTIGONIDS, who ruled the kingdom until the conquest by ROME in 168 BC. (83)

Macedonian Emperors Imperial family of BYZANTIUM, founded in 867 by Basil I the Macedonian. His descendants ruled, sometimes jointly with other families, until the mid-11th century. (1c)

Madagascar Island which now constitutes the Malagasy Republic. There were various tribal kingdoms in Madagascar prior to the 19th century, at the beginning of which the MERINA rulers extended their highland state to dominate the whole island. In the late 19th century, the French gained control of the kingdom, which they annexed in 1896. (134)

Madurai Ancient city in the extreme south of India, traditional capital of the PANDYAS until the Muslim conquest in the early 14th century. The city became the centre of a small and precarious independent sultanate for nearly half a century, falling to VIJAYANAGAR in 1378. On the break-up of the Vijayanagar empire, a local NAYYAK dynasty established its independence, ruling until 1736, when the state was conquered by the Nawab of ARCOT. (223a–d)

Maghrawa Zenata Berber clan and dynasty which ruled a kingdom in MOROCCO, based on Fez, in the 10th/11th centuries AD. Their state was annexed by the ALMORAVIDS. (112c)

Maghrib The 'West', the Arab name for North Africa west of Egypt, now divided into the modern states of LIBYA, TUNISIA, ALGERIA and MOROCCO, but historically sometimes a single political unit under one state or dynasty – see CARTHAGE, FATIMIDS, ALMORAVIDS, ALMOHADS. (105–112)

Maguindanao Area in southern Mindanao in the Philippines, a Muslim sultanate from the mid-17th century which long resisted Spanish conquest, but was finally subdued in the late 19th century. (248b)

Maharashtra Province of India, the north-western part of the Deccan, ruled by various Hindu and Muslim dynasties. (217)

Mahdi The 'Rightly Guided Imam', a divinely-appointed leader expected by the SHI'A Muslim sect. There have been many claimants to this office in Muslim history, of whom the best-known in recent times was the Sudanese leader Muhammad Ahmad, whose forces conquered large areas of the eastern Sudan in 1881–1885 and killed General Gordon at Khartoum. The Mahdi himself died in 1885, and his successor (Khalifah, see CALIPH) 'Abdullah was overthrown by the British in 1898.

Mahdids Dynasty of the YEMEN, rulers at ZABID in the later 12th century AD after the NAJAHIDS. Their state was one of those which fell to the AYYUBID conqueror Turan Shah in 1173–1174. (172d)

Ma'in Early kingdom in the YEMEN, eventually absorbed by SABA. Its chronology is very uncertain, and theories as to its date of origin range from 1200 BC to 400 BC – see Albright, BASOR (Bibliography). (171a)

Maitraka dynasty RAJPUT family who ruled GUJARAT and SAURASHTRA, establishing their state in the late 5th century AD on the break-up of the GUPTA empire. Their capital was at Vallabhi in Saurashtra, destroyed with their state in the mid-8th century, probably by Arab invaders from Sind. (208a)

Majapahit A powerful kingdom based in JAVA, founded in the late 13th century in succession to the short-lived SINGOSARI state. Its rulers probably exercised some control over parts of Sumatra and Borneo at the zenith of their prosperity. The empire collapsed in the late 15th century as Muslim rule spread over Java with the rise of DEMAK and BANTAM. (246a)

Majorca Like the other Balearic Islands, Majorca was part of the Roman empire and was later ruled by the Spanish UMAYYADS, on the break-up of whose state it came under the control of the MUJAHIDS of DENIA. The island was ruled by independent Amirs from 1075 and then by the BANU GHANIYA, at first as a viceroyalty under their relatives the ALMORAVIDS and later as a base for the struggle against the ALMOHADS, who conquered the island early in the 13th century. In the middle of that century, Majorca was seized by James I of ARAGON, whose younger son succeeded him as its king – his line ruled until 1343, when the kingdom was annexed to Aragon. (50)

Malacca City in Malaya, centre of a sultanate established at the beginning of the 15th century by a ruler perhaps belonging to the SAILENDRA royal house of SRIVIJAYA. The state became very powerful, dominating the Malacca Straits, but the city fell to a Portuguese attack in 1511, passing to the Dutch in 1641 and the British in 1795. The last sultan of Malacca and his relatives founded the sultanates of JOHORE, PAHANG and PERAK in the late 15th and early 16th centuries. (244a)

Malaga City of southern Spain, ruled by a branch of the HAMMUDID dynasty in the 11th century AD. (See REYES DE TAIFAS). Their state was annexed by the ZIRIDS of GRANADA. (48h)

Malagasy Republic See MADAGASCAR.

Malatya Ancient Melitene in southeastern Turkey, capital of one of the DANISHMENDID Amirates in the 12th century AD and later of the DHU'L-QADR Amirate in the 14th/16th centuries. (139b, 142j)

Malaya Very little is known about the history of the Malay Peninsula before the rise of the MALACCA Sultanate around 1400 AD, though KEDAH appears to have been a Hindu kingdom whose rulers became Muslims in the 12th century. On the fall of Malacca to the Portuguese in 1511, various sultanates were established under branches of its ruling dynasty, and more states emerged in the 18th/19th centuries – see also BUGIS. The peninsula came under British control during the course of the 19th century, becoming independent in 1957 as the main component of MALAYSIA. (244)

Malaysia Modern federal state and elective monarchy consisting of the peninsula of MALAYA and territories in North Borneo, established in 1957. The rulers of the Malay states in the federation elect one of their number as monarch (Yang Di-

Pertuan Agong) for a five-year term. (244m)

Maldive Islands A Muslim sultanate was established in the islands in medieval times, but fell briefly to Portuguese conquest in the mid-16th century. The sultanate was re-established in 1573 on the expulsion of the Portuguese and survived into the present century, though the islands were subdued for a short time by the 'ALI RAJAS of CANNANORE in the mid-18th century. British suzerainty was accepted in 1887. The sultanate was temporarily abolished in 1952–54 and finally abolished in 1968; the Maldives became a republic. (224e)

Mali Modern republic in the western SUDAN, but also the name of a medieval empire in much the same region, founded in the early 13th century after the collapse of the GHANA empire. It was a large and powerful state until the 15th century, when largely supplanted by the new empire of its formal vassals, the rulers of SONGHAI. (119a)

Malla dynasty Rulers of NEPAL in the 13th/18th centuries, in succession to the THAKURIS, though temporarily subject to the KARNATAKAS in the 14th century. In about 1482, the kingdom was divided into several smaller states under branches of the dynasty, based in the cities of Katmandu, Bhatgaon and Patan, and in the mid-18th century all the Malla lands were conquered by the Gurkha ruler Prithvi Narayan Shah, who thus founded the modern kingdom of Nepal. (211c–f)

Malwa Extensive region of central India and often an independent kingdom. It was ruled by the KSHATRAPAS in the 2nd/4th centuries AD and the PARAMARAS from the 9th century until the conquest of the area by the ruler of DELHI in 1305. At the end of the 14th century, on the break-up of the Delhi sultanate, Malwa became an independent sultanate under the GHURIDS and then the KHALJIS, being conquered by GUJARAT in 1531 and shortly afterwards absorbed into the MOGHUL empire. On the disintegration of Moghul control in the 18th century, two important princely states emerged in the region, INDORE and BHOPAL, both of which were incorporated into the Republic of India in 1948. (207)

Mamikonids Armenian princely family which ruled various territories in ARMENIA from ancient times, some of its members serving as viceroys for BYZANTIUM or IRAN. In the later 8th century, the Mamikonids led a series of revolts against the 'ABBASID Caliphs, and in consequence lost much of their power to other families, notably the BAGRATIDS, though branches of the dynasty survived into later times. (146e)

Mamluks The name means 'owned' and originally indicated slaves trained as soldiers, particular by the AYYUBID rulers of EGYPT, who were eventually supplanted by a series of Mamluk sultans of Egypt and SYRIA. These in turn continued to recruit their troops from Turkish and Caucasian slaves imported for the purpose, some of who became sultans themselves. The Mamluk rulers are usually divided into the BAHRIS, who ruled until the late 14th century, and among whom there was some hereditary succession, and the BURJIS, among whom there was no such succession, and who were overthrown in 1517 by OSMANLI Turkish conquest. (103a–b)

Ma'munids Family which briefly ruled as KHWARIZM-Shahs in the late 10th/early 11th centuries AD, overthrowing the ancient dynasty of the AFRIGHIDS. Shortly afterwards, in 1017, Khwarizm was conquered by the GHAZNAVIDS. (199a)

Man, Isle of In the VIKING period, various Jarls ruled the island before the emergence of the dynasty founded by Godred Crovan in the late 11th century, which ruled (with interruptions) until Man was acquired by Scotland and then by England in the late 13th century. The Stanley family, Earls of Derby, were Lords of Man 1404–1736. (7)

Manchuria/Manchus This large region and its people have been subjected to Chinese influence for many centuries, and its southern parts were ruled by various Chinese dynasties, later falling under the control of the Koguryo kingdom of northern KOREA. In the late 7th century AD southern Manchuria constituted the kingdom of P'O-HAI until the conquest of that state by the LIAO (Khitan) in 927. The Juchen, a people initially subject to the Liao, overthrew the Khitan empire and established the CHIN empire in the 12th century, and their later relatives the Manchus established a state in Manchuria in the 17th century, its ruling dynasty at first taking the title of Later Chin, soon changed to CH'ING. On the collapse of the MING regime in CHINA in the mid-17th century, the Manchus conquered China, continuing to control their homeland also until the fall of their empire in 1912. In 1934, the Japanese occupied Manchuria and set up the puppet state of Manchukuo under the last of the Ch'ing emperors – the region was re-annexed by China in 1945. (233)

Mangit family See HAIDARIDS.

Ma'nid dynasty Amirs of LEBANON under the OSMANLI Sultans from the Turkish conquest of 1516 until succeeded by their SHIHABID relatives in the late 17th century. (168b)

Mantua Ancient Italian city of Etruscan foundation, ruled by the GONZAGAS from the early 14th century, at first as captains-general and later as margraves and dukes, until their state was annexed by the HABSBURGS in 1708. (67d)

Marathas People of the western DECCAN, India, whose leader Shivaji BHONSLA led a revolt against BIJAPUR and later against the MOGHUL conquerors of the Deccan, establishing a state which came to dominate vast areas of central India as the Moghul empire disintegrated. Early in the 18th century, real control of the Maratha empire came into the hands of the PESHWAS, hereditary chief ministers of the BHONSLA kings. On the annexation of the Peshwa dominions by the British in 1818, the Bhonslas continued to rule the small states of SATARA and KOLHAPUR, while other Maratha chiefs ruled in BARODA, GWALIOR, INDORE, NAGPUR. (217)

Marche, La See LA MARCHE.

Mardin Town in south-eastern Turkey, capital of a small state under a branch of the ARTUQID dynasty from the beginning of the 12th century AD until its conquest by the QARA-QOYUNLI three centuries later. (185f)

Marinid dynasty Zenata Berber family which supplanted the ALMOHADS in MOROCCO in the mid-13th century and made repeated but unsuccessful efforts to recover their predecessors' dominions in SPAIN. They were succeeded in the mid-15th century by their relatives the WATTASIDS. (112f)

Mark General term in German-speaking lands for a frontier-district ('March'), ruled by a Margrave (Mark-graf). Also the specific name of a region in north-western Germany, a feudal county from the early 13th century under a family related to the counts of BERG. In 1461, the count of Mark inherited CLEVES, with which duchy the county was thereafter united. (39d)

Marwanids Kurdish dynasty of DIYAR BAKR, established at the end of the 10th century AD. Their lands were conquered by the SELJUKS in 1085. (185d)

Marwar Kingdom in RAJASTAN, in modern time often known by the name of its capital, JODHPUR, founded in the late 14th century by a branch of the RATHOR Rajput clan, which ruled the state until its absorption into the Republic of India in 1949. (206b)

Matabele people See NDEBELE.

Mataram Sultanate which dominated JAVA in the 17th century. Founded in about 1582, it fell under Dutch influence in the 18th century and split in 1755 into the two states of SURAKARTA and JOGJAKARTA. (246d)

Mauretania Modern state in north-western Africa, though the name was used for the region of MOROCCO and western Algeria in classical times, when it constituted a kingdom under various client-rulers subject to Roman control from the 2nd century BC until its annexation by ROME in the mid-1st century AD.

Mauryas Earliest imperial dynasty of India, founded *c.*320 BC, shortly after Alexander's invasion of the Punjab and probably as a result of the disruption caused by the Macedonian victories. The Mauryas rapidly extended their empire to include all India except the far south, plus part of Afghanistan, the best-known ruler of the family being Asoka, a powerful and benevolent promoter of Buddhism.

After his death *c*.232 BC, the empire was divided among his sons and grandsons, and soon collapsed, his last successor in the imperial capital, Pataliputra (modern Patna), being supplanted by the SUNGAS in the early 2nd century BC at the time of the great invasion from the north-west by the Greek rulers of BACTRIA. A branch of the dynasty may have survived for a while in KASHMIR. (200a)

Mayas People of Central America who established a civilization in the region in the 1st millennium BC and flourished for many centuries. Various city-states and kingdoms rose and fell during this long period, but the surviving records are too patchy and difficult of interpretation to provide any lists of rulers. Some of the Maya states still existed up to the Spanish conquest of the region in the 16th century. See also TOLTECS and MEXICO.

Mayyafaraqin Ancient Martyropolis (modern Meyferkin) in south-eastern Turkey, capital of a small AYYUBID principality founded in the late 12th century and conquered by the ILKHANS in 1260. (185l)

Mazandaran Modern province of Iran, the region along the southern coast of the Caspian Sea, incorporating the historical regions of Tabaristan and Gurgan and closely linked in history with the neighbouring GILAN. This area of mountains and dense forest long remained beyond the effective control of the rulers of Iran, and various independent princes held out there after the Muslim conquest of the SASANID empire in the mid-7th century AD, notably the DABUYIDS, who were eventually crushed by the 'ABBASIDS in 761. Their BAVANDID and BADUSPANID colleagues survived as minor rulers for several centuries longer, though Mazandaran also became a refuge for 'ALID rebels who attempted with varying success to establish SHI'A states in the region. In the late 11th century, the Shi'a leader Hasan-i Sabbah founded the ASSASSIN state at ALAMUT. The area was finally brought under central Iranian control by the SAFAVIDS in the 16th century. See also DAYLAM. (189)

Mazovia Region of POLAND around Warsaw. It became a principality under a branch of the PIASTS when Poland was divided in the 12th century, and was not finally re-united to the Polish crown until the early 16th century. (87e)

Mazrui dynasty Shaikhs of MOMBASA (in modern Kenya) in the 18th and early 19th centuries. They were installed in the city by the YA'RUBIDS after the 'Umani conquest of Mombasa from the Portuguese at the end of the 17th century, and ruled until the AL-BU-SA'ID sultan of 'UMAN took Mombasa in 1836. (125b)

Mazyadids Arab dynasty which established a small principality based on HILLAH in southern 'Iraq on the decline of the 'ABBASIDS. Their lands were eventually annexed by the SELJUKS some two centuries later, in about 1150, shortly afterwards falling to the reviving 'Abbasid state. (185c)

Meath Modern county in Eire and name of a former kingdom covering a substantially larger area which was ruled by a branch of the O'NEILL dynasty from the 5th century AD until the area fell into Anglo-Norman hands in 1173. Several rulers of Meath were also HIGH KINGS of Ireland. (14e)

Mecca (Makkah), most holy city of the Islamic world, located in the HIJAZ region of Arabia, and home of the QURAISH clan to which Muhammad the Prophet belonged. It was controlled by the UMAYYAD and early 'ABBASID Caliphs, but in the 10th century AD came under the rule of Amirs, usually called SHARIFS, belonging to the HASHIMID branch of the Quraish. From the beginning of the 13th century, Mecca was ruled by the BANU QITADA line of this family, usually acknowledging the overlordship of the MAMLUK and later the OSMANLI sultans, until the revolt of Sharif Husain against the Osmanlis during the First World War. He took the title King of the Hijaz in 1916, but the new state was conquered by 'Abdul-'Aziz AL-SA'UD in 1924–1925 and Mecca annexed to Sa'udi Arabia. (173)

Mecklenburg Region of northern Germany. In early medieval times the area was inhabited by the Slav Obodrites, whose princes eventually submitted to the German kings, remaining as vassal rulers. During the later Middle Ages,

Mecklenburg was subdivided among branches of the dynasty, two of the main divisions becoming duchies in 1348. After further rearrangements, two well-defined states were established in the 17th/18th centuries, Mecklenburg-Schwerin and Mecklenburg-Strelitz, and these became grand duchies in 1815. They were both abolished in 1918. (30)

Medes An Indo-European people who settled in IRAN with other related tribes in about 1000 BC. In the 7th century, they were united into a strong state which took a leading part in the destruction of ASSYRIA, and their kings then built up an extensive empire which included much of Iran, Armenia and eastern Asia Minor. In 550 BC, the ruler of the vassal Persian state of Parsa (FARS), Cyrus the Great, overthrew the Median king, annexed his lands and thus founded the ACHAEMENID empire. The Medes remained joint masters with the Persians of the new realm. (187a)

Medici Ruling family of Florence and Tuscany, the first of the dynasty becoming Lord of Florence in the mid-15th century. His successors were made dukes of Florence and later grand dukes of Tuscany, the last of the line dying in 1737, to be succeeded by Francis III of LORRAINE, later Holy Roman Emperor. (65b)

Menteshe One of the ANATOLIAN AMIRATES of the 14th/early 15th centuries, located in south-western Asia Minor in the area anciently called Caria. It was conquered by the OSMANLI Turkish sultans for the second and final time in 1426. (142d)

Mercia Early English kingdom in the Midlands, founded by the ICLINGS, a family which claimed descent from the kings of the Angles in Schleswig. Their state emerged as a powerful kingdom in about 600 AD, to dominate England south of the Humber in the 7th and 8th centuries. It was destroyed by VIKING invaders in the late 9th century and its territory was later annexed by WESSEX as that state extended northwards. (5c)

Merinas People and dynasty of MADAGASCAR who established a small highland kingdom in the centre of the island. At the beginning of the 19th century, its able

rulers extended their authority throughout Madagascar. The last monarch of the dynasty was deposed by the French, who annexed her kingdom in 1896. (134)

Mermnads Ruling family of LYDIA in Asia Minor, who supplanted the HERACLIDS early in the 7th century BC. They built up an extensive kingdom which included most of the peninsula west of the Halys (Kizil Irmak) river under the last of the dynasty, Croesus of fabled wealth, who was overthrown by Cyrus the ACHAEMENID in 547 BC. Lydia then became a province of the Persian empire. (137a)

Meroe Sudanese kingdom in the Nile valley, virtually a continuation of NAPATA, from the 4th century BC to the 4th century AD, eventually destroyed by AXUM. The names and dates of the rulers are partially known, and a list may be found in Shinnie, P.L. (see Bibliography).

Merovingians Frankish ruling dynasty, originally kings of a section of the Salian FRANKS. Clovis (d.511) united all the Frankish territories of the Rhineland and conquered most of France, creating the strongest of the successor-states of the Western Roman Empire, but his family repeatedly divided the kingdom among themselves, the later history of the dynasty being remarkable for fratricidal treachery and atrocity. In the 7th century, real power fell into the hands of a series of ministers called Mayors of the Palace, one of whom eventually seized the throne to found the CAROLINGIAN dynasty. (3a)

Mesopotamia The land 'between the rivers', name for ancient 'IRAQ and more specifically for the northern section, as opposed to BABYLONIA/CHALDAEA in the south, in later times called al-Jazirah ('the island') by the Arabs. The early kingdoms of MITANNI and ASSYRIA were centred in this region, where several later Muslim dynasties ruled small states.

Mewar Former kingdom in RAJASTAN, better known in modern times by the name of its capital, Udaipur. It was the most ancient of the RAJPUT states, founded by the GUHILA clan in the 8th century AD, its ruler bearing the distinctive title of Rana (Maharana). During the 15th and early 16th centuries, the Rana of Mewar was the dominant ruler in Rajastan, and the dynasty had a long record of resistance to the Muslim rulers in northern India, their ancient capital Chitor being stormed by Muslim armies after lengthy resistance in 1303, 1534 and 1568. Badly weakened but never completely subdued by the MOGHULS, the Ranas recovered some of their territories in the 17th/18th centuries and were recognized as the premier princes in Rajastan under British rule. Their state was absorbed into the Republic of India in 1949. (206a)

Mexico Civilization flourished in central Mexico (and neighbouring Yucatan – see MAYAS) from the 1st millennium BC, but virtually nothing of its history is known before the rise of the TOLTEC empire in medieval times. That kingdom broke up into a number of city-states in the Valley of Mexico in the 12th century AD, and the city of Tenochtitlan, founded by the new and initially obscure migrant AZTECS in the 14th century, rose rapidly to dominate the region in the next century, as the leading partner in a federation with the older states of TEXCOCO and Tlacopan. Tenochtitlan (modern Mexico City) was captured by the Spanish army of Cortes in 1521 and the country soon converted into a colonial viceroyalty of HABSBURG Spain. After the establishment of Mexican independence in 1821, the country twice became an empire between republican regimes, in 1822–23 and 1864–67, on the latter occasion under Maximilian of Habsburg, captured and shot in 1867. (250)

Midrarids One of the earliest independent Muslim dynasties, leaders of a dissident Berber sect, who established a small state at SIJILMASA in the TAFILALT region of Morocco in the late 8th century AD. They survived temporary FATIMID conquest but were suppressed by the MAGHRAWA in the late 10th century. (112a)

Milan Ancient Mediolanum, an important city of the Later Roman Empire and sometimes an imperial headquarters. In medieval times it remained the most important city of Lombardy and led resistance to the HOHENSTAUFFEN emperors. Early in the 14th century, the VISCONTI

family became rulers of the city and its surrounding areas, being created dukes in 1395. They were succeeded by the SFORZAS, whose claim was contested by the ORLEANS branch of the VALOIS – in the early 16th century, Milan was twice in French hands before the last Sforza duke was succeeded by the Emperor Charles V and the duchy thus annexed to the HABSBURG lands (63)

Min One of the TEN KINGDOMS in 10th century CHINA, located in Fukien province. In 945 it was annexed by SOUTHERN T'ANG. (231i)

Minaeans See MA'IN.

Minamoto Earliest of the SHOGUN families of JAPAN, descendants of the Emperor Seiwa (859–877). They acquired effective control of the Japanese state as the result of a series of civil wars in the late 12th century AD. (236b)

Ming Last native imperial Chinese dynasty, founded by a rebel against the YUAN Mongol regime in the mid-14th century AD. The Ming expelled the Mongols from CHINA and at the height of their power were recognized as overlords of various neighbouring states, extending their influence also into South-East Asia by naval expeditions. The dynasty collapsed amid internal disorder, their capital falling to a rebel leader in 1644, whereupon the MANCHUS invaded the country to establish the CH'ING regime. (227x)

Mingrelia A principality in western GEORGIA which became virtually independent of the kingdom of IMERETI at the end of the 15th century under the DADIANI family. It was annexed by the Russians in 1866. (154a)

Mirdasids Arab dynasty of ALEPPO, who seized the city soon after its conquest by the FATIMIDS from the HAMDANIDS in the early 11th century. They held Aleppo, with two FATIMID interludes, until it was captured by the 'UQAILIDS in 1079. (166b)

Mitanni Early kingdom in northern 'Iraq established in the 16th century BC by Indo-European invaders. It dominated the region for some two hundred years, its lands being eventually annexed by Assyria in the mid-13th century. (181)

Mithridatids Iranian ruling dynasty of PONTUS in Asia Minor, founded at the end of the 4th century BC during the wars of the DIADOCHI. Late in the 2nd century, the kingdom was raised to great power by Mithridates VI (the Great), who added to his domains the BOSPHORUS kingdom before embarking on his long and determined struggle against ROME. Eventually he was driven from Pontus and withdrew to his Bosphoran lands, where he was killed in a revolt. Members of the dynasty ruled in the Bosphoran kingdom until the beginning of the 1st century AD. (90c, 137d)

Modena Ancient Mutina, Italian city acquired by the ESTE family in 1288. After their loss of FERRARA, annexed to the PAPAL STATES in 1597, they retained Modena as a duchy until the last of the family was driven out by the French in 1797. His HABSBURG heirs recovered the city in 1814, and a branch of that dynasty ruled Modena until it was incorporated into the kingdom of Italy in the mid-19th century. (66)

Moghuls Imperial family of India, a branch of the TIMURID dynasty. Babur, founder of the Moghul empire, was driven from his ancestral FARGHANA by the SHAIBANIDS in 1501 and established himself at Kabul. He defeated and killed the last LODI ruler of DELHI in 1526 and seized control of much of northern India. His successor was temporarily driven out by the SURIDS but later recovered his lands. Under the next four rulers, the empire was extended to incorporate all northern India and most of the DECCAN, plus part of AFGHANISTAN. After the death of Aurangzib in 1707, however, the Moghul state distintegrated rapidly, Muslim provincial governors and Hindu rebels setting up as independent rulers. In the mid-18th century, Delhi itself was taken and sacked by Nadir Shah AFSHAR of Iran, and thereafter the Moghul emperors held only a small territory around their capital. The last of the dynasty was deposed by the British for his involvement in the Mutiny of 1857. (202)

Moldavia Region between the Carpathians and the Dniestr river, now divided between RUMANIA and the U.S.S.R. Late in the 13th century AD, Rumanian migrants from TRANSYLVANIA established a principality in the area, at first under Hungarian and later under Polish overlordship. In the 15th/16th centuries, the state was gradually brought under OSMANLI Turkish control, and from the 17th century its rulers were virtually Turkish officials. In 1859, after the expulsion of the Turks by the Russians and the Austrians, Moldavia was united with WALLACHIA to form the principality (later the kingdom) of Rumania. (77)

Mombasa Town on the coast of Kenya, founded by Arab settlers in medieval times. It was of major importance by the 16th century, when the Portuguese captured it after several attempts – when they were driven from East Africa by the YA'RUBID rulers of 'UMAN, who took Mombasa in 1698 after a three-year siege, the city was placed under the MAZRUI Shaikhs as 'Umani vassals, and they ruled in virtual independence until the early 19th century. In 1836, Mombasa was captured by Sa'id ibn Sultan, the AL-BU-SA'ID ruler of 'Uman and ZANZIBAR, and the British acquired control of it in 1887. (125b)

Monaco A sovereign principality in southeastern France, ruled by the GRIMALDI dynasty, a family of Genoese origin who established themselves as lords of Monaco in the 14th century and obtained the title of prince in 1612. They were expelled during the period of the French Revolution but restored in 1814. (25)

Mongolia/Mongols In its widest historical sense, Mongolia meant the whole eastern steppelands from the Gates of ZUNGARIA to the Manchurian steppes, including not only the modern Mongolian Republic but vast areas now part of China. Until the 19th century, this huge region was dominated by successive nomadic empires, the earliest of these being that of the HSIUNG-NU, established at the beginning of the 2nd century BC. After the division and collapse of this realm, the eastern steppes were controlled by various tribes until the rise of the JUAN-JUAN khanate in the 5th century AD, these people being overthrown by their vassals the T'U-CHUEH (Turks), whose first great ruler extended his authority far into the western steppelands also, though his kingdom soon split into an eastern and a western khanate. The T'ANG emperors of China destroyed the eastern T'u-Chueh state temporarily in the 7th century, and its revived regime was supplanted by the UIGHUR khanate in the middle of the following century, the Uighurs themselves falling victim to the Kirghiz in 840. The Khitan of Manchuria, who founded the LIAO empire in northern China, were of Turko-Mongol origin and controlled much of the eastern steppelands, though the grip of their successors, the Juchen (see CHIN), stronger in China, was weaker in the steppes and did not prevent the minor tribe of the Mongols building up its power under its leader Temuchin, proclaimed ruler of a great confederation of nomadic peoples in 1206 under the title of Chingis Khan. During the 13th century, the new state grew into an immense empire stretching across Eurasia from Korea to the Danube and through Iran into Asia Minor, incorporating the whole of China, where the Mongol Great Khans ruled as the YUAN dynasty, nominal overlords of various other khanates under branches of the CHINGIS KHANID family. After losing China to the MING in the mid-14th century, the Yuan line survived as khans in Mongolia until the 17th century, when the MANCHU emperors extended Chinese control, since largely maintained, into the steppelands. See also ZUNGAR KALMAKS. (225)

Monomotapas See MWENE MUTAPA dynasty.

Mons A people of southern BURMA, related to the Khmers of CAMBODIA and now largely absorbed into the Burmese population. There were various early Mon states in Burma and Indo-China, notably that based on the city of PEGU, which was annexed by the founders of the Burmese PAGAN kingdom in the 11th century AD. On the fall of Pagan, a new Pegu kingdom was established in the late 13th century and survived until its conquest by the TOUNGOO rulers of Burma. A final attempt by the Mons to recover independence on

the fall of the Toungoo state was eventually crushed by ALAUNGPAYA, founder of the last Burmese kingdom, in the mid-18th century. (237g)

Montefeltri Italian family, originally counts of Montefeltro, who became rulers of URBINO by imperial appointment in the 13th century. They held the town, with interruptions, as counts and later as dukes, establishing a small but prosperous state which was inherited on the death of the last of the Montefeltri in 1508 by his nephew of the ROVERESCHI family. (67h)

Montenegro In Slavonic, Crnagora, a region of south-western YUGOSLAVIA known in medieval times as Zeta. It formed part of the Serbian NEMANJICH empire, and on the disintegration of that state it became an independent principality under the BALSHICHI family in the mid-14th century. On the extinction of that dynasty, some of their territory fell to VENICE and the rest to the CRNOJEVICHI, who carried on a struggle against the OSMANLI Turks from the early 15th century until 1516, when the last of the family abdicated and the people elected a prince-bishop to rule them and maintain their independence. At the end of the 17th century, this office became hereditary in the PETROVICH dynasty, who abandoned their ecclesiastical functions in the mid-19th century to rule as lay princes. The last Petrovich sovereign proclaimed himself king of Montenegro in 1910, but was deposed in 1918, when his state was brought into the new Yugoslav kingdom. (75)

Montferrat Monferrato, a region in north-western Italy which became a margravate under the ALERAMID family in the 10th century AD. They developed important interests in the eastern Mediterranean lands, where one of the dynasty ruled briefly as king of JERUSALEM and another became king of THESSALONICA as a result of the Fourth Crusade. They inter-married with Byzantine royalty and in 1305 their margravate was inherited by a branch of the PALAEOLOGI – on the extinction of that line, Montferrat was acquired by the GONZAGAS of MANTUA and united with that duchy in the mid-16th century. (67b–c, 85c)

Moravia A region of Czechoslovakia in which arose an important early Slav state after the destruction of the AVAR kingdom at the end of the 8th century AD. Known to history as Greater Moravia, it extended into western Hungary and perhaps exercised suzerainty over the earliest dukes of BOHEMIA, but was overwhelmed by the invading Magyars (see HUNGARY) in the first years of the 10th century. Moravia later formed a margravate attached to the crown of Bohemia. (70)

Morea Medieval name for the Peloponnesian Peninsula of Greece, also name commonly used for the CRUSADER STATE formally entitled the principality of Achaea, which controlled most of the peninsula from its establishment in 1205. It was ruled by the VILHARDOUIN and other families, gradually losing territory to the Byzantines, who reconquered its last remnants in the mid-15th century, just before the whole of Greece fell under OSMANLI Turkish rule. (85h)

Morocco The most westerly region of the MAGHRIB, its modern name deriving from one of its most important cities, Marrakesh – for its pre-Islamic history, see MAURETANIA. It came under UMAYYAD rule in the 7th century AD, but was never effectively controlled by their 'ABBASID successors, being far from Baghdad and much closer to the realm of the surviving Umayyads in Spain, who at times controlled part of the area. However, some of the earliest independent minor Muslim dynasties arose in Morocco, the IDRISIDS at Fez and the MIDRARIDS beyond the Atlas. Indeed the western Maghrib was exceptionally suited by its isolation and the proximity of the Sahara to be a refuge and launching-ground for dissident Muslim sects and religious movements. Morocco was briefly part of the FATIMID empire in the 10th century and later the centre of the ALMORAVID and ALMOHAD states, the latter dynasty being supplanted there in the mid-13th century by the MARINIDS, who were in turn succeeded by their WATTASID relatives. On the collapse of the Wattasid regime in the mid-16th century, order was restored by an 'ALID family from the TAFILALT region, the SA'DIDS, who built up a powerful sultanate which extended Moroccan rule into the western Sudan with the conquest of the SONGHAI state. After a further period of disorder in the 17th century, the Sa'dids were succeeded by their remote cousins the 'ALAWIDS, who survived under a French protectorate during the first half of the present century and became independent sovereigns again in 1956. (112)

Moscow Traditional capital of RUSSIA since the 14th century, though partially replaced under the later Romanovs by St Petersburg (Leningrad). The original Kremlin fortress was built in 1156 by the prince of SUZDAL, and early in the 14th century, Moscow became a separate principality under a branch of the RIURIKIDS who proved more skilful in dealing with their overlords of the GOLDEN HORDE than the other Russian princes, rapidly coming to dominate the Russian lands not within the western kingdom of POLAND-LITHUANIA. In the late 15th century, the Muscovite rulers annexed NOVGOROD and formally repudiated Mongol suzerainty, their state emerging as a major power in Eastern Europe. For the later history of the Muscovite realm, see ROMANOVS. (93)

Mosul (Mawsil), city in northern 'Iraq on the Tigris, close to the site of Nineveh, capital of ASSYRIA. In medieval times the headquarters of several Muslim dynasties. (185a-b, g, j)

Mrohaung (Myohaung), town in ARAKAN and capital of the last ruling family of that kingdom, who are therefore known as the Mrohaung dynasty. They were assisted into power by the sultan of BENGAL in the early 15th century and ruled for nearly 400 years, until their state was conquered by the ALAUNGPAYA kings of BURMA in 1785. (238g)

Muhammad 'Ali dynasty Rulers of EGYPT from the early 19th century until the abolition of the Egyptian monarchy in 1953. Muhammad 'Ali himself was of Albanian origin and established himself as governor of the country under nominal OSMANLI Turkish overlordship. His successors obtained the title of Khedive (an old Iranian princely title) in 1866 and proclaimed their independence in 1917 as sultans (kings from 1922). (104)

Mukalla See SHIHR and MUKALLA.

Multan City of the PUNJAB, now in Pakistan, brought under Muslim rule in the 8th century AD and autonomous under various amirs until its capture by the GHAZNAVIDS in 1010. The city became independent on the break-up of the DELHI sultanate in the 15th century (see LANGAH dynasty) but was seized in 1528 by the ARGHUNS of Sind and shortly afterwards annexed by the MOGHULS. (203b)

Munster Province of Ireland and former kingdom, ruled from the 5th century AD by various branches of the EOGANACHT dynasty and finally by the O'BRIENS. Part of the kingdom was annexed by Anglo-Norman invaders in the late 12th century, and the remainder split into a number of minor chieftainships. (14a)

Murabitids See ALMORAVIDS.

Muradid dynasty Beys of TUNIS during most of the 17th century, formally as governors for the OSMANLI sultans but largely autonomous. At the beginning of the 18th century they were succeeded by the HUSAINIDS. (111a)

Musafirids Family from DAYLAM which ruled lands in AZERBAIJAN and GILAN in the 10th/11th centuries. They were supplanted in Azerbaijan by the RAWWADIDS, and their principality in the TARUM area in Gilan was probably extinguished by the ASSASSINS. (188d, 189d)

Muscat Modern capital of 'Uman, a town which became important in the early 17th century as a Portuguese naval base. It was captured from Portugal in 1648 by the YA'RUBIDS and became capital of the state under the AL-BU-SA'IDS. (179)

Muscovy See MOSCOW and RUSSIA.

Mutawakkilite Kingdom of Yemen See YEMEN and QASIMIDS.

Muwahhid dynasty See ALMOHADS.

Muzaffarids Name of two Muslim dynasties:

1 Sultans of GUJARAT, their founder establishing his independence in the late 14th century on the break-up of the DELHI sultanate. His successors annexed the CHUDSAMA kingdom in SAURASHTRA in the following century, and temporarily conquered the neighbouring MALWA sultanate in 1531. The last of the dynasty lost his lands to the MOGHULS in 1573, though he made an attempt, only briefly successful, to recover Gujarat a decade later. (208e)

2 A family which ruled in western Iran during most of the 14th century, rising to power on the collapse of the ILKHAN state. The founder obtained control of ISFAHAN and KIRMAN and gradually conquered FARS from the INJU'IDS. His sons and grandsons ruled these lands jointly, the most powerful of them at the time of the TIMURID expansion, Shah Mansur, being killed in battle against Timur in 1393. The Muzaffarid lands were then annexed to the Timurid domains. (190e)

Mwene Mutapa dynasty (Monomotapas), a family which established an extensive empire in the regions south of the Zambezi (modern Zimbabwe and Mozambique) in the mid-15th century, probably as the successor of an earlier state based at old Zimbabwe. Their realm remained an important power for some two centuries, sometimes under strong Portuguese influence, but then declined into a minor chieftainship which survived into the present century. 'Mwene Mutapa' was the formal title of the monarch. (130)

Myinsaing and Pinya Towns in Upper BURMA, successive capitals of a small SHAN kingdom of the late 13th/early 14th centuries. Myinsaing survived a major MONGOL siege in 1301, and the state was united with neighbouring SAGAING in 1364 to form the core of the powerful kingdom of AVA. (237b)

Mysore (Maisur), city and province which constitutes the southern section of the DECCAN plateau, India. It was controlled by the MAURYAS in the 3rd century BC and its northern section later formed the KADAMBA kingdom until conquered by the CHALUKYA rulers of the Deccan at the beginning of the 7th century AD. The southern parts were ruled by the Western GANGA kings from the 4th to the early 11th centuries, when that state was over-thrown by the CHOLAS. On the decline of CHOLAS and Later Chalukyas, the HOYSALA dynasty rose to power in Mysore. The last Hoysala kings fell before Muslim invaders in the early 14th century, though perhaps contributing to the foundation of the great VIJAYANAGAR empire which dominated southern India from late medieval times until its distintegration in the late 16th century. The WADIYAR dynasty, vassals of Vijayanagar in Mysore, then became independent, as also did the NAYYAKS of IKKERI. Around 1755, HAIDAR 'ALI, a Muslim adventurer, gained effective power in the Wadiyar realm, and annexed Ikkeri, building up a strong state which came into collision with the rising British power in India. Tipu Sultan, successor of Haidar 'Ali, was killed in 1799 when the British stormed his capital, and the Wadiyar maharajas were then restored. Their state was absorbed into the Republic of India in 1949. (219)

N

Nabataeans (al-Anbat), ancient Arab people who dominated north-western Arabia from the middle of the 1st millennium BC, though little is known of their kingdom or its rulers until the 2nd century BC. From around 85 BC they controlled DAMASCUS, though their capital remained the famous rock-hewn city of Petra, in modern Jordan, and they fell under Roman overlordship soon after-wards. The Nabataean state was annexed by ROME in 105 AD. (169)

Nagpur Town and former state in the DECCAN, India, the kingdom being estab-lished by a MARATHA general, Rhaguji BHONSLA in the mid-18th century. It was annexed by the British in 1853. (2170)

Najahid dynasty Rulers of Ethiopian origin who controlled a state based at ZABID in the YEMEN in the 11th/12th centuries AD. They succeeded the ZIYADIDS and were themselves followed by the MAHDIDS. (172c)

Najd Region of central ARABIA, briefly the centre of the KINDAH realm in the 5th/6th centuries AD, and from the mid-18th century the power-base of the Wahhabi sect of Islam led by the AL-SA'UD dynasty. It is now part of Sa'udi Arabia, its main town Riyadh being the capital of that kingdom. (174, 176)

Namgyal dynasty (Rnam-rgyal), a family of Tibetan origin who established a kingdom in SIKKIM in the mid-17th century. The last ruler ('Chogyal') was deposed in 1975, and his state annexed to the Republic of India. (212)

Namur City and province of Belgium which formed a county from the 10th century, becoming a margravate in 1088. The VALOIS rulers of Burgundy acquired it by purchase in the 15th century. (20d)

Nan Chao Medieval kingdom in what is now Yunnan province, south-western China, founded in the 7th century AD. The ethnic composition of its population is uncertain, but probably included a sub-stantial THAI element. The state usually acknowledged nominal Chinese over-lordship, but was in practice independent until conquered by the MONGOL rulers of China in the 13th century. (234)

Nan Yueh Ancient kingdom in southern CHINA, with its capital at Canton and ruled by the CHAO dynasty. It was founded by a general of the CH'IN empire as that state collapsed in the last years of the 3rd century BC, and was conquered by the HAN in 111 BC. Nan Yueh included TONKIN and it is also regarded as a Vietnamese kingdom. (228q)

Napata Capital of the early kingdom of NUBIA in the eastern Sudan, its first rulers, conquerors of EGYPT, constituting the Egyptian Dynasty XXV of the 8th/7th centuries BC. Their successors continued to rule at Napata after the loss of Egypt until the end of the 4th century BC, when the centre of power in Nubia shifted to MEROE. (113)

Naples Ancient Neapolis, Italian city founded by Greek colonists in the 7th/6th century BC and an important town in Roman times. When most of Italy was lost to the LOMBARDS, Naples remained

THE DYNASTIES OF NASSAU AND ORANGE-NASSAU

Rupert, Count of Nassau, d.1124

Walramian Line:
Counts of Idstein, Weilburg, etc.

Ottonian Line:
Counts of Siegen, Dillenburg, etc.

Counts of
Nassau-Weilburg

Princes of Orange,
Stadtholders of
the Netherlands
1572–1702

Counts of
Nassau-Dietz

Princes of
Nassau-Weilburg
from 1688

Princes of Orange,
Stadtholders of
the Netherlands
1747–1795

Dukes of Nassau 1816–1866

Kings of the Netherlands since 1813

Grand Dukes of Luxemburg
since 1890

under the control of BYZANTIUM, though its governors gradually became more or less independent over the centuries, until the city was annexed to the HAUTEVILLE kingdom of SICILY in 1139. On the ANGEVIN conquest of southern Italy from the HOHENSTAUFFEN in 1266, Naples became their capital, and they continued to rule a 'Kingdom of Naples', when Sicily was lost to the ARAGONESE (who acquired Naples also in the mid-15th century). Naples thereafter remained the capital of the state of Naples and Sicily, except during the several periods in later times when the two regions were divided, until the incorporation of that state into the kingdom of Italy in the mid-19th century. (62)

Nasrid dynasty On the fall of ALMOHAD rule in Spain after the great Christian victory at Las Navas de Tolosa in 1212, most of the Muslim regions were overrun gradually by the victors, but Muhammad the Nasrid established a small kingdom based on GRANADA, which survived rather precariously as a Muslim enclave until its conquest by Ferdinand and Isabella of ARAGON/CASTILE in the same year (1492) as they sent Columbus on his voyage of discovery. (52)

Nassau Region of north-western Germany which formed a county from the mid-12th century, much divided among various branches of its ruling dynasty in later times. The family lands were re-united at the beginning of the 19th century to form the duchy of Nassau, annexed by PRUSSIA in 1866. Its dispossessed ruler inherited the grand duchy of LUXEMBURG in 1890. The Netherlands House of ORANGE is a branch of the Nassau dynasty. (32)

Navarre Region of northern Spain, formerly a kingdom originally founded by a local dynasty shortly after the Muslim conquest of Visigothic Spain. In the 11th century AD, Sancho III the Great ruled much of northern Spain, but divided his lands among his sons, forming the kingdoms of CASTILE and ARAGON, with the result that Navarre was cut off from Muslim territory and did not expand vastly by conquests in the south like the other states. In the 13th century, the kingdom was inherited by the counts of CHAMPAGNE, and later by other French families, and most of it was annexed by united Spain in 1516, though a remnant remained independent until its ruler succeeded to the throne of France as Henry IV (see BOURBON dynasty) in 1589. (46)

Naxos The main island of the Cyclades group in the Aegean Sea. As a result of the Fourth Crusade, the islands were seized early in the 13th century by the Venetian SANUDI family, who established the duchy of Naxos (see CRUSADER STATES) and ruled it until supplanted by their relatives the CRISPI in 1383. The duchy was eventually annexed to the OSMANLI empire in the late 16th century. (85i)

Nayyak dynasties On the break-up of the VIJAYANAGAR empire in southern India in the mid-16th century, several provincial governors ('Nayyaks') became independent, including the rulers of MADURAI, TANJORE and IKKERI, whose families controlled their respective states for several generations. Tanjore was acquired by a branch of the Maratha BHONSLAS in 1674, and both Madurai and Ikkeri fell to Muslim conquest in the 18th century. (219f, 223d–e)

Ndebele (Matabele), a people of Zimbabwe, in origin a section of the ZULU army which broke away and fled north under Mzilikaze in the 1820s, settled temporarily in the Transvaal and finally established a kingdom in the Shona lands south of the Zambezi. The state was conquered by the British in 1893. (133c)

Negri Sembilan The 'Nine States', a federation of small chieftainships in western MALAYA populated by immigrants from Sumatra. The chiefs elected a supreme ruler in 1773 and his successors have continued to head the state thus formed, which is now part of the larger federation of MALAYSIA. (244i)

Nemanjich dynasty Family descended from Stephen Nemanja, founder of the medieval state of Serbia in the late 12th century AD. His successor became a king in 1217, and the most powerful of the dynasty, Stephen Dushan, built up a great Balkan domain, claiming the title of emperor in 1345. However, on his death the Serbian empire broke up, various princes seizing the different provinces, though a smaller Serbian state survived under other families. (72a)

Neopatras Modern Loutra Ipatis in THESSALY, capital of a duchy under a branch of the DUCAS family of EPIRUS in the 13th/14th centuries. On the extinction of its rulers in 1318, the town was acquired by the duchy of ATHENS, though most of the northern lands of the state, which included much of Thessaly, fell to BYZANTIUM. (85f)

Nepal Independent kingdom on the southern slopes of the Himalayas. The valley called Nepal in ancient times was only a small part of the modern state, ruled by various dynasties including the MALLAS, who acquired power in the 13th century AD. Late in the 15th century, the kingdom was divided into several smaller states under branches of the Malla family, all of which were conquered in 1768–69 by the ruler of the small hill-state of GURKHA, who thus founded the present state. (211)

Netherlands In its widest sense the region including both Belgium and the kingdom of the Netherlands (Holland), though nowadays mainly used to indicate the latter state. In medieval times it was divided into various duchies and counties mostly under the suzerainty of the German empire, most of which were gradually acquired in the 14th and 15th centuries by the VALOIS dukes of BURGUNDY and inherited by the HABSBURGS in 1477. The region rose in revolt against Spanish Habsburg rule about a century later and the northern provinces established their independence under the House of ORANGE, who ruled with interruptions until expelled by the French Revolutionary armies. The southern region remained under Spanish and later Austrian rule. Louis BONAPARTE reigned briefly as king of Holland in 1806–10, and on the fall of Napoleon, all the Netherlands were constituted a kingdom under the ORANGE dynasty, but the southern provinces broke away to become the kingdom of BELGIUM in 1831. The Orange dynasty, a branch of the NASSAU family, still rules the modern Netherlands state. (19–20)

Ngo dynasty Ruling family of VIET-NAM whose founder led the revolt which finally freed the country from Chinese rule in the 10th century after a thousand years punctuated by unsuccessful rebellion. However, his dynasty was soon supplanted by the DINH. (243b)

Nguyen dynasty Ruling family of VIET-NAM. When power at Hanoi was seized from the Later LE emperors by the MAC family in the early 16th century, the Nguyen established their effective independence at HUE and continued to recognize puppet Le sovereigns, though in conflict with the TRINH family, who eventually restored the Le emperors at Hanoi but remained the real rulers in the northern province of TONKIN. Both Nguyen and Trinh were overthrown by the TAY-SON brothers in the late 18th century, and a member of the Nguyen family then began a long struggle, with some French help, to recover power. In 1802, he completed his task by making himself emperor of VIET-NAM, and his descendants ruled until the present century, for a while under French control. The monarchy was abolished in 1955. (243l–m)

Nicaea Modern Iznik in north-western Turkey, meeting-place of a major council of the Christian Church in 325 AD. When Constantinople fell to the Fourth Crusade in 1204, a relative of the Byzantine imperial family, Theodore Lascaris, organized a state based on Nicaea and rapidly recovered control of much of western Asia Minor, claiming to be the legitimate Byzantine emperor, as did several other contenders. However, his successors vindicated their claim in 1261 by the recapture of the old imperial capital, and re-established the Byzantine empire, though only as a shadow of its former self. (1e)

Niebla City in Spain, centre of the small state ruled by the BANU YAHYA, one of the 11th century REYES DE TAIFAS states. Their lands were annexed by the 'ABBADIDS of Seville in 1051. (48f)

Nigeria Large and populous African state in which two regions with mostly separate histories are combined. The north is part of the central SUDAN – see HAUSA, FULANI, KANEM-BORNU – while the south was the area of the powerful kingdoms of OYO and BENIN.

Nizam Shahi dynasty Rulers of AHMADNAGAR, one of the DECCAN SULTANATES, from the late 15th century. The Nizam Shahis annexed neighbouring BERAR in 1572, but their state was itself conquered by the MOGHULS in 1633. (217i)

Nkore (Nkole, Ankole), former kingdom in south-western Uganda, ruled by a branch of the BAHINDA dynasty from its establishment in the 15th century until its

abolition by independent Uganda in 1967. (127a)

Normandy Duchy established in north-western France by Norwegian VIKINGS in the early 10th century. By his conquest of England in 1066, William of Normandy linked the duchy with the English crown (with interruptions) until it was seized by the CAPET rulers of France in 1204. Thereafter, it remained under the close control of the French kings, apart from periods in English hands during the Hundred Years War of the 14th/15th centuries (See also NORMANS). (24a)

Normans The 'Northmen' of NORMANDY, Norwegian VIKINGS who established a state in northern France in the 10th century AD, though they rapidly adopted the French language and feudal cutoms. Their dukes were descended from Scandinavian Jarls and related to the Earls of ORKNEY – they acquired the English throne in 1066 and were succeeded in all their lands by the ANGEVIN Henry II in the mid-12th century. A separate Norman family, the HAUTEVILLES, migrated to southern Italy, where they established the duchy of APULIA and the kingdom of SICILY (and later the principality of ANTIOCH in Syria). A third family ruled CAPUA in the 11th/12th centuries. (6b, 24a, 62a, 68d–e, 167b)

Northern For dynasties thus named, see the main dynastic name – Northern YUAN, Northern HAN, etc.

Northumbria English kingdom formed in the late 6th century AD by the union of BERNICIA and DEIRA. It dominated England north of the Humber and part of south-eastern Scotland, but was overwhelmed by the great VIKING invasion of the mid-9th century. The southern section formed the Scandinavian kingdom of YORK thereafter, though English leaders held out at Bamborough, controlling some of the old Bernician lands and recognizing the suzerainty of the rulers of WESSEX. (5f)

Norway In the 9th century AD, the YNGLING Jarl of Westfold, Harald Fairhair, conquered the other small states of Norway and became its first king. His dynasty ruled amid repeated quarrels and murders until succeeded by the FOLKUNGS in 1319. At the end of the 14th century, the crown was acquired by Margaret I of DENMARK, ruler of all three Scandinavian kingdoms, and Norway shared a king with Denmark until 1814, when it was seized by SWEDEN. It became independent by negotiation in 1905 under a member of the OLDENBURG dynasty of Denmark. (17)

Novgorod 'New City', one of the oldest trading settlements in RUSSIA and centre of the power of Riurik, founder of the RIURIKID dynasty, though his successors moved their capital to KIEV. It became a separate principality in the 11th century and soon for practical purposes a republic, ceasing to elect even nominal princes after the MONGOL invasion which had little effect upon Novgorod. The city and its extensive northern territories were annexed by MOSCOW in 1478. (92d)

Nubia Ancient name for the Nile valley south of Egypt to the junction of the Blue and White Niles, now in the Sudanese Republic. The kingdoms of NAPATA (8th/4th centuries BC) and its successor MEROE were based in this area, as were the later Christian kingdoms of Dongola and Alwa, conquered respectively by the MAMLUKS in the 14th century and the FUNG in the 16th.

Numidia Ancient North African state in the eastern MAGHRIB which rose to importance as an ally of ROME against CARTHAGE in the late 3rd century BC. It was a Roman client-state for virtually the whole of its existence, despite the efforts of one of its kings, Jugurtha, to throw off Roman control in the late 2nd century, and was annexed by Rome in 46 BC. (107)

Nupe A state founded under a HAUSA dynasty in the 16th century – its rulers became Muslims in the 18th century, and the kingdom was taken over by a FULANI dynasty in 1832 as a vassal amirate of the SOKOTO sultanate. It is now part of NIGERIA. (116c, 118g)

Obrenovichi See KARAGEORGEVICHI and OBRENOVICHI.

O'Brien In the late 10th century AD, the throne of MUNSTER was seized from the EOGANACHT dynasty by the Dal Cais family, who rose to great power under Brian Boru, HIGH KING of Ireland, killed at the battle of Clontarf in 1014. His descendants, the O'Briens, ruled in Munster until the Anglo-Norman invasion and remained minor princes in Thomond until the 16th century, when they became Earls of Thomond. (14a)

O'Connor Kings of CONNAUGHT from the 9th century AD, some of them being also HIGH KINGS of Ireland, until the Anglo-Norman conquest of the 12th/13th centuries. They were a branch of the CONNACHTA dynasty. (14d)

Oiscings Kings of KENT, descendants of Oisc, allegedly the son of Hengest, founder of the kingdom. They ruled from the 5th to at least the mid-8th century AD, the descent of the later kings of Kent being uncertain. (5a)

Oldenburg dynasty Originally counts of Oldenburg in north-western Germany from the 12th century. They acquired the thrones of DENMARK and NORWAY in 1448, and reigned intermittently in SWEDEN in the late 15th/early 16th centuries. Though they were obliged to cede Norway to Sweden in 1814, a member of the Danish dynasty was elected king of independent Norway in 1905, and the Oldenburgs still reign in both countries. Branches of the family continued to rule in Oldenburg, which became a grand duchy in 1829, until that state was abolished in 1918. Other junior lines ruled in parts of SCHLESWIG and HOLSTEIN, one of which succeeded the main line on the throne of Denmark in 1863, whilst another, that of the important duchy of Holstein-Gottorp, provided kings of Sweden in 1751–1818 and acquired the throne of RUSSIA in the mid-18th century, the later ROMANOVS being Oldenburgs in the male line. A branch of the Danish Oldenburgs ruled GREECE from 1863 until the disappearance of the Greek monarchy, and the present Prince of Wales is an Oldenburg by male descent through that line. (16b, 17c, 18f, 28, 86, 94)

Oman See 'UMAN.

THE OLDENBURG DYNASTY – MALE LINES

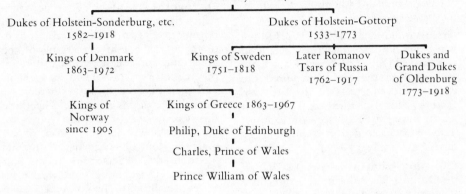

Christian, Count of Oldenburg, d.1167

Counts of Oldenburg to 1667

Kings of Denmark 1448–1863
and of Norway to 1814

Dukes of Holstein-Sonderburg, etc.
1582–1918

Dukes of Holstein-Gottorp
1533–1773

Kings of Denmark
1863–1972

Kings of Sweden
1751–1818

Later Romanov
Tsars of Russia
1762–1917

Dukes and
Grand Dukes
of Oldenburg
1773–1918

Kings of
Norway
since 1905

Kings of Greece 1863–1967

Philip, Duke of Edinburgh

Charles, Prince of Wales

Prince William of Wales

Omayyads See UMAYYADS.

O'Neill Descendants of Niall Noigiallach, a scion of the CONNACHTA dynasty and first HIGH KING of Ireland in the early 5th century AD. The High Kingship soon became an object of contention between two branches of the O'Neills, a southern line in MEATH and a northern line in AILECH – a contest in which the O'BRIENS and O'CONNORS later joined. The northern O'Neills survived the Anglo-Norman conquest as minor princes and later became Earls of Tyrone. (13, 14e–f)

Orange, House of Ruling dynasty of the NETHERLANDS, a branch of the NASSAU dynasty. In the 16th century, William the Silent of the Nassau-Dillenburg line inherited the principality of Orange, in southern France, but his main interests were in the Netherlands, where he was at first a provincial governor for the HABSBURGS and then the leader of the Dutch revolt against Philip II of Spain. Members of his family ruled the Dutch state with interruptions until expelled by the French Revolutionary armies in 1795, and were restored in 1813 as kings of all the Netherlands and grand dukes of LUXEMBURG. In 1830, the southern region broke away as the independent kingdom of BELGIUM, and in 1890, on the failure of male heirs in the Orange dynasty, the grand duchy was inherited by the Nassau-Weilburg branch, distant relatives of the Orange family (which still rules the modern Netherlands kingdom, where three successive queens have reigned since 1890). (19b, d)

Orissa Eastern coastal region of India, ruled by various Hindu dynasties from ancient times, notably the GANGAS. In the mid-16th century, the kingdom was conquered by the Muslim ruler of Bengal, though Hindu chiefs continued to control some areas. (216)

Orkney Nothing much is known of the history of these islands until the emergence of a Norwegian VIKING earldom of Orkney in the 9th century, its rulers related to the dukes of NORMANDY. The earls recognized the overlordship of NORWAY, some of them also ruling Caithness as Scottish vassals. The dynasty became extinct in the 14th century, and various other families later held the earldom, though less independently. (12a)

Orleans Ancient Aurelianum, French city on the Loire usually under the direct control of the CAPET kings in medieval times, though briefly a separate duchy under the members of the VALOIS dynasty in the 14th and 15th centuries. The title was later held nominally by a branch of the BOURBONS, one of whom became king in France in the mid-19th century. (24h)

Orontids Ancient dynasty of ARMENIA, established under the later ACHAEMENIDS as satraps – they survived the fall of the Persian empire to Alexander the Great, but were supplanted in about 200 BC by the ARTAXIADS. (146a)

Orsinis Important family of Papal Rome which provided several Popes – its head was entitled Duke of Gravina from 1435. A branch of the family acquired the county of CEPHALONIA in the late 12th century and also ruled as Despots of EPIRUS during part of the 14th century. They were succeeded in Cephalonia by the TOCCO family. (85b, e)

Osmanlis Ruling dynasty and people of the Ottoman Turkish empire, originally a small ANATOLIAN AMIRATE founded in the late 13th century by Osman ('Uthman), leader of a migrant group of Turks from Central Asia. Located on the frontier with BYZANTIUM in north-western Asia Minor, this state grew rapidly under a series of very able rulers into a powerful multi-national empire, suffering no more than a temporary set-back when most of its Anatolian lands were overrun by Timur after the Osmanli defeat at Ankara in 1402. The sultans extinguished the last remnants of the Byzantine state, taking Constantinople (thereafter Istanbul, their capital) in 1453, and extended their rule over EGYPT and SYRIA, all the Balkan lands and much of HUNGARY. The khans of the CRIMEA were Osmanli vassals, as were the Sharifs of MECCA, and Turkish governors ruled in Algiers, Budapest and Baghdad. HABSBURG Vienna was twice besieged in vain by Osmanli armies, in 1529 and 1683. Decline set in during the 17th/18th centuries, resulting in great losses of territory to Austria and Russia, and in the 19th century the European powers combined on various occasions to secure the independence of GREECE, RUMANIA, SERBIA and BULGARIA. Egypt and North Africa also broke away during this period, and the remaining Arab lands were lost as a result of the First World War. The Osmanli sultanate was abolished in 1922, when the present Republic of Turkey was established. (143)

Osrhoene Ancient name for the region around Edessa (modern Urfa, in southeastern Turkey), a kingdom under the Arab ABGARID dynasty from the 2nd century BC until its annexation by ROME in 242 AD. (164)

Ostrogoths One of the two sections into which the GOTHS were divided in the 4th century AD. For a time they became subject to the HUNS, but at the urging of the government of the Eastern Roman Empire, they conquered ITALY from its previous barbarian rulers in the late 5th century. Their leader in this enterprise, Theodoric the Great, was the most powerful Germanic king of his time, also exercising practical control over the Visigothic kingdom in Gaul and Spain, but after his death the Ostrogothic state weakened, and eventually fell to Byzantine reconquest in the mid-6th century. (57)

Ottoman Turks See OSMANLIS.

Oudh See AVADH.

Oyo Town in south-western Nigeria, centre of a former powerful state which in the 17th and 18th centuries dominated neighbouring states, including DAHOMEY. Its importance faded away in the mid-19th century, though its line of rulers, entitled Alafins, has continued to the present day, their role within the Republic of Nigeria being purely ceremonial. (121b)

P

Padua Ancient Patavium, city in Italy which became an independent lordship under the CARRARESI, who ruled it for most of the 14th century. In 1405 Padua was annexed by VENICE. (67f)

Paekche Early kingdom in central KOREA, traditionally founded in 18 BC, though there is no evidence for its real existence before about the 4th century AD. In the 7th century, it became involved in the major struggle between the Chinese and the much stronger north Korean state of Koguryo, and fell victim to a T'ANG seaborne invasion, its lands passing shortly afterwards to SILLA. When Silla collapsed in the late 9th/early 10th centuries, there was an attempt to revive Paekche, but the new state was soon incorporated into united Korea by the founder of the WANG dynasty. (235b, e)

Pagan Town in Upper BURMA, capital of the earliest fully historical Burmese kingdom, founded by Anawrahta in the mid-11th century. His dynasty ruled both Upper and Lower Burma until the 13th century, when PEGU regained independence in the south and MONGOL attacks weakened the last kings of Pagan, who fell to SHAN conquest. (237a)

Pahang Sultanate in MALAYA, founded by a member of the MALACCA dynasty in the 15th century. On the extinction of its ruling family in 1641, the state was united with JOHORE, but from the beginning of the 19th century the Pahang chief ministers became virtually independent, taking the title of sultan themselves in 1884 – they were descended from an earlier Johore ruler and related to the ministerial family of Johore who also became sultans of that state in 1885. Pahang is now part of the MALAYSIA federation. (244d)

Pahlavi dynasty The last monarchical family of IRAN, founded by an army officer in 1925 after the deposition of the QAJAR dynasty. He and his son made considerable efforts to modernize and westernize Iran, but Muhammad Reza Pahlavi was obliged to go into exile in 1979 by revolutionaries who abolished the monarchy. (187n)

Pakistan From an historical viewpoint, the Indian sub-continent is best considered as a whole – see INDIA.

Palaeologi Last imperial family of BYZANTIUM, its first emperor deposing the Vatatzes ruler at NICAEA in the mid-13th century and shortly afterwards recovering Constantinople, extinguishing the LATIN EMPIRE. The family quarrels among his successors much weakened the state, and Byzantine territory shrank rapidly in the 14th century until it consisted of only the capital city and the MOREA, isolated amid the empire of the OSMANLI Turks, who took Constantinople in 1453. The last Byzantine emperor was killed during the final assault. A branch of the Palaeologi ruled Montferrat until 1533. (1f, 67c)

Palas Buddhist dynasty which ruled BENGAL and neighbouring areas of north-eastern India in the 8th/12th centuries AD, surviving in Bihar until the Muslim conquest, though supplanted in Bengal by the Hindu SENA family. (214a)

Palatinate of the Rhine The Count Palatine of the Rhine, originally an important official in the early HOLY ROMAN EMPIRE, became the ruler of a feudal state with territory on both sides of the middle Rhine and also in northern BAVARIA. In the 13th century, these lands were acquired by the WITTELSBACHS and soon subdivided among several branches of the family, the title of Count Palatine being held by the senior line, who became Electors (see ELECTORATE) in the following century. The Palatine dynasty lost their Bavarian territory to their cousins the Bavarian Wittelsbachs in the 17th century, but inherited Bavaria itself in the late 18th century and thus brought together all the lands of their family. One branch of the Rhine dynasty provided kings for SWEDEN in the 17th/18th centuries, and one Count Palatine briefly ruled in BOHEMIA. (35)

Palembang Town and region in southeastern Sumatra, an important centre in the SRIVIJAYA empire and later a Muslim sultanate annexed by the Dutch in 1823. (245b)

Palestine See JUDAEA and JERUSALEM.

Pallava dynasty A ruling family of early southern India, whose capital was the ancient city of Kanchipuram. Their origins are obscure and controversial, extending back to at least the 4th century AD, but in the 7th century they became the dominant power in the CARNATIC, suppressing the CHOLA kingdom and reducing other southern states to subjection. Their empire was extinguished by a revived Chola state in the late 9th century. (221a)

Pandyas A TAMIL people who inhabited the southern tip of India from ancient times, their traditional capital being MADURAI. The names of some very early Pandya kings are known, but the history of their state is very sketchy until the emergence of a dynasty of rulers at the end of the 6th century AD. The Pandya kingdom was conquered by the CHOLA kings in about 920, the last ruler being obliged to flee to Ceylon. On the decline of the Chola power at the end of the 12th century, a Later Pandya line of kings arose and became for a short period the major power in the CARNATIC, but their capital was taken by the sultan of DELHI in 1310 and the region annexed to his realm, though minor Pandya princes survived in the area for several centuries. (223a–b)

Papacy/Papal States The earliest Roman Popes were solely religious leaders, bishops of Rome with no official standing and sometimes fugitives from the imperial authorities, many being martyred. Under the Christian emperors in the 4th century AD, they became important officials, and after the fall of the Western Roman Empire began to exercise some political leadership and control in Rome and its surrounding area. In the mid-8th century, the LOMBARD ruler of Italy was obliged to recognize Papal rule in extensive lands in the centre of the peninsula. During later medieval times, both the area of this state and the real degree of Papal control varied very greatly, the Popes at times being expelled from Rome and many of their towns coming under the rule of local lords. By the early 16th century, the Popes had achieved effective sovereignty over a large block of territory across central Italy and were able to increase it later by annexations (e.g. FERRARA and URBINO). Most of this territory was seized by the new kingdom of Italy in the mid-19th century and Rome itself in 1870. However, in 1929 the sovereignty of the Pope was recognized in the small Vatican City area of Rome, which is technically an independent state. (2)

Paramara dynasty A RAJPUT family which ruled MALWA and at times wider areas of central India in the 9th/13th centuries. Its kingdom was conquered by the sultan of DELHI at the beginning of the 14th century. (207b)

Parhae See P'O-HAI.

Parin dynasty A family which ruled ARAKAN during part of the 12th century AD. (238c)

Parma Ancient city of Etruscan foundation in northern Italy. It was separated from the PAPAL STATES (with Piacenza) as a duchy for the son of Pope Paul III, Pier Luigi FARNESE, whose family ruled the two towns until succeeded by a branch of the related BOURBONS of Spain, who were expelled by Napoleon BONAPARTE in 1802. On Napoleon's fall, the duchy was allotted to his empress, Marie-Louise of HABSBURG, and recovered only after her death by the Bourbon heirs. The state was annexed to the kingdom of Italy in the mid-19th century. (64)

Parthia/Parthians The region was an ancient province of eastern IRAN, roughly corresponding with modern KHURASAN. Nomadic invaders related to the Scythians established a kingdom in the area in the mid-3rd century BC, soon becoming known as Parthians. Their kings, the ARSACIDS, gradually conquered Iran and 'IRAQ from the SELEUCIDS and became a major imperial dynasty in Western Asia, blocking the expansion of ROME in the east. The Parthian empire was overthrown in the early 3rd century AD by the SASANIDS. See also INDO-PARTHIANS. (187c)

Patani (Pattani), town in the northern area of the Malay Peninsula, now in THAILAND, formerly centre of a Malay state from the mid-16th century until Thai annexation in 1729. (244b)

Patiala Town in the PUNJAB, formerly centre of a state founded by a SIKH family in the mid-18th century and absorbed into the Republic of India in 1948. (203d)

Pegu Town near Rangoon in BURMA, capital of a MON kingdom from its foundation in the 9th century AD, though little is known about this early state, conquered by the PAGAN rulers in the 11th century. On the collapse of the Pagan state, Pegu again became independent until the unification of Burma in the 16th century by the TOUNGOO kings, under some of whom the city was capital of the realm. An attempt to revive the Mon kingdom on the fall of the Toungoo dynasty was only briefly successful, the new state being conquered in 1757 by ALAUNGPAYA. (237g)

Peloponnese The peninsular region of southern Greece, the medieval MOREA. See also SPARTA.

Perak Sultanate in MALAYA, founded by a member of the dispossessed dynasty of MALACCA in the early 16th century. The state is still ruled by his descendants, now as part of the MALAYSIA Federation. (244f)

Pereyaslavl Ancient town on the Dniepr river, RUSSIA, centre of a RIURIKID principality from the division of the KIEV state in the 11th century AD until the early 13th century, initially one of the most important of the Russian states, though it later declined into obscurity. (92c)

Pergamum (Pergamon, modern Bergama), ancient city in western Asia Minor and capital of a kingdom under the ATTALID dynasty. The founder became virtually independent during the wars of the DIADOCHI, from early in the 3rd century BC, and his successors built up an extensive and prosperous state which the last of the family bequeathed to ROME in 133 BC. The region then became the Roman province of Asia. (137f)

Perigord Region of central France which formed a feudal county from the 9th century under a family closely related to the counts of ANGOULEME. The county was seized by the French crown in 1399. (24n)

Perlis State in MALAYA, part of KEDAH until the temporary THAI annexation of that sultanate in the early 19th century. On the Thai withdrawal, Perlis was made a separate state under a Raja. It is now part of the MALAYSIA Federation. (244l)

Persia See IRAN.

Peru Civilized towns and kingdoms existed in Peru for many centuries before the rise of the INCAS, but relatively little is known of their political history. The Inca state was established in the 12th century AD as a small highland kingdom, but in the 15th century expanded rapidly by military conquest to control vast territories including the whole of the modern state of Peru plus parts of Ecuador and Chile. A Spanish force led by Francisco Pizarro and clearly inspired by the successful campaign of Cortes in MEXICO conquered most of this empire in 1532–3, though the Inca ruling dynasty held out in the remote Andes for a further forty years. Peru thereafter remained part of the Spanish American empire until the early 19th century, when it became an independent republic. (252)

Petrovich dynasty Ruling family of MONTENEGRO, at first as hereditary bishops and leaders of their small state in its efforts to remain free of OSMANLI Turkish rule in the 18th century. In the mid-19th century, the ruler abandoned his religious role and became a lay prince, his successor taking the title of king in 1910. However, after the First World War, Montenegro was incorporated into the new YUGOSLAV monarchy, its own sovereign being deposed. (75c)

Pharaoh Traditional title of the rulers of ancient EGYPT, meaning literally 'Great House'. During the 3000 years of Egyptian history prior to the Roman annexation in 30 BC, there were more than two hundred Pharaohs, customarily divided into 33 dynasties (I–XXXIII), an arrangement devised by the Egyptian historian Manetho for the lengthy king-lists he drew up in the 3rd century BC. By his time the earliest Pharaohs were much more remote to him than he is to us, and modern archaeologists have drastically revised his lists. However, his dynastic numbering system is now too entrenched to be changed, though in various ways unsatisfactory, and historians do not in any case have enough information to rearrange it properly – in many cases the relationships, if any, between the various rulers in the dynasties are uncertain or unknown, and accession dates are often inexact. (98)

Philippines See MAGUINDANAO and SULU.

Piast dynasty Rulers of the earliest state in POLAND, from the 10th century AD. Their realm became a strong power in Eastern Europe until its division between the sons of Boleslav III in 1138 under a system whereby they were to be senior rulers in succession. In fact Poland soon broke up into several principalities under branches of the Piasts and was in consequence very weak until most of the Piast lands were re-united in the early 13th century. The last Piast king died in 1370, succeeded by his nephew the ANGEVIN king of Hungary. MAZOVIA was not acquired by the kingdom until the 16th

THE PIAST DYNASTY OF POLAND

Piast, legendary Polish leader
↓
Mieszko I of Poland, d.992 AD
↓
Boleslav III of Poland, d.1138

Princes of Silesia from 1138	Princes of Great Poland 1138–1296	Princes of Kujavia and Mazovia	
Silesian Ducal lines of Wroclaw, Legnica, etc. to 1675		Princes of Kujavia to 1320	Princes of Mazovia to 1526
		Kings of Poland 1320–1370	

century and SILESIA was lost to Poland until 1945. (87a–g)

Picts A people who inhabited most of SCOTLAND in ancient times, named 'Painted Folk' (Picti) by the Romans, whose efforts to conquer their lands they successfully resisted. Nothing is known of their political history until the emergence of a Pictish kingdom in central and northern Scotland in the 6th century AD. It was annexed in the mid-9th century by Kenneth mac Alpin of DALRIADA, who thus created the kingdom of Scotland. (9)

Piedmont Region of north-western Italy ruled by the dukes of SAVOY from the 11th century, except for a period in the 13th/14th centuries when it formed a separate principality under a branch of the dynasty, reverting to the main line in 1418. (59b)

P'ing Southern P'ing or Ching-Nan was one of the 10th century TEN KINGDOMS in CHINA, located in Hupeh province. It was conquered by the imperial SUNG in 963 AD. (231h)

Pinya See MYINSAING.

Plantagenets See ANGEVINS.

P'o-Hai (Parhae), medieval kingdom in southern MANCHURIA and northern KOREA, founded at the end of the 7th century AD, largely Korean both culturally and ethnically, and to some extent the successor of the Koguryo state suppressed by T'ANG China some decades earlier. P'o-Hai was conquered by the LIAO rulers of the Khitan empire in 927. (233a)

Poitiers and Poitou City and region of southern France, a feudal county held in the early Middle Ages by the dukes of AQUITAINE and in fact the centre of their power. It passed with the duchy to the ANGEVINS in 1152 and to the French crown in the early 13th century. (24s)

Poland The earliest Polish state was established by the PIAST family in the 10th century AD and was a major power in Eastern Europe under the early rulers of the dynasty, until the division of their lands into several principalities in 1138. Early in the 14th century, most of the Piast territories were combined under Vladislav IV to constitute a new Polish kingdom, though MAZOVIA was not reabsorbed until the 16th century and SILESIA was not regained by Poland until 1945. On the death of the last Piast king in 1370, the throne passed to his ANGEVIN heir and then to the JAGIELLON dynasty of LITHUANIA, whose extensive grand duchy was united with Poland to form a vast and powerful state, dominant in Eastern Europe in the 15th/16th centuries. On the extinction of the Jagiellons in 1572, the crown of Poland-Lithuania became elective, though the state remained important under the VASA kings until the mid-17th century. Thereafter it declined rapidly amid internal dissent and constitutional obstruction, until removed from the map in a series of partitions, the last in 1795, its territory split between RUSSIA, PRUSSIA and AUSTRIA. Napoleon BONAPARTE established a Grand Duchy of

Warsaw under the king of SAXONY in the early 19th century, overrun by the Russians in 1813. While the ROMANOV Tsars called themselves kings of Poland, the country did not reappear as an independent state until after the First World War. (87)

Polentani Family which ruled as lords of RAVENNA from the late 13th to the mid-15th century, when their state was annexed by VENICE. (67g)

Polotsk City in north-western Russia which became a RIURIKID principality in the 11th century, though its history is very obscure.

Pomerania Coastal region of the Baltic Sea, now partly in Poland and partly in East Germany, ruled from the 12th to the 17th century by a Slav family who divided their territory repeatedly among various branches of the dynasty, the two main duchies being Stettin (Szczecin) and Wolgast. On the extinction of the family in 1637, Pomerania was split between SWEDEN and PRUSSIA (which obtained the Swedish part also in 1815). (88)

Pontus Originally Pontic Cappadocia, the north-eastern coastal region of Asia Minor, which became a kingdom at the end of the 4th century BC during the wars of the DIADOCHI, under an Iranian dynasty, the MITHRIDATIDS. The ablest of the family, Mithridates VI the Great, proved the most determined and persistent opponent of ROME in the Hellenistic World, at the zenith of his power controlling most of Asia Minor and part of Greece as well as the BOSPHORUS kingdom in the CRIMEA. He was finally driven from Pontus in 66 BC, taking refuge in Bosphorus, and the Romans appointed various client-kings in Pontus until its annexation to the empire in the mid-1st century AD. (137d–e)

Popes See PAPACY/PAPAL STATES.

Portugal The early history of Portugal is part of that of the Spanish Peninsula in general, under Roman, Visigoth and Muslim rule, though its northern regions formed part of the kingdom of the SUEBI in the 5th/6th centuries AD. This northern area broke away from CASTILE-LEON in the late 11th century as an independent county under a branch of the CAPET line of Burgundy. It became a kingdom in 1139 and extended its frontiers southwards by conquests from the Muslims, reaching roughly its present borders within a few decades. Under the AVIZ dynasty the Portuguese acquired vast overseas possessions in the 16th century in Africa, the Indian Ocean and BRAZIL, all of which were inherited with the kingdom by the HABSBURGS of Spain in 1580. The country recovered its independence by revolt under the BRAGANZAS in the 17th century, and that dynasty ruled until the abolition of the monarchy in 1910. (54)

Powys Principality in north-central WALES from early post-Roman times, united with GWYNEDD in the 9th century AD but again independent in 1075. It split into northern and southern sections in 1160 and was further subdivided and absorbed into the English system of marcher lordships in the 13th century. (8c)

Pratihara dynasty RAJPUT rulers of a kingdom which extended over much of northern India at the zenith of their power in the 9th century AD. Their state declined in the following century, and their capital, KANAUJ, was taken by the Muslim invader Mahmud of GHAZNA in 1018, the dynasty being extinguished a few years later. (200f)

Premyslids Earliest ruling dynasty of BOHEMIA, which emerged as a state in the 9th century AD. They were obliged to recognize the suzerainty of the German emperors, ruling as dukes until they acquired the kingly title in the 12th century. The neighbouring region of MORAVIA was part of their state, which at the height of their power under Premysl Ottakar II also controlled the Austrian duchies (lost to the HABSBURGS in 1276). On the extinction of the dynasty in 1306, the succession to the kingdom was disputed, but eventually fell to the LUXEMBURG family. (69a)

Provence The 'Provincia' of the Romans, in southern France, centre of one of the kingdoms into which the Carolingian empire broke up in the 9th century AD. However, it was absorbed into the kingdom of BURGUNDY in 933 and a county of

Provence established. The county was acquired by the rulers of BARCELONA in the 12th century, and passed from a branch of that family to the ANGEVIN branch of the CAPETS in the next century. In 1481, it fell to the French crown. (3b, 24t)

Prussia Baltic coastal region now largely within POLAND, inhabited in early medieval times by the Old Prussians, a heathen Baltic tribe. In the 13th century it was conquered by the knights of the Teutonic Order, who were obliged in the 15th century to cede the western region to Poland. At the Reformation, the last Grand Master of the Order became a Lutheran and made himself hereditary duke of (eastern) Prussia – he was a member of the HOHENZOLLERN family, whose main line of BRANDENBURG inherited the duchy in 1618 and converted it to a kingdom in 1701 – though the name 'Prussia' soon came to signify the whole Hohenzollern state in northern Germany. Western Prussia was added to their dominions as a result of the partitions of Poland. The kingdom of Prussia was abolished on the fall of the German empire, of which it formed the core, in 1918. (27c–d)

Ptolemies (Lagids), rulers of EGYPT. The dynasty was founded by Ptolemy, son of Lagus, a Macedonian general appointed governor of Egypt on the death of Alexander the Great in 323 BC and soon an independent sovereign. He also acquired control of CYRENE, CYPRUS and southern SYRIA (Palestine and Phoenicia). The Ptolemaic kingdom was a major power in the eastern Mediterranean area in the 3rd/2nd centuries BC but came increasingly under the dominance of ROME, despite the efforts of Cleopatra, last of the dynasty, to re-establish Ptolemaic power. Egypt was annexed by Rome in 30 BC. Though they adopted the titles and position of PHARAOH, the Ptolemies remained essentially a Greek dynasty, and a son of the first of the line ruled briefly in MACEDONIA. (99)

Punjab The 'Five Rivers' region of north-western India, now divided between Pakistan and the Republic of India. It was invaded by Alexander the Great and shortly afterwards incorporated into the MAURYA empire in the late 4th century BC. Thereafter, it fell to the Greek kings of BACTRIA and then to successive invaders from the north-west, forming part of the GHAZNAVID and GHURID empires and the DELHI sultanate. On the break-up of the latter realm, MULTAN became independent, but the whole region was absorbed into the MOGHUL state until that empire also fell apart in the 18th century. Then the Punjab was overrun by the DURRANI rulers of Afghanistan, expelled by the SIKH leader Ranjit Singh of LAHORE, who founded a state covering most of the area in the early 19th century, though various smaller states also arose, notably PATIALA and BAHAWALPUR. After two hard-fought campaigns in the 1840s, the Lahore kingdom was annexed by the British. (203)

Pushpabhuti dynasty (Pushyabhutis), see HARSHA.

Pyinsa dynasties Two families which briefly ruled the kingdom of ARAKAN, in the 11th and 12th/13th centuries, known respectively as the First and Second Pyinsa dynasties. (238b, e)

Qajar dynasty Ruling family of IRAN, originally leaders of the Turkoman Qajar tribe in northern Iran, who rose to power in a long struggle with the ZANDS during the 18th century. The last Qajar Shah was deposed in 1925, to be succeeded by Reza Shah PAHLAVI. (187m)

Qara-Khanids Family of Qarluq Turkish origin which ruled in Central Asia in the 10th/12th centuries AD. The dynasty habitually divided its lands among its members, with two main branches, the western based at BUKHARA and the eastern at Balasaghun and KASHGAR. The sequence, dates and relationships of the rulers are in some cases very uncertain. The Qara-Khanids were obliged at times to recognise the overlordship of the SELJUKS and later of the QARA-KHITAI. Both branches were extinguished in the early 13th century, the western by the ANUSHTIGINIDS of Khwarizm and the eastern by the ruler of Qara-Khitai, Kuchlug Khan. (198a–b)

Qara-Khitai When the LIAO empire of the Khitan in northern China fell to the JUCHEN in the early 12th century AD, a member of the ruling family led part of the Khitan west into Central Asia, and there set up an extensive empire which dominated the region for nearly a hundred years under rulers known to Chinese historians as the Western Liao dynasty. Early in the 13th century, the empire began to break up, and its last ruler was supplanted by the Naiman leader Kuchlug Khan, an opponent of Chingis Khan driven from the eastern steppelands, who eventually fell victim to MONGOL conquest in 1218. (198c)

Qara-Qoyunli ('Black Sheep'), Turkoman tribe and dynasty of western IRAN which rose to power in AZERBAIJAN on the break-up of the ILKHAN state in the 14th century. Though temporarily crushed by the TIMURIDS, they ruled all western Iran in the mid-15th century, until overthrown by their rivals, the AQ-QOYUNLI, in 1467–68. The founder of the QUTB-SHAHI sultanate in the DECCAN claimed descent from this dynasty. (188e)

Qarabagh Now the Karabakhskaya region of Soviet AZERBAIJAN, a khanate in the 18th/early 19th centuries, annexed by Russia in 1822. (158c)

Qaramanids Two Muslim Turkish dynasties:
  1 Amirs of Qaraman, one of the strongest of the ANATOLIAN AMIRATES, founded in the later 13th century and incorporating much of south-western Asia Minor. The Qaramanids were the most persistent opponents of the OSMANLIS, who finally extinguished their state in 1483. (142a)
  2 Rulers of Libyan TRIPOLI, originally as OSMANLI governors, who established virtual independence early in the 18th century. Their state was reconquered by the Osmanli government in 1835. (106b)

Qasimids Name of several Muslim dynasties:
  1 Rulers of ALPUENTE, one of the 11th century REYES DE TAIFAS states in Spain, known also as BANU QASIM. Their small kingdom was annexed by the ALMORAVIDS. (48d)

  2 Imams of SAN'A, who controlled much of the YEMEN intermittently in the 17th to mid-20th centuries, descendants of the earlier RASSID Imams. They contested rule of the country with the OSMANLIS at various times, and gained recognition as kings of the Yemen early in the present century. Their monarchy was abolished in 1962. (172l)
  3 Family which rules two of the UNITED ARAB EMIRATES, the main line in SHARJAH, with a branch in RAS-AL-KHAIMAH. A further branch ruled independently at KALBA until 1951. (178a–c)

Qatar Peninsula and state in the Persian Gulf, ruled since the mid-19th century by the AL-THANI family, at first under OSMANLI suzerainty but now as an independent monarchy. (177c)

Qu'aiti dynasty Rulers of SHIHR AND MUKALLA, most important state in the eastern section of the former ADEN PROTECTORATE. The family founded the sultanate in the mid-19th century by seizure of the town of Shihr from the Kathiri rulers – their state was abolished by the independent government of South Yemen in 1967. (172n)

Quraishi dynasties The Quraish family was the ruling clan of MECCA in the time of Muhammad the Prophet, who belonged to one of its branches, though initially opposed by his most influential relatives. Many Muslim dynasties descend or have claimed descent from members of the Quraish, the UMAYYADS and 'ABBASIDS from cousins of Muhammad and most others from the Prophet himself via his daughter Fatima – see 'ALIDS and HASHIMIDS, SHARIF and SAYYID.

Qutb-Shahi dynasty Rulers of GOLKUNDA, one of the DECCAN SULTANATES, founded at the beginning of the 16th century by a descendant of the QARA-QOYUNLI dynasty of Iran. It was the last of the Deccan states annexed by the MOGHULS, its capital HYDERABAD falling in 1687. (218g)

Qutlugh-Khanids Rulers of KIRMAN under the suzerainty of the ILKHANS in the 13th century. The founder was an officer of the QARA-KHITAI dynasty who estab-

MAIN QURAISHI DYNASTIES

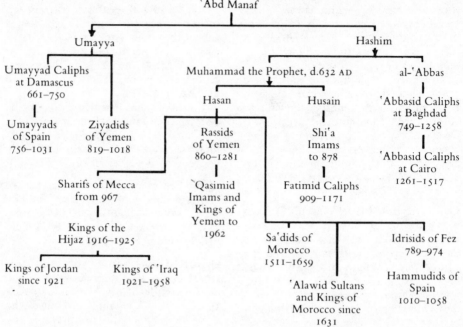

lished control in Kirman on the collapse of the ANUSHTIGINID regime in eastern Iran. On the extinction of his line at the beginning of the 14th century, their lands were brought under direct Ilkhan rule. (192b)

R

Rabeh Zubair An adventurer from the eastern Sudan who established a short-lived state centred on BORNU, which he conquered temporarily from the SHEHUS. However, he came into conflict with the French and was killed by them in battle in 1900, as was his son and successor in the following year. (115c)

Raghavadevas Dynasty of NEPAL which succeeded the LICCHAVIS in the late 9th century AD. They were succeeded in turn by the THAKURI family in the mid-11th century. (211a)

Rajastan (Rajputana), region of north-western India long dominated by the RAJPUTS and until recently divided among various princely states, of which the most important were MEWAR, MARWAR, AMBER (Jaipur), BUNDI, KOTAH, JAISALMER and BIKANIR, most of which have long histories and legendary origins. They were often obliged to recognize stronger powers as suzerains, the sultans of DELHI, the MOGHULS and the MARATHAS, and readily entered into friendly relations with the British in the early 19th century. Certain non-Rajput states also became established in the region on the break-up of the Moghul empire – see BHARATPUR and TONK. (206)

Rajputs The origins of the various Rajput clans of northern and central India have been much discussed and disputed – they claim genealogical connections with peoples and families of the ancient Hindu epics, but emerged into history only in the early medieval period, after much of northern India had been overrun for centuries by a succession of invaders of Iranian and Turkish origins, the Scythians, INDO-PARTHIANS, KUSHANS and Ephthalites. It seems highly likely that the Rajputs ('kings' sons') are to a considerable extent descended from these peoples –

since about the 7th century AD, a very large proportion of the non-Muslim dynasties of the north and the Deccan have been or claimed to be Rajputs, the stronghold of their power being RAJASTAN, almost exclusively a land of Rajput principalities until these were absorbed into the Republic of India in 1949.

Rakoczy dynasty Hungarian family which provided several princes of TRANSYLVANIA in the 17th centuries. In the 18th century Francis Rakoczy led a rebellion in Transylvania against the HABSBURGS and controlled the region for some years. (76)

Ramadan-Oghlu Rulers of CILICIA, their state being founded by a governor for the MAMLUKS after the fall of the kingdom of Lesser ARMENIA in the late 14th century. They later became OSMANLI vassals, and their state was annexed to the Osmanli empire early in the 17th century. (142k)

Ras-al-Khaimah One of the UNITED ARAB EMIRATES, ruled by a branch of the QASIMID family of SHARJAH which broke away independently in the mid-19th century. (178b)

Rashtrakuta dynasty Hindu family, originally vassals of the Early CHALUKYAS of the DECCAN, who overthrew their suzerains in the mid-8th century AD and became, at the height of their power, one of the most important ruling dynasties in India. In the later 10th century, they were in turn overthrown by a descendant of the Chalukyas, who founded the Later Chalukya kingdom. (217d)

Rassids An early 'ALID dynasty in the YEMEN, rulers of a highland state based at Sa'da, though they sometimes also controlled SAN'A. Their power collapsed through internal dissension, but was revived by their QASIMID descendants in the late 16th century. (172e)

Rasulids Successors of the AYYUBIDS as rulers of the YEMEN and overlords of the HIJAZ in the mid-13th century AD. Some two hundred years later they were supplanted by the TAHIRIDS. (172j)

Rathors RAJPUT clan to which the GAHADAVALA dynasty belonged, and whose later leaders were the ruling family

of MARWAR (Jodhpur) and its junior branch of BIKANER, both states of RAJASTAN incorporated into the Republic of India in 1949. (204, 206b–c)

Ravenna Ancient Italian city and important Roman naval base (being at that time accessible from the sea), later the headquarters of the Exarch (Byzantine governor) in Italy until taken by the LOMBARDS in the 8th century. From the later 13th century, the city was an independent lordship under the POLENTANI, from whom it was acquired by VENICE. It became part of the PAPAL STATES half-a-century later, in 1509. (67g)

Rawwadid dynasty Kurdish family which ruled (Persian) AZERBAIJAN in the 10th/11th centuries AD, annexing the lands held by the MUSAFIRIDS in that region. They were suppressed by the SELJUKS in 1071. (188b)

Reddi dynasty Rulers of a state based on KONDAVIDU in ANDHRA PRADESH, effectively the successors of the KAKATIYAS after the temporary conquest of the region by the DELHI sultans in the early 14th century. Their lands were annexed a hundred years later by the BAHMANID rulers of the Deccan. (218f)

Reyes de Taifas (Muluk at-Tawa'if, the 'party kings'), various minor rulers in southern and central SPAIN in the 11th century AD. On the collapse of the Spanish UMAYYAD dynasty, many Muslim leaders established themselves as independent rulers of cities and provinces, some founding short-lived dynasties and several, notably the 'ABBADIDS of Seville, increasing their territory and power by conquest of their neighbours. Literature and the arts flourished in Muslim Spain during this period, but the main gainers from the weakness and dissension were the Christian kingdom of the north, which began to advance their frontiers southwards. On the fall of TOLEDO to CASTILE in 1085, the Muslim princes called upon the ALMORAVID sultan of Morocco for help, and within a few years, he had not only turned back the Christian advance but also annexed nearly all the remaining Muslim principalities. The HUDIDS of Zaragoza lost their capital but survived in

THE RIURIKID DYNASTY OF RUSSIA

Riurik, Prince of Novgorod, ?Danish Viking
9th century AD
|
Princes of Kiev from 880

Princes of Galicia to 1187	Princes of Volynia	Princes of Chernigov to 1245	Princes of Smolensk to 1404	Princes of Pereyaslavl to 1215

Princes and Kings of Galicia 1188–1325   Princes of Riazan to 1520

Princes of Suzdal-Vladimir from 1125

Princes of Moscow from 1283   Princes of Tver 1246–1485   Princes of Suzdal

Tsars of Russia 1547–1610   Princes Shuisky

Romanov Tsars of Russia 1613–1917
(descent in female line)

part of their territory, and VALENCIA resisted the Almoravids for some years under a new master, Rodrigo de Bivar (El Cid), falling to the invaders only after his death. (48)

Rhine Palatinate See PALATINATE of the Rhine.

Riau-Lingga Archipelago Group of islands off the east coast of Sumatra, a sultanate from the early 19th century until its annexation by the Dutch in 1911, under the former ruling dynasty of JOHORE after the loss of their mainland dominions to the ministerial family of the Temenggongs. (244k)

Riazan Russian city, centre of a RIURIKID principality from the end of the 11th century. Its lands were the first Russian territory to be devastated by the MONGOLS, who almost wiped out its ruling dynasty in 1237, though a branch survived to rule under Mongol overlordship. Riazan was eventually annexed by MOSCOW in the early 16th century. (92g)

Riurikid dynasty Ruling family of medieval RUSSIA, its semi-legendary founder Riurik being ruler of NOVGOROD in the 9th century and probably of VIKING origin. His successors moved their capital to KIEV and made that city the centre of a vast realm controlling much of European Russia. However, in the mid-11th century,

their lands were divided among several members of the dynasty and soon became further subdivided between many branches, often in conflict among themselves, though the ruler of Kiev at first retained a vague seniority. In the 12th century, the states of SUZDAL-VLADIMIR in the north-east and GALICIA in the west became dominant, but in 1237–40, most of the Russian principalities were overrun with enormous slaughter by the MONGOLS and the surviving states reduced to vassalage under the GOLDEN HORDE. Western Russia was gradually taken over during the 14th century by LITHUANIA, while the originally minor MOSCOW principality gained predominance in the east, swallowing the other Riurikid states and gaining independence from Mongol suzerainty. In the mid-16th century, the Muscovite rulers conquered the Mongol khanates of KAZAN and ASTRAKHAN and began the colonization of Siberia, adopting the title of Tsar in 1547. In the early 17th century, the Riurikid line of Moscow died out, to be succeeded by the ROMANOVS, but many minor branches of the Riurikids continued to flourish among the Russian nobility into modern times. (91–93)

Roche, De la French family which ruled the duchy of ATHENS from the early 13th century (see CRUSADER STATES) until its last heir, Walter of BRIENNE, was killed in battle by the GRAND CATALAN COMPANY in 1311. (85g)

Romania See RUMANIA.

Romanov dynasty Rulers of RUSSIA in modern times, the first of the line being chosen to rule after the extinction of the RIURIKID line of MOSCOW and a period of disorder and foreign invasion in the early 17th century. Under his successors, notably Peter the Great and Catherine the Great, the Russian empire vastly increased in size and power by conquests and annexations in Siberia, Central Asia, Transcaucasia and the Baltic regions, also acquiring a large part of POLAND at the end of the 18th century. By the mid-19th century, the frontiers of the Romanov empire approximately coincided with those of the modern U.S.S.R. The later Romanovs were in fact OLDENBURGS by male descent from the dukes of Holstein-Gottorp – the last Tsar was deposed in 1917 and the Russian monarchy abolished. (94)

Roman Empire/Rome According to tradition, the city of Rome was founded in the 8th century BC and ruled by kings until the establishment of a republic in 509 BC, growing from a small city-state to control most of Italy by the 3rd century BC and the whole Mediterranean world by the 1st century BC. Late in that century, Augustus Caesar became in fact, though not in name, monarchical ruler of the state, founding an empire which endured more or less intact until it split into eastern and western halves in the late 4th century AD. After the extinction of the JULIO-CLAUDIANS in 68 AD, no family held the throne for more than two or three generations – see FLAVIANS, ANTONINES, SEVERI. The western section of the empire was overrun by Germanic and other invaders and extinguished in the 5th century. For the later Eastern Roman Empire see BYZANTIUM. (1a–b)

Rovereschi (Della Rovere), family to which belonged Pope Julius II, and which inherited the duchy of URBINO from the MONTEFELTRI early in the 16th century. The last of the dynasty ceded his duchy to the PAPAL STATES in 1626. (67i)

Rubenids Armenian family who founded a state in Cilicia and the Taurus range (see ARMENIA, LESSER) in the late 11th century, after the conquest of Armenia by the SELJUKS and the collapse of Byzantine rule in Asia Minor following the battle of Manzikert (see BYZANTIUM). The Byzantines temporarily recovered control of the area in the next century, but the Rubenids re-established their independence – they were succeeded by the related HETHUMIDS in the early 13th century. (140a)

Rum (i.e. 'Rome'), name generally used for Asia Minor by the Arabs and Turks. After the defeat of the Byzantines at Manzikert in 1071, Turkish tribesmen overran the interior of the peninsula and settled there, and although the sultans of the main SELJUK line did not annex the region, a branch of the dynasty hostile to the sultans established an independent state there. The Seljuks of Rum were badly weakened when the army of the First Crusade forced a crossing of their territory, and the Byzantines then recovered large areas of their lost lands, but their advance was reversed at Myriocephalon in 1176. In the late 13th century, the power of the Rum sultanate was broken by the MONGOLS, and their lands were divided among the ANATOLIAN AMIRATES. (138)

Rumania The racial origins of the Rumanians have been much disputed, they themselves claiming descent from the Roman settlers in DACIA but some historians regarding them as migrants of medieval times from more southerly areas of the Balkan region. In the late 13th century, a Rumanian state emerged in WALLACHIA, at first under Hungarian suzerainty, and in the middle of the next century, a second state, MOLDAVIA, was also established, both principalities under rulers with the title of Voivode (commander, governor). These states maintained a large degree of independence of their more powerful neighbours until the 16th century, resisting OSMANLI Turkish attacks with some success, but eventually had to accept Osmanli suzerainty, their rulers nominated by the sultans and becoming virtually provincial governors. In the mid-19th century, the European powers obliged the Osmanlis to grant autonomy to the two regions, which elected the same prince as their ruler – on his deposition in 1866, a member of a junior branch of the HOHENZOLLERN dynasty was chosen as prince, and became an independent king before the end of the century. After the First World War, the size of Rumania was greatly increased by the addition of the former Austro-Hungarian province of TRANSYLVANIA, inhabited largely by Rumanian-speakers, and by Bessarabia – though the latter region was later re-annexed by Russia. The Rumanian monarchy was abolished in 1947. (76–79)

Russia Though the name is now generally used as a synonym for the U.S.S.R., historic Russia was a much smaller (but nevertheless very extensive) region, the mainly forested area north of the European steppelands between the Urals in the east and the Baltic lands in the west. While the steppes were dominated by a succession of nomadic peoples, Slav tribes inhabited the forests from ancient times, and during the early medieval period, major trade routes developed across their territory, linking the Baltic, Black and Caspian seas. In the 9th century AD, the powerful KIEV state grew up along these routes under the RIURIKIDS, a family of perhaps VIKING origin but soon completely Slavonicized. Their lands fragmented among many branches of the dynasty in the 11th/12th centuries and were reduced to vassalage by the GOLDEN HORDE, from which the Russians freed themselves under the leadership of the MOSCOW Riurikids in the 15th century. Since that time, the Russian state has grown steadily, with the conquest of the western Russian-speaking lands from POLAND-LITHUANIA, the occupation of Siberia, the annexation of the western steppelands from various khanates and Central Asia from other local rulers, the seizure of much of Transcaucasia and the coastlands of the eastern Baltic. By the mid-19th century, the Russian empire, under the ROMANOVS, controlled approximately the same territories as the modern U.S.S.R. The monarchy was abolished in 1917 and the last Tsar executed in 1918. (91–97)

Rustamids One of the earliest Muslim dynasties to establish independence from the CALIPHS, founded by members of the Kharijite sect in the 8th century AD in what is now Algeria. They ruled a small state centred on TAHART, which was annexed by the FATIMIDS when that family conquered the MAGHRIB at the beginning of the 10th century. (110a)

Rwanda Highland state in central Africa, formerly a kingdom founded by a TUTSI dynasty in the 14th century AD. The state came under German control in the late 19th century and passed to Belgium after the First World War, the monarchy surviving until 1961. Rwanda is now an independent republic. (129a)

 S

Saba The Biblical Sheba, an early kingdom in YEMEN concerning the dating of which there is much uncertainty. It emerged in the earlier part of the 1st millennium BC and was at first ruled by priest-kings called Mukarrib, though later by temporal monarchs, who conquered the neighbouring kingdom of Ma'in around 100 BC. After a period of disorder in the late 1st century BC, Saba was united with Dhu Raidan to form HIMYAR. (171b)

Sa'did dynasty Ruling family of MOROCCO, who first rose to power in the TAFILALT region and extended their control over the rest of the country – they extinguished the WATTASID regime in the early 16th century. At the height of their power later in the same century, the Sa'dids conquered a large area of the western SUDAN from SONGHAI, but family quarrels weakened them and divided their lands. Like their distant relatives the 'ALAWIDS, who succeeded them in the mid-17th century, they were 'ALIDS by descent. (112h)

Safavids Major dynasty of IRAN, originally leaders of a SHI'A sect in AZERBAIJAN, where Shah Isma'il Safavi established a kingdom by crushing the AQ-QOYUNLI at the beginning of the 16th century. He soon conquered the rest of Iran, and his successors ruled a strong and prosperous state in the 16th/17th centuries, though in constant conflict with the OSMANLI Turks.

The last independent ruler of the dynasty was deposed by GHILZAI Afghan invaders in 1722, but several puppet Safavids were installed later in the century by the various rulers struggling for supremacy in Iran. (187i)

Saffarids Ya'qub as-Saffar ('the copper-smith') rose to power in SISTAN in the mid-9th century AD, and annexed much of the TAHIRID territory in eastern Iran, his brother and successor extending the Saffarid state still further until overthrown by the SAMANIDS in 901. The dynasty long maintained itself in Sistan, however, usually under the suzerainty of stronger neighbouring powers, and vanished only at the end of the 15th century. (193)

Sagaing Town in Upper BURMA, capital of a SHAN kingdom of the 14th century founded by a member of the ruling family of MYINSAING. It was united with the latter state in 1364 to form the new and powerful AVA kingdom. (237c)

Saifawa dynasty Ancient ruling family of KANEM-BORNU, traditionally established in Kanem from about the 8th century AD as kings with the title of Mai (though they formally adopted that of Sultan in the 11th century). In the 14th century they were obliged to abandon Kanem and shift their power-base across Lake Chad into Bornu, though they greatly increased their influence and recovered their original lands in the 16th century. The effective rule of the dynasty was ended after more than a thousand years by FULANI invasion at the beginning of the 19th century, though they held office nominally under the SHEHU family until the last of them tried to regain full control of Bornu and was killed in battle by the Shehus in 1846. (115a)

Sailendras A Buddhist dynasty of Javanese origin which ruled the empire of SRIVIJAYA in Sumatra from the 9th century AD, its power severely weakened in the early 11th century by a great CHOLA naval raid from India. The kingdom and dynasty vanished on the rise of the MAJAPAHIT empire in the 13th century, and few names (and practically no dates) of its rulers are known. The founder of MALACCA may have been a Sailendra.

Sajid dynasty Rulers of AZERBAIJAN, nominally for the 'ABBASID Caliphs but in fact independently, in the 9th/10th centuries. After the extinction of the family, their lands soon fell to the RAWWADIDS and MUSAFIRIDS. (188a)

Sakyas A series of religious leaders who ruled TIBET as viceroys for the MONGOL Great Khans in the 13th/14th centuries until supplanted by the founder of the second Tibetan kingdom in 1358. (226b)

Salankayanas A Hindu dynasty which ruled the VENGI region of ANDHRA PRADESH, India, after the IKSHVAKUS, during the 4th and early 5th centuries AD. They vanished with the CHALUKYA conquest of the area. (218b)

Salerno Ancient Salernum, city in southern Italy which was the centre of a LOMBARD principality, a section of the duchy of BENEVENTO which became independent in 840 AD. It was annexed to the HAUTEVILLE domains in 1075. (68c)

Salghurid dynasty An ATABEG family of FARS who established themselves as rulers in the mid-12th century on the decline of the SELJUK empire. Their lands were annexed by the ILKHANS in 1270. (191a)

Saltuqids Dynasty which ruled a small principality centred on ERZERUM in Armenia from the beginning of the 12th century AD until the SELJUK capture of their capital in 1201. (148b)

Saluvas A family which ruled briefly in VIJAYANAGAR at the end of the 15th century, deposing the YADAVAS. They were soon supplanted in turn by the TULUVAS. (222b)

Saluzzo City in north-western Italy, capital of an extensive margravate of the same name established in the 12th century under a branch of the ALERAMID family. It was annexed by the French in the mid-16th century and soon afterwards incorporated into the duchy of SAVOY. (67a)

Samanid dynasty Iranian Muslim family who became important in TRANSOXANIA under the TAHIRIDS and acquired their dominions after the brief rule of the SAFFARIDS in eastern Iran. During the 10th century AD, the Samanids were an important power, ruling much of the eastern part of the nominal 'ABBASID realm with their capital at BUKHARA. However, at the end of that century, KHURASAN was conquered by the GHAZNAVIDS and Transoxania by the QARA-KHANIDS, the last Samanid being killed during an attempt to recover power in 1005. (194b)

Samarkand Ancient Maracanda, city now in Uzbekistan, capital of the ACHAE-MENID province of Soghdiana and of various dynasties of TRANSOXANIA, including particularly the TIMURIDS. (198g–h)

Samma dynasty Muslim rulers of SIND from the mid-14th century AD in succession to the SUMRAS. They were overthrown by the Afghan ARGHUN dynasty, who annexed their dominions in 1521. (205c)

San'a Ancient city in the YEMEN, most important centre in the highlands and capital of various dynasties, particularly the QASIMIDS. (172)

Sanudi A Venetian family who ruled the duchy of NAXOS (see CRUSADER STATES) in the 13th/14th centuries. The founder took part in the Fourth Crusade and later conquered the Cyclades islands – in 1383, his dynasty was supplanted by the CRISPI. (85i)

Sanusis Members of a Muslim religious movement based in LIBYA and the central SUDAN, founded in the early 19th century. The family of its founder claimed descent from the IDRISIDS of Morocco and exercised considerable political power, particularly in opposing Italian rule in Libya during the early part of the present century. In 1951, the Sanusi leader became king of Libya, but was deposed in 1969, when a republic was established. (106d)

Saragossa See ZARAGOZA.

Sarawak Extensive province of northern Borneo, formerly a state founded in the mid-19th century by an English adventurer, James BROOKE, who obtained appointment as governor of part of the region under the sultan of BRUNEI and soon established his independence as Raja of Sarawak. The state accepted British protection in 1888 and was ceded to Britain by the last Brooke ruler in 1946. It is now part of MALAYSIA. (247b)

Sarbadarids A series of rulers in KHURASAN in the 14th century, mostly unrelated to each other, whose title of Sarbadar ('head-on-the-block') indicated their original status as rebels against the ILKHAN regime. Their state was annexed by Timur (see TIMURID dynasty) in 1381. (194c)

Sardinia The island was a Roman province and later came under the rule of Genoa and Pisa, passing in 1326 to ARAGON and thus eventually to the Spanish HABSBURGS. In 1720 it was made a kingdom for the duke of SAVOY in exchange for SICILY, of which he had been briefly the ruler. In reality, Sardinia remained a minor appendage of the mainland domains of the Savoy dynasty except in the early 19th century, when they were expelled from Italy by the French and retained only their island kingdom. It was absorbed into the new kingdom of Italy in 1861. (59c)

Sargonids Last ruling dynasty of ASSYRIA, though their founder may in fact have been closely related to previous Assyrian kings. He took the title of Sharrukin II (Sargon) in reference to the founder of the kingdom of AKKAD many centuries earlier. His immediate successors, Sennacherib, Esarhaddon and Ashurbanipal, whose reigns spanned almost the entire 7th century BC, were among the most famous and powerful of Assyrian rulers, but the empire began to collapse at the end of Ashurbanipal's reign and the last of the dynasty perished at the fall of Nineveh in 612 BC (though one more king, whose relationship, if any, with the Sargonids is unknown, maintained himself for several years longer at Harran in the west). (183)

Sarukhan One of the ANATOLIAN AMIRATES, on the western coast of Asia Minor, which broke away from the GERMIYAN amirate in the early 14th century and was eventually annexed by the OSMANLI sultans in 1410. (142f)

Sasanid dynasty Imperial family of IRAN, originally rulers of the kingdom of Parsa (FARS) under the suzerainty of the ARSACIDS, whom they overthrew early in the 3rd century AD, establishing a powerful state which probably extinguished the KUSHAN regime in the east and held the Euphrates frontier against the Romans in the west. At the end of the 6th century, Khusraw II overran Asia Minor, Syria and Egypt, only to suffer a Roman counter-attack which caused his downfall. Shortly afterwards, the Sasanid domains were conquered by the Muslims and the last of the dynasty was killed in TRANSOXANIA in 651. (187d)

Satara Town in MAHARASHTRA, India, capital of the BHONSLA descendants of the founder of MARATHA power, Shivaji. Their authority passed in reality to their ministers, the PESHWAS, but they continued to reign nominally and on the collapse of the Maratha power were recognized by the British as minor princes at Satara – their state was annexed by the British in 1848. (217m)

Satavahana dynasty (also known as the Satakarni or Andhra dynasty), an early ruling family of the DECCAN, India. Their dates are uncertain and controversial, but they rose to power after the collapse of the MAURYA empire and dealt the final blow to the KANVA successors of the Mauryas in the north-east. Temporarily weakened by the establishment of an INDO-PARTHIAN viceroyalty in MAHARASHTRA, they eventually conquered it in the 1st/2nd century AD. Their empire broke up in the 2nd/3rd centuries. (217a)

Sa'udi Arabia Kingdom which incorporates the greater part of the Arabian peninsula, established in 1932 by 'Abdul-'Aziz AL-SA'UD, ruler of NAJD, who conquered the AL-RASHID lands and the HASHIMID kingdom of the HIJAZ in the 1920s. (176)

Saurashtra (Kathiawar), a peninsular region of western India which has in general been under the control or influence of the rulers of GUJARAT during most of its history, though it formed a kingdom under the CHUDSAMAS in medieval times. There were numerous minor states in Saurashtra in the 19th century, some of them established much earlier – see particularly KACHH. (208)

Savoy dynasty Rulers from the 11th century of Savoy, now a region of France but in medieval times a county in the HOLY ROMAN EMPIRE. The family soon acquired extensive lands in north-western

ITALY, and PIEDMONT, a principality under a separate branch of the dynasty in the 13th/14th centuries, was reunited with Savoy in the early 15th century, when their original lands became a duchy and their territory reached the coast at Nice. In 1720, having ruled briefly as king of SICILY, the duke of Savoy obtained SARDINIA with the royal title, and although the family was expelled from its mainland possessions in the Napoleonic period, these were restored and increased after the fall of Napoleon. In the mid-19th century, the ruler of this 'Kingdom of Sardinia' obtained the sovereignty of united Italy, though at the price of ceding Savoy itself, with Nice, to France. The House of Savoy ruled Italy until the abolition of their monarchy in 1946. (59–60)

Saxe-Coburg See WETTIN and COBURG.

Saxe-Wittenberg In the mid-13th century, the ASCANIAN dukes of SAXONY divided their lands into the small duchies of Wittenberg and Lauenburg, the former becoming an ELECTORATE in 1356 – on the extinction of the Wittenberg line in 1422, their lands passed to the WETTINS. (33a–b)

Saxony A region of northern Germany inhabited in the early Middle Ages by the Saxon tribes. It was conquered by the CAROLINGIAN Charlemagne and became one of the major duchies of the German kingdom, its dukes obtaining the imperial crown in the 10th century. The WELFS ruled Saxony in the 12th century but forfeited the duchy to the crown – it passed to the ASCANIANS, but the Welfs retained great local possessions, soon converted into the separate duchy of BRUNSWICK. In 1356, the Ascanian duchy of SAXE-WITTENBERG became an ELECTORATE and was later acquired by the WETTINS of Meissen and Thuringia, whose lands gradually became a new 'Saxony' in eastern Germany. In 1806, the Albertine branch of the Wettins obtained the royal title for their lands, and this kingdom of Saxony was abolished in 1918. Old Saxony was divided among various states, the most important being the Welf duchy of Brunswick-Luneburg, later the kingdom of HANOVER, though the area is today known as Lower Saxony. (33)

Sayyid A Muslim title accorded to descendants of Muhammad the Prophet, and more particularly to those of his grandson Husain (see also SHARIF and ῾ALIDS), but borne by two particular dynasties:

I A family which acquired the former territories of the BAVANDIDS in MAZAND-ARAN in the 14th century and ruled in the region until the rise of the SAFAVIDS in the 16th century. (189g)

2 Rulers of DELHI in the early part of the 15th century, successors of the last TUGHLUQS. They controlled little more than the city itself and were supplanted by the LODIS. (201d)

Scaligeri (Della Scala), lords of Verona from the mid-13th century and rulers of an extensive area of north-eastern Italy early in the next century, though their territories were later acquired by the VISCONTI of Milan. (67e)

Schleswig (Slesvig), region on the present Danish-German border, ruled in medieval times by the Danish kings or Danish royal dukes as a fief of the German empire and annexed by DENMARK in 1721. Together with neighbouring HOLSTEIN, Schleswig became the subject of a lengthy dispute between Denmark and Germany in the 19th century, eventually settled by a partition in 1920.

Scotland In Roman times, the main people of Scotland were the PICTS, whose lands in the central and northern regions of the country remained beyond the imperial frontier, though after the collapse of Rome in the 5th century AD, the south-east formed part of the English state of NORTHUMBRIA and the south-west developed into a British kingdom, STRATH-CLYDE. Meanwhile, the rulers of the small principality of DALRIADA in Ulster began to colonize lands in Argyll, and when they lost their Irish territory, the name was transferred to their Scottish kingdom. A strong Pictish state emerged in the north and east in the 6th century, but was conquered in the mid-9th century by Kenneth mac Alpin of Dalriada, who founded the kingdom of Scotland. His successors extended their rule to Strathclyde and Lothian – on the extinction of

the main line of kings in 1290, the English rulers made a prolonged effort to annex the country, but its independence was secured under the BRUCE family, succeeded by the STUARTS in the late 14th century. See also ORKNEY and the ISLES. The succession of James VI of Scotland to the English throne in 1603 brought about the dynastic union of the two kingdoms, an arrangement made permanent and constitutional in 1707. (9–12)

Selangor Sultanate in MALAYA, founded in the mid-18th century by the leaders of the BUGIS and still under the rule of their dynasty. It is now part of the Federation of MALAYSIA. (244h)

Seleucid dynasty Macedonian family founded by Seleucus Nicator, a general of Alexander the Great, who eventually acquired most of Alexander's conquests in Asia during the wars of the DIADOCHI at the end of the 4th century BC. However, his successors soon began to lose their Iranian lands to the PARTHIANS and the independent kings of BACTRIA, while various rulers made themselves autonomous in Asia Minor. 'Iraq too fell to the Parthians in the 2nd century BC and early in the next century the remaining Seleucid lands in Syria were temporarily overrun by the ARTAXIAD king of Armenia, being annexed by ROME shortly afterwards. (162)

Seljuks Turkish family, originally leaders of marauders who conquered KHURASAN from the GHAZNAVIDS and rapidly extended their domains westwards, extinguishing the BUYID realm and taking control of the puppet 'ABBASID Caliphs at Baghdad. BYZANTIUM never fully recovered from the defeat inflicted by the Seljuks at Manzikert in Armenia in 1071, as a result of which large areas of Asia Minor were overrun by freelance Turkish bands. The Seljuk empire was ruled by a line of 'Great Seljuk' sultans of whom the last died in 1157, but branches of the dynasty established themselves in western IRAN/'IRAQ and KIRMAN until the late 12th century, and in SYRIA until 1117, while cousins hostile to the main line set up an independent sultanate of RUM in Asia Minor that survived until the beginning of the 14th century. A branch of the latter

THE SELJUK DYNASTY

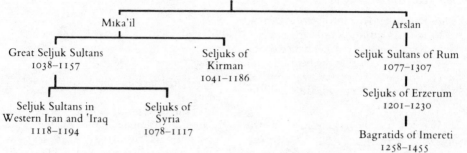

Seljuk, Oghuz Turkish chief, 10th century AD

Mıka'il

Arslan

Great Seljuk Sultans
1038–1157

Seljuks of
Kirman
1041–1186

Seljuk Sultans of Rum
1077–1307

Seljuk Sultans in
Western Iran and 'Iraq
1118–1194

Seljuks of
Syria
1078–1117

Seljuks of Erzerum
1201–1230

Bagratids of Imereti
1258–1455

line ruled at ERZERUM, one of its members marrying Queen Rusudan of GEORGIA, with the result that the early BAGRATID kings of IMERETI were Seljuks by male descent. (138, 148c, 166c, 187f–g, 192a)

Senas A Hindu dynasty which rose to power in BENGAL on the decline of the PALAS in the late 11th century. It vanished with Muslim conquest of the region in the 13th century. (214b)

Sennar Town on the Blue Nile in the Sudanese Republic, formerly the capital of a sultanate ruled by the FUNG dynasty. Their state replaced an earlier Nubian Christian kingdom in the 16th century and soon became an important power, though declining rapidly in the 18th century. Sennar was annexed by MUHAMMAD 'ALI of Egypt in 1821. (114a)

Serbia Region of YUGOSLAVIA settled by the Serbs in early medieval times and established as a kingdom under the NEMANJICH family in the 12th century. In the 14th century Stephan Dushan built up an extensive Serbian empire which was briefly the dominant power in the Balkans, but broke up after his death – the Serbs were crushingly defeated by the OSMANLI Turks at Kossovo in 1389, and their state annexed by the Turks in the next century. Not until the beginning of the 19th century did Serbia again achieve independence, at first temporarily under Kara George and later as an autonomous principality under Milosh Obrenovich. The KARAGEORGEVICHI AND OBRENOVICHI families alternated by coup and assassination upon the throne, the state becoming

a kingdom in 1882, until the murder of the last Obrenovich ruler in 1903. Thereafter, the Karageorgevichi retained the crown of Serbia and later that of the enlarged state renamed Yugoslavia which was established after the First World War. (72)

Severi Imperial family of ROME in the late 2nd/early 3rd centuries AD, brought to power by Septimius Severus in a civil war. After the assassination of his son, two of his Syrian wife's relatives ruled in succession, both also assassinated. (1a)

Seville City in southern Spain, capital of the most powerful of the 11th century REYES DE TAIFAS dynasties, the 'ABBADIDS. The rulers were patrons of literature and art, and extended their control over several neighbouring kingdoms, but were deposed by the ALMORAVIDS, who annexed their lands in 1091. (48a)

Sforza family Rulers of MILAN, the first of the line being a son-in-law of the last VISCONTI duke who acquired the duchy after a short republican interlude in the mid-15th century. Early in the following century, his successors twice lost their lands to the French but were eventually succeeded by the HABSBURGS. (63b)

Shaddadids Kurdish dynasty which succeeded the MUSAFIRIDS in ARRAN and eastern Armenia, based at GANJA and Dvin with a minor branch at Ani. Their main territories fell under SELJUK control in the late 11th century, though Shaddadids ruled at Ani for a further hundred years. (155)

Shah-Armanid dynasty Turkish family

which seized control of much of ARMENIA, ruling from Akhlat on Lake Van throughout the 12th century until suppressed by the AYYUBIDS in 1207. (148a)

Shah-Rukhids Khans of KHOKAND in FARGHANA, a CHINGIS KHANID dynasty which established its independence of the JANIDS of Transoxania at the beginning of the 18th century. Their state was annexed by the Russians after considerable fighting in 1876. (198k)

Shaibānids Family descended from the CHINGIS KHANID prince Shaiban, son of Juchi (see JUCHIDS). Muhammad Shaibani Khan conquered TRANSOXANIA from the TIMURIDS at the end of the 15th century and established a strong state dominated by his Uzbeg tribesmen. A hundred years later, the Shaibanids were succeeded by their relatives the JANIDS. (198h)

Shang (Yin) dynasty The earliest historical ruling family of CHINA, successors of the legendary HSIA kings in the mid-2nd millennium BC. They ruled a state in the plain of the Yellow River and were overthrown by the CHOU, traditionally in 1122 BC but perhaps in fact some decades later. A branch of the dynasty was permitted to survive as rulers of the small vassal state of SUNG under Chou overlordship. (227a)

Shans The Shan and Thai peoples, closely connected by language and origins, inhabited southern China in ancient times, spreading westwards and southwards. The Shans played an important role in the history of BURMA, extinguishing the PAGAN state and expelling the Mongols from the region of Upper Burma in the late 13th century. Under the leadership of the 'Three Shan Brothers' they established kingdoms at MYINSAING/Pinya and later at SAGAING, united in 1364 to form the AVA kingdom which controlled Upper Burma until its conquest by the TOUNGOO rulers in the mid-16th century. Tribal Shan states existed in eastern Burma until modern times. Shan rulers also established the AHOM state in ASSAM. (237b–d)

Sharif A Muslim title accorded to descendants of Muhammad the Prophet, and more particularly to those of his grandson Hasan (see also SAYYID and

'ALIDS). Various dynasties were or are of Sharifian origin, including the present ruling house of Morocco (the 'ALAWIDS) and the HASHIMID family of the HIJAZ, generally known as the Sharifs of MECCA.

Sharjah One of the UNITED ARAB EMIRATES, ruled since the mid-18th century by the QASIMID family. (178a)

Sharqi dynasties Two Muslim ruling families:

1 Sultans of JAUNPUR in northern India, a kingdom founded on the collapse of the TUGHLUQS of Delhi in the late 14th century. Their state was re-annexed to the Delhi sultanate by the LODIS nearly a century later. (204c)

2 Rulers of FUJAIRAH, one of the UNITED ARAB EMIRATES, who gained formal recognition of their independence of SHARJAH in 1952. (178h)

Sharvashidze dynasty Georgian family so named from an alleged link with the SHIRVANshahs. They were rulers of ABKHAZIA from the 12th century and virtually independent princes from the 15th century, but their history is ill-recorded and no complete list of them is available. Their state was annexed by Russia in 1864.

Sheka Modern Nukha in ARRAN, Soviet AZERBAIJAN, centre of a short-lived khanate of the 18th/19th centuries, annexed by Russia in 1818. (158b)

Shi'a Major Muslim sect, the largest Islamic group other than the SUNNI (Orthodox) majority, though now much fragmented by doctrinal and other issues. In origin it consisted of those who believed that the office of CALIPH should not be elective as it first was but belonged to the descendants of Muhammad the Prophet, the 'ALIDS. Most Shi'ites recognize twelve successive Imams, the last of whom disappeared in 878 AD, though early dissident groups split away. At all stages in Islamic history, Shi'a leaders have attempted with varying success to seize political power, especially in remoter regions such as YEMEN, MAZANDARAN and MOROCCO. In the 10th century, the FATIMIDS came close to success, though very briefly, in their effort to supplant the 'ABBASIDS as formal leaders of the Islamic world.

Shihabids Amirs of LEBANON in the 18th/ 19th centuries, successors of their relatives the MA῾NIDS. After the temporary conquest of Syria by the Egyptians in the mid-19th century, the OSMANLI sultans suppressed the amirate. (168c)

Shihr and Mukalla Most important sultanate in the eastern ADEN PROTECTOR- ATE, established by the QU῾AITI family in the mid-19th century. It was abolished by the newly independent government of South Yemen in 1967. (172n)

Shirvan Region of Soviet AZERBAIJAN, in medieval times a kingdom whose rulers bore the traditional title of Shirvan-Shah. Soon after the Muslim conquest of the area, the Arab YAZIDID dynasty established their rule in Shirvan (in the mid-9th century AD) and maintained their hold with varying fortunes until the mid-16th century, when their state was annexed by the SAFAVIDS. Thereafter, the region was disputed between Iran and the OSMANLI Turks until conquered by Russia in 1820. (157)

Shishmanovich family Kings of Bulgaria in the 14th century, the first of the line being chosen as ruler on the extinction of the TERTER family. The last kings of the dynasty split the kingdom into two parts, based on Vidin and Trnovo, both overrun by the OSMANLI Turks in the last decade of the century. (80f)

Shoa Central region of ETHIOPIA, around Addis Ababa. On the break-up of the Ethiopian kingdom in the 18th century, it became a separate state under a branch of the SOLOMONIC dynasty. In 1889, its ruler Menyelek obtained the Ethiopian throne and Shoa was thus reabsorbed into the main kingdom. (123a)

Shogun dynasties Several families which successively ruled JAPAN, formally on behalf of the emperors, who remained in fact powerless, from the late 12th century until the imperial dynasty was restored to power in 1868. The main Shogun families, the MINAMOTO, ASHIKAGA and TOKUGAWA, were all remotely descended from the 9th century Emperor Seiwa. (236b–f)

Shu Traditional name for the modern Szechuan province of CHINA and also the name of several dynasties which have ruled there:

1 Shu-Han dynasty. See HAN **3**.

2 Earlier Shu. Rulers of one of the 10th century TEN KINGDOMS, whose state was re-annexed to the Chinese empire by the Later T῾ANG in 925. (231f)

3 Later Shu. Another ruling family of the TEN KINGDOMS period, who became independent in Szechuan in 934 but whose state was annexed by the imperial SUNG in 965. (231g)

Shutrukids Ruling family of ELAM in the 12th century BC, successors of the IGEHAL- KIDS. Under these kings, Elam reached the zenith of its power, dominating southern ῾Iraq until the end of the century, though the circumstances in which the dynasty disappeared are obscure. (186c)

Siak Sultanate in central SUMATRA which became an important power in the early 18th century under a ruler who seized the throne of JOHORE for a few years. His successors were eventually brought under Dutch suzerainty. (245c)

Siam See THAILAND.

Sicily In ancient times, the island was divided between CARTHAGE and various Greek colonial city-states, the most im- portant of the latter being SYRACUSE, at times controlling much of Sicily and ruled by a number of tyrants and kings with republican intervals. ROME took over most of the island after the First Punic War in the 3rd century BC, and in the Second Punic War captured Syracuse, a Carthaginian ally, in 211 BC. Early in the 9th century AD, the Muslim AGHLABIDS of the MAGHRIB conquered Sicily from the Byzantines, and it then fell to their FATIMID successors, whose governors of the KALBID family became independent in the mid-10th century. A hundred years later, their amirate broke up among various rulers, an arrangement which enabled the HAUTEVILLES of APULIA to invade the island, suppressing all resistance by 1091. Count Roger II became king of Sicily in 1130, ruling a state which also included southern Italy, and this kingdom was annexed in 1194 by the HOHENSTAUFFEN of Germany, becoming the power-base of the Emperor Frederick II in his struggle against the PAPACY in the early part of the 13th century. Soon after his death, the realm was conquered by the French ANGEVIN family, but Sicily rebelled in 1282, installing the ARAGONESE dynasty, which later also acquired the mainland area of the kingdom (the 'Kingdom of NAPLES') and both territories were inherited by the HABSBURGS, being ruled from Spain until the extinction of the Spanish branch of that family. Sicily was briefly ruled by the duke of SAVOY in the early 18th century, but later passed with Naples to a branch of the Spanish BOURBONS, who temporarily lost the mainland area during the Napoleonic Wars, and were finally expelled in the mid-19th century, when their kingdom was absorbed into united Italy. (61–62)

Sidon Ancient city-kingdom of Phoenicia (LEBANON) from around the mid-2nd millennium BC until the period of the PTOLEMIES, recognizing when necessary the overlordship of the major rulers of Western Asia (see also TYRE). The names and dates of some of its kings are known, but a continuous list is not available.

Sijilmasa A town in the oases of the TAFILALT trans-Atlas region of MOROCCO, important in medieval times as a caravan-terminus. It was the capital of the MIDRARIDS, one of the earliest Muslim dynasties independent of the CALIPHS, from the late 8th century AD – the FATIMIDS made repeated efforts to suppress the Midrarids, who were, however, ultimately supplanted by the MAGHRAWA in the late 10th century. (112a)

Sikhs Adherents of an Indian religion, in origin a sect of Hinduism, based in the PUNJAB. Originally founded as a peaceful movement in the 15th century, the sect developed into a rebellious military power under the last effective MOGHUL emperors in the early 18th century. A number of minor Sikh states arose, the most important being PATIALA, and in 1799 Ranjit Singh was confirmed in possession of LAHORE by the DURRANI Afghan ruler, soon building up a powerful independent kingdom which included not only most of the Punjab but also KASHMIR and

Jammu. After his death, the Sikhs fought two wars with the British, the second resulting in the annexation of the state to British India in 1849. Kashmir and Jammu were recognized as a separate state under a Sikh ruler in 1846. (203c–d)

Sikkim Himalayan state established by the Tibetan NAMGYAL dynasty in the mid-17th century. In 1975 the last ruler was deposed and the state absorbed into the Republic of India. (212)

Silesia Valley of the Upper Oder river, part of the early Polish state of the PIASTS, under a branch of which dynasty it formed a principality after the division of POLAND in 1138. Unlike the other Piast lands, it was never re-absorbed into the later Polish kingdom but became largely Germanized and much subdivided into small duchies. Overlordship of these states was acquired by BOHEMIA in the 14th century and passed with the Bohemian crown to the HABSBURGS, from whom Silesia was seized by PRUSSIA in 1740. The region was transferred from German to Polish rule in 1945. (87f)

Silla Early kingdom in southern KOREA, traditionally founded in 57 BC, though there is no evidence for its real existence before the 4th century AD. Assisting the T'ANG rulers of China to destroy the rival Korean states of PAEKCHE and Koguryo in the mid-7th century, the Sillan kings then expelled the Chinese and gained control of most of the peninsula. In the late 9th century, Silla disintegrated, to be replaced by the WANG dynasty, founders of the later Korean state. (235c)

Sind Region of the Lower Indus valley in Pakistan, one of the main centres of the pre-historic Indus Civilization. However, very little is known of its subsequent history prior to the Muslim conquest – in the mid-7th century AD a Buddhist dynasty was replaced by the Hindu CHACH family as rulers, but Sind was the only part of the Indian peninsula to be overrun during the early expansion of Islam in the 7th/8th centuries. Occupied by UMAYYAD forces shortly before the fall of the latter dynasty, the region was never effectively controlled by the 'ABBASID Caliphs, and soon fell to various independent families.

The SUMRAS and SAMMAS ruled in succession *c*.1025–1521, the Sammas falling before the ARGHUNS, an Afghan ruling family driven south by the MOGHUL founder Babur, whose grandson annexed the province in 1591. (205)

Sindhia family Maharajas of GWALIOR, a MARATHA dynasty founded by Ranoji Rao Sindhia in the early 18th century and later among the most important ruling families of India. Their state is now part of the Republic of India. (204e)

Singosari A short-lived but important kingdom based in eastern JAVA in the 13th century, which laid the foundations for the succeeding empire of MAJAPAHIT. (246a)

Sinjar Town in north-western 'IRAQ, capital of a small principality under a branch of the ZANGID dynasty in the late 12th/early 13th centuries. Their state was annexed by the AYYUBIDS. (185h)

Sisodias See GUHILAS.

Sistan (Seistan, Sijistan), ancient Sakastene, region in eastern Iran where the SAFFARIDS rose to power in the 9th century AD. Though their extensive realm in Iran soon vanished, the family continued to rule in Sistan, submitting to the suzerainty of stronger neighbouring powers when necessary, until the end of the 15th century. (193)

Sitawake Kingdom in CEYLON in the 16th century – it broke away from the main Sinhalese state (based at KOTTE) under a branch of the royal dynasty. Its territory came under Portuguese control at the end of the century. (224c)

Siunia A region of south-eastern Armenia, ruled by the HAYKID dynasty from ancient times. It became a kingdom in the 10th century but ceased to be of importance in the 12th century, when its ruling line became extinct. (147a)

Sivas Ancient Sebastea, town in north-eastern Turkey, an important Byzantine fortress which later became the centre of a principality under the DANISHMENDIDS in the 11th/12th centuries. In the 14th century it was the capital of the ERETNID state until the OSMANLI conquest. (139a, 142c)

Sixteen Kingdoms The Western CHIN rulers, having reunified CHINA in 280 AD, soon lost control of much of the north to various barbarian invaders, who set up a number of small states, slightly more than the traditional sixteen, though some succeeded or conquered others and no more than about eight existed at any one time during the 4th and early 5th century. Fu Chien (Shih Tsu) of the Earlier CH'IN temporarily united these northern areas, but was heavily defeated by the southern imperial government in 383, whereupon his state broke up. In the mid-5th century, the Northern WEI completed the conquest of the north, apart from those states re-annexed by the Eastern Chin emperors of the south. (230)

Skioldungs See YNGLINGS.

Slave dynasty Founding dynasty of the sultanate of DELHI, so named because the first of its rulers was a former slave of the GHURIDS and his two most important successors were of similar origin. He was viceroy in northern India for the last major Ghurid sultan, on whose death in 1206 he declared his independence. The state soon became the dominant power in the north, the Slave dynasty ruling during most of the 13th century, until succeeded by the KHALJIS in 1290. (201a)

Smolensk Ancient city in north-western RUSSIA, capital of a principality under a branch of the RIURIKIDS after the break-up of the KIEV state in the 11th century AD. It was eventually annexed by POLAND-LITHUANIA at the end of the 14th century and changed hands between the latter state and MOSCOW several times before being finally secured by Russia in the 17th century. (92e)

Sokoto Sultanate in Northern Nigeria established by the FULANI leader 'Uthman dan Fodio at the beginning of the 19th century. Following the Fulani conquest of the HAUSA states, the sultans became overlords of various amirates, the Sokoto central territory being largely in the former kingdom of GOBIR. At the beginning of the present century, the sultanate came under British control and is now part of independent Nigeria. (117)

Solanki dynasty See CHAULUKYAS.

Solomonic dynasty Ruling dynasty of ETHIOPIA which claimed descent from King Solomon of Judah-Israel and the Queen of Sheba, via the kings of AXUM (who were connected with SABA in southern Arabia). The dynasty was overthrown by the ZAGWE family, who ruled Ethiopia in the 12th/13th century but were in turn supplanted by a representative of the old ruling line in 1268. The restored dynasty survived into modern times, on occasion very powerful, though it was brought close to ruin by Muslim invasion in the 16th century, and in the 18th century its kings became puppets in the hands of various provincial rulers. In the later 19th century, several of these rulers usurped the throne in succession, until Menyelek of SHOA, member of a junior line of the Solomonic dynasty, acquired power in 1889. Emperor Haile Selassie, temporarily expelled by the Italians in 1936–41, was deposed in 1974 and the Solomonic monarchy abolished. (122b, 123a)

Somalia Coastal region of the Horn of Africa, now an independent state created by the union of the former colonial territories of British and Italian Somaliland. Various Muslim states have existed in the region since the conversion of much of it to Islam in medieval times, though its history is very obscure. Mogadishu, the present capital, was a sultanate for several centuries, and part of the north was included in the WALASMA' state of AWFAT. (124)

Somavamsi dynasty Family which ruled in ORISSA, India, in the 10th/11th centuries AD. Their state was conquered by the GANGAS early in the 12th century. (216a)

Songhai Originally a small state on the Niger, centred on the town of Gao in what is now eastern Mali and subject to the MALI empire until the mid-15th century. The last major ruler of its long-established SUNNI (or Sonni) dynasty became independent and greatly extended the territory of his state, absorbing much of the rapidly declining Mali realm. In 1493, the ASKIYA family seized power and ruled until a Moroccan invasion in 1591 virtually destroyed the Songhai empire,

though members of the dynasty survived in the Dendi region, further down the Niger, for another half-century. (119b–c)

Sonni dynasty of SONGHAI See SUNNI.

Sophene Ancient name for the region of DIYAR BAKR in south-eastern Turkey. It was a kingdom under the little-known ZARIADRID family in the 2nd/1st centuries BC until annexed by the ARTAXIADS of Armenia, and sometimes constituted a client-kingdom under the early Roman Empire.

Southern For dynasties thus named, see the main dynastic name – Southern HAN, Southern LIANG, etc.

Soviet Union Extensive modern state which is in constitutional structure a federation of more than a dozen republics, though by far the largest is the R.S.F.S.R. (Russian Republic). The territory of the Soviet Union corresponds closely, except for its Polish frontier, with the ROMANOV empire which fell in 1917, and which had vastly expanded its area in the 18th and 19th centuries, annexing lands with long histories of their own and little or no previous connection with RUSSIA – the Transcaucasian regions of GEORGIA, ARMENIA and what is now Soviet AZERBAIJAN, and the former khanates of Central Asia (see TRANSOXANIA, KHWARIZM, KAZAKHS). Other areas more conveniently considered separately from Russia from a historical viewpoint are LITHUANIA, KURLAND and the CRIMEA.

Spain The Spanish peninsula formed part of the Roman empire until early in the 5th century AD, when it was overrun by the VANDALS, Alans and SUEBI. Later in the century, the VISIGOTHS conquered most of the country, confining the Suebi to a small kingdom in the north-west and establishing a strong state soon centred on TOLEDO (the Suebian state was eventually conquered in the late 6th century). In 711, a Muslim Arab army under an UMAYYAD general invaded Spain and quickly overthrew the Visigothic kingdom, though the northern coastal and Pyrenean areas were never brought under Muslim control, remaining in the hands of independent Christian leaders. When the UMAYYAD Caliphate was overthrown in the mid-8th century by the ʿABBASIDS, a member of the fallen dynasty succeeded in reviving the family fortunes in Spain, founding an independent amirate which controlled most of the peninsula and was proclaimed a CALIPHATE in 929, a century before its disintegration and replacement by numerous minor local rulers, the REYES DE TAIFAS. In the north, the small Christian states of CASTILE-LEON, NAVARRE, ARAGON and BARCELONA had developed and now began to expand, despite temporary set-backs at the hands of the ALMORAVIDS and the ALMOHADS, Moroccan powers called in by the Spanish Muslims. In the 13th century, the Christian states overran all Muslim territory except for the small kingdom of GRANADA. Much the largest of the Spanish kingdoms was Castile-Leon, though Aragon, united with Barcelona in 1162, controlled much of eastern Spain and also a Mediterranean empire which by the late 15th century included the Balearic Islands, Sardinia and Corsica, NAPLES and SICILY. By the marriage of Isabella of Castile and Ferdinand of Aragon and their conquest of GRANADA in 1492, most of the peninsula became united, though PORTUGAL had broken away from Castile in the 12th century as an independent kingdom. Most of Navarre was conquered in 1516, and the combined kingdom, together with its new possessions in the Americas, fell to the HABSBURGS by inheritance, as did Portugal later, in 1580. However, the whole peninsula remained under one ruler only until 1640, when Portugal again broke away, and the Spanish Habsburg line became extinct in 1700, giving way to a branch of the BOURBONS who have ruled Spain, with various interruptions, until the present time – these interruptions include the rule of Joseph BONAPARTE in the early 19th century and the Republican and Franco regimes during 1931–1975. (43–53)

Sparta Ancient Greek city-state in the PELOPONNESE, main rival of ATHENS in the 5th century BC. It was a double monarchy, two kings ruling simultaneously from the two royal dynasties, EURYPONTIDS and AGIADS, traditionally from the 11th century BC, though evidence for the historicity and dates of the kings is flimsy prior to the 6th century. The powers of these rulers were very limited and their role largely military – the kingship lapsed in 192 BC with the assassination of the usurper Nabis. (82)

Spartocids Kings of BOSPHORUS from the late 5th century BC, successors of the ARCHAEANACTIDS and rulers of a strong, prosperous state until the 2nd century BC, when attacks upon their lands by the nomadic peoples of the Pontic steppes weakened them and obliged the last of the dynasty to seek aid from Mithridates VI of PONTUS, who took over the kingdom in about 109 BC (see MITHRIDATIDS). (90b)

Spoleto Ancient Spoletum, a city in central Italy which became the capital of an important LOMBARD duchy at the end of the 6th century AD This state survived the fall of the Lombard kingdom in the north, and in the CAROLINGIAN period provided two kings of Italy. Its importance declined in the 10th century and it was eventually incorporated into the PAPAL STATES. (68a)

Sri Lanka See CEYLON.

Srivijaya State based in southern SUMATRA, its main centre being PALEMBANG. Though it flourished from the 6th to the 13th century AD, very little is known about its political history and no list of the names and dates of its rulers is available. At the zenith of its power, Srivijaya dominated the Malacca Straits and controlled parts of the Malay Peninsula as well as much of Sumatra and probably some of JAVA. In the 9th century, the Javanese SAILENDRA dynasty came to the throne, suffering a major blow in the early 11th century, when a CHOLA fleet from India plundered the most important cities of the kingdom. Eventually the remnants of the empire were absorbed into MAJAPAHIT, though the founder of the MALACCA sultanate may have been a Sailendra prince.

Strathclyde Early British kingdom in south-western SCOTLAND, founded in the 6th century AD. On the extinction of its ruling dynasty in the 10th century, various members of the Scottish royal family ruled under the suzerainty of the

Scottish kings until the final absorption of Strathclyde into the national state in the following century. Very little is known of its history and a full list of the kings and their dates is not available.

Stuarts (or Stewarts), a family which came originally from BRITTANY to England with the Normans and later settled in SCOTLAND, becoming hereditary High Stewards of the kingdom. The 7th High Steward inherited the throne from the BRUCE family in 1371, and in 1603 his descendant James VI acquired the throne of England as the heir of the TUDORS, thus uniting the two realms. The male Stuart line was temporarily expelled from Britain in the mid-17th century, during the period of the Commonwealth under Oliver Cromwell, and was finally dispossessed in 1688, though female Stuarts ruled until 1714, when the throne passed to the WELFS of Hanover. The Stuarts were an unlucky or perhaps simply an unwise family – of their fourteen sovereigns, six died violently and a seventh in exile. (6d, 11b)

Styria (Steiermark), region of AUSTRIA, a margravate from the early 11th century and a duchy from 1180, acquired by the BABENBERGS and united with their other Austria lands, all of which were obtained by the HABSBURGS in 1276. Various members of the Habsburg family ruled independently in Styria on occasion until its final union with their imperial lands in 1619. (40c, e)

Sudan The 'black land', a savanna belt which extends across Africa south of the Sahara – the modern Republic of the Sudan includes only part of this vast geographical region, which can for historical purposes be divided into three sections:

1 Eastern Sudan, the northern half of the modern republic, bisected by the Nile valley – see NUBIA, SENNAR and DARFUR. This whole area was ruled by the MAHDI Muhammad Ahmad and his successor in the late 19th century.

2 Central Sudan, the southern parts of Chad and Niger, and the northern region of NIGERIA – see WADAI, BAGIRMI, KANEM-BORNU, HAUSA and FULANI.

3 Western Sudan, Senegal and part of MALI and MAURETANIA, dominated by three successive empires in medieval and early modern times, GHANA, Mali and SONGHAI, though many smaller states have existed in the area at various periods.

Suebi An ancient Germanic people after whom the region of SWABIA in Germany is named. At the beginning of the 5th century AD, they invaded Roman Gaul and later SPAIN, where they established a kingdom centred in what are now GALICIA and northern PORTUGAL. This state was ultimately conquered in the late 6th century after persistent efforts by the VISIGOTH kings of Spain. (43b)

Sui dynasty Imperial dynasty of CHINA whose founder reunited the country after several centuries of division in 589 AD – he usurped the Northern CHOU throne and conquered the Southern CH'EN realm. His successor proved to be a clever but extravagant and tyrannical ruler under whom the central government eventually collapsed amid disorders from which the T'ANG emerged as masters of the empire after 618. (227n)

Sukhothai City in northern THAILAND, capital of an early Thai kingdom of the same name whose founder took the city from CAMBODIA in the mid-13th century – the most powerful of his successors, Rama Khamheng, ruled an extensive state which included much of Thailand and perhaps parts of neighbouring regions, but the kingdom declined rapidly and was annexed to AYUTHIA in the 15th century. (239a)

Sulayhids Ruling dynasty of YEMEN, nominally as FATIMID viceroys, from the mid-11th century. They ruled at SAN'A and intermittently controlled ZABID, being supplanted by the HAMDANIDS. (172f)

Sulibawa family Amirs of KATSINA, Nigeria, since early in the present century, successors of the DALLAZAWA dynasty. (118e)

Sulu The Sulu Archipelago, lying between Borneo and the Philippines, formed a sultanate founded in the 15th century and for long the major centre of piracy in Indonesian waters. The Spanish government in the Philippines made repeated but unsuccessful efforts to suppress the sultanate, their American successors annexing the islands in 1915. (248a)

Sumatra From the 6th to the 13th century AD, the most important power in Sumatra was the SRIVIJAYA empire based in the PALEMBANG area, but Islam began to spread rapidly through the island in late medieval times, and the strong sultanate of ACHIN arose in the north at the end of the 15th century, while various other Muslim states developed in the more southerly regions – see PALEMBANG and SIAK. In the late 19th century, the Dutch brought the whole island under their control, and it is now part of the Indonesian Republic. (245)

Sumer Ancient name for the southern region of 'IRAQ, land of the Sumerian founders of the earliest civilization in Western Asia. Very early city-states flourished in this region and lists of semi-mythical kings of uncertain date exist for Kish, Uruk, Lagash, UR and other towns. The region was incorporated into the empire of AKKAD in the 24th century BC.

Sumra dynasty Muslim rulers of SIND in the 11th/14th centuries. The dates and genealogy of the rulers are uncertain, as indeed are those of their successors, the SAMMA family. (205b)

Sung Name of an ancient state and of several dynasties in CHINA:
  1 One of the most ancient of the CHOU STATES, in the eastern Yellow River plain, its ruling house claiming descent from the SHANG dynasty, predecessors of the CHOU. It was conquered by CH'I in 286 BC (228c)
  2 Early Sung, an imperial dynasty of the 5th century AD founded by a general of the preceding Eastern CHIN rulers and supplanted by the Southern CH'I. (227j)
  3 Northern Sung and Southern Sung, successive lines of the same family, who ruled from the mid-10th to the late 13th century. The founder deposed the last ruler of the Later CHOU and reconquered the surviving TEN KINGDOMS states but was unable to recover the provinces north of the Yellow river, where the LIAO (Khitan) state became established. When the Liao were overthrown by the CHIN (Juchen) early in the 12th century, the new rulers of the north at once attacked the Sung lands, taking the imperial capital and pushing south to the Yangtze river. The later Sung emperors saw the invaders in turn attacked and destroyed in a long struggle with the MONGOLS, who then embarked on a further prolonged contest with the Sung themselves in the later 13th century, completing the conquest of China and extinguishing the dynasty in 1279. Traditional Chinese civilization perhaps reached its finest flower under the stable and capable Sung administration. (227u–v)

Sungas Dynasty which supplanted the last MAURYA ruler in what remained of the Maurya empire in the early 2nd century BC. Little is known of the Sungas, who probably bore the brunt of the invasions by the Greek rulers of BACTRIA and were in turn overthrown by the KANVAS after about a century on the throne. (200b)

Sunni Islamic term for the 'orthodox' majority of Muslims and also the name of a Sudanese dynasty:
  1 In origin, the Sunnis were those who accepted the leadership of elected CALIPHS, as opposed to the SHI'A, though other theological differences soon developed between these two major Islamic sects.
  2 The Sunni or Sonni dynasty were rulers of SONGHAI, originally a small vassal state of the MALI empire in the western SUDAN, but the last important king of the family, Sunni 'Ali, made himself independent and took over much of the former Mali territory, founding a new empire. Soon after his death in 1492, his dynasty was supplanted by the ASKIYAS. (119b)

Surakarta City in JAVA, former capital of one of the two states into which MATARAM split in 1755 (the other being JOGJAKARTA). The ruler of Surakarta retained the Mataram title of Susuhunan, his rival taking that of Sultan. The state was absorbed into the Republic of Indonesia in 1949 after the end of Dutch colonial rule. (246f)

Surid dynasty A short-lived ruling house in northern India, founded by Shir Shah Sur, an Afghan who rose to power in BENGAL in the mid-16th century and soon expelled the MOGHUL emperor Humayun from India, ruling much of the north until his death in a siege in 1545. His successors proved incompetent and Humayun reconquered his empire within a decade. (201f)

Suzdal-Vladimir RIURIKID state in northern RUSSIA founded in the early 12th century, based successively on Rostov, Suzdal and Vladimir, all towns to the north and east of MOSCOW. It soon became the dominant principality in north-eastern Russia, its rulers taking the title of Great Prince and claiming suzerainty over neighbouring Riurikid states, though they were compelled to submit to MONGOL overlordship as vassals of the GOLDEN HORDE in the mid-13th century. In the next century, the Grand Ducal title and possession of Vladimir was the object of a fierce struggle between two branches of the Suzdal dynasty, the princes of TVER and those of a hitherto minor power, Moscow, in which the latter line prevailed and merged Vladimir with their own state, thus gaining an increase in power and authority which made their dominance in eastern Russia secure. Suzdal had meanwhile become a minor principality under another Riurikid line, also later annexed by Moscow. (92h)

Swabia Region of southern Germany which takes its name from the ancient Germanic tribe called SUEBI. Under the early German kings, it formed one of the several large duchies into which the country was divided, ruled in the 11th/13th centuries by members of the HOHENSTAUFFEN family, on whose extinction it was split into smaller feudal states. (39b)

Swati dynasty Sultans of KASHMIR, the founder of the line being a Muslim adventurer from Swat who seized the throne from the last Hindu ruler of medieval times in the mid-14th century. His family were temporarily dispossessed by Haidar Mirza DUGHLAT in the mid-16th century, and finally supplanted by the CHAKS soon after their restoration. (209d)

Swazis/Swaziland Bantu people and modern kingdom of southern Africa. The state was founded during the upheavals associated with the ZULU conquests in the early 19th century and came under

British protection at the end of that century, but is now independent, its late king having reigned since 1899. (133d)

Sweden Before the late 10th century AD, very little indeed is known by way of firm historical fact about Sweden, though legend and saga provide the names of many rulers, particularly those of the SKIOLDUNG family of Uppsala, ancestors of the first few historic kings – hence the numerals adopted for the rulers named Erik and Karl. Various families held the crown after the extinction of the SKIOLDUNGS, in particular the FOLKUNGS, who came to power in Sweden in the mid-13th century and later acquired the throne of NORWAY too, being succeeded in both countries by Margaret I of DENMARK, under whom all Scandinavia was united. However, her successors proved unable to hold Sweden, which was ruled only intermittently by the OLDENBURGS in the later 15th and early 16th centuries, until a national revolt brought the VASA dynasty to power. This latter family made the country a great and aggressive state with an extensive Baltic empire, becoming involved in wars with RUSSIA and later with POLAND and in Germany. Under their WITTELSBACH successors, Sweden eventually suffered a series of military disasters in the early 18th century and ceased to be a major power – in 1751, a branch of the OLDENBURGS inherited the throne, and in 1818 the French Marshal BERNADOTTE, previously chosen as crown prince, succeeded as Karl XIV. His family still reigns. (18)

Syracuse Ancient city in SICILY founded by Greek colonists. It became the most important city-state on the island, often controlling much of eastern Sicily and taking the lead in the persistent struggle against CARTHAGE in the 5th century BC and later. Syracuse was ruled by various tyrants and kings with republican intervals, and in the 3rd century joined ROME against Carthage, becoming a Roman client-state when the Romans gained control of Sicily. Its last king went over to Carthage, though shortly afterwards assassinated, and after a long siege the Romans conquered the city in 211 BC. (56)

Syria Now the name of a modern state,

but in its widest historical meaning the whole region of settled land between the Middle Euphrates and the Sinai peninsula, including modern Syria, LEBANON, Israel and parts of JORDAN, plus the Antakya region (see ANTIOCH) of Turkey. This is one of the oldest civilized areas of the world, forming a cross-road between EGYPT, 'IRAQ and ASIA MINOR, and numerous city-states flourished there from early times – see ALEPPO, SIDON, TYRE. Syria was disputed between Egypt and the HITTITES in the 13th century BC, and in the early 1st millennium BC was divided between small Hittite kingdoms in the north, Phoenician city-states on the coast, the powerful Aramean kingdom of DAMASCUS and the southern Hebrew states of Israel and Judah, all of which were annexed or made tributary by ASSYRIA in the 8th/7th centuries. The region formed part of the ACHAEMENID empire, and during the wars of the DIADOCHI the south fell to the PTOLEMIES while the north was acquired by the SELEUCIDS and soon became the centre of their great but short-lived empire. In the 1st century BC, ROME annexed the remains of the Seleucid state and reduced the kingdom of JUDAEA to client status, the entire area remaining part of the Roman empire for some 700 years. In the mid-7th century AD, it was conquered by the Muslim Arabs and Damascus became the capital of the vast realm of the UMAYYADS, the land still forming an important province of the 'ABBASID Caliphate until that state broke up and various Muslim dynasties arose in parts of Syria in the 10th/11th centuries. In 1098–99, much of the coast and part of inland Syria was conquered in the First Crusade, and several CRUSADER STATES were established, to be gradually annexed over the next two centuries by the AYYUBIDS and their MAMLUK successors. The whole region fell under the rule of the OSMANLI Turks in the early 16th century and was freed from Turkish control only after the First World War. An attempt to establish a member of the HASHIMID family of Mecca as king of Syria in 1920 failed, though his brother was eventually recognized as ruler of Transjordan (see JORDAN), and the republics of Syria and LEBANON were then set up. (159–170)

T

Tabaristan See MAZANDARAN.

Tafilalt Region of MOROCCO beyond the Atlas Mountains, an oasis area in which lay SIJILMASA, capital of the early Muslim state of the MIDRARIDS. In later centuries, both the SA'DID and the present 'ALAWID dynasties of Morocco first rose to power in this region. (112a)

Tahart (Tagdempt, Tiaret), town in Algeria, capital of the state established in the late 8th century by the RUSTAMIDS, Kharijite sectarian leaders whose kingdom was annexed by the FATIMIDS in 909. (110a)

Tahirids Name of two Muslim dynasties:
1 Rulers of KHURASAN under the 'ABBASIDS for much of the 9th century AD. They were a Persian family who established a realm that was in reality more or less independent, their authority extending over parts of Transoxania and large areas of eastern Iran at the height of their power. The last of the dynasty was dispossessed by the SAFFARIDS, but most of the Tahirid lands soon fell to the SAMANIDS. (194a)
2 Ruling family in YEMEN in the late 15th century, successors of the RASULIDS – their state was conquered by the MAMLUKS just before the latter rulers were themselves overthrown by the OSMANLIS. (172k)

Tahiti Largest of the Society Islands group in the South Pacific. In the late 18th century a local chief gained control of the island and those near by, founding a kingdom which was eventually annexed by the French in 1880. (249b)

Tai One of the SIXTEEN KINGDOMS of the 4th century AD in CHINA, founded by the T'o-Pa nomads. It was conquered by the Earlier CH'IN in 377, but its ruling family revived their state a decade later as the kingdom of Northern WEI, going on to extend their rule over most of northern China. (230f)

Tamil kingdoms In ancient times, the most southerly region of India was divided among three Tamil states and peoples, though very little is known by way of firm historical fact about the CHOLA, PANDYA and Chera kingdoms prior to the rise of the PALLAVAS, who dominated the south in the 7th/9th centuries. For the Cheras see KERALA and KULASEKHARA. Following the overthrow of the Pallavas, the Cholas and Pandyas both controlled large areas of the CARNATIC during their respective later periods of dominance. (223)

T'ang Name of several dynasties of CHINA:

1 Imperial dynasty of the 7th/9th centuries, probably the most powerful and famous of the native Chinese ruling lines, claiming descent from the Western LIANG family of the SIXTEEN KINGDOMS period. On the collapse of SUI authority, the duke of T'ang was one of those leaders who contended for power, and with the aid of his son, later the second ruler of the dynasty and perhaps the greatest of Chinese emperors, eventually gained control of the whole empire. Under the early T'ang, the Chinese established their control over much of Central Asia and reaffirmed suzerainty over neighbouring states, but in the 8th century a prolonged and widespread rebellion greatly weakened the dynasty, though it survived until deposed by the Later LIANG in 907 AD. (2270)

2 Later T'ang, a short-lived dynasty founded by a Sha-t'o Turkish leader who supplanted the Later LIANG in the early 10th century AD. (227q)

3 Southern T'ang, one of the TEN KINGDOMS families, which supplanted the WU rulers in Kiangsu in the mid-10th century. Their state was re-annexed to the empire by the SUNG in 975 AD. (231c)

Tanguts See Western HSIA.

Tanjore (Tanjavur), ancient city in southern India, capital of the CHOLA kings and later the centre of a state which broke away from the disintegrating VIJAYANAGAR empire in the 16th century under a NAYYAK dynasty. In 1674, the city was seized by a half-brother of the MARATHA leader Shivaji and remained under a branch of the BHONSLA family until 1855, though most of their territory had been annexed by the British at the end of the 18th century. On the extinction of the ruling line, Tanjore came under direct British rule. (221b, 223e–f)

Tara Site of a very ancient settlement and ceremonial centre in MEATH, Ireland, which gave the HIGH KINGS of Ireland their formal title of 'King of Tara', though in historic times it had only symbolic importance. (13)

Tarum The valley of the middle Safid Rud river in GILAN, Iran, centre of power of the MUSAFIRID dynasty in the 10th and 11th centuries AD. (189d)

Tay-Son family In 1776 the NGUYEN rulers of southern VIET-NAM were overthrown in a revolt led by three brothers from the Tay-Son district, who then also overran the TRINH dominions in the north and put an end to the puppet Later LE emperors, the eldest brother taking the imperial throne himself. However, a survivor of the Nguyen then reopened the struggle in the south and slowly overcame the Tay-Son, taking Hanoi in 1802 and extinguishing their rule. (243k)

Teke One of the ANATOLIAN AMIRATES, ruled by a branch of the HAMID dynasty with their capital at ANTALYA. It was finally annexed by the OSMANLIS in 1423. (142h)

Ten Kingdoms On the collapse of T'ANG rule in CHINA at the beginning of the 10th century AD, much of the imperial territory was lost to various local independent kingdoms – ten in all, though not all were contemporaneous. The survivors were conquered by the SUNG within two decades of that dynasty's seizure of the imperial throne in 960. (231)

Ternate A small island in the Moluccas, Indonesia, which was the centre of a commercial state controlling much of the spice trade in the 16th and 17th centuries, in constant rivalry with TIDORE. It was eventually brought under Dutch control.

Terter dynasty Ruling family of BULGARIA in the late 13th/early 14th centuries after the extinction of the ASEN dynasty. They in turn were followed by the SHISHMANOVICHI. (80e)

Texcoco City in MEXICO, ruled from about 1300 AD by a Chichimec dynasty. In the early 15th century, the kings entered into an alliance with the AZTECS of Tenochtitlan and the city of Tlacopan, and this federation rapidly came to dominate a large area of central Mexico, though the Aztecs in fact were by far the strongest partners. With the conquest of the empire by the Spaniards in 1521, the Texcoco kingdom ceased to exist in reality, though Spanish puppets were appointed to rule for some years. (250b)

Thailand/Thai people The early Thais were closely related to the SHANS and both peoples occupied much of southern China in ancient times. There was probably a strong Thai/Shan element in the population of the NAN CHAO kingdom in Yunnan. However, much of northern Indo-China was also settled by Thais, though the date and circumstances of these settlements are obscure. The Thais of LAOS and what is now northern Thailand came into conflict with the kings of CAMBODIA in the 13th century, when the Lao state of LAN CHANG and the SUKHOTHAI kingdom arose, and at the end of the century CHIANG MAI emerged as a power further north. However, the direct predecessor of the modern Thai state was the kingdom of AYUTHIA (a city near modern Bangkok) which was founded in 1350 and soon annexed Sukhothai (and later Chiang Mai also), extending its control over the northern part of the Malay peninsula and conquering much of the Cambodian kingdom (though the capital was sacked in 1569 in a disastrous war with BURMA.) The kingdom flourished greatly in the 17th century, entering into relations with European powers, but fell victim to another great Burmese invasion in 1767, when Ayuthia again suffered capture and major damage. The Burmese were expelled by a new ruler who shifted the capital to Bangkok and was succeeded by the founder of the present CHAKRI dynasty of Thailand in 1782. The country was alone among those of South-East Asia in maintaining its independence during the 19th century, when the rest of the region came under European control. (239)

Thakuri dynasty Rulers of NEPAL in the 11th/12th centuries in succession to the RAGHAVADEVAS. They were supplanted by the MALLAS. (211b)

Thessalonica Major city in northern Greece, founded in honour of a half-sister of Alexander the Great. After the fall of Constantinople to the Fourth Crusade in 1204, Thessalonica was allotted to Boniface of MONTFERRAT as a kingdom (see CRUSADER STATES) but was captured in 1225 by Theodore DUCAS of EPIRUS, whose successors ruled there as emperors and later as despots until the annexation of their state by NICAEA in 1246. (85c–d)

Thessaly Region of central Greece, briefly an important power in the 4th century BC under Jason of Pherae, after which it became a kind of sub-kingdom attached to MACEDONIA until the Roman conquest. In the late 13th century AD it became an independent state, the duchy of NEO-PATRAS, under a branch of the DUCAS family of EPIRUS. (85f)

Thrace Ancient name for Turkey-in-Europe and south-eastern Bulgaria, ruled in early classical times by Thracian tribal kings, though its coasts were lined with Greek colonial cities. Philip II of MACEDONIA conquered the region, which fell to Lysimachus on the death of Alexander the Great and became the centre of a large Lysimachid kingdom during the wars of the DIADOCHI, until the defeat and death of its founder in 281 BC. The local Thracian kings then re-established themselves, later becoming clients of ROME, which annexed Thrace in the 1st century AD.

Three Kingdoms At the end of the 2nd century AD, the last HAN emperor of CHINA became a puppet under one of his generals, while other military leaders became independent in the south and west. In 220 AD, on the death of the puppet-master, his son deposed the puppet and founded the WEI dynasty, whereupon the Sun family set up the WU kingdom in the south, and an alleged remote relative of the Han established the state of SHU-Han in Szechuan. Wei conquered Shu-Han in 263 but were themselves supplanted by the Western CHIN soon afterwards – this new dynasty conquered Wu in 280 and thus reunified China. (229)

Tibet Nothing much is known of Tibetan history before the beginning of the 7th century AD, when the ruler of YAR-LUN established himself as king of the country.

Under his dynasty, Tibet became a powerful and aggressive state, on occasion invading India and China, until it broke up in the mid-9th century. The MONGOLS conquered the country in the 13th century and appointed a series of religious leaders, the SAKYAS, as viceroys – these were supplanted by the founder of a new Tibetan kingdom in 1358. In the 17th century, the ruler of the Qosot Mongols installed the DALAI LAMAS, hitherto simply religious leaders, as temporal masters of the country, though various khans continued to act as overlords. The CH'ING emperors of CHINA imposed effective suzerainty in the 18th century but the Dalai Lamas regained control on the collapse of the Chinese empire at the beginning of the present century. The Chinese invaded Tibet in 1950, and the Dalai Lama fled to India in 1959. (226)

Tidore A small island in the Moluccas, Indonesia, centre of a trading state constantly in opposition to TERNATE, its near neighbour. Tidore fell under Spanish influence in the 17th century until 1654, when Dutch control was imposed on it.

Timurid dynasty Barlas Turkish family founded by Timur (Tamerlane), who rose to power in the mid-14th century in TRANSOXANIA and spent his long reign in far-ranging and immensely destructive campaigns, overrunning IRAN, 'IRAQ, ASIA MINOR and the domains of the GOLDEN HORDE in southern Russia. He sacked DELHI in 1398 and temporarily broke the power of the OSMANLI Turks at Ankara in 1402. On his death, his large empire in Iran and Transoxania became divided among his descendants and shrank rapidly over the 15th century amid family quarrels. The last minor prince of the dynasty, Babur, was expelled from FARGHANA by the SHAIBANIDS, conquerors of Transoxania, and established himself at Kabul – in 1526, he defeated and killed the LODI sultan of Delhi, becoming master of much of northern India and founding the MOGHUL empire. (198g, 202)

Tlemcen (Tilimsan), town in Algeria, capital of a state under the ZAYYANIDS ('Abdul-Wadids), who established their independence on the break-up of the ALMOHAD empire in the mid-13th century. The Zayyanids came under repeated attack by their neighbours in the east and the west, HAFSIDS and MARINIDS respectively, losing their capital several times to invaders, but survived until the mid-16th century, when their state was annexed by the OSMANLI Turks. (110c)

Tocco family Counts of CEPHALONIA, who succeeded the related ORSINI line in the mid-14th century and also at times controlled parts of neighbouring EPIRUS. In the late 15th century, their domains were overrun by the OSMANLI Turks but soon fell to VENICE. (85b)

Tokugawa family A SHOGUN dynasty whose founder rose to supreme power in JAPAN after the death of the *de facto* ruler Hideyoshi at the end of the 16th century. The Tokugawa rulers introduced the system under which practically all contact with the outside world was prohibited. The last Shogun was obliged to abdicate as a result of the events leading to the Meiji Revolution of 1868 and the beginning of modernization in Japan. (236f)

Toledo Ancient Toletum, an important city in the centre of SPAIN, capital of the later VISIGOTH kings and of the REYES DE TAIFAS state of the DHU'L-NUNID dynasty. The king of CASTILE captured the city in 1085 and it at once became capital of the kingdom, yielding place to Madrid only in the mid-16th century. (48g)

Toltecs Ruling race of an extensive empire in central MEXICO in early medieval times – the names of a series of Toltec kings are known, but their dates and the extent of their dominions are very uncertain. The Toltec state broke up into a number of city-states in the 12th century.

Tonga Pacific island group of which the various ancient Polynesian chieftainships were united in the mid-19th century by George Tubou I, whose dynasty still rules the modern kingdom. (249c)

Tonk Town in RAJASTAN, capital of a princely state established by the Pindari (Muslim freebooter) leader Amir Khan at the end of the 18th century and recognized by the British in 1817. The state was absorbed into the Republic of India in 1948. (206i)

Tonkin (Tongking), the northern part of VIET-NAM, region of the Red River delta. For many centuries the Vietnamese people and state were confined to this area, at first as a province of the Chinese empire and from the 10th century AD as an independent kingdom. Only with the conquest of CHAMPA in the 15th century did the state expand into what are now the central Vietnamese provinces and later into the south. In the 16th century, the TRINH family seized control of Tonkin in the name of puppet Later LE emperors, carrying on a struggle with the NGUYEN of the south until their power was extinguished by the TAY-SON brothers. (243j)

Toulouse Ancient Tolosa, major city of southern France, capital of the early VISIGOTH kingdom until it fell to the FRANKS in 508. From the mid-9th century it was the centre of an extensive feudal county under a family which also provided the ruling dynasty of Lebanese TRIPOLI (see CRUSADER STATES). The counts of Toulouse were supporters of the Albigensian heretics in the early 13th century and suffered heavily from the anti-Albigensian crusade – the last of the line was obliged to marry his daughter to a member of the CAPET family, who succeeded him but died without heirs, the county then being annexed to the French crown. (24r)

Toungoo dynasty Initially rulers of the small state of Toungoo in BURMA, who rose to great power in the early 16th century, conquering AVA and PEGU to unite the country. The greatest of the dynasty, Bayin Naung, captured AYUTHIA in 1569 and brought much of Thailand under his rule. In the 18th century, the power of the Toungoo kings waned, and their state was extinguished by the revived Pegu kingdom, which however soon fell victim to ALAUNGPAYA, creator of a new Burmese empire. (237e)

Tran dynasty Rulers of VIET-NAM from the early 13th century in succession to the Later LI – they soon had to face prolonged and determined invasion by the MONGOLS, who took the capital Hanoi on three successive occasions, but each time proved unable to hold it against Vietnamese counter-attack. The Tran were deposed by the HO family in 1400, briefly restored with MING Chinese aid and finally suppressed by Chinese occupation (eventually brought to an end by the Later LE). (243f)

Transjordan See JORDAN.

Transoxania The land 'beyond the Oxus', a somewhat vague term meaning the region between Oxus and Jaxartes but often used to include northern Afghanistan, these being the ancient regions of Soghdiana and BACTRIA under the ACHAEMENID empire. After the fall of the Bactrian Greek state, the area came under the rule of various invaders, including the KUSHANS. In the 8th century AD, the armies of the UMAYYAD Caliphs conquered Transoxania, clashing briefly with T'ANG Chinese forces which were obliged to withdraw – the region passed to the 'ABBASIDS and then to their TAHIRID viceroys before becoming the centre of the SAMANID realm in the 10th century. It then fell to the QARA-KHANIDS and later suffered immense devastation during the MONGOL conquest in the early 13th century, becoming part of the CHAGHATAI khanate until the rise of the TIMURIDS. Timur made Transoxania the centre of a vast but short-lived empire, his successors being supplanted by the SHAIBANIDS at the end of the 15th century, who were in turn succeeded by the JANIDS. Under this latter dynasty, the Transoxanian realm shrank to the khanate of BUKHARA, a breakaway state being established at KHOKAND by the SHAH-RUKHID family and the area south of the Oxus was seized by the founders of the DURRANI kingdom of Afghanistan. The HAIDARIDS supplanted the Janids late in the 18th century and Bukhara was obliged to accept Russian overlordship nearly a hundred years later, its last ruler being deposed by Soviet revolutionaries in 1920. Khokand had been annexed to the Russian empire in 1876. (198)

Transylvania Mountainous region of RUMANIA formed by the eastern bend of the Carpathians. It constituted the major part of the Roman province of DACIA –

after the abandonment of the province by Rome, its history is very obscure until its incorporation into the kingdom of HUNGARY around 1000 AD. The population was and remains very mixed, with Rumanian-speaking and Magyar-speaking groups, some Slavs, and colonies of Germans settled in the region by medieval Hungarian kings, and the tendency of Transylvania to autonomy was much strengthened when Hungary was conquered by the OSMANLI Turks in the early 16th century. While the HABSBURGS maintained a claim to the Hungarian crown, a separate principality was established in Transylvania by another claimant to the throne, John Zapolya, whose family was succeeded by other rulers until the late 17th century. At that time, the Habsburgs expelled the Turks from Hungary and annexed Transylvania to their empire – it remained under their rule until the break-up of the Austro-Hungarian state, when it was transferred to Rumania. (76)

Travancore (Tiruvarankodu), southern KERALA. In the mid-18th century, the ruler of the small but ancient state of VENAD gradually united this region to create a strong new kingdom, and his successors allied themselves with the British against the Muslim rulers of MYSORE, HAIDAR ʿALI and Tipu Sultan, further securing their position when the latter king was defeated and killed in 1799. Their state, thereafter dominant in Kerala, was absorbed into the Republic of India in 1949. (220d)

Trebizond Trabzon, ancient Trapezus, an early Greek settlement on the northeastern coast of Asia Minor. On the fall of Constantinople to the Fourth Crusade, members of the former imperial COMNENI family set up an independent state based on the city of Trebizond and controlling a strip of coast around it. The dynasty claimed, like several rival Greek families, to be the legitimate heirs of BYZANTIUM, but were able to do no more than maintain their small kingdom's independence until the OSMANLI Turks conquered it in 1461. (141)

Trengganu Sultanate of northern MALAYA, ruled by a dynasty founded in the early 18th century by a brother of a sultan of JOHORE. It is now one of the states of the Federation of MALAYSIA. (244g)

Trieu dynasty Vietnamese name for the CHAO family, rulers of a state in southern CHINA and northern VIET-NAM in the 2nd century BC. (228q)

Trinh dynasty On the deposition of the Later LE family of VIET-NAM by the MAC in the early 16th century, the Trinh and Nguyen families launched a revolt to restore the Le, but later quarrelled, the Nguyen establishing an autonomous state in the south and the Trinh gradually recovering TONKIN. They took Hanoi in 1592 and extinguished the Mac in 1677, ruling in the name of Le puppets until the late 18th century, when the Trinh state was conquered by the TAY-SON brothers. (243j)

Tripoli (in Lebanon) Ancient port which became the centre of an independent Amirate under the BANU ʿAMMAR family as FATIMID control of the area weakened in the late 11th century AD. During the First Crusade of 1098–99, Raymond IV of TOULOUSE formed a county in the LEBANON region, and his heirs took Tripoli, after a long siege, in 1109, making it their capital. The county passed to the rulers of ANTIOCH in 1187. In 1289, Tripoli, one of the last Christian fortresses in Syria-Palestine, fell to the MAMLUK sultan of Egypt. See CRUSADER STATES. (167c, 168a)

Tripoli (in Libya) Ancient Oea, a North African port which rose to importance during medieval times and was briefly held by the HAUTEVILLE rulers of SICILY in the 12th century. Two hundred years later it formed the centre of a small state ruled by the BANU ʿAMMAR (unrelated to the earlier dynasty of the same name in Lebanese Tripoli) until conquered by the HAFSIDS of Tunis in 1401. The city was captured by the Spaniards and then by the OSMANLI Turks in the 16th century, and in 1711 the QARAMANID family, Turkish governors, established a virtually independent state in the area which survived until Osmanli reconquest in 1835. The city is now capital of the Republic of Libya. (106a–b)

Trucial States See UNITED ARAB EMIRATES.

Ts'ai Minor CHOU STATE in Honan, established in the 9th century BC. It was conquered by CH'U in 447 BC. (2280)

Ts'ao Minor CHOU STATE in Honan, established in the 10th century BC. It was annexed by SUNG in 487 BC. (228p)

T'u-Chueh Chinese name for the early TURKS, who overthrew the JUAN-JUAN masters of MONGOLIA in the 6th century AD and established a vast empire spreading across both eastern and western steppe-lands to the Volga and beyond. Almost immediately, however, this state split into western and eastern khanates, the history of the western state being confused and obscure – it broke up in the mid-7th century. The history of the eastern khanate is somewhat better chronicled, and although it was crushed by the powerful early T'ANG rulers of China, it was revived in the late 7th century, again dominating the eastern steppelands until overthrown by the UIGHURS in 745. (225e)

Tudors From Welsh Tewdwr (Theo-dore), ruling family of England 1485–1603. They were descended in the female line from the princes of DEHEUBARTH, but the founder of the family's importance was Owen Tudor, who married Catherine of VALOIS, widow of Henry V – a son of this union married a Beaufort descendant of Edward III, and a son of that marriage in turn became the candidate of the Lan-castrian party after the elimination of most other claimants to the throne in the Wars of the Roses. With his decisive victory at Bosworth in 1485, Henry VII secured the crown. During most of the 16th century, England was ruled by two remarkable monarchs, Henry VIII and Elizabeth I, under whom the kingdom became Protestant and began the maritime and overseas activity which led ultimately to the development of the British Empire. In 1603, Elizabeth was succeeded by her relative James VI of Scotland, a STUART. (6c)

Tughluq dynasty Sultans of DELHI in the 14th century, in succession to the KHALJIS. Under the able but eccentric Muhammad Tughluq, the sultanate reached the zenith of its power, but his activities did much to hasten the decline after his death, and several independent Muslim states arose in former Tughluq territory, while Delhi itself was taken and sacked by Timur (see TIMURIDS) in 1398. The dynasty was succeeded in 1414 by the SAYYIDS as rulers of what remained of the kingdom, a district around the capital. (201c)

Tujibids Spanish Muslim family which seized power at ZARAGOZA on the dis-integration of the UMAYYAD Caliphate in Spain in the early 11th century AD (see REYES DE TAIFAS). Within two decades they were succeeded by the HUDIDS. (48m)

Tulunids First independent Muslim dynasty of EGYPT, in the later 9th century AD, nominally as governors for the 'ABBASIDS, who suppressed the dynasty and regained control over the country in 905 (only to lose it again permanently thirty years later, initially to the IKHSHIDIDS). (100a)

Tuluvas Third ruling dynasty of VIJAYANAGAR – the founder seized power from the SALUVAS at the end of the 15th century, and his son Krishna Devaraya was the most able of the Vijayanagar kings. From 1542, real power was exercised by the ARAVIDU family, who did not, how-ever, formally supplant the Tuluvas until shortly after the ruin of the empire's military strength at the battle of Talikota in 1565. (222c)

Tunis/Tunisia For the early history of Tunisia, see CARTHAGE and VANDALS. Tunis existed in ancient times but became the capital of the region only in the 13th century. Tunisia was conquered by the Muslim Arabs in the 7th century AD and in the 9th century formed the core of the AGHLABID kingdom – it also constituted the original power-base of the FATIMIDS from 909 until the dynasty shifted to EGYPT, leaving the ZIRIDS as their viceroys in the area. This latter family soon became independent, ruling until the mid-12th century, when the HAUTEVILLES of Sicily put an end to their regime. Tunisia then passed to the ALMOHADS, whose governors the HAFSIDS became independent at Tunis in the early 13th century. The Hafsids ruled an extensive and often prosperous state for some three centuries, eventually siding with Spain when the realm was threatened by the OSMANLI Turks and their corsair allies – who finally acquired Tunis in 1574. In the following century, the MURADID Beys established practical independence of the Osmanli sultans and were succeeded in 1705 by the HUSAINIDS, who came under French control in 1881 and were deposed by newly independent Tunisia in 1957. (109, 111a–b)

Turkestan A vague geographical term signifying Central Asia, both Russian (TRANSOXANIA, KHWARIZM/KHIVA, FARGHANA etc.) and Chinese (KASHGARIA and ZUNGARIA). See the various regions for detailed information.

Turkey See ASIA MINOR, RUM, OSMANLIS.

Turks Major ethno-linguistic group of peoples originating from the eastern steppelands of Eurasia, including the founders of the T'U-CHUEH khanates and perhaps several early nomadic peoples of uncertain origins – HUNS, AVARS, BULGARS, KHAZARS and others. After the break-up of the western T'u-Chueh khanate, various Turkish tribes entered the Muslim world as mercenaries and conquerors, notably the SELJUKS and the early OSMANLIS. The bulk of the MONGOL armies which overran Iran and Russia were ethnically Turks, and many dynasties of Turkish origin ruled in various parts of the Islamic world from India to North Africa. The Osmanli Turks, the ruling people of the Ottoman empire, were in fact a complex mixture with a relatively small Turkish racial element, though Turkish-speaking, by the time their empire reached its zenith.

Tuscany Ancient ETRURIA, region of central Italy where many Etruscan city-states flourished. From the 9th century AD it formed a margravate nominally subject to the HOLY ROMAN EMPIRE until its various cities asserted their independence, notably Florence, Pisa and Sienna. Under the MEDICI, Florentine rule was extended over much of the region in the 15th century, and the dynasty obtained the title of Grand Duke of Tuscany in 1569. In the mid-18th century, the last Medici ruler was succeeded by Francis (III) of Lorraine, later Emperor Francis I, and by a branch of his HABSBURG descendants, who temporarily lost Tuscany to Napoleonic

puppets – the BOURBON 'Kings of Etruria' until 1807 and Eliza BONAPARTE as grand duchess until the Habsburg restoration in 1814. The Tuscan state was annexed to the new kingdom of Italy in the mid-19th century. (65)

Tutsi (Watutsi), people of central Africa who established themselves as rulers in the 14th century AD in RWANDA and somewhat later in BURUNDI, dominating the Hutu population. The Tutsi royal dynasties in both kingdoms were overthrown in the 1960s, when the two countries became independent after a period of German and later Belgian control. (129)

Tver (modern Kalinin), city in RUSSIA which became the centre of a RIURIKID principality in the 13th century and whose rulers fought a brief but determined contest with MOSCOW for the throne of SUZDAL-VLADIMIR – they lost the struggle and their lands were later annexed by Moscow in the 15th century. (92i)

Tyre Most famous of the ancient city-kingdoms of Phoenicia (see LEBANON), which flourished from the mid-2nd millennium BC, surviving sieges by the Assyrians and Nebuchadrezzar II of BABYLON, and falling to Alexander the Great after a long and famous siege in 332 BC. The names and dates of some kings of Tyre are known, but a complete list is not available.

Tyrol Alpine region now divided between Austria and Italy. From the 11th century AD it formed a feudal county which was acquired in 1363 by the HABSBURGS and thereafter formed part of the Austrian lands of that dynasty, though sometimes ruled independently until 1665. (40a, e)

U

Udaipur See MEWAR.

Uganda See BUGANDA, BUNYORO, NKORE.

Uighurs Nomadic people who overthrew the eastern T'U-CHUEH khanate in MONGOLIA in the mid-8th century AD and established a state which, unlike most steppe khanates, proved able to co-operate with the Chinese empire – indeed the

Uighur rulers provided troops on more than one occasion to assist the T'ANG government suppress internal disorder in China. In 840, the Uighur supremacy in Mongolia was overthrown by the Kirghiz, but Uighur refugees then established a smaller realm in ZUNGARIA which survived into MONGOL times. (225f)

Ulaid See ULSTER.

Ulster Most northerly of the ancient provinces of Ireland, the major part of it now forming the Northern Ireland region of the United Kingdom. The kingdom of Ulaid, in the eastern area of the province, existed from ancient times until its conquest by the Anglo-Normans in the late 12th century. The west was dominated by the O'NEILL kings of AILECH from the 5th century AD – they survived as minor princes to become Earls of Tyrone in the 16th century. (14b, f)

'Uman (Oman), region of south-eastern Arabia, the major part of which forms the sultanate of 'Uman, whilst the former Trucial 'Uman is now known as the UNITED ARAB EMIRATES. In ancient times the area was sometimes under Persian control before being absorbed into the realm of the CALIPHS in the 7th century AD. In the following century, an independent elective Imamate was established in the region by the Kharijite sect and survived with varying fortunes into the 16th century, when the Portuguese secured a number of coastal strongholds in the area. The YA'RUBID Imams rose to power in the early 17th century, expelling the Portuguese not only from 'Uman but from ZANZIBAR and most of the East African coast also. In 1741 they were succeeded by the AL-BU-SA'ID dynasty, under whose greatest ruler, Sa'id ibn Sultan, 'Umani control was extended over much of the coast of Kenya and Tanzania, including Zanzibar and MOMBASA. On his death in 1856, his realm was split into an East African sultanate based on Zanzibar and abolished in 1964, and an Arabian sultanate which still survives as a monarchy. (179)

Umayyads First Islamic dynasty and the only one to rule the entire Muslim world. They were the dominant branch of the QURAISH clan at Mecca in the time of Muhammad the Prophet and at first hostile to his preaching but eventually became converts to Islam. One member of the family, 'Uthman ibn 'Affan, was an early convert and became the third Orthodox CALIPH, upon whose assassination his relative Mu'awiya ibn Abi Sufyan contested the Caliphate with 'Ali ibn Abi Talib (see 'ALIDS) and founded the Umayyad regime, becoming undisputed CALIPH in 661 AD. Under him and his successors, the Muslim state expanded to control an empire stretching from SPAIN to TRANSOXANIA, though their efforts to take Constantinople and complete the destruction of the Byzantine empire proved unsuccessful. The 'ABBASIDS, closer relatives of the Prophet, rose in revolt in the mid-8th century and rapidly destroyed Umayyad power, almost exterminating the fallen dynasty, but one survivor reached SPAIN and led a counter-revolt, establishing a state independent of the Caliphate. The Spanish Umayyad regime lasted for nearly three centuries, collapsing in the early part of the 11th century, when its lands became divided among the REYES DE TAIFAS. The ZIYADIDS, rulers in the YEMEN in the 9th/10th centuries, also claimed descent from the Umayyads. (44a, 135b, 172a)

Umm-al-Qawain One of the UNITED ARAB EMIRATES, ruled by the AL-'ALI family since about 1800. (178g)

Union of Soviet Socialist Republics See RUSSIA.

United Arab Emirates A federation of small states in south-eastern Arabia, formerly known as the Trucial States. Most were established in the late 18th or early 19th century, and were brought under British protection by treaty in 1892. This status lapsed with their federation as an independent state in 1971. (178)

United Kingdom of Great Britain and Northern Ireland The whole of the British Isles came under a single monarch in 1603, when the STUART king of SCOTLAND succeeded to the kingdoms of ENGLAND and IRELAND. A constitutional union of these states was negotiated in

1707, and the dynasty of HANOVER/ WINDSOR ruled as monarchs of 'Great Britain and Ireland' until the establishment of the Irish Republic (Eire) in the present century. (6d–e)

United States of America The USA is not of course a monarchy, though its presidents do have some of the characteristics of constitutional sovereigns, and when the presidency was established in 1789, several years after rebellion and war had secured the independence of these former colonies from Britain, it was seriously proposed that the first holder of the office, George Washington, should be addressed as 'Your Majesty' – an idea Congress rejected. The list of presidents is included in this work for the convenience of users. (254)

'Uqailids Arab dynasty of which various members and branches ruled a number of towns in northern 'Iraq. The most important line was that of MOSUL, which succeeded the HAMDANIDS at the end of the 10th century AD and was dispossessed by the SELJUKS in 1096. (185b)

Ur Very ancient city of SUMER (southern 'Iraq), ruled by kings from early in the 3rd millennium BC, though the names and dates of its first and second lines of rulers are uncertain. The Third Dynasty of Ur succeeded to the power of AKKAD around 2100 BC, but its power collapsed a century later and the dynasty was finally extinguished by an attack from ELAM. (180b)

Urartu Earliest kingdom in ARMENIA, its name being preserved in 'Ararat'. It was a powerful state, constantly in conflict with ASSYRIA, whose rulers repeatedly invaded but never conquered the region. The kingdom suffered severely from nomadic invasions from the north, and was eventually overrun by the MEDES at the beginning of the 6th century BC. (145)

Urbino Ancient Urbinum, a city in north-central Italy which was granted by Emperor Frederick II of HOHENSTAUFFEN as a county to the MONTEFELTRO family in 1213. Under the last two rulers of the dynasty it became a duchy and a centre of Renaissance culture. The related ROVERESCHI acquired the duchy in 1508, the last of this latter line bequeathing

Urbino to the Pope in 1626. Thereafter it remained part of the PAPAL STATES. (67h–i)

Urfa See EDESSA.

Urtuqids See ARTUQIDS.

Utpalas Hindu dynasty of KASHMIR, successors of the KARKOTAS, rulers of the kingdom from the mid-9th to the early 10th century AD. (209b)

Uttar Pradesh One of the most fertile and populous regions of India, the plain of the middle Ganges and Jumna rivers, central area of most of the major states of the north, including the MAURYA, GUPTA and PRATIHARA empires, the sultanate of DELHI and the MOGHUL empire. Numerous minor dynasties have also ruled in the region – see particularly JAUNPUR and AVADH (Oudh). (200–202, 204)

V

Vaghelas RAJPUT clan which provided a ruling dynasty in GUJARAT in the 13th century, in succession to the CHAULUKYAS. Their state was conquered by the KHALJIS of DELHI at the beginning of the 14th century. The rulers of Rewa in Baghelkhand, central India, were a later branch of the Vaghelas. (208c)

Vakatakas Dynasty which rose to power in the northern DECCAN in the 3rd century AD, after the fall of the SATAVAHANAS, and ruled an extensive state until the early 6th century. (217b)

Valencia Ancient Valentia, city in eastern Spain, capital of one of the 11th century REYES DE TAIFAS kingdoms under the AMIRIDS. At the end of that century, the city fell into the hands of Rodrigo de Bivar (El Cid), who ruled it until his death in 1099, after which it was captured by the ALMORAVIDS. It was annexed to ARAGON in 1238. (48c)

Valois dynasty A branch of the CAPET family, originally counts of Valois, who inherited the throne of FRANCE in 1328. Their claim was disputed by the kings of ENGLAND, giving rise to the Hundred Years' War. Under the last Valois, France became a major European power in the 16th century – they were succeeded in

1589 by a remote BOURBON cousin, Henry of NAVARRE. Branches of the family ruled at various times in BURGUNDY, ORLEANS, ANJOU and PROVENCE. (22a, 24c, h–i, t)

Vandals A Germanic people settled in the 4th century AD in eastern Europe (where SILESIA still bears the name of one section of the Vandals, the Silings). In the early 5th century, they invaded Roman Gaul and Spain with other tribes (probably leaving another trace of their presence in the name of Andalusia), and then crossed over to Africa under the leadership of one of the ablest rulers of the age, Gaiseric (d.477). They captured CARTHAGE and established a kingdom based in what is now Tunisia but extended by naval power to include for a while SICILY, SARDINIA and other islands – they sacked ROME itself in 455. However, the later Vandal kings proved unable to maintain their power, and their dominions were reconquered by a Byzantine expedition in 534. (108)

Vasa dynasty Ruling family of SWEDEN in the 16th/17th centuries. The founder of the line led a revolt which expelled the Danish OLDENBURG kings from the country, and under his grandson Gustav II Adolf Sweden reached a zenith of power and influence in the Baltic, intervening with major effect in Germany during the Thirty Years' War. In 1654, the last of the line, Queen Christina, abdicated in favour of a WITTELSBACH cousin. An elder branch of the dynasty, dispossessed of the Swedish throne in 1604, ruled POLAND until 1668. (18d, 87i)

Vaspurakan A region of eastern ARMENIA ruled from ancient times by the family of the ARTSRUNIDS, who made their domains a kingdom at the beginning of the 10th century AD. The last of the dynasty ceded his lands to BYZANTIUM in 1021. (147b)

Venad Small state in southern KERALA whose rulers claimed to be the heirs of the KULASEKHARA kings of Kerala from the 12th century. In the mid-18th century, the Raja of Venad extended his control over a large territory, establishing an important kingdom thereafter known as TRAVANCORE. (220b)

Vengi Region of the eastern DECCAN between the lower Godavari and Krishna rivers which formed a small kingdom in early times, ruled in particular by the Eastern CHALUKYA dynasty from the 7th century AD until its absorption into the CHOLA empire in the 11th century. (218)

Venice Italian city founded at the time of the fall of the Roman Empire in the west and for some centuries loosely attached to BYZANTIUM, though always autonomous. By the time of the Crusades it had become an important naval and commercial power, acquiring various ports and islands in the eastern Mediterranean, especially as a result of the Fourth Crusade. At its zenith in the 14th/15th centuries, the Venetian empire included CYPRUS and CRETE, Euboea, the Ionian Islands and much of the Dalmatian coast, as well as extensive territory in northern Italy. The Doges (Dukes) of Venice were elected and the city was for practical purposes a republic. During a long period of decline to the end of the 18th century, Venice gradually lost its eastern possessions to the OSMANLI sultans, fighting obstinately but in vain to hold Cyprus in the 16th century and Crete in the 17th, and to recover southern Greece still later. In 1797, the city was seized by Napoleon BONAPARTE, and then passed to the HABSBURGS, becoming part of united Italy in the mid-19th century.

Verona Ancient city in northern Italy which became the centre of an important though short-lived state in the 14th century under the SCALIGERI family. It was annexed by the VISCONTI of Milan in 1387. (67e)

Vien Chang (Vientiane), town in LAOS, capital of the modern state. At the beginning of the 18th century, the kingdom of LAN CHANG split into two states based on Vien Chang and LUANG PRABANG – the Vien Chang kingdom was annexed by THAILAND in 1828, though its territory was later recovered for Laos by the French. (240b)

Vienne Town of south-eastern FRANCE, on the Rhone, centre of the district of Viennois, part of the kingdom of BURGUNDY which became a county nominally subject to the HOLY ROMAN EMPIRE from the 11th century. The rulers adopted the distinctive title of Dauphin, and when the last of the line ceded his lands to the VALOIS family, that title became traditional for the heir to the French throne, the county being known as Dauphiné. (24 o)

Viet-Nam The region of TONKIN, the early home of the Vietnamese, was part of the southern Chinese state of NAN-YUEH, conquered by the imperial HAN regime in 111 BC. Thereafter, Tonkin remained under the control of various Chinese dynasties for about a thousand years, apart from a brief period of independence under the Earlier LI in the 6th century AD. The NGO family led a more permanent break-away from Chinese control in the 10th century, though the first enduring dynasty was the Later Li, succeeded in the 13th century by the TRAN, who beat off repeated efforts by YUAN MONGOL armies to subdue the country. The MING rulers of China temporarily occupied the region in the early 15th century, to be expelled by the Later LE dynasty, who also settled the long Vietnamese duel with the kingdom of CHAMPA by conquering that state (now central Viet-Nam). In 1527, they were deposed by the MAC family, against whom two other powerful families, the TRINH and NGUYEN at once rebelled in the name of Le puppets. The Mac were driven from the capital, Hanoi, in 1592 and confined to a small territory on the Chinese border, Tonkin being controlled by the Trinh and the southern provinces by the Nguyen (who pushed on with southward expansion into the Mekong delta region, COCHIN CHINA, at the expense of CAMBODIA). Both dynasties were swept away by the TAY-SON rebels at the end of the 18th century, but a Nguyen survivor eventually established himself as emperor of all the Vietnamese lands, his family ruling the country at first independently and then under a French protectorate until the monarchy was abolished in 1955. (243)

Vijayanagar Hindu empire of the 14th/17th centuries in southern India, founded after the destruction of the HOYSALA and PANDYA states by Muslim invaders. It was a powerful state, controlling the southern DECCAN, CARNATIC and KERALA, ruled originally by the YADAVA dynasty and

later by other families. In 1565, however, a major advance against the DECCAN SULTANATES ended in a shattering defeat at Talikota and the sacking of Vijayanagar City – the state began to break up, losing northern territory to BIJAPUR and GOLKUNDA and the south to NAYYAK dynasties – the last ARAVIDU kings were only minor rulers. (222)

Vikings Scandinavian sea-raiders who operated in European waters and the North Atlantic in the 9th to 12th centuries AD, at first led by independent chiefs but later very often by the kings of NORWAY, DENMARK and SWEDEN. Viking leaders founded several overseas states – the kingdoms of YORK and DUBLIN, the Earldom of ORKNEY, the Duchy of NORMANDY, the kingdom of MAN and probably the Lordship of the ISLES and the RIURIKID realm in Russia. Viking monarchs ruled briefly in EAST ANGLIA and later occupied the throne of ENGLAND.

Vilhardouins Family of CHAMPAGNE, two of whose members took part in the Fourth Crusade, one later writing the chronicle of the expedition and the other acquiring the principality of Achaea (MOREA) in 1209 (see CRUSADER STATES). On the death of the last of the Morea line in 1278, his state passed to the ANGEVINS of Naples. (85h)

Visconti family Lords of MILAN from the early 14th century and dukes from 1396, a particularly ruthless and fratricidal dynasty which built up an extensive and powerful state in northern Italy before its extinction in 1447. After a brief republican interval at Milan, the related SFORZAS succeeded to the duchy. (63a)

Vishnukundin dynasty Rulers of VENGI in the eastern DECCAN in the 6th and early 7th centuries. AD – their genealogy and chronology is somewhat uncertain. Their lands eventually passed to the Eastern CHALUKYAS. (218c)

Visigoths One of the two divisions of the GOTHS. Under their great king Alaric, they invaded Greece and then Italy, capturing ROME in 410 AD. Later they settled in southern Gaul with their capital at TOULOUSE, conquering most of SPAIN, to which they withdrew after losing nearly all their French territory to the FRANKS. Ruling from TOLEDO, they controlled the Spanish peninsula until the Muslim invasion of 711 – Gothic kings held out against the Arabs for another decade at Narbonne, and Gothic nobles founded the small state of ASTURIAS in 718. (43a)

Vladimir Russian city east of Moscow, successor of Suzdal as the capital of the RIURIKID principality of SUZDAL-VLADIMIR, eventually annexed by MOSCOW. (92h)

Volynia A region of RUSSIA on the Polish frontier which became a RIURIKID principality after the break-up of the KIEV state in the 11th century AD. Its rulers later acquired GALICIA, with which Volynia was merged at the beginning of the 14th century. (92b)

Wadai Region of the SUDAN now part of the Republic of Chad, formerly a sultanate established in the 17th century and a power of considerable importance in the 19th century. It was conquered by the French in 1912 after some years of intermittent fighting. (114c)

Wadiyar dynasty Maharajas of MYSORE, India, whose state was founded at the end of the 14th century and became independent in the late 16th century, on the disintegration of the VIJAYANAGAR empire. For several decades, HAIDAR 'ALI and his son Tipu Sultan reduced the Wadiyar rulers to puppet status, but the dynasty was restored by the British on the fall of Tipu in 1799. In the mid-19th century, Mysore was placed under direct British administration for a while, but again restored to the Wadiyars, whose state was absorbed into India in 1949. (219c)

Walasma' dynasty Family which ruled the sultanate of AWFAT in eastern Ethiopia and northern Somalia from the 13th century – their state was briefly conquered by ETHIOPIA at the beginning of the 15th century, but soon regained its independence, thereafter being generally called Adal. The dynasty was finally overthrown by the Imam Ahmad Gran – see HARAR. (124)

Wales Various small principalities emerged in Wales after the collapse of Roman rule in Britain in the 5th century AD, including that of GWYNEDD in the north, whose ruler Rhodri the Great united all Wales for a brief period in the 9th century. On his death in 878, his lands were divided, one branch of his descendants ruling Gwynedd and another DEHEUBARTH in the south, while a third line later held POWYS independently. The south fell under Anglo-Norman control in the 12th century, though Gwynedd remained largely independent until its conquest by Edward I in the late 13th century. Since that time, the title Prince of Wales has been held by the eldest son of the monarch of England/Great Britain. (8)

Wallachia Region between the Carpathians and the lower Danube, now part of RUMANIA. It emerged as a state in the late 13th century, at first under Hungarian overlordship but soon virtually independent under rulers who resisted the advance of the OSMANLI Turks with success for a while but were gradually subdued in the 15th/16th centuries – the later princes were no more than Turkish provincial governors. Following the expulsion of the Osmanlis from the region by Russia and Austria in the mid-19th century, Wallachia was united with MOLDAVIA to form the principality (later the kingdom) of Rumania. (78)

Wang dynasty Family which rose to power in KOREA in the early 10th century AD on the collapse of the kingdom of SILLA. Korea was attacked and subdued by the MONGOLS after a long struggle in the 13th century, but the Wang dynasty survived and recovered its independence, being overthrown by the YI family in 1392. (235f)

Wangchuk family Until the present century, BHUTAN was ruled jointly by spiritual and temporal leaders (Dharma Raja and Deb Raja) but the system broke down and in 1907 the first of the Wangchuk dynasty was chosen as king under a monarchical regime which still prevails. (213)

Warangal Town in ANDHRA PRADESH, India, capital of the KAKATIYA dynasty which succeeded the CHALUKYAS in the eastern DECCAN in the 12th century. Their state was conquered by the DELHI sultans in the early 14th century, but the independence of the region was almost at once re-established by the REDDI dynasty. (218e)

Warsaw Capital of POLAND since the end of the 16th century and previously one of the main cities of the PIAST principality of MAZOVIA. On the disappearance of the Polish state in 1795 it fell under Russian rule, but Napoleon BONAPARTE created a grand duchy of Warsaw for the WETTIN king of Saxony in 1807, re-annexed by Russia in 1813. The city remained the capital of Russian Poland until the reappearance of the Polish state in 1918. (87e, j)

Wattasid dynasty Sultans of MOROCCO, succeeding their relatives the MARINIDS, for whom they had acted for some time as regents, in 1472. They controlled only the northern plains, however, and early in the next century came into conflict with the SAʿDID family, who took their capital, Fez, in 1549 and extinguished their regime. (112g)

Wei Name of an ancient state and of several dynasties in CHINA:

1 A CHOU STATE in southern Shansi, one of the three kingdoms into which the older state of CHIN was divided at the end of the 5th century BC. It was conquered by CH'IN in 225 BC. (228j)

2 Dynasty and state of the THREE KINGDOMS period, controlling China north of the Yangtze river in the mid-3rd century AD. It was founded by the son of Ts'ao Ts'ao, who had been the real ruler under the last HAN emperor. The Wei were supplanted by the Western CHIN, who later reunited China. (229a)

3 Northern Wei, T'o-Pa (Tabgach Turko-Mongol) dynasty whose founder was a member of the ruling family of the short-lived TAI state, one of the SIXTEEN KINGDOMS – he revived the regime under a new title, and by the mid-5th century AD his successors had conquered much of northern China. In 535 the kingdom split into two parts under the Eastern and Western Wei branches of the dynasty, but

both regimes were soon supplanted by other families, the Northern CH'I and the Northern CHOU respectively. (232a)

Welf dynasty One of the major ruling families of GERMANY from early medieval times, descended from a 9th century Count Welf in BAVARIA – the lands of his family were inherited in 1055 by Welf of ESTE, later duke of Bavaria and brother of the ancestor of the Este dynasty of FERRARA. The Bavarian line ruled intermittently in both Bavaria and SAXONY until both duchies were confiscated from Henry the Lion in 1180. The family retained extensive lands in Saxony, and provided a HOLY ROMAN EMPEROR, Otto IV, for whose nephew a new duchy of Brunswick was created in 1235. For the later history of the dynasty, see BRUNSWICK, HANOVER and HANOVER/WINDSOR. (33a, e–f, 38b)

Western For dynasties thus named, see the main dynastic name – Western LIANG, Western GANGAS, etc.

Western Roman Empire See ROME.

Wessex Early English kingdom in south-western England, founded in the early 6th century AD, though its beginnings are very obscure. In the 9th century, it was the only English state to survive the VIKING invasions, and its rulers gradually extended their control over all of England, completing the effective unification of the country by the annexation of the kingdom of YORK in 954. The exact date from which the kings of Wessex can be regarded as kings of ENGLAND is debatable. (5b)

Westphalia (Westfalen), region of north-western Germany and the name of a short-lived kingdom established in the area by Napoleon BONAPARTE for his brother Jerome in 1807. The state was abolished in 1813, on the disappearance of Napoleonic power east of the Rhine. (33g)

Wettin dynasty German ruling family, originally in Meissen and Thuringia, who acquired the ELECTORATE of SAXE-WITTENBERG in 1423 on the extinction of its ASCANIAN Electors. In the late 15th century, the Wettin lands were divided between the Albertine (Meissen) and Ernestine (Thuringia) branches of the dynasty, the latter holding the electoral

THE WELF AND ESTE DYNASTIES – MALE LINES

Alberto Azzo, Margrave of Este, d.1097

Dukes of Bavaria and Saxony
to 1180

Margraves of Este, Lords
and Dukes of Ferrara to 1597 and
Modena to 1797

Dukes of Brunswick from 1235

Ducal lines of Grubenhagen, Luneburg, Wolfenbuttel, etc.

Electors and Kings of Hanover 1692–1837
Kings of Great Britain 1714–1837

Dukes of Brunswick
1735–1884

Kings of Hanover 1837–1866

Duke of Brunswick 1913–1918

THE WETTIN DYNASTY – MALE LINES

Conrad of Wettin, Margrave of Meissen, d.1157

Margraves of Meissen and Landgraves of Thuringia
Electors of Saxony from 1423

Ernestine Line:
Electors of Saxony to 1547

Albertine Line:
Electors of Saxony from 1547
Kings of Poland 1697–1763

Ducal lines of Weimar, Coburg
Gotha, Meiningen, etc. to 1918

Kings of Saxony 1806–1918
Grand Duke of Warsaw 1807–13

Coburg line

Kings of Great Britain
1901–1952

Kings of Belgium
since 1831

Kings of Portugal
1853–1910

Kings of
Bulgaria
1887–1946

THE WITTELSBACH DYNASTY

Otto of Wittelsbach, Duke of Bavaria, d.1183

Bavarian Line:
Dukes and Electors of Bavaria
1180–1777

Palatine Line:

Counts Palatine of the
Rhine 1214–1559

Counts of
Simmern and
Zweibrucken

Margraves of
Brandenburg
1324–1373

Counts of
Hainault
and Holland
1346–1417

Kings of Sweden
1654–1751

Counts Palatine
of the Rhine
from 1559

Electors and Kings of Bavaria 1777–1918

King of Greece 1832–1862

title until 1547, when it passed to the Albertines, who maintained the unity of their lands and in 1806 adopted the title of King of SAXONY – they also provided two kings of POLAND and a grand duke of WARSAW. The Ernestine lands were divided and redivided into various small duchies – Weimar, Gotha, Coburg, Meiningen and others. Members of the COBURG line founded royal dynasties in BELGIUM and BULGARIA, whilst others of the same branch are the male ancestors of the later BRAGANZA and HANOVER/WINDSOR monarchs. Both the kingdom of Saxony and the Saxon Duchies were abolished in 1918. (33c–d)

White Horde Khanate in western Siberia established in the mid-13th century by the senior line of the JUCHIDS. Very little is known of its history. In 1378, the ruler of the White Horde seized the throne of the GOLDEN HORDE, briefly uniting the two khanates, but the new state at once came into conflict with Timur (see TIMURIDS) and was severely weakened in the long struggle, after which other members of the family founded the KAZAKH khanate in the old White Horde territory. (96a)

Windsor See HANOVER/WINDSOR.

Wittelsbach dynasty Major German ruling family from the 12th/13th centuries, when they acquired the duchy of BAVARIA and the PALATINATE of the Rhine, soon ruled by separate branches of the family who both subdivided their lands among various members on several occasions. The Bavarian line provided a HOLY ROMAN EMPEROR, Ludwig IV and for a while in late medieval times ruled in HAINAULT and BRANDENBURG, Bavaria itself becoming an ELECTORATE in 1623 – another of its rulers was emperor as Charles VII in the 18th century. The Palatine line also provided an emperor, Rupert of the Rhine (d.1410), a king of BOHEMIA and a dynasty of SWEDEN, and eventually inherited the Bavarian lands in 1777. Bavaria became a kingdom in 1806, its monarchy being abolished in 1918. In the mid-19th century, a Wittelsbach ruled for several decades in GREECE. (35, 38c–e)

Wu Name of several states and dynasties in CHINA:

1 One of the CHOU STATES, established in Chekiang province in the 9th century

BC, though its early history is very obscure. It was conquered by its southern neighbour YUEH in 473 BC. (228m)

2 One of the THREE KINGDOMS which became independent on the fall of the HAN empire in the early 3rd century AD. It was conquered in 280 by the Western CHIN. (229b)

3 One of the TEN KINGDOMS of the 10th century AD, based in Kiangsu province, its ruling family being supplanted by the Southern T'ANG in 937. (231a)

Wu-Yueh One of the TEN KINGDOMS in 10th century CHINA, based in Chekiang province, re-annexed to the empire by the SUNG in 978 AD. (231b)

Wurttemberg Region of south-western Germany, former state which was established as a small county in the 11th century, but grew in size and importance after the break-up of the duchy of SWABIA. It became a duchy in 1495 and a kingdom at the beginning of the 19th century. On the fall of the German Empire in 1918, the Wurttemberg monarchy was abolished. (37)

Y

Yadavas Name of two Hindu dynasties:

1 Rulers of MAHARASHTRA in the 12th/13th centuries, successors of the CHALUKYAS in their northern lands. The Yadava state was conquered by the KHALJI sultans of DELHI at the beginning of the 14th century. (217g)

2 First dynasty of VIJAYANAGAR, established in the mid-14th century after the sultans of DELHI had destroyed the Hindu kingdoms of the southern DECCAN and the CARNATIC. The Muslims proved unable to hold their most southerly conquests, however, and the Yadava family rapidly built up a powerful empire which, after overcoming the isolated sultanate of MADURAI, controlled all India south of the BAHMANID state. The family was supplanted by the SALUVAS in 1486. (222a)

Ya'furids Early Arab dynasty which ruled a state centred on SAN'A in the YEMEN from the mid-9th century AD until the end of the next century. (172b)

Yar-Lun dynasty Originally rulers of the small state of Yar-Lun in TIBET, who became kings of the whole country in about 600 AD. Under their rule, Tibet became an important power, invading the borderlands of India and China. The last of the line was a persecutor of Buddhism, being introduced into Tibet at this time, and was assassinated in 842, whereupon the kingdom broke up. Shortly afterwards, a member of the dynasty founded the small state of LADAKH, though the dates and genealogy of its kings are uncertain until the 16th century. (226a)

Ya'rubids Imams of 'UMAN in the 17th/18th centuries. They expelled the Portuguese from MUSCAT and later from much of the East African coast, establishing 'Umani suzerainty over ZANZIBAR and ports on the near-by mainland. They were succeeded by the AL-BU-SA'ID dynasty. (179a)

Yazidids Dynasty of Arab origin which established itself in SHIRVAN (now part of Soviet Azerbaijan) soon after the Muslim conquest of Iran. They assumed the ancient title of Shirvan-Shah and survived with varying fortunes from the mid-9th century AD to the SAFAVID conquest of the region in the 16th century. (157)

Yemen Region of south-western Arabia now divided between the republics of North Yemen and South Yemen. The date at which organized kingdoms first appeared in the area is uncertain, but the states of MA'IN and SABA, with other smaller kingdoms, flourished in the 1st millennium BC. Ma'in was eventually absorbed by Saba, which in combination with the minor state of Dhu Raidan became the kingdom of HIMYAR in the 1st century AD. This realm dominated the whole region until the 6th century, when it became the object of a struggle between the SASANIDS of Iran and the kings of AXUM in Ethiopia. The last Persian viceroy surrendered to the Muslims in 628 AD. However, the 'ABBASID Caliphs soon lost effective control of the Yemen, remote and difficult to administer, as all subsequent conquerors discovered. Very few later rulers, foreign or indigenous, were able to exercise control over the whole region, which became a refuge for SHI'A dynasties. SAN'A in the mountains and ZABID in the plains, and sometimes ADEN also, served as capitals for various regimes usually in conflict. In the late 12th century, the AYYUBID Turan Shah, brother of Saladin, overran the country and briefly united it, but his successors were supplanted by their RASULID viceroys, followed in the mid-15th century by the TAHIRIDS. The OSMANLI Turks held the Yemen from the early 16th to the mid-17th century and again for a short period at the end of the 19th century. Imams of the Zaidi Shi'a sect, the RASSIDS and later the QASIMIDS, intermittently controlled San'a and other regions from medieval times, and at the beginning of the present century a ruler of the latter dynasty established himself as king of the Yemen (the area which now constitutes North Yemen). This monarchy, formally entitled the Mutawakkilite Kingdom, was overthrown by republicans in 1962. Southern Yemen had come into British hands during the 19th century – see ADEN/ADEN PROTECTORATE. (171–172)

Yen Name of an ancient state and several dynasties in CHINA:

1 One of the CHOU STATES, established in the 9th century BC in northern Hopeh province and responsible for the early spread of Chinese influence and culture into Korea and southern Manchuria. It was conquered by CH'IN in 222 BC. (228e)

2 Group of dynasties of Hsien-Pi Turko-Mongol nomad origin who established states in Hopeh/Shansi/Shantung provinces during the SIXTEEN KINGDOMS period of the 4th/early 5th centuries AD. The Earlier Yen supplanted the Later CHAO but fell to the Earlier CH'IN. The Western Yen fell to the Later Yen, themselves supplanted by the Northern Yen. The Southern Yen dominions in Shantung were re-annexed to the Chinese empire by the Eastern CHIN in 410 AD. (230e, i–j, o)

3 Northern Yen, another of the SIXTEEN KINGDOMS, established by a Chinese dynasty in Hopeh in the early 5th century AD. It was annexed by the Northern WEI in 436. (230r)

Yi dynasty Ruling family of KOREA. They supplanted the WANG dynasty in

1392 and survived a determined attempt by JAPAN to conquer their kingdom at the end of the 16th century. However, the Japanese resumed their efforts to gain control of the country some three centuries later and annexed Korea in 1910, abolishing the monarchy. (235g)

Yin dynasty See SHANG.

Ynglings and Skioldungs Legendary interrelated Scandinavian dynasties from which certain historical ruling families were allegedly descended. One branch was that of the ancient kings of Uppsala, the last few of whom were certainly historical and ruled all SWEDEN until their line died out in the mid-11th century AD. The Jarls of Westfold, ancestors of the first royal dynasty of NORWAY, claimed Yngling descent, though the paternity of two 12th-century kings, and thus the Yngling blood of their successors is suspect. Yngling/Skioldung connections were also claimed for the Scandinavian kings of DUBLIN and YORK, the RIURIKIDS of Russia and the GORM dynasty of DENMARK. (17a, 18a)

York English city, ancient Eboracum, headquarters of the Roman Sixth Legion. It was the capital of NORTHUMBRIA in the 7th/9th centuries and then of the VIKING kingdom of York, founded by a son of the legendary Ragnar Lothbrok and ruled by kings of various origins, including a rebel member of the WESSEX dynasty, several kings of DUBLIN and an exiled king of NORWAY. It was finally annexed to the English crown in 954 AD. (5g)

York, House of See ANGEVINS.

Yuan dynasty Dynastic name assumed by the Great Khans of the MONGOLS (see CHINGIS-KHANIDS) in CHINA, formally back-dated to the proclamation of Chingis Khan as ruler of the Mongols in 1206, though his grandsons did not complete the conquest of China until late in the 13th century. The Yuan were expelled from China in 1368 by the MING, but continued to rule as khans in Mongolia until the 17th century, the later line being known to Chinese historians as the Northern Yuan. (225g–h, 227w)

Yueh One of the CHOU STATES, founded in the 6th century BC in Fukien province among people regarded as barbarians by the Chinese of the north. Thus Yueh was not considered a legitimate member of the community of Chou States. Its rulers conquered WU in 473 BC but were themselves overthrown and their lands annexed by CH'U in the next century. (228n)

Yugoslavia (i.e. 'South' Slavia), the name adopted for the large new state formed after the First World War in the western Balkans. It incorporated the kingdom of SERBIA, whose KARA-GEORGEVICH dynasty became its rulers, the provinces and former medieval kingdoms of CROATIA and BOSNIA, the kingdom of MONTENEGRO, whose PETROVICH dynasty was deposed, and other areas. The Yugoslav monarchy was abolished in 1945. (72c)

Z

Zabid Town on the coastal plain of YEMEN, capital of various Muslim dynasties which ruled all or part of the country. (172)

Zagwe dynasty Ruling family of ETHIOPIA in the 12th/13th centuries. Very little is known of its origins and history, though it appears to have supplanted an earlier SOLOMONIC dynasty, one of whose descendants overthrew the Zagwe in the mid-13th century. (122a)

Zahringen dynasty Ruling house of BADEN in south-western Germany, descended from Berchtold of Zahringen, duke of CARINTHIA in the 11th century. The senior line of the family, dukes of Zahringen, soon became extinct, but the margraves of Baden grew increasingly important in the later Middle Ages. In 1527, their lands were divided into two states, Baden-Baden and Baden-Durlach, re-united in the 18th century. Baden became a grand duchy in 1806, but the state was abolished in 1918. (36)

Zand dynasty Chiefs of the Zand tribe and rulers of IRAN (with opposition) in the later 18th century. Karim Khan Zand seized power on the collapse of the AFSHARID regime and proved a very able ruler, but after his death the dynasty was soon overthrown by the QAJARS. (187l)

Zangids Dynasty founded by the ATABEG Zangi, ruler of MOSUL in the early 12th century, who threw off SELJUK control. He conquered the CRUSADER STATE of EDESSA and extended his rule over northern Syria. His sons divided his realm into two sections, one ruled by a Mosul branch of the dynasty, supplanted by the LU'LU family in 1222, and the other based at DAMASCUS and ALEPPO, suppressed by the AYYUBIDS in 1183. Minor Zangid branches ruled at SINJAR and JAZIRAH IBN 'UMAR. (166e, 185g–i)

Zanzibar Like much of the coast of East Africa, the island of Zanzibar had very ancient cultural and commercial links with southern Arabia and was ruled by local Muslim families from medieval times, though little is known of its history before the Portuguese conquest at the beginning of the 16th century. When the Portuguese were driven from most of East Africa by the YA'RUBIDS of 'UMAN at the end of the next century, Zanzibar came under 'Umani overlordship, and in 1828 the AL-BU-SA'ID ruler of 'Uman, Sa'id ibn Sultan, shifted the capital of his maritime empire to the island. On his death in 1856, the domains of the dynasty were split into an Arabian and an East African sultanate, the latter becoming a British protectorate in 1890. Independent Zanzibar abolished its sultanate in 1964. (125c)

Zaragoza (Saragossa, Roman Caesaraugusta), city of north-eastern Spain, capital of one of the REYES DE TAIFAS states of the 11th century, at first under the TUJIBIDS and then the HUDIDS. Later it became the capital of the kingdom of ARAGON. (48m–n)

Zaria Town and Amirate in northern Nigeria, a HAUSA kingdom from medieval times (when the region was called Zazzau). Zaria was conquered by the FULANI at the beginning of the 19th century and became an amirate subject to SOKOTO. However, the former ruling family maintained their independence in part of their lands, which became the small state of ABUJA. (116e, 118b)

Zariadrid dynasty Family which ruled SOPHENE from about 200 BC until their state was annexed by the ARTAXIADS of ARMENIA in the 1st century BC. The names and dates of only some of the rulers are known.

Zayyanids ('Abdul-Wadids), Zenata Berber dynasty of TLEMCEN, centre of a small state in what is now Algeria. They established their independence in the mid-13th century on the break-up of the ALMOHAD empire, and survived repeated efforts to conquer their lands by MARINIDS and HAFSIDS. The kingdom was finally extinguished in the mid-16th century by the OSMANLI Turks. (110c)

Zirids Sanhaja Berber dynasty which rose to power in TUNISIA as viceroys for the FATIMIDS in the 10th century AD but soon became independent. A branch of the family, the HAMMADIDS, broke away as rulers of part of the central MAGHRIB, while another line established a kingdom centred on GRANADA in Spain, one of the REYES DE TAIFAS states. The Spanish state was conquered by the ALMORAVIDS in 1090, and the two North African kingdoms by the ALMOHADS in the middle of the following century. (48l, 109b, 110b)

Ziyadids A family which claimed to be of UMAYYAD descent and ruled much of the YEMEN from ZABID from the early 9th century AD, nominally under 'ABBASID suzerainty. They were supplanted by the NAJAHIDS in the early 11th century. (172a)

Ziyarids Dynasty of DAYLAMI origin whose founder created an extensive but short-lived kingdom in central Iran in the early 10th century at the expense of the SAMANIDS. After his death, the BUYID brothers, originally officers in his service, took over most of his lands, and his successors ruled only a small state in MAZANDARAN, extinguished by the ASSASSINS at the end of the 11th century. (189e)

Zulus Bantu people of South Africa. Originally they were a small tribe, one of many in the area of Natal now called Zululand, until in the early 19th century an outstanding chief, Shaka, began to build a large military empire which extended over most of Natal by the time of his assassination in 1828. His successors became involved in conflicts with the

European settlers in South Africa, and after a hard-fought war the kingdom was annexed by the British in 1879. (133b)

Zungar Kalmaks (Calmucks), federation of steppe nomads which arose in the early 17th century in ZUNGARIA and the Ili region, and dominated neighbouring areas, including western MONGOLIA and the eastern KAZAKH lands until the middle of the next century, when the last Zungar khan was overthrown by the MANCHU rulers of CHINA, who annexed most of his territory. (225i)

Zungaria Region of Central Asia between the Altai and T'ien Shan ranges, historically and strategically important on account of the famous Zungarian Gate pass at its western extremity – the easiest route between the Russian and Mongolian steppelands, used on innumerable occasions by nomadic invaders moving (almost invariably) westward, from the HUNS to the Kalmaks, today a vital border area on the China/U.S.S.R. frontier. A branch of the CHAGHATAI dynasty ruled in Zungaria after the suppression of the main Chaghatai khanate by the TIMURIDS, their control extending at times over KASHGAR and the Tarim Basin. This state broke up in the 16th century, and early in the next century, the khanate of the ZUNGAR KALMAKS arose in the region, its lands being eventually annexed by CHINA. (198e, 225i)

Zuray'ids Arab dynasty of the YEMEN who supplanted the SULAYHIDS in the south, their capital being ADEN. In the late 11th/early 12th centuries, two branches of the dynasty ruled jointly, until one suppressed the other in 1138. The Zuray'id state fell to Turan Shah the AYYUBID in 1173. (172g)

SECTION II

Dynastic Lists

Any list not found immediately by direct use of this table may be located via the number given at the end of the appropriate alphabetical entry in Section I. For ease of usage certain section-titles in the table have been abbreviated. Full headings giving royal titles and date ranges are given within the lists themselves. The principles by which the lists have been organized are explained in the Introduction, p. 8. Abbreviations are listed on p. 158.

EUROPE	*Page*
1 **Rome and Byzantium**	159
2 **The Popes**	163
3 **The Merovingians and the Carolingians**	169
4 **Holy Roman Emperors/German Kings**	171
5 **Britain** Early English Kingdoms	172
6 **Britain** Kings of England/Great Britain	175
7 **Britain** Isle of Man	177
8 **Britain** Wales	177
9 **Britain** The Picts	179
10 **Britain** Dalriada	179
11 **Britain** Kings of Scotland	180
12 **Britain** Orkney and the Isles	181
13 **Ireland** High Kings of Tara	183
14 **Ireland** Provincial Kingdoms	184
15 **Ireland** Kings of Dublin	192
16 **Scandinavia** Denmark	193
17 **Scandinavia** Norway	194
18 **Scandinavia** Sweden	195
19 **Benelux Region** Netherlands	196
20 **Benelux Region** Belgium	197
21 **Benelux Region** Luxemburg	200
22 **France** Kings	201
23 **France** Kings of Burgundy	202
24 **France** Feudal States	202
25 **Monaco** Grimaldi Dynasty	212
26 **Germany** Hohenzollern Emperors	213
27 **Germany** Brandenburg and Prussia	213
28 **Germany** Oldenburg	214
29 **Germany** Holstein	214
30 **Germany** Mecklenburg	214
31 **Germany** Anhalt	215
32 **Germany** Nassau	215
33 **Germany** Saxony, Brunswick and Hanover	215
34 **Germany** Hesse	217
35 **Germany** Counts Palatine of the Rhine	218
36 **Germany** Baden	219
37 **Germany** Wurttemberg	220
38 **Germany** Bavaria	221

		page
39	**Germany** Medieval States	223
40	**Austria** Medieval Rulers	227
41	**Austria** Emperors	228
42	**Liechtenstein** Princes	229
43	**Spain** Visigothic and Suebian Kings	229
44	**Spain** Amirs and Caliphs	230
45	**Spain** Early Asturias and Leon	231
46	**Spain** Navarre	231
47	**Spain** Early Counties	232
48	**Spain** Minor Muslim Kingdoms	233
49	**Spain** Kingdom of Aragon	235
50	**Spain** Rulers of Majorca	235
51	**Spain** Kingdom of Castile-Leon	235
52	**Spain** Nasrids of Granada	236
53	**Spain** Habsburg and Bourbon Kings	237
54	**Portugal** Kings	237
55	**Italy** Early Kings of Rome	238
56	**Italy** Tyrants and Kings of Syracuse	238
57	**Italy** Ostrogothic Kings	239
58	**Italy** Lombard Kings	239
59	**Italy** House of Savoy in Savoy, Piedmont and Sardinia	240
60	**Italy** Modern Kings	241
61	**Italy** Kalbid Amirs of Sicily	241
62	**Italy** Kings of Naples and Sicily	241
63	**Italy** Rulers of Milan	242
64	**Italy** Rulers of Parma	243
65	**Italy** Rulers of Tuscany	243
66	**Italy** Rulers of Ferrara and Modena	244
67	**Italy** Medieval States in the north	245
68	**Italy** Medieval States in the south	248
69	**Czechoslovakia** Rulers of Bohemia	251
70	**Czechoslovakia** Princes of Greater Moravia	252
71	**Hungary** Kings	253
72	**Yugoslavia** Serbia	254
73	**Yugoslavia** Bosnia	254
74	**Yugoslavia** Croatia	255
75	**Yugoslavia** Montenegro	255
76	**Rumania** Transylvania	256
77	**Rumania** Moldavia	256
78	**Rumania** Wallachia	258
79	**Rumania** Modern Rulers	259
80	**Bulgaria** Rulers	259
81	**Albania** Kingdom	260
82	**Greece** Sparta	261
83	**Greece** Kingdom of Macedonia	262
84	**Greece** Kingdom of Epirus	263
85	**Greece** Medieval States	263

page

86 **Greece** Modern Kings   266
87 **Poland** Princes and Kings.   266
88 **Poland** Pomerania   269
89 **Lithuania and Kurland**   270
90 **Russia** Kingdom of Bosphorus   271
91 **Russia** Princes of Kiev   272
92 **Russia** Medieval Principalities   274
93 **Russia** Princes and Tsars of Moscow   279
94 **Russia** Romanov Dynasty   279
95 **Russia** Golden Horde   280
96 **Russia** Successor-States of the Golden Horde   281
97 **Russia** Khanate of Krim (Crimea)   282

AFRICA

98   **Egypt** Pharaonic Dynasties   285
99   **Egypt** Ptolemies   290
100 **Egypt** Tulunids and Ikhshidids   291
101 **Egypt** Fatimid Caliphs   291
102 **Egypt** Ayyubid Sultans   291
103 **Egypt** Mamluk Sultans   292
104 **Egypt** Dynasty of Muhammad 'Ali   293
105 **Libya** Battiad Dynasty of Cyrene   294
106 **Libya** Muslim Dynasties   294
107 **Maghrib** Kings of Numidia   295
108 **Maghrib** Vandal Kings   295
109 **Maghrib** Muslim Dynasties in Tunisia   295
110 **Maghrib** Muslim Dynasties in Algeria   296
111 **Maghrib** Beys of Tunis and Deys of Algiers   298
112 **Maghrib** Muslim Dynasties in Morocco   299
113 **Sudan** Kings of Napata   302
114 **Sudan** Eastern Sultanates   303
115 **Sudan** Kanem-Bornu   304
116 **Sudan** Hausa Kingdoms of Nigeria   306
117 **Sudan** Sultanate of Sokoto   310
118 **Sudan** Fulani Amirates of Nigeria   310
119 **Sudan** Mali and Songhai   313
120 **West Africa** Ashanti and Dagomba   313
121 **West Africa** Benin, Oyo and Dahomey   315
122 **Ethiopia** Imperial Dynasties   317
123 **Ethiopia** Shoa and Harar   319
124 **Somalia** Awfat and Adal   320
125 **East Africa** Muslim States   320
126 **East Africa** Bunyoro   322
127 **East Africa** Nkore and Karagwe   323
128 **East Africa** Buganda   324
129 **East Africa** Rwanda and Burundi   324
130 **Central Africa** Mwene Mutapa Dynasty   325
131 **Central Africa** Kongo Kingdom   326

page

132 **Central Africa** Luba and Lunda States 327
133 **Southern Africa** Bantu kingdoms 328
134 **Madagascar** Merina Rulers 329

ASIA

135 **The Caliphs** Orthodox, Umayyad, 'Abbasid 330
136 **Asia Minor** Hittite Kingdom 331
137 **Asia Minor** Classical Kingdoms 332
138 **Asia Minor** Seljuk Sultans 333
139 **Asia Minor** Danishmendid Amirates 334
140 **Asia Minor** Kingdom of Lesser Armenia 334
141 **Asia Minor** Empire of Trebizond 335
142 **Asia Minor** Anatolian Amirates 336
143 **Asia Minor** Osmanli Sultans of Turkey 338
144 **Cyprus** Lusignan Kingdom 339
145 **Armenia** Kingdom of Urartu 340
146 **Armenia** Kings and Princes 340
147 **Armenia** Minor States 342
148 **Armenia** Muslim Dynasties 343
149 **Georgia** Early Dynasties of Iberia 343
150 **Georgia** Princes and Kings of Iberia 344
151 **Georgia** Abkhazia and Kakheti 345
152 **Georgia** Bagratid Kings 346
153 **Georgia** Later Bagratid Kingdoms 346
154 **Georgia** Mingrelia and Guria 349
155 **Azerbaijan (Soviet)** Shaddadid Dynasty 350
156 **Azerbaijan (Soviet)** Hashimids of Derbend 350
157 **Azerbaijan (Soviet)** Yazidids of Shirvan 350
158 **Azerbaijan (Soviet)** Khanates of Arran 351
159 **Syria-Palestine** Kingdom of Aleppo 352
160 **Syria-Palestine** Kingdom of Damascus 352
161 **Syria-Palestine** Hebrew Kingdoms 352
162 **Syria-Palestine** Seleucid Dynasty 353
163 **Syria-Palestine** Kings of Judaea 354
164 **Syria-Palestine** Kings of Osrhoene 354
165 **Syria-Palestine** Ghassanid Dynasty 355
166 **Syria-Palestine** Muslim Dynasties 355
167 **Syria-Palestine** Crusader States 357
168 **Lebanon** Muslim Dynasties 358
169 **Jordan** Nabataean Kingdom 359
170 **Jordan** Hashimid Kingdom 359
171 **Yemen** Early Kingdoms 359
172 **Yemen** Muslim Dynasties 361
173 **Hijaz** Sharifs of Mecca 365
174 **Central Arabia** Kings of Kindah 367
175 **Central Arabia** Al-Rashid Dynasty 367
176 **Central Arabia** Al-Sa'ud Dynasty 367
177 **Gulf States** Kuwait, Bahrain, Qatar 368

page

178 **Gulf States** United Arab Emirates   369
179 **'Uman** Rulers   370
180 **'Iraq** Early Kingdoms   371
181 **'Iraq** Kings of Mitanni   372
182 **'Iraq** Kings of Babylon   372
183 **'Iraq** Kings of Assyria   375
184 **'Iraq** Lakhmid Kings of Hirah   376
185 **'Iraq and Kurdistan** Muslim Dynasties   377
186 **Iran** Kings of Elam   379
187 **Iran** Imperial Dynasties   381
188 **Iran** Azerbaijan (Persian)   385
189 **Iran** Mazandaran and Gilan   386
190 **Iran** Jibal   389
191 **Iran** Fars   390
192 **Iran** Kirman   390
193 **Iran** Sistan   391
194 **Iran** Khurasan   392
195 **Afghanistan and Northern India**   392
    Bactrian Greek Kings
196 **Indo-Scythians, Indo-Parthians and Kushans**   393
197 **Afghanistan** Muslim Dynasties   394
198 **Transoxania–Turkestan** Rulers   396
199 **Khwarizm/Khiva** Rulers   400
200 **India** Imperial Dynasties of the North   401
201 **India** Sultans of Delhi   403
202 **India** Timurid Moghul Emperors   404
203 **India** The Punjab   404
204 **India** North-Eastern Plain   405
205 **India** Sind and Baluchistan   407
206 **India** Rajastan   408
207 **India** Malwa   414
208 **India** Gujarat and Saurashtra   416
209 **India** Kashmir   419
210 **India** Ladakh   421
211 **India** Nepal   422
212 **India** Sikkim   424
213 **India** Bhutan   424
214 **India** Bengal   425
215 **India** Assam   426
216 **India** Orissa   428
217 **India** Maharashtra   429
218 **India** Andhra Pradesh   433
219 **India** Mysore   436
220 **India** Kerala   438
221 **India** Pallava and Chola Empires   441
222 **India** Vijayanagar Empire   442
223 **India** The Carnatic   443
224 **Ceylon and Maldives** Rulers   445

page

225 **Mongolia** Rulers   450
226 **Tibet** Rulers   453
227 **China** Imperial Dynasties   454
228 **China** Ancient Chinese States   460
229 **China** The Three Kingdoms   469
230 **China** The Sixteen Kingdoms   469
231 **China** The Ten Kingdoms   471
232 **China** Northern Dynasties   473
233 **China** Manchuria   474
234 **China** Kingdom of Nan Chao   475
235 **Korea** Kingdoms and Dynasties   476
236 **Japan** Emperors and Shoguns   480
237 **Burma** Kings   483
238 **Burma** Kingdom of Arakan   486
239 **Thailand** Thai Kingdoms   489
240 **Laos** Laotian Kingdoms   490
241 **Cambodia** Kings   491
242 **Champa** Kings   493
243 **Viet-Nam** Dynasties   495
244 **Malaya** Malay States   498
245 **Sumatra** Sultanates   502
246 **Java** Kingdoms and Sultanates   504
247 **Borneo** Brunei and Sarawak   505
248 **Philippines** Sulu and Maguindanao   506

PACIFIC ISLANDS

249 **Polynesia** Kingdoms   508

THE AMERICAS

250 **Mexico** Rulers   509
251 **Haiti** Kings and Emperors   509
252 **Peru** Incas   510
253 **Brazil** Braganza Emperors   510
254 **United States of America** Presidents   510

A   Adopted (will precede other abbreviations, e.g. AS = Adopted son)
B   Brother
BD   Brother's daughter
BGD   Brother's grandchild via daughter
BGS   Brother's grandchild via son
BS   Brother's son
D   Daughter
DT   Descendant (distant or uncertain link)
DTB   Descendant of brother
F   Father
FB   Father's brother
FBGS   Father's brother's grandchild via son
FBS   Father's brother's son
GD   Grandchild via daughter
GG   Great-grandchild
GS   Grandchild via son
3G/4G/   Great-great-grandchild/Great-great-
5G etc.   great-grandchild, etc.
H   Husband
HBD   Husband of brother's daughter
HD   Husband of daughter (son-in-law)
HGD   Husband of granddaughter via daughter
HSTD   Husband of sister's daughter
HST   Husband of sister
M   Mother
MB   Mother's brother
MSTD   Mother's sister's daughter
MSTS   Mother's sister's son
MST   Mother's sister
N   Nephew (exact link uncertain)
R   Relative (distant or uncertain link)
S   Son
STGD   Sister's grandchild via daughter
STGS   Sister's grandchild via son
STS   Sister's son
ST   Sister
UB   Uterine brother
W   Wife
WB   Wife's brother
WS   Wife's son (stepson)
WSTGD   Wife's sister's grandchild via daughter

Female rulers are marked with an asterisk – e.g. Wu Hou★. In the case of most dynasties, it is possible to draw up a family tree in traditional form from the information given in the right-hand column, and a key to the letter-symbols used is given here. For each ruler is shown his or her relationship (if any and if known) to predecessors in the same list. For example 'S4' means 'son of ruler No. 4 in the same list', and 'B5' means 'brother of No. 5'. It should be specially noted that 'GS' and 'GD' mean, respectively, 'grand*child* via son' and 'grand*child* via daughter' – thus Queen Victoria★ is GS54, grandchild via son of George III, ruler No. 54 of England/Great Britain. Close relationship with the rulers in another list is sometimes indicated to show dynastic origin – Haakon VII of Norway, elected king in 1905, was a son of Frederick VIII of Denmark and is marked 'S49 Denmark'. Some relationships are of course more complicated or more distant – the Roman Emperor Heliogabalus was the grandson, via a daughter, of the sister of Julia Domna, wife of Septimius Severus (WSTGD24), yet the relationship was enough to gain him the throne. James VI of Scotland was a great-great-grandson of Henry VII of England (3G40), his claim to succeed as James I in 1603. Where a ruler has the name of another state in brackets added to his name in a list – e.g. '(of Burgundy)' – this indicates that he also ruled the other state at some stage. Additions without brackets – e.g. 'of Burgundy' – simply indicate family name, origin or nickname.

1 ROME AND BYZANTIUM

a *Emperors* 30 BC–395 AD

1 (C. Julius Caesar – Dictator)	(49–44 BC)	
2 C. Julius Caesar Octavianus *Augustus*	30 BC–14 AD	STGD1
3 *Tiberius* Claudius Nero	14–37 AD	WS2
4 C. Claudius Nero Germanicus *(Caligula)*	37–41	BGS3
5 Tiberius *Claudius* Nero Drusus	41–54	BS3
6 L. Domitius Claudius *Nero*	54–68	WS5
7 Ser. Sulpicius *Galba*	68–69	
8 M. Salvius *Otho*	69.	
9 A. *Vitellius*	69.	
10 T. Flavius *Vespasianus*	69–79	
11 *Titus* Flavius Vespasianus	79–81	S10
12 T. Flavius *Domitianus*	81–96	S10
13 M. Cocceius *Nerva*	96–98	
14 M. Ulpius *Trajanus*	98–117	AS13
15 P. Aelius *Hadrianus*	117–138	AS14
16 T. Aurelius *Antoninus Pius*	138–161	AS15
17 *Marcus Aurelius* Verus	161–180	AS16
18 L. Aurelius *Verus*	161–169	
19 M. Aurelius Antoninus *Commodus*	180–192	S17
20 P. Helvius *Pertinax*	193.	
21 M. *Didius Julianus*	193.	
22 C. *Pescennius Niger*	193–194	
23 D. *Clodius Albinus*	193–197	
24 L. *Septimius Severus*	193–211	
25 M. Aurelius Antoninus *Caracalla*	211–217	S24
26 P. Septimius *Geta*	211–212	S24
27 M. Opellius *Macrinus*	217–218	
28 M. Aurelius Antoninus *Heliogabalus*	218–222	WSTGD24
29 M. Aurelius *Severus Alexander*	222–235	MSTS28
30 C. Julius *Maximinus*	235–238	
31 M. Antonius *Gordianus I*	238.	
32 M. Antonius *Gordianus II*	238.	S31
33 M. Clodius *Pupienus*	238.	
34 D. Caelius *Balbinus*	238.	
35 M. Antonius *Gordianus III*	238–244	GD31
36 M. Julius *Philippus Arabs*	244–249	

37	C. Messius Trajanus *Decius*	249–251	
38	C. Vibius *Trebonianus Gallus*	251–253	
39	C. Vibius *Volusianus*	251–253	S38
40	M. Aemilius *Aemilianus*	253.	
41	P. Licinius *Valerianus*	253–260	
42	P. Licinius Egnatius *Gallienus*	253–268	S41
43	M. Latinius *Postumus* (Gaul)	260–269	
44	T. Fulvius *Macrianus*	260–261	
45	T. Fulvius Quietus	260–261	B44
46	M. Aurelius *Claudius Gothicus*	268–270	
47	L. Aelianus (Gaul)	269.	
48	M. *Aurelius Marius* (Gaul)	269.	
49	M. Piavonius *Victorinus* (Gaul)	269–270	
50	M. Aurelius *Quintillus*	270.	
51	L. Domitius *Aurelianus*	270–275	
52	C. Pius *Tetricus I* (Gaul)	270–274	
53	C. Pius *Tetricus II* (Gaul)	274.	
54	M. Claudius *Tacitus*	275–276	
55	M. Annius *Florianus*	276.	
56	M. Aurelius *Probus*	276–282	
57	M. Aurelius *Carus*	282–283	
58	M. Aurelius *Carinus*	283–285	S57
59	M. Aurelius *Numerianus*	283–284	S57
60	C. Aurelius *Diocletianus*	284–305	
61	M. Aurelius *Maximianus* (1)	286–305	
62	M. Aurelius *Carausius* (Britain)	286–293	
63	*Allectus* (Britain)	293–296	
64	M. Flavius *Constantius Chlorus*	305–306	
65	C. *Galerius* Valerius	305–311	
66	Flavius Valerius *Severus*	306–307	
	M. Aurelius *Maximianus* (2)	306–308	
67	M. Aurelius *Maxentius*	306–312	S61
68	Flavius Valerius *Constantinus I*	306–337	S64
69	C. Flavius Valerius *Licinius*	307–324	
70	Galerius Valerius *Maximinus Daia*	308–313	
71	Flavius Valerius Claudius *Constantinus II*	337–340	S68
72	Flavius Valerius Julius *Constans*	337–350	S68
73	Flavius Valerius Julius *Constantius II*	337–361	S68
74	Flavius Magnus *Magnentius*	350–353	
75	Flavius Claudius *Julianus*	360–363	BS68
76	Flavius Claudius *Jovianus*	363–364	
77	Flavius *Valentinianus I* (West)	364–375	
78	Flavius *Valens* (East)	364–378	B77
79	Flavius *Gratianus* (West)	367–383	S77
80	Flavius *Valentinianus II* (West)	375–392	S77
81	Flavius *Theodosius I*	379–395	
82	Magnus Clemens *Maximus* (West)	383–388	
83	*Eugenius* (West)	392–394	

b *Western Emperors* 395–476

1	Flavius *Honorius*	395–423	s81
2	Flavius Claudius *Constantinus III*	407–411	
3	Flavius *Constantius III*	421.	HD81
4	*Johannes*	423–425	
5	Flavius Placidius *Valentinianus III*	425–455	s3
6	Flavius Ancius *Petronius Maximus*	455.	
7	Flavius Maecilius Eparchius *Avitus*	455–456	
8	Julius Valerius *Majorianus*	457–461	
9	Libius Severianus *Severus*	461–465	
10	Procopius *Anthemius*	467–472	
11	Anicius *Olybrius*	472.	HD5
12	Flavius *Glycerius*	473–474	
13	*Julius Nepos* (in Dalmatia 475–480)	474–475	
14	Flavius Momyllus *Romulus Augustulus*	475–476	

C. = Gaius, L. = Lucius, Ser. = Servius,
M. = Marcus, T. = Titus, A. = Aulus, P. = Publius,
·D. = Decimus

c *Byzantine Emperors* 395–1204

1	Arcadius	395	s81
2	Theodosius II	408	s1
3	Marcianus	450	HD1
4	Leo I	457	
5	Leo II	474	s6
6	Zeno	474–491	HD4
7	Basiliscus	475–476	WB4
8	Anastasius I	491	HD4
9	Justinus I	518	
10	Justinian I	527	STS9
11	Justinus II	565	STS10
12	Tiberius II	578	
13	Mauricius	582	
14	Phocas	602	
15	Heraclius	610	
16	Constantine III	641	s15
17	Heracleonas	641	s15
18	Constans II	641	s16
19	Constantine IV Pogonatus	668	s18
20	Justinian II (1)	685	s19
21	Leontius	695	
22	Tiberius III Apsimar	698	
	Justinian II (2)	705	
23	Philippicus	711	
24	Anastasius II	713	
25	Theodosius III	715	
26	Leo III Isauricus	717	
27	Constantine V Copronymus	741	s26
28	Leo IV	775	s27

29	Constantine VI	780	S28
30	Irene★	797	W28
31	Nicephorus I	802	
32	Stauracius	811	S31
33	Michael I	811	HD31
34	Leo V the Armenian	813	
35	Michael II	820	HD29
36	Theophilus	829	S35
37	Michael III	842	S36
38	Basil I the Macedonian	867	
39	Leo VI	886	S38
40	Alexander	912–913	S38
41	Constantine VII Porphyrogenitus	912–959	S39
42	Romanus I Lecapenus	920–944	
43	Romanus II	959–963	S41
44	Nicephorus II Phocas	963–969	
45	John I Tzimisces	969–976	
46	Basil II Bulgaroctonos	976–1025	S43
47	Constantine VIII	976–1028	S43
48	Zoe★	1028–1050	D47
49	Romanus III Argyrus	1028–1034	H48
50	Michael IV the Paphlagonian	1034–1041	H48
51	Michael V Calaphates	1041–1042	STS50
52	Constantine IX Monomachus	1042–1055	H48
53	Theodora★	1042–1056	D47
54	Michael VI Stratioticus	1056–1057	
55	Isaac I Comnenus	1057–1059	
56	Constantine X Ducas	1059–1067	
57	Romanus IV Diogenes	1068–1071	
58	Michael VII Ducas	1071–1078	S56
59	Nicephorus III Botaniates	1078–1081	
60	Alexius I Comnenus	1081	BS55
61	John II	1118	S60
62	Manuel I	1143	S61
63	Alexius II	1180	S62
64	Andronicus I	1183	BS61
65	Isaac II Angelus (1)	1185	GG60
66	Alexius III	1195	B65
	Isaac II Angelus (2)	1203–1204	
67	Alexius IV	1203–1204	S65
68	Alexius V Ducas	1204.	HD66

d *Latin Emperors at Constantinople 1204–1261*

1	Baldwin I (of Flanders)	1204	
2	Henry	1205	B1
3	Peter of Courtenay	1216	H4
4	Yolande★	1217	ST1
5	Robert	1219	S3/4
6	Baldwin II	1228–1261	B5
7	John of Brienne (K. Jerusalem)	1231–1237	

e *Emperors at Nicaea* 1204–1261

69	Theodore I Lascaris	1204	HD66
70	John III Vatatzes	1222	HD69
71	Theodore II	1254	S70
72	John IV	1258–1261	S71
73	Michael VIII Palaeologus	1259–(1261)	GG66

f *Byzantine Emperors – Palaeologi* 1261–1453

73	Michael VIII (of Nicaea)	1261–1282	
74	Andronicus II	1282–1328	S73
75	Michael IX	1295–1320	S74
76	Andronicus III	1328–1341	S75
77	John V	1341–1391	S76
78	John VI Cantacuzene	1347–1354	
79	Andronicus IV	1376–1379	S77
80	John VII (1)	1390.	S79
81	Manuel II	1391–1425	S77
	John VII (2)	1399–1402	
82	John VIII	1425–1448	s81
83	Constantine XI	1448–1453	s81

2 THE POPES   (A) = Anti-Pope

1	Peter	c.40 AD
2	Linus	c.67
3	Anacletus I	c.76
4	Clement I	c.88
5	Evaristus	c.97
6	Alexander I	c.105
7	Sixtus I	c.115
8	Telesphorus	c.125
9	Hyginus	c.136
10	Pius I	c.140
11	Anicetus	c.155
12	Soter	c.166
13	Eleuterus	c.175
14	Victor I	189
15	Zephyrinus	199
16	Calixtus I	217
17	Urban I	222–230
18	Hippolytus (A)	222–235
19	Pontian	230–235
20	Anterus	235
21	Fabian	236
22	Cornelius	251–253
23	Novatian (A)	251–c.258
24	Lucius	253–254
25	Stephen I	254–257
26	Sixtus II	257–258

27	Dionysius	260
28	Felix I	269
29	Eutychian	275
30	Caius	283
31	Marcellinus	296–304
32	Marcellus I	308
33	Eusebius	309
34	Miltiades	311
35	Sylvester I	314
36	Marcus	335
37	Julius I	337
38	Liberius	352–366
39	Felix II (A)	353–365
40	Damasus I	366–383
41	Ursinus (A)	366–367
42	Siricius	384
43	Anastasius I	399
44	Innocent I	401
45	Zosimus	417
46	Boniface I	418–422
47	Eulalius (A)	418–419
48	Celestine I	422
49	Sixtus III	432
50	Leo I	440
51	Hilarius	461
52	Simplicius	468
53	Felix III	483
54	Gelasius I	492
55	Anastasius II	496
56	Symmachus	498–514
57	Laurentius (A)	498–505
58	Hormisdas	514
59	John I	523
60	Felix IV	526
61	Boniface II	530–532
62	Dioscurus (A)	530.
63	John II	533
64	Agapetus I	535
65	Silverius	536
66	Vigilius	537
67	Pelagius I	556
68	John III	561
69	Benedict I	575
70	Pelagius II	579
71	Gregory I	590
72	Sabinian	604
73	Boniface III	607
74	Boniface IV	608
75	Deusdedit	615
76	Boniface V	619

77	Honorius I	625–638
78	Severinus	640
79	John IV	640
80	Theodore I	642
81	Martin I	649
82	Eugenius I	655
83	Vitalian	657
84	Adeodatus	672
85	Donus	676
86	Agatho	678
87	Leo II	681
88	Benedict II	684
89	John V	685
90	Conon	686–687
91	Theodore II (A)	687.
92	Paschal I (A)	687–692
93	Sergius I	687–701
94	John VI	701
95	John VII	705
96	Sisinnius	708
97	Constantine	708
98	Gregory II	715
99	Gregory III	731
100	Zacharias	741
101	Stephen II	752
102	Paul I	757
103	Constantine (A)	767
104	Philip (A)	767
105	Stephen III	767
106	Adrian I	772
107	Leo III	795
108	Stephen IV	816
109	Paschal I	817
110	Eugenius II	824
111	Valentine	827
112	Gregory IV	827
113	John VIII (A)	844
114	Sergius II	844
115	Leo IV	847
116	Benedict III	855–858
117	Anastasius III (A)	855.
118	Nicholas I	858
119	Adrian II	867
120	John VIII	872
121	Marinus I	882
122	Adrian III	884
123	Stephen V	885
124	Formosus	891
125	Boniface VI	896
126	Stephen VI	896

127	Romanus	897
128	Theodore II	897
129	John IX	898
130	Benedict IV	900
131	Leo V	903
132	Christopher	903
133	Sergius III	904
134	Anastasius III	911
135	Lando	913
136	John X	914
137	Leo VI	928
138	Stephen VII	929
139	John XI	931
140	Leo VII	936
141	Stephen IX	939
142	Marinus II	942
143	Agapetus II	946
144	John XII	955
145	Leo VIII	963
146	Benedict V	964
147	John XIII	965
148	Benedict VI	973
149	Benedict VII	974
150	John XIV	983
151	Boniface VII	984
152	John XV	985
153	Gregory V	996–999
154	John XVI (A)	996–998
155	Sylvester II	999
156	John XVII	1003
157	John XVIII	1003
158	Sergius IV	1009
159	Benedict VIII	1012–1024
160	Gregory VI (A)	1012.
161	John XIX	1024
162	Benedict IX	1033
163	Sylvester III	1045
164	Gregory VI	1045
165	Clement II	1046
166	Damasus II	1048
167	Leo IX (Bruno of Toul)	1049
168	Victor II (Gebhard of Hirschberg)	1055
169	Stephen X (Frederick of Lorraine)	1057
170	Benedict X (John of Tusculum)	1058
171	Nicholas II (Gerhard of Burgundy)	1058
172	Alexander II (Anselmo da Baggio)	1061–1073
173	Honorius II (A) (Peter Cadalus)	1061–1064
174	Gregory VII (Hildebrand)	1073–1085
175	Clement III (A) (Guibert of Ravenna)	1080–1100
176	Victor III (Desiderius)	1086–1087

177	Urban II (Odo of Chatillon)	1088–1099
178	Paschal II (Raniero da Bieda)	1099–1118
179	Theodoric (A)	1100–1102
180	Albert (A)	1102.
181	Sylvester IV (A)	1105.
182	Gelasius II (John Coniolo)	1118–1119
183	Gregory VIII (A) (Maurice of Braga)	1118–1121
184	Calixtus II (Guy of Burgundy)	1119–1124
185	Honorius II (Lamberto dei Fagnani)	1124–1130
186	Celestine II (A)	1124.
187	Innocent II (Gregory Papareschi)	1130–1143
188	Anacletus II (A)	1130–1138
189	Victor IV (A)	1138.
190	Celestine II (Guido di Castello)	1143
191	Lucius II (Gherardo Caccianemici)	1144
192	Eugenius III (Bernado Paganelli)	1145
193	Anastasius IV (Corrado della Subarra)	1153
194	Adrian IV (Nicholas Breakspear)	1154
195	Alexander III (Orlando Bandinelli)	1159–1181
196	Victor IV (Ottaviano di Monticelli) (A)	1159–1164
197	Paschal III (Guido of Crema) (A)	1164–1168
198	Calixtus III (John of Struma) (A)	1168–1178
199	Innocent III (Lando da Sessa) (A)	1179–1180
200	Lucius III (Ubaldo Allucingoli)	1181
201	Urban III (Uberto Crivelli)	1185
202	Gregory VIII (Alberto del Morra)	1187
203	Clement III (Paolo Scolari)	1187
204	Celestine III (Giacinto Boboni-Orsini)	1191
205	Innocent III (Lotario di Segni)	1198
206	Honorius III (Cencio Savelli)	1216
207	Gregory IX (Ugolino di Segni)	1227
208	Celestine IV (Goffredo Castiglione)	1241
209	Innocent IV (Sinibaldo de' Fieschi)	1243
210	Alexander IV (Rinaldo di Segni)	1254
211	Urban IV (Jacques Pantaleon)	1261
212	Clement IV (Guy le Gros Foulques)	1265–1268
213	Gregory X (Tebaldo Visconti)	1271
214	Innocent V (Pierre de Champagni)	1276
215	Adrian V (Ottobono Fieschi)	1276
216	John XXI (Pietro Rebuli-Giuliani)	1276
217	Nicholas III (Giovanni Gaetano Orsini)	1277
218	Martin IV (Simon Mompitie)	1281
219	Honorius IV (Giacomo Savelli)	1285
220	Nicholas IV (Girolamo Masci)	1288–1292
221	Celestine V (Pietro Angelari da Murrone)	1294
222	Boniface VIII (Benedetto Gaetani)	1294
223	Benedict XI (Niccolo Boccasini)	1303
224	Clement V (Raymond Bertrand de Got)	1305
225	John XXII (Jacques Dueze)	1316–1334
226	Nicholas V (Pietro di Corbara) (A)	1328–1330

227	Benedict XII (Jacques Fournier)	1334
228	Clement VI (Pierre Roger de Beaufort)	1342
229	Innocent VI (Etienne Aubert)	1352
230	Urban V (William de Grimord)	1362
231	Gregory XI (Pierre Roger de Beaufort)	1370
232	Urban VI (Bartolemeo Prignano)	1378–1389
233	Clement VII (Robert of Geneva) (A)	1378–1394
234	Boniface IX (Pietro Tomacelli)	1389–1404
235	Benedict XIII (Pedro de Luna) (A)	1394–1423
236	Innocent VII (Cosmato de' Migliorati)	1404–1406
237	Gregory XII (Angelo Correr)	1406–1415
238	Alexander V (Petros Philargi) (A)	1409–1410
239	John XXIII (Baldassare Cossa) (A)	1410–1415
240	Martin V (Ottone Colonna)	1417–1431
241	Clement VIII (Gil Sanchez Muñoz) (A)	1423–1429
242	Benedict XIV (Bernard Garnier) (A)	1424.
243	Eugenius IV (Gabriele Condulmer)	1431–1447
244	Felix V (Amadeus VIII of Savoy) (A)	1439–1449
245	Nicholas V (Tommaso Parentucelli)	1447–1455
246	Calixtus III (Alonso Borgia)	1455
247	Pius II (Aeneas Silvio de' Piccolomini)	1458
248	Paul II (Pietro Barbo)	1464
249	Sixtus IV (Francesco della Rovere)	1471
250	Innocent VIII (Giovanni Battista Cibo)	1484
251	Alexander VI (Rodrigo Borgia)	1492
252	Pius III (Francesco Todoeschini-Piccolomini)	1503
253	Julius II (Giuliano della Rovere)	1503
254	Leo X (Giovanni de' Medici)	1513
255	Adrian VI (Hadrian Florensz)	1522
256	Clement VII (Giulio de' Medici)	1523
257	Paul III (Alessandro Farnese)	1534
258	Julius III (Giovanni Maria Ciocchi del Monte)	1550
259	Marcellus II (Marcello Cervini)	1555
260	Paul IV (Gian Pietro Caraffa)	1555
261	Pius IV (Giovanni Angelo de' Medici)	1559
262	Pius V (Antonio Michele Ghislieri)	1566
263	Gregory XIII (Ugo Buoncompagni)	1572
264	Sixtus V (Felice Peretti)	1585
265	Urban VII (Giambattista Castagna)	1590
266	Gregory XIV (Niccolo Sfondrati)	1590
267	Innocent IX (Gian Antonio Facchinetti)	1591
268	Clement VIII (Ippolito Aldobrandini)	1592
269	Leo XI (Alessandro de' Medici-Ottaiano)	1605
270	Paul V (Camillo Borghese)	1605
271	Gregory XV (Alessandro Ludovisi)	1621
272	Urban VIII (Maffeo Barberini)	1623
273	Innocent X (Giambattista Pamfili)	1644
274	Alexander VII (Fabio Chigi)	1655
275	Clement IX (Giulio Rospigliosi)	1667
276	Clement X (Emilio Altieri)	1670

277	Innocent XI (Benedetto Odescalchi)	1676
278	Alexander VIII (Pietro Ottoboni)	1689
279	Innocent XII (Antonio Pignatelli)	1691
280	Clement XI (Gian Francesco Albani)	1700
281	Innocent XIII (Michelangelo dei Conti)	1721
282	Benedict XIII (Pietro Francesco Orsini)	1724
283	Clement XII (Lorenzo Corsini)	1730
284	Benedict XIV (Prospero Lambertini)	1740
285	Clement XIII (Carlo Rezzonico)	1758
286	Clement XIV (Lorenzo Ganganelli)	1769
287	Pius VI (Gianangelo Braschi)	1775
288	Pius VII (Luigi Barnaba Chiaramonti)	1800
289	Leo XII (Annibale della Genga)	1823
290	Pius VIII (Francesco Saverio Castiglioni)	1829
291	Gregory XVI (Bartolemeo Alberto Cappellari)	1831
292	Pius IX (Giovanni Mastai-Ferretti)	1846
293	Leo XIII (Gioacchino Pecci)	1878
294	Pius X (Giuseppe Sarto)	1903
295	Benedict XV (Giacomo della Chiesa)	1914
296	Pius XI (Achille Ratti)	1922
297	Pius XII (Eugenio Pacelli)	1939
298	John XXIII (Angelo Roncalli)	1958
299	Paul VI (Giovanni Battista Montini)	1963
300	John Paul I (Albino Luciani)	1978
301	John Paul II (Karol Wojtyla)	1978

3 THE MEROVINGIANS AND THE CAROLINGIANS

a *The Merovingian Dynasty (France and Rhineland) c. 457–751*

1	Childeric I	c.457	
2	Clovis I	481	S1
3	Theodoric I (Rheims)	511–534	S2
4	Chlodomir (Orleans)	511–524	S2
5	Childebert (Paris)	511–558	S2
6	Chlotar I (Soissons; sole king 558)	511–561	S2
7	Theodebert I (Austrasia)	534–548	S3
8	Theodebald (Austrasia)	548–555	S7
9	Charibert I (Paris)	561–567	S6
10	Guntram (Burgundy)	561–592	S6
11	Sigebert (Metz)	561–575	S6
12	Chilperic I (Soissons)	561–584	S6
13	Childebert II (Austrasia; Burgundy 593)	575–595	S11
14	Chlotar II (Soissons; sole king 613–23)	584–629	S12
15	Theodebert II (Austrasia)	595–612	S13
16	Theodoric II (Burgundy; Austrasia 612)	595–613	S13
17	Dagobert I (Austrasia 623–34; Neustria 632–39)	623–639	S14
18	Charibert II (Aquitaine)	629–632	S14
19	Sigebert II (Austrasia)	634–656	S17
20	Clovis II (Neustria and Burgundy)	639–656	S17

21 Dagobert II (Austrasia) (1)	656–661	S19
22 Chlotar III (Neustria)	657–673	S20
23 Childeric II (Austrasia)	661–675	S20
24 Theodoric III (Neustria; Austrasia 679)	673–690	S20
Dagobert II (Austrasia) (2)	676–679	
25 Clovis III	690–694	S24
26 Childebert III	694–711	S24
27 Dagobert III	711–715	S26
28 Chilperic II (Neustria)	715–721	S23
29 Chlotar IV (Austrasia)	718–719	?S22
30 Theodoric IV	721–737	S27
31 Childeric III	743–751	?S28

b *The Carolingians: Kings in France, Germany and Italy 751–1012*
(including several rulers distantly related or unrelated to the dynasty)

1 Pepin the Short	751–768	
2 Carloman	768–771	S1
3 Charlemagne (Charles I; Emperor 800)	768–814	S1
4 Charles (France and Saxony)	781–811	S3
5 Pepin (Italy and Bavaria)	781–810	S3
6 Louis I (Aquitaine; Emperor 813)	781–840	S3
7 Bernard (Italy)	813–817	S5
8 Louis (Germany)	817–876	S6
9 Lothair I (Lotharingia and Italy; Emperor 840)	817–855	S6
10 Pepin I (Aquitaine)	817–838	S6
11 Pepin II (Aquitaine)	838–848	S10
12 Charles II (France; Emperor 875)	840–877	S6
13 Louis II (Italy; Emperor 855)	855–875	S9
14 Lothair II (Lotharingia)	855–869	S9
15 Charles (Provence)	855–863	S9
16 Carloman (Bavaria)	876–880	S8
17 Louis (Saxony)	876–882	S8
18 Charles III (Swabia; Emperor 884)	876–887	S8
19 Louis II (France)	877–879	S12
20 Louis III (France)	879–882	S19
21 Carloman (France)	879–884	S19
22 Boso of Vienne (Provence)	879–887	HD13
23 Arnulf (Germany) (Emperor 896)	887–899	S16
24 Berengar I of Friuli (Italy) (1)	888–889	GD6
25 Louis (Provence; Italy 900–2; Emperor 901)	887–928	S22
26 Odo (France)	887–898	
27 Guy (of Spoleto) (Italy; Emperor 891)	889–894	
28 Lambert (of Spoleto) (Italy; Emperor 894)	894–898	S27
29 Zwentibold (Lotharingia)	895–900	S23
30 Charles the Simple (France)	898–922	S19
31 Louis the Child (Germany)	899–911	S23
Berengar I (Italy; Emperor 915) (2)	898–924	
32 Robert I (France)	922–923	B26
33 Raoul (France)	923–936	HD32
34 Rudolf (II of Burgundy) (Italy)	922–926	

35 Hugh of Arles (Italy)	925–947	GD14
36 Louis IV (France)	936–954	S30
37 Lothair of Arles (Italy)	947–950	S35
38 Berengar II of Ivrea (Italy)	950–961	GD24
39 Adalbert of Ivrea (Italy)	950–961	S38
40 Lothair (France)	954–986	S36
41 Charles (Duke of Lower Lorraine)	978–991	S36
42 Louis V (France)	986–987	S40
43 Odo (Duke of Lower Lorraine)	991–1012	S41

4 HOLY ROMAN EMPERORS/GERMAN KINGS   (A = Anti-king)

1 Conrad I (of Franconia)	911	
2 Henry I the Fowler (of Saxony)	919	
3 Otto I the Great	936	S2
4 Otto II	973	S3
5 Otto III	983	S4
6 Henry II (of Bavaria)	1002	GG2
7 Conrad II (of Franconia)	1024	3G3
8 Henry III	1039	S7
9 Henry IV	1056–1106	S8
10 Rudolf (of Swabia) (A)	1077–1080	HD8
11 Herman (of Salm; s3 Luxemburg) (A)	1081–1093	
12 Conrad of Franconia (A)	1093–1101	S9
13 Henry V	1106–1125	S9
14 Lothair III of Supplinburg	1125–1137	
15 Conrad III of Hohenstauffen (D. Franconia)	1138–1152	GD9
16 Frederick I Barbarossa (D. Swabia)	1152–1190	BS15
17 Henry VI	1190–1197	S16
18 Philip (of Swabia)	1198–1208	S16
19 Otto IV of Saxony	1198–1218	
20 Frederick II (of Sicily)	1212–1250	S17
21 Henry Raspe (of Thuringia) (A)	1246–1247	
22 William (II of Holland) (A)	1247–1256	
23 Conrad IV	1250–1254	S20
24 Richard of Cornwall (s28 England)	1257–1272	
25 Alfonso (X of Castile)	1257–1273	
26 Rudolf I of Habsburg	1273–1291	
27 Adolf (of Nassau)	1292–1298	
28 Albert I (of Austria)	1298–1308	S26
29 Henry VII (IV of Luxemburg)	1308–1313	
30 Ludwig the Bavarian (of Upper Bavaria)	1314–1347	
31 Frederick (II of Austria) (A)	1314–1330	S28
32 Charles IV (of Luxemburg)	1346–1378	GS29
33 Gunther (of Schwarzburg) (A)	1349.	
34 Wenceslas (of Bohemia)	1378–1400	S32
35 Frederick (of Brunswick-Luneburg) (A)	1400.	
36 Rupert (III of the Palatinate)	1400–1410	
37 Sigismund (of Bohemia-Hungary)	1410–1437	S32
38 Jobst (of Moravia) (A)	1410–1411	BS32

39	Albert II (V of Austria)	1437–1439	3G28
40	Frederick III (of Styria)	1440	3G28
41	Maximilian I	1493	S40
42	Charles V (I of Spain)	1519	GS41
43	Ferdinand I	1558	B42
44	Maximilian II	1564	S43
45	Rudolf II	1576	S44
46	Matthias	1612	S44
47	Ferdinand II (of Styria)	1619	BS44
48	Ferdinand III	1637	S47
49	Leopold I	1658	S48
50	Joseph I	1705	S49
51	Charles VI	1711–1740	S49
52	Charles VII (of Bavaria)	1742	HD50
53	Francis I (III of Lorraine)	1745	HD51
54	Joseph II	1765	S53
55	Leopold II	1790	S53
56	Francis II	1792–1806	S55

5 **BRITAIN** EARLY ENGLISH KINGDOMS

a *Kings of Kent c. 450–825*

1	Hengest	c.450	
2	Oisc	c.488	?S1
3	Octa	c.512	S2
4	Eormanric	?	S3
5	Ethelbert I	560	S4
6	Eadbald	616	S5
7	Earconbert	640	S6
8	Egbert I	664	S7
9	Hlothere	673	S7
10	Eadric	685–686	S8
11	Wihtred	690–725	S8
12	Ethelbert II	725–762	S11
13	Eadbert I	725–?761	S11
14	Egbert II	c.765–780	
15	Ealhmund (F18 Wessex)	c.784–?	
16	Eadbert II Praen	796–798	
17	Cuthred (B12 Mercia)	798–807	
18	Baldred	?–825	

b *Kings of Wessex c.519–829*

1	Cerdic	c.519	
2	Cynric	534	S1/GS1
3	Ceawlin	560	S2
4	Coelric	593	GS2
5	Ceolwulf	597	B4
6	Cynegils	611	S5
7	Cenwalh	643	S6

8 Seaxburh★	672	W7
9 Aescwine	674	DT2
10 Centwine	676	S6
11 Caedwalla	685	DT3
12 Ine	688	DT3
13 Aethelheard	726	DTI
14 Cuthred	740	DTI
15 Sigebert	756	DTI
16 Cynewulf	757	DTI
17 Beorhtric	786	DTI
18 Egbert (K. England 829; s15 Kent)	802–(839)	DTB12

c *Kings of Mercia c.606–880*

1 Cearl	c.606	
2 Penda	626–654	
3 Eowa	626–642	B2
4 Wulfhere	657	S2
5 Ethelred	674	S2
6 Coenred	704	S4
7 Ceolred	709	S5
8 Ethelbald	716	GS3
9 Beornred	757	
10 Offa	757	3G3
11 Ecgfrith	796	S10
12 Coenwulf	796	DTB2
13 Ceolwulf I	821	B11
14 Beornwulf	823	
15 Ludecan	825	
16 Wiglaf	827	
17 Beorhtwulf	840	
18 Burgred	852	
19 Ceolwulf II	874–c.880	

d *Kings of Essex c.600–825*

1 Saebert	c.600	
2 Sexred	c.616–617	S1
3 Saeward	c.616–617	S1
4 Sigebert I	c.617–653	S3
5 Sigebert II	c.653–?	
6 Swithelm	?	
7 Sighere	c.664–680	S4
8 Sebbe	c.664–694	
9 Sigeheard	c.694–?	S8
10 Swaefred	c.694–?	S8
11 Offa	?–c.709	S7
12 Saelred	c.709–746	S5
13 Swithred	c.746–?	DT8
14 Sigeric	?–c.799	S12
15 Sigered	c.799–825	S14

e *Kings of East Anglia c.600–902*

1	Redwald	c.600–616	
2	Earpwald	c.616–627	S1
3	Sigebert	c.630–?	
4	Ecgric	?	
5	Anna	?–654	BS1
6	Ethelhere	654.	B5
7	Ethelwold	654–664	B5
8	Aldwulf	664–713	?S6
9	Alfwold	713–749	S8
10	Beorna	c.749–?	
11	Ethelred	?	
12	Ethelbert	?–794	S11
13	Eadwald	c.819–828	
14	Athelstan	c.828–837	
15	Ethelweard	c.837–850	
16	Edmund	855–870	
17	Guthrum	880–890	
18	Eric	890–902	S17

f *Kings of Northumbria c.547–878*

1	Ida (Bernicia)	c.547–568	
2	Aelle (Deira)	c.560–588	
3	Ethelric (Bernicia)	568–572	S1
4	Ethelfrith	593–616	S3
5	Edwin	616–632	S2
6	Eanfrith (Bernicia)	632–633	S4
7	Osric (Deira)	632–633	BS2
8	Oswald	633	S4
9	Oswiu	641	S4
10	Ecgfrith	670	S9
11	Aldfrith	685	S9
12	Osred I	704	S11
13	Cenred	716	DT1
14	Osric	718	?S11
15	Ceolwulf	729	B13
16	Eadbert	737	FBS13
17	Oswulf	758	S16
18	Ethelwald Moll	758	
19	Alhred	765	DT1
20	Ethelred I (1)	774	S18
21	Elfwald I	779	S17
22	Osred II	788	S19
	Ethelred I (2)	790	
23	Osbald	796	
24	Eardwulf	796	
25	Elfwald II	806	
26	Eanred	808	S24

27	Ethelred II	840	s26
28	Osbert	849	
29	Aelle II	862	
30	Egbert I	867	
31	Ricsig	873	
32	Egbert II	876–c.878	

g *Kings of York 875–954*

1	Halfdan Ragnarson (of Dublin)	875	
2	Guthred	883	
3	Siegfred	894	
4	Ethelwald (s5 England)	c.899	
5	Halfdan II	902–909	
6	Eowils	902–909	B5
7	Ivar	902–909	B5
8	Ragnald	919	BGS1
9	Sitric Caoch (of Dublin)	921	B8(?)
10	Guthfrith (of Dublin)	927	B9
11	Athelstan (of England)	927	
12	Anlaf Guthfrithson (of Dublin)	939	S10
13	Anlaf Sitricson (of Dublin) (1)	941	S9
14	Ragnald Guthfrithson	943	S10
15	Edmund (of England)	944	
16	Edred (of England)	946	
17	Eric Bloodaxe (of Norway) (1)	948	
	Anlaf Sitricson (2)	949	
	Eric Bloodaxe (2)	952–954	

6 **BRITAIN** KINGS OF ENGLAND/GREAT BRITAIN

a *Saxon and Danish Kings 829–1066*

1	Egbert (of Wessex)	829	
2	Ethelwulf	839–858	S1
3	Ethelbald	855–860	S2
4	Ethelbert	858–866	S2
5	Ethelred I	866	S2
6	Alfred the Great	871	S2
7	Edward the Elder	899	s6
8	Athelstan	925	S7
9	Edmund	939	S7
10	Edred	946	S7
11	Edwy	955	S9
12	Edgar (K. in Mercia 957–959)	959	S9
13	Edward the Martyr	975	S12
14	Ethelred II Redeless ('Unready') (1)	978	S12
15	Sweyn (Sven Forkbeard of Denmark)	1013	
	Ethelred II (2)	1014	
16	Edmund Ironside	1016	S14
17	Canute (Knut the Great of Denmark)	1016	S15

18	Harold I Harefoot	1035	S17
19	Hardecnut (Harthacnut of Denmark)	1040	S17
20	Edward the Confessor	1042	S14
21	Harold II Godwinson	1066.	WB20

b *Norman and Plantagenet Kings 1066–1485*

22	William I the Conqueror (of Normandy)	1066	
23	William II Rufus	1087	S22
24	Henry I	1100	S22
25	Stephen of Boulogne	1135	GD22
26	Henry II Plantagenet (of Anjou)	1154	GD24
27	Richard I Lionheart	1189	S26
28	John	1199	S26
29	Henry III	1216	S28
30	Edward I	1272	S29
31	Edward II	1307	S30
32	Edward III	1327	S31
33	Richard II	1377	GS32
34	Henry IV of Lancaster	1399	GS32
35	Henry V	1413	S34
36	Henry VI (1)	1422	S35
37	Edward IV (1) of York	1461	3G32
	Henry VI (2)	1471	
	Edward IV (2)	1471	
38	Edward V	1483	S37
39	Richard III	1483–1485	B37

c *Tudor Dynasty 1485–1603*

40	Henry VII	1485	4G32
41	Henry VIII	1509	S40
42	Edward VI	1547	S41
43	Mary I★	1553	D41
44	Elizabeth I★	1558–1603	D41

d *Stuart Dynasty 1603–1714*

45	James I (VI of Scotland)	1603	3G40
46	Charles I	1625–1649	S45
	(Commonwealth)	——	
47	Charles II	1660	S46
48	James II	1685	S46
49	William III of Orange	1689–1702	GD46/H50
50	Mary II★	1689–1694	D48
51	Anne★	1702–1714	D48

e *House of Hanover/Windsor since 1714*

52	George I (of Hanover)	1714	GG45
53	George II	1727	S52
54	George III	1760	GS53
55	George IV	1820	S54

56	William IV	1830	S54
57	Victoria★	1837	GS54
58	Edward VII	1901	S57
59	George V	1910	S58
60	Edward VIII	1936	S59
61	George VI	1936	S59
62	Elizabeth II★	1952	D61

7 **BRITAIN** ISLE OF MAN – KINGS OF MAN 1079–1265

1	Godred I Crovan	1079	
2	Lagman	1095	S1
3	Donald	1096	
4	Magnus (III of Norway)	1098	
5	Olaf I	1103	S1
6	Godred II (1)	1152	S5
7	Somerled (of the Isles)	1158	
	Godred II (2)	1164	
8	Reginald I	1187	S6
9	Olaf II	1226	S6
10	Harald I	1237	S9
11	Reginald II	1249	S9
12	Harald II	1249–1250	
13	Magnus II	1252–1265	S9

8 **BRITAIN** WALES

a *Princes of Gwynedd c.500–1283*

1	Cadwallon Lawhir	c.500	
2	Maelgwn Hir	c.517	S1
3	Rhun Hir	547	S2
4	Beli ap Rhun	?–599	S3
5	Iago ap Beli	?–616	S4
6	Cadfan ab Iago	616	S5
7	Cadwallon ap Cadfan	625	S6
8	Cadafael Cadomedd	633	
9	Cadwaladr Fendigaid	654	S7
10	Idwal Iwrch	664	S9
11	Rhodri Molwynog	?–754	S10
12	Hywel ap Rhodri	754–825	S11
13	Cynan Tindaethwy	754–816	S11
14	Merfyn Frych	825	GD13
15	Rhodri Mawr	844	S14
16	Anarawd	878	S15
17	Idwal Foel	916	S16
18	Hywel Dda (of Deheubarth)	942	
19	Iago ab Idwal	950–979	S17
20	Idwal ab Idwal	950–969	S17

21	Hywel ab Idwal	979	S20
22	Cadwallon ab Idwal	985	S20
23	Maredudd ab Owain (of Deheubarth)	986	
24	Llywelyn ap Seisyll	999	GG16
25	Rhydderch ab Iestyn (of Deheubarth)	1023	
26	Iago ab Idwal	1033	GG17
27	Gruffydd ap Llywelyn	1039	S24
28	Bleddyn ap Cynfyn (of Powys)	1063	GD23
29	Trahaern ap Caradog (of Arwystli)	1075	
30	Gruffydd ap Cynan	1081	GS26
31	Owain Gwynedd	1137	S30
32	Iorwerth Drwyndwn	1170	S31
33	Dafydd ab Owain	1174	S31
34	Llywelyn Fawr	1194	S32
35	Dafydd ap Llywelyn	1240	S34
36	Llywelyn ap Gruffydd	1246	GS34
37	Dafydd ap Gruffydd	1282–1283	B36

b *Princes of Deheubarth 872–1201*

1	Rhodri Mawr (of Gwynedd)	872	
2	Cadell ap Rhodri	878	S1
3	Hywel Dda	909	S2
4	Rhodri ap Hywel	950–953	S3
5	Edwin ap Hywel	950–954	S3
6	Owain ap Hywel	950–988	S3
7	Maredudd ab Owain	988	S6
8	Llywelyn ap Seisyll (of Gwynedd)	999	
9	Rhydderch ab Iestyn	1023	
10	Hywel ab Edwin	1033–1044	GG6
11	Maredudd ab Edwin	1033–1035	B10
12	Gruffydd ap Llywelyn (of Gwynedd)	1044–1063	S8
13	Gruffydd ap Rhydderch	1044–1055	S9
14	Maredudd ab Owain	1063	BS10
15	Rhys ab Owain	1072	B14
16	Rhys ap Tewdwr	1078–1093	3G6
		————	
17	Gruffydd ap Rhys	1135	S16
18	Anarawd ap Gruffydd	1137	S17
19	Cadell ap Gruffydd	1143	S17
20	Maredudd ap Gruffydd	1153–1155	S17
21	Rhys ap Gruffydd	1153–1197	S17
22	Gruffydd ap Rhys	1197–1201	S21

c *Princes of Powys 1063–1269*

1	Bleddyn ap Cynfyn (of Gwynedd)	1063–1075	
2	Madog ap Bleddyn	1075–1088	S1
3	Iorwerth ap Bleddyn	1075–1103	S1
4	Cadwgan ap Bleddyn	1075–1111	S1
5	Owain ap Cadwgan	1111–1116	S4
6	Maredudd ap Bleddyn	1116–1132	S1

7 Madog ap Maredudd	1132–1160	S6
8 Gruffydd Maelor I (N. Powys)	1160–1191	S7
9 Owain Cynfeiliog (S. Powys)	1160–1195	GS6
10 Madog ap Gruffydd (N. Powys)	1191–1236	S8
11 Gwenwynwyn ap Owain (S. Powys)	1195–1208	S9
12 Gruffydd Maelor II (N. Powys)	1236–1269	S10

9 **BRITAIN** KINGS OF THE PICTS *c.*556–848

1 Bridei I (?s2 Gwynedd)	*c.*556	
2 Gartnart	*c.*586–597	STS1
3 Nectu	?	STS2
4 Cinioch	?–631	STS2
5 Garnard	631	STS4
6 Bridei II	635	B5
7 Talorc	641	B5
8 Talorcen (s6 Northumbria)	653	STS7
9 Gartnait	657	STS8
10 Drest I	663	B9
11 Bridei III	671	STS10
12 Taran	692	STS11
13 Bridei IV	696	STS10
14 Nechton	706	B13
15 Drest II	724	STS14
16 Alpin I	726	B15
17 Onuist	728	STS12
18 Bridei V	761	B17
19 Ciniod	763	STS17
20 Alpin II	775	STS19
21 Drest III	780	STS20
22 Talorcan	781	STS20
23 Talorgen I	785	S17
24 Canaul	787	STS20
23 Constantine	789	STS20
26 Unuist	820	B25
27 Drest IV	834–837	S25
28 Talorgen II	834–837	STS25
29 Uuen (Eoganan of Dalriada)	837	S26
30 Uurad	839	STS25
31 Bred	842	S30
32 Kineth	842	S30
33 Brude	843	STS30
34 Drust	845–848	S30

10 **BRITAIN** KINGS OF DALRIADA *c.*500–843

1 Fergus Mor mac Erc	?*c.*500	
2 Domangart mac Fergus	*c.*500	S1
3 Comgall	*c.*506	S2
4 Gabran	*c.*538	S2

5	Conall mac Comgall	559	S3
6	Aedan	574	S4
7	Eochaid Buide	608	S6
8	Connad Cerr	629	S5
9	Ferchar mac Connad	?	S8
10	Domnall Brecc	629	S7
11	Conall Crandomna	642–660	S7
12	Dunchad mac Duban	642–660	
13	Domangart mac Domnall	660	S10
14	Mael Duin	673	S11
15	Domnall Donn	689	S11
16	Ferchar Fota	?676	DTB1
17	Eochaid mac Domangart	697	S13
18	Ainbcellach	697	S16
19	Fiannamail	698	
20	Selbach	700–723	S16
21	Eochaid Angbaid	?–733	S17
22	Dungal	?–726	S20
23	Alpin mac Eochaid	?733–736	S17
24	Muiredach	?733–736	S18
25	Onuist (K. Picts)	741–748	
26	Aed Find	?748–778	S21
27	Fergus mac Eochaid	778	S21
28	Domnall	781	
29	Conall mac Tadg (Canaul, K. Picts)	805	
30	Conall mac Aedan	807	
31	Constantine (K. Picts)	811	S27
32	Angus (Unuist, K. Picts)	820–834	S27
33	Aed mac Boanta	?–839	
34	Eoganan mac Angus	?826–839	S32
35	Alpin mac Eochaid	839–842	GS26
36	Eoganan	?842	
37	Kenneth mac Alpin (K. Scotland)	843–(858)	S35

II **BRITAIN** KINGS OF SCOTLAND

a *Dynasties of MacAlpin and Dunkeld/Canmore 843–1290*

1	Kenneth mac Alpin (of Dalriada)	843	
2	Donald I	858	B1
3	Constantine I	862	S1
4	Aed	877	S1
5	Eochaid	878	STS4
6	Donald II	889	S3
7	Constantine II	903	S4
8	Malcolm I	943	S6
9	Indulf	954	S7
10	Dub	962	S8
11	Culen	966	S9
12	Kenneth II	971	S8

13	Constantine III	995	S11
14	Kenneth III	997	S10
15	Malcolm II	1005	S12
16	Duncan I of Dunkeld	1034	GD15
17	MacBeth	1040	GD12
18	Lulach	1057	GG12
19	Malcolm III Canmore	1058	S16
20	Donald III Bane (1)	1093	S16
21	Duncan II	1094	S19
	Donald III Bane (2)	1094	
22	Edgar	1097	S19
23	Alexander I	1107	S19
24	David I	1124	S19
25	Malcolm IV	1153	GS24
26	William the Lion	1165	B25
27	Alexander II	1214	S26
28	Alexander III	1249	S27
29	Margaret★	1286–1290	GD28

b *Dynasties of Balliol, Bruce and Stuart 1292–1603*

30	John Balliol	1292–1296	4G24
31	Robert I Bruce	1306	5G24
32	David II (1)	1329	S31
33	Edward Balliol	1332	S30
	David II (2)	1334	
34	Robert II Stuart	1371	GD31
35	Robert III	1390	S34
36	James I	1406	S35
37	James II	1437	S36
38	James III	1460	S37
39	James IV	1488	S38
40	James V	1513	S39
41	Mary ('Queen of Scots')★	1542	D40
42	James VI (I of England)	1567–(1625)	S41

12 **BRITAIN** ORKNEY AND THE ISLES

a *Earls (Jarls) of Orkney c.874–1329*

1	Ragnvald I	c.874	
2	Sigurd I	c.875	B1
3	Guthorm	c.892	S2
4	Hallad	c.893	S1
5	Torf Einar I (B1 Normandy)	c.894	S1
6	Arnkel	c.910–954	S5
7	Erlend I	c.910–954	S5
8	Thorfinn I	c.910–977	S5
9	Arnfinn	c.977	S8
10	Havard	?	S8

11	Liot	?	s8
12	Hlodve	?–c.988	s8
13	Sigurd II	c.988	s12
14	Somerled	1014–1053	s13
15	Brusi	1014–c.1030	s13
16	Einar II	1014–1020	s13
17	Thorfinn II	1018–c.1065	s13
18	Ragnvald II	1038–1046	s15
19	Paul I	c.1065–1098	s17
20	Erlend II	c.1065–1098	s17
21	Sigurd III (I of Norway)	1098–1105	
22	Haakon	1105–c.1126	s19
23	Magnus I	1108–c.1117	s20
24	Paul II	c.1126–1137	s22
25	Harald I	c.1126–1131	s22
26	Ragnvald III	c.1137–1157	GD23
27	Erlend III	1154–1156	s25
28	Harald II	1139–1206	GD22
29	David	1206–1214	s28
30	John I	1206–1231	s28
31	Magnus II	1231	
32	Gilbert	1239	
33	Magnus III	1256	s32
34	Magnus IV	1276	s33
35	John II	1284	s33
36	Magnus V	c.1312–1329	s35

b *Lords of the Isles c.*1140–1493

1	Somerled (King of the Isles)	c.1140	
2	Reginar	c.1164	s1
3	Donald I	c.1210	s2
4	Angus Mor mac Donald	?	s3
5	Alexander I	c.1296	s4
6	Angus Og	c.1299	s4
7	John I	c.1330	s6
8	Donald II	1387	s7
9	Alexander II	1423	s8
10	John II	1449–1493	s9

Note on Irish kingdoms
Both the High Kingship and the provincial thrones
were often contested, and changed hands with great
frequency, there sometimes being several contestants in
the field. Reigns cannot be dated exactly in many
cases, and the date of a ruler's death or final
deposition or abdication is the only date given for
most kings (dep. = deposition; abd. = abdication).

13 IRELAND HIGH KINGS OF TARA *c*.450–1186 AD

1	Niall Noigiallach	d.*c*.450 AD	
2	Nath Í	?	BS1
3	Loeguire	d.*c*.463	S1
4	Ailill Molt (of Connaught)	d.*c*.482	S2
5	Lugaid	d.*c*.507	S3
6	Muirchertach mac Erc (of Ailech)	d.534	GG1
7	Tuathal Maelgarb	d.*c*.544	GG1
8	Diarmait mac Cerrbel (of Meath)	d.565	GG1
9	Forrgus (of Ailech)	d.566	S6
10	Domnall Ilchegach (of Ailech)	d.566	S6
11	Ainmuire mac Setnae	d.569	GG1
12	Baetan mac Muirchertach (of Ailech)	d.572	S6
13	Eochaid (of Ailech)	d.572	S10
14	Baetan mac Ninnid	d.586	3G1
15	Aed mac Ainmuire	d.598	S11
16	Aed Slaine (of Brega)	d.604	S8
17	Colman Rimid (of Ailech)	d.604	S12
18	Aed Allan mac Domnall (Aed Uaridnach of Ailech)	d.612	S10
19	Mael Cobo	d.615	S15
20	Suibne Menn (of Ailech)	d.628	5G1
21	Domnall mac Aed	d.642	S15
22	Conall Cael	d.654	S19
23	Cellach	d.658	S19
24	Diarmait mac Aed (of Brega)	d.665	S16
25	Blathmac mac Aed (of Brega)	d.665	S16
26	Sechnussach (of Brega)	d.671	S25
27	Cenn Faelad (of Brega)	d.675	S25
28	Finsnechta Fledach (of Brega)	d.695	GS16
29	Loingsech	d.703	GS21
30	Congal Cennmagair	d.710	GS21
31	Fergal (of Ailech)	d.722	GG18
32	Fogartach	d.724	GG24
33	Cinaed (of Brega)	d.728	3G16
34	Aed Allan mac Fergal (of Ailech)	d.743	S31
35	Flaithbertach	dep. 734	S29
36	Domnall Midi (of Meath)	d.763	5G8
37	Niall Frossach (of Ailech)	d.778	S31
38	Donnchad Midi (of Meath)	d.797	S36
39	Aed Oirnide (of Ailech)	d.819	BS37
40	Conchobar (of Meath)	d.833	S38
41	Niall Caille (of Ailech)	d.846	S39
42	Mael Sechnaill I (of Meath)	d.862	GS38
43	Aed Findliath (of Ailech)	d.879	S41
44	Flann Sinna (of Meath)	d.916	S42
45	Niall Glundub (of Ailech)	d.919	S43
46	Donnchad Donn (of Meath)	d.944	S44
47	Congalach Cnoba (of Brega)	d.956	9G16
48	Domnall Ua Niall (of Ailech)	d.980	GS45

49	Mael Sechnaill II (of Meath) (1)	980–997	GS46
50	Brian Boruma (of Munster)	997–1014	
	Mael Sechnaill II (2)	1014–1022	
		———	
51	Tairrdelbach Ua Briain (Turlough O'Brien of Munster)	1072–1086	GS50
52	Muirchertach Ua Briain (Murtough O'Brien of Munster)	1086–1114	S51
53	Domnall Ua Lochlainn (Donnell O'Loughlin of Ailech)	1090–1121	6G43
54	Tairrdelbach Ua Conchobar (Turlough O'Connor of Connaught)	1118–1156	
55	Muirchertach mac Lochlainn (Murtough MacLoughlin of Ailech)	1150–1166	GS53
56	Ruaidri Ua Conchobar (Rory O'Connor of Connaught)	1166–1186	S54

14 IRELAND PROVINCIAL KINGDOMS

a *Eoganacht and O'Brien Kings of Cashel and Munster c.450–1194*

1	Conall Corc	?c.450	
2	Nad Froich		S1
3	Oengus	c.490	S2
4	Daui Iarlaithe		GG1
5	Eochaid		S3
6	Feidlimid mac Oengus		S3
7	Dub-Gilcach		S3
8	Crimthann Srem		S5
9	Coirpre Cromm	d.c.580	S8
10	Fergus Scandal	d.583	GS5
11	Feidlimid mac Coirpre		S9
12	Feidlimid mac Tigernaig	d.c.590	5G1
13	Amalgaid		3G2
14	Gabran		B13
15	Fingen	d.619	GG6
16	Aed Bennan	d.c.619	GG4
17	Cathal mac Aed	d.628	GS9
18	Failbe Fland	d.c.637	B13
19	Cuan	d.641	S13
20	Maenach	d.662	S15
21	Cathal Cu-cen-mathair	d.665	S17
22	Colgu	d.678	S18
23	Finguine	d.c.695	S21
24	Ailill	d.c.698	S21
25	Eterscel	d.721	GS19
26	Cormac	d.713	GS20
27	Cathal mac Finguine	d.742	S23
28	Cathussach	d.770	S25
29	Mael Duin	d.786	3G16

30 Olchobar mac Flann	d.*c*.796	
31 Olchobar mac Dub-Indrecht	d.805	4G19
32 Artri	d.821	S27
33 Tuathal	d.820	S32
34 Tnuthgal		GS18
35 Feidlimid mac Crimthann	d.847	4G15
36 Olchobar mac Cinaed	d.851	GG29
37 Ailgenan	d.853	GS34
38 Mael Gualae	d.859	B37
39 Cenn Faelad	d.872	6G5
40 Dunchad	d.888	5G22
41 Dub Lachtna	d.895	S38
42 Finguine Cenn Ngecan	d.902	BS40
43 Cormac	d.908	10G3
44 Flaithbertach	d.944	
45 Lorcan		8G22
46 Cellachan Caisil	d.954	7G22
47 Mael Fathardaig	d.957	9G15
48 Dub-da-Bairenn	d.959	15G1
49 Fergraid	d.961	GS37
50 Donnchad mac Cellachan	d.963	S46
51 Mathgamain mac Cennetig (of Thomond)	d.976	
52 Maelmuad mac Bran	d.978	DT12
53 Brian Boruma (High King)	d.1014	B51
54 Dungal	d.1025	S47
55 Donnchad mac Brian	d.1064	S53
56 Murchad	d.1068	S55
57 Tairrdelbach mac Tadg (High King)	d.1086	GS53
58 Muirchertach (High King)	d.1119	S57
59 Tadg	d.1086	S57
60 Domnall	d.1115	S59
61 Diarmait	d.1118	S57
62 Tairrdelbach mac Diarmait	d.1167	S61
63 Brian mac Murchad	d.1118	S56
64 Tadg Glae	d.1154	S61
65 Tadg mac Carrthach	d.1124	3G50
66 Cormac mac Carrthach	d.1138	B65
67 Domnall Mor	d.1194	S62

b *Kings of Ulaid (Ulster) c.500–1201*

1 Muiredach Muinderg	d.*c*.500	
2 Eochaid mac Muiredach	d.507	S1
3 Cairell mac Muiredach	d.525	S1
4 Eochaid mac Condlae	d.553	
5 Fergnae mac Oengus	d.557	BS1
6 Demman	d.572	S3
7 Baetan	d.581	S3
8 Aed Dub	d.588	
9 Fiachnae Lurgan	d.626	GS4
10 Fiachnae mac Demman	d.627	S6

11	Congal Claen	d.637	GS9
12	Dunchad	d.644	S10
13	Mael Cobo	d.647	S10
14	Blathmac	d.670	S13
15	Congal Cendfota	d.674	S12
16	Fergus	d.692	
17	Becc Bairrche	abd.707	S14
18	Cu Chuaran	d.708	5G4
19	Aed Roin	d.735	S17
20	Cathussach	d.749	BS18
21	Bressal	d.750	S19
22	Fiachnae mac Aed Roin	d.789	S19
23	Tommaltach	d.790	3G9
24	Eochaid mac Fiachnae	d.810	S22
25	Cairell mac Fiachnae	d.819	S22
26	Mael Bressail	d.825	3G16
27	Muiredach mac Eochaid	d.839	S24
28	Matudan mac Muiredach	d.857	S27
29	Lethlobar	d.873	GS23
30	Ainbith	d.882	GS24
31	Eochocan	d.883	B30
32	Airemon	d.886	B30
33	Fiachnae mac Ainbith	d.886	S30
34	Becc	d.893	S32
35	Muiredach mac Eochocan	d.896	S31
36	Aitith	d.898	5G16
37	Cenn Etig	d.900	S29
38	Aed mac Eochocan	d.919	S31
39	Dubgall	d.925	S38
40	Loingsech	d.932	S37
41	Eochaid mac Conall	d.937	
42	Matudan mac Aed	d.950	S38
43	Ardgal	d.970	S42
44	Niall mac Aed	d.971	S38
45	Aed mac Loingsech	d.972	S40
46	Eochaid mac Ardgal	d.1004	S43
47	Gilla Comgaill	d.1005	S43
48	Mael Ruanaid	d.1007	S43
49	Matudan mac Domnall	d.1007	
50	Dub Tuinne	d.1007	S46
51	Domnall	d.1007	S50
52	Muiredach mac Matudan	d.1008	S49
53	Niall mac Dub Tuinne	d.1016	S50
54	Niall mac Eochaid	d.1063	S46
55	Eochaid mac Niall	d.1062	S54
56	Donnchad Ua Mathgamain	d.1065	
57	Cu Ulad Ua Flaithri	d.1072	
58	Lochlainn	d.1071	GS48
59	Donn Sleibe	d.1091	S55
60	Aed Meranach	d.1083	

61	Goll na Gorta	d.1081	
62	Donnchad mac Donn Sleibe	dep.1113	s59
63	Eochaid mac Donn Sleibe	d.1108	s59
64	Eochaid Ua Mathgamain	d.1127	
65	Aed mac Donn Sleibe	d.1127	s59
66	Ragnall	d.1131	
67	Cu Ulad mac Conchobar	d.1157	GS59
68	Aed mac Cu Ulad	d.1158	s67
69	Eochaid mac Cu Ulad	dep.1166	s67
70	Magnus	d.1171	s67
71	Donn Sleibe mac Cu Ulad	d.1172	s67
72	Ruaidri	d.1201	s67

c *Kings of Laigin (Leinster) c.436–1171*

1	Bressal Belach	d.c.436	
2	Enna Cennsalach	d.c.444	GS1
3	Crimthann mac Enna Cennsalach	d.483	s2
4	Findchad	d.485	
5	Froech	d.495	s4
6	Illann	d.527	GG1
7	Ailill mac Dunlaing	d.c.530	B6
8	Cormac	d.c.539	s7
9	Coirpre	d.c.550	s8
10	Colman Mar	d.c.580	s9
11	Aed Dibchine	d.c.595	
12	Brandub	d.c.605	4G2
13	Ronan	d.c.624	3G3
14	Crimthann mac Aed Dubchine	d.633	s11
15	Crundmael	d.656	s13
16	Faelan mac Colman Mar	d.666	s10
17	Fianamail	d.680	GG11
18	Bran Mut	d.693	GS16
19	Cellach Cualann	d.c.715	3G11
20	Murchad mac Bran Mut	d.727	s18
21	Dunchad	d.728	s20
22	Faelan mac Murchad	d.738	s20
23	Bran Bec	d.738	s20
24	Aed mac Colcu	d.738	3G15
25	Muiredach mac Murchad	d.760	s20
26	Cellach mac Dunchad	d.776	s21
27	Ruaidri	d.785	s22
28	Bran Ardchenn	d.795	s25
29	Finsnechta Cetharderc	d.808	s26
30	Muiredach mac Ruaidri	d.829	s27
31	Cellach mac Bran Ardchenn	d.834	s28
32	Bran mac Faelan	d.838	GS29
33	Ruarc	dep.846	s32
34	Lorcan mac Cellach	d.851	s31
35	Tuathal mac Muiredach	d.854	BS31
36	Muirecan	d.863	GS27

37	Dunlaing	d.869	B35
38	Ailill mac Dunlaing	d.871	S37
39	Domnall	d.884	S36
40	Muiredach mac Bran	d.885	S32
41	Cerball	d.909	S36
42	Augaire mac Ailill	d.917	S38
43	Faelan mac Muiredach	d.942	S40
44	Lorcan mac Faelan	d.943	S43
45	Broen mac Maelmorda	d.947	GS36
46	Tuathal mac Augaire	d.958	S42
47	Cellach mac Faelan	d.966	S43
48	Murchad mac Finn	d.972	BS45
49	Augaire mac Tuathal	d.978	S46
50	Domnall Cloen	d.984	S44
51	Donnchad mac Domnall Cloen	dep.1003	S50
52	Maelmorda	d.1014	S48
53	Dunlaing mac Tuathal	d.1014	S46
54	Donncuan	d.1016	S53
55	Bran mac Maelmorda	dep.1018	S52
56	Augaire mac Dunlaing	d.1024	S53
57	Donnchad mac Dunlaing	d.1036	S53
58	Murchad mac Dunlaing	d.1042	S53
59	Diarmait mac Mael na mBo	d.1072	14G3
60	Murchad mac Diarmait	d.1070	S59
61	Domnall mac Murchad	d.1075	S60
62	Donnchad mac Domnall	d.1089	BS59
63	Enna mac Diarmait	d.1092	S59
64	Diarmait mac Enna	d.1098	S63
65	Donnchad mac Murchad	d.1115	S60
66	Diarmait mac Enna	d.1117	GS60
67	Enna mac Donnchad	d.1126	S65
68	Diarmait mac Murchad (Dermot MacMurrough)	d.1171	S65

d *Kings of Connaught c.459–1224*

1	Amalgaid (B2 High King)	?c.450	
2	Ailill Molt (High King)	d.c.482	
3	Daui Tenga Uma	d.502	FBS1
4	Eogan Bel	d.c.543	GS2
5	Ailill Inbanda	d.550	S4
6	Echu Tirmcharna		3G3
7	Feradach		BGG1
8	Aed mac Echu	d.577	S6
9	Uatu	d.c.601	S8
10	Mael Cothaid		GS7
11	Colman mac Cobthach	d.622	4GB2
12	Rogallach	d.649	S9
13	Laidgnen	d.655	S11
14	Guaire Aidne	d.663	S11
15	Muirchertach Nar	d.668	S14

16	Cenn Faelad	d.682	3G3
17	Dunchad	d.683	3GB2
18	Fergal Aidne	d.696	GS14
19	Muiredach Muillethan	d.702	GS12
20	Cellach	d.705	S12
21	Indrechtach mac Dunchad	d.707	S17
22	Indrechtach mac Muiredach	d.723	S19
23	Domnall	d.728	S20
24	Cathal mac Muiredach	d.735	S19
25	Aed Balb	d.742	S22
26	Fergus mac Cellach	d.756	S20
27	Ailill Medraige	d.764	S21
28	Dub-Indrecht	d.768	S24
29	Donn Cothaid	d.773	GG17
30	Flaithri	abd.777	S23
31	Artgal	abd.782	S24
32	Tipraite	d.786	GS22
33	Muirgius	d.815	GG22
34	Cinaed	d.792	S31
35	Colla	d.796	S26
36	Mael Cothaid mac Fagartach		GS24
37	Diarmait	d.833	B33
38	Cathal mac Muirgius	d.839	S33
39	Murchad mac Aed	d.840	BS36
40	Fergus mac Fothad	d.843	GS28
41	Finsnechta	d.848	B33
42	Conchobar mac Tadg Mor	d.882	GS33
43	Mugron	d.872	S36
44	Aed mac Conchobar	d.888	S42
45	Tadg mac Conchobar	d.900	S42
46	Cathal mac Conchobar	d.925	S42
47	Tadg mac Cathal	d.956	S46
48	Fergal Ua Ruairc	d.c.966	DT3
49	Conchobar mac Tadg	d.973	S47
50	Cathal mac Tadg	d.973	S45
51	Cathal mac Conchobar	d.1010	S49
52	Tadg in Eich Gil	d.1030	S51
53	Art Uallach	d.1046	GS48
54	Aed in Gai Bernaig	d.1067	S52
55	Aed mac Art	d.1087	S53
56	Ruaidri na Saide Buide	dep.1092	S54
57	Flaithbertach	d.1098	
58	Tadg mac Ruaidri	d.1097	S56
59	Domnall mac Tigernan	d.1102	3G53
60	Domnall mac Ruaidri	dep.1106	S56
61	Tairrdelbach Ua Conchobar (High King)	d.1156	S56
62	Ruaidri Ua Conchobar (High King)	dep.1186	S61
63	Conchobar Maenmaige	d.1189	S62
64	Cathal Crobderg	d.1224	S61

e *Kings of Meath c.450–1173*

1	Conall Cremthainne (s1 High King)	?c.450	
2	Fiachu mac Niall		B1
3	Ardgal		S1
4	Maine mac Cerrbel	d.c.538	GS1
5	Diarmait mac Cerrbel (High King)	d.c.565	B4
6	Colman Mar	d.558	S5
7	Colman Bec	d.574	S5
8	Suibne	d.600	S6
9	Fergus mac Colman Mar	d.618	S6
10	Oengus mac Colman Mar	d.625	S6
11	Conall Guthbind	d.635	S8
12	Mael Doid	d.653	S8
13	Diarmait mac Airmedach	d.689	GS11
14	Murchad mac Diarmait	d.715	S13
15	Domnall mac Murchad (High King)	d.763	S14
16	Niall mac Diarmait	d.765	S13
17	Murchad mac Domnall	d.765	S15
18	Donnchad mac Domnall (High King)	d.797	S15
19	Domnall mac Donnchad	d.799	S18
20	Ailill mac Donnchad	d.803	S18
21	Conchobar mac Donnchad (High King)	d.833	S18
22	Mael Runaid	d.843	S18
23	Flaithbertach	d.845	S22
24	Mael Sechnaill I (High King)	d.862	S22
25	Lorcan mac Cathal	d.864	
26	Donnchad	d.876	GS21
27	Flann Sinna (High King)	d.916	S24
28	Conchobar mac Mael Sechnaill	d.919	S24
29	Domnall mac Flann	d.921	S27
30	Donnchad Donn (High King)	d.944	S27
31	Oengus mac Donnchad	d.945	S30
32	Donnchad mac Domnall	d.950	S29
33	Aed mac Mael Runaid	d.951	
34	Domnall mac Donnchad	d.952	S30
35	Carlus mac Conn	d.960	GS30
36	Muiredach mac Aed	d.974	GS27
37	Domnall mac Congalach (s47 High King)	d.976	DT5
38	Mael Sechnaill II (High King)	d.1022	S34
39	Mael Sechnaill Got	d.1025	
40	Roen mac Murchad	d.1027	
41	Domnall mac Mael Sechnaill	d.1030	S38
42	Conchobar mac Domnall	d.1073	S41
43	Murchad mac Flann	d.1076	GS41
44	Mael Sechnaill mac Conchobar	d.1087	S42
45	Domnall mac Flann	d.1094	B43
46	Donnchad mac Murchad	d.1105	S43
47	Conchobar mac Mael Sechnaill	d.1105	S44
48	Muirchetach mac Domnall	d.1106	S45

49	Murchad mac Domnall	d.1153	S45
50	Mael Sechnaill mac Murchad	d.1155	S49
51	Donnchad mac Domnall	d.1160	GS45
52	Diarmait mac Domnall	d.1169	B51
53	Domnall Breagach	d.1173	BS52

f *Kings of Ailech c.450–1170*

1	Eogan mac Niall (S1 High King)	d.466	
2	Muiredach	?	S1
3	Muirchertach mac Erc	d.536	S2
4	Forrgus (High King)	d.566	S3
5	Domnall Ilchegach (High King)	d.566	S3
6	Baetan mac Muirchertach (High King)	d.572	S3
7	Eochaid (High King)	d.572	S5
8	Colcu	d.580	S5
9	Colman Rimid (High King)	d.604	S6
10	Aed Uaridnach (High King)	d.612	S5
11	Suibne Menn (High King)	d.628	BGS3
12	Mael Fithrich	d.630	S10
13	Crunnmael	?	S11
14	Mael Duin mac Mael Fithrich	d.681	S12
15	Fergal (High King)	d.722	S14
16	Aed Allan (High King)	d.743	S15
17	Niall Frossach (High King)	d.778	S15
18	Mael Duin mac Aed Allan	d.788	S16
19	Aed Oirnide (High King)	d.819	S17
20	Murchad mac Mael Duin	dep.823	S18
21	Niall Caille (High King)	d.846	S19
22	Mael Duin mac Aed Oirnide	d.867	S19
23	Aed Finliath (High King)	d.879	S21
24	Murchad mac Mael Duin	d.887	S22
25	Flaithbertach mac Murchad	d.896	S24
26	Domnall mac Aed	d.915	S23
27	Niall Glundub (High King)	d.919	S23
28	Flaithbertach mac Domnall	d.919	S26
29	Fergal mac Domnall	d.938	S26
30	Muirchertach mac Niall	d.943	S27
31	Domnall Ua Niall (High King) (1)		S30
32	Flaithbertach mac Conchobar	d.962	BS29
33	Tadg mac Conchobar	d.962	B32
34	Conn mac Conchobar	d.962	B32
35	Murchad mac Flaithbertach	dep.972	S28
	Domnall Ua Niall (2)	d.980	
36	Fergal mac Domnall	dep.989	BGS30
37	Aed mac Domnall	d.1004	S31
38	Flaithbertach mac Muirchertach (1)	?	BS37
39	Aed mac Flaithbertach	?	S38
	Flaithbertach mac Muirchertach (2)	?	
40	Niall mac Mael Sechnaill	d.1061	GG26
41	Ardgar	d.1064	BGS37

42	Aed Ua Hualgairg	d.1067	
43	Domnall mac Niall	d.1068	S40
44	Aed mac Niall (1)	?	S40
45	Conchobar O'Brien	d.1078	
	Aed mac Niall (2)	d.1083	
46	Donnchad	d.1083	S40
47	Domnall Ua Lochlainn (High King)	d.1121	S41
48	Conchobar mac Domnall (1)	?	S47
49	Magnus	?	S41
	Conchobar mac Domnall (2)	d.1136	
50	Muirchertach mac Lochlainn (1) (High King)	?	BS48
51	Domnall Ua Gairmledaig	d.1160	
	Muirchertach mac Lochlainn (2)	d.1166	
52	Conchobar mac Muirchertach	d.1170	S50
		....	

15 IRELAND KINGS OF DUBLIN 856–1170 AD

1	Olaf I	856	
2	Ivar I Ragnarson the Boneless	871	
3	Eystein Olafson	873	S1
4	Halfdan Ragnarson	875	B2
5	Bard	877	
6	Sigfrid Ivarson	881	S2
7	Sitric I Ivarson	888	S2
8	Ivar II	896–902	GS2
9	Sitric II Caoch	917	GS2
10	Guthfrith	920	B9
11	Olaf II Guthfrithson	934	S10
12	Blacar Guthfrithson	941	S10
13	Olaf III Sitricson (1)	945	S9
14	Guthfrith Sitricson	948	S9
	Olaf III Sitricson (2)	953	
15	Gluniaran Olafson	981	S13
16	Sitric III Olafson (1)	989	S13
17	Ivar III Ivarson	994	
	Sitric III Olafson (2)	995	
18	Margad Ragnaldson (1)	1035	GS11
19	Ivar IV Haraldson	1038	GS11
	Margad Ragnaldson (2)	1046–1052	
20	Gudrod Sitricson	1072–1075	
21	Thorfinn Thorkellson	1118–1124	
22	Ragnald Thorkellson	1136–1146	
23	Ottar Ottarson	1142–1148	
24	Brodar Thorkellson	1148–1160	
25	Astell Ragnaldson	1160–1170	

16 SCANDINAVIA KINGS OF DENMARK

a *Gorm Dynasty c.900–1448*

1 Gorm the Old	c.900	
2 Harald I Bluetooth	c.950	S1
3 Sven I Forkbeard (K. England)	985	S2
4 Harald II	1014	S3
5 Knut the Great (K. England)	1019	S3
6 Harthacnut (K. England)	1035	S5
7 Magnus the Good (of Norway)	1042	
8 Sven II Astridson	1047	STS5
9 Harald III	1076	S8
10 Knut IV	1080	S8
11 Olaf IV	1086	S8
12 Erik I	1095	S8
13 Niels	1104	S8
14 Erik II	1134	S12
15 Erik III	1137	STS14
16 Sven III	1147–1157	S14
17 Knut V	1147–1157	GS13
18 Valdemar I	1157	GS12
19 Knut VI	1182	S18
20 Valdemar II	1202	S18
21 Erik IV	1241	S20
22 Abel	1250	S20
23 Christopher I	1252	S20
24 Erik V	1259	S23
25 Erik VI	1286	S24
26 Christopher II	1320–1332	S24
27 Valdemar III (IV)	1340	S26
28 Olaf V	1375	S29
29 Margaret I*	1387	D27
30 Erik VII (s9 Pomerania-Wolgast)	1412	GG27
31 Christopher III (BS11 C. Palatine)	1439–1448	STS30

b *Oldenburg Dynasty since 1448*

32 Christian I (of Oldenburg)	1448	DT18
33 John	1481	S32
34 Christian II	1513	S33
35 Frederick I	1523	S32
36 Christian III	1534	S35
37 Frederick II	1559	S36
38 Christian IV	1588	S37
39 Frederick III	1648	S38
40 Christian V	1670	S39
41 Frederick IV	1699	S40
42 Christian VI	1730	S41
43 Frederick V	1746	S42
44 Christian VII	1766	S43

45	Frederick VI	1808	S44
46	Christian VIII	1839	GS43
47	Frederick VII	1848	S46
48	Christian IX	1863	GG43
49	Frederick VIII	1906	S48
50	Christian X	1912	S49
51	Frederick IX	1947	S50
52	Margaret II★	1972	D51

17 SCANDINAVIA KINGS OF NORWAY

a *Yngling Dynasty c.870–1319*

1	Harald Fairhair	*c.*870–940	
2	Erik Bloodaxe	*c.*940	S1
3	Haakon I	*c.*945	S1
4	Harald II	*c.*960	S2
5	Haakon Jarl of Lade	*c.*970	GG1
6	Olaf Tryggvesson	*c.*995	GG1
7	Erik Jarl of Lade	1000	S5
8	Olaf II Haraldsson	1015	GG1
9	Sven Knutsson (S5 Denmark)	1028	
10	Magnus the Good	1035	S8
11	Harald III Hardraade	1047	UB8/DT1
12	Olaf III Kyrre	1066–1093	S11
13	Magnus II	1066–1069	S11
14	Magnus III Barefoot	1093–1103	S12
15	Eystein I	1103–1122	S14
16	Sigurd I	1103–1130	S14
17	Olaf Magnusson	1103–1115	S14
18	Magnus IV	1130–1135	S16
19	Harald IV Gille	1130–1136	?S14
20	Inge I	1136–1161	S19
21	Sigurd II	1136–1155	S19
22	Eystein II	1142–1157	S19
23	Haakon II	1161–1162	S21
24	Magnus V Erlingsson	1162–1184	GD16
25	Sverre	1184–1202	?S21
26	Haakon III	1202–1204	S25
27	Gutorm Sigurdsson	1204.	BS26
28	Inge II Baardsson	1204–1217	GD21
29	Haakon IV	1217–1263	S26
30	Magnus VI	1263–1280	S29
31	Erik II	1280–1299	S30
32	Haakon V	1299–1319	S30

b *Folkung Dynasty 1319–1387*

33	Magnus VII (IV of Sweden)	1319–1355	GD32
34	Haakon VI	1343–1380	S33

35 Olaf IV (V of Denmark)	1380–1387	S34
36 Margaret (of Denmark)★	1387–(1412)	M35

c *Oldenburg Dynasty since* 1905

37 Haakon VII (S49 Denmark)	1905	
38 Olaf V	1957	S37

18 **SCANDINAVIA** KINGS OF SWEDEN

a *Early Kings c.*970–1250

1 Erik (VIII)	*c.*970	
2 Olaf Skotkonung	*c.*995	S1
3 Anund Jakob	*c.*1022	S2
4 Emund	*c.*1050	S2
5 Stenkil Ragnvaldson	*c.*1060–1066	HD14
6 Halsten	?*c.*1080–1110	S5
7 Inge I	?*c.*1080–1112	S5
8 Blot-Sven	?*c.*1081–1083	
9 Philip	*c.*1112–1118	S6
10 Inge II	*c.*1112–1125	S6
11 Magnus I (S13 Denmark)	*c.*1129	GD7
12 Sverker I	*c.*1134	GS8
13 Erik IX	*c.*1156	GD8
14 Magnus II	1160	GG7
15 Karl (VII)	1161	S12
16 Knut I	1167	S13
17 Sverker II	1196	S15
18 Erik X	1208	S16
19 John I	1216	S17
20 Erik XI (1)	1222	S18
21 Knut II	1229	GG13/HD18
Erik XI (2)	1234–1250	

b *Folkung Dynasty* 1250–1389

22 Valdemar I	1250	STS20
23 Magnus III	1275	B22
24 Birger	1290	S23
25 Magnus IV	1319–1365	BS24
26 Erik XII	1356–1359	S25
27 Albert of Mecklenburg	1365–1389	STS25

c *Kings* 1389–1521

28 Margaret (of Denmark)★	1389	
29 Erik XIII of Pomerania (K. Denmark)	1412	BGD27
30 Christopher of Bavaria (K. Denmark)	1440	STS29
31 Karl VIII (1)	1448	
32 Christian I (of Denmark)	1457	
Karl VIII (2)	1464–1465	

Karl VIII (3)	1467–1470	
33 John II (of Denmark)	1497–1501	S32
34 Christian II (of Denmark)	1520–1521	S33

d *Vasa Dynasty 1523–1654*

35 Gustav I	1523	
36 Erik XIV	1560	S35
37 John III	1568	S35
38 Sigismund (III of Poland)	1592	S37
39 Karl IX (Regent 1599)	1604	S35
40 Gustav II Adolf	1611	S39
41 Christina★	1632–1654	D40

e *Palatinate Dynasty 1654–1751*

42 Karl X Gustav (DT10 C. Palatine)	1654	GD39
43 Karl XI	1660	S42
44 Karl XII	1697	S43
45 Ulrika Eleonora★	1718	D43
46 Frederick (of Hesse-Cassel)	1720–1751	H45

f *Holstein-Gottorp Dynasty 1751–1818*

47 Adolf Frederick (BS7 Holstein-Gottorp)	1751	4G39
48 Gustav III	1771	S47
49 Gustav IV Adolf	1792	S48
50 Karl XIII	1809–1818	S47

g *Bernadotte Dynasty since 1818*

51 Karl XIV (Marshal Bernadotte)	1818	
52 Oscar I	1844	S51
53 Karl XV	1859	S52
54 Oscar II	1872	S52
55 Gustav V	1907	S54
56 Gustav VI Adolf	1950	S55
57 Karl XVI Gustav	1973	GS56

19 BENELUX REGION NETHERLANDS

a *Counts of Holland c.920–1304*

1 Dirk I	c.920	
2 Dirk II	c.940	S1
3 Arnulf	988	S2
4 Dirk III	993	S3
5 Dirk IV	1039	S4
6 Floris I	1049	S4
7 Robert (I of Flanders)	1061	
8 Godfrey (V of Lower Lorraine)	1071	

9	Dirk V	1076	s6
10	Floris II	1091	s9
11	Dirk VI	1122	s10
12	Floris III	1157	s11
13	Dirk VII	1190	s12
14	William I	1203	s12
15	Floris IV	1222	s14
16	William II (German King 1247)	1234	s15
17	Floris V	1256	s16
18	John I	1296	s17
19	John II of Avesnes (C. Hainault)	1300–1304	GD15
	(Union with Hainault)		

b *Stadtholders of the Netherlands – House of Orange* 1572–1795

1	William the Silent of Nassau (P. Orange)	1572	
2	Maurice	1584	s1
3	Frederick Henry	1625	s1
4	William II	1647–1650	s3
5	William III (K. England)	1672–1702	s4
6	William IV	1747	3G3
7	William V	1751–1795	s6

c *Kingdom of Holland*

1	Louis Bonaparte (B34 France)	1806–1810	

d *Kings of the Netherlands – House of Orange since* 1813

8	William I	1813	s7
9	William II	1840	s8
10	William III	1849	s9
11	Wilhelmina★	1890	D10
12	Juliana★	1948	D11
13	Beatrix★	1980	D12

20 **BENELUX REGION** BELGIUM

a *Dukes of Lower Lorraine/Brabant* 959–1430

1	Godfrey I	959	
2	Godfrey II	964	
3	Charles (Carolingian)	978	
4	Odo (Carolingian)	991	s3
5	Godfrey III of Verdun (s7 Hainault)	1012	
6	Gozelo I	1023	B5
7	Gozelo II	1044	s6
8	Frederick (s2 Luxemburg)	1046	
9	Godfrey IV (of Lorraine)	1065	s6
10	Godfrey V	1070	s9
11	Conrad of Franconia (s9 Germany)	1076	

12	Godfrey VI (Jerusalem 1099)	1088	GD9/STS10
13	Henry (of Limburg)	1101	GD8
14	Godfrey VII of Louvain (1)	1106	DT3
15	Waleran (II of Limburg)	1128	S13
	Godfrey VII (2)	1139	
16	Godfrey VIII	1140	S14
17	Godfrey IX	1142	S16
18	Henry I	1183	S17
19	Henry II	1235	S18
20	Henry III	1248	S19
21	Henry IV	1261	S20
22	John I	1267	S20
23	John II	1294	S22
24	John III	1312	S23
25	Joanna★	1355–1406	D24
26	Wenceslas (I of Luxemburg)	1355–1383	H25
27	Anthony of Burgundy	1406	GG24
28	John IV	1415	S27
29	Philip	1427	S27
30	Philip the Good (of Burgundy)	1430–(1467)	3G24
	(Union with Burgundy)		

b *Counts of Flanders 862–1405*

1	Baldwin I Iron-Arm	862	
2	Baldwin II	879	S1
3	Arnulf I	918–964	S2
4	Baldwin III	958–962	S3
5	Arnulf II	964	S4
6	Baldwin IV	988	S5
7	Baldwin V	1035	S6
8	Baldwin VI	1067	S7
9	Arnulf III	1070	S8
10	Robert I	1071	S7
11	Robert II	1093	S10
12	Baldwin VII	1111	S11
13	Charles	1119	GD10
14	Dietrich (S11 Lorraine)	1128	GD10
15	Philip	1168	S14
16	Margaret I★	1191–1194	D14
17	Baldwin VIII (V of Hainault)	1191–1195	H16
18	Baldwin IX (VI of Hainault; Latin Emperor)	1195	S16/17
19	Joanna (of Hainault)★	1205–1244	D18
20	Ferdinand (S3 Portugal)	1212–1233	H19
21	Thomas of Savoy (II of Piedmont)	1237–1244	H19
22	Margaret II (of Hainault)★	1244–1280	D18
23	William of Dampierre	1246–1251	S22
24	Guy of Dampierre	1278–1304	S22
25	Robert III	1305	S24
26	Louis I	1322	GS25
27	Louis II	1346	S26

28	Margaret III★	1384	D27
29	John the Fearless (of Burgundy)	1405–(1419)	S28
	(Union with Burgundy)		

c *Counts of Hainault 875–1433 (and Holland from 1300)*

1	Reginar I	875	
2	Reginar II	916	S1
3	Reginar III	932	S2
4	Richer	958	
5	Garnier	965–973	S4
6	Renard	965–973	S4
7	Godfrey of Verdun	973–998	
8	Arnulf of Cambrai	973–977	
9	Reginar IV	998	S3
10	Reginar V	1013	S9
11	Richilda★	1036–1083	D10
12	Hermann of Saxony	1036–1050	H11
13	Baldwin I (VI of Flanders)	1052–1070	H11
14	Baldwin II	1071	S11/13
15	Baldwin III	1098	S14
16	Baldwin IV	1120	S15
17	Baldwin V	1171	S16
18	Baldwin VI (Latin Emperor 1204)	1195	S17
19	Joanna★	1205–1244	D18
20	Ferdinand (s3 Portugal)	1212–1233	H19
21	Thomas of Savoy (II of Piedmont)	1237–1244	H19
22	Margaret (of Flanders)★	1244–1280	D18
23	John I of Avesnes	1246–1257	S22
24	John II (C. Holland 1300)	1257–1304	S23
25	William (III of Holland)	1304	S24
26	William IV	1337	S25
27	Margaret II★	1346–1356	D25
28	Lewis the Bavarian (German King 1314)	1346–1347	H27
29	William V (I of Bavaria)	1356–1389	S27/28
30	Albert (I of Bavaria)	1389–1404	S27
31	William VI (II of Bavaria)	1404–1417	S30
32	Jacqueline★	1417–1433	D31
33	John III (IV of Brabant)	1418–1422	H32
34	Humphrey of Gloucester	1422–1426	H32
35	Philip the Good (of Burgundy)	1433–(1467)	GD30
	(Union with Burgundy)		

d *Counts and Margraves of Namur 907–1429*

1	Berenger	907–932	
2	Robert I	960–973	S1
3	Albert I	973–1000	S2
4	Robert II	?–1013	S3
5	Albert II	1016–1037	S3
6	Albert III (Margrave 1088)	1037–1105	S5
7	Godfrey	1101–1139	S6

8	Henry I	1139–1196	S7
9	Baldwin I (V of Hainault)	1189–1195	GD7
10	Philip I	1196–1212	S9
11	Yolanda (Latin Empress)★	1212–1217	D9
12	Peter of Courtenay (Latin Emperor)	1212–1217	HII
13	Philip II	1217–1226	SII/12
14	Henry II	1226–1229	SII/12
15	Margaret★	1229–1237	DII/12
16	Henry III of Vianden	1229–1237	HI5
17	Baldwin II (Latin Emperor)	1237–1256	SII/12
18	Henry IV (II of Luxemburg)	1256–1263	GD8
19	Guy of Dampierre (C. Flanders)	1263–1297	GG9
20	John I	1297	SI9
21	John II	1331	S20
22	Guy II	1335	S20
23	Philip III	1336	S20
24	William I	1337	S20
25	William II	1391	S24
26	John III	1418	S24
27	Philip the Good (of Burgundy)	1429–(1467)	
	(Union with Burgundy)		

e *Counts and Dukes of Limburg* 1064–1288

1	Waleran I	1064	
2	Henry I	1081	SI
3	Waleran II	1119	S2
4	Henry II (Duke 1155)	1139	S3
5	Henry III	1167	S4
6	Waleran III	1221	S5
7	Henry IV	1226	S6
8	Waleran IV	1247	S7
9	Ermengard★	1280–1282	D8
10	Rainald (I of Gelders)	1280–1288	H9
	(Union with Brabant)		

f *Kings of Belgium (House of Coburg) since* 1831

1	Leopold I of Coburg (DT29 Saxony)	1831	
2	Leopold II	1865	SI
3	Albert	1909	BS2
4	Leopold III	1934	S3
5	Badouin	1951	S4

21 BENELUX REGION LUXEMBURG

a *Counts and Dukes of Luxemburg* 963–1443

1	Siegfried	963	
2	Frederick	998	SI
3	Giselbert	1019–1055	S2
4	Conrad I	1060	S3

5	William	1086–1127	S4
6	Conrad II	1130	S5
7	Henry I (of Namur)	1136	GD4
8	Ermesinda★	1196–1247	D7
9	Theobald (I of Bar)	1196–1214	H8
10	Henry II of Limburg	1247–1281	S8
11	Henry III	1281	S10
12	Henry IV (VII of Germany)	1288	S11
13	John (of Bohemia)	1313	S12
14	Charles (IV of Germany)	1346	S13
15	Wenceslas I (Duke 1354)	1353	S13
16	Wenceslas II (of Germany)	1383	S14
17	Jobst (of Moravia; German King)	1388	BS14
18	Anthony (of Brabant)	1411	H19
19	Elizabeth of Gorlitz★(1)	1415	BD16
20	John (II of Bavaria)	1418	H19
	Elizabeth of Gorlitz★ (2)	1425	
21	Philip the Good (of Burgundy)	1443–(1467)	
	(Union with Burgundy)		

b *Grand Dukes of Luxemburg (House of Nassau) since 1890*

1	Adolf (D. Nassau)	1890	
2	William	1905	S1
3	Marie-Adelaide★	1912	D2
4	Charlotte★	1919	D2
5	John	1964	S4

22 **FRANCE** KINGS

a *Capet and Valois Dynasties 987–1589*

1	Hugh Capet (GS32 Carolingian)	987	
2	Robert II	996	S1
3	Henry I	1031	S2
4	Philip I	1060	S3
5	Louis VI	1108	S4
6	Louis VII	1137	S5
7	Philip II Augustus	1180	S6
8	Louis VIII	1223	S7
9	Louis IX	1226	S8
10	Philip III	1270	S9
11	Philip IV	1285	S10
12	Louis X	1314	S11
13	John I	1316	S12
14	Philip V	1316	S11
15	Charles IV	1322	S11
16	Philip VI (C. Valois)	1328	GS10
17	John II	1350	S16
18	Charles V	1364	S17
19	Charles VI	1380	S18

20	Charles VII	1422	S19
21	Louis XI	1461	S20
22	Charles VIII	1483	S21
23	Louis XII	1498	GG18
24	Francis I	1515	3G18
25	Henry II	1547	S24
26	Francis II	1559	S25
27	Charles IX	1560	S25
28	Henry III	1574–1589	S25

b *Bourbon and Bonaparte Dynasties* 1589–1870

29	Henry IV (of Navarre)	1589	DT9
30	Louis XIII	1610	S29
31	Louis XIV	1643	S30
32	Louis XV	1715	GG31
33	Louis XVI	1774–1792	GS32
34	Napoleon I Bonaparte (Emperor)	1804	
35	Louis XVIII	1814	B33
36	Charles X	1824	B33
37	Louis-Philippe	1830–1848	DT30
38	Napoleon III (Emperor)	1852–1870	BS34

23 FRANCE KINGS OF BURGUNDY

a *Burgundian Kings* 411–532

1	Gundicar	411	
2	Gunderic	436	S1
3	Chilperic	473–486	S2
4	Godegisel	473–500	S2
5	Gundobad	473–516	S2
6	Sigismund	516–524	S5
7	Gundimar	524–532	S5

b *Kings of Burgundy* 888–1032

1	Rudolf I	888	
2	Rudolf II	911	S1
3	Conrad	937	S2
4	Rudolf III	993–1032	S3

24 FRANCE FEUDAL STATES

a *Dukes of Normandy* 911–1204

1	Rolf the Ganger (B5 Orkney)	911	
2	William I	932	S1
3	Richard I	942	S2
4	Richard II	996	S3

5	Richard III	1027	S4
6	Robert I	1028	S4
7	William II (I of England)	1035	S6
8	Robert II	1087	S7
9	Henry I (of England)	1106–1135	S7
10	Geoffrey (V of Anjou)	1144	HD9
11	Henry II (of England)	1150	S10
12	Richard IV (I of England)	1189	S11
13	John (of England)	1199–1204	S11

b *Counts and Dukes of Brittany 826–1514*

1	Nominoe	826	
2	Erispoe	851	S1
3	Salomon	857–874	BS1
4	Alan I	888–908	
5	Alan II	937–952	GD4
6	Drogo	952–958	S5
7	Conan I	987	GG2
8	Geoffrey I	992	S7
9	Alan III	1008	S8
10	Odo of Penthievre	1040	S8
11	Conan II	1056	S9
12	Hoel of Nantes	1066	HD9
13	Alan IV	1084	S12
14	Conan III	1112	S13
15	Odo II of Porhoet	1148	HD14
16	Conan IV	1156	S14
17	Geoffrey II Plantagenet (S26 England)	1170	HD16
18	Arthur I	1186–1203	S17
19	Peter I of Dreux (GG5 France)	1213	HGD16
20	John I	1237	S19
21	John II (Duke 1297)	1286	S20
22	Arthur II	1305	S21
23	John III	1312	S22
24	Charles (S18 Blois)	1341–64	HBD23
25	John IV of Montfort	1341–99	GS22
26	John V	1399	S25
27	Francis I	1442	S26
28	Peter II	1450	S26
29	Arthur III	1457	S25
30	Francis II	1458	BS29
31	Anne (Q. France)★	1488–1514	D30

c *Counts and Dukes of Anjou c.870–1480*

1	Ingelger	c.870	
2	Fulk I	898	S1
3	Fulk II	941	S2
4	Geoffrey I	958	S3

5 Fulk III Nerra	987	s4
6 Geoffrey II Martel	1040	s5
7 Geoffrey III	1060	GD5
8 Fulk IV Rechin	1067–1109	B7
9 Geoffrey IV	1098–1106	s8
10 Fulk V (K. Jerusalem 1131)	1106–1129	s8
11 Geoffrey V Plantagenet	1129	s10
12 Henry (II of England)	1151	s11
13 Richard (I of England)	1189	s12
14 John (of England)	1199–1204	s12
	———	
15 Charles I (of Naples; s8 France)	1246	
16 Charles II (of Naples)	1285	s15
17 Charles III (C. Valois; s10 France)	1290	HD16
18 Philip (VI of France)	1325	s17
19 John (II of France)	1332	s18
20 Louis I (Duke 1360)	1356	s19
21 Louis II	1384	s20
22 Louis III	1417	s21
23 Rene	1434–1480	s21

d *Counts of Champagne c.942–1316*

1 Herbert I (C. Vermandois)	?–942	
2 Robert (Troyes)	942–966	s1
3 Herbert II (Meaux; Troyes 966)	942–982	s1
4 Hugh (Rheims)	940–949	s1
5 Herbert III	983–995	s2
6 Odo I (of Blois)	983–996	GD1
7 Stephen I	996–1023	s5
8 Odo II (of Blois)	996–1037	s6
9 Stephen II	1037–1047	s8
10 Odo III	1047–1063	s9
11 Theobald I (of Blois)	1063–1089	s8
12 Stephen III (of Blois) (Meaux)	1089–1102	s11
13 Odo IV (Troyes)	1089–1093	s11
14 Hugh II (Troyes)	1093–1125	s11
15 Theobald II (of Blois) (Meaux; Troyes 1125)	1102–1152	s12
16 Henry I	1152	s15
17 Henry II (K. Jerusalem)	1181	s16
18 Theobald III	1197	s16
19 Theobald IV (I of Navarre)	1201	s18
20 Theobald V (II of Navarre)	1253	s19
21 Henry III (I of Navarre)	1270	s19
22 Joanna (of Navarre)★	1274	D21
23 Louis (X of France)	1304–1316	s22

e *Counts of Blois and Chartres c.975–1391*

1 Theobald I	?–975	
2 Odo I	975	s1
3 Theobald II	996	s2

4	Odo II	1004	S2
5	Theobald III	1037	S4
6	Stephen	1089	S5
7	Theobald IV	1102	S6
8	Theobald V	1152	S7
9	Louis I	1191	S8
10	Theobald VI	1205	S9
11	Margaret★	1218–1230	D8
12	Gauthier of Avesnes	1218–1230	H11
13	Mary★	1230–1241	D11/12
14	Hugh of Chatillon	1230–1241	H13
15	John I	1241	S13/14
16	Joanna★	1279	D15
17	Hugh II	1292	BS15
18	Guy I	1307	S17
19	Louis II	1342	S18
20	Louis III	1346	S19
21	John II	1372	S19
22	Guy II	1381–1391	S19
23	Louis IV (D. Orleans)	1391–(1407)	

f *Dukes of Lorraine 928–1766*

1	Giselbert	928–939	
2	Otto	941	
3	Conrad (II of Franconia)	944	
4	Bruno of Saxony	954	
5	Frederick (of Bar)	959	
6	Dietrich (of Bar)	978	S5
7	Frederick II (of Bar)	1026	S6
8	Gozelo (I of Lower Lorraine)	1033	
9	Godfrey	1044–1046	S8
10	Gerard of Alsace	1048	
11	Dietrich II	1070	S10
12	Simon I	1115	S11
13	Matthew I	1139	S12
14	Simon II	1176	S13
15	Frederick I	1205	S13
16	Frederick II	1208	S15
17	Theobald I	1213	S16
18	Matthew II	1220	S16
19	Frederick III	1250	S18
20	Theobald II	1303	S19
21	Frederick IV	1312	S20
22	Raoul	1329	S21
23	John I	1346	S22
24	Charles II	1390	S23
25	Rene I (of Anjou)	1431	HD24
26	John II	1453	S25
27	Nicholas	1470	S26
28	Rene II of Vaudemont	1473	3G23

29	Anthony	1508	S28
30	Francis I	1544	S29
31	Charles III	1545	S30
32	Henry	1608	S31
33	Francis II	1624	S31
34	Charles IV (1)	1624	S33
35	Nicholas Francis	1633–1634	S33
	Charles IV (2)	1661–1670	
36	Charles V (Nominal Duke and Imperial General)		S35
37	Leopold	1697	S36
38	Francis III (I as Emperor 1745)	1729	S37
39	Stanislav Leszczynski (K. Poland)	1736–1766	

g *Counts and Dukes of Bar 951–1431*

1	Frederick I	951	
2	Dietrich I	978	S1
3	Frederick II	1026	S2
4	Sophia★	1033–1093	D3
5	Louis (of Montbeliard)	1033–1065	H4
6	Dietrich II	1093	S4/5
7	Dietrich III	1104	S6
8	Renard I	1104	S6
9	Renard II	1150	S8
10	Henry I	1170	S9
11	Theobald I	1191	S9
12	Henry II	1214	S11
13	Theobald II	1240	S12
14	Henry III	1296	S13
15	Edward I	1302	S14
16	Henry IV	1337	S15
17	Edward II	1344	S16
18	Robert (Duke 1355)	1352	S16
19	Edward III	1411	S18
20	Louis	1415	S18
21	Rene (of Anjou)	1419–(1480)	GG18
	(Union with Lorraine)		

h *Dukes of Orleans 1344–1498*

1	Philip of Valois (S16 France)	1344–1375	
2	Louis I of Valois (S18 France)	1392	
3	Charles	1407	S2
4	Louis II (XII of France 1498)	1465–(1515)	S3

i *Dukes of Burgundy 1032–1477*

1	Robert I Capet (S2 France)	1032	
2	Hugh I	1076	GS1

3	Odo I	1079	B2
4	Hugh II	1102	S3
5	Odo II	1143	S4
6	Hugh III	1162	S5
7	Odo III	1192	S6
8	Hugh IV	1218	S7
9	Robert II	1273	S8
10	Hugh V	1305	S9
11	Odo IV	1315	S9
12	Philip of Rouvres	1349–1361	GS11
		———	
13	Philip the Bold of Valois (S17 France)	1363	
14	John the Fearless	1404	S13
13	Philip the Good	1419	S14
16	Charles the Rash	1467–1477	S15

j Counts of Burgundy (Franche Comté) 985–1405

1	Otto-William (S39 Carolingian)	985	
2	Renard I	1026	S1
3	William I	1057	S2
4	Renard II	1087	S3
5	William II	1097	S4
6	William III	1125	S5
7	Renard III	1127	BS4
8	Beatrix I★	1148–1184	D7
9	Frederick (I of Germany)	1156–1189	H8
10	Otto I	1189	S8/9
11	Beatrix II★	1200–1231	D10
12	Otto II of Andechs	1208–1234	H11
13	Otto III	1234	S11/12
14	Alice★	1248–1278	D11/12
15	Hugh of Chalons	1248–1266	H14
16	Philip (of Savoy)	1267–1278	H14
17	Otto IV	1279–1303	S14/15
18	Robert	1303–1315	S17
19	Joanna I★	1315–1330	D17
20	Philip (V of France)	1315–1322	H19
21	Joanna II★	1330–1347	D19/20
22	Odo (IV, D. Burgundy)	1330–1347	H21
23	Philip (D. Burgundy)	1347–1361	GS21
24	Margaret I★	1361–1382	D19/20
25	Louis (II of Flanders)	1382–1384	S24
26	Margaret II (III of Flanders)★	1384–1405	D25
27	Philip the Bold (D. Burgundy)	1384–1404	H26
	(*Union with Duchy of Burgundy*)		

k Dukes of Bourbon 1327–1523

1	Louis I (GS9 France)	1327	
2	Peter I	1341	S1
3	Louis II	1356	S2

4 John I	1410	S3
5 Charles I	1434	S4
6 John II	1456	S5
7 Peter II	1488	S5
8 Suzanne★	1503–1521	D7
9 Charles II of Montpensier	1505–1523	H8/GG4

l *Counts of Auvergne 886–1524*

1 William I	886	
2 William II	918	STS1
3 Acfred	926	B2
4 Ebles (of Aquitaine)	928	
5 Raymond-Pons (of Toulouse)	932	
6 William III (of Aquitaine)	950	
7 William IV (I of Toulouse)	963	
8 Guy I	979	
9 William V	989	B8
10 Robert I	1016	S9
11 William VI	1032	S10
12 Robert II	1060	S11
13 William VII	1096	S12
14 Robert III	1136	S13
15 William VIII	1143	S14
16 William IX	1155	S13
17 Robert IV	1182	S16
18 William X	1194	S17
19 Guy II	1195	S17
20 William XI	1224	S19
21 Robert V	1246	S20
22 William XII	1277	S21
23 Robert VI	1279	S21
24 Robert VII	1314	S23
25 William XIII	1326	S24
26 Joanna I★	1332	D25
27 Philip (of Burgundy)	1360	S26
28 John I	1361	S24
29 John II	1386	S28
30 Joanna II★	1394–1422	D29
31 John III (D. Berry)	1394–1416	H30
32 George of La Tremoille	1416–1422	H30
33 Mary★	1422	BD28
34 Bertrand I of La Tour	1437	S33
35 Bertrand II	1461	S34
36 John IV	1494	S35
37 Anne★	1501–1524	D36

m *Dauphins of Auvergne 1155–1436*

1 William I (VIII as Count)	1155	
2 Robert I	1169	S1
3 William II	1234	S2

4	Robert II	1239	S3
5	Robert III	1262	S4
6	Robert IV	1282	S5
7	John	1324	S6
8	Beraud I	1351	S7
9	Beraud II	1356	S8
10	Beraud III	1400	S9
11	Joanna★	1426–1436	D10

n *Counts of Perigord 866–1399*

1	Wulgrin (of Angouleme)	866	
2	William I	886	S1
3	Bernard	920	S2
4	Boso I (of La Marche)	?	HD2
5	Helias I	968	S4
6	Aldebert I	975	S4
7	Helias II	995	BS6
8	Aldebert II	1031	S7
9	Helias III	1080	S8
10	Helias IV	1117	S9
11	Boso II	1146	S8
12	Helias V	1166	S11
13	Archambald I	1205	S12
14	Archambald II	1212	S12
15	Helias VI	1245	S14
16	Archambald III	1251	S15
17	Helias VII	1294	S16
18	Archambald IV	1311	S17
19	Roger-Bernard	1336	S17
20	Archambald V	1369	S19
21	Archambald VI	1398–1399	S20

o *Dauphins of Vienne 1044–1364*

1	Guigues I	1044	
2	Guigues II	1063	S1
3	Guigues III	1080	S2
4	Guigues IV	1098	S3
5	Guigues V	1142	S4
6	Beatrix★	1162	D5
7	Andre-Guigues VI	1228	S6
8	Guigues VII	1237	S7
9	John I	1269	S8
10	Anne★	1281–1296	D8
11	Humbert I of La Tour	1281–1307	H10
12	John II	1307	S10/11
13	Guigues VIII	1319	S12
14	Humbert II	1333	S12
15	Charles (V of France)	1349–(1364)	

p *Counts of La Marche 944–1308*

1	Boso I	944	
2	Boso II	968	S1
3	Bernard I (s6 Perigord)	1006	BS2
4	Aldebert I	1047	S3
5	Boso III	1088	S4
6	Almodis★	1091–1116	D4
7	Roger of Montgomery	1091–1123	H6
8	Aldebert II	1123–1143	S6/7
9	Odo	1123–1135	S6/7
10	Boso IV	1123–1128	S6/7
11	Bernard II	1143	S8
12	Aldebert III	1150–1177	S11
		—	
13	Hugh I (IX of Lusignan)	1199	
14	Hugh II	1219	S13
15	Hugh III	1249	S14
16	Hugh IV	1260	S15
17	Hugh V	1282	S16
18	Guy	1302–1308	S16

q *Counts of Angouleme 866–1249*

1	Wulgrin I	866	
2	Alduin I	886	S1
3	William I	916	S2
4	Arnold I	962	GG1
5	Arnold II	975	S3
6	William II	987	S5
7	Alduin II	1028	S6
8	Geoffrey	1032	S6
9	Fulk	1048	S8
10	William III	1089	S9
11	Wulgrin II	1118	S10
12	William IV	1140	S11
13	Wulgrin III	1178	S12
14	William V	1181–1188	S12
15	Ademar	1181–1218	S12
16	Matilda★	1181–1208	D13
17	Hugh (II of La Marche)	1218–(1249)	S16
	(*Union with La Marche*)		

r *Counts of Toulouse 852–1271*

1	Raymond I	852	
2	Bernard	864	S1
3	Odo	875	S1
4	Raymond II	918	S3
5	Raymond III	923	S4
6	William I	950	S5
7	Pons	1037	S6

8	William II	1060	S7
9	Raymond IV (C. Tripoli 1101)	1088	S7
10	Bertrand	1105	S9
11	Alfonso-Jordan (of Tripoli)	1112	S9
12	Raymond V	1148–1194	S11
13	Alfonso II	1148–?	S11
14	Raymond VI	1194	S12
15	Raymond VII	1222	S14
16	Joanna★	1249–1271	D15
17	Alfonso III (S8 France)	1249–1271	H16

s *Dukes of Aquitaine (and Counts of Poitiers) 867–1199*

1	Rainulf (of Poitiers; Duke 889)	867	
2	Ebles (1)	890	S1
3	William I (of Auvergne)	893	
4	William II (of Auvergne)	918	
	Ebles (2)	926	
5	William III	935	S2
6	William IV	963	S5
7	William V	990	S6
8	William VI	1029	S7
9	Odo	1038	S7
10	William VII Peter	1039	S7
11	William VIII Geoffrey	1058	S7
12	William IX	1086	S11
13	William X	1127	S12
14	Eleanor★	1137–(1204)	D13
15	Louis (VII of France)	1137–1152	H14
16	Henry (II of England)	1152–1169	H14
17	Richard (I of England)	1169–1199	D14/16
	(Union with England)		

t *Counts of Provence 926–1481*

1	Boso I	926	
2	Boso II	948	
3	William I	968	S2
4	Rotbold	992	S2
5	William II	1008	S3
6	William III	1018–1037	S4
7	Bertrand I	1018–1054	S5
8	Geoffrey	1018–1063	S5
9	Bertrand II	1063–1090	S8
10	Stephanie★	1090–1100	W8
11	Gerberga★	1100–1112	D8
12	Gilbert	1100–1108	H11
13	Raymond-Berengar I (III of Barcelona)	1112–1131	H14
14	Dulcia I★	1112–1131	D11/12
15	Alfonso-Jordan (of Toulouse)	1125–1148	3G4
16	Berengar-Raymond	1131–1144	S14/13
17	Raymond-Berengar II	1144–1166	S16

18 Dulcia II★	1166–1167	D17
19 Alfonso (II of Aragon)	1167–1196	BS16
20 Raymond-Berengar III	1168–1181	B19
21 Sancho	1181–1185	B19
22 Alfonso II	1196–1209	S19
23 Raymond-Berengar IV	1209–1245	S22
24 Beatrix★	1245–1267	D23
25 Charles I (of Naples)	1246–1285	H24
26 Charles II (of Naples)	1285–1309	S24/25
27 Robert (of Naples)	1309–1343	S26
28 Joanna (I of Naples)★	1343–1382	GS27
29 Louis I (of Anjou)	1382–1384	3G26
30 Louis II (of Anjou)	1384–1417	S29
31 Louis III (of Anjou)	1417–1434	S30
32 Rene (of Anjou)	1434–1480	S30
33 Charles III (C. Maine)	1480–1481	BS32

25 MONACO LORDS AND PRINCES OF THE GRIMALDI DYNASTY since 1297

1 Rainier I (Lord of Cagnes)	1297	
2 Charles I (Cagnes; Lord of Monaco 1331)	1314	S1
3 Rainier II	1357–1407	S2
4 John I	1419	S3
5 Catalan	1454	S4
6 Claudine★	1457	D5
7 Lambert of Antibes	1458	H6/3G1
8 John II	1494	s6
9 Lucien	1505	B8
10 Augustin	1523	B8
11 Honore I	1532	S9
12 Charles II	1581	S11
13 Hercule	1589	S11
14 Honore II (Prince 1612)	1604	S13
15 Louis I	1662	GS14
16 Antoine	1701	S15
17 Louise-Hyppolyte★	1731	D16
18 Jacques of Torrigny	1731	H17
19 Honore III	1733–1793	S17/18
20 Honore IV	1814	S19
21 Honore V	1819	S20
22 Florestan	1841	S20
23 Charles III	1856	S22
24 Albert	1889	S23
25 Louis II	1922	S24
26 Rainier III	1949	GD25

26 GERMANY HOHENZOLLERN EMPERORS 1871–1918

1 William I (of Prussia)	1871	
2 Frederick (III of Prussia)	1888	S1
3 William II (of Prussia)	1888–1918	S2

27 GERMANY BRANDENBURG AND PRUSSIA

a *Margraves of Brandenburg 1134–1415*

1 Albert the Bear	1134	
2 Otto I	1170	S1
3 Otto II	1184	S2
4 Albert II	1205	S2
5 John I	1220	S4
6 John II	1266–1281	S5
7 Otto III	1266–1308	S5
8 Conrad	1266–1304	S5
9 John III	1286–1305	S8
10 Otto IV	1291–1297	S8
11 Henry I	1293–1318	S5
12 Waldemar	1304–1319	S8
13 Henry II	1319–1320	BS8
14 Ludwig I of Wittelsbach (V of Bavaria)	1324–1351	
15 Ludwig II (VI of Bavaria)	1351–1365	
16 Otto V (of Bavaria)	1366–1373	
17 Wenceslas of Luxemburg (K. Germany)	1373–1378	
18 Sigismund of Luxemburg (1)	1378–1395	B17
19 Jobst (of Moravia; German King)	1397–1411	
Sigismund (of Germany) (2)	1411–1415	

b *Hohenzollern Electors of Brandenburg 1415–(1701)*

1 Frederick I of Nuremberg	1415	
2 Frederick II	1440	S1
3 Albert Achilles	1471	S1
4 John Cicero	1486	S3
5 Joachim I	1499	S4
6 Joachim II	1535	S5
7 John George	1571	S6
8 Joachim Frederick	1598	S7
9 John Sigismund (D. Prussia 1618)	1608	S8
10 George William	1620	S9
11 Frederick William	1640	S10
12 Frederick III (K. Prussia 1701)	1688–(1713)	S11

c *Hohenzollern Dukes of Prussia 1525–(1618)*

1 Albert (GS3 Brandenburg)	1525	
2 Albert Frederick	1568	S1
3 John Sigismund (of Brandenburg)	1618–(1620)	

d *Hohenzollern Kings of Prussia* 1701–1918

12	Frederick I (III of Brandenburg)	1701	
13	Frederick William I	1713	S12
14	Frederick II the Great	1740	S13
15	Frederick William II	1786	BS14
16	Frederick William III	1797	S15
17	Frederick William IV	1840	S16
18	William I (German Emperor 1871)	1861	S16
19	Frederick III (Emperor)	1888	S18
20	William II (Emperor)	1888–1918	S19

28 **GERMANY** COUNTS AND DUKES OF OLDENBURG
1440–1918

1	Christian (I of Denmark)	1440	
2	Gerhard	1454	B1
3	John I	1483	S2
4	John II	1526	S3
5	Anton	1529	S3
6	Anton Gunther	1603–1667	S5
7	Frederick Augustus I (BS7 Gottorp; Duke 1777)	1773	DT1
8	William (1)	1785–1810	S7
	William (2)	1815	
9	Peter I	1823	BS7
10	Augustus (Grand Duke)	1829	S9
11	Peter II	1853	S10
12	Frederick Augustus II	1900–1918	S11

29 **GERMANY** DUKES OF HOLSTEIN-GOTTORP 1490–1773

1	Frederick I (of Denmark)	1490	
2	Adolf	1533	S1
3	Frederick II	1586	S2
4	John Adolf	1587	S2
5	Frederick III	1616	S4
6	Christian Albert	1659	S5
7	Frederick IV	1694	S6
8	Karl Frederick	1702	S7
9	Karl Peter Ulrich (Peter III of Russia)	1739	S8
10	Paul (of Russia)	1762–1773	S9

30 **GERMANY** MECKLENBURG

a *Dukes and Grand Dukes of Mecklenburg-Schwerin* 1611–1918

1	Adolf-Frederick I	1611	
2	Christian-Ludwig I	1658	S1
3	Frederick-William	1692	BS2

4	Charles-Leopold	1713	B3
5	Christian-Ludwig II	1747	B3
6	Frederick	1756	S5
7	Frederick-Franz I (Grand Duke 1815)	1785	BS6
8	Paul-Frederick	1837	GS7
9	Frederick-Franz II	1842	S8
10	Frederick-Franz III	1883	S9
11	Frederick-Franz IV	1897–1918	S10

b *Dukes and Grand Dukes of Mecklenburg-Strelitz* 1701–1918

1	Adolf-Frederick II (S1 Schwerin)	1701	
2	Adolf-Frederick III	1708	S1
3	Adolf-Frederick IV	1752	BS2
4	Charles (Grand Duke 1815)	1794	B3
5	George	1816	S4
6	Frederick-William	1860	S5
7	Adolf-Frederick V	1904	S6
8	Adolf-Frederick VI	1914–1918	S7

31 GERMANY DUKES OF ANHALT 1863–1918

1	Leopold (IV of Anhalt-Dessau)	1863	
2	Frederick I	1871	S1
3	Frederick II	1904	S2
4	Edward	1918	S2
5	Joachim-Ernst	1918.	S4

32 GERMANY DUKES OF NASSAU 1816–1866

1	William (of Nassau-Weilburg)	1816	
2	Adolf (G. Duke of Luxemburg 1890)	1839–1866	S1

33 GERMANY SAXONY, BRUNSWICK AND HANOVER

a *Dukes of Saxony* 850–1260

1	Ludolf	850	
2	Bruno	866	S1
3	Otto I	880	S1
4	Henry (I of Germany)	912	S3
5	Otto II (I of Germany)	936	S4
6	Hermann Billung	961	
7	Bernard I	973	S6
8	Bernard II	1011	S7
9	Orthulf	1059	S8
10	Magnus	1072	S9
11	Lothair of Supplinburg (K. Germany)	1106	
12	Henry the Proud (X of Bavaria)	1137	GD10
13	Albert the Bear (of Brandenburg)	1138	GD10
14	Henry the Lion (XII of Bavaria)	1142	S12

15	Bernard III	1180	S13
16	Albert II	1212–1260	S15

b *Ascanian Dukes and Electors of Saxe-Wittenberg 1260–1422*

17	Albert III	1260	S16
18	Rudolf I	1298	S17
19	Rudolf II (Elector)	1356	S18
20	Wenceslas	1370	S18
21	Rudolf III	1388	S20
22	Albert IV	1419–1422	S20

c *Wettin Electors of Saxony 1423–1806*

23	Frederick I (of Meissen)	1423	
24	Frederick II	1428	S23
25	Ernest	1464–1486	S24
26	Albert V	1464–1485	S24
27	Frederick III	1486	S25
28	John	1525	S25
29	John-Frederick	1532	S28
30	Maurice	1547	GS26
31	Augustus	1553	B30
32	Christian I	1586	S31
33	Christian II	1591	S32
34	John-George I	1611	S32
35	John-George II	1656	S34
36	John-George III	1680	S35
37	John-George IV	1691	S36
38	Frederick-Augustus I (K. Poland)	1694	S36
39	Frederick-Augustus II (K. Poland)	1733	S38
40	Frederick-Christian	1763	S39
41	Frederick-Augustus III (G. D. Warsaw; King of Saxony 1806)	1763–(1827)	S40

d *Kings of Saxony – Wettin Dynasty 1806–1918*

41	Frederick-Augustus I	1806	S40
42	Anton	1827	S40
43	Frederick-Augustus II	1836	BS41
44	John	1854	B43
45	Albert	1873	S44
46	George	1902	S44
47	Frederick-Augustus III	1904–1918	S46

e *Electors and Kings of Hanover – Welf Dynasty 1692–1866*

1	Ernest-Augustus (of Brunswick-Luneburg)	1692	
2	George I (of G. Britain)	1698	S1
3	George II (of G. Britain)	1727	S2
4	George III (of G. Britain) (K. Hanover 1814)	1760	GS3
5	George IV (of G. Britain)	1820	S4
6	William (IV of G. Britain)	1830	S4
7	Ernest Augustus	1837	S4

8 George V   1851–1866 S7

f *Dukes of Brunswick* 1735–1918 – Welf Dynasty

1 Charles I   1735
2 Charles II   1780–1806 S1

3 Frederick-William   1813   S2
4 Charles III   1815   S3
5 William   1830–1884 S3

6 Ernest Augustus (GS8 Hanover)   1913–1918

g *King of Westphalia*

1 Jerome Bonaparte (B34 France)   1807–1813

34 **GERMANY** HESSE

a *Landgraves of Hesse* 1265–1567

1   Henry I (S19 Brabant)   1265
2   Otto (Upper Hesse; Lower Hesse 1311)   1308–1328 S1
3   John (Lower Hesse)   1308–1311 S1
4   Henry II   1328   S2
5   Hermann   1376   GS2
6   Ludwig I   1413   S5
7   Ludwig II (Cassel)   1458–1471 S6
8   Henry III (Marburg)   1458–1483 S6
9   William I (Cassel)   1471–1493 S7
10 Ludwig III (Marburg)   1474–1478 S8
11 William II (Cassel)   1483–1509 S7
12 William III (Marburg)   1483–1500 S8
13 Philip   1509–1567 BS11

b *Landgraves of Hesse-Darmstadt/Grand Dukes of Hesse* 1567–1918

1   George I (Landgrave; S13 Hesse)   1567
2   Ludwig V   1596   S1
3   George II   1626   S2
4   Ludwig VI   1661   S3
5   Ludwig VII   1678   S4
6   Ernest-Ludwig   1678   S4
7   Ludwig VIII   1739   S6
8   Ludwig IX   1768   S7
9   Ludwig X (I as Grand Duke 1806)   1790   S8
10 Ludwig II   1830   S9
11 Ludwig III   1848   S10
12 Ludwig IV   1877   BS11
13 Ernest-Ludwig   1892–1918 S12

c *Landgraves of Hesse-Cassel/Electors of Hesse* 1567–1866

1	William IV (Landgrave; s13 Hesse)	1567	
2	Maurice	1592	S1
3	William V	1627	S2
4	William VI	1637	S3
5	William VII	1663	S4
6	Charles	1670	S4
7	Frederick I (K. Sweden)	1730	S6
8	William VIII	1751	S6
9	Frederick II	1760	S8
10	William IX (I as Elector 1803)	1785	S9
11	William II	1821	S10
12	Frederick-William	1831–1866	S11

35 **GERMANY** COUNTS PALATINE OF THE RHINE

Wittelsbach dynasty 1214–1799

1	Ludwig I (of Bavaria)	1214	
2	Otto (II of Bavaria)	1227	S1
3	Ludwig II (of Upper Bavaria)	1253–1294	S2
4	Henry (of Lower Bavaria)	1253–1255	S2
5	Rudolf I (of Upper Bavaria)	1294–1317	S3
6	Ludwig III (IV of Germany)	1294–1329	S3
7	Rudolf II	1329	S5
8	Rupert I	1353	S5
9	Rupert II	1390	GS5
10	Rupert III (K. Germany)	1398	S9
11	Ludwig IV	1410	S10
12	Ludwig V	1436	S11
13	Frederick I	1449	S11
14	Philip	1476	S12
15	Ludwig VI	1508	S14
16	Frederick II	1544	S14
17	Otto Henry	1556	BS16
18	Frederick III of Simmern	1559	4G10
19	Ludwig VII	1576	S18
20	Frederick IV	1583	S19
21	Frederick V (K. Bohemia 1619–20)	1610–1623	S20
		———	
22	Charles Ludwig	1649	S21
23	Charles	1680	S22
24	Philip William of Neuberg	1685	7G10
25	John William	1690	S24
26	Charles Philip	1716	S24
27	Charles Theodore of Sulzbach (Elector of Bavaria 1777)	1742–1799	10G10

36 GERMANY BADEN

Zahringen dynasty

a *Margraves of Baden c.*1100–1527

1	Hermann I of Zahringen	*c.*1100	
2	Hermann II	1130	S1
3	Hermann III	1160	S2
4	Hermann IV	1190	S3
5	Hermann V	1243	S4
6	Frederick I	1250	S5
7	Rudolf I	1268	S4
8	Rudolf II	1288	S7
9	Hesso	1295	S7
10	Rudolf III	1297	S7
11	Rudolf Hesso	1332	S10
12	Rudolf IV	1335	GS7
13	Frederick II	1348	S12
14	Rudolf V	1353	S13
15	Rudolf VI	1372	S14
16	Bernard I	1391	S14
17	Jacob I	1431	S16
18	Charles I	1453	S17
19	Christopher I	1475–1527	S18

b *Margraves of Baden-Baden* 1527–1771

1	Bernard II	1527	S19
2	Philibert	1536	S1
3	Philip	1569	S2
4	Edward Fortunatus	1588–1596	BS2
		———	
5	William	1622	S4
6	Ludwig-William	1677	GS5
7	Ludwig-George	1707	S6
8	Augustus-George	1761–1771	S6

c *Margraves of Baden-Durlach* 1527–1806

1	Ernest	1527	S19
2	Charles II	1553	S1
3	Ernest-Frederick	1577–1604	S2
4	Jacob II	1577–1590	S2
5	George-Frederick	1577–1622	S2
6	Frederick III (1)	1622–1634	S5
		———	
	Frederick III (2)	1648	
7	Frederick IV	1659	S6
8	Frederick V	1677	S7
9	Charles III	1709	S8
10	Charles-Frederick (Baden-Baden 1771)	1738–1806	GS9

d *Grand Dukes of Baden* 1806–1918

1	Charles-Frederick (of Baden-Durlach)	1806	
2	Charles	1811	GS1
3	Ludwig I	1818	S1
4	Leopold	1830	S1
5	Ludwig II	1852	S4
6	Frederick I	1858	S4
7	Frederick II	1907–1918	S6

37 GERMANY WURTTEMBERG

a *Counts and Dukes of Wurttemberg* 1083–1806

1	Conrad I	1083–1105	
2	Conrad II	1110–1122	STS1
3	Ludwig I	1134–1158	S2
4	Ludwig II	1166–1181	S3
5	Ludwig III	1201–1228	S4
6	Eberhard I	1236	S5
7	Ulrich I	1241	S5
8	Ulrich II	1265	S7
9	Eberhard II	1279	S7
10	Ulrich III	1325	S9
11	Eberhard III	1344–1392	S10
12	Ulrich IV	1344–1366	S10
13	Eberhard IV	1392–1417	GS12
14	Eberhard V	1417–1419	S13
15	Ludwig IV (Urach only from 1441)	1419–1450	S14
16	Ulrich V (Stuttgart)	1441–1480	S14
17	Ludwig V (Urach)	1450–1457	S15
18	Eberhard VI (Urach; Duke 1495)	1450–1496	S15
19	Eberhard VII (Stuttgart; Duke 1495)	1480–1504	S16
20	Ulrich VI (1)	1504–1519	BS19
	Ulrich VI (2)	1534	
21	Christopher	1550	S20
22	Ludwig VI	1568	S21
23	Frederick I	1593	BS20
24	John-Frederick	1608	S23
25	Eberhard VIII	1628	S24
26	William-Ludwig	1674	S25
27	Eberhard-Ludwig	1677	S26
28	Charles-Alexander	1733	BS26
29	Charles-Eugene	1737	S28
30	Ludwig-Eugene	1793	S28
31	Frederick-Eugene	1795	S28
32	Frederick II (King 1806)	1797–(1816)	S31

b *Kings of Wurttemberg 1806–1918*

32	Frederick I	1806	
33	William I	1816	s32
34	Charles	1864	s33
35	William II	1891–1918	GG32

38 GERMANY BAVARIA

a *Agilulfing Dukes of Bavaria c.555–788*

1	Garibald I	c.555	
2	Tassilo I	596	s1
3	Garibald II	611	s2
4	Theodo I	660	s3
5	Theudebald	717	s4
6	Theudebert	722	s4
7	Grimwald	722–729	s4
8	Tassilo II	?	s4
9	Hugbert	729–737	s6
10	Otilo	737–748	s8
11	Tassilo III	748–788	s10
12	Theodo II	777–788	s11

b *Dukes of Bavaria 911–1180*

1	Arnulf (1)	911	
2	Conrad I (K. Germany)	914	
	Arnulf (2)	919	
3	Eberhard	937	s1
4	Berchtold	938	B1
5	Henry I (s2 Germany)	947	HD1
6	Henry II (1)	955	s5
7	Otto I (of Swabia)	976	
8	Henry III	983	s4
	Henry II (2)	985	
9	Henry IV (II of Germany) (1)	995	s6
10	Henry V (1) (s1 Luxemburg)	1004	
	Henry IV (2)	1009	
	Henry V (2)	1018	
11	Conrad II (K. Germany)	1026	
12	Henry VI (III of Germany) (1)	1027	s11
13	Henry VII (s2 Luxemburg)	1042	
	Henry VI (2)	1047	
14	Conrad III of Zutphen	1049	
15	Henry VIII (IV of Germany) (1)	1053	s12
16	Conrad IV	1054	s12
17	Agnes of Poitiers★	1055	W12
18	Otto II of Nordheim	1061	
19	Welf I of Este (1)	1070	
	Henry VIII (2)	1077	
	Welf I (2)	1096	

20	Welf II	1101	S19
21	Henry IX the Black	1120	S19
22	Henry X the Proud	1126	S21
23	Leopold (IV of Austria)	1139	
24	Conrad V (III of Germany)	1141	
25	Henry XI (II of Austria)	1142	B23
26	Henry XII the Lion (of Saxony)	1156–1180	S22

c *Dukes of Bavaria – Wittelsbach Dynasty* 1180–1623

1	Otto I of Wittelsbach	1180	
2	Ludwig I	1183	S1
3	Otto II	1231	S2
4	Ludwig II (Upper Bavaria)	1253–1294	S3
5	Henry I (Lower Bavaria)	1253–1290	S3
6	Otto III (Lower Bavaria)	1290–1312	S5
7	Rudolf I (Upper Bavaria)	1294–1317	S4
8	Ludwig III (Lower Bavaria)	1294–1296	S5
9	Stephen I (Lower Bavaria)	1294–1310	S5
10	Ludwig IV (Upper Bavaria; K. Germany)	1294–1347	S4
11	Henry II (Lower Bavaria)	1310–1339	S9
12	Otto IV (Lower Bavaria)	1312–1334	S9
13	Henry III (Lower Bavaria)	1312–1333	S6
14	John I (Lower Bavaria)	1339–1340	S11
15	Ludwig V (Upper Bavaria)	1347–1361	S10
16	Stephen II (Landshut)	1347–1375	S10
17	William I (Straubing)	1347–1358	S10
18	Ludwig VI (Upper Bavaria)	1347–1351	S10
19	Albert I (Straubing)	1347–1404	S10
20	Otto V (Upper Bavaria)	1347–1379	S10
21	Meinhard (Upper Bavaria)	1361–1363	S15
22	Stephen III (Ingolstadt)	1375–1413	S16
23	Frederick (Landshut)	1375–1393	S16
24	John II (Munich)	1375–1397	S16
25	Henry IV (Landshut; Ingolstadt 1445)	1393–1450	S23
26	Ernest (Munich)	1397–1438	S24
27	William II (Munich)	1397–1435	S24
28	William III (Straubing)	1404–1417	S19
29	Ludwig VII (Ingolstadt)	1413–1443	S22
30	John III (Straubing)	1417–1425	S19
31	Adolf (Munich)	1435–1440	S27
32	Albert II (Munich)	1438–1460	S26
33	Ludwig VIII (Ingolstadt)	1443–1445	S29
34	Ludwig IX (Landshut/Ingolstadt)	1450–1479	S25
35	John IV (Munich)	1460–1463	S32
36	Sigismund (Munich)	1460–1467	S32
37	Albert III (Munich; Landshut/Ingolstadt 1503)	1463–1508	S32
38	George (Landshut/Ingolstadt)	1479–1503	S34
39	William IV	1508–1550	S37
40	Ludwig X (Landshut)	1516–1545	S37
41	Albert IV	1550–1579	S39

42	William V	1579–1598	S41
43	Maximilian I (Elector 1623)	1598–(1651)	S42

d *Electors of Bavaria 1623–1806 – Wittelsbach dynasty*

43	Maximilian I	1623–1651	
44	Ferdinand	1651–1679	S43
45	Maximilian II Emanuel (1)	1679–1706	S44
	Maximilian II Emanuel (2)	1714	
46	Charles (VII of Germany)	1726	S45
47	Maximilian III Joseph	1745	S46
48	Charles Theodore (C. Palatine)	1777	DT4
49	Maximilian IV Joseph (C. Zweibrucken) (King 1806)	1799–(1825)	DT4

e *Kings of Bavaria 1806–1918 – Wittelsbach dynasty*

49	Maximilian I Joseph	1806	
50	Ludwig I	1825	S49
51	Maximilian II	1848	S50
52	Ludwig II	1864	S51
53	Otto	1886	S51
54	Ludwig III	1913–1918	BS51

39 GERMANY MEDIEVAL STATES

a *Dukes of Franconia 906–1196*

1	Conrad I (of Germany)	906	
2	Eberhard	912	BI
3	Conrad II	939	GDI
4	Otto (1)	955	S3
5	Henry I (II of Bavaria)	985	
	Otto (2)	995	
6	Conrad III	1004	S4
7	Conrad IV	1011	S5
8	Conrad V (II of Germany)	1030	BS6
9	Henry II (III of Germany)	1039	S8
10	Henry III (IV of Germany)	1056	S9
11	Henry IV (V of Germany)	1106	S10
12	Conrad VI (III of Germany)	1115	GD10
13	Frederick of Rothenburg (D. Swabia)	1152	S12
14	Conrad VII (s16 Germany)	1167–1196	

b *Dukes of Swabia 917–1268*

1	Burkhard I	917	
2	Hermann I	926	
3	Ludolf (s3 Germany)	949	HD2
4	Burkhard II	954	SI
5	Otto I	973	S3
6	Conrad I	982	BS2

7	Hermann II	997	s6
8	Hermann III	1003	s7
9	Ernest I of Babenberg (s1 Austria)	1012	HD7
10	Ernest II	1015	s9
11	Hermann IV	1030	s9
12	Henry I (III of Germany)	1038	UB11
13	Otto II (C. Palatine)	1045	
14	Otto III of Schweinfurt	1048	
15	Rudolf of Rheinfelden (German King)	1057	HD12
16	Berchtold	1079	s15
17	Frederick I of Hohenstauffen	1079	
18	Frederick II	1105	s17
19	Frederick III (I of Germany)	1147	s18
20	Frederick IV of Rothenburg	1152	BS18
21	Frederick V	1167	s19
22	Conrad II (VII of Franconia)	1191	s19
23	Philip (of Germany)	1196	s19
24	Frederick VI (II of Germany)	1208	BS23
25	Henry II	1216	s24
26	Conrad III (IV of Germany)	1235	s24
27	Conradin	1254–1268	s26

c *Counts and Dukes of Berg* 1101–1423

1	Adolf I	1101	
2	Adolf II	1152	s1
3	Eberhard	1160	s2
4	Engelbert I	1166	s2
5	Adolf III	1189	s4
6	Engelbert II	1218	s4
7	Henry (IV of Limburg)	1225	HD4
8	Adolf IV	1247	s7
9	Adolf V	1259	s8
10	William I	1296	s8
11	Adolf VI	1308	BS9
12	Gerard of Julich	1348	HSTD11
13	William II (Duke 1380)	1360	s12
14	Adolf VII (D. Julich 1423)	1408–(1437)	s13
	(Union with Julich)		

d *Counts of Mark* 1203–1461

1	Adolf I of Altena	1203	
2	Engelbert I	1249	s1
3	Eberhard I	1277	s2
4	Engelbert II	1308	s3
5	Adolf II	1328	s4
6	Engelbert III	1347	s5
7	Adolf III (I of Cleves)	1391	s5
8	Dietrich	1393	s7
9	Adolf IV (II of Cleves)	1398	s7
10	Gerard	1422	s7

11	John (I of Cleves)	1461–(1481)	S9

(Union with Cleves)

e *Counts and Dukes of Cleves* 1092–1524

1	Dietrich I	1092	
2	Arnold I	1119	
3	Dietrich II	1150	S2
4	Dietrich III	1176	S3
5	Dietrich IV	1188	S4
6	Arnold II	1191	S4
7	Dietrich V	1202	S6
8	Dietrich VI	1260	S7
9	Dietrich VII	1275	S8
10	Otto	1305	S9
11	Dietrich VIII	1311	S9
12	John	1347	S9
13	Adolf I	1368	GD11
14	Adolf II (Duke 1417)	1394	S13
15	John I	1448	S14
16	John II	1481	S15
17	John III (D. Julich 1524)	1521–(1539)	S16

(Union with Julich)

f *Counts and Dukes of Julich* 1081–1609

1	Gerard I	1081	
2	Gerard II	1102	S1
3	Gerard III	1126	S2
4	Gerard IV	1141	S3
5	William I	1154	GS1
6	William II	1176–1207	S5
7	Gerard V	1185–1203	S5
8	William III	1207	GD5
9	William IV	1219	S8
10	Walram	1278	S9
11	Gerard VI	1297	S9
12	William V (I as Duke 1356)	1329	S11
13	William II	1361	S12
14	William III	1393	S13
15	Reinhard	1402	S13
16	Adolf (VII of Berg)	1423	GG12
17	Gerard VII	1437	BS16
18	William IV	1474	S17
19	Sibylla of Brandenburg★	1511	W18
20	John (III of Cleves)	1524	HD18
21	William V	1539	S20
22	John-William	1592–1609	S21

g *Counts and Dukes of Gelders* 1096–1543

1	Gerard I	1096	
2	Gerard II	1118	S1

3	Henry	1131	S2
4	Otto I	1182	S3
5	Gerard III	1207	S4
6	Otto II	1229	S5
7	Rainald I	1271	S6
8	Rainald II (Duke 1339)	1326	S7
9	Rainald III (1)	1343	S8
10	Edward	1361	S8
	Rainald III (2)	1371	
11	John (II of Blois)	1372	HD8
12	William (II of Julich)	1379	GD8
13	Rainald IV (Reinhard of Julich)	1402	B12
14	Arnold of Egmont	1423	STGD13
15	Charles the Rash (of Burgundy)	1472	
15	Adolf of Egmont	1477	S14
16	Charles of Egmont (1)	1477	S15
17	Maximilian of Habsburg (I of Germany)	1483	
	Charles of Egmont (2)	1492	
18	William (V of Julich)	1538–1543	

40 **AUSTRIA** MEDIEVAL RULERS

a *Counts of Tyrol* 1055–1363

1	Albert I	1055–1124	
2	Albert II	1101–1165	S1
3	Berchtold	1165	S1
4	Henry I	1180	
5	Albert III	1202	S4
6	Meinhard (III of Goritz)	1253	HD5
7	Meinhard IV	1258	S6
8	Otto	1295	S7
9	Henry II	1310	S7
10	Margaret Maultasch★	1335–1363	D9
11	John-Henry of Moravia	1335–1341	H10
12	Ludwig (V of Bavaria)	1342–1361	H10
13	Meinhard V	1361–1363	S10/12
14	Rudolf of Habsburg (IV of Austria)	1363–(1365)	GG7

b *Dukes of Carinthia* 976–1335

1	Henry I (III of Bavaria) (1)	976	
2	Otto I (of Franconia) (1)	978	
	Henry I (2)	982–989	
	Otto I (2)	995	
3	Conrad I (of Franconia)	1004	S2
4	Adalbert of Eppenstein	1012	
5	Conrad II (of Franconia)	1036–1039	S3
6	Welf of Altdorf	1047	

7	Conrad III	1056	
8	Berchtold of Zahringen	1061	
9	Markwald	1072	S4
10	Leopold	1077	S9
11	Henry II	1090	S9
12	Henry III of Spanheim	1122	STS10
13	Engelbert	1124	B12
14	Ulrich I	1134	S13
15	Henry IV	1144	S14
16	Hermann	1161	S14
17	Ulrich II	1181	S16
18	Bernard	1202	S16
19	Ulrich III	1256	S18
20	Ottakar (II of Bohemia)	1269	
21	Rudolf (I of Germany)	1276	
22	Meinhard (IV of Tyrol)	1286	
23	Otto II (of Tyrol)	1295–1310	S22
24	Ludwig	1295–1305	B23
25	Henry V (II of Tyrol)	1295–1335	B23
26	Albert of Habsburg (II of Austria)	1335–(1358)	

c *Margraves and Dukes of Styria* 1035–1276

1	Arnold of Lambach	1035	
2	Ottakar I of Steyr	c.1055	
3	Aldalbert	c.1064	S2
4	Ottakar II	1082	S2
5	Leopold I	1122	S4
6	Ottakar III	1129	S5
7	Ottakar IV (Duke 1180)	1164	S6
8	Leopold II (V of Austria)	1192	
9	Leopold III (VI of Austria)	1194	
10	Frederick (II of Austria)	1230–1246	
		——	
11	Ottakar V (II of Bohemia)	1259–1276	

d *Margraves and Dukes of Austria – Babenbergs* 976–1276

1	Leopold I	976	
2	Henry I	994	S1
3	Adalbert	1018	S1
4	Ernest	1055	S3
5	Leopold II	1075	S4
6	Leopold III	1096	S5
7	Leopold IV	1136	S6
8	Henry II Jasomirgott (Duke 1156)	1141	S6
9	Leopold V	1177	S8
10	Frederick I	1194	S9
11	Leopold VI	1198	S9
12	Frederick II	1230–1246	S11
		——	

13 Ottokar (II of Bohemia)	1251–1276	GG5

e *Habsburg Dynasty in Austria, Styria, Carinthia, Tyrol 1276–1665*

1 Rudolf I (Austria and Styria) (K. Germany)	1276–1282	
2 Albert I (of Germany)	1282–1298	S1
3 Rudolf II	1282–1290	S1
4 Rudolf III (K. Bohemia 1306)	1298–1307	S2
5 Frederick II	1298–1330	S2
6 Leopold I	1298–1326	S2
7 Albert II (Carinthia 1335)	1298–1358	S2
8 Otto	1298–1339	S2
9 Rudolf IV (Tyrol 1363)	1358–1365	S7
10 Frederick III	1358–1362	S7
11 Leopold II (Styria, Carinthia and Tyrol)	1358–1386	S7
12 Albert III (Austria)	1358–1395	S7
13 William (Styria)	1386–1406	S11
14 Leopold III (Styria)	1386–1411	S11
15 Ernest (Styria)	1386–1424	S11
16 Frederick IV (Tyrol)	1386–1439	S11
17 Albert IV (Austria)	1395–1404	S12
18 Albert V (Austria) (II of Germany)	1404–1439	S17
19 Albert VI (Styria)	1424–1463	S15
20 Frederick V (Styria; Austria 1457; III of Germany)	1424–1493	S15
21 Sigismund (Tyrol)	1439–1496	S16
22 Ladislas (Austria) (K. Bohemia and Hungary)	1439–1457	S18
23 Maximilian I (all lands; K. Germany)	1493–1519	S20
24 Charles (V of Germany)	1519–1522	GS23
25 Ferdinand (I of Germany)	1522–1564	B24
26 Maximilian II (of Germany) (Austria)	1564–1576	S25
27 Ferdinand (Tyrol)	1564–1595	S25
28 Charles (Styria and Carinthia)	1564–1590	S25
29 Rudolf (II of Germany) (Austria; Tyrol 1595–1612)	1576–1608	S26
30 Matthias (of Germany) (Austria)	1608–1619	S26
31 Ferdinand (II of Germany)	1590–1637	S28
(Styria and Carinthia; Austria 1619; Tyrol 1621–25)		
32 Maximilian (Tyrol)	1612–1618	S26
33 Albert (Tyrol)	1620–1621	S26
34 Leopold (Tyrol)	1625–1632	S28
35 Ferdinand-Charles (Tyrol)	1632–1662	S34
36 Sigismund-Francis (Tyrol)	1662–1665	S34

41 **AUSTRIA** HABSBURG EMPERORS 1804–1918

1 Francis (II as Holy Roman Emperor)	1804	
2 Ferdinand	1835	S1
3 Francis Joseph (Emperor of Austria-Hungary from 1867)	1848	BS2
4 Charles	1916–1918	BGS3

42 PRINCES OF LIECHTENSTEIN since 1719

1 Anton-Florian	1719	
2 Joseph	1721	S1
3 John-Charles	1732	S2
4 Joseph-Wenceslas-Lorenz	1748	BS1
5 Francis-Joseph I	1772	BS4
6 Alois I	1781	S5
7 John I (1)	1805	S5
8 Charles	1807	S7
John I (2)	1813	
9 Alois II	1836	S7
10 John II	1858	S9
11 Francis	1929	S9
12 Francis-Joseph II	1938	3G7

43 SPAIN VISIGOTHIC AND SUEBIAN KINGS

a *Visigoth Kings in Gaul and Spain 395–c.720*

1 Alaric I	395	
2 Athaulf	410	B1
3 Wallia	415	
4 Theodoric I	419	HD1
5 Thorismund	451	S4
6 Theodoric II	453	S4
7 Euric	466	S4
8 Alaric II	484	S7
9 Gesalaric	507	s8
10 Amalaric	511	s8
11 Theudis	531	
12 Theudigisel	548	
13 Agila	549–555	
14 Athanagild	551–568	
15 Liuva I	568–572	
16 Leovigild I	569–586	B15
17 Reccared I	586	S16
18 Liuva II	601	S17
19 Witteric	603	
20 Gundemar	610	
21 Sisebut	612	
22 Reccared II	621	S21
23 Swinthila	621	
24 Sisenand	631	
25 Chintila	636	
26 Tulga	640	S25
27 Chindaswinth	642–653	
28 Recceswinth	649–672	S27
29 Wamba	672	
30 Erwig	680	
31 Egica	687–702	

32	Witiza	700–710	S31
33	Roderic	710–711	
34	Achila (Narbonne)	710–*c.*714	S32
35	Ardo (Narbonne)	*c.*714–720	

    b *Suebian Kings in N.W. Spain 409–585*

1	Hermeric	409	
2	Rechila	438	S1
3	Rechiar	448	S2
4	Aioulf	456	
5	Maldras	457	
6	Frumar (South)	460–*c.*465	
7	Richimund (North)	460–*c.*463	
8	Remisund	*c.*463–?	
		....	
9	Carriaric	*c.*550	
10	Theodimir	559	S9
11	Miro	570	S10
12	Eboric	582	S11
13	Andeca	584–585	HD11

44 **SPAIN** AMIRS AND CALIPHS

    a *Umayyad Dynasty 756–1031*

1	'Abdul-Rahman I (GS10 Damascus; Amir)	756	
2	Hisham I	788	S1
3	al-Hakam I	796	S2
4	'Abdul-Rahman II	822	S3
5	Muhammad I	852	S4
6	al-Mundhir	886	S5
7	'Abdullah	888	S5
8	'Abdul-Rahman III (Caliph 929)	912	GS7
9	al-Hakam II	961	S8
10	Hisham II (1)	976	S9
11	Muhammad II (1)	1009	BGS9
12	Sulayman (1)	1009	BGS9
	Muhammad II (2)	1010	
	Hisham II (2)	1010	
	Sulayman (2)	1013–1016	
		———	
13	'Abdul-Rahman IV	1018.	BGS9
		———	
14	'Abdul-Rahman V	1023	B11
15	Muhammad III	1024–1025	BGS9
		———	
16	Hisham III	1027–1031	B13

    b *Hammudid Dynasty – Caliphs 1016–1027*

1	'Ali ibn Hammud (of Malaga)	1016–1018	

2 al-Qasim (1) (of Malaga)	1018–1021	BI
3 Yahya (1) (of Malaga)	1021–1022	SI
al-Qasim (2)	1022–1023	
Yahya (2)	1025–1027	

45 **SPAIN** EARLY ASTURIAS AND LEON KINGS 718–1037

1 Pelayo	718	
2 Fafila	737	SI
3 Alfonso I	739	HDI
4 Fruela I	757	S3
5 Aurelius	768	BS3
6 Silo	774	HD3
7 Mauregatus	783	S3
8 Vermudo I	788	B5
9 Alfonso II	791	S4
10 Ramiro I	842	S8
11 Ordoño I	850	S10
12 Alfonso III	866	S11
13 Garcia I (Leon)	910–914	S12
14 Ordoño II (Galicia)	910–925	S12
15 Fruela II (Asturias)	910–925	S12
16 Alfonso IV	925	S14
17 Ramiro II	931	S14
18 Ordoño III	951	S17
19 Sancho I	956–966	S17
20 Ordoño IV	958–960	S16
21 Ramiro III	966	S19
22 Vermudo II	982	S18
23 Alfonso V	999	S22
24 Vermudo III	1028–1037	S23

46 **SPAIN** KINGS OF NAVARRE *c.*810–1589

1 Iñigo Arista	*c.*810	
2 Garcia Iñiguez	*c.*851	SI
3 Fortun Garces	*c.*880	S2
4 Sancho I	905	S2
5 Garcia II	926	S4
6 Sancho II	970	S5
7 Garcia III	994	S6
8 Sancho III the Great	1000	S7
9 Garcia IV	1035	S8
10 Sancho IV	1054	S9
11 Sancho V (of Aragon)	1076	BS9
12 Peter (I of Aragon)	1094	SII
13 Alfonso (I of Aragon)	1104	SII
14 Garcia V	1134	BGS10

15	Sancho VI	1150	S14
16	Sancho VII	1194	S15
17	Theobald I (IV of Champagne)	1234	STS16
18	Theobald II (V of Champagne)	1253	S17
19	Henry I (III of Champagne)	1270	S17
20	Joanna I★	1274–1304	D19
21	Philip I (IV of France)	1285–1314	H20
22	Louis (X of France)	1314–1316	S20/21
23	John I (of France)	1316.	S22
24	Philip II (V of France)	1316–1322	S20/21
25	Charles I (IV of France)	1322–1328	S20/21
26	Joanna II★	1328–1349	D22
27	Philip III of Evreux	1328–1343	H26/BS21
28	Charles II	1349–1387	S26/27
29	Charles III	1387–1425	S28
30	Blanche★	1425–1441	D29
31	John II (of Aragon)	1425–1479	H30
32	Eleanor★	1479.	D30/31
33	Francis-Phoebus (of Foix)	1479	GS32
34	Catherine★	1483–1517	ST33
35	John III of Albret	1484–1516	H34
36	Henry II (Lower Navarre)	1516–1555	S34/35
37	Joanna III (Lower Navarre)★	1555–1572	D36
38	Anthony of Bourbon (Lower Navarre)	1555–1562	H37
39	Henry III (IV of France 1589)	1572–(1610)	S37/38

47 **SPAIN** EARLY COUNTIES

a *Counts of Castile 923–1035*

1	Fernan Gonzalez	923	
2	Garcia I	970	S1
3	Sancho I	995	S2
4	Garcia II	1021	S3
5	Sancho II (III of Navarre)	1028	HD3
6	Ferdinand (King of Castile 1035)	1029–(1065)	S5

b *Counts of Aragon c.809–922*

1	Aznar I Galindo	c.809	
2	Galindo I Aznarez	c.844	S1
3	Aznar II Galindo	867	S2
4	Galindo II Aznarez	893–922	S3

c *Counts of Barcelona 873–1162*

1	Wilfred	873	
2	Wilfred Borrell I	898	S1
3	Sunyer	912	PS1
4	Borrell II	954	S3
5	Ramon Borrell	992	S4
6	Berengar-Ramon I	1018	S5

7 Ramon-Berengar I	1035	s6
8 Ramon-Berengar II	1076–1082	s7
9 Berengar–Ramon II	1076–1096	s7
10 Ramon-Berengar III	1096	s8
11 Ramon-Berengar IV	1131	s10
12 Alfonso (II of Aragon)	1162–(1196)	s11

48 SPAIN MINOR MUSLIM KINGDOMS

a 'Abbadid Dynasty of Seville 1023–1091

1 Muhammad I ibn Isma'il	1023	
2 'Abbad al-Mu'tadid	1042	s1
3 Muhammad II al-Mu'tamid	1069–1091	s2

b Aftasid Dynasty of Badajoz 1022–1094

1 'Abdullah al-Mansur	1022	
2 Muhammad al-Muzaffar	1045	s1
3 'Umar al-Mutawakkil	1068–1094	s2

c 'Amirid Dynasty of Valencia 1021–1096

1 'Abdul-'Aziz al-Mansur	1021	
2 'Abdul-Malik al-Muzaffar	1061	s1
3 Yahya al-Ma'mun (of Toledo)	1065	
4 Abu-Bakr	1075	s1
5 al-Qadi 'Uthman	1085	s4
6 Yahya al-Qadir (of Toledo)	1085	
7 al-Qadi Ja'far	1090–1096	

d Banu Qasim Dynasty of Alpuente c.1029–1092

1 Nizam-ud-Dawlah 'Abdullah I ibn al-Qasim	c.1029	
2 Yamin-ud-Dawlah Muhammad	1030	s1
3 'Adud-ud-Dawlah Ahmad	1048	s1
4 Jannah-ud-Dawlah 'Abdullah II	1048–1092	s2

e Banu Sumadih Dynasty of Almeria 1041–1091

1 Abu'l-Ahwaz Ma'an ibn Muhammad	1041	
2 Muhammad al-Mu'tasim	1051	s1
3 'Izz-ud-Dawlah Ahmad	1087–1091	s2

f Banu Yahya Dynasty of Niebla 1023–1051

1 Ahmad ibn Yahya	1023	
2 Muhammad	1041	B1
3 Fath ibn Khalaf	?–1051	Bs1

g Dhu'l-Nunid Dynasty of Toledo 1028–1085

1 Isma'il az-Zafir	1028	
2 Yahya al-Ma'mun	1043	s1
3 Yahya al-Qadir	1075–1085	gs2

h *Hammudid Dynasty of Malaga* 1010–1057

1	'Ali an-Nasir ibn Hammud	1010	5G2 Idrisid
2	al-Qasim I al-Ma'mun (1)	1016	B1
3	Yahya I al-Mu'tali (1)	1021	S1
	al-Qasim I (2)	1023	
	Yahya I (2)	1023	
4	Idris I al-Muta'ayyid	1036	S1
5	Yahya II	1039	S4
6	Hasan al-Mustansir	1039	S3
7	Idris II al-'Ali (1)	1043	S3
8	Muhammad al-Mahdi (of Algeciras)	1046	
9	Muhammad II al-Mu'tasim	1048	S4
10	al-Qasim al-Wathiq (of Algeciras)	1048	
11	Idris III al-Muwaffaq	1054	S5
	Idris II al-'Ali (2)	1054	
12	Muhammad III al-Musta'li	1055–1057	S4

i *Hammudid Dynasty of Algeciras* 1035–1058

1	Muhammad al-Mahdi (s2 Malaga)	1035	
2	al-Qasim al Wathiq	1048–1058	S1

j *Jahwarid Dynasty of Cordoba* 1031–1069

1	Jahwar ibn Muhammad	1031	
2	Muhammad al-Rashid	1043	S1
3	'Abdul-Malik	1058–1069	S2

k *Mujahid Dynasty of Denia (and Majorca)* 1018–1075

1	Mujahid ibn Yusuf	1018–1041	
2	'Ali Iqbal-ud-Dawlah	1045–1075	S1

l *Zirid Dynasty of Granada* 1012–1090

1	Zawi ibn Ziri (B1 Tunisia)	1012	
2	Habbus al-Muzaffar	1019	BS1
3	Badis	1038	S2
4	'Abdullah Saif-ud-Dawlah	1073–1090	GS3

m *Tujibid Dynasty of Zaragoza* 1019–1039

1	Mundhir I al-Mansur	1019	
2	Yahya al-Muzaffar	1023	S1
3	Mu'izz-ud-Dawlah Mundhir II	1029–1039	S2

n *Hudid Dynasty of Zaragoza* 1039–1142

1	Sulayman al-Musta'in ibn Hud	1039	
2	Ahmad I al-Muqtadir	1046	S1
3	Yusuf al-Mu'tamin	1081	S2
4	Ahmad II al-Musta'in	1085	S3
5	'Imad-ud-Dawlah 'Abdul-Malik (at Rueda	1110	S4
6	Ahmad III al-Mustansir de Jalon)	1130–1142	S5

49 **SPAIN** KINGS OF ARAGON 1035–1516

1 Ramiro I (s8 Navarre)	1035	
2 Sancho	1063	S1
3 Peter I	1094	S2
4 Alfonso I	1104	S2
5 Ramiro II	1134	S2
6 Petronilla★	1137	D5
7 Alfonso II	1162	s6
8 Peter II	1196	S7
9 James I the Conqueror	1213	s8
10 Peter III (I of Sicily)	1276	S9
11 Alfonso III	1285	S10
12 James II (of Sicily)	1291	S10
13 Alfonso IV	1327	S12
14 Peter IV	1336	S13
15 John I	1387	S14
16 Martin (II of Sicily)	1395–1410	S14
17 Ferdinand (s18 Castile)	1412	GD14
18 Alfonso V	1416	S17
19 John II	1458	S17
20 Ferdinand II (V of Castile)	1479	S19
21 Charles (V of Germany)	1516–(1556)	GD20

50 **RULERS OF MAJORCA**

a *Amirs of Majorca* 1075–1115

1 'Abdullah al-Murtada	1075	
2 Munbashir ibn Sulayman	1093	
3 Abu Rabi' Sulayman	1115.	

b *Banu Ghaniya Dynasty* 1126–1203

1 Muhammad ibn 'Ali	1126	
2 Ishaq ibn Muhammad	1156	S1
3 Muhammad ibn Ishaq	1183	S2
4 'Ali ibn Ishaq	1184	S2
5 Yahya ibn Ishaq	1188–1203	S2

c *Kings of Majorca* 1230–1343

1 James I the Conqueror (of Aragon)	1230	
2 James II	1276	S1
3 Sancho	1311	S2
4 James III	1324–1343	BS3

51 **SPAIN** KINGS OF CASTILE-LEON 1035–1516

1 Ferdinand I (Castile; Leon 1037) (S8 Navarre)	1035	
2 Sancho II (Castile)	1065–1072	S1
3 Alfonso VI (Leon; Castile 1072)	1065–1109	S1

4	Urraca★	1109–1126	D3
5	Alfonso VII	1126–1157	S4
6	Sancho III (Castile)	1157–1158	S5
7	Ferdinand II (Leon)	1157–1188	S5
8	Alfonso VIII (Castile)	1158–1214	S6
9	Alfonso IX (Leon)	1188–1230	S7
10	Henry I (Castile)	1214–1217	S8
11	Ferdinand III (Castile; Leon 1230)	1217–1252	S9
12	Alfonso X (K. Germany 1257)	1252–1284	S11
13	Sancho IV	1284	S12
14	Ferdinand IV	1295	S13
15	Alfonso XI	1312	S14
16	Peter the Cruel (1)	1350	S15
17	Henry II of Trastamara (1)	1366	S15
	Peter the Cruel (2)	1367	
	Henry II (2)	1369	
18	John I	1379	S17
19	Henry III	1390	S18
20	John II	1406	S19
21	Henry IV	1454	S20
22	Isabella★	1474	D20
23	Joanna★	1504–1516	D22
24	Philip I of Habsburg	1504–1506	H23
25	Ferdinand V (II of Aragon)	1506–1516	H22/F23
26	Charles I (V of Germany)	1516–(1556)	S23/24

52 SPAIN NASRID KINGS OF GRANADA 1230–1492

1	Muhammad I al-Ghalib	1230	
2	Muhammad II al-Faqih	1272	S1
3	Muhammad III al-Makhlu'	1302	S2
4	Nasr	1308	S2
5	Isma'il I	1313	BGS1
6	Muhammad IV	1325	S5
7	Yusuf I	1333	S5
8	Muhammad V al-Ghani (1)	1354	S7
9	Isma'il II	1359	S7
10	Muhammad VI	1360	BGS5
	Muhammad V al-Ghani (2)	1362	
11	Yusuf II	1391	S8
12	Muhammad VII al-Musta'in	1395	S11
13	Yusuf III	1407	S11
14	Muhammad VIII al-Mutamassik (1)	1417	S13
15	Muhammad IX as-Saghir	1428	BS11
	Muhammad VIII al-Mutamassik (2)	1430	
16	Yusuf IV	1432	S10
	Muhammad VIII al-Mutamassik (3)	1432	
17	Muhammad X al-Ahnaf (1)	1444	BS14
18	Sa'd al-Musta'in (1)	1445	BS13
	Muhammad X al-Ahnaf (2)	1446	

Sa'd al-Musta'in (2)	1453	
19 'Ali (1)	1462	S18
20 Abu 'Abdullah Muhammad XI (Boabdil) (1)	1482	S19
'Ali (2)	1483	
21 Muhammad XII az-Zaghal	1485	S18
Muhammad XI (2)	1487–1492	

53 SPAIN HABSBURG AND BOURBON KINGS

a *Habsburg Dynasty* 1516–1700

1 Charles I (V of Germany)	1516	
2 Philip II	1556	S1
3 Philip III	1598	S2
4 Philip IV	1621	S3
5 Charles II	1665–1700	S4

b *Bourbon Dynasty since* 1700

6 Philip V (1) (GS31 France)	1700	GG4
7 Luis	1724	S6
Philip V (2)	1724	
8 Ferdinand VI	1746	S6
9 Charles III (of Naples)	1759	S6
10 Charles IV	1788	S9
11 Ferdinand VII (1)	1808	S10
12 Joseph Bonaparte (B34 France)	1808	
Ferdinand VII (2)	1814	
13 Isabella II★	1833–1868	D11
14 Amadeus of Savoy (S1 Italy)	1870–1873	
15 Alfonso XII	1874–1885	S13
16 Alfonso XIII	1886–1931	S15
17 Juan Carlos	1975	GS16

54 PORTUGAL KINGS

a *Burgundian Dynasty* 1095–1383

1 Henry of Burgundy (Count; B2 Burgundy)	1095	
2 Alfonso I (King 1139)	1112	S1
3 Sancho I	1185	S2
4 Alfonso II	1211	S3
5 Sancho II	1223	S4
6 Alfonso III	1245	S4
7 Diniz	1279	S6
8 Alfonso IV	1325	S7
9 Peter I	1357	S8
10 Ferdinand	1367–1383	S9

b *Aviz Dynasty* 1385–1580

11	John I of Aviz	1385	S9
12	Edward	1433	S11
13	Alfonso V	1438	S12
14	John II	1481	S13
15	Manuel I	1495	BS13
16	John III	1521	S15
17	Sebastian	1557	GS16
18	Henry	1578–1580	S15

c *Habsburg Dynasty* 1580–1640

19	Philip I (II of Spain)	1580	HD16
20	Philip II (III of Spain)	1598	S19
21	Philip III (IV of Spain)	1621–1640	S20

d *Braganza Dynasty* 1640–1910

22	John IV of Braganza	1640	3GI5
23	Alfonso VI	1656	S22
24	Peter II	1683	S22
25	John V	1706	S24
26	Joseph	1750	S25
27	Maria I★	1777–1816	D26
28	Peter III	1777–1786	S25/H27
29	John VI	1816	S27/28
30	Peter IV (I of Brazil)	1826	S29
31	Maria II★ (1)	1826	D30
32	Miguel	1828	S29
	Maria II★ (2)	1834	
33	Peter V	1853	S31
34	Luis	1861	S31
35	Charles	1889	S34
36	Manuel II	1908–1910	S35

55 **ITALY** EARLY KINGS OF ROME 753–509 BC

1	Romulus	753 BC	
2	Numa Pompilius	716	
3	Tullus Hostilius	672	
4	Ancus Marcius	640	
5	Lucius Tarquinius Priscus	616	
6	Servius Tullius	578	HD5
7	Lucius Tarquinius Superbus	534–509	S5

56 **ITALY** TYRANTS AND KINGS OF SYRACUSE 485–214 BC

1	Gelon	485 BC	
2	Hiero I	478	BI
3	Thrasybulus	466.	BI

4	Dionysius I	405	
5	Dionysius II (1)	367	S4
6	Dion	356	HD4
7	Callippus	354	
8	Hipparinus	352	S4
9	Nysaeus	350	S4
	Dionysius II (2)	347–344	
10	Agathocles	317–289	
11	Hiero II	*c.*270	
12	Hieronymus	215–214 BC	GS11

57 **ITALY** OSTROGOTHIC KINGS 489–553 AD

1	Theodoric the Great	489	
2	Athalaric	526	GD1
3	Theodahad	534	STS1
4	Witigis	536	
5	Hildibad	540	
6	Euraric	540	
7	Totila	541	BS5
8	Teias	552–553	

58 **ITALY** LOMBARD KINGS 568–774 AD

1	Alboin	568	
2	Cleph	572–574	
3	Authari	584	S2
4	Agilulf	590	
5	Adalwald	615	S4
6	Ariwald	624	
7	Rothari	636	
8	Aribert I (GS1 Bavaria)	653	
9	Godebert	661	S8
10	Grimwald (I of Benevento)	662	HD8
11	Garibald	671	S10
12	Perctarit	672	S8
13	Cunincbert	688	S12
14	Raginbert	700	S9
15	Aribert II	701	S14
16	Luitprand	712	
17	Hildebrand	744	BS16
18	Ratchis	744	
19	Aistulf	749	B18
20	Desiderius	756–774	
21	Adelgis	758–774	S20

59 ITALY HOUSE OF SAVOY IN SAVOY, PIEDMONT AND SARDINIA

a *Counts and Dukes of Savoy 1034–1720*

1	Humbert I	1034	
2	Amadeus I	1049	S1
3	Otto	1056	S1
4	Peter I	1057	S3
5	Amadeus II	1078	S3
6	Humbert II	1080	S5
7	Amadeus III	1103	S6
8	Humbert III	1149	S7
9	Thomas I	1189	S8
10	Amadeus IV	1233	S9
11	Boniface	1253	S10
12	Peter II	1263	S9
13	Philip I	1268	S9
14	Amadeus V	1285	BS13
15	Edward	1323	S14
16	Aimone	1329	S14
17	Amadeus VI	1343	S16
18	Amadeus VII	1383	S17
19	Amadeus VIII (Duke 1416; Pope Felix V)	1391	S18
20	Louis	1434	S19
21	Amadeus IX	1465	S20
22	Philibert I	1472	S21
23	Charles I	1482	S21
24	Charles II	1490	S23
25	Philip II	1496	S20
26	Philibert II	1497	S25
27	Charles III	1504	S25
28	Emanuel-Philibert	1553	S27
29	Charles-Emanuel I	1580	S28
30	Victor-Amadeus I	1630	S29
31	Francis-Hyacinth	1637	S30
32	Charles-Emanuel II	1638	S30
33	Victor-Amadeus II (K. Sicily; K. Sardinia 1720)	1675–(1730)	S32

b *Princes of Piedmont 1233–1418*

1	Thomas II (S9 Savoy)	1233	
2	Thomas III	1259	S1
3	Philip	1282	S2
4	James	1334	S3
5	Amadeus	1367	S4
6	Louis	1402–1418	S4

c *Kings of Sardinia (and Dukes of Savoy) 1720–1861*

1	Victor-Amadeus II (of Savoy)	1720	
2	Charles-Emanuel III	1730	S1
3	Victor-Amadeus III	1773	S2

4	Charles-Emanuel IV	1796	S3
5	Victor-Emanuel I	1802	S3
6	Charles-Felix	1821	S3
7	Charles-Albert	1831	6G29
8	Victor-Emanuel II (K. Italy 1861)	1849–(1878)	S7

60 **ITALY** MODERN KINGS 1861–1946

1	Victor-Emanuel II (of Sardinia-Savoy)	1861	
2	Humbert I	1878	S1
3	Victor-Emanuel III	1900	S2
4	Humbert II	1946.	S3

61 **ITALY** KALBID AMIRS OF SICILY 948–1062

1	Hasan I	948	
2	Ahmad I	953	S1
3	'Ali	970	S1
4	Jabir	982	S3
5	Ja'far I	983	BS4
6	'Abdullah	985	B5
7	Yusuf	986	S6
8	Ja'far II	998	S7
9	Ahmad II al-Akhal	1019	S7
10	Hasan II as-Samsam	1040	S7
11	Muhammad ath-Thumna	1053–1062	

62 **ITALY** KINGS OF NAPLES AND SICILY

a *Hauteville Dynasty 1072–1194*

1	Roger of Hauteville (Count; B4 Apulia)	1072	
2	Simon (Count)	1101	S1
3	Roger II (King 1130)	1105	S1
4	William I	1154	S3
5	William II	1166	S4
6	Tancred	1189	BS4
7	William III	1194.	S6

b *Hohenstauffen Dynasty 1194–1266*

1	Henry (VI of Germany)	1194	HD3 above
2	Frederick (II of Germany)	1197	S1
3	Conrad (IV of Germany)	1250–1254	S2
4	Manfred	1258–1266	S2

c *Angevin Dynasty of Naples 1266–1435*

1	Charles I (of Anjou; Sicily to 1282)	1266	
2	Charles II	1285	S1

3	Robert	1309	S2
4	Joanna I★	1343	GS3
5	Charles III	1382	GG2
6	Ladislas	1386	S5
7	Joanna II★	1414–1435	D5

d *Aragonese Dynasty of Sicily (and Naples from 1435) 1282–1501*

1	Peter I (III of Aragon)	1282	
2	James (II of Aragon)	1285	S1
3	Frederick II	1295	S1
4	Peter II	1337	S3
5	Louis	1342	S4
6	Frederick III	1355	S4
7	Maria★	1377–1402	D6
8	Martin I	1391–1409	H7
9	Martin II (of Aragon)	1409–1410	F8

10	Ferdinand (I of Aragon)	1412	GG4
11	Alfonso I (V of Aragon; Naples 1435)	1416	S10
12	John (II of Aragon) (Sicily)	1458–1479	S10
13	Ferdinand I (Naples)	1458–1494	S11
14	Ferdinand (II of Aragon) (Sicily; Naples 1501)	1479–(1516)	S12
15	Alfonso II (Naples)	1494–1495	S13
16	Ferdinand II (Naples)	1495–1496	S15
17	Frederick IV (Naples)	1496–1501	S13

e *House of Savoy 1713–1718*

1	Victor-Amadeus (II of Savoy; Sicily)	1713–1718	

f *Bourbon and Bonaparte Dynasties 1734–1860*

1	Charles (III of Spain)	1734	
2	Ferdinand I (Sicily only 1806–1815)	1759–1825	S1
3	Joseph Bonaparte (Naples; B34 France)	1806–1808	
4	Joachim Murat (Naples)	1808–1815	HST3
5	Francis I	1825	S2
6	Ferdinand II	1830	S5
7	Francis II	1859–1860	S6

63 **ITALY** RULERS OF MILAN

a *Visconti Dynasty 1310–1447*

1	Matteo I	1310	
2	Galeazzo I	1322	S1
3	Azzo	1328	S2
4	Lucchino	1339	S1
5	Giovanni	1349	S1
6	Matteo II	1354–1355	BS5
7	Bernabo	1354–1385	B6
8	Galeazzo II	1354–1378	B6

9 Gian Galeazzo (Duke 1396)	1378–1402	S8
10 Giovanni Maria (Milan)	1402–1412	S9
11 Filippo Maria (Pavia; Milan 1412)	1402–1447	S9

b *Sforza Dynasty* 1450–1535

12 Francesco	1450	HD11
13 Galeazzo Maria	1466	S12
14 Gian Galeazzo	1476	S13
15 Ludovico	1494	S12
16 Louis XII of France	1499	STGS11
17 Massimiliano	1512	S15
18 Francis I of France	1515	
19 Francesco Maria	1521	S15
20 Charles (V of Germany)	1535–(1556)	

64 **ITALY** DUKES OF PARMA

a *Farnese Dynasty* 1545–1731

1 Pier Luigi	1545–1547	
2 Ottavio	1550	S1
3 Alessandro	1586	S2
4 Ranuccio I	1592	S3
5 Odoardo	1622	S4
6 Ranuccio II	1646	S5
7 Francesco	1694	S6
8 Antonio	1727–1731	S6

b *Bourbon Dynasty* 1731–1859

9 Charles I (III of Spain)	1731–1735	GG6
10 Philip	1748	B9
11 Ferdinand	1765–1799	S10
12 Marie-Louise of Habsburg★ (w34 France)	1814	
13 Charles II	1847	GS11
14 Charles III	1849	S13
15 Robert	1854–1859	S14

65 **ITALY** RULERS OF TUSCANY

a *Margraves of Tuscany* 812–1115

1 Boniface I	812–813
2 Boniface II	828–834
3 Aganus	835–845
4 Adalbert I	847–884
5 Adalbert II	890
6 Guy	917
7 Lambert	929

8	Boso	931	
9	Humbert	936	
10	Hugh	961	
11	Boniface III	1001–1012	
12	Ranier	1014	
13	Boniface IV of Canossa	1027	
14	Frederick	1052–1053	S13
15	Beatrice of Bar★	1052–1076	W13
16	Matilda★	1052–1115	D13

b *Medici Dynasty* 1434–1737

1	Cosimo (Lord of Florence)	1434	
2	Piero I	1464	S1
3	Lorenzo the Magnificent	1469–1492	S2
4	Giuliano	1469–1478	S2
5	Piero II	1492–1494	S3
		———	
6	Lorenzo II	1512–1519	S5
		———	
7	Alessandro (1)	1523–1527	S6
		———	
	Alessandro (2) (Duke of Florence 1531)	1530	
8	Cosimo I (Grand Duke of Tuscany 1569)	1537	3GB1
9	Francesco I	1574	S8
10	Ferdinand I	1587	S8
11	Cosimo II	1609	S10
12	Ferdinand II	1621	S11
13	Cosimo III	1670	S12
14	Gian Gastone	1723–1737	S13

c *Habsburg-Lorraine Dynasty* 1737–1859 – *Grand Dukes*

15	Francis (I as Emperor)	1737	
16	Leopold (II as Emperor)	1765	S15
17	Ferdinand III (1)	1790–1801	S16
		———	
18	(Eliza Bonaparte)★ (ST34 France)	1809–1814	
	Ferdinand III (2)	1814–1824	
19	Leopold II	1824–1859	S17

d *Kings of Etruria* 1801–1807

1	Louis of Bourbon-Parma (S11 Parma)	1801	
2	Charles (D. Parma 1847)	1803–1807	S1

66 ITALY RULERS OF FERRARA AND MODENA

a *Este Dynasty – Ferrara* 1209–1597 *and Modena* 1288–1797

1	Azzo I (Lord of Ferrara)	1209	
2	Aldobrandino I	1212	S1
3	Azzo II (1)	1215–1222	S1

	Azzo II (2)	1240	
4	Obizzo I (Modena 1288)	1264	GS3
5	Azzo III	1293	S4
6	Aldobrandino II	1308–1326	S4
7	Niccolo I	1317–1344	S6
8	Obizzo II	1317–1352	S6
9	Rinaldo I	1317–1335	S6
10	Aldobrandino III	1352–1361	S8
11	Niccolo II	1361–1388	S8
12	Alberto	1361–1393	S8
13	Niccolo III	1393	S12
14	Leonello	1441	S13
15	Borso (Duke Modena 1452, Ferrara 1471)	1450	S13
16	Ercole I	1471	S13
17	Alfonso I	1505	S16
18	Ercole II	1534	S17
19	Alfonso II	1559	S18
20	Cesare (Modena only)	1597	GS17
21	Alfonso III	1628	S20
22	Francesco I	1629	S21
23	Alfonso IV	1658	S22
24	Francesco II	1662	S23
25	Rinaldo II	1694	S22
26	Francesco III	1737	S25
27	Ercole III	1780–1797	S26

b *Habsburg Dukes of Modena 1814–1859*

28	Francesco IV (BS16 Tuscany)	1814	GD27
29	Francesco V	1846–1859	S28

67 **ITALY** MEDIEVAL STATES IN THE NORTH

a *Margraves of Saluzzo – Aleramid Dynasty 1142–1548*

1	Manfred I (4G1 Montferrat)	1142	
2	Manfred II	1175	S1
3	Manfred III	1215	GS2
4	Thomas I	1244	S3
5	Manfred IV	1296	S4
6	Frederick I	1334	S5
7	Thomas II (1)	1336	S6
8	Manfred V	1341	S5
	Thomas II (2)	1346	
9	Frederick II	1357	S7
10	Thomas III	1396	S9
11	Louis I	1416	S10
12	Louis II	1475	S11
13	Michael-Anthony	1504	S12
14	John-Louis	1528	S12
15	Francis	1529	S12
16	Gabriel	1537–1548	S12

b *Margraves of Montferrat – Aleramid Dynasty 967–1305*

1	Aleram	967	
2	Otto I	?	S1
3	William I	990	S2
4	Henry	c.1032	S3
5	Otto II	c.1040	S3
6	William II	1084	S5
7	Ranier	c.1100	S6
8	William III	c.1140	S7
9	Conrad (K. Jerusalem)	1188	S8
10	Boniface I (K. Thessalonica)	1192	S9
11	William IV	1207	S10
12	Boniface II	1225	S11
13	William V	1253	S12
14	John I	1290–1305	S13

c *Margraves of Montferrat – Palaeologi 1306–1533*

15	Theodore I (S74 Byzantium)	1306	GD13
16	John II	1338	S15
17	Otto III	1372	S16
18	John III	1378	S16
19	Theodore II	1381	S16
20	John-Jacob	1418	S19
21	John IV	1445	S20
22	William VI	1464	S20
23	Boniface III	1483	S20
24	William VII	1493	S23
25	Boniface IV	1518	S24
26	John-George	1530–1533	S23

d *Gonzaga Dynasty of Mantua 1328–1708*

1	Luigi I (Captain-General)	1328	
2	Guido	1360	S1
3	Luigi II	1369	S2
4	Francesco I	1382	S3
5	Gian-Francesco (Margrave 1433)	1407	S4
6	Luigi III	1444	S5
7	Federigo I	1478	S6
8	Francesco II	1484	S7
9	Federigo II (Duke 1530)	1519	S8
10	Francesco III	1540	S9
11	Gugliemo	1550	S9
12	Vincenzo I	1587	S11
13	Francesco IV	1612	S12
14	Ferdinando	1612	S12
15	Vincenzo II	1626	S12
16	Carlo I	1627	GS9
17	Carlo II	1637	GS16
18	Ferdinando-Carlo	1665–1708	S17

e *Scaligeri Dynasty of Verona* 1262–1387

1	Mastino I della Scala (Captain-General)	1262	
2	Alberto I	1277	B1
3	Bartolomeo I	1301	S2
4	Alboino	1304	S2
5	Cangrande I (Imperial Vicar)	1311	S2
6	Alberto II	1329–1352	S4
7	Mastino II	1329–1351	S4
8	Cangrande II	1351–1359	S7
9	Paolo-Alboino	1351–1365	S7
10	Cansignorio	1351–1375	S7
11	Bartolomeo II	1375–1381	S10
12	Antonio	1375–1387	S10

f *Carraresi Dynasty, Lords of Padua* 1318–1405

1	Giacomo da Carrara	1318	
2	Marsiglio I	1324	
3	Ubertino	1338	
4	Marsiglio II	1345	
5	Giacomo II	1345	
6	Giacomino	1350	B5
7	Francesco I	1355	S5
8	(Gian Galeazzo of Milan)	1388	
9	Francesco II	1390–1405	S7

g *Polentano Dynasty, Lords of Ravenna* 1275–1441

1	Guido da Polenta	1275	
2	Lamberto I	1297	S1
3	Guido II	1316	GS1
4	Ostasio I	1322	GS1
5	Bernadino I (1)	1346	S4
6	Pandolfo	1347	S4
7	Lamberto II	1347	S4
	Bernadino I (2)	1347	
8	Guido III	1359	S5
9	Azzo	1390–1394	S8
10	Ostasio II	1390–1396	S8
11	Bernadino II	1390–1400	S8
12	Pietro	1390–1404	S8
13	Aldobrandino	1390–1406	S8
14	Obizzo	1390–1431	S8
15	Ostasio III	1431–1441	S14

h *Counts and Dukes of Urbino – Montefeltro Dynasty* 1213–1508

1	Buonconte	1213	
2	Montefeltrano	1241	S1
3	Guido I (1)	1255–1286	S2
	Guido I (2)	1292	

4	Federigo I	1296	S3
5	Guido II	1323–1341	S4
6	Nolfo	1323–1359	S4
7	Antonio	1377	GS6
8	Guidantonio	1404	S7
9	Oddantonio	1443	S8
10	Federigo II (Duke 1474)	1444	S8
11	Guidobaldo I	1482–1508	S10

i *Dukes of Urbino – Della Rovere* 1508–1626

12	Francesco-Maria I	1508	STS11
13	Guidobaldo II	1538	S12
14	Francesco-Maria II (1)	1574	S13
15	Federigo-Ubaldo	1621	S14
	Francesco-Maria II (2)	1623–1626	

68 ITALY MEDIEVAL STATES IN THE SOUTH

a *Dukes of Spoleto* 570–999

1	Farwald I	570	
2	Ariulf	592	
3	Theudelap	602	
4	Atto	650	
5	Trasamund I	665	
6	Farwald II	703	
7	Trasamund II (1)	724	
8	Hilderic	739	
	Trasamund II (2)	739	
9	Asprand	742	
10	Lupus	745	
11	Unnolfo	752	
12	Alboin	757	
13	Gisulf	758	
14	Theodicius	763	
15	Hildebrand	774	
16	Winigis	789	
17	Suppo I	822	
18	Adalard	824	
19	Mauring	824	
20	Berengar	836	
21	Guy I	842	
22	Lambert I (1)	860	S21
23	Suppo II	871	
	Lambert I (2)	875–879	
24	Guy II	876–882	S21
25	Guy III (Emperor 891)	880–894	S22
26	Lambert II (Emperor 894)	894–898	S25

27	Guy IV	895–898	
28	Alberic	898	
29	Boniface I	923–928	
30	Theodebald I	933	s29
31	Anscar of Ivrea	936	
32	Sarlio	940	
33	Humbert (of Tuscany)	943	
34	Boniface II	946–953	s30
35	Theodebald II	953–959	s34
36	Trasamund III	959	
37	Pandulf (I of Benevento)	967	
38	Trasamund IV (of Camerino)	982	
39	Hugh (of Tuscany)	989–999	
		….	

b *Dukes of Benevento* 571–1074

1	Zotto	571	
2	Arichis	594	
3	Ago I	641	s2
4	Radwald	642	
5	Grimwald I (K. Italy)	647	B4
6	Romwald I	662	s5
7	Grimwald II	677	s6
8	Gisulf I	686	s6
9	Romwald II	703	s8
10	Audelais	729	s8
11	Gregorius	732	
12	Gottschalk	738	
13	Gisulf II	742	s9
14	Luitprand	750	s13
15	Arichis II	758	
16	Grimwald III	788	s15
17	Grimwald IV	806	
18	Sico	817	
19	Sicard	832	s18
20	Radelchis I	839	
21	Radelgar	851	s20
22	Adelchis	854	s20
23	Gaideris	878	s21
24	Radelchis II (1)	881	s22
25	Ago II	884	s22
26	Ursus	890–891	s25
27	Guy (IV of Spoleto)	895	
	Radelchis II (2)	897	
28	Atenulf I (of Capua)	900–910	
29	Landulf I	901–943	s28
30	Atenulf II	911–940	s28
31	Atenulf III	933–943	s29

32	Landulf II	940–961	S29
33	Pandulf I Iron-head	943–981	S32
34	Landulf III	959–968	S32
35	Landulf IV	968–981	S33
36	Pandulf II	981–1014	S34
37	Landulf V	987–1033	S36
38	Pandulf III (1)	1012–1053	S37
39	Landulf VI (1)	1038–1053	S38
40	Rudolf	1053–1054	
	Pandulf III (2)	1054–1059	
	Landulf VI (2)	1054–1077	
41	Pandulf IV	1056–1074	S39

c *Princes of Salerno 840–1075*

1	Siconulf	840	
2	Sico	851–853	SI
3	Petrus	852–856	
4	Ademar	852–861	S3
5	Gaifar	856–880	
6	Gaimar I	877–901	S5
7	Gaimar II	893–933	S6
8	Gisulf I (1)	933–972	S7
9	Landulf I (S30 Benevento)	972–974	
10	Landulf II	972–974	S9
	Gisulf I (2)	974–978	
11	Pandulf I (of Benevento)	978–981	
12	Pandulf II	974–981	SII
13	Manso of Amalfi	981–983	
14	John I	981–983	
15	John II Lambert	983–994	
16	Guy	983–988	SI5
17	Gaimar III	988–1031	SI5
18	Gaimar IV	1018–1052	SI7
19	John III	1038–1042	SI8
20	Guy of Sorrento	1040–?	SI7
21	Gisulf II	1042–1075	SI8

d *Princes of Capua 840–1156*

1	Landulf I	840	
2	Lando I	842	SI
3	Lando II	861	S2
4	Pando	861	SI
5	Pandenulf (1)	862	S4
6	Landulf II	862	SI
	Pandenulf (2)	879	
7	Lando III	882	BS2
8	Landenulf I	885	B7
9	Atenulf (I as D. Benevento 900)	887–(910)	B7
	(Union with Benevento)		
10	Aloara★ (w33 Benevento)	982–992	

11	Landenulf II (s33 Benevento)	982–993	S10
12	Laidulf	993	B11
13	Ademar	999	
14	Landulf VII (s34 Benevento)	999	
15	Pandulf II	1007–1022	S14
16	Pandulf III (II of Benevento)	1009–1014	B14
17	Pandulf IV (1)	1016–1022	S16
18	Pandulf V (1)	1020–1022	S17
19	Pandulf VI	1022–1026	BS12
20	John	1022–1026	S19
	Pandulf IV (2)	1026–1038	
	Pandulf V (2)	1026–1038	
21	Gaimar (IV of Salerno)	1038–1047	GD16
	Pandulf IV (3)	1047–1050	
	Pandulf V (3)	1047–1057	
22	Landulf VIII	1047–1058	S18
23	Richard I (C. Aversa)	1058	
24	Jordan I	1078	S23
25	Lando IV	1091	
26	Richard II	1098	S24
27	Robert I	1107	S24
28	Richard III	1120	S27
29	Jordan II	1120	S24
30	Robert II (1)	1127	S29
31	Anfuso	1137	
32	William (I of Sicily)	1144	
	Robert II (2)	1155–1156	

e *Counts and Dukes of Apulia 1043–1127 – Hauteville Dynasty*

1	William of Hauteville	1043	
2	Drogo	1046	B1
3	Humphrey	1051	B1
4	Robert Guiscard (Duke 1059)	1057	B1
5	Roger Borsa	1085	S4
6	William II	1111–1127	S5

69 CZECHOSLOVAKIA RULERS OF BOHEMIA

a *Premyslid Dynasty 873–1306 – Dukes, later Kings*

1	Borzhivoi I (Duke)	873(?)	
2	Spitihnev I	895–912	S1
3	Vratislav I	895–921	S1
4	Vaclav I (St Wenceslas)	921	S3
5	Boleslav I	929	S3
6	Boleslav II	967	S5
7	Boleslav III (1)	999	S6
8	Vladivoi	1002	STS6
	Boleslav III (2)	1003	
9	Jaromir	1003	S6

10	Odalrich	1012	S6
11	Bretislav I	1034	S10
12	Spitihnev II	1055	S11
13	Vratislav II (King 1086)	1061	S11
14	Conrad (Duke)	1092	S11
15	Bretislav II	1092	S13
16	Borzhivoi II (1)	1100	S13
17	Svatopluk	1107	BS13
18	Vladislav I (1)	1109	S13
	Borzhivoi II (2)	1117	
	Vladislav I (2)	1120	
19	Sobeslav I	1125	S13
20	Vladislav II (King 1158)	1140	S18
21	Sobeslav II (Duke)	1173	S19
22	Frederick	1179	S20
23	Conrad-Otto	1189	GG14
24	Vaclav II	1191	S19
25	Premysl Ottakar I (1)	1192	S20
26	Bretislav-Henry	1193	BS20
27	Vladislav III	1197	S20
	Premysl Ottakar I (2) (King 1198)	1197	
28	Vaclav I	1230	S25
29	Premysl Ottakar II	1253	S28
30	Vaclav II	1278	S29
31	Vaclav III	1305–1306	S30

b *Kings of Bohemia 1306–1526*

32	Rudolf (III of Austria)	1306	
33	Henry (V of Carinthia)	1307	HD30
34	John of Luxemburg	1310	HD30
35	Charles (IV of Germany)	1346	S34
36	Vaclav IV (Wenceslas, K. Germany)	1378	S35
37	Sigismund (of Hungary and Germany)	1419	S35
38	Albert (II of Germany)	1437	HD37
39	Ladislas (V of Hungary)	1440	S38
40	George Podiebrad	1457	
41	Vladislav Jagiellon	1471	STS39
42	Louis (II of Hungary)	1516	S41
43	Ferdinand (I of Germany)	1526–(1564)	HD41

70 CZECHOSLOVAKIA PRINCES OF GREATER MORAVIA
c.820–906

1	Moimir I	*c.*820	
2	Rostislav	*c.*846	BS1
3	Svatopluk I	869	BS2
4	Moimir II	894–*c.*906	S3
5	Svatopluk II	894–*c.*895	S3

71 **HUNGARY** KINGS

a *Arpad Dynasty 896–1301 – Kings from 1000*

1	Arpad (Duke)	896	
2	Zsolt	907	S1
3	Taksony	947	S2
4	Geza	972	S3
5	Stephen I (King 1000)	997	S4
6	Peter Orseolo (1)	1038	STS5
7	Samuel Aba	1041	HD4
	Peter Orseolo (2)	1044	
8	Andrew I	1046	GG3
9	Bela I	1060	B8
10	Salomon	1063	S8
11	Geza I	1074	S9
12	Ladislas I	1077	S9
13	Koloman	1095	S11
14	Stephen II	1116	S13
15	Bela II	1131	BS13
16	Geza II	1141	S15
17	Stephen III	1162–1172	S16
18	Ladislas II	1162–1163	S15
19	Stephen IV	1163–1165	S15
20	Bela III	1172	S16
21	Emeric	1196	S20
22	Ladislas III	1204	S21
23	Andrew II	1205	S20
24	Bela IV	1235	S23
25	Stephen V	1270	S24
26	Ladislas IV	1272	S25
27	Andrew III	1290–1301	GS23

b *Kings of Hungary 1301–1540*

28	Vaclav (III of Bohemia)	1301	4G20
29	Otto (III of Bavaria)	1305	STS25
30	Charles Robert of Anjou (GS2 Naples)	1308	GG25
31	Louis I the Great (K. Poland 1370)	1342	S30
32	Mary★	1382–1395	D31
33	Sigismund of Luxemburg (Emperor)	1387–1437	H32
34	Albert (II of Germany)	1437–1439	HD33
35	Vladislav Jagiellon (VI of Poland)	1440–1444	
36	Ladislas V	1444–1457	S34
37	Matthias Corvinus	1458	
38	Vladislav II Jagiellon (of Bohemia)	1490	BS35
39	Louis II (K. Bohemia)	1516	S38
40	John Zapolya	1526–1540	
41	Ferdinand (I of Germany)	1526–(1564)	HD38

72 **YUGOSLAVIA** RULERS OF SERBIA

a *Nemanjich Dynasty* 1168–1371

1	Stephen Nemanja (Grand Zhupan)	1168	
2	Stephen Nemanjich (King 1217)	1196	S1
3	Stephen Radoslav	1227	S2
4	Stephen Vladislav	1234	S2
5	Stephen Urosh I	1243	S2
6	Stephen Dragutin	1276	S5
7	Stephen Urosh II Miliutin	1282	S5
8	Stephen Urosh III	1321	S7
9	Stephen Urosh IV Dushan (Emperor 1345)	1331	S8
10	Stephen Urosh V	1355–1371	S9
11	Simeon Urosh (Thessaly)	1356–1371	S8
12	Vukashin (Macedonia)	1365–1371	

b *Princes of Serbia* 1371–1459

1	Lazar I Hrebeljanovich	1371	
2	Stephen	1389	S1
3	George Brankovich	1427	
4	Lazar II	1456	S3
5	Stephen Tomashevich (of Bosnia)	1458–1459	HD4

c *Karageorgevich and Obrenovich Dynasties* 1804–1945

1	Kara George Petrovich (Hospodar of Serbia)	1804–1813	
2	Milosh Obrenovich (Prince of Serbia) (1)	1815	
3	Milan I	1839	S2
4	Michael (1)	1839	S2
5	Alexander I	1842	S1
	Milosh Obrenovich (2)	1858	
	Michael (2)	1860	
6	Milan II (King of Serbia 1882)	1868	BGS2
7	Alexander II	1889	S6
8	Peter I (K. of the Serbs, Croats and Slovenes 1918)	1903	S5
9	Alexander (III) (King of Yugoslavia 1929)	1921	S8
10	Peter II	1934–1945	S9

73 **YUGOSLAVIA** BANS AND KINGS OF BOSNIA 1180–1463

1	Kulin (Ban)	1180	
2	Stephen	1204	
3	Matei Ninoslav	1232	
4	Prijesda I	1250	
5	Prijesda II	1287–1290	
6	Stephen Kotroman	1287–1302	
7	Paul Subich	1299–1312	
8	Mladen Subich	1312	S7
9	Stephen Kotromanich	1322	S6
10	Stephen Tvrtko I (King 1376)	1353	GS6

11	Stephen Dabisha	1391	B10
12	Helena★	1395	W11
13	Stephen Ostoja (1)	1398	S10
14	Stephen Tvrtko II (1)	1404	S10
	Stephen Ostoja (2)	1408	
15	Stephen Ostojich	1418	S13
	Stephen Tvrtko II (2)	1421	
16	Stephen Thomas Ostojich	1443	S13
17	Stephen Tomashevich	1461–1463	S16

74 **YUGOSLAVIA** BANS AND KINGS OF CROATIA 810–1095

1	Borna (Ban)	810
2	Vladislav	821
3	Mislav	835
4	Trpimir I	845
5	Domagoi	864
6	Iliko	876
7	Zdeslav	878
8	Branimir	879
9	Mutimir	892
10	Kresimir I	900
11	Miroslav	908
12	Pribunia	912
13	Tomislav (King 924)	913
14	Kresimir II	930
15	Stephen Drzhislav	969
16	Svetoslav	997
17	Kresimir III	c.1000–1030
18	Goislav	1000–1020
19	Stephen I	1030
20	Peter Kresimir	1058
21	Dimitar Zvonimir	1076
22	Stephen II	1089
23	Almos (S11 Hungary)	1091–1095

75 **YUGOSLAVIA** RULERS OF MONTENEGRO

a *Balshich Dynasty* 1356–1421

1	Balsha I	1356	
2	Stracimir	1368	S1
3	George I	1373–1379	S1
4	Balsha II	1373–1385	S1
5	George II	1373–1403	S2
6	Balsha III	1403–1421	S5

b *Crnojevich Dynasty* 1427–1516

1	Stephen I	1427

2	Ivan I	1466	S1
3	George III	1490	S2
4	Stephen II	1496–99	
		———	
5	Ivan II	1515	
6	George IV	1515–1516	S2

c *Petrovich Dynasty* 1696–1918

1	Danilo (Vladika)	1696	
2	Sava	1735–1781	FBS1
3	Vasil	1750–1756	BS1
4	Peter I	1782	BGS1
5	Peter II	1830	BS4
6	Danilo II (Prince)	1851	BGS4
7	Nicholas (King 1910)	1860–1918	BS6

76 RUMANIA PRINCES OF TRANSYLVANIA 1526–1691

1	John Zapolya (K. Hungary)	1526	
2	John Sigismund (1)	1540	S1
3	Ferdinand (I of Germany)	1551	
	John Sigismund (2)	1556	
4	Stephen Bathory (K. Poland 1575)	1571	
5	Christopher Bathory	1576	B4
6	Sigismund Bathory (1)	1581	S5
7	Andrew Bathory	1599	BS5
8	Michael the Brave (of Wallachia)	1599	
	Sigismund Bathory (2)	1601–1602	
		———	
9	Stephen Bocskay	1605	
10	Sigismund Rakoczy	1607	
11	Gabriel Bathory	1608	BS7
12	Gabriel Bethlen	1613	
13	Catherine of Brandenburg★	1629	W12
14	Stephen Bethlen	1630	B12
15	George Rakoczy I	1630	S10
16	George Rakoczy II	1648	S15
17	Michael Apafi I	1661	
18	Michael Apafi II	1690–1691	S17

77 RUMANIA VOIVODES OF MOLDAVIA 1352–1615

1	Dragosh	1352	
2	Sas	1354	
3	Balc	1359	
4	Bogdan I	1359	
5	Latzcu	1365	S4
6	Costea	1373	
7	Peter I	1375	S6
8	Roman I	1391	S6

9	Stephen I	1394	S7
10	Iuga	1399	S8
11	Alexander I	1400	S8
12	Ilias I (1)	1432	S11
13	Stephen II (1)	1433	S11
	Ilias I (2)	1435–1442	
	Stephen II (2)	1436–1447	
14	Peter II (1)	1447	S11
15	Roman II	1447	S12
	Peter II (2)	1448	
16	Alexandrel (1)	1449	S12
17	Bogdan II	1449	S11
18	Peter Aaron (1)	1451	S11
	Alexandrel (2)	1452	
	Peter Aaron (2)	1454	
	Alexandrel (3)	1455	
	Peter Aaron (3)	1455	
19	Stephen III the Great	1457	S17
20	Bogdan III	1504	S19
21	Stephenitsa	1517	S20
22	Peter III (1)	1527	S19
23	Stephen IV	1538	BS20
24	Alexander II	1540	
	Peter III (2)	1541	
25	Ilias II	1546	S22
26	Stephen V	1551	S22
27	John I	1552	
28	Alexander III (1)	1552	S20
29	John Jacob	1561	
30	Stephen VI	1563	
	Alexander III (2)	1564	
31	Bogdan IV	1568	S28
32	John II	1572	S21
33	Peter IV (1) (of Wallachia)	1574	
34	John III	1577	S21
	Peter IV (2)	1578	
35	Iancul Sasul	1579	
	Peter IV (3)	1582	
36	Aaron (1)	1591	
37	Peter V	1592	S32
	Aaron (2)	1592	
38	Stephen VII	1595	
39	Ieremei Movila (1)	1595	
40	Michael the Brave (of Wallachia)	1600	
	Ieremei Movila (2)	1600	
41	Simeon Movila (of Wallachia)	1606	B39
42	Michael Movila (1)	1607	
43	Constantine (1)	1607	
	Michael Movila (2)	1607	
	Constantine (2)	1607	

| 44 Stephen VIII | 1611–1615 |
| | .... |

78 RUMANIA VOIVODES OF WALLACHIA *c.*1277–1611

1	Barbat	*c.*1277	
2	Tihomir	*c.*1290	
3	Basarab I	*c.*1310	
4	Nicholas Alexander	1352	s3
5	Vladislav I	1364	s4
6	Radu I Negru	*c.*1377	s4
7	Dan I	*c.*1383	s6
8	Mircea I the Old (1)	1386	s6
9	Vlad I	1394	
	Mircea I (2)	1397	
10	Michael I	1418	s8
11	Dan II	1420–1431	s7
12	Radu II	1421–1427	
13	Alexander I	1431	
14	Vlad II Dracul (1)	1436	s8
15	Mircea II	1442	
16	Basarab II	1442	
	Vlad II Dracul (2)	1443	
17	Vladislav II (1)	1447	
18	Vlad III the Impaler (1)	1448	s14
	Vladislav II (2)	1448	
	Vlad III (2)	1456	
19	Radu III	1462–1475	s14
20	Basarab III	1473–1477	s19
21	Basarab IV	1477–1482	
22	Mircea III	1481	
23	Vlad IV	1481	
24	Radu IV	1495	s18
25	Mihnea I	1508	s24
26	Mircea IV	1509	
27	Vlad V	1510	
28	Neagoe Basarab	1512	s20
29	Theodosius (1)	1521	s28
30	Vlad Radu	1521	
	Theodosius (2)	1521	
31	Radu V (1)	1522	s24
32	Vladislav III (1)	1523	
33	Radu VI	1523	
	Radu V (2)	1524–1529	
	Vladislav III (2)	1524–1525	
34	Moses	1529	
35	Vlad VI	1530	
36	Vlad VII	1532	
37	Peter I	1535	
38	Mircea V (1)	1545	

39	Radu VII	1552	
	Mircea V (2)	1552	
40	Patrascu	1554	
41	Peter II	1559	
42	Alexander II	1568	
43	Mihnea II (1)	1577	
44	Peter III	1583	S40
	Mihnea II (2)	1585	
45	Stephen	1591	
46	Alexander III	1592	
47	Michael II the Brave	1593–1601	S40
48	Nicholas Patrascu	1599–1600	S47
49	Simeon Movila	1600–1602	
50	Radu Mihnea	1601–1602	
51	Radu VIII	1602–1611	
		....	

79 RUMANIA MODERN RULERS 1859–1947

1	Alexander Couza (Prince)	1859	
2	Carol I of Hohenzollern-Sigmaringen (King 1881)	1866	
3	Ferdinand	1914	BS2
4	Michael (1)	1927	S5
5	Carol II	1930	S3
	Michael (2)	1940–1947	

80 BULGARIA RULERS

a *Bulgarian Khans 681–803*

1	Asparuch	681	
2	Tervel	702	
3	(Unknown)	718	
4	Sevar	725	
5	Kormisosh	740	
6	Vinech	756	
7	Telets	762	
8	Sabin	765	
9	Umar	767	
10	Toktu	767	
11	Pagan	772	
12	Telerig	c.772	
13	Kardam	777–803	

b *Krum Dynasty 803–972*

14	Krum Khan	803	
15	Omortag	814	S14
16	Malamir	831	S15
17	Presijan	836	
18	Boris I Michael (King)	852	BS16

19	Vladimir	889	S18
20	Simeon (Emperor 925)	893	S18
21	Peter	927	S20
22	Boris II	969–972	S21

c *Macedonian Bulgarian Kingdom 979–1018*

23	Samuel (with brothers; alone *c*.987)	976	
24	Gabriel Radomir	1014	S23
25	John Vladislav	1015–1018	BS23

d *Asen Dynasty 1187–1280 – Kings*

26	Asen I	1187	
27	Peter	1196	B26
28	Kalojan	1197	B26
29	Boril	1207	BS26
30	John Asen II	1218	S26
31	Koloman	1241	S30
32	Michael Asen	1246	S30
33	Constantine Tich	1257	
34	Ivailo	1277	
35	John Asen III	1279–1280	BS32

e *Terter Dynasty 1280–1323 – Kings*

36	George I	1280	STH35
37	Smilets	1292	
38	Chaka	1299	
39	Theodore Svetoslav	1300	S36
40	George II	1322–1323	S39

f *Shishmanovich Dynasty 1323–1396 – Kings*

41	Michael Shishman	1323	
42	John Stephen	1330	S41
43	John Alexander	1331–1371	BS41
44	John Shishman (Trnovo)	1371–1393	S43
45	John Stracimir (Vidin)	*c*.1360–1396	S43

g *Princes and Kings of Bulgaria 1879–1946*

46	Alexander of Battenberg (Prince)	1879	
47	Ferdinand of Coburg (Prince; King 1908)	1887	
48	Boris III	1918	S47
49	Simeon II	1943–1946	S48

81 ALBANIA KINGS

1	Ahmad Zog	1928–1939	
2	Victor Emmanuel (III of Italy)	1939–1943	

82· GREECE SPARTA (DOUBLE KINGSHIP)

*Agiad Dynasty c.*815–215 BC

1	Agesilaus I	c.815 BC	
2	Archilaus	c.785	S1
3	Teleclus	c.760	S2
4	Alcmenes	c.740	S3
5	Polydorus	c.700	S4
6	Eurycrates	c.665	S5
7	Anaxander	c.640	S6
8	Eurycratides	c.615	S7
9	Leon	c.590	S8
10	Anaxandridas	c.560	S9
11	Cleomenes I	c.520	S10
12	Leonidas I	c.489	S10
13	Pleistarchus	480	S12
14	Pleistoanax	c.458	BGS12
15	Pausanias	444	S14
16	Agesipolis I	394	S15
17	Cleombrotus I	380	S15
18	Agesipolis II	371	S17
19	Cleomenes II	369	S17
20	Areus I	309	GS19
21	Acrotatus	264	S20
22	Areus II	c.262	S21
23	Leonidas II (1)	254	GS19
24	Cleombrotus II	242	HD23
	Leonidas II (2)	241	
25	Cleomenes III	235–221	S23
26	Euclidas	227–221	S23
		———	
27	Agesipolis III	219–215	GS24

*Eurypontid Dynasty c.*775–192 BC

1	Charillus	c.775 BC	
2	Nicander	c.750	S1
3	Theopompus	c.720	S2
4	Anaxandridas I	c.675	S3
5	Zeuxidamus	c.645	GS4
6	Anaxidamus	c.625	S5
7	Archidamus I	c.600	S6
8	Agasicles	c.575	S7
9	Ariston	c.550	S8
10	Demaratus	c.515	S9
11	Leotychidas	c.491	DT4
12	Archidamus II	469	GS11
13	Agis II	427	S12
14	Agesilaus II	398	S12
15	Archidamus III	361	S14
16	Agis III	338	S15

17	Eudamidas I	331	S15
18	Archidamus IV	c.300	S17
19	Eudamidas II	?	S18
20	Agis IV	c.245	S19
21	Eudamidas III	241	S20
22	Archidamus V	228–227	S19
23	Lycurgus	219	?DT13
24	Pelops	210	S23
25	Nabis	206–192	?DT10

83 **GREECE** KINGDOM OF MACEDONIA

a *Argead Dynasty c.650–310 BC*

1	Perdiccas I	c.650 BC	
2	Argaeus I	c.630	S1
3	Philip I	c.620	S2
4	Aeropus I	c.590	S3
5	Alcetas	c.570	S4
6	Amyntas I	c.540	S5
7	Alexander I	c.495	S6
8	Perdiccas II	c.452	S7
9	Archelaus	c.413	S8
10	Orestes	c.399	S9
11	Aeropus II	c.398	?S8
12	Amyntas II	c.395	?GS7
13	Pausanias	c.394	S12
14	Amyntas III (1)	c.393	GS7
15	Argaeus II	c.393	?S9
	Amyntas III (2)	c.392	
16	Alexander II	369	S14
17	Ptolemy I	368	?S12
18	Perdiccas III	365	S14
19	Philip II	359	S14
20	Alexander III the Great	336	S19
21	Philip III Arrhidaeus	323–317	S19
22	Alexander IV	323–310	S20

b *Antipatrid Dynasty 310–294 BC*

23	Cassander	310 BC	HD19
24	Philip IV	297	S23
25	Antipater (East)	297–294	S23
26	Alexander V (West)	297–294	S23

c *Antigonid Dynasty and others in Macedonia and Asia Minor 306–168 BC*

1	Antigonus I Monophthalmus (Asia Minor and Syria)	306–301 BC
2	Lysimachus (Thrace; Asia Minor 301, Macedonia 288)	306–381

3	Demetrius I Poliorcetes (Asia Minor and Syria 306–301, Macedonia 294–288 etc.)	306–285	s1
4	Pyrrhus (I of Epirus; Macedonia) (1)	288–285	
5	Antigonus II Gonatas (Greece; Macedonia 276–274 and from 272)	285–239	s3
6	Ptolemy II Ceraunus (Macedonia; s1 Egypt)	281–279	
	Pyrrhus of Epirus (Macedonia) (2)	274–272	
7	Demetrius II (Macedonia and Greece)	239–229	s5
8	Antigonus III Doson	229–221	BS5
9	Philip V	221–179	s7
10	Perseus	179–168	s9

84 GREECE KINGDOM OF EPIRUS

Aeacid Dynasty c.400–235 BC

1	Alcetas I	c.400 BC	
2	Neoptolemus I	?	s1
3	Arybbas (1)	360	s1
4	Alexander I	342	s2
5	Neoptolemus II (1)	331–313	s4
	Arybbas (2)	323–322	
6	Aeacides (1)	322–317	s3
	Aeacides (2)	313.	
7	Alcetas II	313–307	s3
8	Pyrrhus I (1)	307–302	s6
	Neoptolemus II (2)	302–295	
	Pyrrhus I (2)	297–272	
9	Alexander II	272–c.240	s8
10	Pyrrhus II	c.240–?	s9
11	Ptolemy	?–235	s9

85 GREECE MEDIEVAL STATES

a *Hafsid Amirs of Crete 828–961*

1	Abu-Hafs 'Umar I	828	
2	Shu'aib I	c.841	s1
3	'Umar II	c.880	s2
4	Muhammad	c.895	s2
5	Yusuf	c.910	s3
6	'Ali I	c.915	s5
7	Ahmad	c.925	s3
8	Shu'aib II	c.940	s7
9	'Ali II	c.943	s7
10	'Abdul-'Aziz	c.949–961	s8

b *Counts of Cephalonia 1194–1483*

| 1 | Matteo Orsini | 1194 | |
| 2 | Ricardo | 1238 | s1 |

3	Giovanni I	1304	S2
4	Niccolo	1317	S3
5	Giovanni II	1323–1324	S3
6	Leonardo I Tocco	1357	GD3
7	Carlo I	*c.*1370	S6
8	Carlo II	1429	BS6
9	Leonardo II	1448	S8
10	Antonio	1481–1483	S8

c *Aleramid Kings of Thessalonica 1204–1225*

1	Boniface (I of Montferrat)	1204	
2	Demetrius	1207–1225	S1

d *Ducas Dynasty of Thessalonica 1225–1246*

1	Theodore (of Epirus; Emperor)	1225	
2	Manuel	1230	B1
3	John (Despot from 1242)	1240	S1
4	Demetrius II	1244–1246	S1

e *Despots of Epirus c.1204–1359*

1	Michael Ducas (GG60 Byzantium)	1204	
2	Theodore (Emp. Thessalonica 1225)	1214	B1
3	Constantine	1225	S1
4	Michael II	1236	S1
5	Nicephorus I	1271	S4
6	Thomas	1296	S5
7	Niccolo Orsini (of Cephalonia)	1318	GD5
8	Giovanni Orsini (of Cephalonia)	1323	B7
9	Nicephorus II (1)	1335–1337	S8
	Nicephorus II (2)	1356–1359	

f *Dukes of Neopatras (Thessaly) 1271–1318*

1	John I Ducas (S4 Epirus)	1271	
2	Constantine	1295	S1
3	John II	1303–1318	S2

g *Dukes of Athens 1205–1460*

1	Othon de la Roche	1205–1225	
2	Guy I	1210–1263	BS1
3	John I	1263	S2
4	William I	1280	S2
5	Guy II	1287	S4
6	Walter of Brienne	1308	GD2
7	Manfred of Aragon (S3 Sicily)	1312	
8	William II	1317	B7
9	John II	1338	B7
10	Frederick I	1348	S9
11	Frederick II (III of Sicily)	1355	BS7

12	Maria★ (of Sicily)	1377	DII
13	Peter (IV of Aragon)	1381	
14	Nerio I Acciajuoli	1388–1394	
15	Antonio I	1402	S14
16	Nerio II (1)	1435	BGS14
17	Antonio II	1439	B16
	Nerio II (2)	1441	
18	Francesco	1451	S16
19	Franco (Thebes only from 1456)	1455–1460	S17

h *Princes of Achaea (Morea)* 1205–1430

1	William I of Champlitte	1205	
2	Geoffrey I of Vilhardouin	1209	
3	Geoffrey II	1218	S2
4	William II	1246	S2
5	Charles I (of Naples)	1278	
6	Charles II (of Naples)	1285	S5
7	Isabella★	1289–1307	D4
8	Florent (S23 Hainault)	1289–1297	H7
9	Philip (of Piedmont)	1301–1307	H7
10	Philip II of Taranto	1307–1313	S6
11	Matilda of Hainault★	1313–1318	D7/8
12	Louis (S9 Burgundy)	1313–1316	H11
13	Robert I (of Naples)	1318	S6
14	John of Gravina	1322	S6
15	Catherine of Valois★	1333–1346	W10
16	Robert II of Taranto	1333–1364	S10
17	Maria of Bourbon★	1364–1370	W16
18	Philip III of Taranto	1364–1373	S10
19	Joanna (I of Naples)★	1374–1376	GS13
20	Jacques of Les Baux	1381–1383	STS19
21	Pedro Bordo of San Superano	1396–1402	
22	Centurione Zaccaria	1404–1430	

i *Dukes of Naxos* 1207–1579

1	Marco I Sanudo	1207	
2	Angelo	1227	S1
3	Marco II	1262	S2
4	Guglielmo I	1303	S3
5	Niccolo I	1323	S4
6	Giovanni I	1341	S4
7	Fiorenza★	1361–1371	D6
8	Niccolo II	1364–1371	H7/GG3
9	Niccolo III dalle Carceri	1371	S7
10	Francesco I Crispo	1383	
11	Giacomo I	1397	S10

12	Giovanni II	1418	s10
13	Giacomo II	1433	s12
14	Gian Giacomo	1447	s13
15	Guglielmo II	1453	s10
16	Francesco II	1463	bs15
17	Giacomo III	1463	s16
18	Giovanni III	1480–1494	s16
19	Francesco III	1500–1511	s18
20	Giovanni IV	1517	s19
21	Giacomo IV	1564–1566	s20
22	Joseph Nasi	1566–1579	

86 GREECE MODERN KINGS 1832–1967

1	Otto of Wittelsbach (s50 Bavaria)	1832–1862	
2	George I (s48 Denmark)	1863	
3	Constantine I (1)	1913	s2
4	Alexander	1917	s3
	Constantine I (2)	1920	
5	George II (1)	1922–1923	s3
	George II (2)	1935	
6	Paul	1947	s3
7	Constantine II	1964–1967	s6

87 POLAND PRINCES AND KINGS

a *Piast Dynasty – Princes and Kings of all Poland c. 960–1138*

1	Mieszko I (Prince)	c.960	
2	Boleslav I the Brave (King 1024)	992	s1
3	Mieszko II (Prince) (1)	1025	s2
4	Bezprim	1031	s2
	Mieszko II (2)	1032–1034	
5	Kasimir I	1034–1058	s3
6	Maslav (Mazovia)	1037–1047	
7	Boleslav II (King 1076)	1058–1079	s5
8	Vladislav I Herman (Prince)	1079–1102	s5
9	Zbigniev	1097–1107	s8
10	Boleslav III	1102–1138	s8

b *Piast Dynasty – Princes of Great Poland 1138–1320*

1	Mieszko III (s10 Poland)	1138–1202	
2	Otto	1179–1202	s1
3	Vladislav I (III)	1202	s1
4	Vladislav II	1231	s2
5	Przemislav I	1239–1257	s4
6	Boleslav	1239–1279	s4

7 Przemislav II (King 1295)	1270–1296	S5
8 Henry (1) (S12 Silesia; Prince)	1296	STS5
9 Vaclav I (II of Bohemia)	1300	HD7
10 Vaclav II (III of Bohemia)	1305	S9
Henry (2)	1306–1309	
11 Vladislav IV (K. Poland 1320)	1314–(1333)	HD6

c *Piast Dynasty – Princes of Little Poland and Krakow* 1138–1320

1 Vladislav (II) (of Silesia; S10 Poland)	1138	
2 Boleslav (IV) (of Mazovia)	1146	B1
3 Mieszko (III) (of Great Poland) (1)	1173	B1
4 Kasimir (II)	1177	B1
5 Leszek (II) (of Mazovia) (1)	1194	S4
Mieszko (III) (2)	1198	
6 Vladislav (III) (of Great Poland)	1202	
Leszek (II) (2)	1206	
7 Boleslav (V)	1227	S5
8 Leszek (III) (of Kujavia)	1279	GG4
9 Henry (IV of Silesia)	1288	
10 Przemislav (II of Great Poland)	1290	
11 Vaclav I (II of Bohemia)	1291	HD10
12 Vaclav II (III of Bohemia)	1305	S11
13 Vladislav IV (K. Poland 1320)	1306–(1333)	B8

d *Piast Dynasty – Princes of Kujavia* 1138–1320

1 Boleslav (IV) (of Mazovia; S10 Poland)	1138	
2 Leszek (I) (of Mazovia)	1173	S1
3 Kasimir (II) (of Little Poland)	1186	B1
4 Leszek (II) (of Mazovia)	1194	S3
5 Conrad I (of Mazovia)	1202	S3
6 Kasimir	1247	S5
7 Leszek III	1267–1288	S6
8 Vladislav IV (K. Poland 1320)	1267–(1333)	S6

e *Piast Dynasty – Princes of Mazovia* 1138–1526

1 Boleslav (IV) (S10 Poland)	1138	
2 Leszek I	1173	S1
3 Kasimir (II) (of Little Poland)	1186	B1
4 Leszek II	1194	S3
5 Conrad I	1202	S3
6 Ziemovit I	1247	S5
7 Boleslav II (Plock)	1262–1313	S6
8 Conrad II (Czersk)	1262–1294	S6
9 Ziemovit II (Sochaczew)	1313–1343	S7
10 Troiden (Warsaw)	1313–1341	S7
11 Vaclav (Plock)	1313–1330	S7
12 Boleslav III (Plock)	1330–1351	S11
13 Ziemovit III (Czersk)	1341–1381	S10
14 Kasimir II (Warsaw)	1341–1354	S10

15 Janusz I (Czersk)	1381–1429	S13
16 Ziemovit IV (Plock)	1381–1426	S13
17 Ziemovit V (Sochaczew)	1426–1442	S16
18 Vladislav I (Plock)	1426–1455	S16
19 Kasimir III (Belz)	1426–1446	S16
20 Boleslav IV (Czersk)	1429–1454	GS15
21 Ziemovit VI (Plock)	1455–1462	S18
22 Vladislav II (Plock)	1455–1462	S18
23 Kasimir IV (Plock)	1462–1475	S20
24 Janusz II (Ciechanow)	1475–1495	S20
25 Boleslav V (Warsaw)	1475–1488	S20
26 Conrad III (Czersk; Plock 1462–1496)	1454–1503	S20
27 Stanislav (Czersk)	1503–1524	S26
28 Janusz III (Czersk)	1503–1526	S26

f *Piast Dynasty – Princes of Silesia* 1138–1290

1 Vladislav (II) (S10 Poland)	1138	
2 Boleslav (IV) (of Mazovia)	1146	BI
3 Boleslav I (Lower Silesia)	1163–1201	SI
4 Mieszko I (Upper Silesia)	1163–1211	SI
5 Henry I (Lower Silesia)	1201–1238	S3
6 Kasimir (Upper Silesia)	1211–1229	S4
7 Henry II (Lower Silesia)	1238–1241	S5
8 Mieszko II (Upper Silesia)	1229–1246	S6
9 Vladislav (Upper Silesia)	1229–1281	S6
10 Boleslav II (Legnica)	1241–1278	S7
11 Henry III (Wroclaw)	1241–1266	S7
12 Conrad (Glogow)	1241–1273	S7
13 Henry IV (Wroclaw)	1266–1290	S11
(further subdivision of Silesian Duchies)		
	....	

g *Piast Dynasty – Kings of Poland* 1320–1370

1 Vladislav IV (of Kujavia)	1320	
2 Kasimir III the Great	1333–1370	SI

h *Angevin and Jagiellon Dynasties* 1370–1572 – *Kings*

3 Louis of Anjou (K. Hungary)	1370	STS2
4 Jadwiga★	1382–1395	D3
5 Vladislav V Jagiellon (of Lithuania)	1386–1434	H4
6 Vladislav VI	1434–1444	S5
7 Kasimir IV (of Lithuania)	1447	S5
8 John Albert	1492	S7
9 Alexander (of Lithuania)	1501	S7
10 Sigismund I	1506	S7
11 Sigismund II Augustus	1548–1572	S10

i *Elected Kings of Poland* 1573–1795

12 Henry (III of France)	1573–1574	
13 Stephen Bathory (of Transylvania)	1576–1586	HD10

14 Sigismund III Vasa (of Sweden)	1587–1632	GD10
15 Vladislav VII	1632–1648	S14
16 John Kasimir	1648–1668	S14
17 Michael Wisniowecki	1669–1673	
18 John Sobieski	1674–1696	
19 (Frederick-) Augustus II (of Saxony) (1)	1697–1704	
20 Stanislav I Leszczynski	1704–1709	
Augustus II (2)	1709–1733	
21 (Frederick-) Augustus III (of Saxony)	1733–1763	S19
22 Stanislav II Poniatowski	1764–1795	

j *Grand Duke of Warsaw*

1 Frederick-Augustus (K. Saxony)	1807–1813	S21 above

88 POLAND POMERANIA

a *Dukes of Pomerania 1124–1295*

1 Vratislav I	1124	
2 Ratibor	1148	B1
3 Bogislav I (Stettin)	1156–1187	S1
4 Kasimir I (Demmin)	1156–1180	S1
5 Bogislav II (Stettin)	1187–1220	S3
6 Kasimir II (Demmin)	1187–1219	S3
7 Vratislav II (Demmin)	1219–1264	S6
8 Barnim I (Stettin; Demmin 1264)	1220–1278	S5
9 Barnim II	1278–1295	S8
10 Bogislav III (Wolgast from 1295)	1278–(1309)	S8
11 Otto I (Stettin from 1295)	1278–(1344)	S8

b *Dukes of Pomerania-Stettin 1295–1637*

1 Otto I	1295	11 above
2 Barnim III	1344	S1
3 Kasimir III	1368–1372	S2
4 Bogislav IV	1368–1404	S2
5 Svantibor	1368–1413	S2
6 Otto II	1413–1428	S5
7 Kasimir IV	1413–1435	S5
8 Joachim	1435	S7
9 Otto III	1451	S8
10 Erik (of Wolgast)	1464	
11 Bogislav V (VIII of Wolgast)	1474	S10
12 Barnim IV	1523	S11
13 John-Frederick (S18 Wolgast)	1569	
14 Barnim V	1600	B13
15 Bogislav VI	1603	B13
16 Philip	1606	S15
17 Franz	1618	S15
18 Bogislav VII	1620–1637	S15

c *Dukes of Pomerania-Wolgast and Rugen 1295–1637*

1	Bogislav III	1295	10 Pomerania
2	Vratislav II	1309	S1
3	Bogislav IV	1326–1373	S2
4	Barnim III	1326–1365	S2
5	Vratislav III	1326–1390	S2
6	Vratislav IV	1365–1394	S4
7	Bogislav V	1365–1393	S4
8	Kasimir III	1374–1377	S3
9	Vratislav V	1374–1394	S3
10	Bogislav VI	1377–1418	S3
11	Barnim IV	1374–1403	S3
12	Barnim V	1394–1405	S6
13	Vratislav VI	1394–1415	S6
14	Vratislav VII	1405–1457	S12
15	Barnim VI	1405–1449	S12
16	Barnim VII	1415–1451	S13
17	Svantibor	1415–1436	S13
18	Bogislav VII	1418–1447	S10
19	Erik	1457–1474	S14
20	Vratislav VIII	1457–1478	S14
21	Bogislav VIII	1478–1523	S19
22	George	1523	S21
23	Philip	1531	S22
24	Ernest-Ludwig	1560	S23
25	Philip-Julius	1592	S24
26	Bogislav IX (VII of Stettin)	1625–1637	

89 LITHUANIA AND KURLAND

a *Grand Dukes of Lithuania c.1235–1569*

1	Mindaugas (King 1251)	*c.*1235	
2	Treniota	1263	
3	Vaishvilkis	1264	S1
4	Shvarnas (s8 Galicia)	1267	HD1
5	Traidenis	1270	
6	Pukuveras	1283	
7	Vitenis	1293	S6
8	Gediminas	1316	S6
9	Jaunutis	1341	S8
10	Algirdas	1345–1377	S8
11	Kestutis	1345–1382	S8
12	Jogaila (Vladislav V of Poland)	1377–1392	S10
13	Vytautas	1392–1430	S11
14	Shvitrigaila	1430–1435	S10
15	Sigismund	1432–1440	S11
16	Kasimir (IV of Poland)	1440	S12
17	Alexander	1492	S16

18 Sigismund (I of Poland)	1506	s16
19 Sigismund II Augustus (of Poland)	1548–(1572)	s18

b *Dukes of Kurland (and Semigallia) 1562–1795*

1 Gotthard Kettler	1562	
2 William	1587	s1
3 Frederick (Semigallia from 1587)	1616	s1
4 Jacob	1641	s2
5 Frederick-Casimir	1682	s4
6 Frederick-William	1698	s5
7 Anne (of Russia)★	1711	w6
8 Ferdinand	1730	s4
9 Ernest-John Biron (1)	1737–1740	
10 Charles of Saxony (s19 Poland)	1758	
Ernest-John Biron (2)	1763	
11 Peter Biron	1769–1795	s9

90 **RUSSIA** KINGDOM OF BOSPHORUS

a *Archaeanactid Dynasty c.480–438 BC*

1 Archaeanax	c.480 BC	
2 Paerisades	?	
3 Leucon	?	
4 Sagaurus	?–438	

b *Spartocid Dynasty 438–109 BC*

5 Spartocus I	438 BC	
6 Satyrus I	433	s5
7 Leucon I	389	s6
8 Spartocus II	349–344	s7
9 Paerisades I	349–310	s7
10 Satyrus II	310–309	s9
11 Eumelus	310–304	s9
12 Prytanis	310–309	s9
13 Spartocus III	304–284	s11
14 Paerisades II	284	s13
15 Spartocus IV	c.245	s14
16 Leucon II	c.240	s14
17 Hygiaenon	c.220	
18 Spartocus V	c.200	s16
19 Paerisades III	c.180	s16
20 Paerisades IV	c.150	s19
21 Paerisades V	c.125–109	s20

c *Mithridatid Dynasty c.109 BC–7AD*

22 Mithridates (VI of Pontus) (1)	c.109 BC	
23 Machares	81	s22
Mithridates (2)	65	

24	Pharnaces (II of Pontus)	63	S22
25	Asander	44	H28
26	Scribonius	17–16	H28
27	Polemo (I of Pontus)	14–8	H28
28	Dynamis★	8 BC–7 AD	D24

d *Aspurgid Dynasty* 10–342 AD

29	Aspurgus	10 AD	H28
30	Gepaepyris★	37	W29
31	Mithridates	39–49	S29
32	Cotys I	46–69	S29
33	Rhescuporis I	69	S32
34	Sauromates I	92	S33
35	Cotys II	124	S34
36	Rhoemetalces	132	
37	Eupator	154	
38	Sauromates II	174	S36
39	Rhescuporis II	211	S38
40	Cotys III	228–234	S39
41	Sauromates III	228–233	
42	Ininthimenos	234.	
43	Rhescuporis III	234–235	
44	Rhescuporis IV	240–253	
45	Pharsanzes	253–254	
46	Rhescuporis V	255	
47	Sauromates IV	276	
48	Teiranes	278	
49	Thothorses	278	
50	Sauromates V	308–312	
51	Rhadamsadius	308–323	
52	Rhescuporis VI	311–342	

91 **RUSSIA** PRINCES OF KIEV

Riurikid Dynasty c.880–1240

1	Oleg	c.880	
2	Igor I	c.912	
3	Olga★	945	W2
4	Sviatoslav I	964	S2/3
5	Yaropolk I	972	S4
6	Vladimir I the Saint	978	S4
7	Sviatopolk I	1015	S6
8	Yaroslav I the Wise	1019	S6
9	Iziaslav I (1)	1054	S8
10	Vseslav (of Polotsk)	1068	BGS8
	Iziaslav I (2)	1069	
11	Sviatoslav II (of Chernigov)	1073	S8
	Iziaslav I (3)	1076	
12	Vsevolod I (of Pereyaslavl)	1078	S8

13	Sviatopolk II (of Novgorod)	1093	S9
14	Vladimir II Monomach (of Smolensk)	1113	S12
15	Mstislav I Harald (of Novgorod)	1125	S14
16	Yaropolk II (of Pereyaslavl)	1132	S14
17	Viacheslav (II of Smolensk)	1139	S14
18	Vsevolod II (of Chernigov)	1139	GS11
19	Igor II	1146	B18
20	Iziaslav II (of Pereyaslavl) (1)	1146	S15
21	Yuri Dolgoruky (of Suzdal-Vladimir) (1)	1149	S14
	Iziaslav II (2)	1150	
	Yuri Dolgoruky (2)	1150	
	Iziaslav II (3)	1150	
22	Rostislav I (of Smolensk) (1)	1154	S15
	Yuri Dolgoruky (3)	1155	
23	Iziaslav III (of Chernigov) (1)	1157	GS11
	Rostislav I (2)	1159	
	Iziaslav III (2)	1161	
	Rostislav I (3)	1161	
24	Mstislav II (of Pereyaslavl)	1167	S20
25	Gleb (of Pereyaslavl)	1169	S21
26	Roman (of Smolensk) (1)	1171	S22
27	Vsevolod III (of Suzdal – Vladimir)	1172	S21
28	Riurik (of Novgorod) (1)	1173	S22
29	Yaroslav II	1174	S20
	Roman (2)	1175	
30	Sviatoslav III (of Chernigov) (1)	1176	S18
	Riurik (2)	1180	
	Sviatoslav III (2)	1181	
	Riurik (3)	1194	
31	Ingvar (of Lutsk)	1200	S29
	Riurik (4)	1203	
32	Rostislav II	1204	S28
	Riurik (5)	1205	
33	Vsevolod IV (of Chernigov)	1206	S30
34	Mstislav III (of Smolensk)	1212	S26
35	Vladimir III	1223	S28
36	Yaroslav III (of Suzdal – Vladimir)	1236	S27
37	Michael (of Chernigov)	1238	S33
38	Daniel (of Galicia)	1240.	GS24

Note

There is no simple and tidy way to set out the
Riurikid rulers of the 11th–13th centuries under the
territories they ruled. From the original division of
the early Russian realm in 1054, there were several
main principalities and an ever-growing number of
minor ones by constant sub-division and re-division.
When an important prince died, there was often a
complete reshuffle of princes, though gradually the

various branches came to regard particular principalities as exclusively theirs. The lists below cover only the states originally or later important.

92 **RUSSIA** MEDIEVAL PRINCIPALITIES

Riurikid Dynasty

a *Princes of Galicia* 1144–1349

1	Vladimirko Volodarich (GS1 Novgorod)	1144	
2	Yaroslav Osmomysl	1153	S1
3	Vladimir I (1)	1187	S2
4	Andrew (II of Hungary) (1)	1187	
5	Roman I (of Volynia) (1)	1188	
	Vladimir I (2)	1189	
	Roman I (2)	1199	
6	Daniel (1)	1205	S5
7	Vladimir II (GS10 Chernigov) (1)	1206	
8	Roman II	1208	B7
9	Rostislav (S28 Kiev)	1210	
	Vladimir II (2)	1210	
	Daniel (2)	1211	
10	Vladislav	1212	
11	Koloman (1)	1214	S4
12	Mstislav (VI of Nogorod (1)	1219	
	Koloman (2)	1219	
	Mstislav (2)	1221	
	Andrew (2)	1228	
	Daniel (3)	1230	
	Andrew (3)	1232	
	Daniel (4)	1233	
13	Rostislav II (S16 Chernigov)	1236	
14	Michael (of Chernigov)	1236	
	Daniel (5) (King 1254)	1238	
15	Leo I	1264	S6
16	Yuri I	1301	S15
17	Leo II	1308	S16
18	Yuri II Boleslav (S10 Mazovia)	1325	HD17
19	Liubart (S7 Lithuania)	1340–1349	

b *Princes of Volynia* 1054–1301

1	Igor (S8 Kiev)	1054–1057	
2	Oleg (S11 Kiev)	*c.*1073	
3	Yaropolk of Turov (S9 Kiev)	1078	
4	David of Dorogobuzh	1085–1086	S1
5	Mstislav I (S13 Kiev)	1097	
	David (2)	1099	
6	Yaroslav I of Brest (S13 Kiev)	1100	
7	Andrei (S14 Kiev)	1123	

8 Iziaslav (of Pereyaslavl; II of Kiev)	1135	
9 Sviatopolk (of Novgorod)	1146	B8
10 Vladimir	1154	B8
11 Yaroslav II (I of Novgorod)	1155	S8
12 Mstislav (of Pereyaslavl)	1157	S8
13 Roman (I of Novgorod)	1170	S12
14 Daniel (of Galicia)	1205	S13
15 Sviatoslav (GS10 Chernigov)	1206	
16 Vasilko	1214	S13
17 Ivan-Vasili	1269	S16
18 Mstislav II	1289	S14
19 Yuri (I of Galicia)	1301–(1308)	

c *Princes of Pereyaslavl 1054–1215*

1 Vsevolod I (S8 Kiev)	1054	
2 Vladimir I Monomach (of Smolensk) (1)	1076	S1
3 Rostislav	1078	S1
Vladimir I Monomach (2)	1094	
4 Yaropolk	1125	S2
5 Vsevolod II (I of Novgorod) (S15 Kiev)	1132	
6 Iziaslav (1)	1132	B5
7 Viacheslav (of Smolensk) (1)	1133	S2
8 Yuri Dolgoruky (of Suzdal-Vladimir)	1133	S2
9 Andrei (of Volynia)	1135	S2
Viacheslav (2)	1142	
Iziaslav (2)	1142	
10 Rostislav II (of Novgorod)	1149	S8
11 Mstislav	1152	S6
12 Gleb	1155	S8
13 Vladimir I	1169	S12
14 Yaroslav I (II of Novgorod)	1180	
15 Yaroslav II (I of Suzdal-Vladimir)	1201	
16 Vladimir II	1213–1215	B15

d *Princes of Novgorod 1036–1263*

1 Vladimir (S8 Kiev)	1036–1052	
2 Iziaslav (I of Kiev)	1054	
3 Gleb (S11 Kiev)	c.1069	
4 Sviatopolk (II of Kiev)	1078	
5 David I	1088	S4
6 Mstislav Harald (of Kiev)	1095	
7 Vsevolod I	1125	S6
8 Sviatoslav I (1) (II of Chernigov)	1136	
9 Rostislav I (1) (S21 Kiev)	1138	
Sviatoslav I (2)	1139	
Rostislav I (2)	1141	
10 Sviatopolk	1142	S6
11 Yaroslav I (S20 Kiev)	1148	
12 Rostislav II	1154	S6
13 David II	1154	S12

14	Mstislav II (s21 Kiev)	1155	
15	Sviatoslav II (1)	1158	s12
16	Mstislav III (1)	1160	s9
	Sviatoslav II (2)	1161	
17	Roman I (s24 Kiev)	1169	
18	Riurik	1170	s12
19	Yuri (s2 Suzdal-Vladimir)	1172	
	Mstislav III (2)	1175	
20	Yaroslav II	1176	s14
	Mstislav III (3)	1177	
21	Yaropolk I	1178	s9
22	Roman II	1179	s12
23	Mstislav IV	1179	s12
24	Vladimir II (s11 Chernigov)	1180	
25	Yaroslav III (1) (s9 Volynia)	1182	
26	Mstislav V	1184	s13
	Yaroslav III (2)	1187	
27	Yaropolk II (s14 Chernigov)	1197	
	Yaroslav III (3)	1198	
28	Vsevolod II (of Suzdal-Vladimir)	1199	
29	Sviatoslav III (of Suzdal-Vladimir)	1200	
30	Constantine (of Suzdal-Vladimir)	1205	
31	Mstislav VI (1)	1209	s23
32	Yaroslav IV (I of Suzdal-Vladimir) (1)	1215	
	Mstislav VI (2)	1216	
33	Sviatoslav IV (s11 Smolensk)	1217	
34	Vsevolod III	1219	B33
35	Vsevolod IV (s5 Suzdal-Vladimir)	1222	
	Yaroslav IV (2)	1223	
36	Michael (of Kiev) (1)	1225	
	Yaroslav IV (2)	1228	
	Michael (2)	1229–1230	
37	Rostislav III	1229–1230	s36
	Yaroslav IV (3)	1230	
38	Alexander Nevsky	1236–1263	s35

e *Princes of Smolensk 1054–1404*

1	Viacheslav I (s8 Kiev)	1054	
2	Igor (of Volynia)	1057–1060	
3	Vladimir Monomach (of Pereyaslavl) (1)	1077	
4	David (s11 Kiev)	1095	
	Vladimir Monomach (2)	1097	
5	Sviatoslav I	1113	s3
6	Viacheslav II	1114	s3
7	Rostislav I (s15 Kiev)	1127	
8	Roman (1)	1159	s7
9	Yaropolk	1171	s8
	Roman (2)	1175	
10	David (II of Novgorod)	1180	s7

11	Mstislav I	1197	s8
12	Mstislav II Feodor	1223	s10
13	Sviatoslav II (IV of Novgorod)	1232	s11
14	Vsevolod (gs24 Kiev)	1239	
15	Rostislav II	1240	s12
16	Gleb I	c.1270	s15
17	Michael	1277	s15
18	Feodor	1280	s15
19	Alexander	1297	s16
20	Ivan	1313	s19
21	Sviatoslav III	1358	s20
21	Yuri (1)	1386	s21
22	Gleb II	1394	s21
23	Yamont	1395	
	Yuri (2)	1401–1404	

f *Princes of Chernigov* 1054–1245

1	Sviatoslav I (s8 Kiev)	1054	
2	Vsevolod I (of Pereyaslavl)	1076	
3	Boris (s1 Smolensk)	1077	
4	Vladimir Monomach (of Pereyaslavl)	1078	
5	Oleg (of Volynia)	1094	s1
6	David (of Smolensk)	1097	s1
7	Yaroslav I (of Riazan)	1123	s1
8	Vsevolod II	1129	s5
9	Iziaslav (III of Kiev)	1139	s6
10	Sviatoslav II (I of Novgorod)	1157	s5
11	Sviatoslav III	1164	s8
12	Yaroslav II	1177	s8
13	Vsevolod III	1202	s11
14	Gleb	1206	s11
15	Mstislav I	1215	s11
16	Michael	1223	s13
17	Mstislav II	1235	s14
18	Andrew	1239–1245	s17

g *Princes of Riazan* 1097–1520

1	Yaroslav I (s1 Chernigov)	1097	
2	Rostislav (1)	1129	s1
3	David	1146	bs2
4	Igor	1147	b3
	Rostislav (2)	1149	
5	Gleb I	c.1155	s2
6	Roman I	1178	s5
7	Yaroslav II (I of Suzdal-Vladimir)	1207	
8	Gleb II	1212	bs6
9	Ingvar I	1217	bs6
10	Yuri	1235	b9
11	Ingvar II	1237	bs10
12	Oleg I	1251	b11

13	Roman II	1258	S12
14	Feodor I	1270	S13
15	Yaroslav III	1294	S13
16	Constantine	1299	S13
17	Ivan I	1301	S15
18	Ivan II	1327	S17
19	Yaroslav Dimitri	1342	GG15
20	Ivan III	1344	B19
21	Oleg II	1351	S20
22	Feodor II	1402	S21
23	Ivan IV	1427	S22
24	Vasili	1456	S23
25	Ivan V	1483	S24
26	Ivan VI	1500–1520	S25

h *Princes of Suzdal-Vladimir 1125–1363*

1	Yuri I Dolgoruky (s14 Kiev)	1125	
2	Andrei I Bogoliubsky	1157	S1
3	Michael I	1175	S1
4	Vsevolod	1176	S1
5	Yuri II (1)	1212	S4
6	Constantine	1216	S4
	Yuri II (2)	1218	
7	Yaroslav I	1238	S4
8	Sviatoslav	1246	S4
9	Michael II	1248	S7
10	Andrei II	1248	S7
11	Alexander Nevsky	1252	S7
12	Yaroslav II (of Tver)	1263	S7
13	Vasili	1272	S7
14	Dimitri I (1)	1276	S11
15	Andrei III (1)	1281	S11
	Dimitri I (2)	1283	
	Andrei III (2)	1294	
16	Michael III (I of Tver)	1304	S12
17	Yuri III (of Moscow)	1318	
18	Dimitri II (of Tver)	1322	S16
19	Alexander II (I of Tver)	1326	S16
20	Ivan I (of Moscow)	1328	
21	Semeon (of Moscow)	1341	
22	Ivan II (of Moscow)	1353	
23	Dimitri III (of Nizhny Novgorod)	1359	GG10
24	Dimitri IV Donskoy (of Moscow)	1363–(1389)	

i *Princes of Tver 1246–1485*

1	Yaroslav (II of Suzdal-Vladimir)	1246	
2	Sviatoslav	1271	S1
3	Michael I	1285	S1
4	Dimitri	1319	S3
5	Alexander I (1)	1325	S3

6 Constantine (1)	1328	S3
Alexander I (2)	1338	
Constantine (2)	1339	
7 Vsevolod	1345	S5
8 Vasili	1365	S3
9 Michael II	1368	S5
10 Ivan	1399	S9
11 Alexander II	1427	S10
12 Boris	1427	S11
13 Michael III	1461–1485	S12

93 **RUSSIA** PRINCES AND TSARS OF MOSCOW

Riurikid

1 Daniel (S11 Suzdal-Vladimir)	1283	
2 Yuri	1303	S1
3 Ivan I	1325	S1
4 Semeon	1341	S3
5 Ivan II	1353	S3
6 Dimitri Donskoy	1359	S5
7 Vasili I	1389	S6
8 Vasili II	1425	S7
9 Ivan III the Great	1462	S8
10 Vasili III	1505	S9
11 Ivan IV the Terrible (Tsar 1547)	1533	S10
12 Feodor I	1584	S11
13 Boris Godunov	1598	
14 Feodor II	1605	S13
15 Dimitri II	1605	??S11
16 Vasili IV Shuisky (DT23 Suzdal-Vladimir)	1606–1610	

94 **RUSSIA** TSARS OF THE ROMANOV DYNASTY 1613–1917

17 Michael	1613	
18 Alexei	1645	S17
19 Feodor III	1676	S18
20 Ivan V	1682–1696	S18
21 Peter I the Great (Emperor 1721)	1682–1725	S18
22 Catherine I★	1725	W21
23 Peter II	1727	GS21
24 Anne★ (of Kurland)	1730	D20
25 Ivan VI	1740	STGD24
26 Elizabeth★	1741	D21
27 Peter III (D. Holstein-Gottorp)	1762	GD21
28 Catherine II the Great★	1762	W27
29 Paul	1796	S27/28
30 Alexander I	1801	S29

31	Nicholas I	1825	S29
32	Alexander II	1855	S31
33	Alexander III	1881	S32
34	Nicholas II	1894–1917	S33

95 RUSSIA KHANS OF THE GOLDEN HORDE 1227–1502

1	Batu (GS Chingis Khan)	1227	
2	Sartak	1255	S1
3	Ulaghchi	1256	S2
4	Berke	1257	B1
5	Mengu Timur	1267	GS1
6	Tuda Mengu	1280	B5
7	Tola Buqa	1287	BS5
8	Toqtu	1290	S5
9	Uzbeg	1312	BS8
10	Tinibeg	1341	S9
11	Janibeg	1342	S9
12	Berdibeg	1357	S11
13	Qulpa	1359	S11
14	Nawruz Beg	1360	S11
15	Khidr	1361	3GB1
16	Timur Khoja	1362	S15
17	Keldibeg	1362	
18	Murid	1362	S15
19	'Aziz Khan	1364	S16
20	'Abdullah	1367	
21	Muhammad Bulak	1370–1378	
22	Urus Khan (of White Horde)	1373–1377	
23	Tokhtamish (of White Horde)	1378	
24	Timur Qutlugh	1395	GS22
25	Shadibeg	1400	B24
26	Pulad Timur	1407	B25
27	Timur Khan	1410	S24
28	Jalal-ud-Din	1412	S23
29	Karim Berdi	1412	S23
30	Kebek	1414	S23
31	Jabbar Berdi	1417	S23
32	Ulugh Muhammad (of Kazan)	1419–1437	DTB1
33	Sayyid Ahmad I	c.1433–c.1465	S23
34	Kuchuk Muhammad	c.1435–c.1465	S27
35	Ahmad Khan	1465–1481	S34
36	Shaikh Ahmad	1481–1502	S35
37	Sayyid Ahmad II	1481–1502	S35
38	Murtada	1481–1499	S35

96 RUSSIA SUCCESSOR-STATES OF THE GOLDEN HORDE

a *Khans of the White Horde 1226–1378*

1 Orda (B1 Golden Horde)	1226	
2 Kochu	1280	S1
3 Bayan	1302	S2
4 Sasibuqa	1309	S3
5 Ilbasan	1315	S4
6 Mubarak Khoja	1320	S4
7 Chimtai	1344	S5
8 Urus	1361	S7
9 Tuqtaqiya	1375	S8
10 Timur Malik	1375	S8
11 Tokhtamish (Kh. Golden Horde 1378)	1376–(1398)	BS8

b *Khans of Kazan 1438–1552*

1 Ulugh Muhammad (of Golden Horde)	1438	
2 Mahmudek	1446	S1
3 Khalil	1466	S2
4 Ibrahim	1467	S2
5 Ilham (1)	1479	S3
6 Muhammad Amin (1)	1485	S3
Ilham (2)	1486	
Muhammad Amin (2)	1487	
7 Mamuk (of Sibir)	1496	
8 'Abdul-Latif	1497	S3
Muhammad Amin (3)	1502	
9 Shah 'Ali (of Kasimov) (1)	1518	
10 Sahib Girai (I of Krim)	1521	
11 Safa Girai (1)	1525	S10
12 Jan 'Ali (of Kasimov)	1532	
Safa Girai (2)	1535	
Shah 'Ali (2)	1546	
Safa Girai (3)	1546	
13 Utemish Girai	1549	S11
Shah 'Ali (3)	1551	
14 Yadigar Muhammad (S4 Astrakhan)	1552.	

c *Khans of Kasimov 1452–1681*

1 Kasim Khan (S1 Kazan)	1452	
2 Daniyar	1469	S1
3 Nur Dawlat (of Krim)	1485	
4 Satilghan	1498	S3
5 Janai	1508	S3
6 Shaikh Awliar (GS34 Golden Horde)	1512	
7 Shah 'Ali (1)	1516	S6
8 Jan 'Ali	1519	S6
Shah 'Ali (2)	1535	
9 Sayin Bulat (BGS36 Golden Horde)	1567	
10 Mustafa 'Ali (GS5 Kazan)	1573–1583	

11 Urus Muhammad (BS12 Kazakh Horde)	1600–1610	
12 Arslan	1614	
13 Sayyid Burhan	1626	S12
14 Fatima Sultan★	1678–1681	W12

d *Khans of Astrakhan 1466–1556*

1 Kasim I (BS35 Golden Horde)	1466	
2 'Abdul-Karim	1490	B1
3 Husain	1504	BS1
4 Kasim II (S37 Golden Horde)	1523	
5 Akkubak (S38 Golden Horde)	1532	
6 'Abdul-Rahman (1)	1534	S2
7 Darwish 'Ali (GS36 Golden Horde) (1)	1537	
'Abdul-Rahman (2)	1538	
8 Yamgurchi	1548	BS5
Darwish 'Ali (2)	1554–1556	

e *Khans of the Kazakh Horde 1395–1718*

1 Koirijak (S8 White Horde)	1395	
2 Borrak	c.1422	S1
3 Girai	1427–?	S2
4 Janibeg	1427–?	S2
5 Berenduk	1488	S3
6 Kasim	1509	S4
7 Mimash	1518	BS6
8 Tagir	1523	B7
9 Uziak Ahmad	1530	S4
10 Ak Nazar	?	S6
11 Shigai	1580	B7
12 Tevkel	c.1582	S11
13 Ishim	1598	S11
14 Jahangir	c.1635	S13
15 Tiavka	c.1644–1718	S14

97 RUSSIA KHANATE OF KRIM (CRIMEA) 1426–1785

1 Hajji Girai (1) (BS1 Kazan)	1426	
2 Haidar Girai	1456	
Hajji Girai (2)	1456	
3 Nur Dawlat Girai (1)	1466	S1
4 Mengli Girai (1)	1466	S1
Nur Dawlat Girai (2)	1474	
Mengli Girai (2)	1475	
Nur Dawlat Girai (3)	1476	
Mengli Girai (3)	1478	
5 Muhammad Girai I	1514	S4
6 Ghazi Girai I	1523	S5
7 Sa'adat Girai I	1524	S4

8	Islam Girai I	1532	S5
9	Sahib Girai I	1532	S4
10	Dawlat Girai I	1551	BS9
11	Muhammad Girai II	1577	S10
12	Islam Girai II	1584	S10
13	Ghazi Girai II (1)	1588	S10
14	Fath Girai I	1596	S10
	Ghazi Girai II (2)	1596	
15	Tokhtamish Girai	1608	S13
16	Salamat Girai I	1608	S11
17	Muhammad Girai III	1610	S11
18	Janibeg Girai (1)	1610	S11
	Muhammad Girai III (2)	1623	
	Janibeg Girai (2)	1627	
19	ʿInayat Girai	1635	S13
20	Bahadur Girai I	1637	S16
21	Muhammad Girai IV (1)	1641	S16
22	Islam Girai III	1644	S16
	Muhammad Girai IV (2)	1654	
23	ʿAdil Girai	1666	GS14
24	Selim Girai I (1)	1671	S20
25	Murad Girai	1678	BS20
26	Hajji Girai II	1683	BS20
	Selim Girai I (2)	1684	
27	Saʿadat Girai II	1691	B26
28	Safa Girai	1691	BS23
	Selim Girai I (3)	1692	
29	Dawlat Girai II (1)	1699	S24
	Selim Girai I (4)	1702	
30	Ghazi Girai III	1704	S24
31	Qaplan Girai I (1)	1707	S24
	Dawlat Girai II (2)	1708	
	Qaplan Girai I (2)	1713	
32	Dawlat Girai III	1716	S23
33	Saʿadat Girai III	1717	S24
34	Mengli Girai II (1)	1724	S24
	Qaplan Girai I (3)	1730	
35	Fath Girai II	1736	S29
	Mengli Girai II (2)	1737	
36	Salamat Girai II	1740	S24
37	Selim Girai II	1743	S31
38	Arslan Girai (1)	1748	S29
39	Halim Girai	1756	S33
40	Kirim Girai (1)	1758	S29
41	Selim Girai III (1)	1764	S35
	Arslan Girai (2)	1767	
42	Maqsud Girai (1)	1767	S36
	Kirim Girai (2)	1768	
43	Dawlat Girai IV (1)	1769	S38
44	Qaplan Girai II	1770	S37

	Selim Girai III (2)	1770	
	Maqsud Girai (2)	1771	
45	Sahib Girai II	1772	BS40
	Dawlat Girai IV (2)	1775	
46	Shahin Girai (1)	1777	B45
47	Bahadur Girai II	1784	S42
	Shahin Girai (2)	1785.	

AFRICA

98 **EGYPT** PHARAONIC DYNASTIES

Dynasty I c.3100–2890 BC

1 Na'rmer
2 'Aha
3 Djer
4 Djet
5 Den
6 'Anedjib
7 Semerkhet
8 Qa'a

Dynasty II c.2890–2686 BC

9 Hetepsekhemwy
10 Re'neb
11 Ninetjer
12 Weneg
13 Sened
14 Peribsen
15 Khasekhem
16 Khasekhemwy

Dynasty III c.2686–2613 BC

17 Sanakhte
18 Netjerikhet (Djoser)
19 Sekhemket
20 Kha'ba
21 Huni

Dynasty IV c.2613–2498 BC

22 Sneferu
23 Khufu (Cheops)
24 Ra 'djedef
25 Kha'fre' (Chephren)
26 Menkaure' (Mycerinus)
27 Shepseskaf

Dynasty V c.2498–2345 BC

28 Userkaf

29 Sahure'
30 Neferirkare'
31 Shepseskare'
32 Neferefre'
33 Niuserre'
34 Menkauhor
35 Djedkare'
36 Unas

Dynasty VI c.2345–2181 BC

37	Teti	
38	Userkare'	
39	Meryre' Piopi I	S37
40	Merenre' Antyemsaf I	S39
41	Neferkare' Piopi II	S40
42	Merenre' Antyemsaf II	S41
43	Netjerykare'	
44	Menkare'	

Dynasties VII–X

Brief period of disorder from *c.*2181 BC until *c.*2040 BC,
when Dynasty XI, rulers of Upper Egypt since
*c.*2133 BC conquered the Delta.

Dynasty XI 2133–1991 BC

45	Mentuhotpe I	2133–2117	
46	Inyotef I	2133–2117	S45
47	Inyotef II	2117	S46
48	Inyotef III	2068	S47
49	Nebhepetre' Mentuhotpe II	2060	S48
50	S'ankhkare' Mentuhotpe III	2009	S49
51	Nebtowere' Mentuhotpe IV	1997–1991	S50

Dynasty XII 1991–1786 BC

52	Shetepibre' Amenemhe I	1991–1962	
53	Kheperkare' Senwosre I	1971–1928	S52
54	Nubkaure' Amenemhe II	1929–1895	S53
55	Kha'kheperre' Senwosre II	1897–1878	S54
56	Kha'kaure' Senwosre III	1878	S55
57	Nema're' Amenemhe III	1842	S56
58	Ma'kherure' Amenemhe IV	1798	S57
59	Sebekkare' Sebeknofru★	1789–1786	D57

Dynasty XIII c.1786–1674 BC (Main rulers only)

60 Sebekhotpe I
61 Sekhemkare' Amenemhe (V)
62 Sehetepibre' Amenemhe (VI)
63 S'ankhibre'
64 Hetepibre'
65 Sebekhotpe II

66 Renseneb
67 Awibre' Hor
68 Sedjefakare'
69 Khutowere'
70 Seneferibre' Senwosre (IV)
71 Userkare' Khendjer
72 Semenkhkare'
73 Sekhemre' Wadjkhau Sobkemsaf
74 Sekhemre' Sewadjtowy Sebekhotpe III
75 Kha'sekhemre' Neferhotep I
76 Kha'neferre' Sebekhotpe IV
77 Kha'ankhre' Sebekhotpe V
78 Mersekhemre' Neferhotep II
79 Kha'hotepre' Sebekhotpe VI
80 Sekhemre' S'ankhtowy Neferhotep III
81 Wahibre' Ia'yeb
82 Merneferre' Iy
83 Merhetepre' Ini
84 Djedneferr'e Dudimose

*Dynasty XIV c.*1786–1603 BC

A minor dynasty in the Western Delta

*Dynasty XV (Great Hyksos) c.*1674–1567 BC

85 Mayebre' Sheshi
86 Meruserre' Yakubher
87 Seweserenre' Khayan
88 'Auserre' Apopi I
89 'Akenenre' Apopi II
90 Asehre' Khamudy

Dynasty XVI
A minor Hyksos dynasty probably contemporary
with XV

*Dynasty XVII c.*1650–1552 BC *(Upper Egypt)*

91 Sekhemre' Wahkha' Ra'hotpe
92 Sekhemre' Wepma'e Inyotef
93 Sekhemre' Herhima'e Intyotef
94 Sekhemre' Shedtowe Sebekemsaf
95 Sekhemre' Smentowe Djehuty
96 S'ankhenre' Mentuhotpe
97 Swadjenre' Nebirierau
98 Neferkare' Nebirierau
99 Semenmedjatre'
100 Seuserenre'
101 Sekhemre' Shedwast
102 Nubkheperre' Inyotef
103 Senakhtenre'
104 Sekenenre' Ta'o I

105	Sekenenre' Ta'o II		S104
106	Wadjkheperre' Kamose		S105

Dynasty XVIII 1552–1305 BC

107	Nebpehtire' 'Ahmose	1552	S105
108	Djeserkare' Amenhotpe I	1527	S107
109	'Akheperkare' Dhutmose I (Tuthmosis)	1506	HD107
110	'Akheperenre' Dhutmose II	1494	S109
111	Ma'kare' Hashepsowe (Hatshepsut)★	1490–1468	D109
112	Menkheperre' Dhutmose III	1490–1436	S110
113	'Akheprure' Amenhotpe II	1438–1412	S112
114	Menkheprure' Dhutmose IV	1412	S113
115	Nebma're' Amenhotpe III	1402	S114
116	Neferkheprure' Wa'enre' Amenhotpe IV (Akhenaten)	1364–1347	S115
117	'Ankheprure' Smenkhkare'	1351–1348	S115
118	Nebkheprure' Tut'ankhamun	1347–1337	
119	Kheperkheprure' Itnute Ay	1337–1333	
120	Djeserkheprure' Haremhab	1333–1305	

Dynasty XIX 1305–1186 BC

121	Menpehtire' Ra'messe I	1305	
122	Menma're' Seti I Merenptah	1303	S121
123	Userma're' Ra'messe II Miamun (Rameses II)	1289	S122
124	Binere' Meryamun Merenptah Hotphima'e	1224	S123
125	Usikheperure' Seti II Merenptah	1204	
126	Menmire' Amenmesse	1200	
127	Akhenre' Merenptah Siptah	1194–1188	
128	Sitre' Meryamun Tewosre★	1194–1186	

Dynasty XX 1186–1069 BC

129	Userkha'ure' Setnakhte	1186	
130	Userma're' Meryamun Ra'messe III	1184	S129
131	Hekama're' Setpenamun Ra'messe IV	1153	S130
132	Userma're' Sekheperenre' Ra'messe V	1146	S131
133	Nebma're' Meryamun Ra'messe VI	1142	S130
134	Userma're' Meryamun Ra'messe VII	1135	S133
135	Userma're' Akhenamun Ra'messe VIII	1129	S130
136	Neferkare' Setpenre' Ra'messe IX	1127	
137	Kheperma're' Setpenre' Ra'messe X	1109	
138	Menma're' Setpenptah Ra'messe XI	1099–1069	

Dynasty XXIA (Tanis) 1069–945 BC

139	Hedjkeperre' Nesbanebded (Smendes)	1069	HD138
140	Neferkare' Hekawise Amenemnisu	1043	S139
141	Akheperre' Psibkha'emne I	1039	S139
142	Userma're' Amenemope	993	S141
143	Nutekheperre' Siamun	978	
144	Titkheprure' Psibkha'emne II	959–945	S151

Dynasty XXIB (Thebes) 1079–945 BC

145	Hrihor	
146	Pi'ankh	S145
147	Pinudjem I	S146
148	Masahert	S147
149	Menkheperre'	S147
150	Nesbanebded	S149
151	Pinudjem II	S149

Dynasty XXII 945–715 BC

152	Hedjkheperre' Shoshenk I	945	
153	Sekhemkheperre' Osorkhon I	924	S152
154	Hekakheperre' Shoshenk II	890	S153
155	Userma're' Takelot I	889	S153
156	Userma're' Osorkhon II	874	S155
157	Hedjkheperre' Takelot II	850	S156
158	Userma're' Shoshenk III	825	S157
159	Userma're' Pimay	773	S158
160	'Akheperre' Shoshenk V	767	S159
161	'Akheperre' Osorkhon IV	730–715	S160

Dynasty XXIII 818–715 BC

162	Userma're' Pedubast	818–793	S157
163	Iuput I	804–783	S162
164	Shoshenk IV	783–777	S163
165	Osorkhon III	777–749	S164
166	Takelot III	754–734	S165
167	Rudamen	734–731	S166
168	Iuput II	731–720	
169	Shoshenk VI	720–715	

Dynasty XXIV (Delta) 730–715 BC

170	Shepsesre' Tefnakhte	730	
171	Wahkare' Bekenrinef	720–715	S170

Dynasty XXV c.760–656 BC *(also Kings of Napata)*

172	Kashta (Meroe)	c.760	
173	Pi'ankhi (Meroe; Thebes c.730)	747	S172
174	Shabako (all Egypt 715)	716	S172
175	Shebitku	702	S173
176	Taharqa	690	S173
177	Tanuatamun	664–656	S175

Dynasty XXVI c.668–525 BC

178	Neko I	c.668	
179	Wahibre' Psamtek I	664	S178
180	Wehemibre' Neko II	610	S179
181	Neferibre' Psamtek II	595	S180
182	Ha'a'ibre' Wahibre'	589	S181

183 Khnemibre' 'Ahmose	570	
184 'Ankhkaenre' Psamtek III	526–525	s183

Dynasty XXVII 525–404 BC

(Achaemenid Kings – see Iran)

Dynasty XXVIII 404–399 BC

185 Amonirdisu

Dynasty XXIX 399–380 BC

186 Nef'aurud	399	
187 Usire' Setpenptah Pshenmut	393	
188 Khnemma'ere' Hakor	393–380	

Dynasty XXX 380–343 BC

189 Kheperkare' Nekhtnebef	380	
190 Irma'enre' Djeho Setpenanhur	362	s189
191 Snedjemibre' Nekhtharehbe	360–343	bs189

Dynasty XXXI 343–332 BC

(Achaemenid Kings – see Iran)

Dynasty XXXII 332–310 BC

(Argead Kings – see Macedonia)

99 EGYPT PTOLEMIES – LAGID DYNASTY 305–30 BC

1 Ptolemy I Soter	305–283	
2 Ptolemy II Philadelphus	285–246	s1
3 Ptolemy III Euergetes	246	s2
4 Ptolemy IV Philopator	222	s3
5 Ptolemy V Epiphanes	204	s4
6 Ptolemy VI Philometor	181–145	s5
7 Ptolemy VII Euergetes (Cyrene; Egypt 145)	163–116	s5
8 Ptolemy VIII Soter (Egypt to 108 and 88–80; Cyprus 108–88)	116–80	s7
9 Ptolemy IX Alexander (Cyprus to 108; Egypt 108–88)	116–88	s7
10 Ptolemy Apion (Cyrene)	116–96	s7
11 Ptolemy X Alexander	80.	s9
12 Ptolemy XI Auletes (1)	80–58	s8
13 Ptolemy (Cyprus)	80–58	s8
14 Berenice★	58–55	d12
Ptolemy XI Auletes (2)	55–51	
15 Ptolemy XII	51–47	s12
16 Cleopatra★	51–30	d12
17 Ptolemy XIII	47–44	s12
18 Ptolemy XIV Caesarion	44–30	s16

100 EGYPT TULUNIDS AND IKHSHIDIDS

a *Tulunid Dynasty 868–905*

1	Ahmad ibn Tulun	868	
2	Khumarawayh	884	S1
3	Jaish	896	S2
4	Harun	896	S2
5	Shaiban	905.	S1

b *Ikhshidid Dynasty 935–969*

1	Muhammad ibn Tughj al-Ikhshid	935	
2	Abu'l-Qasim Unujur	946	S1
3	'Ali	961	S1
4	Abu'l-Misk Kafur	966	
5	Ahmad	968–969	S3

101 EGYPT FATIMID DYNASTY CALIPHS IN MAGHRIB AND EGYPT 909–1171

1	al-Mahdi (at Qairawan)	909	
2	al-Qa'im	934	S1
3	al-Mansur	946	S2
4	al-Mu'izz (Egypt from 969)	953	S3
5	al-'Aziz	975	S4
6	al-Hakim	996	S5
7	az-Zahir	1021	S6
8	al-Mustansir	1036	S7
9	al-Musta'li	1094	S8
10	al-Amir	1101	S9
11	al-Hafiz	1130	GS8
12	az-Zafir	1149	S11
13	al-Fa'iz	1154	S12
14	al-'Adid	1160–1171	GS11

102 EGYPT AYYUBID SULTANS 1169–1252

1	an-Nasir Salah-ud-Din Yusuf (Saladin)	1169	
2	al-'Aziz 'Imad-ud-Din 'Uthman	1193	S1
3	al-Mansur Nasir-ud-Din Muhammad	1198	S2
4	al-'Adil Saif-ud-Din Abu-Bakr I	1200	B1
5	al-Kamil Nasir-ud-Din Muhammad	1218	S4
6	al-'Adil Saif-ud-Din Abu-Bakr II	1238	S5
7	as-Salih Najm-ud-Din Ayyub	1240	S5
8	al-Mu'azzam Turan Shah	1249	S7
9	al-Ashraf Muzaffar-ud-Din Musa (s6 Yemen)	1250–1252	BS7

103 **EGYPT** MAMLUK SULTANS

a *Bahri Sultans* 1250–1390

1	al-Mu'izz 'Izz-ud-Din Aibak	1250	
2	al-Mansur Nur-ud-Din 'Ali	1257	S1
3	al-Muzaffar Saif-ud-Din Qutuz	1259	
4	az-Zahir Rukn-ud-Din Baibars I	1260	
5	as-Sa'id Nasir -ud-Din Baraka Khan	1277	S4
6	al-'Adil Badr-ud-Din Salamish	1280	S4
7	al-Mansur Saif-ud-Din Qala'un	1280	
8	al-Ashraf Salah-ud-Din Khalil	1290	S7
9	an-Nasir Nasir-ud-Din Muhammad (1)	1294	S7
10	al-'Adil Zain-ud-Din Kitbugha	1295	
11	al-Mansur Husam-ud-Din Lajin	1297	
	an-Nasir Nasir-ud-Din Muhammad (2)	1299	
12	al-Muzaffar Rukn-ud-Din Baibars II	1309	
	an-Nasir Nasir-ud-Din Muhammad (3)	1309	
13	al-Mansur Saif-ud-Din Abu-Bakr	1340	S9
14	al-Ashraf 'Ala-ud-Din Kujuk	1341	S9
15	an-Nasir Shihab-ud-Din Ahmad	1342	S9
16	as-Salih 'Imad-ud-Din Isma'il	1342	S9
17	al-Kamil Saif-ud-Din Sha'ban I	1345	S9
18	al-Muzaffar Saif-ud-Din Hajji I	1346	S9
19	an-Nasir Nasir-ud-Din Hasan (1)	1347	S9
20	as-Salih Salah-ud-Din Salih	1351	S9
	an-Nasir Nasir-ud Din Hasan (2)	1354	
21	al-Mansur Salah-ud-Din Muhammad	1361	S18
22	al-Ashraf Nasir-ud-Din Sha'ban II	1363	BS20
23	al-Mansur 'Ala-ud-Din 'Ali	1376	S22
24	as-Salih Salah-ud-Din Hajji II (1)	1382.	S22
	as-Salih Salah-ud-Din Hajji II (2)	1389–1390	

b *Burji Sultans* 1382–1517

1	az-Zahir Saif-ud-Din Barquq (1)	1382–1389
	az-Zahir Saif-ud-Din Barquq (2)	1390
2	an-Nasir Nasir-ud-Din Faraj (1)	1399
3	al-Mansur 'Izz-ud-Din 'Abdul-'Aziz	1405
	an-Nasir Nasir-ud-Din Faraj (2)	1405
4	al-'Adil al-Musta'in ('Abbasid Caliph)	1412
5	al-Mu'ayyad Saif-ud-Din Shaikh	1412
6	al-Muzaffar Ahmad	1421
7	az-Zahir Saif-ud-Din Tatar	1421
8	as-Salih Nasir-ud-Din Muhammad	1421
9	al-Ashraf Saif-ud-Din Barsbay	1422
10	al-'Aziz Jamal-ud-Din Yusuf	1437
11	az-Zahir Saif-ud-Din Jaqmaq	1438
12	al-Mansur Fakhr-ud-Din 'Uthman	1453
13	al-Ashraf Saif-ud-Din Inal	1453

14	al-Mu'ayyad Shihab-ud-Din Ahmad	1461	
15	az-Zahir Saif-ud-Din Khushqadam	1461	
16	az-Zahir Saif-ud-Din Bilbay	1467	
17	az-Zahir Timurbugha	1468	
18	al-Ashraf Saif-ud-Din Qa'it Bay	1468	
19	an-Nasir Muhammad	1496	
20	az-Zahir Qansuh	1498	
21	al-Ashraf Janbalat	1500	
22	al-'Adil Saif-ud-Din Tuman Bay	1501	
23	al-Ashraf Qansuh al-Ghawri	1501	
24	al-Ashraf Tuman Bay	1517.	

c *'Abbasid Caliphs at Cairo* 1261–1517

1	al-Mustansir (S35 Baghdad)	1261	
2	al-Hakim I (DT29 Baghdad)	1261	
3	al-Mustakfi I	1302	S2
4	al-Wathiq I	1340	BS2
5	al-Hakim II	1341	S3
6	al-Mu'tadid I	1352	S3
7	al-Mutawakkil I (1)	1362	S6
8	al-Musta'sim (1)	1377	BS4
	al-Mutawakkil I (2)	1377	
9	al-Wathiq II	1383	B8
	al-Musta'sim (2)	1386	
	al-Mutawakkil I (3)	1389	
10	al-Musta'in	1406	S7
11	al-Mu'tadid II	1414	S7
12	al-Mustakfi II	1441	S7
13	al-Qa'im	1451	S7
14	al-Mustanjid	1455	S7
15	al-Mutawakkil II	1479	S10
16	al-Mustamsik (1)	1497	S15
17	al-Mutawakkil III (1)	1508	S16
	al-Mustamsik (2)	1516	
	al-Mutawakkil III (2)	1517.	

104 **EGYPT** DYNASTY OF MUHAMMAD 'ALI 1805–1953

1	Muhammad 'Ali Pasha	1805	
2	Ibrahim	1848	S1
3	'Abbas I	1848	BS2
4	Sa'id	1854	S1
5	Isma'il (Khedive 1866)	1863	S2
6	Tawfiq	1879	S5
7	'Abbas II Hilmi	1892	S6
8	Husain Kamil (Sultan 1917)	1914	S5
9	Ahmad Fu'ad I (King 1922)	1917	S5
10	Faruq	1936	S9
11	Ahmad Fu'ad II	1952–1953	S10

105 **LIBYA** BATTIAD DYNASTY OF CYRENE *c.*639–439 BC

1	Aristoteles Battus I	*c.*639 BC	
2	Argesilaus I	*c.*599	S1
3	Battus II	*c.*583	S2
4	Argesilaus II	*c.*554	S3
5	Learchus	*c.*550	
6	Battus III	*c.*550	S4
7	Argesilaus III	*c.*526	S6
8	Battus IV	*c.*515	S7
9	Argesilaus IV	*c.*466–439	S8

106 **LIBYA** MUSLIM DYNASTIES

a *Banu 'Ammar Dynasty of Tripoli 1327–1401*

1	Thabit I ibn 'Ammar	1327	
2	Muhammad	1327	S1
3	Thabit II	1348–1355	S2
4	Abu-Bakr	1371	S2
5	'Ali ibn 'Ammar	1392	BS4
6	Yahya	1397–1401	S4
7	'Abdul-Wahid	1397–1401	S4

b *Awlad Muhammad Dynasty of Fezzan c.1577–1842*

1	al-Muntasir ibn Muhammad	?–1577	
2	an-Nasir	1582	S1
3	al-Mansur	1599	S2
4	Tahir I	1613	S2
5	Muhammad I	1626	BS3
6	Jehim	1658	S5
7	Najib	1682	S5
8	Muhammad II Nasir (1)	1682	S5
9	Temmam	1689	
10	Muhammad III	1689	S6
	Muhammad II Nasir (2)	1691	
11	Ahmad I	1718	S8
12	Tahir II	1767	S11
13	Ahmad II	1775	
14	Muhammad IV al-Hakim	1789	B13
15	Muhammad V al-Muntasir	1804	B13
16	Muhammad VI al-Muqni	1811	
17	'Abdul-Jalil	1831–1842	

c *Qaramanid Dynasty of Tripoli 1711–1835*

1	Ahmad I	1711	
2	Muhammad	1745	S1
3	'Ali I (1)	1754	S2
4	'Ali Burghul	1793	
	'Ali I (2)	1795	

5 Ahmad II	1795	s3
6 Yusuf	1795	s3
7 'Ali II	1832–1835	s6

d *Sanusi Dynasty* 1837–1969

1 Sayyid Muhammad al-Sanusi	1837	
2 Sayyid al-Mahdi	1859	s1
3 Sayyid Ahmad ash-Sharif	1902	BS2
4 Sayyid Muhammad Idris (King of Libya 1951)	1918–1969	s2

107 **MAGHRIB** KINGS OF NUMIDIA 201–46 BC

1 Masinissa	201 BC	
2 Micipsa	148–118	s1
3 Gulussa	148–?	s1
4 Mastanabal	148–?	s1
5 Adherbal	118–112	s2
6 Hiempsal I	118–117	s2
7 Jugurtha	118–105	s4
8 Gauda	105–?	s4
9 Hiempsal II	c.88–62	s8
10 Juba	c.62–46	s9

108 **MAGHRIB** VANDAL KINGS 429–534

1 Gaiseric	429 AD	
2 Huneric	477	s1
3 Gunthamund	484	BS2
4 Thrasamund	496	B3
5 Hilderic	523	s2
6 Gelimer	530–534	BS3

109 **MAGHRIB** MUSLIM DYNASTIES IN TUNISIA

a *Aghlabid Dynasty* 800–909

1 Ibrahim ibn al-Aghlab	800	
2 'Abdullah I	812	s1
3 Ziyadat-Allah I	817	s1
4 Abu-'Iqal al-Aghlab	838	s1
5 Muhammad I	841	s4
6 Ahmad	856	s5
7 Ziyadat-Allah II	863	s5
8 Muhammad II	863	s6
9 Ibrahim II	875	s6
10 'Abdullah II	902	s9
11 Ziyadat-Allah III	903–909	s10

b *Zirid Dynasty* 972–1148

1	Yusuf Buluggin ibn Ziri (B1 Granada)	972	
2	al-Mansur	984	S1
3	Nasir-ud-Dawlah Badis	996	S2
4	Sharaf-ud-Dawlah al-Mu'izz	1016	S3
5	Abu-Tahir Tamim	1062	S4
6	Abu-Tahir Yahya	1108	S5
7	'Ali	1116	S6
8	Abu-Yahya Hasan	1121–1148	S7

c *Hafsid Dynasty* 1228–1574

1	Abu-Zakariya Yahya I	1228	
2	Muhammad I al-Mustansir	1249	S1
3	Yahya II al-Wathiq	1277	S2
4	Abu-Ishaq Ibrahim I	1279	S1
5	Ahmad ibn Abu-'Umara	1282	
6	Abu-Hafs 'Umar I (Tunis)	1284–1295	S1
7	Abu-Zakariya Yahya III (Bougie)	1285–1299	S4
8	Muhammad II al-Muntasir	1295–1309	S3
9	Abu-Bakr I ash-Shahid	1309	S1
10	Khalid I an-Nasir	1309	S7
11	Zakariya I al-Lihyani	1311	BGS1
12	Muhammad III al-Mustansir	1317	S11
13	Abu-Bakr II al-Mutawakkil	1318	S7
14	Abu-Hafs 'Umar II	1346–1348	S13
15	Ahmad I al-Fadl	1349	S13
16	Ibrahim II al-Mustansir (1)	1350–1357	S13
	Ibrahim II al-Mustansir (2)	1359	
17	Abu'l-Baqa Khalid II	1369	S16
18	Ahmad II al-Mustansir	1370	BS15
19	'Abdul-'Aziz al-Mutawakkil	1394	S18
20	Muhammad IV al-Muntasir	1434	GS19
21	Abu-'Umar 'Uthman	1435	B20
22	Abu-Zakariya Yahya IV	1488	GS21
23	'Abdul-Mu'min	1489	BS20
24	Abu-Yahya Zakariya II	1490	S22
25	Abu-'Abdullah Muhammad V	1494	BS22
26	Muhammad Hasan	1526	S25
27	Ahmad III	1543–1569	S26
28	Abu-'Abdullah Muhammad VI	1573–1574	S26

110 **MAGHRIB** MUSLIM DYNASTIES IN ALGERIA

a *Rustamid Dynasty of Tahart* 777–909

1	'Abdul-Rahman ibn Rustam	777	
2	'Abdul-Wahhab	784	S1

3	Abu-Sa'id Aflah	823	S2
4	Abu-Bakr	872	S3
5	Abu'l-Yaqzan Muhammad	?	S3
6	Abu-Hatim Yusuf (1)	894	S5
7	Ya'qub	897	S3
	Abu-Hatim Yusuf (2)	901	
8	Yaqzan	907–909	S5

b *Hammadid Dynasty* 1015–1152

1	Hammad ibn Buluggin (S1 Zirids)	1015	
2	al-Qa'id	1028	S1
3	Muhsin	1054	S2
4	Buluggin	1055	BS2
5	an-Nasir	1062	BS2
6	al-Mansur	1088	S5
7	Badis	1105	S6
8	al-'Aziz	1105	S6
9	Yahya	c.1121–1152	S8

c *Zayyanid ('Abdul-Wadid) Dynasty of Tlemcen* 1235–1553

1	Abu-Yahya Yaghmurasan	1235	
2	Abu-Sa'id 'Uthman I	1282	S1
3	Abu-Zayyan Muhammad I	1303	S2
4	Abu-Hammu Musa I	1307	S2
5	Abu-Tashufin 'Abdul-Rahman I	1318–1337	S4
6	Abu-Sa'id 'Uthman II	1348–1352	GG1
7	Abu-Thabit	1348–1352	B6
8	Abu-Hammu Musa II	1358	BS6
9	Abu-Tashufin 'Abdul-Rahman II	1388	S8
10	Abu-Thabit Yusuf I	1393	S9
11	Abu-Hajjaj Yusuf II	1393	S8
12	Abu-Zayyan Muhammad II	1394	S8
13	Abu-Muhammad 'Abdullah	1399	S8
14	Abu-'Abdullah Muhammad	1401	S8
15	'Abdul-Rahman III	1411	S14
16	Sa'id ibn Musa	1411	S8
17	Abu-Malik 'Abdul-Wahid (1)	1411	S8
18	Abu-'Abdullah Muhammad IV	1423	S9
	Abu-Malik 'Abdul-Wahid (2)	1427	
19	Ahmad al-Mu'tasim	1430	S8
20	Muhammad V al-Mutawakkil	1461	BGS11
21	Muhammad VI al-Thabiti	1468	S20
22	Abu-'Abdullah Muhammad VII	1505	S21
23	Abu-Hammu Musa III	1516	S20
24	Abu-Muhammad 'Abdullah II	1526	S20
25	Abu-'Abdullah Muhammad VIII	1540	S24
26	Abu-Zayyan Ahmad	1540	S24
27	Hasan ibn 'Abdullah	1550–1553	S24

III **MAGHRIB** BEYS OF TUNIS AND DEYS OF ALGIERS

a *Muradid Beys of Tunis* 1628–1705

1	Murad I	1628	
2	Muhammad I	1631	S1
3	Murad II	1662	S2
4	Muhammad II (1)	1675	S3
5	'Ali (1)	1675	S3
6	Muhammad III	1675	S2
	Muhammad II (2)	1675	
	'Ali (2)	1676	
	Muhammad II (3)	1688	
7	Ramadan	1695	S3
8	Murad III	1698	S5
9	Ibrahim ash-Sharif	1702–1705	

b *Husainid Beys of Tunis* 1705–1957

1	Husain I	1705	
2	'Ali I	1735	BS1
3	Muhammad I	1756	S1
4	'Ali II	1759	S1
5	Hammuda	1782	S4
6	'Uthman	1814	S4
7	Mahmud	1814	S3
8	Husain II	1824	S7
9	Mustafa	1835	S7
10	Ahmad I	1837·	S9
11	Muhammad II	1855	S8
12	Muhammad III as-Sadiq	1859	S8
13	'Ali Muddat	1882	S8
14	Muhammad IV al-Hadi	1902	S13
15	Muhammad V an-Nasir	1906	S11
16	Muhammad VI al-Habib	1922	GS8
17	Ahmad II	1929	S13
18	Muhammad VII al-Munsif	1942	S15
19	Muhammad VIII al-Amin	1943–1957	S16

c *Deys of Algiers* 1671–1830

1	Muhammad I	1671
2	Hasan I	1682
3	Husain I	1683
4	Sha'ban	1689
5	Ahmad I	1695
6	Hasan II	1698
7	Mustafa I	1700
8	Husain II Khoja	1705
9	Muhammad II Bektash	1707
10	Ibrahim I	1710
11	'Ali I	1710
12	Muhammad III	1718

13 Kurd 'Abdi	1724	
14 Ibrahim II	1732	
15 Kuchuk Ibrahim III	1745	
16 Muhammad IV	1748	
17 'Ali II	1754	
18 Muhammad V	1766	
19 Hasan III	1791	
20 Mustafa II	1798	
21 Ahmad II	1805	
22 'Ali III ar-Rasul	1808	
23 'Ali IV	1809	
24 Muhammad VI	1815	
25 'Umar	1815	
26 'Ali V Khoja	1817	
27 Husain III	1818–1830	

112 **MAGHRIB** MUSLIM DYNASTIES IN MOROCCO

a *Midrarid Dynasty of Sijilmasa 772–976*

1 Abu'l-Qasim Samghun ibn Wasul	772	
2 Abu'l-Wizir Ilyas	783	S1
3 Abu'l-Mansur Ilyasa'	790	S1
4 Midrar al-Muntasir	823	S3
5 'Abdul-Rahman Maimun	867	S4
6 Maimun al-Amir	867	S4
7 Muhammad I	876	S6
8 Ilyasa' al-Muntasir	883–909	S4
9 al-Fath Wasul	911	S6
10 Ahmad	912	S6
11 Muhammad II	922	BS5
12 Abu'l-Muntasir Muhammad III	933	GS11
13 Muhammad IV ash-Shakir	933	S9
14 al-Muntasir	958	S13
15 Abu-Muhammad al-Mu'tazz	963–976	S13

b *Idrisid Dynasty 789–974*

1 Idris I ibn 'Abdullah	789	
2 Idris II	791	S1
3 Muhammad al-Muntasir	828	S2
4 'Ali I	836	S3
5 Yahya I	849	S3
6 Yahya II	863	S5
7 'Ali II ibn 'Umar	866	GS2
8 Yahya III al-Miqdam	?	GS2
9 Yahya IV	905–920	BS7
10 Hasan al-Hajjam	925–927	BS8

11	al-Qasim Gannun	937	BIO
12	Abu'l-'Aish Ahmad	948	SII
13	Hasan II	954–974	SII

c *Maghrawa Dynasty of Fez 987–1070*

1	Ziri ibn 'Atiya	987	
2	al-Mu'izz	1001	SI
3	Hamama	1026	BSI
4	Dunas	1040	S3
5	al-Futuh	1060	S4
6	Mu'ansar	1063	BGS3
7	Tammim	1068–1070	S6

d *Almoravid (Murabitid) Dynasty 1056–1147*

1	Abu-Bakr ibn 'Umar	1056	
2	Yusuf ibn Tashufin	1061	FBGSI
3	'Ali	1106	S2
4	Tashufin	1142	S3
5	Ibrahim	1146	S4
6	Ishaq	1146–1147	S3

e *Almohad (Muwahhid) Dynasty 1130–1269*

1	'Abdul-Mu'min	1130	
2	Abu-Ya'qub Yusuf I	1163	SI
3	Ya'qub al-Mansur	1184	S2
4	Muhammad an-Nasir	1199	S3
5	Yusuf II al-Mustansir	1214	S4
6	'Abdul-Wahid I al-Makhlu'	1224	S2
7	'Abdullah al-'Adil	1224	S3
8	Yahya al-Mu'tasim	1227	S4
9	Idris al-Ma'mun	1229	S3
10	'Abdul-Wahid ar-Rashid	1232	S9
11	'Ali as-Sa'id	1242	S9
12	'Umar al-Murtada	1248	BS3
13	Abu'l-'Ula al-Wathiq	1266–1269	BGS2

f *Marinid Dynasty 1196–1465*

1	Abu-Muhammad 'Abdul-Haqq I	1196	
2	'Uthman I	1217	SI
3	Muhammad I	1240	SI
4	Abu-Yahya Abu-Bakr	1244	SI
5	Abu-Yusuf Ya'qub	1258	SI
6	Abu-Ya'qub Yusuf	1286	S5
7	Abu-Thabit 'Amir	1307	GS6
8	Abu'l-Rabi' Sulayman	1308	B7
9	Abu-Sa'id 'Uthman II	1310	S5
10	Abu'l-Hasan 'Ali I	1331	S9
11	Abu-'Inan Faris	1348	SIO
12	Muhammad II as-Sa'id	1359	SII
13	Abu-Salim 'Ali II	1359	SIO

14	Abu-'Umar Tashufin	1361	S10
15	'Abdul-Halim	1361	BS10
16	Abu-Zayyan Muhammad III	1362	BS14
17	Abu'l-Faris 'Abdul-'Aziz I	1366	S10
18	Abu-Zayyan Muhammad IV	1372	S17
19	Abu'l-'Abbas Ahmad (1)	1374	S13
20	Musa	1384	S11
21	Abu-Zayyan Muhammad V	1386	S19
22	Muhammad VI	1386	BS11
	Abu'l-'Abbas Ahmad (2)	1387	
23	Abu'l-Faris	1393	S19
24	'Abdul-'Aziz II	1397	S19
25	'Abdullah	1398	S19
26	Abu-Sa'id 'Uthman III	1399–1420	S19
27	Abu-Muhammad 'Abdul-Haqq II	1428–1465	S26

g *Wattasid Dynasty* 1472–1549

1	Muhammad ash-Shaikh	1472	
2	Muhammad II al-Burtuqali	1505	S1
3	Ahmad al-Wattasi (1)	1524	S2
4	Muhammad III al-Qasri	1545	S3
	Ahmad al-Wattasi (2)	1547–1549	

h *Sa'did Dynasty* 1511–1659

1	Muhammad I al-Qa'im (Sus)	1511	
2	Ahmad I al-A'raj (Marrakesh 1524)	1517	S1
3	Muhammad II al-Mahdi (Marrakesh; Fez 1549)	1540	S1
4	'Abdullah al-Ghalib	1557	S3
5	Muhammad III al-Mutawakkil	1574	S4
6	'Abdul-Malik I al-Ghazi	1576	S3
7	Ahmad II al-Mansur	1578	S3
8	Zaydan an-Nasir (Marrakesh)	1603–1628	S7
9	Muhammad IV al-Ma'mun (Fez)	1610–1613	S7
10	'Abdullah II (Fez)	1613–1624	S9
11	'Abdul-Malik II (Marrakesh)	1623–1631	S8
12	'Abdul-Malik III (Fez)	1624–1626	S10
13	al-Walid (Marrakesh)	1631–1636	S8
14	Muhammad V al-Asghar (Marrakesh)	1636–1654	S8
15	Ahmad III al-'Abbas (Marrakesh)	1654–1659	S14

i *'Alawid (Filali) Dynasty since* 1631

1	Muhammad I ash-Sharif	1631	
2	Muhammad II	1635	S1
3	ar-Rashid	1664	S1
4	Isma'il as-Samin	1672	S1
5	Ahmad adh-Dhahabi	1727	S4
6	'Abdullah (1)	1729	S4
7	'Ali ibn Isma'il	1735	S4
	'Abdullah (2)	1737	

8	al-Mustadi ibn Isma'il	1738	S4
	'Abdullah (3)	1740	
9	Zain-ul-'Abidin	1745	S4
	'Abdullah (4)	1745	
10	Muhammad III	1757	S6
11	Yazid	1790	S10
12	Hisham	1792	S10
13	Sulayman	1793	S10
14	'Abdul-Rahman	1822	S12
15	Muhammad IV	1859	S14
16	Hasan I	1873	S15
17	'Abdul-'Aziz	1894	S16
18	'Abdul-Hafiz	1907	S16
19	Yusuf	1912	S16
20	Muhammad V (1)	1927	S19
21	Muhammad VI	1953	BS16
	Muhammad V (2) (King 1957)	1955	
22	Hasan II	1962	S20

113 SUDAN KINGS OF NAPATA *c.*760–310 BC

1	Kashta		*c.*760 BC
2	Pi'ankhi		751
3	Shabako	(Dynasty XXV	716
4	Shebitku	of Egypt)	701
5	Taharqa		689
6	Tanuatamun		664
7	Atlanersa		653
8	Senkamanisken		643
9	Anlamani		623
10	Aspelta		593
11	Amtalqa		568
12	Malenaqen		555
13	Analmaye		542
14	Amani-nataki-lebte		538
15	Karkamani		519
16	Amaniastabarqa		510
17	Siaspiqa		487
18	Nasakhma		468
19	Malewiebamani		463
20	Talakhamani		435
21	Amani-nete-yerike		431
22	Baskakeren		405
23	Harsiotef		404
24	(Unknown)		369
25	Akhraten		350
26	Nastasen		335–310

114 **SUDAN** EASTERN SULTANATES

a *Fung Dynasty of Sennar c.1504–1821*

1	'Amara Dunqas	c.1504	
2	Nail	c.1546	S1
3	'Abdul-Qadir I	1550	S1
4	'Amara Abu-Sakaykin	1557	?S1
5	Dekin	1568	S2
6	Tabl I	c.1580	S3
7	Unsa I	c.1590	S6
8	'Abdul-Qadir II	1603	S7
9	'Adlan I	1606	S7
10	Badi I Sid-al-Qum	1611	S8
11	Rubat	1616	S10
12	Badi II Abu-Daqan	1644	S11
13	Unsa II	1680	BS12
14	Badi III al-Ahmar	1692	S13
15	Unsa III	1716	S14
16	Nul	1720	
17	Badi IV Abu-Shulukh	1724	S16
18	Nasir	1762	S17
19	Isma'il	1769	S17
20	'Adlan II	1777	S17
21	Awkal	1789	
22	Tabl II	1789	
23	Badi V	1789	
24	Hasan Rabbihi	1789	
25	Nowwar	1790	
26	Badi VI (1)	1790	S22
27	Ranfi	c.1796	
	Badi VI (2)	1803–1821	

b *Kayra Dynasty of Darfur c.1640–1916*

1	Sulayman Solong	c.1640	
2	Musa	c.1670	S1
3	Ahmad Bakr	1682	S2
4	Muhammad I Dawra	1722	S3
5	'Umar Lele	1732	S4
6	Abu'l-Qasim	1739	S3
7	Muhammad II Tairab	1756	S3
8	'Abdul-Rahman ar-Rashid	1787	S3
9	Muhammad III al-Fadl	1801	S8
10	Muhammad IV Husain	1839	S9
11	Ibrahim	1873–1874	S10
12	'Ali Dinar ibn Zakariyya	1898–1916	GS9

c *Sultans of Wadai c.*1635–1912

1	'Abdul-Karim	c.1635	
2	Kharut al-Kabir	1655	S1
3	Kharif	1678	S2
4	Ya'qub 'Arus	1681	S2
5	Kharut as-Saghir	1707	S4
6	Joda Kharif at-Timan	1745	S5
7	Salih Derret	1795	S6
8	'Abdul-Karim Sabun	1803	S7
9	Yusuf Kharifain	1814	S8
10	Rakib	1829	S9
11	'Abdul-'Aziz	1830	BGS7
12	Muhammad Sharif	1835	S7
13	'Ali	1858	S12
14	Yusuf	1874	
15	Ibrahim	1898	
16	Abu-Ghazali	1901	
17	Dudmurra	1902	
18	'Asil	1911–1912	

d *Kenga Dynasty of Bagirmi* 1522–1935

1	Birni Besse	1522	
2	Lubatko	1536	S1
3	Malo	1548	S2
4	'Abdullah	1568	S2
5	'Umar	1608	S4
6	Dalai	1625	S4
7	Burkomanda I	1635	S5
8	'Abdul-Rahman I	1665	S7
9	Dalo Birni	1674	S8
10	'Abdul-Qadir I	1680	S9
11	Bar	1707	S10
12	Wanja	1722	S9
13	Burkomanda II Tad Lele	1736	S12
14	Loel	1741	S13
15	Hajji Muhammad al-Amin	1751	S10
16	'Abdul-Rahman II Gauranga	1785	S15
17	Ngarba Bira	1806	S16
18	Burkomanda III	1807	S16
19	'Abdul-Qadir II	1846	S18
20	Abu-Sekkin Muhammad	1858	S19
21	'Abdul-Rahman III	1871	BS18
22	'Abdul-Qadir III	1918–1935	

115 SUDAN KANEM-BORNU

a *Saifawa Sultans* 1086–1846

1	Umme ibn 'Abdul-Jalil	1086	
2	Dunama I	1098	S1

3	Biri I	1151	S2
4	'Abdullah I	1177	GS3
5	'Abdul-Jalil	1194	B4
6	Dunama II Dubalemi	1221	S5
7	'Abdul-Kadim	1259	S6
8	Biri II Ibrahim	1288	S6
9	Ibrahim I	1307	S8
10	'Abdullah II	1326	S7
11	Selma	1346	S10
12	Kure Ghana as-Saghir	1350	S10
13	Kure Kura al-Kabir	1351	S10
14	Muhammad I	1352	S10
15	Idris I Nigalemi	1353	S9
16	Da'ud Nigalemi	1377	S9
17	'Uthman I	1387	S16
18	'Uthman II	1391	S15
19	Abu-Bakr Liyatu	1392	S16
20	'Umar I	1393	S15
21	Sa'id	1398	S19
22	Kade Afunu	1399	S15
23	Biri III	1400	S15
24	'Uthman III Kaliwama	1432	S16
25	Dunama III	1433	S20
26	'Abdullah III Dakumuni	1435	S20
27	Ibrahim II	1442	S17
28	Kadai	1450	S24
29	Ahmad Dunama IV	1451	S23
30	Muhammad II	1455	
31	'Amr	1456	GD18
32	Muhammad III	1456	S28
33	Ghaji	1456	S31
34	'Uthman IV	1461	S28
35	'Umar II	1466	S26
36	Muhammad IV	1467	S32
37	'Ali Ghajideni	1472	S29
38	Idris II Katakarmabi	1505	S37
39	Muhammad V Aminami	1526	S38
40	'Ali II Zainami	1545	S38
41	Dunama V Ngumaramma	1546	S39
42	'Abdullah IV	1564	S41
43	Idris III Aloma	1571	S40
44	Muhammad VI Bukalmarami	1603	S43
45	Ibrahim III	1618	S43
46	'Umar III	1625	S43
47	'Ali III	1645	S46
48	Idris IV	1685	S47
49	Dunama VI	1704	S47
50	Hamdan	1723	S49
51	Muhammad VII Erghamma	1737	S50
52	Dunama VII Ghana	1752	S51

53	'Ali IV	1755	S51
54	Ahmad	1793	S53
55	Dunama VIII Lafiami (1)	1808	S54
56	Muhammad VIII	1811	
	Dunama VIII Lafiami (2)	1814	
57	Ibrahim IV	1817	S54
58	'Ali V Dalatumi	1846.	S57

b *Shehu Shaikhs 1808–1893 and since 1902*

1	Muhammad al-Amin al-Kanemi	1808	
2	'Umar (1)	1837	S1
3	'Abdul-Rahman	1853	S1
	'Umar (2)	1854	
4	Bukar	1881	S2
5	Ibrahim	1884	S2
6	Hashim	1885	S2
7	Kiyari Muhammad al-Amin	1893	S4
8	Sanda Wudoroma	1893.	S4
9	Bukar Garbai	1902	S5
10	'Umar Sanda Kura	1922	S5
11	'Umar Sanda Kiyarimi	1937	S7
12	'Umar Baba Ya Mairami	1969	S9

c *Rabeh Dynasty 1893–1901*

1	Rabeh Zubair	1893	
2	Fadl-Allah	1900–1901	S1

116 SUDAN HAUSA KINGDOMS OF NIGERIA

a *Habe Kings of Kano 998–1807*

1	Bagauda	998	
2	Warisi	1063	S1
3	Gijimasu	1095	S2
4	Nawata	1133–1135	S3
5	Gawata	1133–1135	S3
6	Yusa	1135	S3
7	Naguji	1193	S6
8	Gugua	1247	S3
9	Shekarau	1290	S6
10	Tsamia	1306	S9
11	Osumanu Zamnagawa	1342	S9
12	Yaji I	1349	S10
13	Bugaya	1385	S10
14	Kanajeji	1389	S12
15	Umaru	1409	S14
16	Dauda	1421	S14
17	Abdullahi Burja	1437	S14
18	Dakauta	1452	S17

19	Atuma	1452	S18
20	Yakubu	1452	S17
21	Mohamma Rimfa	1462	S20
22	Abdullahi	1498	S21
23	Mohamma Kisoki	1508	S22
24	Yakufu	1564	S23
25	Dauda Abasama I	1565	S24
26	Abu-Bakr Kado	1565	S21
27	Mohamma Shashere	1572	S24
28	Mohamma Zaki	1582	S23
29	Mohamma Nazaki	1617	S28
30	Kutumbi	1622	S29
31	al-Hajj	1648	S30
32	Shekkarau	1649	S31
33	Mohamma Kukuna (1)	1650	S31
34	Soyaki	1651	S32
	Mohamma Kukuna (2)	1651	
35	Bawa	1659	S33
36	Dadi	1670	S35
37	Mohamma Sharefa	1702	S36
38	Kumbari	1730	S37
39	al-Hajj Kabe	1743	S38
40	Yaji II	1752	S36
41	Babba Zaki	1768	S40
42	Dauda Abasuma II	1776	S40
43	Mihamma Alwali	1780–1807	S40

b *Habe Kings of Katsina 1554–1806*

1	Ali Marabus	1554
2	Muhammad Toya Rero I	1568
3	Ali Karya Giwa I	1572
4	Uthman Tsagarana	1585
5	Ali Jan Hazo I	1589
6	Muhammad Mai-sa-maza-gudu	1595
7	Ali Jan Hazo II	1612
8	Maje Ibrahim	1614
9	Abdul-Karim	1631
10	Ashafa	1634
11	Ibrahim Gamdu	1634
12	Muhammad Wari I	1644
13	Sulayman	1655
14	Uthman Na-yi-Nawa	1667
15	Muhammad Toya Rero II	1684
16	Muhammad Wari II	1701
17	Muhammad dan Wari	1704
18	Karya Giwa II	1706
19	Jan Hazo III	1715
20	Tsagarana Hasan	1728
21	Muhammad Kabiya	1740
22	Tsagarana Yahya	1750

23 Karya Giwa III	1751	
24 Muhammad Wari III	1758	
25 Karya Giwa IV	1767	
26 Agwaragi	1784	
27 Tsagarana Gwozo	1801	
28 Bawa dan Gima	1801	
29 Mare Mawa Mahmud	1804	
30 Magajin Halid	1805–1806	

c *Kings of Nupe* 1531–1835

1 Tsoede	1531	
2 Shaba	1591	
3 Zavunla	1600	
4 Jigba	1625	
5 Mamma Wari	1670	
6 Abdu Waliyi	1679	
7 Aliyu	1700	
8 Ganamace	1710	
9 Ibrahim	1713	
10 Idirisu I	1717	
11 Tsado	1721	
12 Abu-Bakr Kolo	1742	
13 Jibrilu	1746	
14 Ma'azu (1)	1759	
15 Majiya I	1767	
16 Ilyasu	1777	
Ma'azu (2)	1778	
17 Ali Kolo Tankari	1795	
18 Mamma	1795	
19 Jimada (East)	1796–1805	
20 Majiya II (1) (West; sole ruler 1805)	1796–1810	
21 Idirisu II	1810–1830	
Majiya II (2)	1830–1835	

d *Kings of Kebbi/Amirs of Argungu since c.*1515

1 Muhammad Kantu	c.1515	
2 Ahmad I	c.1561	S1
3 Dawud	c.1596	S2
4 Ibrahim I	c.1619	S1
5 Sulayman I	c.1621	S3
6 Muhammad	c.1636	S1
7 Maliki	c.1649	S4
8 'Umar Giwa	c.1662	S2
9 Muhammad Kaye	c.1674	S5
10 Ibrahim II	c.1676	S9
11 Muhammad Na Sifawa	c.1684	S8
12 Ahmad II	c.1686	GS1
13 Tomo	c.1696	S4
14 Muhammad Dan Giwa	c.1700	S8
15 Sumail I Ta-Gandu	c.1717	S11

16	Muhammad Dan Ta-Gandu	c.1750	S15
17	'Abdullah Toga I	c.1754	S15
18	Sulayman II	c.1775	S17
19	Abu Bakr	1803	S18
20	Muhammad Hodi	1803	S18
21	Sumail II (Amir of Argungu)	1826–1831	S18
22	Yakubu Nabame	1849	S21
23	Yusufu Mainassara	1854	S21
24	Muhammad Ba Are	1859	S22
25	'Abdullah Toga II	1860	S21
26	Samail I	1883	S22
27	Sulayman III	1915	S22
28	Muhammad Sama	1920	S26
29	Muhammad Sani	1934	S28
30	Samail II	1942	DT14
31	Muhammad Shefe	1953	S28
32	Muhammad Mera	1959	S29

e *Kings of Zaria/Amirs of Abuja from c.1505*

1	Monan Abu	c.1505
2	Gidan dan Masukanan	c.1530
3	Nohir	c.1532
4	Kawanissa	c.1535
5	Bakwa Tunkuru★	c.1536
6	Ibrahim I	c.1539
7	Karama	c.1566
8	Kafo	c.1576
9	Bako I	c.1578
10	'Aliyu I	c.1581
11	Isma'il	c.1587
12	Musa	c.1598
13	Gadi	c.1598
14	Hamza	c.1601
15	'Abdullah	c.1601
16	Burema I	c.1610
17	'Aliyu II	c.1613
18	Muhama Rabo	c.1640
19	Ibrahim II Basuki	c.1641
20	Bako II	c.1654
21	Sukana	c.1657
22	'Aliyu III	c.1658
23	Ibrahim III	c.1665
24	Muhamman Abu	c.1668
25	Sayo 'Ali	c.1686
26	Bako III dan Musa	c.1696
27	Ishaq	c.1701
28	Burema II Ashakuka	c.1703
29	Bako IV dan Sunkuru	c.1704
30	Muhammad dan Gunguma	c.1715

31	Uban Bawa	*c.*1726	
32	Muhammad Gani	*c.*1733	
33	Abu Muham Gani	*c.*1734	
34	Dan Ashakuka	*c.*1734	
35	Muhama Abu	*c.*1737	
36	Bawo	*c.*1757	
37	Yunusa	*c.*1759	
38	Ya'qub	*c.*1764	
39	'Aliyu IV	*c.*1767	
40	Chikkoku	*c.*1773	
41	Muhama Maigamo	*c.*1779	
42	Ishaq II Jatau	1782	
43	Muhamman Makau	1802–1804	S42
	(at Zuba)	1804–1825	
	(Amirs of Abuja)		
44	Abu Ja	1825	S42
45	Abu Kakwa	1851	S59
46	Ibrahim IV Iyalai	1877	S44
47	Muhamman Gani	1902	S45
48	Musa Angulu	1917	S46
49	Sulayman Barau	1944	S47

117 **SUDAN** SULTANATE OF SOKOTO SINCE 1804

1	'Uthman dan Fodio	1804	
2	Muhammad Bello	1817	SI
3	Abu-Bakr Atiku I	1837	SI
4	'Aliyu Babba	1842	S2
5	Ahmad Atiku	1859	S3
6	'Aliyu Karami	1866	S2
7	Ahmad Rufai	1867	SI
8	Abu-Bakr Atiku II	1873	S2
9	Mu'azu	1877	S2
10	'Umar	1881	S4
11	'Abdul-Rahman	1891	S3
12	Attahiru Ahmad	1902	S5
13	Muhammad Attahiru	1903	S4
14	Muhammad Maiturare	1915	S5
15	Muhammad Tambari	1924	SI4
16	Hasan	1931	S9
17	Siddiq Abu-Bakr	1938	BSI6

118 **SUDAN** FULANI AMIRATES OF NIGERIA

a *Amirs of Kano since* 1807

1	Sulayman	1807	
2	Ibrahim Dabo	1819	
3	'Uthman I	1846	S2
4	'Abdullah	1855	S2

5	Muhammad Bello	1883	S2
6	Tukur	1893	S5
7	'Aliyu Babba	1894	S4
8	Muhammad 'Abbas	1903	S4
9	'Uthman II	1919	S4
10	'Abdullah Bayero	1926	S8
11	Muhammad Sanusi	1953	S10
12	Muhammad Inuwa 'Abbas	1963	S8
13	Ado Bayero	1963	S12

b *Amirs of Zaria since* 1804

1	Malam Musa	1804	
2	Yamusa	1821	
3	'Abdul-Karim	1834	
4	Hamada	1846	S2
5	Mamman Sani	1846	S2
6	Sidi 'Abdul-Qadir	1853	S1
7	'Abdul-Salam	1854	
8	'Abdullah (1)	1857	S4
9	Abu Bakr	1871	S1
	'Abdullah (2)	1874	
10	Sambo	1879	S3
11	Yero	1888	S8
12	Kwassau	1897	S11
13	'Aliyu	1903	S6
14	Dallatu	1920	S11
15	Ibrahim	1924	S12
16	Ja'far	1937	GS8
17	Muhammad Amin	1959	BS10

c *Amirs of Bauchi since* 1805

1	Ya'qub I	1805	
2	Ibrahim	1845	S1
3	'Uthman	1877	S2
4	'Umar	1883	GS1
5	Muhammad	1902	S2
6	Hasan	1903	GS1
7	Ya'qub II	1907	S3
8	Ya'qub III	1941	S4
9	Adamu Jumba	1954	S8

d *Dallazawa Amirs of Katsina* 1806–1906

1	'Umar Dallaji	1806	
2	Siddiq	1835	S1
3	Muhammad Bello	1844	S1
4	Ahmad Rufai	1869	S1
5	Ibrahim	1870	S3
6	Musa	1882	S1
7	Abu-Bakr	1887	S5
8	Yero	1904–1906	S6

e *Sulibawa Amirs of Katsina since* 1906

9	Muhammad Dikko	1906	
10	'Uthman Nagogo	1944	S9

f *Amirs of Gwandu since* 1808

1	'Abdullah (B1 Sokoto)	1808	
2	Muhammad I	1828	S1
3	Khalil	1833	S1
4	Haliru I	1858	S1
5	'Aliyu	1860	S1
6	'Abdul-Qadir	1864	S1
7	Mustafa	1868	S2
8	Hanufi	1875	S3
9	Malik	1876	S2
10	'Umar Bakatara	1888	S3
11	'Abdullah Bayero	1897	S2
12	Bayero 'Aliyu	1898	S5
13	Muhammad II	1903	S5
14	Haliru II	1906	BGS6
15	Muhammad Bashir	1915	S14
16	'Uthman	1918	S14
17	Yahya	1938	S14
18	Harun	1954	S15

g *Amirs of Nupe since* 1832

1	'Uthman Zaki (1)	1832	
2	Masaba (1)	1841	B1
3	'Umar Bahaushe	1847	
	'Uthman Zaki (2)	1856	
	Masaba (2)	1859	
4	'Umar Majigi	1873	BS1
5	Malik	1884	S1
6	Abu-Bakr	1895	S2
7	Muhammad	1901	S4
8	Bello	1916	S5
9	Sa'id	1926	BS6
10	Muhammad Ndayako	1935	S7
11	'Uthman Sarki	1962	S9

h *Amirs of Ilorin since* c.1830

1	'Abdul-Salam	c.1830	
2	Shi'ta	1842	B1
3	Zubair	1860	S1
4	Shi'ta 'Aliyu	1868	S2
5	Moma	1891	S3
6	Sulayman	1896	S4
7	Shu'aib	1915	S3
8	'Abdul-Qadir	1919	S7
9	Sulu Gambari	1959	BS8

119 **SUDAN** MALI AND SONGHAI

a *Kings of Mali* 1230–*c*.1390

1 Mari Jata I (Sundiata Keita)	1230	
2 Uli	1255	SI
3 Wati	1270	SI
4 Khalifa	1274	SI
5 Abu-Bakr	1274	GDI
6 Sakura	1285	
7 Qu	1300	S2
8 Muhammad	1305	S7
9 Musa I	1312	BGSI
10 Magha I	1337	S9
11 Sulayman	1341	B9
12 Qasa	1360	SII
13 Mari Jata II	1360	SIO
14 Musa II	1374	SI3
15 Magha II	1387	SI3
16 Sandaki	1388	
17 Mahmud	1390–?	S7

....

b *Sunni Dynasty of Songhai c.1464–1493*

1 Sunni Silman Dandi	?–1464	
2 Sunni 'Ali	1464	
3 Sunni Baro	1492–1493	

c *Askiya Dynasty of Songhai 1493–1640*

1 Muhammad ibn Abu-Bakr	1493	
2 Musa	1528	SI
3 Muhammad Benkan	1531	BSI
4 Isma'il	1537	SI
5 Ishaq I	1539	SI
6 Dawud I	1549	SI
7 al-Hajj	1582	S6
8 Muhammad Bana	1586	S6
9 Ishaq II	1588	S6
10 Muhammad Gao	1591	S6
11 Nuh	1591	S6
12 Harun (in Dendi)	1599	S6
13 al-Amin	1612	S6
14 Dawud II	1618–1640	

120 **WEST AFRICA** ASHANTI AND DAGOMBA

a *Kings of Ashanti c.1630–1896*

1 Oti Akenten	c.1630	
2 Obiri Yeboa	1660	STSI
3 Osei Tutu	1697	BS2

4	Opoku Ware	1731	STGD3
5	Kwasi Obodum	1742	STS3
6	Osei Kojo	1752	STS3
7	Osei Kwamina	1781	STGD6
8	Opoku Fofie	1797	B7
9	Osei Bonsu	1800	B7
10	Osei Yaw	1824	B7
11	Kwaku Dua I	1838	STS7
12	Kofi Karikari	1867	BGS11
13	Mensa Bonsu	1874	B12
14	Kwaku Dua II	1884	BS13
15	Kwaku Dua III Prempeh	1888–1896	B14

b *Kings of Dagomba since c.1500*

1	Nyagse	c.1500(?)	
2	Zulande		S1
3	Nagalogu		S2
4	Datorli		S2
5	Buruguyomda		S2
6	Zoligu		S4
7	Zonman		S6
8	Ninmitoni		S6
9	Dimani		S6
10	Yanzo		S6
11	Dariziegu		S7
12	Luro	c.1660	S6
13	Tutugri		S12
14	Zagale		S12
15	Zokuli		S12
16	Gungobili		S12
17	Zangina	c.1700	S13
18	Andani Sigili		S14
19	Ziblim Bunbiogo		S17
20	Gariba	c.1740	S17
21	Ziblim Na Saa		S18
22	Ziblim Bandamda		S20
23	Andani I		S20
24	Mahama I		S22
25	Ziblim Kulunku	c.1820	S23
26	Sumani Zoli		S24
27	Yakubu I	c.1850	S23
28	Abudulai I		S27
29	Andani II		S27
30	Darimani	1899	S27
31	al-Hasan	1900	S28
32	Abudulai II	1920	S31
33	Mahama II	1938	S29
34	Mahama III	1948	S31
35	Abudulai III	1953	S34
36	Andani III	1968	S33

37	Muhammad Abudulai IV	1969	s35
38	Yakubu II	1974	s36

121 **WEST AFRICA** BENIN, OYO AND DAHOMEY

a *Obas of Benin since c.1176*

1	Oranmiyan	c.1176	
2	Eweka I	c.1200	s1
3	Uwakhuahen		s2
4	Ehenmihen		s2
5	Ewedo	c.1255	s4
6	Oguola	c.1280	s5
7	Edoni	c.1295	s6
8	Udagbedo	c.1299	s6
9	Ohen	c.1334	s6
10	Egbeka	c.1370	s9
11	Orobiru		s9
12	Uwaifiokun		s9
13	Ewuare	c.1440	s9
14	Ezoti	c.1473	s13
15	Olua	c.1473	s13
16	Ozolua	c.1481	s13
17	Esigie	c.1504	s16
18	Orhogbua	c.1550	s17
19	Ehengbuda	c.1578	s18
20	Ohuan	c.1608	s19
21	Ohenzae	c.1641	GG18
22	Akenzae	c.1661	
23	Akengboi	c.1669	
24	Akenkpaye	c.1675	
25	Akengbedo	c.1684	
26	Ore-Oghenen	c.1689	
27	Ewuakpe	c.1700	
28	Ozuere	c.1712	s27
29	Akenzua I	c.1713	s27
30	Eresoyen	c.1735	s29
31	Akengbuda	c.1750	s30
32	Obanosa	c.1804	s31
33	Ogbebo	c.1816	s32
34	Osemwede	c.1816	s32
35	Adolo	c.1848	s34
36	Ovonramwen	c.1888–1897	s35
		———	
37	Eweka II	1914	s36
38	Akenzua II	1933	s37

b *Alafins of Oyo since c.1400*

1	Oranyan	c.1400(?)
2	Ajaka (1)	

3	Sango	
	Ajaka (2)	
4	Aganju	
5	Kori	
6	Oluaso	
7	Onigbogi	
8	Ofiran	
9	Eguguojo	
10	Orompoto	
11	Ajiboyede	
12	Abipa	*c.*1600
13	Obalokum	
14	Oluodo	
15	Ajagbo	
16	Odarawu	
17	Kanran	
18	Jayin	
19	Ayibi	
20	Osiyago	
21	Ojigi	*c.*1720
22	Gberu	*c.*1730
23	Amuniwaiye	
24	Onisile	
25	Labisi	*c.*1754
26	Awonbioju	
27	Agbolouje	
28	Majeogbe	
29	Abiodun	*c.*1770
30	Awole	*c.*1789
31	Adebo	*c.*1796
32	Maku	*c.*1796.

33	Majotu	*c.*1802
34	Amodo	*c.*1830
35	Oluewu	*c.*1833
36	Atiba	*c.*1837
37	Adelu	1859
38	Adeyemi I	1876
39	Lawani	1905
40	Ladigbolu I	1911
41	Adeniran	1945
42	Ladigbolu II	1956–1969

43	Lamidi Adeyemi II	1971

c *Aladahonu Kings of Dahomey c.1625–1894*

1	Dakpodunu	*c.*1625	
2	Wegbaja	*c.*1650	S1
3	Akaba	*c.*1680	S2
4	Agaja	*c.*1708	S2

5	Tegbesu	*c.*1730	S4
6	Kpengla	1775	S4
7	Agonglo	1789	S6
8	Adandozan	1797	S7
9	Gezo	1818	S7
10	Glele	1858	S9
11	Behanzin	1889–1894	S10

122 **ETHIOPIA** IMPERIAL DYNASTIES

a *Zagwe Dynasty* 1117–1268

1	Marari	1117	
2	Yemrehana Krestos	1133	S1
3	Gebra Maskal Lalibela	1172	BS2
4	Na'akueto La'ab	1212	S3
5	Yetbarak	1260–1268	S4

b *Solomonic Dynasty* 1268–1974

1	Yekuno Amlak	1268	
2	Yagbe'a Seyon	1285	S1
3	Senfa Ar'ed	1294	S2
4	Hezba Asgad	1295	S2
5	Kedma Asgad	1296	S2
6	Jin Asgad	1297	S2
7	Saba Asgad	1298	S2
8	Wedem Ar'ed	1299	S1
9	'Amda Seyon I	1314	S8
10	Newaya Krestos	1344	S9
11	Newaya Maryam	1372	S10
12	Dawit I	1382	S10
13	Tewoderos I	1411	S12
14	Yeshak	1414	S12
15	Endreyas	1429	S14
16	Takla Maryam	1430	S12
17	Sarwe Iyasus	1433	S16
18	'Amda Iyasus	1433	S16
19	Zara Ya'kob Constantine	1434	S12
20	Ba'eda Maryam I	1468	S19
21	Eskandar	1478	S20
22	'Amda Seyon II	1494	S21
23	Na'od	1494	S20
24	Lebna Dengel Dawit II	1508	S23
25	Galawdewos	1540	S24
26	Minas	1559	S24
27	Sarsa Dengel	1563	S26
28	Ya'kob (1)	1597	S27
29	Za Dengel	1603	BS27
	Ya'kob (2)	1604	
30	Susenyos	1607	BGS26

31	Fasiladas	1632	S30
32	Yohannes I	1667	S31
33	Iyasu I	1682	S32
34	Takla Haymanot I	1706	S33
35	Tewoflos	1708	S32
36	Yostos	1711	GG32
37	Dawit III	1716	S33
38	Asma Giyorgis	1721	S33
39	Iyasu II	1730	S38
40	Iyo'as I	1755	S39
41	Yohannes II	1769	S33
42	Takla Haymanot II	1769	S41
43	Salomon	1777	GS39
44	Takla Giyorgis (1)	1779	S41
45	Iyasu III	1784	GS39
	Takla Giyorgis (2)	1788	
46	Hezekiyas	1789	S39
	Takla Giyorgis (3)	1794	
47	Ba'eda Maryam II	1795	S43
	Takla Giyorgis (4)	1795	
48	Walda Salomon (1)	1796	S42
49	Yonas	1797	DT31
	Takla Giyorgis (5)	1798	
	Walda Salomon (2)	1799	
50	Demetros (1)	1799	DT31
	Takla Giyorgis (6)	1800	
	Demetros (2)	1800	
51	'Egwala Seyon	1801	S46
52	Iyo'as II	1818	S46
53	Gigar (1)	1821	DT31
54	Ba'eda Maryam III	1826	
	Gigar (2)	1826	
55	Iyasu IV	1830	S48
56	Gabra Krestos (1)	1832	
57	Sahla Dengel (1)	1832	DT31
	Gabra Krestos (2)	1832	
	Sahla Dengel (2)	1832	
58	Yohannes III (1)	1840	S44
	Sahla Dengel (3)	1841	
	Yohannes III (2)	1850	
	Sahla Dengel (4)	1851	
59	Tewoderos II	1855	
60	Takla Giyorgis II	1868	
61	Yohannes IV	1871	
62	Menyelek II (of Shoa)	1889	DT28
63	Lej Iyasu	1913	GD62
64	Zawditu★	1916	D62
65	Haile Selassie (1) (GG7 Shoa)	1930–1936	
	Haile Selassie (2)	1941–1974	

123 ETHIOPIA SHOA AND HARAR

a *Solomonic Dynasty of Shoa c.*1700–1889

1	Negassie (DT24 Ethiopia)	c.1700	
2	Sibeste	1703	S1
3	Abiye	1720	S2
4	Amha Iyasu	1745	S3
5	Asfa Wossen	1775	S4
6	Wossen Sagad	1808	S5
7	Sahle Selassie	1813	S6
8	Haile Malakot	1847	S7
9	Menyelek (1)	1855.	S8
	Menyelek (2) (Emperor of Ethiopia 1889)	1865–(1913)	

b *Amirs of Harar* 1525–1887

1	Ahmad Gran ibn Ibrahim	1525–1543	
2	Nur ibn Mujahid	1552	BS1
3	'Uthman al-Habashi	1567	
4	Talha ibn al-'Abbas	1569	
5	Nasir ibn 'Uthman	1571	
6	Muhammad ibn Nasir	1573	
7	Mansur ibn Muhammad	1576	
8	Muhammad ibn Ibrahim	1576–1583	
9	'Ali ibn Da'ud	1647	
10	Hashim	1653	
11	'Abdullah	1671	
12	Talha	1700	
13	Abu-Bakr	1721	
14	Khalaf	1732	
15	Hamid	1733	
16	Yusuf	1747	
17	Ahmad ibn Abu-Bakr	1756	
18	Muhammad	1783	
19	'Abdul-Shakur ibn Yusuf	1783	
20	Ahmad ibn Muhammad	1794	
21	'Abdul-Rahman ibn Muhammad	1821	B20
22	'Abdul-Karim ibn Muhammad	1826	B20
23	Abu-Bakr ibn 'Abdul-Mannan	1834	BS22
24	Ahmad ibn Abu-Bakr	1852	S23
25	Muhammad ibn 'Ali	1856–1875	HD22
26	'Abdullah ibn Muhammad	1885–1887	S25

124 **SOMALIA** AWFAT AND ADAL

a *Walasma' Dynasty of Awfat c.1270–1403*

1	'Umar ibn Dunyahuz	c.1270	
2	Jaziwi		
3	Haqq-ud-Din I	c.1321	
4	Husain		
5	Nasir		
6	al-Mansur I		
7	Jamal-ud-Din I		
8	Abut		
9	Zubair		
10	Ma'at Laila★		
11	Sabr-ud-Din I		
12	Kat 'Ali		
13	Harbi Ar'ed		
14	Haqq-ud-Din II		
15	Sa'd-ud-Din Ahmad	1373–1403	

b *Walasma' Dynasty of Adal 1409–1526*

16	Sabr-ud-Din II	1409	S15
17	al-Mansur II	1418	S15
18	Jamal-ud-Din II	1425	S15
19	Badlai	1433	S15
20	Muhammad I	1445	S19
21	Ibrahim I	1471	S20
22	Shams-ud-Din	1472	S20
23	Ibrahim II	1487	
24	Muhammad II	1488	3G15
25	'Ali	1518	GG19
26	Fakhr-ud-Din	1519	
27	Abu-Bakr	1520–1526	

125 **EAST AFRICA** MUSLIM STATES

a *Sultans of Kilwa 957–1513*

1	'Ali I ibn Husain	957	
2	'Ali II ibn Bashat	996	GS1
3	Da'ud I ibn 'Ali	999	S1
4	Khalid I ibn Bakr	1003	
5	Hasan I ibn Sulayman	1005	GS1
6	'Ali III ibn Da'ud	1042	S3
7	'Ali IV ibn Da'ud	1100	S3
8	Hasan II ibn Da'ud	1106	S3
9	Sulayman I	1129	DT1
10	Da'ud II ibn Sulayman	1131	S9
11	Sulayman II Hasan ibn Da'ud	1170	S10
12	Da'ud III ibn Sulayman	1188	S11

13	Talut I ibn Sulayman	1190	S11
14	Hasan III ibn Sulayman	1191	S11
15	Khalid II	1215	S11
16	(Unknown) ibn Sulayman	1225	S11
17	'Ali V ibn Da'ud	1263	S12
18	Hasan IV ibn Talut	1277	GS17
19	Sulayman III ibn Hasan	1294	S18
20	Da'ud IV ibn Sulayman (1)	1308	S19
21	Hasan V ibn Sulayman	1310	S19
	Da'ud IV (2)	1333	
22	Sulayman IV ibn Da'ud	1356	S20
23	Husain I ibn Sulayman	1356	S19
24	Talut II ibn Husain	1362	S23
25	Sulayman V ibn Husain	1364	S23
26	Sulayman VI ibn Hasan	1366	S19
27	Husain II ibn Sulayman	1389	S26
28	Muhammad I ibn Sulayman	1412	S26
29	Sulayman VII ibn Muhammad	1421	S28
30	Isma'il ibn Husain	1442	S23
31	Muhammad II Yabik	1454	
32	Ahmad ibn Sulayman	1455	S29
33	Hasan VI ibn Isma'il	1456	S30
34	Sa'id I ibn Hasan	1466	S33
35	Sulayman VIII ibn Muhammad	1476	S31
36	'Abdullah ibn Hasan	1477	S33
37	'Ali VI ibn Hasan	1478	S33
38	Hasan VII ibn Sulayman (1)	1479	S35
39	Sabhat ibn Muhammad	1485	S28
	Hasan VII (2)	1486	
40	Ibrahim I ibn Muhammad	1490	S28
41	Fudail ibn Sulayman	1495	S29
42	Ibrahim II ibn Sulayman (1)	1499	S35
43	Muhammad III	1505	
44	'Ali Hasan	1506	
45	Muhammad IV Mikatu	1507	
	Ibrahim II (2)	1507	
46	Sa'id II ibn Sulayman	?	S35
47	Muhammad V ibn Husain	1513–?	GS29

(**Note:** It has been suggested that Nos. 9–17 are
imaginary, arising from duplication in the chronicles,
and that Nos. 1–8 ruled during the period c.1200–1300)

b *Mazrui Shaikhs of Mombasa c.1698–1836*

1	Nasir ibn 'Abdullah	c.1698	
2	Muhammad ibn 'Uthman	1730	BS1
3	'Ali ibn 'Uthman	1744	B2
4	Mas'ud ibn Nasir	1754	S1
5	'Abdullah ibn Muhammad	1779	S2
6	Ahmad ibn Muhammad	1782	S2

7	'Abdullah ibn Ahmad	1814	s6
8	Sulayman ibn 'Ali	1823	s3
9	Salim ibn Ahmad	1825	s6
10	Rashid ibn Salim	1835–1836	s9

c *Al-Bu-Sa'id Sultans of Zanzibar* 1806–1964

1	Sa'id ibn Sultan (of 'Uman)	1806	
2	Majid ibn Sa'id	1856	s1
3	Barghash ibn Sa'id	1870	s1
4	Khalifa ibn Barghash	1888	s3
5	'Ali ibn Sa'id	1890	s1
6	Hamid ibn Thuwaini (s7 'Uman)	1893	GS1
7	Hammud ibn Muhammad	1896	BS4
8	'Ali ibn Hammud	1902	s7
9	Khalifa ibn Harub	1911	BS6
10	'Abdullah ibn Khalifa	1960	s9
11	Jamshid ibn 'Abdullah	1963–1964	s10

126 **EAST AFRICA** OMUKAMAS OF BUNYORO

*Babito Dynasty c.*1450–1967

1	Rukidi Mpugu	c.1450(?)	
2	Ocaki Rwangirra		s1
3	Oyo Nyimba		s1
4	Winyi I Rubembeka		s3
5	Olimi I Kalimbi		s4
6	Nyabongo I Rulemu		s5
7	Winyi II Rubagiramasega		s6
8	Olimi II Ruhundwangeye		s7
9	Nyarwa Omuzarra Kyaro		s8
10	Chwa I Mali Rumoma Mahanga		s8
11	Mashamba★		D8
12	Kyebambe I Omuzikya		s10
13	Winyi III Ruguruka		s12
14	Nyaika		s13
15	Kyebambe II Bikaju		s13
16	Olimi III Isansa	c.1710	s15
17	Duhaga I Chwa Mujwiga	1731	s16
18	Olimi IV Kasoma	c.1782	s17
19	Kyebambe III Nyamutukura	1786	s17
20	Nyabongo II Mugenyi	1835	s19
21	Olimi V Rwakabale	1848	s20
22	Kyebambe IV Kamurasi	1852	s20
23	Kabigumere	1869	s22
24	Chwa II Kabarega	1870	s22
25	Kitahimbwa Karukare	1898	s24
26	Duhaga II Bisereko	1902	s24
27	Winyi IV Tito Gafabusa	1924–1967	s24

127 **EAST AFRICA** NKORE AND KARAGWE

Bahinda Dynasty

a *Omugabes of Nkore (Ankole) c.1430–1967*

1	Ruhinda (of Karagwe)	c.1430(?)	
2	Nkuba	c.1446	S1
3	Nyaika	c.1475	S2
4	Nyabugaro Ntare I	c.1503	S3
5	Rushango	c.1531	S4
6	Ntare II Kagwejegyerera	c.1559	S5
7	Ntare III Rugamba	c.1587	S6
8	Kasasira	c.1615	S7
9	Kitera	c.1643	S8
10	Rumongye		S8
11	Mirindi	c.1671	S10
12	Ntare IV Kitabanyoro	c.1699	S11
13	Macwa	c.1727	S12
14	Rwabirere	c.1755	S13
15	Karara		S13
16	Karaiga		S13
17	Kahaya I		S13
18	Nyakashaija	c.1783	S17
19	Bwarenga		S17
20	Rwebishengye		S17
21	Kayunga	c.1811	S20
22	Gasiyonga I		S20
23	Mutambuka	c.1839	S22
24	Ntare V	c.1867	GS23
25	Kahaya II	1895	BS24
26	Gasiyonga II	1944–1967	GG23

b *Omugabes of Karagwe c.1450–1963*

1	Ruhinda Kizarabagabe	c.1450(?)	
2	Ntare I	c.1490	
3	Ruhinda II	c.1520	
4	Ntare II	c.1550	
5	Ruhinda III	c.1575	
6	Ntare III	c.1595	
7	Ruhinda IV	c.1620	
8	Ntare IV	c.1645	
9	Ruhinda V	c.1675	
10	Rusatira	c.1700	
11	Mehiga	c.1725	
12	Kalemera Bwirangenda	c.1750	
13	Ntare V Kiitabanyoro	c.1775	
14	Ruhinda VI Orushongo	c.1795	
15	Ndagara I	c.1820	S14
16	Rumanyika I	1853	S15
17	Kayenje Kalemera II	1883	S16

18	Nyamukuba Ndagara II	1886	S17
19	Kanyorozi Ntare VI	1893	S18
20	Rumanyika II	1916	S19
21	Ruhinda VII	1939–1963	GG16

128 EAST AFRICA KABAKAS OF BUGANDA *c.*1400–1967

1	Kintu		
2	Chwa I		
3	Kimera	*c.*1420	
4	Tembo	*c.*1447	S3
5	Kiggala	*c.*1474	S4
6	Kiyimba	*c.*1501	S5
7	Kayima	*c.*1528	BS6
8	Nakibinge	*c.*1555	S7
9	Mulondo		S8
10	Jemba	*c.*1582	S8
11	Suuna I		S8
12	Sekamaanya		S11
13	Kimbugwe	*c.*1609	S11
14	Kateregga	*c.*1636	S11
15	Mutebi I		S14
16	Juuko	*c.*1663	S14
17	Kayemba		S14
18	Tebandeke		S15
19	Ndawula	*c.*1690	S16
20	Kagulu		S19
21	Kikulwe	*c.*1717	S19
22	Mawanda		S19
23	Mwanga I		BS22
24	Namugala	*c.*1744	B23
25	Kyabaggu		B23
26	Junju		S25
27	Semakookiro	*c.*1771	S25
28	Kamaanya	*c.*1798	S27
29	Suuna II	*c.*1825	S28
30	Mutesa I	1852	S29
31	Mwanga II (1)	1884	S30
32	Kiwewa Mutebi II	1888	S30
33	Kalema	1888	S30
	Mwanga II (2)	1890	
34	Daudi Chwa II	1897	S31
35	Mutesa II	1939–1967	S34

129 EAST AFRICA RWANDA AND BURUNDI

a *Mwamis of Rwanda c.*1350–1961

1	Ndahiro Ruyange	*c.*1350	
2	Ndoba	*c.*1386	S1

3	Samembe	c.1410	S2
4	Nsoro Samukondo	c.1434	S3
5	Ruganza Bwimba	c.1458	S4
6	Cyilima Rugwe	c.1482	S4
7	Kigeri I Mukobanya	c.1506	
8	Mibambwe I Mutabaazi	c.1528	B7
9	Yuhi I Gahima	c.1552	S8
10	Ndahiro II Cyaamatare	c.1576	S9
11	Ruganza II Ndoori	c.1600	
12	Mutara I Seemugeshi	c.1624	S11
13	Kigeri II Nyamuheshera	c.1648	S12
14	Mibambwe II Gisanura	c.1672	S13
15	Yuhi II Mazimpaka	c.1696	S14
16	Karemeera Rwaaka	c.1720	S15
17	Cyilima II Rujugira	c.1744	S15
18	Kigeri III Ndabarasa	c.1768	S17
19	Mibambwe III Seentaabyo	c.1792	S18
20	Yuhi III Gahindiro	c.1797	S19
21	Mutara II Rwoogera	c.1830	S20
22	Kigeri IV Rwabugiri	1853	S21
23	Mibambwe IV Rutulindwa	1895	S22
24	Yuhi IV Musinga	1896	S23
25	Mutara III Rudahigwa	1931	S24
26	Kigeri V Ndahundirwa	1959–1961	S25

b *Mwamis of Burundi c.1675–1966*

1	Ntare I Rushatsi	c.1675	
2	Mwezi I	c.1705	
3	Mutaga I Seenyamwiiza	c.1735	
4	Mwambutsa I	c.1765	S3
5	Ntare II Rugaamba	c.1795	S4
6	Mwezi II Kisabo	1852	S5
7	Mutaga II	1908	S6
8	Mwambutsa II	1916	S7
9	Ntare III Ndizeye	1966.	S8

130 CENTRAL AFRICA MWENE MUTAPA DYNASTY
c. 1440–1917

1	Nyatsimba Mutota	c.1440	
2	Matope Nyanhehwe Nebedza	c.1450	S1
3	Mavura Maobwe	1480	S2
4	Nyahuma Mukombero	1480	S2
5	Changamire	1490	
6	Chikuyo Chisamarengu	1494	S4
7	Neshangwe Munembire	1530	GS3
8	Chivere Nyasoro	1550	S6
9	Negomo Chisamhuru	1560	S8
10	Gatsi Rusere	1589	S7
11	Nyambu Kapararidze	1623	S10

12	Mavura Mhande Philip	1629	S9
13	Siti Kazurukamusapa	1652	S12
14	Kamharapasu Mukombwe	1663	S12
15	Nyakambira	1692	
16	Nyamaende Mhande	1694	S14
17	Nyenyedzi Zenda	1707	S14
18	Boroma Dangwarangwa	1711	S14
19	Samatambira Nyamhandu I	1719	S14
20	Nyatsutsu	1735	S18
21	Dehwe Mupunzagutu	1740	S19
22	Changara	1759	S20
23	Nyamhandu II	1785	BS21
24	Chiwayo	1790	S21
25	Nyasoro	1810	S24
26	Kataruza	1835	GS23
27	Kandeya	1868	S26
28	Dzuda	1870	GG23
29	Chioko	1887–1917	S26

131 CENTRAL AFRICA KONGO KINGDOM *c.*1490–1718

1	Nzinga Kuwu	*c.*1490	
2	Nzinga Mvemba Alfonso I	1506	
3	Pedro I Nkang Mvemba	1543	S2
4	Diego I	1545	BS3
5	Alfonso II	1561	
6	Bernado I	1561	S4
7	Henry I	1566	
8	Alvaro I	1567	
9	Alvaro II	1576	S8
10	Bernado II	1614	S8
11	Alvaro III	1615	S9
12	Pedro II	1622	
13	Garcia I	1624	S12
14	Ambrosio	1626	
15	Alvaro IV	1631	S11
16	Alvaro V	1636	
17	Alvaro VI	1636	
18	Garcia II	1641	
19	Antonio I	1661	
20	Alvaro VII	1665	
21	Alvaro VIII	1666	
22	Alfonso III	1666	
23	Pedro III	1667–1683	
24	Rafael	1669–1674	
25	Alvaro IX	1669–?	
26	Daniel	1674–1678	
27	John	1683–1717	
28	Pedro IV	1709–1718	
29	Pedro V	1718–?	

132 CENTRAL AFRICA LUBA AND LUNDA STATES

a Luba Kings c. 1620–1885

1	Ilunga Walwefu	c.1620
2	Kasongo Mwine Kibanza	
3	Ngoi Sanza	
4	Kasongo Kabundulu	
5	Kumwimba Mputu	
6	Kasongo Bonswe	
7	Mwine Kombe Dai	
8	Kadilo	c.1740
9	Kekenya	
10	Kaumbo	
11	Miketo	
12	Ilunga Sunga	c.1780
13	Kumwimba Ngombe	c.1810
14	Ndai a Mujinga	c.1840
15	Ilunga Kabala	c.1840
16	Muloba	c.1870
17	Kitamba	
18	Kasongo Kolombo	?–c.1885

b Lunda Kings c.1600–1907

1	Nkonda Matit	
2	Cibind Yirung (B1 Luba)	c.1600
3	Yavu a Yirung	c.1630
4	Yavu a Nawej	c.1660
5	Mbal Iyavu	c.1690
6	Mukaz Munying Kabalond	c.1720
7	Muteba Kat Kateng	c.1720
8	Mukaz Waranankong	c.1750
9	Nawej Mufa Muchimbunj	c.1767
10	Chikombi Iyavu	c.1775
11	Nawej Ditend	c.1800
12	Mulaji Namwan	1852
13	Muteba Chikombu	1857
14	Mbala Kamong Isot	1873
15	Mbumb Muteba Kat	1874
16	Chimbindu Kasang	1883
17	Kangapu Nawej	1884
18	Mudib	1884
19	Mutand Mukaz	1886
20	Mbala Kalong	1887
21	Mushidi	1887–1907

c Kazembe Luapula Kings c.1710–1899

1	Kazembe I Nganda Bilonda	c.1710	
2	Kazembe II Kaniembo	c.1740	B1
3	Kazembe III Ilunga	c.1760	S2
4	Kazembe IV Kibangu Keleka	c.1805	S3

5	Kazembe V Mwongo Mfwama	c.1850	S3
6	Kazembe VI Cinyanta Munona	1854	S3
7	Kazembe VII Mwonga Nsemba	1862	
8	Kazembe VIII Cinkonkole Kafuti	1870	S4
9	Kazembe IX Lukwesa Mpanga	1872	S4
10	Kazembe X Kaniembo Ntemena	1885–1899	S4

133 SOUTHERN AFRICA BANTU KINGDOMS

a Lozi (Barotse) Kings c.1600–1964

1	Mboo	c.1600	
2	Inyambo		BI
3	Yeta I		MBI
4	Ngalama		BSI
5	Yeta II		S4
6	Ngombela		S4
7	Yubia		GS6
8	Musanawina		B7
9	Musananyanda		S8
10	Mulambwa	c.1780	S8
11	Silumelume	c.1835	SIO
12	Mubukwanu	c.1840	SIO
13	Sebitwane	c.1840	
14	Mamocesane★	c.1851	DI3
15	Sekeletu	c.1851	
16	Sepopa	1864	SIO
17	Mwanawina I	1874	SI2
18	Lewanika	1878	BSI6
19	Yeta III	1916	SI8
20	Imwiko Lewanika	1945	SI8
21	Mwanawina II	1948–1964	SI8

b Zulu Kings c.1781–1879

1	Senzangakhona	c.1781	
2	Shaka	1816	SI
3	Dingane	1828	SI
4	Mpande	1840	SI
5	Cetshwayo	1872–1879	S4

c Ndebele (Matabele) Kings 1837–1893

1	Mzilikaze	1837	
2	Lobengula	1868–1893	SI

d Swazi Kings since c.1820

1	Sobhuza I	c.1820	
2	Mswazi	1839	SI
3	Ludvonga	1868	S2
4	Mbandzeni	1874	S2
5	Bhunu (Ngwane)	1889	S4

6	Sobhuza II	1899	s5

e *Lesotho (Basuto) Kings since* 1823

1	Moshoeshoe I	1823	
2	Letsie I	1870	s1
3	Lerotholi	1891	s2
4	Letsie II	1905	s3
5	Griffith	1913	s3
6	Seeiso	1939	s5
7	Mansebo★ (regent)	1940	w6
8	Moshoeshoe II	1960	s6

134 MADAGASCAR MERINA RULERS 1810–1896

1	Radama I	1810	
2	Ranavalona I★	1828	w1
3	Radama II	1861	s2
4	Rasoaherina★	1863	MSD2
5	Ranavalona II★	1868	MSD2
6	Ranavalona III★	1883–1896	R5

ASIA

135 THE CALIPHS ORTHODOX, UMAYYAD, 'ABBASID

a *Orthodox Caliphs 632–661*

1 Abu-Bakr as-Saddiq	632	
2 'Umar ibn al-Khattab	634	
3 'Uthman ibn 'Affan	644	
4 'Ali ibn Abi-Talib	656–661	

b *Umayyad Dynasty of Damascus 661–750*

1 Mu'awiya I	661	GG Umayya
2 Yazid I	680	S1
3 Mu'awiya II	683	S2
4 Marwan I	684	GG Umayya
5 'Abdul-Malik	685	S4
6 al-Walid I	705	S5
7 Sulayman	715	S5
8 'Umar II	717	GS4
9 Yazid II	720	S5
10 Hisham	724	S5
11 al-Walid II	743	S9
12 Yazid III	744	S6
13 Ibrahim	744	S6
14 Marwan II	744–750	GS4

c *'Abbasid Dynasty of Baghdad 749–1258*

1 as-Saffah	749	3G al-'Abbas
2 al-Mansur	754	B1
3 al-Mahdi	775	S2
4 al-Hadi	785	S3
5 (Harun) ar-Rashid	786	S3
6 al-Amin	809	S5
7 al-Ma'mun	813	S5
8 al-Mu'tasim	833	S5
9 al-Wathiq	842	S8
10 al-Mutawakkil	847	S8
11 al-Muntasir	861	S10
12 al-Musta'in	862	GS8
13 al-Mu'tazz	866	S10
14 al-Muhtadi	869	S9

15	al-Mu'tamid	870	S10
16	al-Mu'tadid	892	GS10
17	al-Muktafi	902	S16
18	al-Muqtadir	908	S16
19	al-Qahir	932	S16
20	ar-Radi	934	S18
21	al-Muttaqi	940	S18
22	al-Mustakfi	944	S17
23	al-Muti'	946	S18
24	at-Ta'i'	974	S23
25	al-Qadir	991	S21
26	al-Qa'im	1031	S25
27	al-Muqtadi	1075	GS26
28	al-Mustazhir	1094	S27
29	al-Mustarshid	1118	S28
30	ar-Rashid	1135	S29
31	al-Muqtafi	1136	S28
32	al-Mustanjid	1160	S31
33	al-Mustadi	1170	S32
34	an-Nasir	1180	S33
35	az-Zahir	1225	S34
36	al-Mustansir	1226	S35
37	al-Musta'sim	1242–1258	S36

136 ASIA MINOR HITTITE KINGDOM *c.*1800–1200 BC

1	Pitkhana	*c.*1800 BC	
2	Anitta		S1
3	Tudkhaliash I		?S2
4	Pu-Sharruma	*c.*1700	S3
5	Labarnash		S4
6	Khattushilish I	*c.*1650	S5
7	Murshilish I		GS6
8	Khantilish I		HST7
9	Zidantash I		S8
10	Ammunash	*c.*1550	S9
11	Khuzziyash I		?S10
12	Telepinush		HST11
13	Alluwamnash	*c.*1500	HD12
14	Khantilish II		
15	Zidantash II		
16	Khuzziyash II	*c.*1450	
17	Tudkhaliash II		
18	Arnuwandash I		S17
19	Khattushilish II	*c.*1400	S17
20	Tudkhaliash III	*c.*1390	S19
21	Shuppiluliumash I	*c.*1380	S20
22	Arnuwandash II	*c.*1346	S21
23	Murshilish II	*c.*1345	S21
24	Muwatallish	*c.*1320	S23

25	Urkhi-Teshub (Murshilish III)	c.1294	S24
26	Khattushilish III	c.1286	S23
27	Tudkhaliash IV	c.1265	S26
28	Arnuwandash III	c.1220	S27
29	Shuppiluliumash II	c.1200(?)	S27

137 ASIA MINOR CLASSICAL KINGDOMS

a *Mermnad Dynasty of Lydia c.687–547 BC*

1	Gyges	c.687 BC	
2	Ardys	c.652	S1
3	Sadyattes	c.629	S2
4	Alyattes	c.610	S3
5	Croesus	560–547	S4

b *Kings of Bithynia c.297–75 BC*

1	Ziboetes	c.297 BC	
2	Nicomedes I	c.279	S1
3	Ziaelas	c.250	S2
4	Prusias I	c.230	S3
5	Prusias II	c.182	S4
6	Nicomedes II	c.149	S5
7	Nicomedes III	c.127	S6
8	Nicomedes IV	c.94–75	S7

c *Kings of Cappadocia c.350 BC–17 AD*

1	Ariarathes I	c.350–322 BC	
2	Ariarathes II	c.301	S1
3	Ariaramnes	c.280–230	S2
4	Ariarathes III	c.250–220	S3
5	Ariarathes IV Eusebes	220	S4
6	Ariarathes V Philopator	163	S5
7	Ariarathes VI Epiphanes	130	S6
8	Ariarathes VII Philometor	c.116	S7
9	Ariarathes VIII (s8 Pontus) (1)	c.101	
10	Ariarathes IX	96	S7
	Ariarathes VIII (2)	c.95–86	
11	Ariobarzanes I Philoromaeus	c.95–62	
12	Ariobarzanes II	62	S11
13	Ariobarzanes III	52	S12
14	Ariarathes X	42	S12
15	Archelaus	36 BC–17 AD	

d *Mithridatid Dynasty of Pontus 302–63 BC*

1	(Mithridates I, ruler of Cius 336–302 BC)		
2	Mithridates II	302 BC	S1
3	Ariobarzanes	266	S2
4	Mithridates III	c.250	S2

5	Pharnaces I	c.185	S4
6	Mithridates IV Philopator	c.170	S4
7	Mithridates V Euergetes	c.150	S5
8	Mithridates VI Eupator (the Great)	121–63	S7

e *Later Kings of Pontus* 63 BC–64 AD

9	Deiotarus (of Galatia)	63 BC	
10	Darius	39	GS8
11	Polemo I	37	
12	Pythodoris★	8 BC–23 AD	WI1
13	Polemo II	38–64 AD	GD11

f *Attalid Dynasty of Pergamum* 282–133 BC

1	Philetaerus	282 BC	
2	Eumenes I	263	BS1
3	Attalus I Soter	241	BGS1
4	Eumenes II Soter	197	S3
5	Attalus II	160	S3
6	Attalus III	139–133	S4

g *Kings of Commagene* c.163 BC–72 AD

1	Ptolemy	c.163 BC	
2	Samus Theosebes	c.130	S1
3	Mithridates I Callinicius	c.100	S2
4	Antiochus I Theos	c.69	S3
5	Antiochus II	c.40	S4
6	Mithridates II	c.38	S4
7	Mithridates III	c.20	GS4
8	Antiochus III	c.12 BC–17 AD	S7
9	Antiochus IV	38–72 AD	S8

138 **ASIA MINOR** SELJUK SULTANS OF RUM 1077–1307

1	Sulayman ibn Qutalmish	1077–1086	GG Seljuk
2	Qilich Arslan I	1092	S1
3	Malik Shah	1107	S2
4	Rukn-ud-Din Mas'ud I	1116	S2
5	'Izz-ud-Din Qilich Arslan II	1156	S4
6	Ghiyath-ud-Din Kai-Khusraw I (1)	1192	S5
7	Rukn-ud-Din Sulayman II	1196	S5
8	'Izz-ud-Din Qilich Arslan III	1204	S7
	Ghiyath-ud-Din Kai-Khusraw I (2)	1204	
9	'Izz-ud-Din Kai-Ka'us I	1210	S6
10	'Ala-ud-Din Kai-Kubadh I	1219	S6
11	Ghiyath-ud-Din Kai-Khusraw II	1237	S10
12	'Izz-ud-Din Kai-Ka'us II	1246–1249	S11
13	Rukn-ud-Din Qilich Arslan IV	1248–1265	S11

14	'Ala-ud-Din Kai-Kubadh II	1249–1257	S11
15	Ghiyath-ud-Din Kai-Khusraw III	1265	S13
16	Ghiyath-ud-Din Mas'ud II (1)	1282	S12
17	'Ala-ud-Din Kai-Kubadh III (1)	1284	BS16
	Ghiyath-ud-Din Mas'ud II (2)	1284	
	'Ala-ud-Din Kai-Kubadh III (2)	1293	
	Ghiyath-ud-Din Mas'ud II (3)	1294	
	'Ala-ud-Din Kai-Kubadh III (3)	1301	
	Ghiyath-ud-Din Mas'ud II (4)	1303	
	'Ala-ud-Din Kai-Kubadh III (4)	1305	
18	Ghiyath-ud-Din Mas'ud III	1307.	S17

139 ASIA MINOR DANISHMENDID AMIRATES

a *Danishmendid Dynasty of Sivas c.1071–1174*

1	Danishmend Ghazi	c.1071	
2	Ghazi Gumushtigin	1084	S1
3	Muhammad	1134	S2
4	'Imad-ud-Din Dhu'l-Nun (1)	1142	S3
5	Nizam-ud-Din Yaghi-Basan	1142	S2
6	Mujahid Jamal-ud-Din Ghazi	1164	S5
7	Shams-ud-Din Ibrahim	1166	S2
8	Shams-ud-Din Isma'il	1166	S7
	Nasir-ud-Din Dhu'l-Nun (2)	1168–1174	

b *Danishmendid Dynasty of Malatya c.1142–1178*

1	'Ain-ud-Din (S2 Sivas)	c.1142	
2	Dhu'l-Qarnain	1152	S1
3	Nasir-ud-Din Muhammad (1)	1162	S2
4	Fakhr-ud-Din Qasim	1170	S2
5	Afridun	1172	S2
	Nasir-ud-Din Muhammad (2)	1175–1178	

140 ASIA MINOR KINGDOM OF LESSER ARMENIA

a *Rubenid Dynasty 1080–1225*

1	Ruben I	1080	
2	Constantine I	1095	S1
3	Thoros I	1100	S2
4	Leo I	1129–1138	S2
5	Thoros II	1145	S4
6	Ruben II	1169	S5
7	Mleh	1170	S4
8	Ruben III	1175	BS7
9	Leo II	1186	B8
10	Isabella★	1219	D9
11	Philip of Antioch	1222–1225	H10

b *Hethumid Dynasty* 1226–1375

12	Hethum I of Lambron	1226	HI0
13	Leo III	1269	S12
14	Hethum II (1)	1289	S13
15	Thoros III	1293	S13
	Hethum II (2)	1294	
16	Smbat	1296	S13
17	Constantine II	1298	S13
	Hethum II (3)	1299	
18	Leo IV	1305	S15
19	Oshin	1308	S13
20	Leo V	1320	S19
21	Guy I of Lusignan (BS8 Cyprus)	1342	STS19
22	Constantine III	1344–1363	BGG12
23	Constantine IV	1365–1373	FBS22
24	Peter (I of Cyprus)	1368–1369	
25	Leo VI of Lusignan	1373–1375	BS21

141 ASIA MINOR EMPIRE OF TREBIZOND

Comnenian Dynasty 1204–1461

1	Alexius I (GS64 Byzantium)	1204	
2	Andronicus I	1222	HD1
3	John I	1235	S1
4	Manuel I	1238	S1
5	Andronicus II	1263	S4
6	George	1266	S4
7	John II	1280–1297	S4
8	Theodora★	1285.	D4
9	Alexius II	1297	S7
10	Andronicus III	1330	S9
11	Manuel II	1332	S10
12	Basil	1332	S9
13	Irene★	1340	W12
14	Anna★	1341–1342	D9
15	Michael (1)	1341.	B9
16	John III	1342	S15
	Michael (2)	1344	
17	Alexius III	1349	S12
18	Manuel III	1390	S17
19	Alexius IV	1417	S18
20	John IV	1429	S19
21	David	1458–1461	S19

142 **ASIA MINOR** ANATOLIAN AMIRATES

a *Qaramanid Dynasty c.1256–1483*

1	Qaraman ibn Nura Sufi	c.1256	
2	Muhammad I	1261	S1
3	Badr-ud-Din Mahmud	1278	S1
4	Burhan-ud-Din Musa	c.1340	S3
5	Fakhr-ud-Din Ahmad	?	BS4
6	Shams-ud-Din	1349	B5
7	'Ala-ud-Din Khalil	1352	S3
8	'Ala-ud-Din ibn Khalil	1381–1390	S7
9	Muhammad II (1)	1403–1419	S8
	Muhammad II (2)	1421	
10	'Ala-ud-Din 'Ali	1424	S8
11	Taj-ud-Din Ibrahim	1424	S9
12	Ishaq	1463	S11
13	Pir Ahmad	1464–1474	S11
14	Qasim	1469–1483	S11

b *Jandarid Dynasty of Kastamuni 1291–1460*

1	Shams-ud-Din Timur Jandar	1291	
2	Shuja-ud-Din Sulayman I	c.1301	S1
3	Ghiyath-ud-Din Ibrahim I	c.1339	S2
4	'Adil Beg	1345	BS2
3	Jalal-ud-Din Bayazid	1374	S4
6	Sulayman II	1385–1393	S5
7	Mubariz-ud-Din Isfandiyar	1403	S5
8	Ibrahim II	1439	S7
9	Kamal-ud-Din Abu'l-Hasan Isma'il	1443–1460	S8

c *Eretnid Dynasty of Sivas 1336–1398*

1	'Ala-ud-Din Eretna ibn Ja'far	1336	
2	Ghiyath-ud-Din Muhammad	1352	S1
3	'Ala-ud-Din 'Ali	1366	S2
4	Muhammad Chelebi	1380	S3
5	Sultan Ahmad Qadi Burhan-ud-Din	1380	
6	Zain-ul-'Abidin Muhammad	1398.	S5

d *Menteshe Dynasty c.1300–1426*

1	Menteshe Beg Mas'ud	c.1300	
2	Shuja-ud-Din Orkhan		S1
3	Ibrahim		S2
4	Muhammad	1354	S3
5	Taj-ud-Din Ahmad Ghazi	1375	S3
6	Muzaffar-ud-Din Ilyas (1)	1391.	S4
	Muzaffar-ud-Din Ilyas (2)	1402	

7 Laith ⎫		s6
8 Uwais ⎬	1421–1426	s6
9 Ahmad ⎭		s6

e *Germiyan Dynasty of Kutahya c.1299–1429*

1 Muzaffar-ud-Din Ya'qub Germiyan Khan	c.1299	
2 Muhammad Beg	c.1330	s1
3 Sulayman Shah	c.1360	s2
4 Ya'qub II (1)	1388–1390	s3
Ya'qub II (2)	1402–1411	
Ya'qub II (3)	1414–1429	

f *Sarukhan Dynasty of Magnesia c.1300–1410*

1 Saru Khan	c.1300	
2 Fakhr-ud-Din Ilyas	1345	s1
3 Muzaffar-ud-Din Ishaq	1374	s2
4 Khidr Shah Beg (1)	1388–1390	s3
Khidr Shah Beg (2)	1403–1410	

g *Aidin Dynasty 1308–1425*

1 Mahmud Beg	1308	
2 'Umar I	1334	s1
3 Khidr	1348	s1
4 'Isa	1360–1390	s1
5 Musa	1402	s4
6 'Umar II	1403	s4
7 Ghazi Junaid (1)	1405–1406	BS4
Ghazi Junaid (2)	1411–1415	
Ghazi Junaid (3)	1422–1425	

h *Hamid dynasty of Teke c.1300–1423*

1 Hamid Beg Ilyas	c.1300	
2 Yunus Beg	?	s1
3 Khidr	c.1330	s2
4 Mahmud	?	s2
5 Mubariz-ud-Din Muhammad	c.1360	s4
6 'Uthman (1)	c.1378–1392	s5
'Uthman (2)	1402–1423	

i *Hamid Dynasty of Egridir c.1300–1391*

1 Hamid Beg Ilyas (of Teke)	c.1300	
2 Falak-ud-Din Dundar	?–1324	s1
3 Najm-ud-Din Ishaq Beg	1328	s2
4 Mustafa	1344	BS3

5	Ilyas Beg	1358	s4
6	Kamal-ud-Din Husain Beg	1375–1391	s5

j *Dhu'l-Qadr Dynasty of Malatya* 1337–1522

1	Zain-ud-Din Karaja Beg	1337	
2	Ghars-ud-Din Khalil	1353	s1
3	Sha'ban Suli	1386	s1
4	Sadaqa	1398	s3
5	Nasir-ud-Din Muhammad	1399	s2
6	Sulayman Beg	1442	s5
7	Malik Arslan Beg	1454	s6
8	Shah Budaq (1)	1465	s6
9	Shah Suwar	1465	s6
	Shah Budaq (2)	1472	
10	'Ala-ud-Dawlah Buzqurd	1479	s6
11	'Ali Beg	1515–1522	s9

k *Ramadan-Oghlu Dynasty of Cilicia* 1379–1608

1	Ahmad	1379	
2	Ibrahim I	1407	s1
3	'Izz-ud-Din Hamza Beg	1416	s2
4	Muhammad Beg	1419–1436	s1
5	'Ali Beg	1419–1436	s1
6	Arslan Da'ud	1436	s2
7	Ghars-ud-Din Khalil Beg	1480–1510	s6
8	Mahmud Beg	1480–?	s6
9	Piri Muhammad Pasha	1510	s7
10	Darwish Beg	1568	s9
11	Ibrahim Beg II	1578	s9
12	Muhammad II	1594–1608	s11

143 ASIA MINOR OSMANLI SULTANS OF TURKEY
1299–1924

1	Osman I	1299	
2	Orkhan	1326	s1
3	Murad I	1359	s2
4	Bayazid I	1389	s3
5	Sulayman I	1403–1410	s4
6	Muhammad I	1403–1421	s4
7	Musa	1410–1413	s4
8	Murad II (1)	1421	s6
9	Muhammad II the Conqueror (1)	1444	s8
	Murad II (2)	1446	
	Muhammad II (2)	1451	
10	Bayazid II	1481	s9
11	Selim I the Grim	1512	s10
12	Sulayman II the Magnificent	1520	s11
13	Selim II	1566	s12
14	Murad III	1574	s13

15	Muhammad III	1595	S14
16	Ahmad I	1603	S15
17	Mustafa I (1)	1617	S15
18	Osman II	1618	S16
	Mustafa I (2)	1622	
19	Murad IV	1623	S16
20	Ibrahim	1640	S16
21	Muhammad IV	1648	S20
22	Sulayman III	1687	S20
23	Ahmad II	1691	S20
24	Mustafa II	1695	S21
25	Ahmad III	1703	S21
26	Mahmud I	1730	S24
27	Osman III	1754	S24
28	Mustafa III	1757	S25
29	'Abdul-Hamid I	1774	S25
30	Selim III	1789	S28
31	Mustafa IV	1807	S29
32	Mahmud II	1808	S29
33	'Abdul-Majid I	1839	S32
34	'Abdul-'Aziz	1861	S32
35	Murad V	1876	S33
36	'Abdul-Hamid II	1876	S33
37	Muhammad V	1909	S33
38	Muhammad VI	1918	S33
39	'Abdul-Majid II (Caliph only)	1922–1924	S34

144 CYPRUS LUSIGNAN DYNASTY 1192–1489

1	Guy of Lusignan (K. Jerusalem) (B13 La Marche)	1192	
2	Amalric (II of Jerusalem) (King 1197)	1194	B1
3	Hugh I	1205	S2
4	Henry I	1218	S3
5	Hugh II	1253	S4
6	Hugh III (GS10 Antioch)	1267	GD2
7	John I	1284	S6
8	Henry II	1285	S6
9	Hugh IV	1324	GS6
10	Peter I	1359	S9
11	Peter II	1369	S10
12	James I	1382	S9
13	Janus	1398	S12
14	John II	1432	S13
15	Charlotte★	1458–1464	D14
16	Louis (S20 Savoy)	1458–1464	H15
17	James II	1460–1473	S14
18	James III	1473–1474	S17
19	Catherine Cornaro★	1473–1489	W17

145 **ARMENIA** KINGDOM OF URARTU *c.*880–590 BC

1	Aramu	*c.*880 BC	
2	Sarduri I	*c.*844	
3	Ishpuini	*c.*828	S2
4	Menua	*c.*810	S3
5	Argishti I	*c.*785	S4
6	Sarduri II	*c.*760	S5
7	Rusa I	*c.*730	s6
8	Argishti II	*c.*714	S7
9	Rusa II	*c.*685	S8
10	Sarduri III	*c.*645	S9
11	Erimena	*c.*625	
12	Rusa III	*c.*605–590	S11

146 **ARMENIA** KINGS AND PRINCES *c.*880–590 BC

a *Orontid Dynasty c.*401–200 BC

1	Orontes I	*c.*401 BC	
2	Orontes II	*c.*344	S1
3	Mithranes	*c.*331	S2
4	Orontes III	*c.*317	?S3
5	Samus	?	?S4
6	Arsames	*c.*260	S5
7	Xerxes	*c.*228	s6
8	Abdissares	*c.*212	?s6
9	Orontes IV	*c.*212–200	s6

b *Artaxiad Dynasty c.*200–1 BC

1	Artaxias I	*c.*200 BC	
2	Tigranes I (Digran)	159	S1
3	Artavazd I	123	S2
4	Tigranes II the Great	95	S2
5	Artavazd II	56	S4
6	Artaxias II	33	S5
7	Tigranes III	20	S5
8	Tigranes IV	*c.*6–1	S7
9	Erato★	*c.*6–1	D7
10	Artavazd III	*c.*6–1	S5

c *Kings of Armenia 2–54 AD*

1	Ariobarzanes (of Atropatene)	2 AD	
2	Artavazd IV (of Atropatene)	4	S1
3	Tigranes V (GS1 Judaea)	6	
4	Vonones (I of Parthia)	12	
5	Orodes (S22 Parthia)	16	
6	Artaxias III (S11 Pontus)	18	
7	Arshak I	34	B5
8	Mihrdat (B10 Iberia)	35	
9	Rhadamist (S10 Iberia)	51–54	

d *Arsacid Dynasty of Armenia 54–428 AD*

1	Tiridat I (S27 Parthia) (1)	54 AD	
2	Tigranes VI	60	BS3 Above
	Tiridat I (2)	63	
3	Axidares (S29 Parthia)	98	
4	Sanatruk (BS33 Parthia)	114	
5	Vologaeses I	117	S4
6	Sohaemus (of Emesa) (1)	140	
7	Pacorus (S33 Parthia)	161	
	Sohaemus (2)	163	
8	Vologaeses II (IV of Parthia)	180	
9	Khusraw I	191	S8
10	Tiridat II	216	S9
11	Hormizd (I of Iran)	252	
12	Nerseh (of Iran; East only from 279)	272–293	
13	Khusraw II (West)	279–287	S10
14	Tiridat III (West; all Armenia 293)	287–298	S10
15	Tiridat IV	298	S13
16	Khusraw III	330	S15
17	Tiridat Arshak II	339	S16
18	Pap	368	S17
19	Varazdat	374	GS17
20	Arshak III (West only from 384)	379–390	S18
21	Valarshak (West only from 384)	379–386	S18
22	Khusraw IV (East)	384–401	S19
23	Vramshapur (East)	401–417	
24	Shahpur (East; S15 Iran)	417–422	
25	Artaxias IV (East)	422–428	S23

e *Viceroys and Ruling Princes of Armenia (Main rulers only) c.442–885*

1	Vasak (I of Siunia)	c.442–451	
2	Vahan Mamikonean	c.485–505	
3	Vard Mamikonean	c.505–514	
4	Mzhezh I Gnuni	518–548	
5	Philip of Siunia	574–576	
6	Varaz-Tirots Bagratuni	c.628–631	
7	Mzhezh II Gnuni	628–635	
8	David Saharuni	635–638	
9	Theodore Rshtuni	638–655	
10	Hamazasp Mamikonean	655–658	
11	Gregory I Mamikonean	c.662–684	
12	Ashot I Bagratuni	c.686–690	GS6
13	Nerseh Kamsarakan	c.689–691	
14	Smbat I Bagratuni	691–711	BS12
15	Ashot II Bagratuni	732–748	BS12
16	Gregory II Mamikonean	748–750	
17	Isaac Bagratuni	c.755–761	BS12
18	Smbat II Bagratuni	761–772	S15
19	Tachat Anjewatsi	c.780–785	

20	Ashot III Bagratuni	806–826	s18
21	Smbat III Bagratuni	826–855	s20
22	Bagrat Bagratuni	830–852	
23	Ashot IV Bagratuni (K. Armenia 885)	856–(890)	s21

f *Bagratid Kings of Armenia 885–1045*

1	Ashot I the Great	885	23 above
2	Smbat I	890	s1
3	Ashot II	914	s2
4	Abas	928	s2
5	Ashot III	952	s4
6	Smbat II	977	s5
7	Gagik I	989	s5
8	John Smbat III	1020–1040	s7
9	Ashot IV	1021–1039	s7
10	Gagik II	1042–1045	s9

147 **ARMENIA** MINOR STATES

a *Haykid Dynasty of Siunia c.800–1116*

1	Vasak III	c.800–821	
2	Isaac II (West)	821–831	s1
3	Philip (East)	821–848	s1
4	Gregory-Supan I (West)	831–851	s2
5	Babgen (East)	848–851	s3
6	Vasak IV (West)	851–859	s4
7	Vasak V (East)	851–892	s3
8	Gregory-Supan II (West)	859–912	s6
9	Ashot (East)	892–908	s3
10	Smbat I (East)	909–c.949	s9
11	Isaac III (West)	c.914–?	s6
12	Vasak VI (West)	914–c.920	s6
13	Smbat II (King c.970)	c.950–998	BS10
14	Vasak VII	c.998–1019	s13
15	Smbat III	c.1019–?	GS8
16	Gregory III	?–c.1072	B15
17	Sennacherib of Gardman	c.1072–1094	DT2/AS16
18	Gregory IV	1094–1116	s11

b *Artsrunid Dynasty of Vaspurakan 762–1021*

1	Hamazasp I	762	
2	Gagik	785	s1
3	Hamazasp II	c.800	s2
4	Ashot I (1)	836	s3
5	Gregory Derenik (1)	857	s4
	Ashot I (2)	868	
	Gregory Derenik (2)	874	
6	Ashot II	887	s5
7	Khachik-Gagik (King 908)	903	s5

8	Derenik-Ashot	936	S7
9	Abusahl-Hamazasp	953	S7
10	Ashot-Isaac	972	S9
11	Gurgen-Khachik	983	S9
12	Sennacherib-John	1003–1021	S9

c *Bagratid Kings of Kars 962–1064*

1	Mushel (s4 Armenia)	962	
2	Abas I	984	S1
3	Gagik-Abas II	1029–1064	S2

d *Bagratid Kings of Lori 982–1081*

1	Gurgen I (s5 Armenia)	982	
2	David	989	S1
3	Gurgen II Kvirike	1046–1081	S2

148 ARMENIA MUSLIM DYNASTIES

a *Shah-Armanid Dynasty 1100–1207*

1	Suqman al-Qutbi	1100	
2	Zahir-ud-Din Ibrahim	1112	S1
3	Ahmad	1127	S1
4	Nasir-ud-Din Suqman II	1128	S2
5	Saif-ud-Din Beg Timur	1185	
6	Badr-ud-Din Aq-Sonqor	1193	S4
7	al-Mansur Muhammad	1198	S5
8	'Izz-ud-Din Balban	1206–1207	

b *Saltuqid Dynasty of Erzerum 1103–1201*

1	'Ali ibn Abu'l-Qasim	1103	
2	'Izz-ud-Din Saltuq	c.1123	S1
3	Nasir-ud-Din Muhammad	1168	S2
4	al-Muzaffar Malik Shah	c.1189	S3
5	'Ala-ud-Din Abu Mansur	c.1197–1201	S4

c *Seljuk Dynasty of Erzerum 1201–1230*

1	Mughith-ud-Din Tughril Shah (s5 Rum)	1201	
2	Rukn-ud-Din Jahan Shah	1225–1230	S1

149 GEORGIA EARLY DYNASTIES OF IBERIA

a *Kings of Iberia 299 BC–189 AD*

1	Parnavaz I	299 BC	
2	Saurmag I	234	S1
3	Mirian I	159	HD2
4	Parnajom	109	S3
5	Arshak I (s3 Armenia)	90	HD3
6	Artog	78	S5
7	Parnavaz II Bartom	63	S6

8	Mirian II	30	S4
9	Arshak II	20	S8
10	Parsman I Aderk	1 AD	GD7
11	Mihrdat I	58	S10
12	Amazasp I	106	S11
13	Parsman II	116	S12
14	Rhadamist	132	S13
15	Parsman III	135	S14
16	Amazasp II	185–189	S15

b *Arsacid Dynasty of Iberia* 189–284

17	Rev the Just (S36 Parthia)	189	GD15
18	Vache	216	S17
19	Bakur I	234	S18
20	Mihrdat II	249–265	S19
21	Amazasp III	260–265	
22	Aspagur	265–284	S20

c *Chosroid Dynasty of Iberia* 284–580

23	Mirian III	284–361	HD22
24	Rev II	345–361	S23
25	Saurmag II	361	S24
26	Bakur II	363	S23
27	Mihrdat III	365	S26
28	Bakur III	380	S27
29	Tirdat	394	S24
30	Parsman IV	406	S28
31	Mihrdat IV	409	S28
32	Archil	411	S31
33	Mihrdat V	435	S32
34	Vakhtang I Gorgasal	447	S33
35	Dachi	522	S34
36	Bakur IV	534	S35
37	Parsman V	547	S36
38	Parsman VI	561	BS37
39	Bakur V	?–580	S38

150 GEORGIA PRINCES AND KINGS OF IBERIA 588–1008

1	Guaram I (GS34 Iberia)	588	
2	Stephen I	590	S1
3	Adarnase I (of Kakheti) (S39 Iberia)	627	
4	Stephen II (I of Kakheti)	c.640	S3
5	Adarnase II (of Kakheti)	c.650	S4
6	Guaram II	684	?S2
7	Guaram III	c.693	?GS6
8	Adarnase III Nersiani	c.748	
9	Nerse	c.760	S8
10	Stephen III	c.779–786	GS7
11	Ashot I Bagratuni (GG15 Armenia)	813–830	GG7

12	Bagrat I	842–876	S11
13	David	876–881	S12
14	Gurgen I	881–891	BS12
15	Adarnase IV (King)	888–923	S13
16	David I (King)	923–937	S15
17	Ashot II	923–954	S15
18	Smbat (King)	937–958	S15
19	Bagrat II (King)	958–994	S18
20	Adarnase V	958–961	BS18
21	David II	990–1000	S20
22	Gurgen II (King)	975–1008	S19
23	Bagrat III (King of Georgia 1008)	1000–(1014)	S22

151 GEORGIA ABKHAZIA AND KAKHETI

a *Anchabad Dynasty, Kings of Abkhazia c.790–1008*

1	Leo I	c.790	
2	Theodosius I	811	S1
3	Demetrius I	837	S1
4	Giorgi I	872	S1
5	John Shavliani	878	
6	Adarnase	880	S5
7	Bagrat I	887	S3
8	Constantine	898	S7
9	Giorgi II	916	S8
10	Leo II	960	S9
11	Demetrius II	969	S9
12	Theodosius II	976	S9
13	Bagrat II (III of Iberia; K. Georgia 1008)	978–(1014)	STS12

b *Chosroid Dynasty of Kakheti 580–807*

1	Adarnase I (S39 Iberia)	580	
2	Stephen I	c.637	S1
3	Adarnase II	c.650	S2
4	Stephen II	c.685	S3
5	Miriani	?	S4
6	Archil	736	S4
7	Juansher	786–807	S6

c *Princes of Kakheti 807–1029*

8	Gregory	807	
9	Dachi	827	
10	Samuel	839	
11	Gabriel	861	
12	Padala I	881	
13	Kvirike I	893	
14	Padala II	918	S13
15	Kvirike II	929	S14

16	David	976	S15
17	Kvirike III (King)	1010–1029	S16

d *Bagratid Kings of Kakheti* 1039–1105

18	Gagik Bagratuni (s2 Lori)	1039	STS17
19	Aghsartan I	1058	S18
20	Kvirike IV	1084	S19
21	Aghsartan II	1102–1105	BS20

152 GEORGIA BAGRATID KINGS 1008–1490

1	Bagrat III (of Iberia and Abkhazia)	1008	
2	Giorgi I	1014	S1
3	Bagrat IV	1027	S2
4	Giorgi II	1072	S3
5	David III	1089	S4
6	Demetrius I (1)	1125	S5
7	David IV	1155	S6
	Demetrius I (2)	1155	
8	Giorgi III	1156–1184	S6
9	Thamar★	1179–1212	D8
10	Giorgi IV	1212–1223	S9
11	Rusudan★	1223–1245	D9
		———	
12	David V (K. Imereti 1258)	1250–1258	S11
13	David VI	1250–1269	S10
		———	
14	Demetrius II	1273	S13
15	Vakhtang II	1289	S12
16	David VII	1292	S14
17	Vakhtang III	1301	S14
18	Giorgi V	1307	S16
19	Giorgi VI	1314	S14
20	David VIII	1346–1360	S19
21	Bagrat V	1355–1395	S20
22	Giorgi VII	1395–1405	S21
23	Constantine I	1405–1412	S21
24	Alexander I	1408–1442	S23
25	Vakhtang IV	1442–1446	S24
26	Demetrius III	1446–1453	S24
27	Giorgi VIII (K. Kakheti 1466)	1446–1465	S24
28	Bagrat VI (II of Imereti)	1465–1478	BS24
29	Constantine II (K. Kartli 1490)	1465–(1505)	S26

153 GEORGIA LATER BAGRATID KINGDOMS

a *Kings of Kartli* 1490–1800

1	Constantine II (of Georgia)	1490	
2	David IX	1505	S1

3 Giorgi IX	1524	S1
4 Luarsab I	1535	S2
5 Simon I (1)	1558	S4
6 David X Da'ud Khan	1569	S4
Simon I (2)	1578	
7 Giorgi X	1600	S5
8 Luarsab II	1603	S7
9 Bagrat VII	1614	S6
10 Simon II	1619	S9
11 Taymuraz I (of Kakheti)	1629	
12 Rustam Mirza	1632	S6
13 Vakhtang V Shah Nawaz I	1658	AS12/DT1
14 Giorgi XI Shah Nawaz II (1)	1676	S13
15 Irakli I Nazar 'Ali Khan	1688	GS11
Giorgi XI (2)	1703	
16 Kai-Khusraw	1709	BS14
17 Vakhtang VI Husain Quli Khan (1)	1711	B16
18 Iesse 'Ali Quli Khan (1)	1714	B16
19 Bakar Shah Nawaz III	1716	S18
Vakhtang VI (2)	1719	
Iesse 'Ali Quli Khan (2)	1724–1727	
20 Archil 'Abdullah Beg	1736–1737	S18
21 Taymuraz II (of Kakheti)	1744	
22 Irakli II (of Kakheti)	1762	
23 Giorgi XII (of Kakheti)	1798–1800	S22

b *Kings of Kakheti* 1466–1800

1 Giorgi I (VIII of Georgia)	1466	
2 Alexander I	1476	S1
3 Giorgi II	1511	S2
4 David I (IX of Kartli)	1513	
5 Levan	1520	S3
6 Alexander II (1)	1574	S5
7 David II	1603	S6
Alexander II (2)	1603	
8 Constantine I	1605	S6
9 Taymuraz I (1)	1605–1614	S7
Taymuraz I (2)	1615–1616	
Taymuraz I (3)	1623–1632	
Taymuraz I (4)	1636–1648	
10 Rustam Mirza (of Kartli)	1648–1656	
11 Archil Shah Nazar Khan (of Imereti)	1664–1675	
12 Irakli I	1675–1676	GS9
13 David III Imam Quli Khan	1703	S12
14 Constantine II Mahmud Quli Khan	1722	S12
15 Taymuraz II (1)	1732	S12
16 Alexander III	1736	S13
Taymuraz II (2)	1738	

17	Irakli II	1744	S15
18	Giorgi III (XII of Kartli)	1798–1800	S17

c *Kings of Imereti 1258–1810*

1	David I (V of Georgia)	1258	
2	Constantine I	1293	S1
3	Michael	1327	S1
4	Bagrat I	1330	S3
5	Alexander I	1372	S4
6	Giorgi I	1389–1392	S4
7	Constantine II	1396	S4
8	Demetrius (Governor)	1401	S5
9	Bagrat II (BS24 Georgia)	1455–1478	GD8
10	Alexander II	1484	S9
11	Bagrat III	1510	S10
12	Giorgi II	1565	S11
13	Constantine III	1585	S11
14	Levan	1585	S12
15	Rustam (1)	1588	S13
16	Bagrat IV	1589	GG10
	Rustam (2)	1590	
17	Giorgi III	1604	S13
18	Alexander III	1639	S17
19	Bagrat V (1)	1660	S18
20	Vakhtang (1)	1661	
21	Archil (1) (S13 Kartli)	1661	
22	Demetrius (of Guria)	1663	
	Bagrat V (2)	1664	
	Vakhtang (2)	1668	
	Bagrat V (3)	1668	
	Archil (2)	1678	
	Bagrat V (4)	1679	
23	Giorgi IV (III of Guria)	1681	
24	Alexander IV (1)	1683	S19
	Archil (3)	1690	
	Alexander IV (2)	1691	
	Archil (4)	1695	
25	Giorgi V	1696	S19
	Archil (5)	1698	
26	Simon	1699	S24
27	Mamia (III of Guria) (1)	1701	
28	Giorgi VI (1)	1702	S25
	Mamia (2)	1711	
	Giorgi VI (2)	1711	
	Mamia (3)	1713	
	Giorgi VI (3)	1713	
29	Giorgi VII (IV of Guria)	1716.	

30	Alexander V	1720	s28
31	Solomon I (1)	1751	s30
32	Taymuraz	1765	BS30
	Solomon I (2)	1768	
33	David II	1784	BS30
34	Solomon II	1789–1810	BS31

154 GEORGIA PRINCES OF MINGRELIA AND GURIA

a *Dadiani Dynasty of Mingrelia 1491–1866*

1	Liparit I	1491	
2	Mamia I	1512	S1
3	Leo I	1532	S2
4	Giorgi I (1)	1546	S3
5	Mamia II	1574	S3
	Giorgi I (2)	1574	
6	Manuchar I	1582	S3
7	Leo II	1611	S6
8	Liparit II	1658	BS7
9	Vameq	1658	BS6
10	Leo III	1660	B8
11	Leo IV	1681	S10
12	Giorgi II	1691	GD18
13	Katsia I	1704	S12
14	Bejan	1710	S12
15	Otia	1728	S14
16	Katsia II	1744	S15
17	Gregory (1)	1788	S16
18	Manuchar II	1791	S16
19	Tariel	1793	S16
	Gregory (2)	1793	
20	Leo V	1804	S17
21	David	1846	S20
22	Nicholas	1853–1866	S21

b *Gurieli Dynasty of Guria 1491–1829*

1	Giorgi I (FBGS1 Mingrelia)	1491	
2	Mamia I	1512	S1
3	Rustam	1534	S2
4	Giorgi II (1)	1564	S3
5	Vakhtang I	1583	S4
	Giorgi II (2)	1587	
6	Mamia II	1600	S4
7	Simon I	1625	S6
8	Kai-Khusraw I	1625	S5
9	Demetrius	1659	S7
10	Giorgi III	1669	S8
11	Malachie (1)	1685	S8
12	Kai-Khusraw II	1685	S10

	Malachie (2)	1689	
13	Mamia III	1689	S10
14	Giorgi IV	1714	S13
15	Mamia IV	1726	S14
16	Giorgi V	1744	S14
17	Simon II	1744	S16
18	Vakhtang II	1792	S16
19	Mamia V	1792	S17
20	David	1826–1829	S19

155 AZERBAIJAN (SOVIET) SHADDADID DYNASTY *c.*951–1075

1	Muhammad ibn Shaddad (Dvin)	*c.*951–954	
2	'Ali Lashkari I (Ganja)	971	S1
3	Marzuban (Ganja)	978	S1
4	Fadl I (Ganja)	985	S1
5	Abu'l-Fath Musa (Ganja)	1031	S4
6	'Ali Lashkari II (Ganja)	1034	S5
7	Anushirvan (Ganja)	1049	S6
8	Abu'l-Asvar Shavur (Ganja; Dvin 1022)	1049	S4
9	Fadl II	1067	S8
10	Fadl III	1073–1075	S9

156 AZERBAIJAN (SOVIET) HASHIMID AMIRS OF DERBEND 869–1077

1	Hashim ibn Suraqa	869	
2	'Amr	885	S1
3	Muhammad I	886	S1
4	'Abdul-Malik I	916	S1
5	Ahmad	939	S4
6	Maimun I	976	S5
7	Muhammad II	997	S5
8	Lashkari	997	S6
9	al-Mansur I	1001	S6
10	'Abdul-Malik II	1034	S9
11	al-Mansur II	1042	S10
12	'Abdul-Malik III	1065	S8
13	Maimun II	?–1077	S11

157 AZERBAIJAN (SOVIET) YAZIDIDS OF SHIRVAN *c.*860–1538

1	al-Haitham ibn Khalid	*c.*860	
2	Muhammad I	?	S1
3	al-Haitham II	?	S2
4	'Ali	*c.*900	S3
5	Abu-Tahir Yazid I	917	BS3
6	Muhammad II	948	S5

7	Ahmad	956	S6
8	Muhammad III	981	S7
9	Yazid II	991	S7
10	Manuchihr I	1027	S9
11	Abu-Mansur 'Ali	1034	S9
12	Kubad	1043	S9
13	Bukhtanassar 'Ali	1049	BS12
14	Sallar	1049	S9
15	Fariburz I	1063	S14
16	Faridun	1094	S15
17	Abu-Muzaffar Manuchihr II	c.1100	S16
18	Akhistan I	c.1155	S17
19	Farrukhzad I	1171	S17
20	Kershasp	1179	S19
21	'Ala-ud-Din Fariburz II	1225	S20
22	Akhistan II	1251	S21
23	Farrukhzad II	1281	S21
24	Kai-Qubadh	1317	S23
25	Kai-Ka'us	1344	S24
26	Hushang	1373	S25
27	Ibrahim Derbendi	1382	BS25
28	Khalil-Allah I	1417	S27
29	Farrukhsiyar	1462	S28
30	Bahram Beg	1500	S29
31	Ghazi Beg	1501	S29
32	Mahmud	1502	S31
33	Ibrahim II	1502	S29
34	Khalil-Allah II	1524	S33
35	Shah Rukh	1535–1538	BS34

158 AZERBAIJAN (SOVIET) KHANATES OF ARRAN

a *Khans of Ganja* 1747–1806

1	Shah Wardi	1747	
2	Muhammad Hasan	1761	
3	Ibrahim Khalil (of Qarabagh)	1781	
4	Hajji Beg	1784	
5	al-Jawwad	1786–1806	

b *Khans of Sheka* 1783–1818

1	Muhammad	1783	
2	Mustafa	1795	
3	Ja'far Quli	1806	
4	Isma'il Khan	1816–1818	S3

c *Khans of Qarabagh* 1763–1822

1	Ibrahim Khalil	1763	
2	Mahdi Quli Khan	1806–1822	S1

159 **SYRIA-PALESTINE** KINGDOM OF ALEPPO *c.*1800–1450 BC

1 Yarimlim I
2 Hammurabi I
3 Abbael I
4 Yarimlim II
5 Niqmiepu' I
6 Irkabtum
7 Hammurabi II
8 Yarimlim III
. . . .
9 Abbael II
10 Ilimilimma I
11 Idrimi
12 Niqmiepu' II
13 Ilimilimma II

160 **SYRIA-PALESTINE** KINGDOM OF DAMASCUS
*c.*950–732 BC

1 Rezon I	*c.*950 BC	
2 Tab-Rimmon	?	
3 Ben Hadad I	*c.*900	S2
4 Ben Hadad II	*c.*860	S3
5 Hazael	843	
6 Ben Hadad III	*c.*796	S5
7 Tab-El	*c.*770	
8 Rezon II	*c.*740–732	S7

161 **SYRIA-PALESTINE** HEBREW KINGDOMS

a *Kings of Judah-Israel c.*1020–922 BC

1 Saul	*c.*1020 BC	
2 David	*c.*1000	
3 Solomon	*c.*961–922	S2

b *Kings of Israel* 922–724 BC

1 Jeroboam I	*c.*922 BC	
2 Nadab	*c.*901	S1
3 Baasha	*c.*900	
4 Elah	*c.*877	S3
5 Zimri	*c.*876	
6 Tibni	*c.*876	
7 Omri	*c.*876	
8 Ahab	*c.*869	S7
9 Ahaziah	*c.*850	S8
10 Jehoram	*c.*849	S8
11 Jehu	*c.*842	
12 Jehoahaz	*c.*815	S11
13 Joash	*c.*801	S12
14 Jeroboam II	*c.*786	S13

15	Zachariah	*c.*746	S14
16	Shallum	*c.*745	
17	Menahem	*c.*745	
18	Pekahiah	*c.*736	S17
19	Pekah	*c.*735	
20	Hoshea	*c.*732–724	

c *Kings of Judah 922–587 BC – House of David*

4	Rehoboam	*c.*922	S3
5	Abijah	*c.*915	S4
6	Asa	*c.*913	S5
7	Jehoshaphat	*c.*873	S6
8	Jehoram	*c.*849	S7
9	Ahaziah	*c.*842	S8
10	Athaliah★	*c.*842	W8
11	Joash	*c.*837	S9
12	Amaziah	*c.*800	S11
13	Uzziah	*c.*783	S12
14	Jotham	*c.*742	S13
15	Ahaz	*c.*735	S14
16	Hezekiah	*c.*715	S15
17	Manasseh	*c.*687	S16
18	Amon	*c.*642	S17
19	Josiah	*c.*640	S18
20	Jehoahaz	609	S19
21	Jehoiakim	609	S19
22	Jehoiachin	597	S21
23	Zedekiah	597–587	S19

162 SYRIA-PALESTINE SELEUCID DYNASTY 305–64 BC

1	Seleucus I Nicator	305 BC	
2	Antiochus I Soter	281	S1
3	Antiochus II Theos	261	S2
4	Seleucus II Callinicus	246	S3
5	Seleucus III Soter	225	S4
6	Antiochus III the Great	223	S4
7	Seleucus IV Philopator	187	S6
8	Antiochus IV Epiphanes	175	S6
9	Antiochus V Eupator	163	S8
10	Demetrius I Soter	162	S7
11	Alexander I Balas	150	
12	Demetrius II Nicator (1)	145–139	S10
13	Antiochus VI Epiphanes	145–142	S11
14	Antiochus VII Sidetes	139–129	S10
	Demetrius II Nicator (2)	129–125	
15	Alexander II Zabinas	128–123	
16	Antiochus VIII Gryphus	125–96	S12
17	Seleucus V	125.	S12
18	Antiochus IX Cyzicenus	115–95	S14

19	Seleucus VI Epiphanes Nicator	96–95	S16
20	Antiochus X Eusebes Philopator	95–83	S18
21	Antiochus XI Philadelphus	92.	S16
22	Philip I Philadelphus	92–83	S16
23	Demetrius III Eukairos Soter	95–88	S16
24	Antiochus XII Dionysus	87–84	S16
25	Tigranes (II of Armenia)	83–69	
26	Antiochus XIII Asiaticus	69–64	S20
27	Philip II	65–64	S22

163 SYRIA-PALESTINE KINGS OF JUDAEA

a *Hasmonean Dynasty* 166–37 BC

1	Judas Maccabaeus	166 BC	
2	Jonathan	161	B1
3	Simon	142	B1
4	John Hyrcanus	134	S3
5	Aristobulus I	104	S4
6	Alexander Jannaeus	103	S4
7	Alexandra Salome★	76	W6
8	Hyrcanus II	67–40	S6
9	Aristobulus II	67–63	S6
10	Antigonus	40–37	S9

b *Herodian Dynasty* 37 BC–*c*.100 AD

1	Herod I the Great (Judea)	37–4 BC	
2	Archelaus (Judaea)	4 BC–6 AD	S1
3	Antipas (Galilee)	4 BC–39 AD	S1
4	Philip (Batanaea)	4 BC–34 AD	S1
5	Herod Agrippa I (Batanaea; Galilee 40 AD Judaea 41 AD)	37–44	GS1
6	Herod II (Chalcis)	41–48	B5
7	Herod Agrippa II (Chalcis; Batanaea 53 AD)	50–*c*.100	S5

164 SYRIA-PALESTINE KINGS OF OSRHOENE

Abgarid Dynasty 132 BC–242 AD

1	Aryu (Osrhoes)	132 BC	
2	'Abdu bar Maz'ur	127	
3	Fradhasht bar Gebar'u	120	
4	Bakru I bar Fradhasht	115	
5	Bakru II bar Bakru	112–92	
6	Ma'nu I	94.	
7	Abgar I Piqa	94–68	
8	Abgar II bar Abgar	68	
9	Ma'nu II	52	
10	Paqor	34	
11	Abgar III	29	
12	Abgar IV Sumaqa	26	

13 Maʿnu III Saphul	23	
14 Abgar V Ukkama bar Maʿnu (1)	4	
15 Maʿnu IV bar Maʿnu	7 AD	
Abgar V Ukkama bar Maʿnu (2)	13	
16 Maʿnu V bar Abgar	50	
17 Maʿnu VI bar Abgar	57	
18 Abgar VI bar Maʿnu	71	
19 Sanatruk (of Adiabene)	91	
20 Abgar VII bar Ezad	109–116	
	———	
21 Yalur	118–122	
22 Parthamaspates (of Parthia)	118–123	
23 Maʿnu VII bar Ezad	123	
24 Maʿnu VIII bar Maʿnu (1)	139	
25 Waʿil bar Sahru	163	
Maʿnu VIII bar Maʿnu (2)	165	
26 Abgar VIII bar Maʿnu the Great	177	
27 Abgar IX Severus bar Abgar	212	
28 Maʿnu IX bar Abgar	214	
29 Abgar X Frahad bar Maʿnu	240–242	

165 SYRIA-PALESTINE GHASSANID DYNASTY
c.529–636 AD

1 al-Harith ibn Jabalah	c.529	
2 al-Mundhir	c.569	S1
3 al-Nuʿman	c.582–584	S2
	———	
4 Jabalah ibn al-Ayham	?–c.636	

166 SYRIA-PALESTINE MUSLIM DYNASTIES

a *Hamdanid Dynasty of Aleppo 945–1004*

1 Saif-ud-Dawlah ʿAli (S1 Mosul)	945	
2 Saʿd-ud-Dawlah Sharif I	967	S1
3 Saʿid-ud-Dawlah Saʿid	991	S2
4 Abuʾl-Hasan ʿAli II	1002	S3
5 Abuʾl-Maʿali Sharif II	1004.	S3

b *Mirdasid Dynasty of Aleppo 1023–1079*

1 Salih ibn Mirdas	1023	
2 Shibl-ud-Dawlah Nasr	1029–1037	S1
	———	
3 Muʿizz-ud-Dawlah Tamal (1)	1042–1057	S1
	———	
4 Rashid-ud-Dawlah Mahmud (1)	1060	S2
Muʿizz-ud-Dawlah Tamal (2)	1061	
5 Abu Duʾaba ʿAtiya	1062	S1
Rashid-ud-Dawlah Mahmud (2)	1062	

6	Jalal-ud-Dawlah Nasr	1075	S4
7	Abu'l-Fada'il Sabiq	1076–1079	S4

c Seljuk Dynasty of Syria 1078–1117

1	Taj-ud-Dawlah Tutush (s2 Iran)	1078	
2	Ridwan (Aleppo)	1095–1113	S1
3	Duqaq (Damascus)	1095–1104	S1
4	Alp-Arslan al-Akhras (Aleppo)	1113–1114	S2
5	Sultan Shah (Aleppo)	1114–1117	S2

d Burid Dynasty of Damascus 1104–1154

1	Saif-ul-Islam Zahir-ud-Din Tughtigin	1104	
2	Taj-ul-Muluk Buri	1128	S1
3	Shams-ul-Muluk Isma'il	1132	S2
4	Shihab-ud-Din Mahmud	1135	S2
5	Jamal-ud-Din Muhammad	1139	S2
6	Mujir-ud-Din Abaq	1140–1154	S5

e Zangid Dynasty of Syria 1128–1183

1	'Imad-ud-Din Zangi (of Mosul)	1128	
2	Nur-ud-Din Mahmud	1146	S1
3	as-Salih Isma'il	1174	S2
4	'Izz-ud-Din Mas'ud (of Mosul)	1181	BS2
5	'Imad-ud-Din Zangi II (of Sinjar)	1182–1183	B4

f Ayyubid Dynasty of Damascus 1174–1238

1	an-Nasir Salah-ud-Din Yusuf (of Egypt)	1174	
2	al-Afdal Nur-ud-Din 'Ali	1186	S1
3	al-'Adil Saif-ud-Din Abu-Bakr (of Aleppo)	1196	B1
4	al-Mu'azzam Sharaf-ud-Din 'Isa	1218	S3
5	an-Nasir Salah-ud-Din Da'ud	1227	S4
6	al-Ashraf Muzaffar-ud-Din Musa	1229	S3
7	as-Salih 'Imad-ud-Din Isma'il (1)	1237	S3
8	al-Kamil Nasir-ud-Din Muhammad (of Egypt)	1238	S3
9	al-'Adil Saif-ud-Din Abu-Bakr II (of Egypt)	1238	s8
10	as-Salih Najm-ud-Din Ayyub (of Egypt) (1)	1239	s8
	as-Salih 'Imad-ud-Din Isma'il (2)	1239	
	as-Salih Najm-ud-Din Ayyub (2)	1245	
11	al-Mu'azzam Turan Shah (of Egypt)	1249	S10
12	an-Nasir Salah-ud-Din Yusuf II (of Aleppo)	1250–1260	BGS2

g Ayyubid Dynasty of Aleppo 1183–1260

1	al-'Adil Saif-ud-Din Abu-Bakr (B1 Damascus)	1183	
2	az-Zahir Ghiyath-ud-Din Ghazi (S1 Damascus)	1186	
3	al-'Aziz Ghiyath-ud-Din Muhammad	1216	S2
4	an-Nasir Salah-ud-Din Yusuf	1236–1260	S3

h Ayyubid Dynasty of Hims 1178–1262

1	al-Qahir Nasir-ud-Din Muhammad (FBS1 Damascus)	1178	

2 al-Mujahid Salah-ud-Din Shirkuh	1185	S1
3 al-Mansur Nasir-ud-Din Ibrahim	1239	S2
4 al-Ashraf Muzaffar-ud-Din Musa	1245–1262	S3

i *Ayyubid Dynasty of Hamah* 1178–1341

1 al-Muzaffar Taqi-ud-Din 'Umar (BS1 Damascus)	1178	
2 al-Mansur Nasir-ud-Din Muhammad I	1191	S1
3 an-Nasir Salah-ud-Din Qilich Arslan	1220	S2
4 al-Muzaffar Taqi-ud-Din Mahmud I	1229	S2
5 al-Mansur Saif-ud-Din Muhammad II	1244	S4
6 al-Muzaffar Taqi-ud-Din Mahmud II	1284–1298	S5
7 al-Mu'ayyad Abu'l-Fida Isma'il	1310	BS5
8 al-Afdal Muhammad III	1332–1341	S7

j *Ayyubid Dynasty of Baalbek* 1173–1230

1 al-Mu'azzam Shams-ud-Din Turan Shah (B1 Damascus)	1173	
2 'Izz-ud-Din Farrukhshah Da'ud (B1 Hamah)	1180	
3 al-Amjad Majd-ud-Din Bahram Shah	1182	S2
4 al-Ashraf Muzaffar-ud-Din Musa (of Damascus)	1230–(1237)	

167 **SYRIA-PALESTINE** CRUSADER STATES

a *Kings of Jerusalem* 1099–1291

1 Godfrey of Bouillon (VI of Lower Lorraine)	1099	
2 Baldwin I (of Edessa)	1100	B1
3 Baldwin II (of Edessa)	1118	STGS2
4 Fulk (V of Anjou)	1131	HD3
5 Baldwin III	1143	S4
6 Amalric I	1162	S4
7 Baldwin IV	1174	S6
8 Baldwin V	1185	STS7
9 Guy of Lusignan (Cyprus 1192)	1186–1192	HD6
10 Conrad (of Montferrat)	1190–1192	HD6
11 Henry I (II of Champagne)	1192	HD6
12 Amalric II (of Cyprus)	1197	HD6
13 Maria★	1205	D1O
14 John of Brienne	1210	H13
15 Frederick (II of Germany)	1225	HD13
16 Conrad II (IV of Germany)	1243	S15
17 Conradin of Hohenstauffen	1254	S16
18 Hugh (III of Cyprus)	1268	STS13
19 John II (I of Cyprus)	1284	S18
29 Henry II (of Cyprus)	1285–1291	S18

b *Princes of Antioch* 1098–1268 – *Hauteville Dynasty*

1 Bohemund I (S4 Apulia)	1098	
2 Tancred	1111	STS1

3	Roger of Salerno	1112	STS2
4	Baldwin (II of Jerusalem)	1119	
5	Bohemund II	1126	S1
6	Constance★	1130–1163	D5
7	Raymond of Poitiers (S12 Aquitaine)	1136–1149	H6
8	Raynald of Chatillon	1153–1160	H6
9	Bohemund III	1160	S6/7
10	Bohemund IV (1) (of Tripoli)	1201	S9
11	Raymond-Ruben	1216	BS10
	Bohemund IV (2)	1219	
12	Bohemund V	1233	S10
13	Bohemund VI	1251–1268	S12

c *Counts of Tripoli* 1101–1287

1	Raymond I (IV of Toulouse)	1101	
2	Alfonso-Jordan	1105	S1
3	Bertrand (of Toulouse)	1109	S1
4	Pons	1112	S3
5	Raymond II	1137	S4
6	Raymond III	1152	S5
7	Bohemund (IV of Antioch)	1187	
8	Bohemund V (of Antioch)	1233	S7
9	Bohemund VI (of Antioch)	1251	S8
10	Bohemund VII	1275–1287	S9

d *Counts of Edessa* 1098–1150

1	Baldwin I of Boulogne	1098	
2	Baldwin II of Rethel	1100	STGS1
3	Joscelin I of Courtenay	1118	MSTS2
4	Joscelin II (at Tell Bashir from 1144)	1131–1150	S3

168 LEBANON MUSLIM DYNASTIES

a *Banu ʿAmmar Dynasty of Tripoli* 1070–1109

1	Amin-ud-Dawlah Hasan ibn ʿAmmar	1070	
2	Jalal-ul-Mulk ʿAli	1072	BS1
3	Fakhr-ul-Mulk ʿAmmar	1099–1109	B2

b *Maʿnid Amirs* 1516–1697

1	Fakhr-ud-Din I	1516	
2	Qurqumaz	1544–1585	S1
3	Fakhr-ud-Din II	1590	S2
4	Mulhim	1635	BS3
5	Ahmad	1657–1697	S4

c *Shihabid Amirs* 1697–1842

1	Bashir I (STS5 Maʿnid)	1697	
2	Haidar (GD5 Maʿnid)	1707	

3	Mulhim	1732	S2
4	Mansur	1754	S2
5	Yusuf	1770	S3
6	Bashir II	1788	BGS3
7	Bashir III	1840–1842	BS5

169 JORDAN NABATAEAN KINGDOM 169 BC–105 AD

1	Harithath I	169 BC
2	Maliku I	144
3	Harithath II	110
4	ʿObidath I	95
5	Rabbil I	87
6	Harithath III	87
7	ʿObidath II	62
8	Maliku II	c.50
9	ʿObidath III	28
10	Harithath IV	9
11	Maliku III	c.40 AD
12	Rabbil II	c.70–105

170 JORDAN HASHIMID KINGDOM since 1921

1	ʿAbdullah ibn Husain (Amir; King 1946; s67 Mecca) 1921	
2	Talal	1951	S1
3	Husain	1952	S2

171 YEMEN EARLY KINGDOMS (Chronology uncertain and much disputed)

a *Kings of Maʿin c.400–100 BC*

1	Ilyafiʿ Yithiʿ	c.400 BC(?)	
2	Hufnu Dharih		S1
3	Ilyafiʿ Riyam		S1
4	Haufi ʿAthta		S3
5	Abyadiʿ Yithiʿ		S3
6	Waqah-il Riyam		S4
7	Hufnu Sidqu		S4
8	Ilyafiʿ Yafash		S7
9	Ilyafiʿ Waqah	c.250 BC(?)	
10	Waqah-il Sidqu		S9
11	Abi-Karib Yathiʿ		S10
12	ʿAmmi-Yathiʿ Nabat		S11
13	Yithʿi-il Sidqu		
14	Waqah-il Yathiʿ	c.150 BC(?)	S13
15	Ilyafaʿ Yashur		S14
16	Hufnum Riyam		S15

17	Waqah-il Nabat		S15
			———
18	Abiyadi' Riyam		
19	Khali-Karib Sidqu		S18
20	Hufnum Yathi'		S19
			———
21	Yith'i-il Riyam		
22	Tubba'-Karib	*c.*100 BC(?)	S21

b *Kings of Saba c.750 (?)–c.25 BC*

1	Samah 'Ali	*c.*750 BC(?)	
2	Yada'-il Dharih		S1
3	Yathi'-amar Watar I		S2
4	Yada'-il Bayin I		S3
5	Yathi'-amar Watar II		BS4
6	Karib-il Bayin		S5
7	Dhamar 'Ali Watar		S6
8	Samah 'Ali Yanif I		S7
9	Yathi'-amar Bayin I		S8
10	Karib-il Watar I	*c.*450 BC(?)	S7
11	Samah 'Ali Dharih		S10
12	Karib-il Watar II		S11
13	Il-Sharah I		S11
14	Yada'-il Bayin II		S12
15	Yakrib Malik Watar		S14
16	Yathi'-amar Bayin II		S15
17	Karib-il Watar III		S16
18	Samah 'Ali Yanif II		S17
19	Il-Sharah II		S18
20	Dhamar 'Ali Bayin I		S18
21	Yada'-il Watar		S20
22	Dhamar 'Ali Bayin II		S21
23	Karib-il Watar IV		S22
24	Il-Karib Yuhan'im		
25	Karib-il Watar V		
26	Wahb-il		
27	Anmar Yuhan'im		S26
28	Dhamar 'Ali Dharih		S27
29	Nash'a-Karib Yuhamin		S28
30	Nasir Yuhan'im		
31	Wahb-il Yahuz		
32	Karib-il Watar Yuhan'im		S31
33	Yarim Aiman I	*c.*80 BC(?)	
34	'Alhan Nahfan	*c.*60	S33
35	Far'um Yanhab		
36	Yarim Aiman II	*c.*35	S34
37	Sha'irum Awtar ⎱		S34
38	Yazil Bayin ⎰	*c.*25 BC	S35
39	Ilasharah Yahdub ⎱		S35

c *Kings of Himyar (Saba and Dhu-Raidan) c.25 BC–577 AD*

1	Ilasharah Yahdub (of Saba)	*c.*25 BC	
2	Nash'a-Karib Yamin Yuharhib		S1
3	Watar Yuhamin		S1
4	Yasir Yuhasdiq		
5	Dhamar 'Ali Yuhabir I		S4
6	Tharan Ya'ubb Yuhan'im		S5
7	Dhamar 'Ali Yuhabir II		S6
8	Dhamar 'Ali Bayin		
9	Karib-il Watar Yuhan'im		S8
10	Halk-amar		S9
11	Dhamar 'Ali Dharih		S9
12	Yada'-il Watar	?*c.*200 AD	S11
13	Il-Adhdh Naufan Yuhasdiq	*c.*245 AD	
14	Yasir Yuhan'im		
15	Shamir Yuhar'ish		S14
16	Yarim Yarhab		
17	Ela Amida (of Aksum)	*c.*340	
18	Malik-Karib Yuhamin	*c.*378	
19	Ab-Karib As'ad	*c.*385	S18
20	Warau-amar Aiman	*c.*420	S18
21	Sharah-bil Ya'fur	*c.*425	S19
22	Ma'ad-Karib		
23	'Abd-Kilal		
24	Sharah-bil Yakuf	464	
25	Nauf		S24
26	Lahi-'athta Yanuf		S24
27	Marthad-ilan Yanuf	496	
28	Ma'adi-Karib Ya'fur		
29	Yusuf Ash'ar Dhu-Nuwas	*c.*515–525	
30	Sumu-Yafa' Ashwa'	526	
31	Abraha	*c.*533	
32	Yaksum	570	S31
33	Mazruq	572	S31
34	Ma'adi-Karib	575–577	

172 **YEMEN** MUSLIM DYNASTIES

a *Ziyadid Dynasty of Zabid 819–1018*

1	Muhammad ibn Ziyad (DTB1 Umayyad Damascus)	819	
2	Ibrahim	859	S1
3	Ziyad	901	S2
4	Abu'l-Jaish Ishaq	903	S2
5	'Abdullah	981–1018	S4

b *Ya'furid Dynasty of San'a 861–997*

1	Ya'fur ibn 'Abdul-Rahman	861	
2	Muhammad ibn Ya'fur	872	S1
3	'Abdul-Qadir ibn Ahmad	892	GS1
4	Ibrahim	892	S2
5	As'ad (1)	898–900	S4
	As'ad (2)	915	
6	Muhammad ibn Ibrahim	943	S4
7	'Abdullah ibn Kahtan	963–997	GS6

c *Najahid Dynasty of Zabid 1022–1159*

1	al-Mu'ayyad Najah	1022–1062	
2	Sa'id al-Ahwal	1080	S1
3	Jayyash	1088	S1
4	al-Fatik I	1105	S3
5	al-Mansur	1109	S4
6	al-Fatik II	1123	S5
7	al-Fatik III	1136–1159	BS5

d *Mahdid Dynasty of Zabid 1159–1173*

1	'Ali ibn al-Mahdi	1159	
2	al-Mahdi	1159	S1
3	'Abdul-Nabi	1162–1173	S1

e *Imams of San'a/Sa'da – Rassid Dynasty c.860–1281*

1	Tarjuman-ud-Din al-Qasim	?	
2	Husain	860	S1
3	Yahya al-Hadi I	893	S2
4	Muhammad al-Murtada	911	S3
5	Ahmad an-Nasir	914	S3
6	Husain al-Muntakhab	?	S5
7	Qasim al-Mukhtar	936	S5
8	Yusuf al-Mansur	?	BS7
9	Qasim al-Mansur	?	3G1
10	Husain al-Mahdi	1003	S9
11	Ja'far	?	S9
12	Hasan al-Mahdi	1035	BGG3
13	Abu'l-Fath an-Nasir	1039–1062	
14	Ahmad al-Mutawakkil	1150–1161	4G5
15	'Abdullah al-Mansur	1198	5G12
16	Yahya al-Hadi II	1217–1248	6G7
17	Muhammad an-Nasir	1217–1226	S15
18	Ahmad al-Mahdi	1248	
19	Shams-ud-Din Ahmad al-Mutawakkil	1258	S15
20	Da'ud al-Muntasir	c.1281	S15

f *Sulayhid Dynasty* 1047–1138

1	'Ali ibn Muhammad	1047	
2	al-Mukarram Ahmad	1067	S1
3	as-Sayyida Arwa★	1084–1138	W2
4	al-Mukarram al-Asghar 'Ali	1084–1091	S2
5	al-Mansur Saba	1091–1099	FBGS1

g *Zuray'id Dynasty of Aden* 1083–1173 *(Double rule (A) and (B) to* 1139*)*

1	Mas'ud ibn al-Karam (A)	1083–1111	
2	'Abbas (B)	1083–?	B1
3	Abu'l-Gharat (A)	?	S1
4	Zuray' (B)	c.1087–1111	S2
5	Muhammad I (A)	?	S3
6	Abu-Su'ud I (B)	?	S4
7	'Ali (A)	?–1139	S3
8	Saba (B)	?–1139	S6
9	'Ali A'azz al-Murtada	1139	S8
10	Muhammad II	1140	S8
11	'Imran	1153	S10
12	Muhammad III	1164–1169	S11
13	Abu-Su'ud II	1164–1173	S11
14	al-Mansur	1164–1173	S11

h *Hamdanid Dynasty of San'a* 1098–1174

1	Hatim ibn al-Ghashim	1098	
2	'Abdullah ibn Hatim	1108	S1
3	Ma'n ibn Hatim	1110	S1
4	Hisham ibn al-Qubaib	1116	
5	al-Humas ibn al-Qubaib	?	B4
6	Hatim ibn al-Humas	1132	S5
7	Hamid-ud-Dawlah Hatim ibn Ahmad	1138	
8	'Ali al-Wahid	1161–1174	S7

i *Ayyubid Dynasty of Yemen* 1173–1229

1	al-Mu'azzam Shams-ud-Din Turan Shah (of Baalbek)	1173	
2	al-'Aziz Zahir-ud-Din Tughtigin	1181	B1
3	Mu'izz-ud-Din Isma'il	1197	S2
4	an-Nasir 'Ayyub	1202	S2
5	al-Muzaffar Sulayman (BS2 Hamah)	1214	
6	al-Mas'ud Salah-ud-Din Yusuf (S5 Egypt)	1215–1229	

j *Rasulid Dynasty* 1229–1442

1	al-Mansur Nur-ud-Din 'Umar I	1229	
2	al-Muzaffar Shams-ud-Din Yusuf I	1250	S1
3	al-Ashraf Mumahhid-ud-Din 'Umar II	1295	S2
4	al-Mu'ayyad Hizabr-ud-Din Da'ud	1296	S2
5	al-Mujahid Saif-ud-Din 'Ali	1322	S4
6	al-Afdal Dirgham-ud-Din al-'Abbas	1363	S5

7	al-Ashraf Mumahhid-ud-Din Isma'il I	1377	S6
8	an-Nasir Salah-ud-Din Ahmad	1400	S7
9	al-Mansur 'Abdullah	1424	S8
10	al-Ashraf Isma'il II	1427	S8
11	az-Zahir Yahya	1428	S7
12	al-Ashraf Isma'il III	1439	S11
13	al-Muzaffar Yusuf II	1442.	BS8

k *Tahirid Dynasty* 1454–1516

1	az-Zafir Salah-ud-Din 'Amir I	1454	
2	al-Mujahid Shams-ud-Din 'Ali	1460	B1
3	al-Mansur Taj-ud-Din 'Abdul-Wahhab	1478	BS2
4	az-Zafir Salah-ud-Din 'Amir II	1489–1516	S3

l *Qasimid Imams of San'a c.*1592–1962

1	al-Qasim Muhammad al-Mansur (DT8 Rassid)	c.1592	
2	Muhammad al-Mu'ayyad I	1620	S1
3	Isma'il al-Mutawakkil	1654	S1
4	Muhammad al-Mu'ayyad II	1676	BS3
5	Muhammad al-Hadi	1681	S3
6	Muhammad al-Mahdi	1686	S4
7	al-Qasim al-Mutawakkil	1716	BS6
8	Husain al-Mansur (1)	1726	S7
9	Muhammad al-Hadi al-Majid	1726	
	Husain al-Mansur (2)	1728	
10	Al-'Abbas al-Mahdi	1747	
11	'Ali al-Mansur I	1776	S10
12	Ahmad al-Mahdi	1806	S11
13	'Abdullah ibn Ahmad	?	S12
14	'Ali al-Mansur II (1)	1834	S13
15	al-Qasim al-Mahdi	1841	S12
	'Ali al-Mansur II (2)	1844	
16	Muhammad Yahya	1845	
	'Ali al-Mansur II (3)	1849.	
		———	
17	Muhammad ibn Yahya Hamid-ud-Din	1891	DT1
18	Yahya al-Mutawakkil (King of Yemen)	1904	S17
19	Saif-ul-Islam Ahmad (King of Yemen)	1948	S18
20	Muhammad al-Badr (King of Yemen)	1962.	S19

m *'Abdali Sultans of Lahej* 1728–1967

1	Fadl I	1728	
2	'Abdul-Karim I	1742	S1
3	'Abdul-Hadi	1753	S2
4	Fadl II	1777	S2
5	Ahmad I	1792	S2
6	Muhsin	1827	S4
7	Ahmad II	1847	S6
8	'Ali I	1849	S6
9	Fadl III (1)	1863	S8

10	Fadl IV	1863	s6
	Fadl III (2)	1874	
11	Ahmad III	1898	s10
12	'Ali II	1914	s7
13	'Abdul-Karim II	1915	s9
14	Fadl V	1947	s13
15	'Ali al-Karim	1952	s13
16	Fadl VI ibn 'Ali ibn Ahmad	1958–1967	BGS9

n *Qu'aiti Sultans of Shihr and Mukalla 1866–1967*

1	Awadh I ibn 'Umar	1866	
2	Ghalib I	1909	s1
3	'Umar	1922	s1
4	Salih	1936	s2
5	Awadh II	1956	s4
6	Ghalib II	1966–1967	s5

173 HIJAZ SHARIFS OF MECCA 967–1925

1	Abu-Muhammad Ja'far ibn Muhammad	967	
2	'Isa ibn Ja'far	980	s1
3	Abu'l-Futuh Hasan (1)	994	s1
4	Abu'l-Tayyib Da'ud	1010	
	Abu'l-Futuh Hasan (2)	1012	
5	Muhammad Shukr ibn Hasan	1039	s3
6	Hamza ibn Wahhas	1061	GS4
7	Abu-Hashim Muhammad ibn Ja'far	1069	
8	Abu-Fulaita al-Qasim	1094	s7
9	Fulaita ibn al-Qasim	1123	s8
10	Hashim ibn Fulaita	1133	s9
11	al-Qasim ibn Hashim	1154	s10
12	'Isa ibn Fulaita	1161	s9
13	Da'ud ibn 'Isa (1)	1174	s12
14	Mukaththir ibn 'Isa (1)	1175	s12
	Da'ud ibn 'Isa (2)	1176	
	Mukaththir ibn 'Isa (2)	1189	
15	al-Mansur ibn Da'ud	1194	s13
16	Abu-'Aziz Qatada ibn Idris	1201	
17	Hasan ibn Qatada	1220	s16
18	Rajih ibn Qatada	1232	s16
19	Abu-Sa'd 'Ali ibn Qatada	1241	s16
20	Idris ibn Qatada	1254–1270	s16
21	Abu-Numay Muhammad ibn 'Ali	1254–1301	s19
22	Rumaitha ibn Abi-Numay	1301–1346	s21
23	Humaida ibn Abi-Numay	1303–1318	s21
24	'Ajlan ibn Rumaitha	1346–1375	s22
25	Shihab-ud-Din Ahmad ibn 'Ajlan	1361–1386	s24
26	'Inan ibn Mughamis	1386–1387	BS24
27	'Ali ibn 'Ajlan	1387–1395	s24

28	Muhammad ibn 'Ajlan	1392–1396	S24
29	Hasan ibn 'Ajlan	1396–1426	S24
30	Barakat ibn Hasan	1407–1455	S29
31	Muhammad ibn Barakat	1455–1497	S30
32	Barakat ibn Muhammad	1497–1525	S31
33	Qa'it Bay ibn Muhammad	1504–1512	S31
34	Abu-Numay Muhammad ibn Barakat	1512–1566	S32
35	Ahmad ibn Muhammad	1539–1554	S34
36	Hasan ibn Muhammad	1554–1602	S34
37	Idris ibn Hasan	1603–1624	S36
38	Muhsin ibn Husain	1603	GS36
39	Mas'ud ibn Idris	1629	S37
40	'Abdullah ibn Hasan	1630	S36
41	Zaid ibn Muhsin	1631	S38
42	Sa'd ibn Zaid (1)	1666	S41
43	Barakat ibn Muhammad	1672	3G34
44	Sa'id ibn Barakat	1682	S44
45	Ahmad ibn Zaid	1684	S41
46	Ahmad ibn Ghalib	1688	BGG37
47	Muhsin ibn Husain	1690	BS37
48	Sa'id ibn Sa'd (1)	1691	S42
	Sa'd ibn Zaid (2)	1692	
49	'Abdullah ibn Hashim	1694	GS40
	Sa'd ibn Zaid (3)	1695	
	Sa'id ibn Sa'd (2)	1702	
50	'Abdul-Karim ibn Muhammad	1704	GS36
	Sa'id ibn Sa'd (3)	1712	
51	'Abdullah ibn Sa'id (1)	1716	S48
52	Yahya ibn Barakat (1)	1718	S43
53	Mubarak ibn Ahmad (1)	1720	S45
	Yahya ibn Barakat (2)	1722	
	Mubarak ibn Ahmad (2)	1723	
	'Abdullah ibn Sa'id (2)	1724	
54	Muhammad ibn 'Abdullah (1)	1730	S51
55	Mas'ud ibn Sa'id (1)	1732	S48
	Muhammad ibn 'Abdullah (2)	1733	
	Mas'ud ibn Sa'id (2)	1734	
56	Masa'id ibn Sa'id	1752	S48
57	Ahmad ibn Sa'id	1770	S48
58	Surur ibn Masa'id	1773	S56
59	Ghalib ibn Masa'id	1788	S56
60	Yahya ibn Surur	1813	S58
61	Muhammad ibn 'Abdul-Mu'in (1)	1827	5G40
62	'Abdul-Muttalib ibn Ghalib (1)	1851	S59
	Muhammad ibn 'Abdul-Mu'in (2)	1856	
63	'Abdullah ibn Muhammad	1858	S61
64	Husain ibn Muhammad	1877	S61
	'Abdul-Muttalib ibn Ghalib (2)	1880	
65	'Aun ar-Rafiq ibn Muhammad	1882	S61
66	'Ali ibn 'Abdullah	1905	S63

| 67 | Husain ibn 'Ali (King of the Hijaz 1916) | 1908 | GS61 |
| 68 | 'Ali ibn Husain (King of the Hijaz) | 1924–1925 | S67 |

174 CENTRAL ARABIA KINGS OF KINDAH *c.460–540*

1	Hujr Akil al-Murar	*c.*460	
2	'Amr al-Maksur	*c.*500	S1
3	al-Harith	*c.*520	S2
4	Hujr ibn al-Harith		S3
5	Shurahbil		S3
6	Salama	*c.*528–540	S3
7	Ma'adi-Karib		S3
8	'Abdullah		S3

175 CENTRAL ARABIA AL-RASHID AMIRS OF HA'IL
1835–1921

1	'Abdullah ibn 'Ali al-Rashid	1835	
2	Talal	1847	S1
3	Mit'ab I	1867	S1
4	Bandar	1869	S2
5	Muhammad I	1872	S1
6	'Abdul-'Aziz	1897	S3
7	Mit'ab II	1906	S6
8	Sultan ibn Hamud	1907	BGS1
9	Sa'ud I	1908	B8
10	Sa'ud II	1908	S6
11	'Abdullah II	1920	S7
12	Muhammad II	1921.	GG2

176 CENTRAL ARABIA AL-SA'UD DYNASTY AMIRS OF NAJD/KINGS OF SA'UDI ARABIA since *c.*1720

1	Sa'ud I (Amir of Najd)	*c.*1720	
2	Muhammad I	1726	S1
3	'Abdul-'Aziz I	1765	S2
4	Sa'ud II	1803	S3
5	'Abdullah I	1814–1818	S4
6	Turki	1823	BS3
7	Faisal I (1)	1834	S6
8	Khalid I	1837	S4
9	'Abdullah II	1841	BGG2
	Faisal I (2)	1843	
10	'Abdullah III (1)	1865	S7
11	Sa'ud III (1)	1871	S7
	'Abdullah III (2)	1871	
	Sa'ud III (2)	1873	
	'Abdullah III (3)	1876	

12	'Abdul-Rahman	1889–1891	s7

13	'Abdul-'Aziz II (K. Hijaz 1926, Sa'udi Arabia 1932)	1901	s12
14	Sa'ud IV	1953	s13
15	Faisal II	1964	s13
16	Khalid II	1975	s13
17	Fahd	1982	s13

177 GULF STATES KUWAIT, BAHRAIN, QATAR

a *Al-Sabah Dynasty of Kuwait since 1756 – Amirs*

1	Sabah I	1756	
2	'Abdullah I	1762	s1
3	Jabir I	1812	s2
4	Sabah II	1859	s3
5	'Abdullah II	1866	s4
6	Muhammad	1892	s4
7	Mubarak	1896	s4
8	Jabir II	1915	s7
9	Salim	1917	s7
10	Ahmad	1921	s8
11	'Abdullah III	1950	s9
12	Sabah III	1965	s9
13	Jabir III	1977	s10

b *Al-Khalifah Dynasty of Bahrain since 1783 – Amirs*

1	Ahmad ibn Khalifah	1783	
2	Salman I	1796–1825	s1
3	'Abdullah	1796–1843	s1
4	Khalifah	1825–1836	s2
5	Muhammad	1834–1868	s4
6	'Ali	1868–1869	s4
7	'Isa I	1869–1935	s6
8	Hamad	1923–1942	s7
9	Salman II	1942	s8
10	'Isa II	1961	s9

c *Al-Thani Dynasty of Qatar since 1868 – Amirs*

1	Muhammad ibn Thani	1868	
2	Ahmad I	1876	s1
3	Qasim	1905	s1
4	'Abdullah	1913	s3
5	'Ali	1949	s4
6	Ahmad II	1960	s5
7	Khalifah	1972	Gs4

178 GULF STATES UNITED ARAB EMIRATES

a *Qasimid Dynasty of Sharjah since c.1727*

1 Rashid ibn Matar	c.1727	
2 Saqr I	1777	S1
3 Sultan I	1803	S2
4 Khalid I	1866	S3
5 Salim	1868	S3
6 Saqr II	1883	S4
7 Khalid II ibn Ahmad	1914	GS3
8 Sultan II	1924	S6
9 Saqr III	1951	S8
10 Khalid III ibn Muhammad	1965	BS8
11 Sultan III	1972	B10

b *Qasimid Dynasty of Ras-al-Khaimah since 1869*

1 Humaid ibn 'Abdullah (GS3 Sharjah)	1869	
2 Khalid ibn Saqr (S6 Sharjah)	1900	
3 Salim ibn Sultan (of Sharjah)	1909	
4 Sultan	1919	S3
5 Saqr ibn Muhammad	1948	BS4

c *Qasimid Dynasty of Kalba 1936–1951*

1 Sa'id ibn Hamad (BGS4 Sharjah)	1936	
2 Hamad	1937–1951	S1

d *Al-Bu-Falah (Al-Nihayyan) Dynasty of Abu Dhabi since c. 1761*

1 Dhiyab I ibn 'Isa	c.1761	
2 Shakhbut I	1793	S1
3 Muhammad	1816	S2
4 Tahnun I	1818	S2
5 Khalifah	1833	S2
6 'Isa ibn Khalid	1845	
7 Dhiyab II ibn 'Isa	1845	
8 Sa'id	1845	S4
9 Zaid I	1855	S5
10 Tahnun II	1909	S9
11 Hamdan	1912	S9
12 Sultan	1922	S9
13 Saqr	1926	S9
14 Shakhbut II	1928	S12
15 Zaid II	1966	S12

e *Al-Bu-Falasah (Al-Maktum) Dynasty of Dubai since 1833*

1 Maktum I ibn Buti	1833	
2 Sa'id I	1852	B1
3 Hashar	1859	S1
4 Rashid I	1886	S1
5 Maktum II	1894	S3
6 Buti ibn Suhail	1906	BS4

7	Sa'id II	1912	S5
8	Rashid II	1958	S7

f *Al-Bu-Khuraiban (Al-Nu'aimi) Dynasty of 'Ajman since c.1820*

1	Rashid I ibn Humaid	c.1820	
2	Humaid I (1)	1838	S1
3	'Abdul-'Aziz I	1841	S1
	Humaid I (2)	1848	
4	Rashid II	1873	S2
5	Humaid II	1891	S4
6	'Abdul-'Aziz II	1900	S2
7	Humaid III	1908	S6
8	Rashid III	1928	S7

g *Al-'Ali (Al-Mu'alla) Dynasty of Umm-al-Qawain since c.1775*

1	Majid	c.1775	
2	Rashid I	?	S1
3	'Abdullah I	1816	S2
4	'Ali	1853	S3
5	Ahmad I	1873	S3
6	Rashid II	1904	S5
7	'Abdullah II	1922	S6
8	Hamad ibn Ibrahim	1923	BS6
9	Ahmad II	1929	S6

h *Sharqi Dynasty of Fujairah since 1952*

1	Muhammad ibn Hamad	1952	
2	Hamad	1974	S1

179 'UMAN RULERS – IMAMS AND SULTANS (also of Zanzibar to 1856)

a *Ya'rubid Dynasty 1625–1741*

1	Nasir ibn Murshid	1625	
2	Sultan I	1649	
3	Abu'l-'Arab	1669	S2
4	Saif I	1711	S2
5	Sultan II	1711	S4
6	Saif II (1)	1719	S5
7	Muhanna	1719	S5
8	Ya'rub	1722	S3
	Saif II (2)	1723	
9	Muhammad ibn Nasir	1725	
	Saif II (3)	1728–1741	
10	Sultan ibn Murshid	1739–1741	

b *Al-Bu-Sa'id Dynasty since 1741*

1	Ahmad ibn Sa'id	1741	
2	Sa'id I	1783	S1

3	Hamid	1786	s2
4	Sultan	1792	s1
5	Salim I	1806	s4
6	Sa'id II	1806	s4
7	Thuwaini	1856	s6
8	Salim II	1866	s7
9	'Azan ibn Qais	1868	3G1
10	Turki	1870	s6
11	Faisal	1888	s10
12	Taimur	1913	s11
13	Sa'id III	1932	s12
14	Qabus	1970	s13

180 'IRAQ EARLY KINGDOMS

a *Kings of Akkad c.2371–2191 BC*

1	Sharrukin (Sargon)	c.2371 BC	
2	Rimush	c.2315	s1
3	Manishtusu	c.2306	s1
4	Naram-Sin	c.2291	s3
5	Shar-kali-sharri	c.2254	s4
6	Dudu	c.2226	
7	Shu-Durul	c.2205–2191	

b *Kings of Ur (Third Dynasty) c.2113–2006 BC*

1	Ur-Nammu	c.2113 BC	
2	Shulgi	c.2095	s1
3	Amar-Sin	c.2047	s2
4	Shu-Sin	c.2038	s2
5	Ibbi-Sin	c.2029–2006	s4

c *Kings of Larsa c.2025–1763 BC*

1	Naplanum	c.2025 BC
2	Emisum	c.2004
3	Samium	c.1976
4	Zabaia	c.1941
5	Gungunum	c.1932
6	Abisare	c.1905
7	Sumuel	c.1894
8	Nur-Adad	c.1865
9	Sin-iddinam	c.1849
10	Sin-eribam	c.1842
11	Sin-iqisham	c.1840
12	Silli-Adad	c.1835
13	Warad-Sin	c.1834
14	Rim-Sin	c.1822–1763

d *Kings of Isin c.2017–1794 BC*

1	Ishbi-Erra	c.2017 BC

2	Shu-ilishu	c.1984	S1
3	Iddin-Dagan	c.1974	S2
4	Ishme-Dagan	c.1953	S3
5	Lipit-Ishtar	c.1934	S4
6	Ur-Ninurta	c.1923	
7	Bur-Sin	c.1895	S6
8	Lipit-Enlil	c.1874	S7
9	Erra-imitti	c.1869	
10	Enlil-bani	c.1861	
11	Zambia	c.1837	
12	Iter-pisha	c.1834	
13	Ur-dukuga	c.1830	
14	Sin-magir	c.1827	
15	Damiq-ilishu	c.1816–1794	

181 'IRAQ KINGS OF MITANNI c.1550–1260 BC

1	Shuttarna I	c.1550 BC	
2	Parattarna		
3	Saustatar	c.1500	
4	Artatama	c.1450	S3
5	Shuttarna II		S4
6	Artashshuwara	c.1400	S5
7	Tushratta	c.1385	S5
8	Shuttarna III	c.1360	
9	Kurtiwaza		S7
10	Shattuara I	c.1300	
11	Wasashatta		
12	Shattuara II	?–1260	

182 'IRAQ KINGS OF BABYLON

a *First Dynasty of Babylon c.1894–1595 BC*

1	Sumuabum	c.1894 BC	
2	Sumulael	c.1880	
3	Sabium	c.1844	S2
4	Apil-Sin	c.1830	S3
5	Sin-muballit	c.1812	S4
6	Hammurabi	c.1792	S5
7	Samsu-iluna	c.1749	S6
8	Abieshu	c.1711	S7
9	Ammiditana	c.1683	S8
10	Ammisaduqa	c.1646	S9
11	Samsu-ditana	c.1625–1595	S10

b *Kassite Dynasty c.1720–1157 BC (in Babylon from c.1550 BC)*

1	Gandash	c.1720 BC	
2	Agum I	c.1700	S1
3	Kashtiliash I		S2

4	Ushshi	c.1650	s3
5	Abirattash		s3
6	Kashtiliash II		
7	Urzigurumash		s6
8	Kharbashikhu	c.1600	
9	Tiptakzi		
10	Agum II	c.1580	s7
11	Burnaburiash I		
12	(Unknown)		
13	Kashtiliash III		s11
14	Ulamburiash		s11
15	Agum III	c.1450	s13
16	Kadashman-kharbe I		
17	Karaindash		
18	Kurigalzu I	c.1400	s16
19	Kadashman-Enlil I		
20	Burnaburiash II	c.1375	
21	Karakhardash	c.1347	
22	Nazibugash		
23	Kurigalzu II	c.1345	
24	Nazimaruttash	c.1323	
25	Kadashman-Turgu	c.1297	s24
26	Kadashman-Enlil II	c.1279	s25
27	Kudur-Enlil	c.1264	
28	Shagarakti-Shuriash	c.1255	s27
29	Kashtiliash IV	c.1242–1235	s28
30	Enlil-nadin-shumi	1227–1225	
31	Kadashman-kharbe II	1227–1225	
32	Adad-shuma-iddina	1224	
33	Adad-shuma-usur	1218	
34	Meli-shikhu	1188	s33
35	Marduk-apla-iddina I	1173	s34
36	Zababa-shuma-iddina	1160	
37	Enlil-nadin-akhi	1159–1157	

c *Kings of Babylon c.*1156–627 BC

1	Marduk-kabit-ahheshu	1156 BC	
2	Itti-Marduk-balatsu	1138	
3	Ninurta-nadin-shumi	1130	
4	Nabu-kudurri-usur I	1124	s3
5	Enlil-nadin-apli	1102	s4
6	Marduk-nadin-ahhe	1098	
7	Marduk-shapik-zeri	1080	
8	Adad-apla-iddina	1067	s2
9	Marduk-ahhe-eriba	1045	
10	Marduk-zer	1044	
11	Nabu-shumu-libur	1032	
12	Simbar-shikhu	1024	
13	Ea-mukin-zeri	1007	

14	Kashshu-nadin-akhi	1006	
15	E-ulmash-shakin-shumi	1003	
16	Ninurta-kudurri-usur I	986	
17	Shirikti-Shuqamuna	984	
18	Mar-biti-apla-usur	983	
19	Nabu-mukin-apli	978	
20	Ninurta-kudurri-usur II	943	
21	Mar-biti-ahhe-iddina	942	
22	Shamash-mudammiq	941	
23	Nabu-shum-ukin I	900	
24	Nabu-apla-iddina	885	s23
25	Marduk-bel-usate	852	s24
26	Marduk-zakir-shumi I	851	s24
27	Marduk-balatsu-iqbi	827	s26
28	Bau-ahhe-iddina	814	
29	Adad-shuma-ibni	811	
30	Marduk-bel-zeri		
31	Marduk-apla-usur		
32	Eriba-Marduk	802	
33	Nabu-shuma-ukin II		
34	Nabu-nasir	747	
35	Nabu-nadin-zeri	735	
36	Nabu-shuma-ukin III	732	
37	Ukin-zer	732	
38	Pulu (Tukulti-apla-esharra III of Assyria)	729	
39	Ululai (Shulmanu-ashared V of Assyria)	727	
40	Marduk-apla-iddina II (Merodach-Baladan) (1)	722	
41	Sharrukin (II of Assyria)	710	
42	Sin-ahhe-eriba (of Assyria) (1)	705	
43	Marduk-zakir-shumi II	703	
	Marduk-apla-iddina II (2)	703	
44	Bel-ibni	702	
45	Ashur-nadin-shumi	700	s42
46	Nergal-ushezib	694	
47	Mushezib-Marduk	693	
	Sin-ahhe-eriba (2)	689	
48	Ashur-ahhe-iddina (of Assyria)	681	
49	Shamash-shuma-ukin	669	s48
50	Kandalanu	648–627	

d *Neo-Babylonian Empire 626–539* BC

1	Nabu-apla-usur (Nabopolassar)	626 BC	
2	Nabu-kudurri-usur II (Nebuchadrezzar)	605	s1
3	Awel-Marduk	562	s2
4	Nergal-shar-usur	559	
5	Labashi-Marduk	556	s4
6	Nabu-Naʿid (Nabonidus)	556–539	

183 'IRAQ KINGS OF ASSYRIA 1813–609 BC

1	Shamshi-Adad I	1813 BC	
2	Ishme-Dagan I	1780	S1
3	Mut-Ashkur		
4	Rimush		
5	Asinum		
6	Puzur-Sin		
7	Ashur-dugul		
8	Ashur-apla-idi		
9	Nasir-Sin		
10	Sin-namir		
11	Ipqi-Ishtar		
12	Adad-shalulu		
13	Adasi		
14	Belubani	1700	
15	Libaia	1690	
16	Sharma-Adad I	1673	
17	Iptar-Sin	1661	
18	Bazaia	1649	
19	Lullaia	1621	
20	Kidin-Ninua	1615	
21	Sharma-Adad II	1601	
22	Erishum	1598	
23	Shamshi-Adad II	1585	
24	Ishme-Dagan II	1579	S23
25	Shamshi-Adad III	1563	S24
26	Ashur-nirari I	1547	S25
27	Puzur-Ashur	1521	S26
28	Enlil-nasir I	1497	S27
29	Nur-ili	1484	S28
30	Ashur-shaduni	1472	S29
31	Ashur-rabi I	1472	S28
32	Ashur-nadin-ahhe I	1452	S31
33	Enlil-nasir II	1432	
34	Ashur-nirari II	1426	S31
35	Ashur-bel-nisheshu	1419	S34
36	Ashur-rim-nisheshu	1410	S34
37	Ashur-nadin-ahhe II	1402	S36
38	Eriba-Adad I	1392	S35
39	Ashur-uballit I	1365	S38
40	Enlil-nirari	1329	S39
41	Arik-den-ili	1319	S40
42	Adad-nirari I	1307	S41
43	Shulmanu-ashared I (Shalmanesar)	1274	S42
44	Tukulti-Ninurta I	1244	S43
45	Ashur-nadin-apli	1207	S44
46	Ashur-nirari III	1203	S45
47	Enlil-kudurri-usur	1197	S44
48	Ninurta-apil-Ekur	1192	DT38

49	Ashur-dan I	1179	s48
50	Ninurta-tukulti-Ashur	?	s49
51	Mutakkil-Nusku	?	s49
52	Ashur-resha-ishi I	1133	s51
53	Tukulti-apil-esharra I (Tiglath-Pilesar)	1115	s52
54	Ashared-apil-Ekur	1076	s53
55	Ashur-bel-kala	1074	s53
56	Eriba-Adad II	1056	
57	Shamshi-Adad IV	1054	s53
58	Ashur-nasir-apli I	1050	s57
59	Shulmanu-ashared II	1031	s58
60	Ashur-nirari IV	1019	
61	Ashur-rabi II	1013	
62	Ashur-resha-ishi II	972	s61
63	Tukulti-apil-esharra II	967	s62
64	Ashur-dan II	935	s63
65	Adad-nirari II	911	s64
66	Tukulti-Ninurta II	890	s65
67	Ashur-nasir-apli II	884	s66
68	Shulmanu-ashared III	859	s67
69	Shamshi-Adad V	824	s68
70	Adad-nirari III	811	s69
71	Shulmanu-ashared IV	782	s70
72	Ashur-dan III	772	s70
73	Ashur-nirari V	754	s70
74	Tukulti-apil-esharra III	745	s70
75	Shulmanu-ashared V	727	s74
76	Sharrukin II (Sargon)	722	
77	Sin-ahhe-eriba (Sennacherib)	705	s76
78	Ashur-ahhe-iddina (Esarhaddon)	681	s77
79	Ashur-bani-apli (Ashurbanipal)	669	s78
80	Ashur-etil-ilani	626–621	s79
81	Sin-shum-lishir	626–621	s79
82	Sin-shar-ishkun	621–612	s79
83	Ashur-uballit II (at Harran)	612–609	

184 'IRAQ LAKHMID KINGS OF HIRAH 380–602 AD

1	Imru'l-Qais	380	
2	Nu'man I	405–433	s1
3	Mundhir I	430–473	s2
4	Aswad	474	s3
5	Mundhir II	494	s3
6	Nu'man II	500	s4
7	Abu-Ya'fur ibn Alqama	503	
8	Mundhir III	505	s6
9	'Amr	554–569	s8
10	Qabus	577	s8
11	Mundhir IV	580–583	s8
12	Nu'man III	582–602	s11

185 'IRAQ AND KURDISTAN MUSLIM DYNASTIES

a *Hamdanid Dynasty of Mosul 905–991*

1 Abu'l-Haija 'Abdullah	905	
2 Nasir-ud-Dawlah Hasan	929	S1
3 'Uddat-ud-Dawlah Abu-Taghlib	969–979	S2
4 Abu-Tahir Ibrahim	981–991	S2
5 Abu-'Abdullah Husain	981–991	S2

b *'Uqailid Dynasty of Mosul c.992–1096*

1 Muhammad	c.992	
2 Husam-ud-Dawlah al-Muqallad	996	B1
3 Mu'tamid-ud-Dawlah Qirwash	1001	S2
4 Za'im-ud-Dawlah Baraka	1050	S2
5 'Alam-ud-Din Quraish	1052	BS4
6 Sharaf-ud-Dawlah Muslim	1061	S5
7 Ibrahim	1085	S5
8 'Ali	1093–1096	S6

c *Mazyadid Dynasty of Hillah c.961–1150*

1 Sana-ud-Dawlah 'Ali ibn Mazyad	c.961	
2 Nur-ud-Dawlah Dubais I	1018	S1
3 Baha-ud-Dawlah Mansur	1081	S2
4 Saif-ud-Dawlah Sadaqa I	1086	S3
5 Nur-ud-Dawlah Dubais II	1108	S4
6 Saif-ud-Dawlah Sadaqa II	1135	S5
7 Muhammad	1138	S5
8 'Ali II	1145–1150	S5

d *Marwanid Dynasty of Diyar Bakr 990–1085*

1 Hasan ibn Marwan	990	
2 Mumahhid-ud-Dawlah Sa'id I	997	B1
3 Nasr-ud-Dawlah Ahmad	1011	B1
4 Nizam-ud-Dawlah Nasr (Mayyafariqin; Amid 1063)	1061–1079	S3
5 Sa'id II (Amid)	1061–1063	S3
6 Mansur	1079–1085	S4

e *Artuqid Dynasty of Hisn Kaifa 1098–1232*

1 Mu'in-ud-Din Sukman I ibn Artuq	1098	
2 Ibrahim	1105	S1
3 Rukn-ud-Dawlah Da'ud	1109	S1
4 Fakhr-ud-Din Qara Arslan	1144	S3
5 Nur-ud-Din Muhammad	1167	S4
6 Qutb-ud-Din Sukman II	1185	S5
7 Nasir-ud-Din Mahmud	1201	S5
8 Rukn-ud-Din Maudud	1222	S7
9 Mas'ud	1232.	

f *Artuqid Dynasty of Mardin* 1104–1408

1	Najm-ud-Din Il-Ghazi I (BI Hisn Kaifa)	1104	
2	Husam-ud-Din Timur Tash	1122	SI
3	Najm-ud-Din Alpi	1152	S2
4	Qutb-ud-Din Il-Ghazi II	1176	S3
5	Husam-ud-Din Yuluk Arslan	1184	S4
6	Nasir-ud-Din Artuq Arslan	1201	S4
7	Najm-ud-Din Ghazi I	1239	S6
8	Qara Arslan al-Muzaffar	1260	S7
9	Shams-ud-Din Da'ud	1292	S8
10	Najm-ud-Din Ghazi II	1294	S8
11	'Imad-ud-Din 'Ali Alpi	1312	S10
12	Shams-ud-Din Salih	1312	S10
13	Ahmad al-Mansur	1364	S12
14	Mahmud as-Salih	1368	S13
15	Da'ud al-Muzaffar	1368	S12
16	Majd-ud-Din 'Isa az-Zahir	1376	S15
17	as-Salih	1406–1408	S15

g *Zangid Dynasty of Mosul* 1127–1222

1	'Imad-ud-Din Zangi ibn Aq Sonqur	1127	
2	Saif-ud-Din Ghazi I	1146	SI
3	Qutb-ud-Din Maudud	1149	SI
4	Saif-ud-Din Ghazi II	1169	S3
5	'Izz-ud-Din Mas'ud I	1176	S3
6	Nur-ud-Din Arslan Shah I	1193	S5
7	'Izz-ud-Din Mas'ud II	1211	S6
8	Nur-ud-Din Arslan Shah II	1218	S7
9	Nasir-ud-Din Mahmud	1219–1222	S7

h *Zangid Dynasty of Sinjar* 1171–1220

1	'Imad-ud-Din Zangi (S3 Mosul)	1171	
2	Qutb-ud-Din Muhammad	1198	SI
3	'Imad-ud-Din Shahanshah	1219	S2
4	Jalal-ud-Din Mahmud	1219–1220	S2

i *Zangid Dynasty of al-Jazirah Ibn 'Umar* 1180–1250

1	Mu'izz-ud-Din Sinjar Shah (S4 Mosul)	1180	
2	Mu'izz-ud-Din Mahmud	1208	
3	Mas'ud	1241–1250	S2

j *Lu'lu Dynasty of Mosul* 1222–1262

1	ar-Rahim Badr-ud-Din Lu'lu	1222	
2	as-Salih Isma'il	1259–1262	SI

k *Begtiginid Dynasty of Irbil* 1145–1233

1	Zain-ud-Din 'Ali Kuchuk ibn Begtigin	1145	
2	Zain-ud-Din Yusuf (Irbil)	1168–1190	SI
3	Muzaffar-ud-Din Kukburi (Harran; Irbil 1190)	1168–1233	SI

l *Ayyubid Dynasty of Mayyafaraqin 1185–1260*

1 an-Nasir Salah-ud-Din Yusuf (of Egypt)	1185–1193	
2 al-'Adil Saif-ud-Din Abu-Bakr (of Aleppo)	1195	
3 al-Awhad Najm-ud-Din Ayyub	1200	S2
4 al-Ashraf Muzaffar-ud-Din Musa	1210	S2
5 al-Muzaffar Shihab-ud-Din Ghazi	1220	S2
6 al-Kamil Nasir-ud-Din Muhammad	1244–1260	S5

m *Ayyubid Dynasty of Hisn Kaifa 1232–c.1470*

1 as-Salih Najm-ud-Din Ayyub (of Egypt)	1232	
2 al-Mu'azzam Turan Shah (of Egypt)	1239	
3 al-Muwahhid Taqi-ud-Din 'Abdullah	1249	S2
4 al-Kamil Muhammad	1283	S3
5 al-'Adil Mujir-ud-Din Muhammad	?	S4
6 al-'Adil Shihab-ud-Din Ghazi	?	S5
7 as-Salih Abu-Bakr	?	S6
8 al-'Adil Fakhr-ud-Din Sulayman I	1378	S6
9 al-Ashraf Sharaf-ud-Din Ahmad I	?	S8
10 as-Salih Salah-ud-Din Khalil I	1433	S9
11 al-Kamil Ahmad II	1452	S10
12 al-'Adil Khalaf	?	BS10
13 Khalil II	1462	BS10
14 Sulayman II	?	S13
15 Husain	?	S13

n *Jalayirid Dynasty of 'Iraq 1336–1432*

1 Taj-ud-Din Hasan Buzurg	1336	
2 Uwais I	1356	S1
3 Jalal-ud-Din Husain I	1374	S2
4 Ghiyath-ud-Din Ahmad	1382–1410	S2
5 Bayazid (Kurdistan)	1382–1383	S2
6 Shah Walad	1410	BS3
7 Mahmud (1)	1411	S6
8 Uwais II	1415	S6
9 Muhammad	1421	S6
Mahmud (2)	1422	
10 Husain II	1424–1432	GS4

o *Hashimid Kings of 'Iraq 1921–1958*

1 Faisal I (S67 Mecca)	1921	
2 Ghazi	1933	S1
3 Faisal II	1939–1958	S2

186 IRAN KINGS OF ELAM

a *Eparti Dynasty c.1850–1505 BC*

1 Epart	c.1850 BC	
2 Silhaha	c.1830	S1
3 Sirktuh	c.1800	STS2

4	Simut-Wartash	*c.*1772	B3
5	Siwe-Palar-Huhpak	*c.*1770	STS4
6	Kuduzulush I	*c.*1745	B5
7	Kuter-Nahhunte I	*c.*1730	
8	Lila-Irtash	*c.*1700	B7
9	Tempt-Agun	*c.*1698	
10	Tan-Uli	*c.*1690	S8
11	Tempt-Halki	*c.*1655	
12	Kuk-Nashur	*c.*1650	STS10
13	Kuter-Silhaha	*c.*1635	B12
14	Tempt-Raptash	*c.*1625	
15	Kuduzulush II	*c.*1605	S14
16	Tata	*c.*1600	
17	Atta-Merra-Halki	*c.*1580	B16
18	Pala-Ishshan	*c.*1570	
19	Kuk-Kirwesh	*c.*1545	
20	Kuk-Nahhunte	*c.*1520	
21	Kuter-Nahhunte II	*c.*1505–?	

b *Igehalkid Dynasty c.*1350–1210 BC

1	Ige-Halki	*c.*1350 BC	
2	Pahir-Ishshan	*c.*1330	S1
3	Attar-Kittah	*c.*1310	S1
4	Humban-Numena	*c.*1300	S3
5	Untash-Napirisha	*c.*1275	S4
6	Unpatar-Napirisha	*c.*1240	BS5
7	Kiten-Hutran	*c.*1235–1210	B6

c *Shutrukid Dynasty c.*1205–1110 BC

1	Hallutush-Inshushinak	*c.*1205 BC	
2	Shutruk-Nahhunte	*c.*1185	S1
3	Kutir-Nahhunte	*c.*1155	S2
4	Shilhak-Inshushinak	*c.*1150	S2
5	Hatelutush-Inshushinak	*c.*1120	S3
6	Shilhana-Hamru-Lagamar	*c.*1110–?	S4

d *Later Kings of Elam c.*760–644 BC

1	Humban-Tahrah	*c.*760	
2	Humban-Nikash I	742	S1
3	Shutur-Nahhunte	717	STS2
4	Hallutush-Inshushinak	699	B3
5	Kudur-Nahhunte	693	S4
6	Humban-Nimena	692	B5
7	Humban-Haltash I	687	B6
8	Shilhak-Inshushinak	680–653	
9	Humban-Haltash II	681–675	
10	Urtaki	674–663	
11	Tempt-Humban-Inshushinak	668–653	S8
12	Atta-Hamiti-Inshushinak	653–648	
13	Humban-Nikash II	653–651	S9

| 14 Tamma-Ritu | 651–649 | |
| 15 Humban-Haltash III | 648–644(?) | S12 |

187 **IRAN** IMPERIAL DYNASTIES

a *Median Kings c.650–550 BC*

1 Kshathrita (Phraortes)	c.650 BC	
2 Uvakhshatra (Cyaxares)	c.625	?S1
3 Arshtivaiga (Astyages)	585–550	S2

b *Achaemenid Dynasty c.700–329 BC*

1 Hakhamanish (Achaemenes)	c.700 BC	
2 Chispish (Teispes)	c.675	S1
3 Kurush I (in Anshan)	c.640–600	S2
4 Ariaramna (in Parsa)	c.640–615	S2
5 Kambujiya I (in Anshan)	c.600–559	S3
6 Arshama (in Parsa)	c.615–?	S4
7 Kurush II (Cyrus the Great)	559	S5
8 Kambujiya II (Cambyses)	530	S7
9 Bardiya-Gaumata (Smerdis)	522	
10 Darayavahush I (Darius the Great)	522	GS6
11 Khshayarsha I (Xerxes)	486	S10
12 Artakhshassa I (Artaxerxes)	465	S11
13 Khshayarsha II	424	S12
14 Darayavahush II	423	S12
15 Artakhshassa II	404	S14
16 Artakhshassa III	359	S15
17 Arsha	338	S16
18 Darayavahush III	336	BGS15
19 Artakhshassa IV (Bessus) (Bactria)	330–329	

c *Arsacid (Parthian) Dynasty c.250 BC–228 AD*

1 Arsaces (Arshak)	c.250 BC	
2 Tiridates I (Tiridat)	c.247	B1
3 Artabanus I (Ardavan)	c.211	S2
4 Priapatius	c.191	S3
5 Phraates I	c.176	S4
6 Mithridates I	c.171	S4
7 Phraates II	c.138	S6
8 Artabanus II	c.128	S4
9 Mithridates II	c.123–87	S8
10 Gotarzes I	c.91–81	
11 Orodes I	c.80–77	
12 Sanatruces (Sanatruk)	c.77–70	
13 Phraates III	c.70–57	S12
14 Orodes II	c.57–37	S13
15 Mithridates III	c.56–55	S13
16 Pacorus I	c.38.	S14
17 Phraates IV	c.38–2 BC	S14

18	Tiridates II	*c.*30–25 BC	
19	Phraates V (Phrataces)	*c.*2 BC–4 AD	S17
20	Orodes III	*c.*4–7 AD	
21	Vonones I	*c.*7–12	S17
22	Artabanus III	*c.*12–38	
23	Tiridates III	*c.*36.	
24	Cinnamus	*c.*37.	
25	Gotarzes II	*c.*39–51	
26	Vardanes	*c.*39–48	
27	Vonones II	*c.*51.	
28	Vologaeses I	*c.*51–80	S27
29	Pacorus II	*c.*78–116	
30	Artabanus IV	*c.*80–81	
31	Osrhoes	*c.*109–128	
32	Parthamaspates	*c.*117.	
33	Vologaeses II	*c.*105–147	
34	Mithridates IV	*c.*128–147	
35	Vologaeses III	148–192	S33
36	Vologaeses IV	191–208	
37	Vologaeses V	208–228	S36
38	Artabanus V	212–224	S36
39	Artavazdes (Artavazd)	*c.*228.	S38

d *Sasanid Dynasty c.*208–651

1	Papak (Parsa)	*c.*208	
2	Shapur (Parsa)	*c.*222	S1
3	Ardashir I (King of Kings 226)	*c.*222	S1
4	Shapur I	241	S3
5	Hormizd I	272	S4
6	Varahran I (Bahram)	273	S4
7	Varahran II	276	s6
8	Varahran III	293	S7
9	Nerseh	293	S4
10	Hormizd II	302	S9
11	Shapur II	309	S10
12	Ardashir II	379	S10
13	Shapur III	383	S11
14	Varahran IV	388	S11
15	Yazdagird I	399	S13
16	Varahran V	420	S15
17	Yazdagird II	438	S16
18	Hormizd III	457	S17
19	Peroz	459	S17
20	Valash	484	S17
21	Kavadh I (1)	488	S19
22	Jamasp	496	S19
	Kavadh I (2)	498	
23	Khusraw I Anushirvan	531	S21
24	Hormizd IV	579	S23
25	Khusraw II Parvez (1)	590	S24

26 Varahran VI Chobin	590	
Khusraw II Parvez (2)	590	
27 Kavadh II	628	S25
28 Ardashir III	628	S27
29 Shahrvaraz	629	
30 Borandukht★	629	D25
31 Hormizd V	630	
32 Yazdagird III	632–651	GS25

e *Buyid Dynasty* 932–1062

1 'Imad-ud-Dawlah 'Ali ibn Buya (Jibal to 947; Fars 934)	932–949	
2 Mu'izz-ud-Dawlah Ahmad (Kirman to 949; 'Iraq 945)	936–967	B1
3 Rukn-ud-Dawlah Hasan (Jibal)	947–977	B1
4 'Adud-ud-Dawlah Fana-Khusraw (Fars/Kirman; 'Iraq 978)	949–983	S3
5 'Izz-ud-Dawlah Bakhtiyar ('Iraq)	967–978	S2
6 Mu'ayyid-ud-Dawlah Buya (Isfahan)	977–983	S3
7 Fakhr-ud-Dawlah 'Ali (Ray; Isfahan 983)	977–997	S3
8 Sharaf-ud-Dawlah Shirzil (Fars; 'Iraq 987–989)	983–990	S4
9 Samsam-ud-Dawlah Marzuban (Kirman/'Iraq to 987; Fars 990)	983–998	S4
10 Baha-ud-Dawlah Firuz ('Iraq; Fars/Kirman 998)	987–1012	S4
11 Majd-ud-Dawlah Rustam (Ray)	997–1029	S7
12 Shams-ud-Dawlah Abu-Tahir (Hamadan)	997–1021	S7
13 Sultan-ud-Dawlah Abu-Shuja (Fars and 'Iraq)	1012–1021	S10
14 Qawam-ud-Dawlah Abu'l-Fawaris (Kirman)	1012–1028	S10
15 Musharrif-ud-Dawlah Hasan ('Iraq; Fars to 1024)	1021–1025	S10
16 Sama-ud-Dawlah Abu'l-Hasan (Hamadan)	1021–1028	S12
17 Muhyi-ud-Din Abu-Kalijar Marzuban (Fars; Kirman 1028; 'Iraq 1044)	1024–1048	S13
18 Jalal-ud-Dawlah Shirzil ('Iraq)	1025–1044	S10
19 ar-Rahim Khusraw-Firuz (Fars and 'Iraq)	1048–1055	S17
20 Abu-Mansur Fulad-Sutun (Fars)	1055–1062	S17

f *Great Seljuk Dynasty* 1038–1157

1 Rukn-ud-Dunya wa'd-Din Tughril ibn Mika'il	1038	GS Seljuk
2 'Adud-ud-Dawlah Alp Arslan ibn Chaghri Beg	1063	BS1
3 Jalal-ud-Dawlah Malik Shah I	1072	S2
4 Nasir-ud-Din Mahmud	1092	S3
5 Rukn-ud-Din Barkiyaruq	1094	S3
6 Mu'izz-ud-Din Malik Shah II	1105	S5
7 Ghiyath-ud-Din Muhammad	1105	S3
8 Mu'izz-ud-Din Sanjar (Khurasan from 1097)	1118–1157	S3

g *Seljuk Dynasty of Western Iran and 'Iraq* 1118–1194

9 Mughith-ud-Din Mahmud II	1118	S7
10 Ghiyath-ud-Din Da'ud	1131	S9
11 Rukn-ud-Din Tughril II	1132	S7

12	Ghiyath-ud-Din Mas'ud	1134	S7
13	Mu'in-ud-Din Malik Shah III	1152	S9
14	Rukn-ud-Din Muhammad II	1153	S9
15	Ghiyath-ud-Din Sulayman Shah	1160	S7
16	Mu'izz-ud-Din Arslan	1161	S11
17	Rukn-ud-Din Tughril III	1176–1194	S16

h *Ilkhan (Mongol) Dynasty 1256–1353*

1	Hulegu (GS Chingis Khan)	1256	
2	Abaqa	1265	S1
3	Ahmad Teguder	1282	S1
4	Arghun	1284	S2
5	Gaikhatu	1291	S2
6	Baidu	1295	BS2
7	Mahmud Ghazan	1295	S4
8	Muhammad Khudabanda Uljaitu	1304	S4
9	Abu-Sa'id	1317	S8
10	Arpa	1335	B3G1
11	Musa	1336–1337	GS6
12	Muhammad	1336–1338	B3G2
13	Tugha-Timur	1336–1353	
14	Jahan-Timur	1339–1340	GS5
15	Sati-Beg Khatun★	1339–1344	D8
16	Sulayman	1339–1344	BGG2
17	Anushirwan	1344–1353	

i *Safavid Dynasty 1501–1753*

1	Isma'il I	1501	
2	Tahmasp I	1524	S1
3	Isma'il II	1576	S2
4	Muhammad Khudabanda	1578	S2
5	'Abbas I	1588	S4
6	Safi	1629	GS5
7	'Abbas II	1642	S6
8	Sulayman I	1666	S7
9	Husain I	1694	S8
10	Tahmasp II	1722	S9
11	'Abbas III	1732–1736	S10
		———	
12	Sulayman II	1749	GD8
13	Isma'il III	1750	STS10
14	Husain II	1753.	S10

j *Ghilzai Afghan Dynasty 1722–1729*

1	Mahmud Khan	1722	
2	Ashraf Khan	1725–1729	FBS1

k *Afsharid Dynasty 1736–1795*

1	Nadir Shah	1736	
2	'Adil Shah	1747	BS1

3	Ibrahim	1748	B2
4	Shah Rukh (Khurasan)	1748–1795	GS1

l *Zand Dynasty* 1750–1794

1	Muhammad Karim Khan	1750	
2	Abu'l-Fath }	1779	S1
3	Muhammad ʿAli }	1779	S1
4	Sadiq (Shiraz)	1779–1781	B1
5	ʿAli Murad (Isfahan)	1779–1785	WS4
6	Jaʿfar	1785–1789	S4
7	Lutf ʿAli	1789–1794	S6

m *Qajar Dynasty* 1779–1925

1	Agha Muhammad	1779	
2	Fath ʿAli	1797	BS1
3	Muhammad	1834	GS2
4	Nasir-ud-Din	1848	S3
5	Muzaffar-ud-Din	1896	S4
6	Muhammad ʿAli	1907	S5
7	Ahmad	1909–1925	S6

n *Pahlavi Dynasty* 1925–1979

1	Reza Shah	1925	
2	Muhammad Reza Shah	1941–1979	S1

188 IRAN AZERBAIJAN (PERSIAN)

a *Sajid Dynasty* 889–929

1	Muhammad ibn Abu'l-Saj	889	
2	Devdad ibn Muhammad	901	S1
3	Yusuf ibn Abu'l-Saj	901	B1
4	Abu'l-Musafir al-Fath	928–929	S1

b *Rawwadid Dynasty* *c.*951–1071

1	Muhammad ibn Husain	?	
2	Husain I	*c.*951	S1
3	Abu'l-Haija Mamlan I	?	
4	Abu-Nasr Husain II	1000	S3
5	Vahsudan	1025	S3
6	Mamlan II	1059–1071	S5

c *Ildegizid Dynasty* 1137–1225

1	Shams-ud-Din Ildegiz	1137	
2	Nusrat-ud-Din Pahlavan Muhammad	1175	S1
3	Muzaffar-ud-Din Qizil Arslan ʿUthman	1186	S1
4	Qutlugh Inanj	1191	S2
5	Nusrat-ud-Din Abu-Bakr	1195	S2
6	Muzaffar-ud-Din Uzbeg	1210–1225	S2

d *Musafirid Dynasty* 941–984

1 Marzuban ibn Muhammad	941	
2 Justan	957	S1
3 Ibrahim	960–984	S1

e *Qara Qoyunli Dynasty* 1380–1468

1 Qara Muhammad Turmush	1380	
2 Qara Yusuf (1)	1389–1400	S1
Qara Yusuf (2)	1406	
3 Iskandar	1420	S2
4 Jihan Shah	1438	S2
5 Hasan 'Ali	1467–1468	S4

f *Aq Qoyunli Dynasty* 1378–1508

1 Qara Yuluk 'Uthman	1378	
2 Hamza	1435–1444	S1
3 'Ali	1435–1438	S1
4 Jihangir	1444	S2
5 Uzun Hasan	1453	S2
6 Khalil	1478	S5
7 Ya'qub	1478	S5
8 Baisonqor	1490	S7
9 Rustam	1493	GS5
10 Ahmad Govde	1497	GS5
11 Murad (Qum; sole ruler 1504)	1497–1508	S7
12 Alwand (Azerbaijan; Jibal/Fars 1500)	1498–1504	GS5
13 Muhammad Mirza (Jibal/Fars)	1498–1500	B12

189 IRAN MAZANDARAN AND GILAN

a *Bavandid Dynasty of Tabaristan* 665–1349

1 Bav ibn Qabus	665	
2 Valash ibn Dadmihr	680	
3 Surkhab I	688	S1
4 Mihr Mardan	717	S3
5 Surkhab II	755	S4
6 Sharvin I	772	S5
7 Shahriyar I	797	S6
8 Shapur	825	S7
9 Qarin I	837	S7
10 Rustam I	867	GS9
11 Sharvin II	895	S10
12 Shahriyar II	930	S11
13 Rustam II	?	S11
14 Dara	966	S13
15 Shahriyar III	969	S14
16 Rustam III	1006	S15
17 Qarin II	1057	BS16

18	Husam-ud-Dawlah Shahriyar IV	1074	S17
19	Najm-ud-Dawlah Qarin III	1110	S18
20	Shams-ul-Muluk Rustam IV	1117	S19
21	'Ala-ud-Dawlah 'Ali I	1118	S18
22	Shah Ghazi Rustam I	1140	S21
23	'Ala-ud-Dawlah Hasan	1163	S22
24	Husam-ud-Dawlah Ardashir I	1172	S23
25	Nasir-ud-Dawlah Shah Ghazi Rustam II	1206–1210	S24
26	Husam-ud-Dawlah Ardashir II	1238	DT18
27	Shams-ul-Muluk Muhammad	1249	S26
28	'Ala-ud-Dawlah 'Ali II	1267	S26
29	Taj-ud-Dawlah Yazdagird	1276	BS28
30	Nasir-ud-Dawlah Shahriyar V	1299	S29
31	Rukn-ud-Dawlah Kai-Khusraw	1314	S29
32	Sharaf-ul-Muluk	1328	S31
33	Fakhr-ud-Dawlah Hasan	1334–1349	S31

b *Baduspanid Dynasty* 660–1476

1	Baduspan I (S1 Dabuyids)	660	
2	Khurzad	694	S1
3	Baduspan II	724	S2
4	Shahriyar I	763	S3
5	Vindad-Umid	792	S3
6	'Abdullah	823	S5
7	Faridun	856	BGG5
8	Baduspan III	?	S7
9	Shahriyar II	872	S8
10	Hazar-Sindan	888	BGS8
11	Shahriyar III	899	FBGS10
12	Shams-ul-Muluk Muhammad I	939	S11
13	Ustundar Abu'l-Fadl	952	S12
14	Husam-ud-Din Zarin-Kemer I	965	BS12
15	Saif-ud-Din Baharb	996	S14
16	Husam-ud-Din Ardashir I	1023	S15
17	Fakhr-ud-Dawlah Namwar I	1047	BS16
18	'Izz-ud-Dawlah Hazarasp I	1078	S17
19	Shahrivash	1116	S18
20	Kai-Ka'us I	1129	S18
21	Hazarasp II	1165	S19
22	Husam-ud-Din Zarin-Kemer II	1210	GS20
23	Sharaf-ud-Din Bisutun	1214	S22
24	Fakhr-ud-Dawlah Namwar II	1223	S23
25	Husam-ud-Dawlah Ardashir II	?	S24
26	Shah Rakim Gaubara	1236	S24
27	Fakhr-ud-Dawlah Namwar III	1272	S26
28	Malik Shah Kai-Khusraw	1302	S26
29	Shams-ul-Muluk Muhammad II	1312	S28
30	Nasir-ud-Din Shahriyar IV	1318	S28
31	Taj-ud-Dawlah Ziyar	1325	S28

32	Jalal-ud-Dawlah Iskandar I	1334	S31
33	Fakhr-ud-Dawlah Shah Ghazi	1360	S31
34	'Adud-ud-Dawlah Qubad	1379	S33
35	Sa'd-ud-Dawlah Tus	1399	S31
36	Kayumarth	1404	BGS35
37	Kai-Ka'us II (Nur)	1453–1476	S36
38	Iskandar II (Kujur)	1453–1475	S36

c *Dabuyid Dynasty c.650–761*

1	Gil Gawbara ibn Farrukhan Gilanshah	c.650	
2	Dabuya	660	S1
3	Khurshid I	676	S1
4	Farrukhan	709	S3
5	Dadburz-Mihr	722	S4
6	Saruya	734	S4
7	Khurshid II	734–761	S5

d *Musafirid Dynasty of Tarum c.910–1060*

1	Muhammad ibn Musafir	c.910	
2	Vahsudan	941	S1
3	Marzuban	966–983	GS2
4	Ibrahim	997	S3
5	Justan	c.1030	S4
6	Musafir	c.1060(?)	S4

e *Ziyarid Dynasty 927–c.1090*

1	Mardawij ibn Ziyar	927	
2	Zahir-ud-Dawlah Vushmagir	935	B1
3	Zahir-ud-Dawlah Bisutun	967	S2
4	Shams-ul-Ma'ali Qabus	978	S2
5	Falak-ul-Ma'ali Manuchihr	1012	S4
6	Sharaf-ul-Ma'ali Anushirvan	1029	S5
7	'Unsur-ul-Ma'ali Kai-Ka'us	1049	BS5
8	Gilan Shah	?–c.1090	S7

f *Assassin Grand Masters – Alamut 1090–1256*

1	Hasan-i-Sabbah	1090	
2	Kiya Buzurg-Ummid	1124–	
3	Muhammad I	1138	S2
4	Hasan II	1162	S3
5	Nur-ud-Din Muhammad II	1166	S4
6	Jalal-ud-Din Hasan III	1210	S5
7	'Ala-ud-Din Muhammad III	1221	S6
8	Rukn-ud-Din Khurshah	1255–1256	S7

g *Sayyid Dynasty 1357–c.1525*

1	Qivam-ud-Din Mar'ashi	1357–1380	
2	'Ali ibn Kamal-ud-Din	1406	GS1

3	al-Murtada	1417	S2
4	Muhammad	1433	S3
5	Abdul-Karim I	1452	S4
6	'Abdullah	1461	S5
7	Zain-ul-'Abidin	1468	GS4
8	'Abdul-Karim II	1475–c.1525	S6

190 **IRAN** JIBAL

a *Dulafid Dynasty c.825–898*

1	Abu-Dulaf Qasim ibn 'Isa	c.825	
2	'Abdul-'Aziz	839	S1
3	Dulaf	873	S2
4	Ahmad	878	S2
5	'Umar	893	S2
6	Abu-Laila Harith	896–898	S2

b *Hasanuyid Dynasty of Hamadan c.959–1015*

1	Hasanuya ibn Husain	c.959	
2	Nasir-ud-Din Badr	979	S1
3	Zahir ibn Hilal	1014–1015	GS2

c *Kakuyid Dynasty 1008–c.1141*

1	'Ala-ud-Dawlah Muhammad	1008	
2	Abu-Mansur Faramurz (Isfahan to 1051; Yazd 1051)	1041–?	S1
3	Abu-Kalijar Garshasp (Hamadan)	1041–c.1048	S1
4	Abu-Mansur 'Ali (Yazd)	?	S2
5	Abu-Kalijar Garshasp II (Yazd)	1095–c.1141	S4

d *Hazaraspid Dynasty of Luristan 1148–1424*

1	Abu-Tahir ibn Muhammad	1148–1160	
2	Nasrat-ud-Din Hazarasp	1204	S1
3	Takla	1252	S2
4	Shams-ud-Din Alp Arghun	1259	S2
5	Yusuf Shah I	1274	S4
6	Afrasiyab I	1288	S5
7	Nasrat-ud-Din Ahmad I	1297	S4
8	Rukn-ud-Din Yusuf Shah II	1333	S7
9	Muzaffar-ud-Din Afrasiyab II	1339	S8
10	Shams-ud-Din Hushang	1355	?GS8
11	Malik Pir Ahmad II	c.1378	S10
12	Abu-Sa'id	1412	S11
13	Husain Shah	c.1417	S12
14	Ghiyath-ud-Din	1424.	BGS11

e *Muzaffarid Dynasty 1314–1393*

| 1 | Mubariz-ud-Din Muhammad ibn Muzaffar | 1314–1364 | |
| 2 | Qutb-ud-Din Shah Mahmud (Isfahan) | 1358–1375 | S1 |

3	Jala-ud-Din Shah Shuja (Fars/Kirman; Isfahan 1375)	1364–1384	S1
4	Mujahid-ud-Din Zain-ul-'Abidin 'Ali (Fars)	1384–1387	S3
5	'Imad-ud-Din Ahmad (Kirman)	1384–1393	S3
6	Nusrat-ud-Din Yahya (Yazd)	1387–1393	BS3
7	Shah Mansur (Fars/Isfahan)	1387–1393	B6

191 IRAN FARS

a *Salghurid Dynasty* 1148–1270

1	Muzaffar-ud-Din Sonqor ibn Mawdud	1148	
2	Muzaffar-ud-Din Zangi	1161	B1
3	Dakla	1175	S2
4	Tughril	1194	S1
5	'Izz-ud-Din Sa'd I	1203	S2
6	Abu-Bakr Qutlugh Khan	1231	S5
7	Sa'd II	1260	S6
8	Muhammad I	1260	S5
9	Muhammad Shah II	1262	BS8
10	Seljuk Shah	1263	B9
11	Abish Khatun★	1265–1270	D7

b *Inju'id Dynasty* 1303–1353

1	Sharaf-ud-Din Mahmud Shah	1303	
2	Ghiyath-ud-Din Kai Khusraw	1336	S1
3	Jalal-ud-Din Mas'ud Shah (1)	1338	S1
4	Shams-ud-Din Muhammad	1339	S1
	Jalal-ud-Din Mas'ud Shah (2)	1340	
5	Abu-Ishaq Jamal-ud-Din	1343–1353	S1

192 IRAN KIRMAN

a *Seljuk Dynasty of Kirman* 1041–1186

1	'Imad-ud-Din Qawurd (B2 Great Seljuk)	1041	
2	Kirman Shah	1073	S1
3	Husain	1074	S2
4	Rukn-ud-Dawlah Sultan Shah	1074	S1
5	Muhyi-ud-Din Turan Shah I	1085	S1
6	Baha-ud-Din Iran Shah	1097	S5
7	Muhyi-ud-Din Arslan Shah I	1101	S2
8	Mughith-ud-Din Muhammad I	1142	S7
9	Muhyi-ud-Din Tughril Shah	1156	S8
10	Bahram Shah	1170	S9
11	Arslan Shah II	1175	S9
12	Turan Shah II	1176	S9
13	Muhammad II	1183–1186	S10

b *Qutlugh Khanid Dynasty* 1222–1303

1	Burak Hajib Qutlugh Khan	1222	
2	Qutb-ud-Din Tayangu (1)	1234	BS1

3	Rukn-ud-Din Mubarak Khwaja	1236	S1
	Qutb-ud-Din Tayangu (2)	1252	
4	Qutlugh Turkhan Khatun★	1257	W2
5	Jalal-ud-Din Suyurghatmish	1282	S2
6	Safwat-ud-Din Padishah Khatun★	1293	D2
7	Jalal-ud-Din Muhammad Shah	1294	BS5
8	Qutb-ud-Din Shah Jahan	1301–1303	S5

193 IRAN SISTAN

Saffarid Dynasty 867–c.1495

1	Ya'qub ibn Laith as-Saffar	867	
2	'Amr ibn Laith	879	B1
3	Tahir I	901	GS2
4	Laith	908	BS2
5	Muhammad I	910	B4
6	'Amr II	912–913	BS3
7	Ahmad I ibn Muhammad	922	DTB1
8	Wali-ud-Dawlah Khalaf I	963–1003	S7
9	Nasr I	1029	S7
10	Baha-ud-Dawlah Tahir II	1073	S9
11	Baha-ud-Dawlah Khalaf II	1090	S9
12	Taj-ud-Din Nasr II	c.1103	GG8
13	Shams-ud-Din Ahmad II	1164	S12
14	Taj-ud-Din Harb	1167	BS13
15	Shams-ud-Din Bahram Shah	1215	GS14
16	Taj-ud-Din Nasr III	1221	S15
17	Rukn-ud-Din Abu-Mansur	1221	S15
18	Shihab-ud-Din Mahmud I	1222	B15
19	'Ali I	1225	B15
20	Shams-ud-Din 'Ali II	1229	DT10
21	Nasr-ud-Din	1254	BS20
22	Nusrat-ud-Din	1328	S21
23	Qutb-ud-Din Muhammad II	1331	BS22
24	Taj-ud-Din I	1346	S23
25	Mahmud II	1350	BS22
26	'Izz-ud-Din	1362	B23
27	Qutb-ud-Din I	1382	S26
28	Taj-ud-Din II	1386	S27
29	Qutb-ud-Din II	1403	S28
30	Shams-ud-Din	1419	S27
31	Nizam-ud-Din Yahya	1438	S30
32	Shams-ud-Din Muhammad III	1480–c.1495	S31

194 IRAN KHURASAN

a *Tahirid Dynasty 821–873*

1	Tahir ibn Husain	821	
2	Talha	822	S1
3	'Abdullah	828	S1
4	Tahir II	845	S3
5	Muhammad	862–873	S4

b *Samanid Dynasty of Khurasan and Transoxania 819–1005*

1	Ahmad ibn Asad ibn Saman	819	
2	Nasr I	864	S1
3	Isma'il I	892	S1
4	Ahmad II	907	S3
5	as-Sa'id Nasr II	914	S4
6	al-Hamid Nuh I	943	S5
7	al-Mu'ayyad 'Abdul-Malik I	954	S6
8	as-Sadid Mansur I	961	S6
9	ar-Rida Nuh II	976	S8
10	Mansur II	997	S9
11	'Abdul-Malik II	999	S9
12	Isma'il II al-Muntasir	1000–1005	S9

c *Sarbadarid Dynasty 1337–1381*

1	'Abdul-Razzaq ibn Fadl-Allah	1337	
2	Wajih-ud-Din Mas'ud	1338	B1
3	Ai-Timur Muhammad	1344	
4	Isfandiyar	1346	
5	Fadl-Allah	1346	B1
6	Shams-ud-Din 'Ali	1347	
7	Yahya	1352	
8	Zahir-ud-Din	1358	
9	Haidar al-Qassab	1359	
10	Lutf-Allah	1359	S2
11	Hasan al-Damighani	1360	
12	'Ali al-Mu'ayyad	1364–1381	

195 AFGHANISTAN AND NORTHERN INDIA BACTRIAN
GREEK KINGS c.256–55 BC

1	Diodotus I	c.256 BC	
2	Diodotus II	c.248	S1
3	Euthydemus I	c.235	
4	Demetrius I	c.200–185	S3
5	Euthydemus II	c.200–190	S3
6	Antimachus I	c.190–180	
7	Pantaleon	c.185–175	S4
8	Agathocles	c.180–165	S4
9	Demetrius II	c.180–165	S6

10	Eucratides I	c.171–155	
11	Heliocles I	c.155–140	S10
12	Plato	c.155–?	S10
13	Menander	c.155–130	S9
14	Eucratides II	c.140–?	S11
15	Zoilus I	?–c.125	S4
16	Polyxenus	?–c.130	
17	Epander	?–c.130	
18	Antimachus II	c.130–125	S9
19	Strato I (1)	c.130–95	S13
20	Archebius	c.130–120	S14
21	Philoxenus	c.125–115	S18
22	Lysias	c.120–110	S15
23	Heliocles II	c.120–115	S11
24	Apollodotus	c.115–95	S13
25	Antialcidas	c.115–100	S23
26	Artemidorus	?–95	
27	Peucolaus	?–95	
28	Diomedes	c.95–85	S25
29	Telephus	c.95–80	S25
30	Nicias	c.95–85	S21
31	Theophilus	?–c.85	S22
32	Zoilus II		S24
33	Dionysius	c.95–80	S24
34	Apollophanes		S24
35	Hippostratus	c.85–70	S30
36	Amyntas	c.85–75	S25
	Strato I (2)	c.80–75	
37	Strato II		S19
38	Hermaeus	c.75–55	S36

Note: The order, dates and relationships of these
kings are very uncertain.

196 INDO-SCYTHIANS, INDO-PARTHIANS AND KUSHANS –
1st century BC to 1st century AD

a *Indo-Scythian Kings*

1	Maues (Moga)	
2	Azes I (Aya)	
3	Azilizes (Ayilisha)	S2
4	Azes II	S3

b *Indo-Parthian Kings*

1	Vonones	
2	Spalirises (Spalirisha)	B1
3	Spalagdames (Spalagadama)	S2
4	Orthagnes (Verethragna)	

5 Gondophares (Vindafarna)   *c*.20–50 AD
6 Pacorus

Note: The dates and territories ruled by these kings
are uncertain, and some certainly overlapped with
others. They controlled parts of Afghanistan, Eastern
Iran and Northern India.

c *Kushan Dynasty*

		Dating A	Dating B	
1	Kujula Kadphises I	*c*.25 BC	*c*.30 AD	
2	Wema Kadphises II	*c*.35 AD	*c*.80	
3	Kanishka I	*c*.78	*c*.103	
4	Vasishka	*c*.102	*c*.126	s3
5	Huvishka I	*c*.111–138	*c*.130	s3
6	Kanishka II	*c*.119	*c*.143	s4
7	Huvishka II			s4
8	Vasudeva I	*c*.152	*c*.166	s6
9	Kanishka III		*c*.200	
10	Vasudeva II		*c*.222–244	

Note: The accession date of Kanishka I is very
uncertain, and the other Kushan dates depend upon
it. The alternatives above are the most widely
accepted but not the only possibilities.

197 **AFGHANISTAN** MUSLIM DYNASTIES

a *Ghaznavid Dynasty 961–1186*

1	Alp-Tigin	961	
2	Abu-Ishaq Ibrahim	963	s1
3	Bilga-Tigin	966	
4	Piri-Tigin	974	
5	Nasir-ud-Dawlah Sabuk-Tigin	977	
6	Isma'il	997	s5
7	Yamin-ud-Dawlah Mahmud	998	s5
8	Jalal-ud-Dawlah Muhammad (1)	1030	s7
9	Shihab-ud-Dawlah Mas'ud I	1031	s7
	Jalal-ud-Dawlah Muhammad (2)	1041	
10	Shihab-ud-Dawlah Mawdud	1041	s9
11	Mas'ud II	1050	s10
12	Baha-ud-Dawlah 'Ali	1050	s9
13	'Izz-ud-Dawlah 'Abdul-Rashid	1050	s7
14	Qiwam-ud-Dawlah Tughril	1053	
15	Jamal-ud-Dawlah Farrukhzad	1053	s9
16	Zahir-ud-Dawlah Ibrahim	1059	s9
17	'Ala-ud-Dawlah Mas'ud III	1099	s16
18	Kamal-ud-Dawlah Shirzad	1115	s17
19	Sultan-ud-Dawlah Arslan Shah	1115	s17
20	Yamin-ud-Dawlah Bahram Shah	1118	s17

21	Mu'izz-ud-Dawlah Khusraw Shah	1152	s20
22	Taj-ud-Dawlah Khusraw Malik	1160–1186	s21

b *Ghurid Dynasty in Ghur and Ghazna c.1100–1215*

1	'Izz-ud-Din Husain I	c.1100	
2	Saif-ud-Din Suri	1146	s1
3	Baha-ud-Din Sam I	1149	s1
4	'Ala-ud-Din Husain II Jahansuz	1149	s1
5	Saif-ud-Din Muhammad I	1161	s4
6	Ghiyath-ud-Din Muhammad II (Ghur)	1163–1203	s3
7	Shihab-ud-Din Muhammad III (Ghazna)	1173–1206	s3
8	Ghiyath-ud-Din Mahmud	1206	s6
9	Baha-ud-Din Sam II	1212	s8
10	'Ala-ud-Din Atsiz	1213	s4
11	'Ala-ud-Din Muhammad IV	1214–1215	BS4

c *Ghurid Dynasty of Bamiyan 1145–1215*

1	Fakhr-ud-Din Mas'ud (s1 Ghur)	1145	
2	Shams-ud-Din Muhammad	1163	s1
3	Baha-ud-Din Sam	1192	s2
4	Jalal-ud-Din 'Ali	1206–1215	s3

d *Kart Dynasty of Herat 1245–1389*

1	Shams-ud-Din I Muhammad	1245–1285	
2	Rukn-ud-Din	1278–1283	s1
3	Fakhr-ud-Din	1285	s2
4	Ghiyath-ud-Din	1308	s2
5	Shams-ud-Din II	1328	s4
6	Hafiz	1329	s4
7	Mu'izz-ud-Din	1331	s4
8	Ghiyath-ud-Din Pir 'Ali	1370–1389	s7

e *Durrani Amirs of Afghanistan 1747–1842*

1	Ahmad Shah Durrani	1747	
2	Timur Shah	1773	s1
3	Zaman Shah	1793	s2
4	Mahmud Shah (1) (Kabul)	1800–1803	s2
5	Shah Shuja (1) (Peshawar; Kabul 1803)	1800–1809	s2
	Mahmud Shah (2) (Herat; Kabul to 1818)	1809–1829	
6	'Ali Shah (Kabul)	1818–1819	s2
		———	
	Shah Shuja (2)	1839	
7	Fath Jang	1842.	s5

f *Barakzai Amirs and Kings of Afghanistan 1819–1973*

1	Dost Muhammad Khan (1) (Ghazna; Kabul 1826)	1819–1839	
		———	
	Dost Muhammad Khan (2)	1842	
2	Shir 'Ali Khan (1)	1863	s1
3	Afdal Khan	1866	s1

	Shir 'Ali Khan (2)	1867	
4	Muhammad Ya'qub Khan	1879	S2
5	'Abdul-Rahman Khan	1880	S3
6	Habib-Allah Khan	1901	S5
7	Aman-Allah Khan (King 1926)	1919	S6
8	Nadir Shah	1929	DTBI
9	Muhammad Zahir Shah	1933–1973	S8

198 TRANSOXANIA-TURKESTAN RULERS

a *Qara-Khanid Dynasty of Kashgar c.955–1211*

1	'Abdul-Karim Satuq Bughra Khan	?–c.955	
2	Shihab-ud-Dawlah Harun Bughra Khan	?–992	GSI
3	'Ali ibn Musa	?	
4	Ahmad Arslan Qara Khan	998	
5	Mansur Arslan Khan	1015	
6	Ahmad Toghan Khan	1024	
7	Yusuf Qadir Khan	1026	S2
8	Sulayman Arslan Khan	1032	
9	Muhammad Khan I	1056	S7
10	Ibrahim Khan I	1057	
11	Mahmud Khan	1059	
12	'Umar Khan	1074	
13	Harun Bughra Khan	1075	S8
14	Ahmad Arslan Khan	1103	S13
15	Ibrahim Khan II	1128	
16	Muhammad Khan II	1158	
17	Yusuf Khan	?	
18	Muhammad Khan III	1211.	

b *Qara-Khanid Dynasty of Bukhara 999–1211*

1	Nasr Khan I	999–1012	GSI Kashgar
2	'Ali Tigin	1020–1034	S2 Kashgar
3	'Ain-ud-Dawlah Muhammad I	1041	
4	Ibrahim I Bori Tigin Tamghach Khan	1052	SI
5	Shams-ul-Mulk Nasr Khan II	1068	S4
6	Khidr Khan	1080	S4
7	Ahmad Khan	1081	S6
8	Ya'qub Tigin	1089	GS7 Kashgar
9	Mas'ud Khan I	1095	
10	Sulayman Khan	1097	GS4
11	Mahmud Tigin I	1097	
12	Harun Khan	1099	GS7 Kashgar
13	Muhammad II Arslan Khan	1102	S10
14	Nasr Khan III	1129	S13
15	Ahmad Qadir Khan	1129	S13
16	Hasan Khan	1130	
17	Ibrahim Khan II	1132	S13
18	Mahmud Khan II	1132	S13

19 Ibrahim III Tamghach Khan	1141	
20 'Ali Chagri Khan	1156	
21 Mas'ud Qilich Tamghach Khan	1161	B20
22 Ibrahim Khan IV	1178	
23 'Uthman Khan	1204–1211	S22

c *Qara-Khitai (Western Liao) Dynasty* 1124–1218

1 Te-Tsung (Yeh-Lu Ta-Shih)	1124	DTI Liao
2 Kan-T'ien Hou★	1144	WI
3 Jen-Tsung	1151	SI
4 Ch'eng-T'ien Hou★	1163	DI
5 Mo-Chu	1178	S3
6 Kuchlug Khan Naiman	1211–1218	HD5

d *Chaghatai Dynasty* 1227–1363

1 Chaghatai (S Chingis Khan)	1227	
2 Qara Hulegu (1)	1242	GSI
3 Yesu Mongke	1247	SI
Qara-Hulegu (2)	1252	
4 Orqina Khatun★	1252	W2
5 Alughu	1261	GSI
6 Mubarak Shah	1266	S2
7 Baraq	1266	BS2
8 Negubai	1271	GSI
9 Tuqa Timur	1272	BS2
10 Duwa	1282	S7
11 Konchek	1306	SIO
12 Taliqu	1308	B9
13 Kebek (1)	1309	SIO
14 Esen Buqa	1309	SIO
Kebek (2)	1318	
15 Eljigidei	1326	SIO
16 Duwa Timur	1326	SIO
17 'Ala-ud-Din Tarmashirin	1326	SIO
18 Changshi	1334	BSI7
19 Buzan	1334	SI6
20 Yesun Timur	1338	BI8
21 Muhammad	1342	GSI1
22 Qazan	1343	BSI7
23 Danishmenji	1346	
24 Bayan Quli	1348	BSI7
25 Shah Timur	1359	S20
26 Tughluq Timur (of Zungaria)	1359–1363	BSI7

e *Chaghatai Dynasty of Zungaria* 1347–1571

1 Tughluq Timur (BSI7 Chaghatai)	1347	
2 Ilyas Khoja	1363	SI
3 Qamar-ud-Din (of Kashgar)	1368–1392	
4 Khidr Khoja	1389–1399	SI
5 Shams-i-Jahan	1399	S4

6	Muhammad Khan	1408	S4
7	Naqsh-i-Jahan	1415	S5
8	Uwais Khan (1)	1418	BS6
9	Shir Muhammad	1421	BS6
	Uwais Khan (2)	1425	
10	Esen Buqa	1429	S8
11	Yunus Khan	1462	S8
12	Mahmud Khan	1487	S11
13	Mansur Khan	1508–1543	BS12
14	Sa'id Khan	1514–1533	B13
15	'Abdul-Rashid	1533–1571	S14

f *Dughlat Dynasty of Kashgar* 1368–1533

1	Qamar-ud-Din	1368	
2	Khudaidad	1392–c.1420	BS1
		———	
3	Sayyid 'Ali	1433	S2
4	Saniz Mirza	1457	S3
5	Muhammad Haidar	1464	S3
6	Muhammad Husain (Kashgar)	1480–1508	S5
7	Abu-Bakr Mirza (Yarkand)	1480–1514	S4
8	Sayyid Muhammad Mirza (Kashgar)	1508–1533	S5

g *Timurid Dynasty* 1370–(1530)

1	Timur	1370–1405	
2	Jalal-ud-Din Miran Shah (Western Iran)	1404–1409	S1
3	Khalil Sultan (Eastern Iran and Turkestan to 1409; Western Iran from 1409)	1405–1414	S2
4	Shah Rukh (Khurasan; Turkestan 1409; Western Iran 1415)	1405–1447	S1
5	'Ayyal (Western Iran)	1414.	S2
6	Ailankar (Western Iran)	1414–1415	BS5
7	Ulugh Beg	1447–1449	S4
8	'Abdul-Latif (Turkestan)	1449–1450	S7
9	Babur ibn Baisonqur (Khurasan)	1449–1457	BS7
10	'Abdullah Mirza (Turkestan)	1450–1451	BS7
11	Abu-Sa'id (Turkestan; Khurasan 1459)	1451–1469	BS3
12	Mahmud ibn Babur (Khurasan)	1457–1459	S9
13	'Umar Shaikh (Farghana)	1465–1494	S11
14	Ahmad (Turkestan)	1469–1494	S11
15	Yadigar Muhammad (Khurasan)	1469–1470	BS9
16	Husain Baiqara (Khurasan)	1470–1506	BGG2
17	Mahmud ibn Abi-Sa'id (Turkestan)	1494–1495	S11
18	Baisonqur (Turkestan)	1495–1497	S17
19	'Ali Mirza (Turkestan)	1498–1500	S17
20	Badi-uz-Zaman (Khurasan)	1506.	S16
21	Muhammad Babur (Farghana to 1501; Kabul 1504; Moghul Emperor 1526)	1494–(1530)	S13

h *Shaibanid Dynasty of Samarkand* 1500–1598

1 Muhammad Shaibani (DTB1 Golden Horde)	1500	
2 Kochkunju	1510	FB1
3 Muzaffar-ud-Din Abu-Sa'id	1531	S2
4 Abu'l-Ghazi 'Ubaidullah	1534	BS1
5 'Abdullah I	1539	S2
6 'Abdul-Latif	1540	S2
7 Nawruz Ahmad	1552	BS2
8 Pir Muhammad I	1556	BGS2
9 Iskandar	1561	B8
10 'Abdullah II	1583	S9
11 'Abdul-Mu'min	1598	S10
12 Pir Muhammad II	1598.	BS9

i *Janid Dynasty* 1598–1785

1 Baqi Muhammad (GD9 Shaibanid) (Bukhara)	1598–1605	DTB35 Golden Horde
2 Wali Muhammad (Balkh; Bukhara 1605)	1598–1608	B1
3 Imam Quli	1608–1650	BS1
4 Nadir Muhammad	1640–1651	B3
5 'Abdul-'Aziz	1647–1680	S4
6 Subhan Quli (Balkh; Bukhara 1680)	1657–1702	S4
7 Makim Khan (Balkh)	1702–1707	GS6
8 'Ubaidullah I (Bukhara)	1702–1705	S6
9 Abu'l-Faid	1705–1747	S6
19 'Abdul-Mu'min	1747	S9
11 'Ubaidullah II	1751	S9
12 Muhammad Rahim	1753	
13 Abu'l-Ghazi	1758–1785	DT3

j *Haidarid Dynasty of Bukhara* 1785–1920

1 Mir Ma'sum Shah Murad (HD13 Janid)	1785	
2 Haidar Tora	1800	S1
3 Husain	1826	S2
4 'Umar	1826	S2
5 Nasr-Allah	1827	S2
6 Muzaffar-ud-Din	1860	S5
7 'Abdul-Ahad	1885	S6
8 'Abdul-Sa'id Mir 'Alim	1910–1920	S7

k *Shah-Rukhid Dynasty of Khokand* c.1700–1876

1 Shah Rukh Beg	c.1700	
2 'Abdul-Rahim		S1
3 'Abdul-Karim		S1
4 Erdeni Beg		S2
5 Sulayman	1770	BS2
6 Shah Rukh II	1770	GS3
7 Narbuta	1770	B6
8 'Alim Khan	1800	S7
9 Muhammad 'Umar	1809	S7

10	Muhammad 'Ali	1822	S9
11	Shir 'Ali	1840	BS7
12	Murad	1845	S8
13	Khudayar (1)	1845	S11
14	Muhammad Malla	1857	S11
15	Shah Murad	1859	BS13
	Khudayar (2)	1861	
16	Muhammad Sultan	1864	S14
	Khudayar (3)	1871	
17	Nasir-ud-Din	1875–1876	S13

199 KHWARIZM/KHIVA RULERS

a *Ma'munid Dynasty c.992–1017*

1	Abu'l-'Ali Ma'mun I	c.992	
2	Abu'l-Hasan 'Ali	997	S1
3	Abu'l-'Abbas Ma'mun II	1009	S1
4	Abu'l-Harith Muhammad ibn 'Ali	1017.	S2

b *Anushtiginid Dynasty c.1077–1231*

1	Anushtigin Gharcha'i	c.1077	
2	Qutb-ud-Din Muhammad I	1097	S1
3	'Ala-ud-Din Atsiz	1127	S2
4	Il Arslan	1156	S3
5	'Ala-ud-Din Tekish	1172–1200	S4
6	Sultan Shah Mahmud (Khurasan)	1172–1193	S4
7	'Ala-ud-Din Muhammad II	1200	S5
8	Jalal-ud-Din Mangubarti	1220–1231	S7

c *'Arab-Shahid Dynasty c.1515–1804*

1	Ilbars Khan I (DTBI Golden Horde)	c.1515	
2	Sultan Hajji	c.1525	FBS1
3	Hasan Quli		FBS1
4	Sufyan Khan		FBS1
5	Bujugha Khan		B4
6	Avanak Khan		B4
7	Kal Khan		B4
8	Agatai Khan	c.1540	B4
9	Dost Khan	1546	S5
10	Hajji Muhammad I	1558	S8
11	'Arab Muhammad I	1602	S10
12	Isfandiyar	1623	S11
13	Abu'l-Ghazi I	1643	S11
14	Anusha Khan	1663	S13
15	Muhammad Arank	1674	S14
16	Ishaq Aqa Shah Niyaz	1688	
17	'Arab Muhammad II	1702	S14
18	Hajji Muhammad II	?	S14
19	Yadigar Khan	1714	S14

20 Arank Khan	1714	
21 Shir Ghazi	1715	
22 Ilbars Khan II	*c.*1732	
23 Abu-Muhammad	1741	S22
24 Abu'l-Ghazi II	1742	
25 Kaip Khan	1745	
26 Abu'l-Ghazi III	*c.*1770–1804	

d *Inakid Dynasty* 1804–1919

1 Iltazar Khan	1804	
2 Muhammad Rahim	1806	B1
3 Allah Quli	1825	S2
4 Rahim Quli	1842	S3
5 Muhammad Amin	1845	S3
6 'Abdullah	1855	BGS2
7 Qutlugh Muhammad	1855	B6
8 Sayyid Muhammad	1856	S2
9 Sayyid Muhammad Rahim	1865	S8
10 Asfandiyar	1910	
11 Sayyid 'Abdullah	1918–1919	

200 **INDIA** IMPERIAL DYNASTIES OF THE NORTH

a *Maurya Dynasty c.*320–187 BC

1 Chandragupta Maurya	*c.*320 BC	
2 Bindusara	*c.*300	S1
3 Ashoka Vardhana	*c.*273	S2
4 Kunala (?Jalauka) (West)	*c.*232–225	S3
5 Dasaratha (East)	*c.*232–225	?S3
6 Samprati	*c.*225	S4
7 Salisuka	?	
8 Devadharma	?	
9 Satamdhanu	?	
10 Brihadratha	*c.*194–187	

b *Sunga Dynasty c.*187–75 BC

1 Pushyamitra Sunga	*c.*187 BC	
2 Agnimitra	*c.*151	S1
3 Vasujyeshtha	*c.*143	S2
4 Vasumitra	*c.*133	S3
5 Andhraka		S4
6 Pulindaka		S5
7 Ghosha		S6
8 Vajramitra		
9 Bhagavata		
10 Devabhumi	*c.*85–75	S9

c *Kanva Dynasty c.*75–30 BC

1 Vasudeva	*c.*75 BC	

2	Bhumimitra	*c.*66	SI
3	Narayana	*c.*52	
4	Susarman	*c.*40–30	

d *Gupta Dynasty c.275–550* AD

1	Gupta	*c.*275	
2	Ghatotkacha	*c.*300	SI
3	Chandragupta I	*c.*320	S2
4	Samudragupta	*c.*350	S3
5	Ramagupta	*c.*370	S4
6	Chandragupta II	*c.*376	S4
7	Kumaragupta I	*c.*415	s6
8	Skandagupta	*c.*455	S7
9	Kumaragupta II	*c.*467	?s8
10	Budhagupta	*c.*477	BS8
11	Chandragupta III	*c.*495	?SI0
12	Vainyagupta	*c.*500	BI0
13	Narasimhagupta	*c.*510	BI0
14	Kumaragupta III	*c.*540	SI3
15	Vishnugupta	*c.*550.	SI4

e *Pushpabhuti Dynasty c.500–647*

1	Naravardhana	*c.*500	
2	Rajyavardhana I		SI
3	Adityavardhana		S2
4	Prabhakaravardhana	*c.*580	S3
5	Rajyavardhana II	*c.*605	S4
6	Harshavardhana	*c.*606–647	S4

f *Pratihara Dynasty c.750–1030*

1	Nagabhata I	*c.*750	
2	Devaraja		BSI
3	Vatsaraja	*c.*783	S2
4	Nagabhata II	*c.*815	S3
5	Ramabhadra	*c.*833	S4
6	Bhoja I	*c.*836	s5
7	Mahendrapala I	*c.*893	s6
8	Mahipala	*c.*914	S7
9	Bhoja II		S7
10	Vinayakapala		S7
11	Mahendrapala II	*c.*946	SI0
12	Devapala	*c.*948	s8
13	Vijayapala	*c.*960	s8
14	Rajyapala		SI3
15	Trilochanapala	*c.*1018–1030	SI4

201 **INDIA** SULTANS OF DELHI

a *Slave Dynasty* 1206–1290

1 Qutb-ud-Din Aibak	1206	
2 Aram Shah	1210	S1
3 Shams-ud-Din Iltutmish	1211	
4 Rukn-ud-Din Firuz Shah	1236	S3
5 Jalalat-ud-Din Radiyya Begum★	1236	D3
6 Mu'izz-ud-Din Bahram Shah	1240	S3
7 'Ala-ud-Din Mas'ud Shah	1242	S4
8 Nasir-ud-Din Mahmud Shah	1246	S3
9 Ghiyath-ud-Din Balban	1266	
10 Mu'izz-ud-Din Kai-Qubadh	1287	GS9
11 Shams-ud-Din Kayumarth	1290.	S10

b *Khalji Dynasty* 1290–1320

1 Jalal-ud-Din Firuz Shah	1290	
2 Rukn-ud-Din Ibrahim Shah	1296	S1
3 'Ala-ud-Din Muhammad Shah	1296	BS1
4 Shihab-ud-Din 'Umar Shah	1316	S3
5 Qutb-ud-Din Mubarak Shah	1316	S3
6 Nasir-ud-Din Khusraw Shah	1320.	

c *Tughluq Dynasty* 1320–1414

1 Ghiyath-ud-Din Tughluq Shah I	1320	
2 Ghiyath-ud-Din Muhammad Shah I	1325	S1
3 Mahmud Shah	1351	S2
4 Firuz Shah	1351	BS1
5 Ghiyath-ud-Din Tughluq Shah II	1388	GS4
6 Abu-Bakr Shah	1389	GS4
7 Nasir-ud-Din Muhammad Shah II	1390	S4
8 'Ala-ud-Din Sikandar Shah	1393	S7
9 Nasir-ud-Din Mahmud Shah	1393–1413	S7
10 Nusrat Shah	1395–1399	B5
11 Dawlat Khan Lodi	1413–1414	

d *Sayyid Dynasty* 1414–1451

1 Khidr Khan	1414	
2 Mu'izz-ud-Din Mubarak Shah	1421	S1
3 Muhammad Shah	1435	BS2
4 'Ala-ud-Din 'Alam Shah	1446–1451	S3

e *Lodi Dynasty* 1451–1526

1 Bahlul Lodi	1451	
2 Nizam Shah Sikandar	1489	S1
3 Ibrahim Lodi	1517–1526	S2

f *Surid Dynasty* 1540–1556

1 Shir Shah Sur (of Bengal)	1540	
2 Islam Shah	1545	S1

3	Muhammad 'Adil Shah	1554–1556	BS1
4	Ibrahim Shah	1554–1556	FBS1
5	Ahmad Khan Sikandar Shah	1555–1556	FBS1

202 INDIA TIMURID MOGHUL EMPERORS 1526–1858

1	Zahir-ud-Din Babur (of Kabul)	1526	(= 198g. No.21)
2	Nasir-ud-Din Humayun (1)	1530–1540	S1
	Nasir-ud-Din Humayun (2)	1555	
3	Jalal-ud-Din Akbar I	1556	S2
4	Nur-ud-Din Jahangir	1605	S3
5	Dawar Bakhsh	1627	GS4
6	Shihab-ud-Din Shah Jahan I	1628	S4
7	Murad Bakhsh (Gujarat)	1657–1658	S6
8	Shah Shuja (Bengal)	1657–1660	S6
9	Muhyi-ud-Din Aurangzib 'Alamgir I	1658–1707	S6
10	A'zam Shah	1707.	S9
11	Kam Bakhsh (Deccan)	1707–1708	S9
12	Shah 'Alam Bahadur Shah I	1707–1712	S9
13	'Azim-ush-Sha'n	1712.	S12
14	Mu'izz-ud-Din Jahandar	1712	S12
15	Farrukhsiyar	1713	S13
16	Shams-ud-Din Rafi-ud-Darajat	1719	BS14
17	Rafi-ud-Dawlah Shah Jahan II	1719	B16
18	Nikusiyar	1719	BS12
19	Nasir-ud-Din Muhammad	1719	BS14
20	Ahmad Shah Bahadur	1748	S19
21	'Aziz-ud-Din 'Alamgir II	1754	S14
22	Shah Jahan III	1760	GS11
23	Jalal-ud-Din 'Ali Jauhar Shah 'Alam II (1)	1760	S21
24	Bidar Bakht	1788	S20
	Shah 'Alam II (2)	1788	
25	Mu'in-ud-Din Akbar II	1806	S23
26	Siraj-ud-Din Bahadur Shah II	1837–1858	S25

203 INDIA THE PUNJAB

a *Hindu Shahi Dynasty of Udabhanda (Waihind) c.850–1026*

1	Lalliya Shahi	c.850	
2	Samantadeva	c.870	
3	Kamaluka	c.900	S1
4	Bhima Shahi	c.940	S3
5	Jayapala	c.965	S4
6	Anandapala	1002	S5
7	Trilochanapala	1012	S6
8	Bhimapala	1021–1026	S7

b *Langah Dynasty of Multan* 1444–1526

1	Qutb-ud-Din Mahmud I Langah	1444	
2	Husain I	1468	S1
3	Mahmud II ibn Firuz	1502	GS2
4	Husain II	1524–1526	S3

c *Maharajas of Lahore* 1799–1849

1	Ranjit Singh	1799	
2	Kharak Singh	1839	S1
3	Nao Nehal Singh	1840	S2
4	Chand Kaur★	1840	W2
5	Sher Singh	1841	S1
6	Dalip Singh	1843–1849	S1

d *Maharajas of Patiala* 1762–1948

1	Ala Singh	1762	
2	Amar Singh	1765	GS1
3	Sahib Singh	1781	S2
4	Karam Singh	1813	S3
5	Narindar Singh	1845	S4
6	Mohindar Singh	1862	S5
7	Rajindar Singh	1876	S6
8	Bhupindar Singh	1900	S7
9	Yadavindar Singh	1938–1948	S8

e *Nawabs of Bahawalpur – Daudputra Dynasty* 1739–1955

1	Sadiq Muhammad Khan I	1739	
2	Muhammad Bahawal Khan I	1746	S1
3	Mubarak Khan	1749	S1
4	Muhammad Bahawal Khan II	1772	BS3
5	Sadiq-Muhammad Khan II	1809	S4
6	Muhammad Bahawal Khan III	1825	S5
7	Sadiq Muhammad Khan III	1852	S6
8	Fateh Muhammad Khan	1853	S6
9	Muhammad Bahawal Khan IV	1858	S8
10	Sadiq Muhammad Khan IV	1866	S9
11	Muhammad Bahawal Khan V	1899	S10
12	Sadiq Muhammad Khan V	1907–1955	S11

204 INDIA NORTH-EASTERN PLAIN (Uttar Pradesh and Bihar etc.)

a *Gahadavala Dynasty of Varanasi (Benares) c.* 1080–1200

1	Chandradeva	c.1080	
2	Madanapala	c.1100	S1
3	Govindachandra	c.1114	S2
4	Vijayachandra	c.1155	S3
5	Jayachandra	c.1170	S4
6	Harischandra	c.1194–1200	S5

b *Chandella Dynasty of Jejakabhukti (Bundelkhand) c.831–1315*

1	Nannuka Chandravarman	c.831	
2	Vakpati		S1
3	Jayasakti	c.850	S2
4	Vijayasakti		S2
5	Rahila		S4
6	Harsha	c.900	S5
7	Yasovarman	c.925	S6
8	Dhanga	c.950	S7
9	Ganda	c.1002	S8
10	Vidyadhara	c.1018	S9
11	Vijayapala	c.1022	S10
12	Devendravarman	c.1051	S11
13	Kirtivarman	c.1070	S11
14	Sallakshanavarman	c.1100	S13
15	Jayavarman	c.1117	S14
16	Prithvivarman	c.1125	S13
17	Madanavarman	c.1129	S16
18	Paramardi	c.1165	GS17
19	Trailokyavarman	c.1202	S18
20	Viravarman I	c.1247	S19
21	Bhojavarman	c.1286	S20
22	Hammiravarman	c.1289	S20
23	Viravarman II	c.1315	

c *Sharqi Sultans of Jaunpur 1394–1479*

1	Malik Sarvar Khwaja Jahan	1394	
2	Mubarak Shah	1399	AS1
3	Shams-ud-Din Ibrahim Shah	1402	B2
4	Mahmud Shah	1440	S3
5	Muhammad Shah	1457	S4
6	Husain Shah	1458–1479	S4

d *Nawabs of Avadh (Oudh) 1722–1856*

1	Burhan-ul-Mulk Muhammad Sa'adat Khan	1722	
2	Muhammad Safdar Jang	1739	STS1
3	Shuja-ud-Dawlah Haidar	1754	S2
4	Asaf-ud-Dawlah	1775	S3
5	Wazir 'Ali	1797	S4
6	Sa'adat 'Ali	1798	
7	Ghazi-ud-Din Haidar	1814	S6
8	Nasir-ud-Din Haidar	1827	S7
9	'Ali Shah	1837	S6
10	Amjad 'Ali Shah	1842	S9
11	Wajid 'Ali Shah	1847–1856	S10

e *Sindhia Maharajas of Gwalior 1726–1948*

1	Ranoji Sindhia	1726	
2	Jayappa	1745	S1

3	Jankoji I	1755	s2
4	Madhava Rao I	1761	s1
5	Daulat Rao	1794	BGS4
6	Jankoji Rao II	1827	s5
7	Jayaji Rao	1843	s6
8	Madhava Rao II	1886	s7
9	Jivaji Rao	1925–1948	s8

205 **INDIA** SIND AND BALUCHISTAN

a *Chach Dynasty of Sind c.643–724*

1	Chach	c.643	
2	Chandar	c.671	B1
3	Dahir	c.679	s1
4	Hullishah	712	s3
5	Sisah	c.724.	

b *Sumra Dynasty c.1025–1336*

1	Sumra	c.1025
2	Bhungar I	c.1053
3	Duda I	c.1068
4	Singhar	c.1092
5	Hamun*	c.1107
6	Pithu	
7	Khaira	
8	Hafif I	
9	'Umar	
10	Duda II	
11	Pahtu	
12	Genhra I	
13	Muhammad Tur	
14	Genhra II	
15	Duda III	c.1190
16	Tai	c.1204
17	Chani Sar	c.1228
18	Bhungar II	c.1246
19	Hafif II	c.1261
20	Duda IV	c.1279
21	'Umar Sumra	c.1304
22	Bhungar III	c.1330
23	Hamir	c.1336.

c *Samma Dynasty 1336–1521*

1	Unar (Afzah)	1336	
2	Juna	1340	B1
3	Banhatiya	1353	s1
4	Timaji	1376	s1
5	Salah-ud-Din	1379	s4
6	Nizam-ud-Din	1391	s5

7	'Ali Shir	1393	S6
8	Fath Khan	1408	
9	Tughluq	1423	B8
10	Mubarak	1449	
11	Sikandar	1449	S8
12	Sanjar	1452	?S7
13	Nizam-ud-Din Nanda	1460	?S7
14	Firuz Salah-ud-Din	1492–1521	S13

d *Arghun Dynasty 1521–1591*

1	Mirza Shah Beg (of Qandahar 1507–1524)	1521	
2	Mirza Husain	1524	S1
3	Mirza Muhammad 'Isa	1556	
4	Mirza Muhammad Baqi	1567	S3
5	Mirza Janibeg	1585–1591	

e *Khans of Kalat c.1666–1948*

1	Mir Hasan Khan Mirwari	?–1666	
2	Sardar Mir Ahmad Khan	1666	
3	Mir Mehrab Khan I	1695	S2
4	Mir Samandar Khan	1695	GS2
5	Mir 'Abdullah Khan	1714	S3
6	Mir Mohabat Khan	1734	S5
7	Mir Nasir Khan I	1749	S5
8	Mir Mahmud Khan I	1817	S7
9	Mir Mehrab Khan II	1831	S8
10	Mir Nasir Khan II	1840	S9
11	Mir Khudadad Khan	1857	S9
12	Mir Mahmud Khan II	1893	S11
13	Mir 'Azam Khan	1931	S11
14	Mir Ahmad Yar Khan	1933–1948	S13

206 **INDIA** RAJASTAN

a *Guhila Ranas/Maharanas of Mewar/Udaipur c.730–1949*

1	Khommana I (Bappa)	c.730	
2	Mattata	c.753	
3	Bhartripatta I		
4	Simha		
5	Khommana II		S4
6	Mahayaka		S5
7	Khommana III		S6
8	Bhartripatta II	c.940	S7
9	Allata	c.950	S8
10	Naravahana	c.960	S9
11	Salivahana	c.971	S10
12	Saktikumara	c.977	S11
13	Ambaprasada		S12
14	Suchivarman		S12

15	Naravarman		S12
16	Anantavarman		S12
17	Kirtivarman		S12
18	Yogaraja		
19	Vairata		
20	Hamsapala		
21	Vairi Singh		
22	Vijaya Singh	c.1108	
23	Ari Singh I		
24	Choda Singh		
25	Vikrama Singh		
26	Rana Singh	c.1168	
27	Kshema Singh		S26
28	Samanta Singh	c.1171	S27
29	Kumara Singh		S27
30	Mathana Singh		
31	Padma Singh		
32	Jaitra Singh	c.1213	
33	Teja Singh	c.1260	S32
34	Samara Singh	c.1273	S33
35	Ratna Singh I	c.1302	S34
36	Lakhana Singh	c.1303	DT26
37	Hammir I	c.1314	BS36
38	Kshetra Singh	c.1378	S37
39	Laksha Singh	c.1405	S38
40	Mokala	c.1420	S39
41	Kumbhakarna	1433	S40
42	Udaya Karan	1468	S41
43	Rayamalla	1473	S41
44	Sangrama Singh I	1509	S43
45	Ratna Singh II	1528	S44
46	Bikramajit	1532	S44
47	Ranbir	1535	BS44
48	Udaya Singh	1537	S44
49	Pratap Singh I	1572	S48
50	Amar Singh I	1597	S49
51	Karan	1620	S50
52	Jagat Singh I	1628	S51
53	Raja Singh I	1652	S52
54	Jaya Singh	1680	S53
55	Amar Singh II	1699	S54
56	Sangrama Singh II	1711	S55
57	Jagat Singh II	1734	S56
58	Pratap Singh II	1752	S57
59	Raja Singh II	1754	S58
60	Ari Singh II	1761	S57
61	Hammir II	1773	S60
62	Bhim Singh	1778	S60
63	Jawan Singh	1828	S62
64	Sardar Singh	1838	AS63

65	Sarup Singh	1842	AB64
66	Sambhu	1861	AN65
67	Sujjan Singh	1874	FBS66
68	Fateh Singh	1884	DT56
69	Bhopal Singh	1930–1949	S68

b *Rathor Rajas/Maharajas of Marwar/Jodhpur 1382–1949*

1	Chunda Rao	1382	
2	Kanha		S1
3	Sata		S1
4	Ranamalla		S1
5	Jodha	1438	S4
6	Satal	1488	S5
7	Suja	1491	S5
8	Ganga	1515	GS7
9	Malladeva	1532	?S8
10	Udaya Singh Raja	1584	S9
11	Sura Singh	1595	S10
12	Gaja Singh	1620	S11
13	Jaswant Singh I	1638	S12
14	Ajit Singh	1680	S13
15	Abhaya Singh (Maharaja)	1725	S14
16	Rama Singh (1)	1750	S15
17	Bakht Singh	1751	S14
18	Vijaya Singh (1)	1752	S17
	Rama Singh (2)	1752	
	Vijaya Singh (2)	1773	
19	Bhim Singh	1792	GS18
20	Man Singh	1803	GS18
21	Takht Singh	1843	DT14
22	Jaswant Singh II	1873	S21
23	Sardar Singh	1895	S22
24	Sumer Singh	1911	S23
25	Umaid Singh	1918	S23
26	Hanwant Singh	1947–1949	S25

c *Rathor Rajas/Maharajas of Bikaner 1465–1949*

1	Bika Rao (S5 Marwar)	1465	
2	Naro	1504	S1
3	Lunkaran	1505	S1
4	Jetsi	1526	S3
5	Kalyan Singh	1542	S4
6	Raya Singh (Raja)	1571	S5
7	Dalpat Singh	1612	S6
8	Sur Singh	1613	S6
9	Karan Singh	1631	S8
10	Anup Singh (Maharaja)	1669	S9
11	Sarup Singh	1698	S10
12	Sujan Singh	1700	S10
13	Zorawar Singh	1736	S12

14	Gaja Singh	1745	BS12
15	Raja Singh	1787	S14
16	Pratap Singh	1787	S15
17	Surat Singh	1787	S14
18	Ratan Singh	1828	S17
19	Sardar Singh	1851	S18
20	Dungar Singh	1872	DT14
21	Ganga Singh	1887	B20
22	Sadul Singh	1943–1949	S21

d *Kachwaha Rajas/Maharajas of Amber/Jaipur c.1128–1949*

1	Dulha Rao	c.1128	
2	Kankal	c.1136	S1
3	Maidal		S2
4	Hunadeva		S3
5	Kantal I		S4
6	Pujanadeva	c.1185	S5
7	Malesi		S6
8	Byala		S7
9	Rajadeva		S8
10	Kilhan		S9
11	Kantal II	1276	S10
12	Jansi		S11
13	Udayakarna		S12
14	Nara Singh		S13
15	Banbir		S14
16	Udha Rao		S15
17	Chandrasena		S16
18	Prithvi I	1502	S17
19	Bhima	1534	S18
20	Ratan		S18
21	Baharmalla	1547	S18
22	Bhagwan Das		S21
23	Man Singh I	1589	S22
24	Jagat Singh I	1614	S23
25	Bhao Singh	1614	S23
26	Jaya Singh I	1622	GS24
27	Rama Singh I	1667	S26
28	Bishan Singh	1688	GS27
29	Sawai Jaya Singh II	1700	S28
30	Ishwari Singh	1743	S29
31	Madhu Singh I	1750	S29
32	Prithvi Singh II	1768	S31
33	Pratap Singh	1778	S31
34	Jagat Singh II	1803	S33
35	Jaya Singh III	1818	S34
36	Rama Singh II	1835	S35
37	Sawai Madhu Singh II	1881	AS36
38	Sawai Man Singh II	1922–1949	AS37

e *Chauhan Raos/Maharaos of Bundi c.*1342–1949

1	Devi Singh	c.1342	
2	Samar Singh		S1
3	Napurji		S2
4	Mahirji		S3
5	Bar Singh		S4
6	Subhand Deva		S5
7	Narain Das	1503	S6
8	Suraj Mal		S7
9	Surthan	1531	S8
10	Arjun		BS7
11	Surjan	1554	S10
12	Bhoja	1585	S11
13	Ratan	1607	S12
14	Chhatra Sal	1631	GS13
15	Bhao Singh	1658	S14
16	Aniruddha Singh	1678	BGS15
17	Budh Singh	1706	S16
18	Dalel Singh	1729	S17
19	Ummed Singh	1748	S18
20	Ajit Singh	1770	S19
21	Bishan Singh	1770	S20
22	Ram Singh	1821	S21
23	Raghubir Singh	1889	AS22
24	Ishwari Singh	1927	BS23
25	Bahadur Singh	1945–1949	AS24

f *Chauhan Raos/Maharaos of Kotah* 1625–1949

1	Madhu Singh (S13 Bundi)	1625	
2	Mokund Singh	1656	S1
3	Jagat Singh	1657	S2
4	Paim Singh	1669	BS2
5	Kishor Singh I	1669	S1
6	Ram Singh I	1685	S5
7	Bhima Singh I	1707	S6
8	Arjun Singh	1719	S7
9	Durjan Sal	1723	S7
10	Ajit Singh	1756	GG6
11	Chhatra Sal I	1759	S10
12	Goman Singh	1765	S10
13	Ummed Singh I	1770	S12
14	Kishor Singh II	1819	S13
15	Ram Singh II	1828	S14
16	Chhatra Sal Singh II	1866	S15
17	Ummed Singh II	1889	AS16
18	Bhima Singh II	1941–1949	S17

g *Bhati Rawals/Maharawals of Jaisalmer c.*1180–1949

1	Jaisal	c.1180	

2	Salivahan I		SI
3	Baijal		S2
4	Kelan		SI
5	Chachigdeva I	c.1219	S4
6	Karan Singh I	c.1250	GS5
7	Lakhasena	c.1278	
8	Punyapala	c.1281	
9	Jait Singh I	c.1281	B6
10	Mulraja I	c.1300.	S9

11	Duda		GG4
12	Ghar Singh	c.1331	BS10
13	Kehar	1361	B12
14	Lakhmana		SI3
15	Bairi Singh	1436	
16	Chachigdeva II	c.1448	SI5
17	Devidas	1467	SI6
18	Jait Singh II	1496	SI7
19	Karan Singh II	1528	SI8
20	Lunkaran	1528	SI7
21	Malladeva	1550	S20
22	Har Raja	1561	S21
23	Bhima	1577	S22
24	Kalyandas	1613	S22
25	Manohardas	1650	S24
26	Sabal Singh	1650	GG21
27	Amar Singh	1661	S26
28	Jaswant Singh	1702	S27
29	Budh Singh	1707	GS28
30	Tej Singh	1721	S28
31	Sawai Singh	1722	S30
32	Akhai Singh	1722	B29
33	Mulraja II	1762	S32
34	Gaja Singh	1819	GS33
35	Ranjit Singh	1846	N34
36	Bairi Sal	1864	B35
37	Salivahan II	1891	AS36
38	Jawahir Singh	1914	DTI
39	Girdhar Singh	1949.	S38

h *Maharajas of Bharatpur* 1722–1948

1	Badan Singh	1722	
2	Suraj Mal	1756	ASI
3	Jawahir Singh	1763	S2
4	Ratan Singh	1768	S2
5	Kesri Singh	1769–1774	S4

6	Ranjit Singh	1785	S2
7	Randhir Singh	1805	S6
8	Baldeo Singh	1823	S6

9	Durjan Sal	1825	FBS8
10	Balwant Singh	1826	S8
11	Jaswant Singh	1853	S10
12	Ram Singh	1893	S11
13	Brijendra Sawai Kishan Singh	1900	S12
14	Brijendra Singh	1929–1948	S13

i *Nawabs of Tonk* 1798–1948

1	Amir Khan	1798	
2	Wazir Muhammad Khan	1834	S1
3	Muhammad 'Ali Khan	1864	S2
4	Hafiz Muhammad Ibrahim 'Ali Khan	1867	S3
5	Hafiz Muhammad Sa'adat 'Ali Khan	1930–1948	S4

207 INDIA MALWA

a *Kshatrapa Dynasty c.*110–395 AD

1	Chashtana	*c.*110	
2	Rudradaman I		GSI
3	Damajadasri I	*c.*170	S2
4	Jivadaman (1)	*c.*175	S3
5	Rudrasimha I (1)	*c.*175	S2
6	Isvaradatta	*c.*188	
	Rudrasimha I (2)	*c.*191	
	Jivadaman (2)	*c.*197	
7	Rudrasena I	*c.*200	S5
8	Sanghadaman	*c.*222	S5
9	Damasena	*c.*223	S5
10	Yasodaman I	*c.*238	S9
11	Vijayasena	*c.*240	S9
12	Damajadasri II	*c.*250	S9
13	Rudrasena II	*c.*255	BS12
14	Visvasimha	*c.*279	S13
15	Bhartridaman	*c.*282	S13
16	Rudrasimha II	*c.*304	
17	Yasodaman II	*c.*316	S16
18	Rudradaman II	*c.*332	
19	Rudrasena III	*c.*348	S18
20	Simhasena	*c.*380	STS19
21	Rudrasena IV	?	S20
22	Rudrasimha III	*c.*388–395	

b *Paramara Dynasty c.*800–1305

1	Upendra	*c.*800	
2	Vairisimha I	*c.*818	S1
3	Siyaka I	*c.*843	S2
4	Vakpati	*c.*893	S3
5	Vairisimha II	*c.*918	S4
6	Siyaka II	*c.*948	S5

7	Vakpatiraja	c.974	s6
8	Sindhuraja	c.995	s6
9	Bhoja I	c.1010	s8
10	Jayasimha I	c.1055	s9
11	Udayaditya	c.1060	s8
12	Lakshmanadeva	c.1087	s11
13	Naravarman	c.1097	s11
14	Yasovarman	c.1134	s13
15	Jayavarman I	c.1142	s14
16	Vindhyavarman	c.1160	s15
17	Subhatavarman	c.1193	s16
18	Arjunavarman I	c.1210	s17
19	Devapala	c.1218	BGS15
20	Jaitugideva	c.1239	s19
21	Jayavarman II	c.1256	s19
22	Jayasimha II	c.1269	
23	Arjunavarman II	c.1274	
24	Bhoja II	c.1283	
25	Mahlakadeva	?–c.1305	

c *Ghurid Sultans of Malwa* 1390–1436

1	Dilavar Khan Husain	1390	
2	Alp Khan Hushang	1405	s1
3	Ghazni Khan Muhammad	1435	s2
4	Mas'ud Khan	1436.	s3

d *Khalji Sultans of Malwa* 1436–1531

1	Mahmud Shah I	1436	
2	Ghiyath Shah	1469	s1
3	Nasir Shah	1500	s2
4	Mahmud Shah II	1511–1531	s3

e *Faruqi Sultans of Khandesh* 1370–1601

1	Malik Raja Faruqi	1370	
2	Nasir Khan	1399	s1
3	'Adil Khan I	1437	s2
4	Miran Mubarak Khan I	1441	s3
5	'Adil Khan II	1457	s4
6	Da'ud Khan	1503	s4
7	Ghazni Khan	1510	s6
8	'Alam Khan	1510	
9	'Adil Khan III	1510	BS3
10	Miran Muhammad I	1520	s9
11	Ahmad Shah	1537	
12	Mubarak Shah II	1537	s9
13	Miran Muhammad II	1566	s12
14	Hasan Shah	1576	s13
15	'Adil Shah IV 'Ali Khan	1577	s12
16	Bahadur Shah	1597–1601	s15

f *Holkar Maharajas of Indore* 1728–1948

1	Malhar Rao Holkar	1728	
2	Malle Rao	1764–1766	GS1
3	Ahalya Bai★	1765–1795	M2
4	Tukoji Holkar	1795	
5	Jaswant Rao I	1798	S4
6	Malhar Rao II	1811	S5
7	Hari Rao	1834	S6
8	Tukoji Rao II	1843	S7
9	Shivaji Rao	1886	S8
10	Tukoji Rao III	1903	S9
11	Jaswant Rao II	1926–1948	S10

g *Nawabs of Bhopal* 1723–1948

1	Dost Muhammad Khan	1723	
2	Muhammad Khan	1740	S1
3	Yar Muhammad Khan	1740	S1
4	Faid Muhammad Khan	1754	S3
5	Hayat Muhammad Khan	1777	S3
6	Wazir Muhammad Khan	1807	BS3
7	Nadhr Muhammad Khan	1816	S6
8	Kudsiyya Begum★	1820	W7/GS5
9	Sikandar Begum★	1844	D7/8
10	Shah Jahan Begum★	1868	D9
11	Sultan Jahan Begum★	1901	D10
12	Hamid-Allah Khan	1926–1948	S11

208 INDIA GUJARAT AND SAURASHTRA

a *Maitraka Dynasty of Vallabhi* c.475–767

1	Bhatarka	c.475	
2	Dharasena I		S1
3	Dronasimha	c.500	S1
4	Dhruvasena I	c.525	S1
5	Dharapatta	c.545	S1
6	Guhasena	c.556	S5
7	Dharasena II	c.570	S6
8	Siladitya I	c.606	S7
9	Kharagraha I	c.616	S7
10	Dharasena III	c.623	S9
11	Dhruvasena II	c.640	S9
12	Dharasena IV	c.644	S11
13	Dhruvasena III	c.651	GS8
14	Kharagraha II	c.656	B13
15	Siladitya II	c.662	BS14
16	Siladitya III		S15
17	Siladitya IV		S16
18	Siladitya V		S17
19	Siladitya VI	c.766–767	S18

b *Chaulukya Dynasty of Anhilavara c.940–1244*

1	Mulraja I	c.940	
2	Chamundaraja	c.995	S1
3	Vallabharaja	c.1010	S2
4	Durlabharaja	c.1010	S2
5	Bhima I	c.1022	BS4
6	Karnadeva	c.1064	S5
7	Jayasimha I	c.1094	S6
8	Kumarapala	c.1145	BGG6
9	Ajayapala	c.1171	BS8
10	Mulraja II	c.1176	S9
11	Bhima II	c.1178–1241	S9
12	Jayasimha II	c.1223.	
13	Tribhuvanapala	c.1241–1244	

c *Vaghela Dynasty of Anhilavara c.1244–1304*

1	Visala	c.1244	
2	Arjuna	c.1262	BS1
3	Sarangadeva	c.1275	S2
4	Karnadeva	c.1297–1304	BS3

d *Chudsama Dynasty of Saurashtra c.845–1472*

1	Chandrachud	c.845	
2	Mulraja	907	GS1
3	Vishvara	915	S2
4	Graharipu	940	S3
5	Kawat I	982	S4
6	Mahipala I	1003–1010	S5
7	Navghan I	1020	S6
8	Khengar I	1044	S7
9	Navghan II	1067	S8
10	Khengar II	1094–1113	S9
11	Navghan III	1125	S10
12	Kawat II	1140	S11
13	Jaya Singh I	1152	S12
14	Raya Singh	1184	S13
15	Mahipala II	1184	S14
16	Jaya Malla	1201	S15
17	Mahipala III	1230	S16
18	Khengar III	1253	S17
19	Mandlik I	1260	S18
20	Navghan IV	1306	S19
21	Mahipala IV	1308	S20
22	Khengar IV	1325	S21
23	Jaya Singh II	1352	S22
24	Mahipala V	1369	S23
25	Mokala Singh	1373	S24

26	Mandlik II	1397	S25
27	Melag	1400	S25
28	Jaya Singh III	1415	S27
29	Mahipala VI	1440	S28
30	Mandlik III	1451–1472	S29

e *Muzaffarid Sultans of Gujarat* 1391–1583

1	Muzaffar Shah I	1391	
2	Ahmad Shah I	1411	GS1
3	Muhammad Karim Shah	1442	S2
4	Qutb-ud-Din Ahmad Shah II	1451	S3
5	Da'ud Shah	1458	S2
6	Mahmud Shah I Begara	1458	S3
7	Muzaffar Shah II	1511	S6
8	Sikandar Shah	1526	S7
9	Nasir Khan Mahmud II	1526	S7
10	Bahadur Shah	1526	S7
11	Miran Muhammad (I of Khandesh)	1537	GD7
12	Mahmud Shah III	1537	BS10
13	Ahmad Shah III	1554	S12
14	Muzaffar Shah III (1)	1561–1573	S12
	Muzaffar Shah III (2)	1583.	

f *Jadeja Raos/Maharaos of Kachh (Cutch)* 1548–1948

1	Khengar I	1548	
2	Bharmal I	1585	S1
3	Bhojaraja	1631	S2
4	Khengar II	1645	GS2
5	Tamachi	1654	B4
6	Rayadhan I	1662	S5
7	Pragmal I	1697	S6
8	Godji I	1715	S7
9	Desal I	1718	S8
10	Lakha	1741	S9
11	Godji II	1760	S10
12	Rayadhan II	1778	S11
13	Bharmal II	1814	S12
14	Desal II	1819	S13
15	Pragmal II	1860	S14
16	Khengar III	1876	S15
17	Vijayaraja	1942	S16
18	Madan Singh	1948.	S17

g *Gaekwar Maharajas of Baroda* 1721–1949

1	Pilaji Rao Gaekwar	1721	
2	Damaji Rao	1732	S1
3	Govind Rao (1)	1768	S2
4	Sayaji Rao I	1771–1789	S2
5	Fateh Singh (Regent)	1771–1789	S2

6	Manaji Rao	1789	S2
	Govind Rao (2)	1793	
7	Anand Rao	1800	S3
8	Sayaji Rao II	1818	S3
9	Ganpat Rao	1847	S8
10	Khande Rao	1856	S8
11	Malhar Rao	1870	S8
12	Sayaji Rao III	1875	AS10
13	Pratap Singh	1939–1949	GS12

209 INDIA KASHMIR

a *Karkota Dynasty 596–857*

1	Durlabhavardhana	596	
2	Durlabhaka	632	
3	Chandrapida	682	
4	Tarapida	682	
5	Muktapida Lalitaditya	695	
6	Kuvalayapida	732	S5
7	Vajraditya Bappiyaka	733	S5
8	Prithivyapida I	740	S7
9	Sangramapida	744	S7
10	Jayapida	751	S7
11	Jajja	782	
12	Lalitapida	785	S10
13	Prithivyapida II	797	S10
14	Chippatajayapida	804	
15	Ajitapida	816	GS7
16	Anangapida		S13
17	Utpalapida	?–857	S15

b *Utpala Dynasty 857–939*

18	Avantivarman	857	
19	Shankaravarman	884	S18
20	Gopalavarman	903	S19
21	Samkatavarman	905	S19
22	Sugandha★	905	W19
23	Nirjitavarman (1)	907	BGS18
24	Partha (1)	907	S23
	Nirjitavarman (2)	923	
25	Chakravarman (1)	924	S23
26	Suravarman I	935	S23
	Partha (2)	936	
	Chakravarman (2)	936	
27	Sambhuvardhana	936	
28	Unmattavanti	938	S24
29	Suravarman II	939.	

c *Hindu Kings* 939–1338

30	Yasaskaradeva	939	
31	Samgramadeva I	948	S30
32	Parvagupta	949	
33	Kshemagupta	950	S32
34	Abhimanyu	958	S33
35	Nandigupta	972	S34
36	Tribhuvana	973	S34
37	Bhimagupta	975	S34
38	Didda★	980	W33
39	Samgramaraja	1003	N38
40	Hariraja	1028	S39
41	Ananta	1028	S39
42	Kalasa	1063	S41
43	Utkarsha	1089	S42
44	Harsha	1089	S42
45	Uchchala	1101–1112	
46	Salhana	1111–1112	B45
47	Sussala (1)	1112	B45
48	Bhikshachara	1120	GS44
	Sussala (2)	1121–1128	
49	Jayasimha (1)	1123–1131	S47
50	Lothana	1131	B45
51	Mallarjuna	1131	S47
	Jayasimha (2)	1132	
52	Paramanuka	1155	S49
53	Vantideva	1165	S52
54	Vuppadeva	1172	
55	Jassaka	1181	B54
56	Jagadeva	1199	S55
57	Rajadeva	1213	S56
58	Samgramadeva II	1236	S57
59	Ramadeva	1252	S58
60	Lakshmanadeva	1273	S59
61	Simhadeva	1286	
62	Suhadeva	1301	B61
63	Rinchana Sadr-ud-Din	1320	H65
64	Udayanadeva	1323	H65
65	Kotadevi★	1338.	D62

d *Swati Sultans of Kashmir* 1339–1561

1	Shams-ud-Din Shah Mirza Swati	1339	
2	Jamshid	1349	S1
3	'Ala-ud-Din 'Ali Shir	1350	S1
4	Shihab-ud-Din Shirashamak	1359	S1
5	Qutb-ud-Din Hindal	1378	S1
6	Sikandar	1394	S5
7	'Ali Mirza Khan	1416	S6
8	Zain-ul-'Abidin Shahi Khan	1420	S6

9	Haidar Shah Hajji Khan	1470	s8
10	Hasan	1471	s9
11	Muhammad (1)	1489	s10
12	Fath Shah (1)	1490	BS9
	Muhammad (2)	1498	
	Fath Shah (2)	1499	
	Muhammad (3)	1500	
13	Ibrahim (1)	1526	S11
14	Nazuk (1)	1627	S12
	Muhammad (4)	1529	
15	Shams-ud-Din II	1533	S11
	Nazuk (2)	1540	
16	Haidar Dughlat (s6 Kashgar)	1540	
	Nazuk (3)	1551	
	Ibrahim (2)	1552	
17	Isma'il	1555	S11
18	Habib	1557–1561	S17

e *Chak Sultans of Kashmir* 1561–1589

20	Ghazi Khan Chak	1561	
21	Nasr-ud-Din Husain	1563	UB & FBS20
22	Zahir-ud-Din 'Ali	1569	B21
23	Nasr-ud-Din Yusuf	1579	S22
24	Ya'qub	1586–1589	S23

f *Doghra Maharajas of Kashmir* 1846–1952

1	Gulab Singh	1846	
2	Ranbir Singh	1857	S1
3	Partab Singh	1885	S2
4	Hari Singh	1925–1952	BS3

210 **INDIA** KINGS OF LADAKH *c.*1555–1842

1	bKra-sis-rnam-rgyal	*c.*1555	
2	Ts'e-dban-rnam-rgyal	*c.*1575	BS1
3	rNam-rgyal-mgon-po	*c.*1595–1600	B2
4	'Jam-dbyangs-rnam-rgyal	*c.*1595–1616	B2
5	Seng-ge-rnam-rgyal (1)	1616	S4
6	Nor-bu-rnam-rgyal	1623	S4
	Seng-ge-rnam-rgyal (2)	1624	
7	bDe-ldan-rnam-rgyal	1642	S5
8	Nyi-ma-rnam-rgyal	1694	GS7
9	bDe-skyong-rnam-rgyal	1729	s8
10	P'un-tsogs-rnam-rgyal	1739	s9
11	Ts'e-dbang-rnam-rgyal	1753	s10
12	Ts'e-brtan-rnam-rgyal	1782	S11
13	Ts'e-dpal-rnam-rgyal (1)	1802–1837	S11
14	Ts'e-dban-rab-brtan-rnam-rgyal	1830–1837	S13

| | Ts'e-dpal-rnam-rgyal (2) | 1839 | |
| 15 | Kun-dga-rnam-rgyal | 1840–1842 | S14 |

211 **INDIA** KINGS OF NEPAL

a *Raghavadeva Dynasty c.879–1046*

1	Raghavadeva	c.879
2	Jayadeva	
3	Vikramadeva	
4	Narendradeva I	
5	Gunakamadeva I	
6	Udayadeva	
7	Nirbhayadeva	c.1008
8	Rudradeva	c.1008
9	Bhoja	c.1015
10	Lakshmikamadeva I	c.1015
11	Jayakamadeva	c.1039–1046

b *Thakuri Dynasty 1046–1201*

1	Bhaskaradeva	1046
2	Baladeva	1059
3	Pradyumnakamadeva	1064
4	Nagarjunadeva	
5	Shankaradeva	1068
6	Vamadeva	1080
7	Harshadeva	1090
8	Sivadeva	1118
9	Indradeva	1128
10	Manadeva	
11	Narendradeva II	
12	Anandadeva	1146
13	Rudradeva	
14	Amritadeva	1176
15	Ratnadeva	
16	Somesvaradeva	
17	Gunakamadeva II	1187
18	Lakshmikamadeva II	1193
19	Vijayakamadeva	1196–1201

c *Malla Kings of Nepal c.1201–1482*

1	Arimalladeva	c.1201
2	Ranasura	c.1216
3	Abhayamalla	c.1216
4	Jayadevamalla	c.1235
5	Jayabhimadeva	c.1258
6	Jayasimhamalla	c.1271
7	Anantamalla	c.1274
8	Jayanandadeva	c.1310
9	Jayarudramalla	c.1320–1326

10	Jayarimalla	c.1320–1344	
11	Jayarajadeva	c.1347	s8
12	Jayarjunamalla	c.1361	S11
13	Jayasthitimalla	c.1382	
14	Jayadharmamalla	c.1395–1408	S13
15	Jayakitimalla	c.1395–1403	S13
16	Jayajyotimalla	c.1395–1428	S13
17	Jayayakshamalla	c.1428–1482	S16

d Malla Kings of Katmandu 1482–1768

1	Ratnamalla (s17 Nepal)	c.1482	
2	Suryamalla	c.1520	SI
3	Amaramalla	c.1530	S2
4	Narendramalla	c.1538	S3
5	Mahendramalla	c.1560	S4
6	Sadasivamalla	c.1574–1583	S5
7	Sivasimhamalla	c.1578–1620	S5
8	Lakshminarasimhamalla	c.1620	GS7
9	Pratapamalla	c.1641	s8
10	Jayanripendramalla	c.1674	S9
11	Parthivendramalla	c.1680	S9
12	Bhupendramalla	c.1687	S11
13	Bhaskaramalla	c.1700	S12
14	Mahendrasimhamalla	c.1714	DT7
15	Jagajjayamalla	1722	BGD11
16	Jayaprakasamalla	1736–1768	S15

e Malla Kings of Bhatgaon 1482–1769

1	Rayamalla (s17 Nepal)	c.1482	
2	Pranamalla	c.1519	GSI
3	Vishvamalla	c.1547	S2
4	Trailokyamalla	c.1560	S3
5	Jagatjyotimalla	c.1613	S4
6	Naresamalla	c.1637	S5
7	Jagatprakasamalla	c.1644	s6
8	Jitamitramalla	c.1673	S7
9	Bhupatindramalla	c.1696	s8
10	Ranjitamalla	1722–1769	S9

f Malla Kings of Patan c.1620–1768

1	Siddhinarasimhamalla (GS7 Katmandu)	c.1620	
2	Srinivasamalla	c.1661	SI
3	Yoganarendramalla	c.1684	S2
4	Lokaprakasamalla	c.1705	GD3
5	Indramalla	c.1706	GD2
6	Mahendramalla	c.1709	S3
7	Hrddhinarasimhamalla	c.1714	GG2
8	Mahendrasimhamalla (of Katmandu)	c.1717	
9	Jayayogaprakasamalla	c.1722	
10	Vishnumalla	c.1729	STS5

11 Rajyaprakasamalla (s15 Katmandu) *c.*1745 HST8
12 Vishvajitamalla *c.*1758
13 Jayaprakasamalla (of Katmandu) *c.*1760
14 Ranjitamalla *c.*1761
15 Dalamardana Shah (B1 Gurkha) 1763
16 Tejanarasimhamalla 1765–1768

g *Karnataka Kings in Nepal c.*1324–1418

1 Harisimha (of Tirhut) *c.*1324
2 Matisimha *c.*1387
4 Saktisimha *c.*1413–1418

h *Gurkha Kings of Nepal since* 1768

1 Prithvi Narayan Shah 1768
2 Pratap Singh Shah 1775 S1
3 Rana Bahadur Shah 1778 S2
4 Girvana Judha Bikram Shah 1799 S3
5 Rajendra Bir Bikram Shah 1816 S4
6 Surendra Bir Bikram Shah 1847 S5
7 Prithvi Bir Bikram Shah 1881 GS6
8 Tribhuvana Bir Bikram Shah 1911 S7
9 Mahendra Bir Bikram Shah 1955 S8
10 Birendra Bir Bikram Shah 1972 S9

212 **INDIA** MAHARAJAS OF SIKKIM

Namgyal Dynasty 1642–1975

1 Phuntsog Namgyal 1642
2 Tensung Namgyal 1670 S1
3 Chador Namgyal 1686 S2
4 Gyurmed Namgyal 1717 S3
5 Namgyal Phuntsog 1733 S4
6 Tenzing Namgyal 1780 S5
7 Tsugphud Namgyal 1793 S6
8 Sidkeong Namgyal I 1863 S7
9 Thutob Namgyal 1874 S7
10 Sidkeong Namgyal II 1914 S9
11 Tashi Namgyal 1914 S9
12 Palden Thondup Namgyal 1963–1975 S11

213 **INDIA** WANGCHUK KINGS OF BHUTAN SINCE 1907

1 Ugyen Wangchuk 1907
2 Jigme Wangchuk 1926 S1
3 Jigme Dorji Wangchuk 1952 S2
4 Jigme Singhi Wangchuk 1972 S3

214 INDIA BENGAL

a *Pala Dynasty c.750–1161*

1	Gopala I	c.750	
2	Dharmapala	c.770	S1
3	Devapala	c.810	S2
4	Vigrahapala I	c.850	BGS2
5	Narayanapala	c.875	S4
6	Rajyapala	c.908	S5
7	Gopala II	c.935	S6
8	Vigrahapala II	c.952	S7
9	Mahipala I	c.988	S8
10	Nayapala	c.1038	S9
11	Vigrahapala III	c.1055	S10
12	Mahipala II	c.1070	S11
13	Shurapala	c.1075	S11
14	Ramapala	c.1077	S11
15	Kumarapala	c.1120	S14
16	Gopala III	c.1125	S15
17	Madanapala	c.1144–1161	S14

b *Sena Dynasty c.1030–1250*

1	Samantasena	?c.1030	
2	Hemantasena		S1
3	Vijayasena	c.1095	S2
4	Ballalasena	c.1159	S3
5	Lakshmanasena	c.1178	S4
6	Vishvarupasena	c.1205	S5
7	Keshavasena	c.1220–1250	S5

c *Sultans of Bengal 1282–1576*

1	Nasir-ud-Din Bughra Khan (s9 Delhi)	1282	
2	Rukn-ud-Din Kai-Ka'us	1291	S1
3	Shams-ud-Din Firuz Shah I	1298	S1
4	Shihab-ud-Din Bughra (West Bengal)	1318–1319	S3
5	Ghiyath-ud-Din Bhadur (East Bengal; West 1319–1323)	1318–1330	S3
6	Nasir-ud-Din Ibrahim (West)	1323–1325	S3
7	Bahram Shah (East)	1324–1336	
8	Qadr Khan (West)	1325–1339	
9	'Izz-ud-Din A'zam-ul-Mulk (Satgaon)	1323–1339	
10	Fakhr-ud-Din Mubarak Shah (East)	1336–1349	
11	'Ala-ud-Din 'Ali Shah (West)	1339–1345	
12	Ikhtiyar-ud-Din Ghazi Shah (East)	1349–1352	S10
13	Shams-ud-Din Ilyas Shah (West; East 1352)	1345–1357	
14	Sikandar Shah I	1358	S13
15	Ghiyath-ud-Din A'zam Shah	1390	S14
16	Saif-ud-Din Hamza Shah	1410	S15
17	Shihab-ud-Din Bayazid Shah I	1412	S16
18	'Ala-ud-Din Firuz Shah II	1414	S17

19	Raja Ganesh	1415	
20	Jalal-ud-Din Muhammad Shah	1418	S19
21	Shams-ud-Din Ahmad Shah	1432	S20
22	Nasir-ud-Din Mahmud Shah I	1437	GS13
23	Rukn-ud-Din Barbak Shah I	1460	S22
24	Shams-ud-Din Yusuf Shah	1474	S23
25	Sikandar Shah II	1481	S24
26	Jalal-ud-Din Fath Shah	1481	S22
27	Sultan Shahzada Barbak Shah II	1487	
28	Saif-ud-Din Firuz Shah III	1487	
29	Nasir-ud-Din Mahmud Shah II	1490	S26
30	Shams-ud-Din Muzaffar Shah	1491	
31	'Ala-ud-Din Husain Shah	1494	
32	Nasir-ud-Din Nusrat Shah	1519	S31
33	'Ala-ud-Din Firuz Shah IV	1532	S32
34	Ghiyath-ud-Din Mahmud Shah III	1533	S31
35	Shir Shah Sur	1539	
36	Khidr Khan	1540	
37	Muhammad Khan Sur	1545	
38	Khidr Khan Bahadur Shah	1555	S37
39	Ghiyath-ud-Din Jalal Shah	1561	S37
40	Sulayman Kararani	1564	
41	Bayazid Shah II	1572	S40
42	Da'ud Shah	1572–1576	S40

d *Nawabs of Bengal* 1703–1770

1	Murshid Quli Ja'far Khan	1703	
2	Shuja-ud-Din	1727	HD1
3	Safaraz Khan	1739	S2
4	'Alivardi Khan	1740	
5	Siraj-ud-Dawlah	1756	GD4
6	Mir Ja'far (1)	1757	
7	Mir Qasim	1760	HD6
	Mir Ja'far (2)	1763	
8	Najm-ud-Dawlah	1765	s6
9	Saif-ud-Dawlah	1766–1770	s6

215 INDIA ASSAM

a *Kings of Kamarupa c.355–1228*

1	Pushyavarman	c.355	
2	Samudravarman	c.380	S1
3	Balavarman I	c.405	S2
4	Kalyanavarman	c.420	S3
5	Ganapativarman	c.440	S4
6	Mahendravarman	c.450	S5
7	Narayanavarman	c.485	s6
8	Bhutivarman	c.510	S7
9	Chandramukhavarman	c.555	s8

10	Sthitivarman	*c*.565	S9
11	Susthitavarman	*c*.585	S10
12	Supratisthitivarman	*c*.593	S11
13	Bhaskaravarman	*c*.594	S11
14	Salastambha	*c*.650	
15	Vigrahastambha	*c*.675	S14
16	Palaka	?	S15
17	Kumara	?	S16
18	Vajradeva	?	S17
19	Harshadeva	*c*.725	S18
20	Balavarman II	*c*.750–765	S19
		————	
21	Salambha	*c*.790	
22	Arathi	*c*.810	B21
23	Harjjaravarman	*c*.815	S22
24	Vanamalavarmadeva	*c*.835	S23
25	Jayamala	*c*.865	S24
26	Balavarman III	*c*.885–910	S25
27	Tyagasimha	*c*.970	
28	Brahmapala	*c*.990	
29	Ratnapala	*c*.1010	S28
30	Indrapala	*c*.1040	GS29
31	Gopala	*c*.1065	S30
32	Harshapala	*c*.1080	S31
33	Dharmapala	*c*.1095	S32
34	Jayapala	*c*.1120	S33
35	Vaidyadeva	*c*.1138	
36	Rayarideva	*c*.1145	
37	Udayakarna	?	S36
38	Vallabhadeva	*c*.1175	S37
39	Vishvasundaradeva	*c*.1195–1228	

b *Ahom Kings* 1228–1838

1	Sukapha	1228	
2	Suteupha	1268	S1
3	Subinpha	1281	S2
4	Sukhangpha	1293	S3
5	Sukhrangpha	1332	S4
6	Sutupha	1364–1376	S4
		————	
7	Tyaokhamti	1380–1389	S4
8	Sudangpha	1397	S7
9	Sujangpha	1407	
10	Suphakpha	1422	
11	Susenpha	1439	S10
12	Suhenpha	1488	S11
13	Supimpha	1493	S12
14	Dihingia Raja	1497	S13

15	Garhgaya Raja	1539	S14
16	Khora Raja	1552	
17	Pratap Singh	1603	
18	Bhaga Raja	1641	
19	Nariya Raja	1644	
20	Jayadhvaj Singh	1648	
21	Chakradhvaj Singh	1663	
22	Udayaditya Singh	1669	
23	Ramdhvaj	1673	
24	Suhung	1675	
25	Gobar Raja	1675	GG14
26	Sujinpha	1675	
27	Sudaipha	1677	
28	Lara Raja	1679	
29	Gadadhar Singh	1681	S25
30	Rudra Singh	1696	S29
31	Siva Singh	1714	S30
32	Pramatta Singh	1744	S30
33	Rajesvar Singh	1751	S30
34	Lakshmi Singh	1769	S30
35	Gaurinath Singh	1780	S34
36	Kamalesvar Singh	1795	3G29
37	Chandrakant Singh (1)	1811	B36
38	Purandar Singh (1)	1817	3G33
	Chandrakant Singh (2)	1819–1821	

Purandar Singh (2) (Upper Assam)	1833–1838	

216 **INDIA** ORISSA

a *Somavamsi Dynasty c.915–1118*

1	Sivagupta	*c.*915	
2	Janamejaya Mahabhavagupta I	*c.*935	S1
3	Yayati Mahasivagupta I	*c.*970	S2
4	Bhimaratha Mahabhavagupta II	*c.*1000	S3
5	Dharmaratha Mahasivagupta II	*c.*1015	S4
6	Nahusha Mahabhavagupta III	*c.*1020	S4
7	Chandihara Yayati Mahasivagupta III	*c.*1025	
8	Uddyotakesari Mahabhavagupta IV	*c.*1055	S7
9	Karnakesari	*c.*1080–1118	

b *Ganga Dynasty c.1118–1434*

1	Anantavarman Chodaganga	*c.*1118	
2	Kamarnava	*c.*1148	S1
3	Raghava	*c.*1157	S1
4	Rajaraja I	*c.*1171	S1
5	Aniyankabhima I	*c.*1192	S1
6	Rajaraja II	*c.*1205	S5
7	Aniyankabhima II	*c.*1216	S6

8	Narasimha I	c.1238	s7
9	Bhanudeva I	c.1264	s8
10	Narasimha II	c.1279	s9
11	Bhanudeva II	c.1306	s10
12	Narasimha III	c.1328	s11
13	Bhanudeva III	c.1352	s12
14	Narasimha IV	c.1378	s13
15	Bhanudeva IV	c.1414–1434	s14

c *Gajapati Dynasty* 1434–1541

1	Kapilendra	1434	
2	Purushottama	1467	s1
3	Prataparudra	1497	s2
4	Kaluadeva	1540	s3
5	Kakharuadeva	1541.	s3

d *Kings of Orissa* 1541–1568

1	Govindaraja Vidyadhara	1541	
2	Chakrapratapa	1549	s1
3	Narasimha Jana	1557	s2
4	Raghurama Chhotra	1558	s2
5	Mukundadeva Harichandana	1560–1568	

217 INDIA MAHARASHTRA

a *Satavahana Dynasty* c.271 BC–174 AD

1	Simuka	c.271 BC
2	Krishna	c.248
3	Satakarni I	c.230
4	Purnotsanga	c.220
5	Skandastambhi	c.202
6	Satakarni II	c.184
7	Lambodara	c.128
8	Apilaka	c.110
9	Meghasvati	c.98
10	Svati	c.80
11	Skandasvati	c.62
12	Mrigendra Svatikarna	c.55
13	Kuntala Svatikarna	c.52
14	Svatikarna	c.44
15	Pulumavi I	c.43
16	Gaurakrishna	c.19
17	Hala	c.6 AD
18	Mandulaka	c.7
19	Purindrasena	c.12
20	Sundara Svatikarni	c.33
21	Chakora Svatikarna	c.34
22	Sivasvati	c.34
23	Gautamiputra Satakarni	c.62

24 Pulumavi II Vasishthiputra	c.86	
25 Siva Sri Satakarni	c.114	
26 Sivaskanda Satakarni	c.121	
27 Yajna Sri Satakarni	c.128	
28 Vijaya	c.157	
29 Chandra Sri Satakarni	c.163	
30 Pulumavi III	c.166–174	

Note: Satavahana chronology is very uncertain and disputed – the above table follows Yazdani (see Bibliography)

b *Vakataka Dynasty c.255–510* AD

1 Vindhyasakti	c.255	
2 Pravarasena	c.275	S1
3 Rudrasena I	c.335	GS2
4 Prithvishena I	c.360	S3
5 Rudrasena II	c.385	S4
6 Divakarasena	c.390	S5
7 Damodarasena	c.403	S5
8 Narendrasena	c.440	BS7
9 Prithvishena II	c.460	S8
10 Harishena	c.480–510	DT2

c *Chalukya Dynasty of Badami* 543–757

1 Pulakesin I	543	
2 Kirtivarman I	566	S1
3 Mangalesa	597	S1
4 Pulakesin II	609–642	S2
	———	
5 Vikramaditya I	655	S4
6 Vinayaditya	680	S5
7 Vijayaditya	696	S6
8 Vikramaditya II	733	S7
9 Kirtivarman II	746–757	S8

d *Rashtrakuta Dynasty* 754–982

1 Dantidurga	754	
2 Krishna I	768	FB1
3 Govinda I	783	S2
4 Dhruva	?	S2
5 Govinda II	793	S4
6 Amoghavarsha I	814	S5
7 Krishna II	877	S6
8 Indra I	915	GS7
9 Amoghavarsha II	917	S8
10 Govinda III	918	S8
11 Amoghavarsha III	934	B8
12 Krishna III	939	S11
13 Khottiga	968	S11

14 Karka Amoghavarsha IV	972	BS13
15 Indra II	973–982	GS12

e *Chalukya Dynasty of Kalyana 973–1200*

1 Taila Ahavamalla (DT7 Badami)	973	
2 Satyasraya Irivabedanga	997	S1
3 Vikramaditya I	1008	BS2
4 Ayyana	1014	B3
5 Jayasimha	1015	B3
6 Somesvara I	1042	S5
7 Somesvara II	1068	S6
8 Vikramaditya II	1076	S6
9 Somesvara III	1127	S8
10 Jagadekamalla	1138	S9
11 Tailapa	1151–1156	S9
12 Somesvara IV	1184–1200	S11

f *Kalachuri Dynasty of Kalyana 1156–1184*

1 Bijjala	1156	
2 Somesvara	1168	S1
3 Sankama	1177	S1
4 Ahavamalla	1180	S1
5 Singhana	1183–1184	S1

g *Yadava Dynasty of Devagiri c.1185–1317*

1 Bhillama	c.1185	
2 Jaitugi	c.1192	S1
3 Singhana	c.1200	S2
4 Krishna	1247	GS3
5 Mahadeva	1261	B4
6 Amana	1271	S5
7 Ramachandra	1271	S4
8 Sankaradeva	1311	S7
9 Harapaladeva	1313–1317	

h *Bahmanid Sultans of the Deccan 1347–1527*

1 'Ala-ud-Din Hasan Bahman Shah	1347	
2 Muhammad Shah I	1358	S1
3 'Ala-ud-Din Mujahid Shah	1375	S2
4 Da'ud Shah	1378	S1
5 Muhammad Shah II	1378	B2
6 Ghiyath-ud-Din	1397	S5
7 Shams-ud-Din	1397	S5
8 Taj-ud-Din Firuz Shah	1397	BS2
9 Ahmad Shah I Wali	1422	B8
10 'Ala-ud-Din Ahmad Shah II	1436	S9
11 'Ala-ud-Din Humayun Zalim Shah	1458	S10
12 Nizam Shah	1461	S11
13 Muhammad Shah III Lashkari	1463	S11

14	Mahmud Shah	1482	S13
15	Ahmad Shah III	1518	S14
16	'Ala-ud-Din	1521	S14
17	Wali-Allah Shah	1522	S14
18	Kalim-Allah Shah	1525–1527	S14

i *Nizam Shahi Dynasty of Ahmadnagar* 1490–1633

1	Malik Ahmad Nizam Shah	1490	
2	Burhan Nizam Shah	1509	S1
3	Husain Shah I	1553	S2
4	Murtaza Shah	1565	S3
5	Miran Husain	1588	S4
6	Isma'il Shah	1589	S7
7	Burhan Shah II	1591	S3
8	Ibrahim Shah	1595	S7
9	Ahmad Shah II	1596	S6
10	Bahadur Shah	1596	S8
11	Murtaza Shah II	1600	BS3
12	Burhan Shah III	1610	S11
13	Husain Shah II	1631–1633	S12

j *'Imad Shahi Dynasty of Berar* 1490–1572

1	Fath-Allah 'Imad-ul-Mulk	1490	
2	'Ala-ud-Din 'Imad Shah	1504	S1
3	Darya 'Imad Shah	1529	S2
4	Burhan 'Imad Shah	1562	S3
5	Tufal Khan Dakhni	1568–1572	

k *Barid Shahi Dynasty of Bidar* 1492–1619

1	Qasim Barid Shah I	1492	
2	Amir Barid Shah I	1504	S1
3	'Ali Barid Shah I	1542	S2
4	Ibrahim Barid Shah	1579	S3
5	Qasim Barid Shah II	1586	S3
6	Amir Barid Shah II	1589	S5
7	Mirza 'Ali Barid Shah	1601	
8	'Ali Barid Shah II	1609–1619	

l *'Adil Shahi Dynasty of Bijapur* 1490–1686

1	Yusuf 'Adil Shah	1490	
2	Isma'il Shah	1510	S1
3	Mallu 'Adil Shah	1534	S2
4	Ibrahim 'Adil Shah I	1534	S2
5	'Ali 'Adil Shah I	1558	S4
6	Ibrahim 'Adil Shah II	1580	BS5
7	Muhammad 'Adil Shah	1627	S6
8	'Ali 'Adil Shah II	1657	S7
9	Sikandar 'Adil Shah	1672–1686	S8

m *Bhonsla Dynasty of Satara* 1674–1848

1	Shivaji I	1674
2	Shambhuji I	1680	S1
3	Rajaram	1689	S1
4	Tara Bai★	1700	W3
5	Shahu I	1708	S2
6	Ramaraja	1749	GS3
7	Shahu II	1777	AS6
8	Pratap Singh	1808	S7
9	Shahji Raja	1839–1848	S7

n *Bhonsla Dynasty of Kolhapur* 1700–1949

1	Shivaji I (s3 Satara)	1700
2	Shambhuji	1712	B1
3	Shivaji II	1760	AS2
4	Shambhu	1812	S3
5	Shahaji I	1821	S3
6	Shivaji III	1837	S5
7	Rajaram I	1866	AS6
8	Shivaji IV	1870	AS7
9	Shahu	1883	AS8
10	Rajaram II	1922–1940	S9
11	Shivaji V	1942	AS10
12	Shahaji II	1947–1949	AS10

o *Bhonsla Dynasty of Nagpur* 1738–1853

1	Raghuji I	1738
2	Janoji	1755	S1
3	Mudhoji I	1772	S1
4	Raghuji II	1788	S3
5	Mudhoji II	1816	BS4
6	Raghuji III	1818–1853	GS4

p *Peshwa Dynasty* 1713–1818

1	Balaji Vishvanath	1713
2	Baji Rao I	1720	S1
3	Balaji Baji Rao	1740	S2
4	Madhava Rao Ballal	1761	S3
5	Narayan Rao	1772	S3
6	Raghunath Rao	1773	S2
7	Madhava Rao Narayan	1774	S5
8	Chimnaji Appa	1796	S6
9	Baji Rao II	1796–1818	S6

218 INDIA ANDHRA PRADESH

a *Ikshvaku Dynasty of Vengi* c.220–295

1	Sri Santamula I	c.220 AD

2	Virapurisadatta	*c.*240	S1
3	Sri Santamula II	*c.*260	S2
4	Rudrapurisadatta	*c.*284–295	S3

b *Salankayana Dynasty of Vengi c.300–450*

1	Hastivarman I	*c.*300	
2	Nandivarman I	*c.*310	S1
3	Vijayadevavarman	*c.*325	S1
4	Hastivarman II	*c.*340	S2
5	Skandavarman I	*c.*370	S4
6	Nandivarman II	*c.*400	BS4
7	Skandavarman II	*c.*425–450	B6

c *Vishnukundin Dynasty c.500–631*

1	Vikramendravarman I	*c.*500	
2	Govindavarman Vikramasraya		S1
3	Madhavavarman Janasraya	*c.*535	S2
4	Vikramendravarman II	*c.*585	S3
5	Indravarman	*c.*590	S4
6	Vikramendravarman III	*c.*620–631	S5

d *Chalukya Dynasty of Vengi c.610–1073*

1	Kubja Vishnuvardhana I (S2 Badami)	*c.*610	
2	Jayasimha I		S1
3	Indra-Bhattaraka		S1
4	Vishnuvardhana II		S3
5	Mangi Yuvaraja		S4
6	Jayasimha II		S5
7	Kokkili		S5
8	Vishnuvardhana III		S5
9	Vijayaditya I		S8
10	Vishnuvardhana IV	*c.*764	S9
11	Vijayaditya II	*c.*799	S10
12	Kali-Vishnuvardhana V	*c.*847	S11
13	Gunaka-Vijayaditya III	*c.*848	S12
14	Chalukya-Bhima I	*c.*890	BS13
15	Vijayaditya IV	*c.*922	S14
16	Amma-Vishnuvardhana VI	*c.*922	S15
17	Beta-Vijayaditya V	*c.*929	S16
18	Tala I	*c.*929	BS13
19	Vikramaditya	*c.*929	S14
20	Bhima II	*c.*929	S16
21	Yuddhamalla	*c.*930	S18
22	Chalukya-Bhima III	*c.*935	S15
23	Amma-Vijayaditya VI	*c.*945–970	S16
24	Badapa	*c.*956	S21
25	Tala II Vishnuvardhana	?	S21
26	Danarnava	*c.*970	S16
27	Jata Choda-Bhima IV	*c.*973	
28	Saktivarman I	*c.*999	S26

29	Vimaladitya	*c.*1011	S26
30	Rajaraja Narendra	*c.*1022	S29
31	Vijayaditya VII (1)	1060	S29
32	Saktivarman II	1061	S31
	Vijayaditya VII (2)	1062	
33	Rajendra (III) Kulottunga (Chola King)	1073–(1122)	S30

e *Kakatiya Dynasty of Warangal c.*1000–1326

1	Beta I	*c.*1000	
2	Prola I	1030	S1
3	Tribhuvanamalla Beta II	1075	S2
4	Prola II	1110	S3
5	Prataparudra I	1158	S4
6	Mahadeva	1195	S4
7	Ganapati	1199	S6
8	Rudramba	1262	S7
9	Prataparudra II	1296–1326	GD8

f *Reddi Dynasty of Kondavidu* 1325–1424

1	Prolaya Vema	1325	
2	Anavota	1353	S1
3	Anavema	1364	S1
4	Kumaragiri	1386	S2
5	Peda Komati Vema	1402	BGS1
6	Rachavema	1420–1424	S5

g *Qutb-Shahi Dynasty of Golkunda* 1512–1687

1	Quli Qutb Shah (3G3 Qara-Qoyunli)	1512	
2	Jamshid Qutb Shah	1543	S1
3	Subhan Quli Qutb Shah	1550	S2
4	Ibrahim Qutb Shah	1550	S1
5	Muhammad Quli Qutb Shah	1580	S4
6	Muhammad Qutb Shah	1612	BS5
7	'Abdullah Qutb Shah	1626	S6
8	Abu'l-Hasan Qutb Shah	1672–1687	HD7

h *Nizams of Hyderabad* 1724–1948

1	Qamar-ud-Din Nizam-ul-Mulk Asaf Jah	1724	
2	Muhammad Nasir Jang	1748	S1
3	Muzaffar Jang	1750	GD1
4	Asaf-ud-Dawlah Salabat Jang	1751	S1
5	Nizam 'Ali	1762	S1
6	Akbar 'Ali Khan Sikandar Jah	1802	S5
7	Nasir-ud-Dawlah Farkhundah 'Ali	1829	S6
8	Afzal-ud-Dawlah	1857	S7
9	Mahbub 'Ali Khan	1869	S8
10	'Uthman 'Ali Khan Bahadur Jang	1911–1948	S9

219 **INDIA** MYSORE

a *Western Ganga Dynasty c.350–1024*

1	Kongunivarman Madhava I	c.350 AD	
2	Madhava II	c.400	
3	Harivarman	c.450	
4	Vishnugopa		
5	Madhava III	c.460	
6	Avinita	c.500	
7	Durvinita	c.540	
8	Mushkara		
9	Sri Vikrama		
10	Bhuvikrama		
11	Sivamara I	c.670	
12	(Unknown)		
13	Sri Purusha	725	
14	Sivamara II	788	S13
15	Rajamalla I	817	BS14
16	Nitimarga I	853	S15
17	Rajamalla II	870	S16
18	Nitimarga II	907	BS17
19	Narasimha	935	S18
20	Rajamalla III	936	S18
21	Butuga	937	S18
22	Maruladeva	960	S21
23	Marasimha	960	S21
24	Rajamalla IV	974	S23
25	Rakkasa Ganga	985–1024	S23

b *Hoysala Dynasty 1022–1346*

1	Nripakama	1022	
2	Vinayaditya	1047–1098	S1
3	Ereyanga	1063–1100	S2
4	Ballala I	1100	S3
5	Vishnuvardhana	1110	S3
6	Narasimha I	1152	S5
7	Ballala II	1173	S6
8	Narasimha II	1220–1238	S7
9	Somesvara	1233–1267	S8
10	Narasimha III	1254–1292	S9
11	Ballala III	1291–1342	S10
12	Virupaksha Ballala IV	1342–1346	S11

c *Wadiyar Maharajas of Mysore 1399–1949*

1	Yadu Raya	1399	
2	Hiriya Bettada Chamaraja I	1423	S1
3	Timmaraja I	1459	S2
4	Hiriya Chamarajasa II	1478	S3
5	Hiriya Bettada Chamaraja III	1513	S4
6	Timmaraja II	1553	S5

7	Bola Chamaraja IV	1572	S5
8	Bettada Devaraja	1576	BS7
9	Raja Wadiyar	1578	S7
10	Chamaraja V	1617	GS9
11	Immadi Raja	1637	S9
12	Kanthirava Narasaraja I	1638	BS9
13	Kempa Devaraja	1659	BS9
14	Chikkadevaraja	1673	BS13
15	Kanthirava Narasaraja II	1704	S14
16	Krishnaraja I	1714	S15
17	Chamaraja VI	1732	AS16
18	Krishnaraja II	1734	AS16
19	Nanjaraja	1766	S18
20	Bettada Chamaraja VII	1770	S18
21	Khasa Chamaraja VIII	1776–1796	AS18
22	Krishnaraja III	1799–1831	S21
23	Chamaraja IX	1881	AS22
24	Krishnaraja IV	1894	S23
25	Jayachamarajendra Bahadur	1940–1949	BS24

d *Dynasty of Haidar ʿAli c.1755–1799*

1	Haidar ʿAli Khan	c.1755	
2	Tipu Sultan	1782–1799	S1

e *Kadamba Dynasty of Vanavasi c.340–610*

1	Mayurasarman	c.340	
2	Kangavarman	c.370	S1
3	Bhagiratha	c.395	S2
4	Raghu	c.420	S3
5	Kakutsthavarman	c.430	S3
6	Santivarman	c.450	S5
7	Krishnavarman I (South)	c.475–485	S5
8	Mrigesavarman (North)	c.475–490	S6
9	Vishnuvarman (South)	c.485–497	S7
10	Mandhatrivarman (North)	c.490–497	BS6
11	Simhavarman (South)	c.497–540	S9
12	Ravivarman (North)	c.497–537	S10
13	Harivarman (North)	c.537–547	S12
14	Krishnavarman II (South; sole king 547)	c.540–565	S11
15	Ajavarman	c.565	S14
16	Bhogivarman	c.606–610	S15

f *Nayyak Dynasty of Ikkeri c.1499–1763*

1	Chaudappa	c.1499	
2	Sadasiva	1513	S1
3	Dodda-Sakanna	1536	S2
4	Chikka-Sakanna	1570–1580	S2
5	Ramaraja	1570–1592	S3

6	Venkatappa I	1592	S3
7	Virabhadra	1629	GS6
8	Sivappa	1645	S6
9	Venkatappa II	1660	S6
10	Bhadrappa	1661	S8
11	Somashekara I	1664	S8
12	Chennamma★	1671	W11
13	Basavappa I	1696	AS12
14	Somashekara II	1714	S13
15	Basavappa II	1739	BS14
16	Chenna-Basavappa	1754	AS15
17	Virammaji★	1757–1763	W16
18	Somashekara III	1757–1763	AS17

g *Haleri Rajas of Coorg c.1633–1834*

1	Muddu Raja I	c.1633	
2	Dodda Virappa	1687	S1
3	Chikka Virappa	1736	GS2
4	Muddu Raja II	1766–1770	DT1
5	Muddaya Raja	1766–1770	DT1
6	Devappa Raja	1770	GS5
7	Linga Raja	1773–1780	B4
		———	
8	Vira Rajendra	1789	S7
9	Devammaji★	1809	D8
10	Linga Rajendra	1811	S7
11	Chikka Vira Rajendra	1820–1834	S10

220 **INDIA** KERALA

a *Kulasekhara (Chera) Dynasty c.800–1102*

1	Kulasekhara Alwar	c.800
2	Rajasekharavarman	c.820
3	Sthanu Ravivarman	844
4	Ramavarma	885
5	Goda Ravivarma	917
6	Indu Kothavarma	944
7	Bhaskara Ravivarman I	962–1019
8	Bhaskara Ravivarman II	979–1021
9	Vira Kerala	1021
10	Rajasimha	1028
11	Bhaskara Ravivarman III	1043
12	Ravi Ramavarma	1082
13	Ramavarma Kulasekhara	1090–1102

b *Rajas of Venad* 1102–1729

1	Kotha Varma	1102
2	Kotha Kerala Varma	1125
3	Vira Ravi Varma	1155

4	Aditya Varma I	1165
5	Udaya Marthanda Varma	1175
6	Vira Rama Varma	1195
7	Vira Rama Kerala Varma	1205
8	Ravi Kerala Varma I	1215
9	Padmanabha Marthanda Varma	1240–1253
10	Ravi Varma Kulasekhara	1299
11	Vira Udaya Marthanda Varma	1314
12	Kunnumel Vira Kerala Varma Tiruvati	1344
13	Iravi Iravi Varma	1350
14	Aditya Varma Sarvanyanatha	1376
15	Chera Udaya Varma	1383
16	Ravi Varma I	1444
17	Sri Vira Rama Marthanda Varma Kulasekhara	1458
18	Kotha Aditya Varma	1469
19	Ravi Ravi Varma	1484
20	Ravi Kerala Varma II	1512
21	Jayasimha Kerala Varma	1514
22	Bhutalavira Sri Vira Udaya Marthanda Varma	1516
23	Bhutalavira Ravi Varma	1535
24	Rama Kerala Varma	?
25	Aditya Varma II	?
26	Sri Vira Kerala Varma	1544
27	Rama Varma I	1545
28	Unni Kerala Varma	1556
29	Sri Vira Udaya Varma	?
30	Sri Vira Ravi Varma	1595
31	Aditya Varma III	1609
32	Rama Varma II	1610
33	Rama Varma III	1610
34	Ravi Varma II	1611
35	Ravi Varma III	1663
36	Aditya Varma IV	1672
37	Ummayama Rani*	1677
38	Ravi Varma IV	1684
39	Aditya Varma V	1714
40	Rama Varma IV	1721
41	Marthanda Varma (of Travancore)	1729–(1758)

c *Rajas of Cochin c.*1500–1949

1	Unni Rama Koil I	c.1500
2	Unni Rama Koil II	1503
3	Vira Kerala Varma I	1537
4	Kesara Rama Varma	1565
5	Vira Kerala Varma II	1601
6	Ravi Varma I	1615
7	Vira Kerala Varma III	1624
8	Goda Varma I	1637
9	Vira Rayira Varma	1645

10	Vira Kerala Varma IV	1646
11	Rama Varma I	1650
12	Gangadhara Lakshmi★	1656
13	Rama Varma II	1658
14	Goda Varma II	1662
15	Vira Kerala Varma V	1663
16	Rama Varma III	1687
17	Ravi Varma II	1693
18	Rama Varma IV	1697
19	Rama Varma V	1701
20	Ravi Varma III	1721
21	Rama Varma VI	1731
22	Kerala Varma I	1746
23	Rama Varma VII	1749
24	Kerala Varma II	1760
25	Rama Varma VIII	1775
26	Rama Varma Saktan Tampuran	1790
27	Rama Varma IX	1805
28	Kerala Varma III	1809
29	Rama Varma X	1828
30	Rama Varma XI	1837
31	Rama Varma XII	1844
32	Kerala Varma IV	1851
33	Ravi Varma IV	1853
34	Rama Varma XIII	1864
35	Kerala Varma V	1888
36	Rama Varma XIV	1895
37	Rama Varma XV	1914
38	Rama Varma XVI	1932
39	Kerala Varma VI	1941
40	Ravi Varma V	1943
41	Kerala Varma VII	1946
42	Rama Varma XVII	1948–1949

d *Maharajas of Travancore* 1729–1949

1	Marthanda Varma (of Venad)	1729
2	Kartika Tirunal Rama Varma	1758
3	Balarama Varma	1798
4	Gouri Lakshmi Bai★	1810
5	Gouri Parvati Bai★	1815
6	Swati Tirunal	1829
7	Utram Tirunal Marthanda Varma	1847
8	Ayilyam Tirunal	1860
9	Rama Varma Visakhan Tirunal	1880
10	Sri Mulam Tirunal Rama Varma	1885
11	Setu Lakshmi Bai★	1924
12	Sri Chitra Tirunal Balarama Varma	1931–1949

e *'Ali Raja Dynasty of Cannanore* 1545–1949

1	'Ali Adi-Raja I	1545

2	Abu Bakr Adi-Raja I	1591
3	Abu Bakr Adi-Raja II	1607
4	Muhammad 'Ali Adi-Raja I	1610
5	Muhammad 'Ali Adi-Raja II	1647
6	Kamal Adi-Raja	1655
7	Muhammad 'Ali Adi-Raja III	1656
8	'Ali Adi-Raja II	1691
9	Kunhi Amsa Adi-Raja I	1704
10	Muhammad 'Ali Adi-Raja IV	1720
11	Harrabichi Kadavube Adi-Raja Bibi★	1728
12	Junumabe Adi-Raja Bibi I★	1732
13	Kunhi Amsa Adi-Raja II	1745
14	Junumabe Adi-Raja Bibi II★	1777
15	Mariambe Adi-Raja Bibi★	1819
16	Hayashabe Adi-Raja Bibi★	1838
17	'Abdul-Rahman 'Ali Adi-Raja I	1852
18	Musa 'Ali Adi-Raja	1870
19	Muhammad 'Ali Adi-Raja V	1899
20	Imbichi Adi-Raja Bibi★	1907
21	Ahmad 'Ali Adi-Raja	1911
22	Ayisha Adi-Raja Bibi★	1921
23	'Abdul-Rahman 'Ali Adi-Raja II	1931
24	Mariyumma Adi-Raja Bibi★	1946–1949

221 INDIA PALLAVA AND CHOLA EMPIRES

a *Pallava Dynasty of Kanchi c.315–897*

1	Simhavarman I	c.315	
2	Skandavarman I	c.345–355	S1
3	Vishnugopa	c.350–355	
4	Kumaravishnu I	c.355	S2
5	Skandavarman II	c.370	S4
6	Viravarman	c.385	S5
7	Skandavarman III	c.400	S6
8	Simhavarman II	c.438	S7
9	Skandavarman IV	c.460	S8
10	Nandivarman I	c.480	S9
11	Kumaravishnu II	c.500	S9
12	Buddhavarman	c.520	S11
13	Kumaravishnu III	c.540	S12
14	Simhavarman III	c.550	DT7
15	Simhavishnu	c.574	S14
16	Mahendravarman I	c.600	S15
17	Narasimhavarman I	630	S16
18	Mahendravarman II	668	S17
19	Paramesvaravarman I	670	S18
20	Narasimhavarman II	680	S19
21	Paramesvaravarman II	720	S20
22	Nandivarman II	731	DT14

23	Dantivarman	795–845	S22
24	Nandivarman III	844–866	S23
25	Nripatungavarman	855–896	S24
26	Aparajita	879–897	S25

b *Chola Dynasty c.846–1279*

1	Vijayalaya	c.846	
2	Aditya I	c.871	S1
3	Parantaka I	907–953	S2
4	Rajaditya I	947–949	S3
5	Gandaraditya	949–957	S3
6	Arinjaya	956–957	S3
7	Parantaka II	956–973	S6
8	Aditya II	956–969	S7
9	Madurantaka Uttama	969–985	S5
10	Rajaraja I	985–1016	S7
11	Rajendra I	1012–1044	S10
12	Rajadhiraja I	1044–1054	S11
13	Rajendradeva II	1052–1064	S11
14	Raja Mahendra	1060–1063	S13
15	Virarajendra	1063–1069	S11
16	Adhirajendra	1067–1070	S15
17	Rajendra III Kulottunga Chola (K. Vengi)	1070–1122	GD11
18	Vikrama Chola	1118–1135	S17
19	Kulottunga Chola II	1133–1150	S18
20	Rajaraja II	1146–1173	S19
21	Rajadhiraja II	1163–1179	GS18
22	Kulottunga III	1178–1218	
23	Rajaraja III	1216–1246	
24	Rajendra IV	1246–1279	

222 **INDIA** VIJAYANAGAR EMPIRE

a *Yadava Dynasty* 1336–1486

1	Harihara I	1336	
2	Bukka I	1354	B1
3	Harihara II	1379	S2
4	Bukka II	1406	S3
5	Devaraya I	1406	S3
6	Vijaya Bukka	1422	S5
7	Devaraya II	1422	S6
8	Mallikarjuna	1446	S7
9	Virupaksha	1465	S7
10	Praudha Devaraya	1485–1486	S9

b *Saluva Dynasty* 1486–1505

1	Saluva Narasimha	1486	
2	Immadi Narasimha	1491–1505	S1

c *Tuluva Dynasty* 1491–*c.*1570

1 Narasa Nayyaka	1491	
2 Vira Narasimha	1503	S1
3 Krishna Devaraya	1509	S1
4 Achyuta Raya	1529	S1
5 Venkata I	1542	S4
6 Sadasiva	1542–*c.*1570	BS4

d *Aravidu Dynasty* 1542–*c.*1670

1 Ramaraja	1542	
2 Tirumala	1570	B1
3 Ranga I	1572	S2
4 Venkata II	1584	S2
5 Ranga II	1614	BS4
6 Rama Devaraya	1614	S5
7 Venkata III	1630	GS1
8 Ranga III	1642–*c.*1670	S7

223 INDIA THE CARNATIC

a *Early Pandya Dynasty c.*590–920

1 Kadungon	*c.*590	
2 Maravarman Avanisulamani	*c.*620	S1
3 Sendan	*c.*645	S2
4 Arikesari Maravarman	*c.*670	S3
5 Kochchadaiyan Ranadhira	*c.*700	S4
6 Maravarman Rajasimha I	*c.*730–765	S5
7 Jatila Parantaka Nedunjadaiyan	*c.*756–815	S6
8 Srimara Srivallabha	*c.*815	S7
9 Varagunavarman	*c.*862	S8
10 Parantaka Viranarayana	*c.*880	S8
11 Maravarman Rajasimha II	*c.*900–920	S10

b *Later Pandya Dynasty* 1190–1310

1 Jatavarman Kulasekhara Pandya	1190
2 Maravarman Sundara Pandya I	1216
3 Maravarman Sundara Pandya II	1238
4 Jatavarman Sundara Pandya	1251
5 Maravarman Kulasekhara Pandya	1268–1310

c *Sultans of Madurai* 1334–1378

1 Jalal-ud-Din Ahsan Shah	1334
2 'Ala-ud-Din Udauji Shah	1339
3 Qutb-ud-Din Firuz Shah	1341
4 Ghiyath-ud-Din Muhammad Shah	1341
5 Nasir-ud-Din Mahmud Ghazi Shah	1345
6 'Adil Shah	1356
7 Fakhr-ud-Din Mubarak Shah	1360
8 'Ala-ud-Din Sikandar Shah	1372–1378

d *Nayyak Dynasty of Madurai* 1529–1736

1	Vishvanatha	1529	
2	Krishnappa I	1564	S1
3	Virappa	1572	S2
4	Krishnappa II	1595	S3
5	Muttu Krishnappa	1601	BS4
6	Muttu Virappa I	1609	S5
7	Tirumala	1623	S5
8	Muttu Virappa II	1659	S7
9	Chokkanatha	1659–1682	S8
10	Muttu Linga	1678.	S8
11	Muttu Virappa III	1682	S9
12	Mangammal★	1689	M11
13	Vijayaranga Chokkanatha	1706	S11
14	Minakshi★	1732–1736	W13

e *Nayyak Dynasty of Tanjore* 1549–1673

1	Sevappa	1549	
2	Achyutappa	1572	S1
3	Raghunatha	1614	S2
4	Vijaya Raghava	?–1673	S3

f *Bhonsla Dynasty of Tanjore* 1674–1855

1	Venkaji (B1 Satara)	1674	
2	Shahji	1686	S1
3	Sarabhoji I	1711	S1
4	Tukoji	1727	S1
5	Bava Sahib	1735	S4
6	Sujana Bai★	1736	W5
7	Sawai Shahji	1738	
8	Sayaji	1738	S4
o	Pratap Singh	1739	S4
10	Tusalji	1763	S9
11	Amar Singh	1787	S9
12	Sarabhoji II	1798	S10
13	Shivaji	1824–1855	S12

g *Nawabs of Arcot* c.1690–1825

1	Zulf'iqar 'Ali Khan	c.1690	
2	Da'ud Khan	1703	
3	Muhammad Sa'adat-Allah Khan I	1710	
4	Dost 'Ali Khan	1732	BS3
5	Safdar 'Ali Khan	1740	S4
6	Sa'adat-Allah Khan II	1742	S5
7	Anwar-ud-Din Muhammad	1744	
8	Wala Jah Muhammad 'Ali	1749	S7
9	'Umdut-ul-Umara	1795	S8
10	'Azim-ud-Dawlah	1801	BS9
11	'Azim Jah	1819–1825	S10

224 CEYLON AND MALDIVES RULERS

a *Kings of Ceylon c.250 BC–1598 AD*

1	Devanampiya Tissa	*c.*250 BC	
2	Uttiya		BI
3	Mahasiva		BI
4	Suratissa		BI
5	Sena		
6	Guttaka		
7	Asela		BI
8	Elara Chola		
9	Dutthagamani	161	DTBI
10	Saddhatissa	137	B9
11	Thulatthana	119	S10
12	Lanjatissa	119	S10
13	Khallata Naga	109	S10
14	Vattagamani Abhaya (1)	103	S10
15	Pulahattha		
16	Bahiya		
17	Panayamara	102	
18	Pilayamara		
19	Dathika		
	Vattagamani Abhaya (2)	89	
20	Mahachuli Mahatissa	76	S14
21	Choranaga	62	S14
22	Tissa	50	S20
23	Anula★	47	W21
24	Kutakannatissa	41	S20
25	Bhatika Abhaya	19	S24
26	Mahadathika Mahanaga	9 AD	S24
27	Amandagamani Abhaya	22	S26
28	Kanirajanu Tissa	31	S26
29	Chulabhaya	34	S27
30	Sivali★	35	D27
31	Ilanaga	35	STS27
32	Chandamukha Siva	44	S31
33	Yasalalaka Tissa	52	S31
34	Subharaja	59	
35	Vasabha	65	
36	Vankanasika Tissa	109	S35
37	Gajabahu I Gamani	112	S36
38	Mahalla Naga	134	GS35
39	Bhatika Tissa	140	S38
40	Kanittha Tissa	164	S38
41	Khujja Naga	192	S40
42	Kuncha Naga	194	S40
43	Sirinaga I	195	S39
44	Voharika Tissa I	214	S43
45	Abhaya Naga	236	S43
46	Sirinaga II	244	S44

47	Vijayakumara	246	s46
48	Samghàtissa I	247	
49	Sirisamghabodhi	251	
50	Gothabhaya	236	s46
51	Jetthatissa I	266	s50
52	Mahasena	276	s50
53	Sirimeghavanna	303	s52
54	Jetthatissa II	331	s52
55	Buddhadasa	340	s54
56	Upatissa I	368	s55
57	Mahanama	410	s55
58	Chattagahaka Jantu	432	HD55
59	Mittasena	432	
60	Pandu	433	
61	Parinda	438	
62	Khudda Parinda	441	
63	Tiritara	456	
64	Dathiya	456	
65	Pithiya	459	
66	Dhatusena	459	
67	Kassapa I	477	s66
68	Moggallana I	495	s66
69	Kumara Dhatusena	512	s68
70	Kittisena	520	s69
71	Siva	521	WB69
72	Upatissa II	522	HD66
73	Silakala	522	s72
74	Dathapabhuti	535	s73
75	Moggallana II	535	s73
76	Kittisirimegha	555	s75
77	Mahanaga	573	
78	Aggabodhi I	575	STS77
79	Aggabodhi II	608	STS78
80	Samghàtissa II	618	B79
81	Moggallana III	618	
82	Silameghavanna	623	
83	Aggabodhi III (1)	632	s82
84	Jetthatissa III	632	s80
	Aggabodhi III (2)	633	
85	Dathopatissa	643	
86	Kassapa II	650	s82
87	Dappula I	659	HD82
88	Hatthadatha I	659	STS85
89	Aggabodhi IV	667	B88
90	Datta	683	
91	Hatthadatha II	684	
92	Manavamma	684	s86
93	Aggabodhi V	718	s92
94	Kassapa III	724	s92
95	Mahinda I	730	s92

96	Aggabodhi VI	733	S95
97	Aggabodhi VII	772	S95
98	Mahinda II	777	S96
99	Udaya I	797	S98
100	Mahinda III	801	S99
101	Aggabodhi VIII	804	B100
102	Dappula II	815	B100
103	Aggabodhi IX	831	S102
104	Sena I	833	S102
105	Sena II	853	BS104
106	Udaya II	887	B105
107	Kassapa IV	898	B105
108	Kassapa V	914	S105
109	Dappula III	923	S105
110	Dappula IV	924	B109
111	Udaya III	935	BS105
112	Sena III	938	B111
113	Udaya IV	946	WB112
114	Sena IV	954	S111
115	Mahinda IV	956	?S111
116	Sena V	972	S115
117	Mahinda V	982	B116
118	Kassapa VI	1029	S117
119	Mahalana Kitti	1040	
120	Vikkama Pandu	1042	
121	Jagatipala	1043	
122	Parakkama Pandu	1046	
123	Lokissara	1048	
124	Kassapa VII	1054	
125	Vijayabahu I	1055	GG116
126	Jayabahu I	1110	B125
127	Vikramabahu I	1111	S125
128	Gajabahu II	1132	S127
129	Parakramabahu I	1153	STGS125
130	Vijayabahu II	1186	STS129
131	Nissamkamalla	1187	
132	Vikramabahu II	1196	B131
133	Chodaganga	1196	STS131
134	Lilavati (1)★	1197	W129
135	Sahassamalla	1200	B131
136	Kalyanavati★	1202	W131
137	Dharmasoka	1208	
138	Anikanga	1209	F137
	Lilavati (2)★	1209	
139	Lokesvara	1210	
	Lilavati (3)★	1211	
140	Parakrama Pandya	1212	
141	Kalinga Magha	1215–1236	
142	Vijayabahu III	1232–1236	
143	Parakramabahu II	1236	S142

144	Vijayabahu IV	1270	S143
145	Bhuvanaikabahu I	1272–1284	S143
146	Parakramabahu III	1287	S144
147	Bhuvanaikabahu II	1293	S145
148	Parakramabahu IV	1302	S147
149	Bhuvanaikabahu III	1326	
150	Vijayabahu V	1335	
151	Bhuvanaikabahu IV	1341	S150
152	Parakramabahu V	1344	B151
153	Vikramabahu III	1357	S152
154	Bhuvanaikabahu V	1372	S151
155	Parakramabahu VI	1412	DT152
156	Jayabahu II	1467	GD155
157	Bhuvanaikabahu VI	1470	
158	Parakramabahu VII	1478	S157
159	Parakramabahu VIII	1484–1518	B157
160	Parakramabahu IX	1508–1528	S159
161	Vijayabahu VI	1509–1521	S159
162	Bhuvanaikabahu VII	1521–1550	S161
163	Dharmapala	1551–1598	GD162

b *Kings of Jaffna 1215–1615*

1	Kalinga Segarajasekaran I	1215	
2	Kulasekhara Pararajasekaran I	1240	S1
3	Kulottunga Segarajasekaran II	1256	S2
4	Vikrama Pararajasekaran II	1279	S3
5	Varothya Segarajasekaran III	1302	S4
6	Marthanda Pararajasekaran III	1325	S5
7	Gunapushana Segarajasekaran IV	1348	S6
8	Virothya Pararajasekaran IV	1371	S7
9	Jayavira Segarajasekaran V	1380	S8
10	Gunavira Pararajasekaran V	1410	S9
11	Kangasuriya Segarajasekaran VI (1)	1440	S10
12	Bhuvanaikabahu (VI of Ceylon)	1450	
	Kangasuriya Segarajasekaran VI (2)	1467	
13	Singai Pararajasekaran VI	1478	S11
14	Sangili Segarajasekaran VII	1519–1565	S13
15	Puviraja Pandaram Pararajasekaran VII	1561–1565	S14
16	Cunchi Nayinar	1565	
17	Periya Pillai Segarajasekaran VIII	1570	
18	Puviraja Pandaram II	1582	
19	Ethirmanasinga Pararajasekaran VIII	1591–1615	S17

c *Kings of Sitawake 1521–1592*

1	Mayadunne	1521–1581	S161 Ceylon
2	Rajasinha	1581–1592	S1

d *Kings of Kandy 1591–1815*

1	Vimala Dharma Surya I	1591

2	Senarat	1604	BS1
3	Rajasinha	1635	S2
4	Vimala Dharma Surya II	1687	S3
5	Narendra Sinha	1707	S4
6	Sri Vijaya Rajasinha	1739	WB5
7	Kirti Sri Rajasinha	1747	WB6
8	Rajadhi Rajasinha	1782	B7
9	Sri Vikrama Rajasinha	1798–1815	SS8

e Sultans of the Maldives 1573–1968

1	Muhammad Tukrufan al-'Alam	1573	
2	Ibrahim ibn Muhammad	1584	S1
3	Husain Famuderi	1609	
4	'Imad-ud-Din Muhammad I	1620	GGB1
5	Ibrahim Iskandar I	1648	S4
6	Muhammad ibn Ibrahim	1687	S5
7	Muhi-ud-Din Muhammad	1691	GS4
8	Shams-ud-Din Muhammad al-Hamawi	1692	
9	Muhammad ibn Hajji 'Ali	1692	
10	'Ali	1700	
11	Hasan ibn 'Ali	1701	S10
12	Muzhir-ud-Din Ibrahim	1701	BS10
13	'Imad-ud-Din Muhammad II	1705	
14	Ibrahim Iskandar II	1721	S13
15	'Imad-ud-Din Muhammad Mukarram	1750–1754	S13
16	'Izz-ud-Din Hasan Ghazi	1760	
17	Ghiyath-ud-Din Muhammad	1766	S14
18	Shams-ud-Din Muhammad	1773	BS16
19	Mu'izz-ud-Din Muhammad	1774	S16
20	Nur-ud-Din Hajji Hasan	1778	S16
21	Mu'in-ud-Din Muhammad	1798	S20
22	'Imad-ud-Din Muhammad III	1834	S21
23	Nur-ud-Din Ibrahim (1)	1882	S22
24	Mu'in-ud-Din Muhammad II	1886	BS23
	Nur-ud-Din Ibrahim (2)	1888	
25	'Imad-ud-Din Muhammad IV	1892	S23
26	Shams-ud-Din Muhammad Iskandar (1)	1893	S23
27	'Imad -ud-Din Muhammad V	1893	BS23
	Shams-ud-Din Muhammad Iskandar (2)	1903	
28	Nur-ud-Din Hasan Iskandar	1935	S27
29	'Abdul-Majid Didi	1945–1952	
30	Muhammad Farid Didi	1954–1968	S29

225 **MONGOLIA** RULERS

a *Shanyus of the Hsiung-Nu (Huns)* 201 BC–47 AD

1	Mao-Tun	201 BC	
2	Lao-Shang	174	S1
3	Chun-Ch'en	160	S2
4	I-Chih-Hsieh	127	S2
5	Wu-Wei	114	S4
6	Wu-Shih-Lu-Erh	104	S5
7	Chiu-Li-Hu	102	S4
8	Chu-Ti-Hou	101	S4
9	Hu-Lu-Ku	96	S8
10	Hu-I-Ti	85	S9
11	Hsiu-Lu-Ch'uan-Ch'u	70	S9
12	Wo-I-Chu-Ti	60	
13	Hu-Han-Yeh	58–31	S11
14	Chih-Chih-Ku-Tu-Hou	56–36	B13
15	Fu-Chu-Lei-Jo-Ti	30	S13
16	Shou-Hsieh-Jo-Ti	20	S13
17	Chu-Ya-Jo-Ti	11	S13
18	Wu-Chu-Liu-Jo-Ti	7	S17
19	Wu-Lei-Jo-Ti	14 AD	S13
20	Hu-Tu-Erh-Shih-Tao-Kao-Jo-Ti	19–47	S13

b *Shanyus of the Northern Hsiung-Nu* 47–123 AD

21	P'u-Nu	47 AD	S19
22	San-Mu-Lou-Chih	84	
23	Yu-Ch'u-Chien	89	
24	Ao-Chien-Jih-Chu-Wang-Fung-Hou	93–123	

c *Shanyus of the Southern Hsiung-Nu* 48–304 AD

1	Hu-Han-Yeh (S18 Above)	48 AD	
2	Ch'u-Fu-Yu-Ti	56	S1
3	I-Fa-Yu-Liu-Ti	58	S1
4	Hsien-Tung-Shih-Chu-Hou-Ti	59	GS1
5	Ch'iu-Ch'u-Chu-Lin-Ti	63	GS1
6	Hou-Yeh-Shih-Chu-Hou-Ti	64	GS1
7	I-T'u-Yu-Liu-Ti	85	
8	Hsiu-Lan-Shih-Chu-Hou-Ti	88	S6
9	An-Kuo	93	S7
10	T'ing-Tu-Shih-Chu-Hou-Ti	94	
11	Wan-Shih-Shih-Chu-Hou-Ti	98	S6
12	Wu-Chi-Hou-Shih-Chu-Ti	124	S6
13	Ch'u-Teh-Jo-Shih-Chu-Tsu	128	S6
14	Ch'e-Niu	140	
15	Hu-Lan-Jo-Shih-Chu-Tsu	143	
16	I-Ling-Shih-Chu-Chiu	147	
17	T'u-Te-Jo-Shih-Chu-Chiu	172	S16
18	Hu-Chen	178	S17
19	Ch'iang-Ch'iu	179	

20	T'e-Chih-Shih-Chu-Hou	188	S19
21	Hu-Shu-Ch'uan	195	S19
22	Liu Pao	216	S20
23	Liu Yuan (Northern Han 1.)	279–(304)	S22

d *Khagans of the Juan-Juan (?Avars) 394–557*

1	She-Lun	394	
2	Ai-Tou-Kai	410	B1
3	Mou-Han-He-Sheng-Kai	415	FBS2
4	Ch'ih-Lien-Ting	430	S3
5	Ch'u-Lo	444	
6	Shou-Lo-Pu Chen	464	
7	Fu-Ming-Tun	485	S6
8	Ho-Ch'i-Fu-Tai-K'u-Che	492	B6
9	T'o-Han	506	S8
10	Tou-Lo-Fu-Pa-Tou	508	S9
11	A-Na-Huai	520	S9
12	T'ieh-Fa	552	
13	Teng-Chu	553	
14	K'u-Ti	553	
15	Yen-Lo-Ch'en	553–557	

e *Khans of the Eastern Turks (T'u-Chueh) 545–682*

1	T'u-Men	545	
2	I-Hsi-Chi	552	S1
3	Mu-Kan	553	
4	T'o-Pei	572	S3
5	Sha-Pei-Liao	582	
6	Yeh-Hu	587	B5
7	Yeh-Chia-Shih-To-Na-Tu-Lan	587	BS5
8	Pu-Ch'ia	599	
9	Ch'i-Min	601	
10	Shih-Pi	609	S9
11	Ch'u-Lo	619	S9
12	Hsieh-Li (Illig Khan)	620–630	S9
13	Elterish Qutlugh Khan	682	DT12
14	Qapaghan Khan	691	B13
15	Bilga Khan	716	S13
16	I-Jan Khan	734	S15
17	Tengri Khan	734	
18	Ku-T'u Yabgu Khan	741	
19	I-T'ieh-I-Shih Khan	743	
20	Ozmish Khan	743	
21	Pei-Mei Khan	744–745	

f *Khans of the Uighurs 744–840*

1	Qutlugh Bilga Kul Khan	744	
2	Bolmish Bilga Khan	747	S1
3	Iltutmish Alp Kulug Bilga Khan	759	S2

4	Alp Qutlugh Bilga Khan	779	BS2
5	Bolmish Kulug Bilga Khan	789	S4
6	Qutlugh Bilga Khan	790	S5
7	Ulugh Bulmish Alp Qutlugh Khan	795	
8	Qut Bulmish Alp Bilga Khan I	808	
9	Ulugh Bulmish Alp Kuchlug Khan	821	
10	Qut Bulmish Alp Bilga Khan II	824	
11	Qut Bulmish Alp Kulug Bilga Khan	832	
12	Wu-Tu Tegin	839–840	

g *Great Khans of the Mongols (Yuan Dynasty of China)* 1206–1370

1	Chingis Khan	1206–1227	
2	Ogodei Khan	1229–1241	S1
3	Guyuk Khan	1246–1248	S2
4	Mengu Khan	1251–1259	BS2
5	Kubilai Khan	1260	B4
6	Temur Oljeitu Khan	1294	GS5
7	Qaishan Guluk Khan	1307	BS6
8	Buyantu Khan	1311	B7
9	Gegen Khan	1320	S8
10	Yesun Temur Khan	1323	BS6
11	Toq Temur Khan (1)	1328	S10
12	Qushila Qutuqtu Khan	1329	S7
	Toq Temur Khan (2)	1329	
13	Irinchinbal Khan	1332	S12
14	Toghan Temur Khan	1332–1370	S12

h *Khans of the Mongols (Northern Yuan Dynasty)* 1370–1634

15	Biliktu Khan	1370	S14
16	Usaqal Khan	1379	S14
17	Engke Soriktu Khan	1389	S16
18	Elbek Khan	1393	S16
19	Gun Temur Khan	1400	S18
20	Oljei Temur Khan	1403	S18
21	Delbek Khan	1411	S20
22	Ajai Taiji Khan	1415	BS18
23	Taisung Khan	1433	S22
24	Akbarji Khan	1451	S22
25	Ukegtu Khan	1454	S23
26	Molon Khan	1465	S23
27	Mandagul Khan	1475	S22
28	Dayan Khan	1479	GG24
29	Bodi Alag Khan	?	GS28
30	Daraisun Kudang Khan	1547	S29
31	Tumen Jasagtu Khan	1557	S30
32	Buyan Taiji Khan	1592	S31
33	Lindan Khan	*c.*1605–1634	S32

i *Khans of the Zungar Kalmaks* 1626–1757

1	Batur Khan	1626

2	Senge Khan	1653	S1
3	Galdan Boshoktu Khan	1671–1697	S1
4	Tsevan Rabdan Khan	1689–1727	BS3
5	Galdan Tseren Khan	1727	S4
6	Tsevan Dorji Khan	1745	S5
7	Lama Dorji Khan	1750	S5
8	Dawa Achi Khan	1753	S5
9	Amursana Khan	1755–1757	GG4

226 TIBET RULERS

a Yar-Lun Dynasty (Kings) c.600–842

1	Nam-ri-srong-brtsan	c.600	
2	Srong-brtsan-sgam-po	c.627	S1
3	Mang-srong-mang-brtsan	649	GS2
4	Dus-srong-mang-po-rje	676	S3
5	Khri-lde-gtsug-brtsan	704	S4
6	Khri-srong-lde-brtsan	754	S5
7	Mu-ne-btsan-po	797	S6
8	Khri-lde-srong-brtsan	c.800	S6
9	Khri-gtsug-lde-brtsan (Ral-pa-can)	815	S8
10	Glang-dar-ma	c.836–842	S8

b Sakya Dynasty (Mongol Viceroys) 1244–1358

1	Sakya Pandit	1244
2	Phags-pa Tisri	1253
3	Rinchen Tisri	1280
4	Dharmapala Rakshita Tisri	1282
5	Yishe Rinchen Tisri	1286
6	Tragpa-Oser Tisri	1295
7	Rinchen Gyantsen Tisri	1303
8	Dorje Pal Tisri	1304
9	Sangye Pal Tisri	1313
10	Kunga Lotro Tisri	1316
11	Kunga Lekpa Chungne Tisri	1327
12	Kunga Gyantsen Tisri	1330–1358

c Kings of Tibet 1358–1750

1	Chang-chub Gyantsen	1358
2	Sakya Gyantsen	1372
3	Trakpa Chang-chub	1386
4	Sonam Trakpa Gyantsen	1388
5	Trakpa Chungne	1440
6	Sangye Gyantsen Pal Zangpo	1465
7	Donyo Dorje	1481
8	Ngawang Namgye	1522
9	Tondup Tseten	1550
10	Karma Tseten	1565
11	Lhawang Dorje	c.1582

12	Phuntso Namgye	*c.*1603
13	Karma Tsen-kyong	1623
14	Gusri Khan Qosot	1642
15	Dayan Khan	1655
16	Tenzin Dalai Khan	1668
17	Tenzin Wangchuk Khan	1696
18	Lhabzang Khan	1697–1717
19	Phola Sonam Tobgye	1728
20	Gyurme Namgyal	1747–1750

d *Dalai Lamas* 1391–1959

1	Gedun Truppa	1391–1475
2	Gedun Gyatso	1475–1542
3	Sonam Gyatso	1543–1588
4	Yonten Gyatso	1589–1617
5	Ngawang Lobzang Gyatso	1617–1682
6	Tsang-yang Gyatso	1683–1706
7	Kezang Gyatso	1708–1757
8	Jampel Gyatso	1758–1804
9	Luntok Gyatso	1806–1815
10	Tshultrim Gyatso	1816–1837
11	Khedrup Gyatso	1838–1856
12	Trinle Gyatso	1856–1875
13	Thupten Gyatso	1876–1933
14	Tenzin Gyatso	1935–1959

227 **CHINA** IMPERIAL DYNASTIES

a *Shang (Yin)* 1766–1122 BC (Traditional dating – probable dates *c.*1600–1050 BC)

1	T'ang (Ta I)	1766 BC	
2	T'ai Chia	1753	GS1
3	Wu Ting	1720	S2
4	Ta Keng	1691	S2
5	Hsiao Chia	1666	S4
6	Yung Chi	1649	S4
7	T'ai Wu	1637	S4
8	Chung Ting	1562	S7
9	Wai Jen	1549	S7
10	Ho T'an Chia	1534	S7
11	Tsu I	1525	S8
12	Tsu Hsin	1506	S11
13	Wu Chia	1490	S11
14	Tsu Ting	1465	S12
15	Nan Keng	1433	S13
16	Yang Chia	1408	S14
17	P'an Keng	1401	S14

18	Hsiao Hsin	1373	S14
19	Hsiao I	1352	S14
20	Wu Ting	1324	S19
21	Tsu Keng	1265	S20
22	Tsu Chia	1258	S20
23	Lin Hsin	1225	S22
24	Keng Ting	1219	S22
25	Wu I	1198	S24
26	T'ai Ting	1194	S25
27	Ti I	1191	S26
28	Chou Hsin	1154–1122	S27

b *Western Chou* 1122–771 BC (Traditional founding date – probable real date *c.*1050 BC)

1	Wu Wang	1122 BC	
2	Ch'eng Wang	1115	S1
3	K'ang Wang	1078	S2
4	Chao Wang	1052	S3
5	Mu Wang	1001	S4
6	Kung Wang	946	S5
7	I Wang	934	S6
8	Hsiao Wang	909	S5
9	I Wang	894	S7
10	Li Wang	878–841	S9
11	Hsuan Wang	827	S10
12	Yu Wang	781–771	S11

c *Eastern Chou* 770–249 BC

13	P'ing Wang	770	S12
14	Huan Wang	719	GS13
15	Chuang Wang	696	S14
16	Hsi Wang	681	S15
17	Hui Wang	676	S16
18	Hsiang Wang	651	S17
19	Ch'ing Wang	618	S18
20	K'uang Wang	612	S19
21	Ting Wang	606	S19
22	Chien Wang	585	S21
23	Ling Wang	571	S22
24	Ching Wang	544	S23
25	Ching Wang	519	S24
26	Yuan Wang	475	S25
27	Chen Ting Wang	468	S26
28	K'ao Wang	440	S27
29	Wei Lieh Wang	425	S28
30	An Wang	401	S29
31	Lieh Wang	375	S30
32	Hsien Wang	368	S30
33	Shen Ching Wang	320	S32

| 34 | Nan Wang | 314 | S33 |
| 35 | Tung Chou Chun | 255–249 | DT27 |

d *Ch'in* 221–206 BC

1	Shih Huang Ti (Cheng Wang of Ch'in)	221 BC	
2	Erh Shih Huang Ti	210	S1
3	Ch'in Wang	207–206	BS2

e *Western Han* 206 BC–8 AD

1	Kao Tsu (Liu Pang)	206 BC	
2	Hui Ti	195	S1
3	Kao Hou★	188	W1
4	Wen Ti	180	S1
5	Ching Ti	157	S4
6	Wu Ti	141	S5
7	Chao Ti	87	S6
8	Hsuan Ti	74	BGS7
9	Yuan Ti	48	S8
10	Ch'eng Ti	33	S9
11	Ai Ti	7	BS10
12	P'ing Ti	1	BS10
13	Ju-Tzu Ying	6–8 AD	BGG9

f *Hsin* 9–23 AD

| 1 | Chia Huang Ti (Wang Mang) | 9–23 AD | |

g *Eastern Han* 25–220 AD

1	Kuang Wu Ti (Liu Hsiu; DT1 W.Han)	25 AD	
2	Ming Ti	57	S1
3	Chang Ti	75	S2
4	Ho Ti	88	S3
5	Shang Ti	106	S4
6	An Ti	106	BS4
7	Shao Ti	125	BGS4
8	Shun Ti	125	S6
9	Ch'ung Ti	144	S8
10	Chih Ti	145	3G3
11	Huan Ti	146	GG3
12	Ling Ti	168	3G3
13	Shao Ti	189	S12
14	Hsien Ti	189–220	S12

h *Western Chin* 266–316

1	Wu Ti (Ssu-Ma Yen)	266	
2	Hui Ti	290	S1
3	Huai Ti	307–11	S1
4	Min Ti	313–316	BS3

i *Eastern Chin* 317–420

1	Yuan Ti (Ssu-Ma Jui; DTFBI W.Chin)	317	
2	Ming Ti	323	S1
3	Ch'eng Ti	325	S2
4	K'ang Ti	342	S2
5	Mu Ti	344	S4
6	Ai Ti	361	S3
7	Ti I (Hai Hsi Kung)	365	S3
8	Chien Wen Ti	372	S1
9	Hsiao Wu Ti	372	S8
10	An Ti	396	S9
11	Kung Ti	419–420	S9

j *Earlier Sung* 420–479

1	Wu Ti (Liu Yu)	420	
2	Shao Ti	422	S1
3	Wen Ti	424	S1
4	Hsiao Wu Ti	453	S3
5	Ch'ien Fei Ti	464	S4
6	Ming Ti	466	S3
7	Hou Fei Ti	472	S6
8	Shun Ti	477–479	S6

k *Southern Ch'i* 479–502

1	Kao Ti (Hsiao Tao-Ch'eng)	479	
2	Wu Ti	482	S1
3	Yu-Lin Wang	493	GS2
4	Hai-Ling Wang	494	B3
5	Ming Ti	494	BS1
6	Tung-Hun Hou	498	S5
7	Ho Ti	501–502	S5

l *Southern Liang* 502–557

1	Wu Ti (Hsiao Yen; FBS1 Southern Ch'i)	502	
2	Chien Wen Ti	549	S1
3	Yu-Chang Wang	551	S1
4	Yuan Ti	552	S1
5	Chen-Yang Hou	555	
6	Ching Ti	555–557	S4

m *Southern Ch'en* 557–589

1	Wu Ti (Ch'en Pa-Hsien)	557	
2	Wen Ti	559	BS1
3	Fei Ti	566	S2
4	Hsuan Ti	568	B2
5	Hou Chu	582–589	S4

n *Sui* 581–618

1	Wen Ti (Yang Chien)	587	

2	Yang Ti	604–618	S1
3	Kung Ti Yu (at Ch'ang An)	617–618	GS2
4	Kung Ti T'ung (at Lo Yang)	618.	B3

o *T'ang* 618–907

1	Kao Tsu (Li Yuan)	618	
2	T'ai Tsung (Li Shih-Min)	626	S1
3	Kao Tsung	649	S2
4	Chung Tsung (1)	683	S3
5	Jui Tsung (1)	684	S3
6	Wu Hou★	690	W3
	Chung Tsung (2)	705	
	Jui Tsung (2)	710	
7	Hsuan Tsung	712	S5
8	Su Tsung	756	S7
9	Tai Tsung	762	S8
10	Te Tsung	779	S9
11	Shun Tsung	805	S10
12	Hsien Tsung	805	S11
13	Mu Tsung	820	S12
14	Ching Tsung	824	S13
15	Wen Tsung	827	S13
16	Wu Tsung	840	S13
17	Hsuan Tsung	846	S12
18	I Tsung	859	S17
19	Hsi Tsung	873	S18
20	Chao Tsung	888	S18
21	Chao Hsuan Ti	904–907	S20

p *Later Liang* 907–923

1	T'ai Tsu (Chu Wen)	907	
2	Ying Wang	912	S1
3	Mo Ti	913–923	S1

q *Later T'ang* 923–936

1	Chuang Tsung (Li Ts'un-Hsu)	923	
2	Ming Tsung	926	AB1
3	Min Ti	933	S2
4	Mo Ti	934–936	AS2

r *Later Chin* 936–947

1	Kao Tsu (Shih Ching-T'ang)	936	
2	Ch'u Ti	942–947	BS1

s *Later Han* 947–951

1	Kao Tsu (Liu Chih-Yuan)	947	
2	Yin Ti	948–951	S1

t *Later Chou* 951–960

1	T'ai Tsu (Kuo Wei)	951	

2	Shih Tsung	954	AS1
3	Kung Ti	959–960	S2

u *Northern Sung* 960–1127

1	T'ai Tsu (Chao K'uang-Yin)	960	
2	T'ai Tsung	976	B1
3	Chen Tsung	997	S2
4	Jen Tsung	1022	S3
5	Ying Tsung	1063	GG2
6	Shen Tsung	1067	S5
7	Che Tsung	1085	S6
8	Hui Tsung	1100	S6
9	Ch'in Tsung	1126–1127	S8

v *Southern Sung* 1127–1279

1	Kao Tsung (s8 N.Sung)	1127	
2	Hsiao Tsung (DT1 N.Sung)	1162	
3	Kuang Tsung	1189	S2
4	Ning Tsung	1194	S3
5	Li Tsung (DT1 N.Sung)	1224	
6	Tu Tsung	1264	BS5
7	Kung Tsung	1274	S6
8	Tuan Tsung	1276	S6
9	Ti Ping	1278–1279	S6

w *Yuan* 1206–1368 *(Mongol Great Khans)*

1	T'ai Tsu (Chingis Khan)	1206–1227	
2	T'ai Tsung (Ogodei)	1229–1241	S1
3	Ting Tsung (Guyuk)	1246–1248	S2
4	Hsien Tsung (Mengu)	1251–1259	BS2
5	Shih Tsu (Kubilai)	1260	B4
6	Ch'eng Tsung	1294	GS5
7	Wu Tsung	1307	BS6
8	Jen Tsung	1311	B7
9	Ying Tsung	1320	S8
10	T'ai Ting Ti	1323	BS6
11	Wen Tsung (1)	1328	S10
12	Ming Tsung	1329	S7
	Wen Tsung (2)	1329	
13	Ning Tsung	1332	S12
14	Shun Ti	1332–1368	S12

x *Ming* 1368–1644

1	T'ai Tsu (Hung Wu) (Chu Yuan-Chang)	1368	
2	Hui Ti (Chien Wen)	1398	GS1
3	Ch'eng Tsu (Yung Lo)	1402	S1
4	Jen Tsung (Hung Hsi)	1424	S3
5	Hsuan Tsung (Hsuan Te)	1425	S4
6	Ying Tsung (Cheng T'ung) (1)	1435	S5
7	Tai Tsung (Ching T'ai)	1449	S5

Ying Tsung (2)	1457	
8 Hsien Tsung (Ch'eng Hua)	1464	S6
9 Hsiao Tsung (Hung Chih)	1487	S8
10 Wu Tsung (Cheng Te)	1505	S9
11 Shih Tsung (Chia Ching)	1521	BS9
12 Mu Tsung (Lung Ch'ing)	1567	S11
13 Shen Tsung (Wan Li)	1572	S12
14 Kuang Tsung (T'ai Ch'ing)	1620	S13
15 Hsi Tsung (T'ien Ch'i)	1620	S14
16 Chuang Lieh Ti (Ch'ung Chen)	1627–1644	S14

y *Ch'ing (Manchu)* 1616–1912

1 T'ai Tsu (T'ien Ming) (Nurhachi)	1616	
2 T'ai Tsung (T'ien Ts'ung/Ch'ung Te)	1626	S1
3 Shih Tsu (Shun Chih)	1643	S2
4 Sheng Tsu (K'ang Hsi)	1661	S3
5 Shih Tsung (Yung Cheng)	1722	S4
6 Kao Tsung (Ch'ien Lung)	1735	S5
7 Jen Tsung (Chia Ch'ing)	1796	S6
8 Hsuan Tsung (Tao Kuang)	1820	S7
9 Wen Tsung (Hsien Feng)	1850	S8
10 Mu Tsung (T'ung Chih)	1861	S9
11 Te Tsung (Kuang Hsu)	1875	BS9
12 Mo Ti (Hsuan T'ung)	1908–1912	BS11

228 **CHINA** ANCIENT CHINESE STATES

a *Rulers of Lu* 1122–255 BC

1 Chou Kung Tan (B1 W. Chou)	1122 BC	
2 Po Ch'in Kung	1115	S1
3 K'ao Kung	1062	S2
4 Yang Kung	1058	S3
5 Yu Kung	998	S4
6 Wei Kung	984	S4
7 Li Kung	934	S6
8 Hsien Kung	897	S6
9 Chen Kung	855	S8
10 Wu Kung	825	S8
11 I Kung	815	S10
11a Po-yu	806	S10
12 Hsiao Kung	795	BS11
13 Hui Kung	768	S12
14 Yin Kung	722	S13
15 Huan Kung	711	S13
16 Chuang Kung	693	S15
17 Min Kung	661	S16
18 Hsi Kung	659	S17
19 Wen Kung	626	S18

20	Hsuan Kung	608	S19
21	Ch'eng Kung	590	S20
22	Hsiang Kung	572	S21
23	Chao Kung	541	S22
24	Ting Kung	509	S22
25	Ai Kung	494	S24
26	Tao Kung	466	S25
27	Yuan Kung	428	S26
28	Mu Kung	407	S27
29	Kung Kung	376	S28
30	K'ang Kung	352	S29
31	Ching Kung	343	S30
32	P'ing Kung	314	S31
33	Wen Kung	295	S32
34	Ch'ing Kung	272–255	S33

b *Rulers of Ch'in 821–221 BC*

1	Chuang Kung	821 BC	
2	Hsiang Kung	777	S1
3	Wen Kung	765	S2
4	Ling Kung	715	GS3
5	Chu Kung	703	S4
6	Wu Kung	697	S4
7	Te Kung	677	S4
8	Hsuan Kung	675	S7
9	Ch'eng Kung	663	S7
10	Mu Kung	659	S7
11	K'ang Kung	620	S10
12	Kung Kung	608	S11
13	Huan Kung	603	S12
14	Ching Kung	576	S13
15	Ai Kung	536	S14
16	Hui Kung	500	BS15
17	Tao Kung	490	S16
18	Li Kung Kung	476	S17
19	Tsao Kung	442	S18
20	Huai Kung	428	S18
21	Ling Kung	424	GS20
22	Chien Kung	414	S20
23	Hui Kung	399	S22
24	Chu-Tzu	386	S23
25	Hsien Kung	384	S21
26	Hsiao Kung	361	S25
27	Hui-Wen Wang	337	S26
28	Wu Wang	310	S27
29	Chao Hsiang Wang	306	S27
30	Hsiao Wen Wang	250	S29
31	Chuang Hsiang Wang	250	S30
32	Cheng Wang (Emperor Shih Huang Ti 221 BC)	246–(209)	S31

c Rulers of Sung 1111–286 BC

1	Wei Tzu Ch'i	1111 BC	
2	Wei Chung	1077	
3	Sung Kung	1053	
4	Ting Kung	1000	
5	Min Kung	935	
6	Yang Kung	908	
7	Li Kung	893	
8	Hsi Kung	858	
9	Hui Kung	830	
10	Tai Kung	799	
11	Wu Kung	765	S10
12	Hsuan Kung	747	S11
13	Mu Kung	728	S11
14	Shang Kung	719	S12
15	Chuang Kung	710	S13
16	Min Kung	691	S15
17	Huan Kung	681	S15
18	Hsiang Kung	650	S17
19	Ch'eng Kung	636	S18
20	Chao Kung	619	S19
21	Wen Kung	610	S19
22	Kung Kung	588	S21
23	P'ing Kung	575	S22
24	Yuan Kung	531	S23
25	Ching Kung	516	S24
26	Chao Kung	450	GS24
27	Tao Kung	403	
28	Hsiu Kung	395	S27
29	Pi Kung	372	S28
30	T'i Ch'eng	369	S29
31	Yen Wang	328–286	S29

d Rulers of Ch'en c.854–479 BC

1	Hu Kung Man		
2	Shen Kung		
3	Huan Kung		
4	Hsiao Kung		
5	Shen Kung		
6	Yu Kung	854	
7	Hsi Kung	831	S6
8	Wu Kung	795	S7
9	I Kung	780	S8
10	P'ing Kung	777	S8
11	Wen Kung	754	S10
12	Huan Kung	744	S11
13	Li Kung	706	S11
14	Chuang Kung	699	S12
15	Hsuan Kung	692	S12

16	Mu Kung	647	S15
17	Kung Kung	631	S16
18	Ling Kung	613	S17
19	Ch'eng Kung	598	S18
20	Ai Kung	568	S19
21	Hui Kung (1)	533–532	BS20
		———	
	Hui Kung (2)	529	
22	Huai Kung	505	S21
23	Min Kung	501–479	S22

e *Rulers of Yen 864–222 BC*

1	Hui Hou	864 BC	
2	Hsi Hou	826	S1
3	Ch'ing Hou	790	S2
4	Ai Hou	766	S3
5	Cheng Hou	764	
6	Mu Hou	728	S5
7	Hsuan Hou	710	S6
8	Huan Kung	697	S7
9	Chuang Kung	690	S8
10	Hsiang Kung	657	S9
11	Huan Kung	617	
12	Hsuan Kung	601	
13	Chao Kung	586	S12
14	Wu Kung	573	S13
15	Wen Kung	554	S14
16	I Kung	548	S15
17	Hui Kung	544	S16
18	Tao Kung	535	S17
19	Kung Kung	528	S18
20	P'ing Kung	523	S19
21	Chien Kung	504	S20
22	Hsien Kung	492	S21
23	Hsiao Kung	464	S22
24	Ch'eng Kung	449	S23
25	Min Kung	433	S24
26	Hsi Kung	402	S25
27	Huan Kung	372	S26
28	Wen Kung	361	S27
29	I Wang	332	S28
30	K'uai Wang	320	S29
31	Chao Wang	311	S30
32	Hui Wang	278	S31
33	Wu-Ch'eng Wang	271	S32
34	Hsiao Wang	257	S33
35	Hsi Wang	254–222	S34

f *Rulers of Cheng 806–375 BC*

1	Huan Kung (S10 W.Chou)	806 BC

2	Wu Kung	770	S1
3	Chuang Kung	743	S2
4	Li Kung (1)	700	S3
5	Chao Kung	696	S3
6	Tzu-Wei	694	S3
7	Tzu-Ying	693	
	Li Kung (2)	679	
9	Wen Kung	672	S4
10	Mu Kung	627	S9
11	Ling Kung	605	S10
12	Hsiang Kung	604	S11
13	Tao Kung	586	S12
14	Ch'eng Kung	584	S13
15	Hsi Kung	570	S14
16	Chien Kung	565	S15
17	Ting Kung	529	S16
18	Hsien Kung	513	S17
19	Sheng Kung	500	S17
20	Ai Kung	463	S19
21	Kung Kung	455	S17
22	Yu Kung	423	S21
23	Hsu Kung	422	S21
24	K'ang Kung	395–375	S21

g *Rulers of Ch'u* 1122–223 BC

1	Hsiung I	1122 BC	
2	Hsiung Ai	1078	
3	Hsiung Tan	1052	
4	Hsiung Sheng	1001	
5	Hsiung Yang	946	
6	Hsiung Ch'u	887	
7	Hsiung Wu-K'ang	?	
8	Hsiung Chih-Hung	877	
9	Hsiung Yen	876	
10	Hsiung Yung	847	
11	Hsiung Yen	837	
12	Hsiung Hsiang	827	
13	Hsiung Hsun	821	
14	Hsiung O	799	
15	Hsiung I	790	
16	Hsiung K'an	762	
17	Hsiung Hsun	757	
18	Wu Wang	740	
19	Wen Wang	689	
20	Hsiung Chien	676	
21	Ch'eng Wang	671	
22	Mu Wang	625	
23	Chuang Wang	613	S22
24	Kung Wang	590	S23
25	K'ang Wang	559	S24

26	Ao Wang	544	S25
27	Ling Wang	540	S24
28	P'ing Wang	528	S24
29	Chao Wang	515	S28
30	Hui Wang	488	S29
31	Chien Wang	431	S30
32	Sheng Wang	407	S31
33	Tao Wang	401	S32
34	Su Wang	380	
35	Hsuan Wang	369	
36	Wei Wang	339	
37	Huai Wang	328	
38	Ch'ing-Hsiang Wang	298	S37
39	K'ao-Lieh Wang	262	
40	Yu Wang	237	
41	Fu-Ch'u Wang	227–223	

h *Rulers of Ch'i* 1122–226 BC

1	T'ai Kung Shang	1122 BC	
2	Ting Kung	1077	
3	I Kung	1051	
4	Kuei Kung	1000	
5	Ai Kung	934	
6	Hu Kung	893	B5
7	Hsien Kung	859	B5
8	Wu Kung	850	S7
9	Li Kung	824	S8
10	Wen Kung	815	S9
11	Ch'eng Kung	803	S10
12	Chuang Kung	794	S11
13	Hsi Kung	730	S12
14	Hsiang Kung	697	S13
15	Huan Kung	685	S13
16	Hsiao Kung	642	S15
17	Chao Kung	632	S15
18	I Kung	612	S15
19	Hui Kung	608	S15
20	Ch'ing Kung	598	S19
21	Ling Kung	581	S20
22	Chuang Kung	553	S21
23	Ching Kung	547	S21
24	Yen Ju-Tzu	489	S23
25	Tao Kung	488	S24
26	Chien Kung	484	S25
27	P'ing Kung	480	S25
28	Hsuan Kung	455	S27
29	K'ang Kung	404	S28
30	T'ai Kung T'ien Ho	386	
31	Huan Kung	384	S30
32	Wei Wang	378	S31

33	Hsuan Wang	342	s32
34	Min Wang	323	s33
35	Hsiang Wang	283	s34
36	Chien Wang	264–226	s35

i *Rulers of Chin c.900–376 BC*

1	Wu Hou	c.900 BC	
2	Ch'eng Hou	c.880	
3	Li Hou	c.860	
4	Ching Hou	858	
5	Hsi Hou	840	
6	Hsien Hou	822	s5
7	Mu Hou	811	s6
8	Shang-Shu	784	s6
9	Wen Hou	780	s8
10	Chao Hou	745	s9
11	Hsiao Hou	739	s10
12	O Hou	723	s11
13	Ai Hou	717	s12
14	Hsiao-Tzu Hou	709	s13
15	Hou-min	706	
16	Wu Kung	678	DT9
17	Hsien Kung	676	s16
18	Hui Kung	650	s17
19	Wen Kung	636	s17
20	Hsiang Kung	627	s19
21	Ling Kung	620	s20
22	Ch'eng Kung	606	s19
23	Ching Kung	599	s22
24	Li Kung	580	s23
25	Tao Kung	572	GS19
26	P'ing Kung	557	s25
27	Chao Kung	531	s26
28	Ch'ing Kung	525	s27
29	Ting Kung	511	s28
30	Ch'u Kung	474	s29
31	Ai Kung	456	GS27
32	Yu Kung	437	s31
33	Lieh Kung	419	s32
34	Hsiao Kung	392	s33
35	Ching Kung	377–376	s34

(Chin divided into Wei, Han and Chao)

j *Rulers of Wei 424–225 BC*

1	Wen Hou	424 BC	
2	Wu Hou	386	s1
3	Hui Wang	370	s2
4	Hsiang Wang	334	
5	Ai Wang	318	
6	Chao Wang	295	s5

7 An-Hsi Wang	276	s6
8 Ching-Min Wang	242	s7
9 Chia Wang	227–225	

k *Rulers of Han* 408–230 BC

1 Ching Hou	408 BC	
2 Lieh Hou	399	
3 Wen Hou	386	s2
4 Ai Hou	376	s3
5 Chuang Hou	370	s4
6 Chao Hou	358	s5
7 Hsuan-Hui Wang	332	s6
8 Hsiang Wang	311	s7
9 Hsi-Chui Wang	295	s8
10 Huan-Hui Wang	272	s9
11 An Wang	238–230	

l *Rulers of Chao* 408–228 BC

1 Lieh Hou	408 BC	
2 Wu Kung	399	B1
3 Ching Kung	386	s1
4 Ch'eng Hou	374	s3
5 Su Hou	349	s4
6 Wu-Ling Wang	325	s5
7 Hui-Wen Wang	298	s6
8 Hsiao-Ch'eng Wang	265	s7
9 Tao-Hsiang Wang	244	s8
10 Ch'ien Wang	235–228	s9

m *Rulers of Wu* 677–473 BC

1 Chiao-I	677 BC
2 Ti-I	653
3 Chieh-Ssu	623
4 Chih-Chi	588
5 Shou-Mang	585
6 Chu-Fan	560
7 Yu-Ts'ai	547
8 Yu-Mei	530
9 Liao	526
10 Ho-Lu	514
11 Fu-Ch'ai	495–473

n *Rulers of Yueh* 510–334 BC

1 Yun-Ch'ang	510 BC
2 Kou-Chien	496
3 Shih-Yu	464
4 Lu-Ying	464
5 Pu-Shou	458
6 Chu-Kou Weng	448
7 Wang I	411

8	Chih-Hou	375	
9	Wu-Chiang	356–334	

o *Rulers of Ts'ai 863–447* BC

1	Wu Hou	863 BC	
2	I Hou	837	S1
3	Hsi Hou	809	S2
4	Kung Hou	761	S3
5	Tai Hou	759	S4
6	Hsuan Hou	749	S5
7	Huan Hou	714	S6
8	Ai Hou	694	S6
9	Mu Hou	674	S8
10	Chuang Hou	645	S9
11	Wen Hou	611	S10
12	Ching Hou	591	S11
13	Ling Hou	542–531	S12
14	P'ing Hou	529	BS13
15	Tao Hou	521	B14
16	Chao Hou	518	B14
17	Ch'eng Hou	490	S16
18	Sheng Hou	471	S17
19	Yuan Hou	456–447	S18

p *Rulers of Ts'ao 934–487* BC

1	Kung Pai	934 BC	
2	Hsiao Pai	894	
3	I Pai	864	
4	Yu Pai	834	S3
5	Tai Pai	825	S3
6	Hui Pai	795	S5
7	Mu Kung	759	S6
8	Huan Kung	756	S7
9	Chuang Kung	701	S8
10	Hsi Kung	670	S9
11	Chao Kung	661	S10
12	Kung Kung	652	S11
13	Wen Kung	617	S12
14	Hsuan Kung	594	S13
15	Ch'eng Kung	577	S13
16	Wu Kung	554	S15
17	P'ing Kung	527	S16
18	Tao Kung	523	S17
19	Hsiang Kung	514	S17
20	Yin Kung	509	S17
21	Ching Kung	505	S17
22	Po-Yang	501–487	S21

q *Chao Dynasty of Nan-Yueh (Trieu of Canton)* 207–111 BC

1	Wu Ti (Vo-De)	207 BC	
2	Wen Wang (Van-Vuong)	136	GS1
3	Ming Wang (Minh-Vuong)	124	S2
4	Ai Wang (Ai Vuong)	112	S3
5	Wei-Yang Wang (Vuong Kien-Duc)	111.	S3

229 **CHINA** THE THREE KINGDOMS

a *Wei* 220–266 AD

1	Wen Ti (Ts'ao P'ei)	220	
2	Ming Ti	226	S1
3	Fei Ti	239	S2
4	Shao Ti	254	AS2
5	Yuan Ti Huan	260–266	BS1

b *Wu* 222–280 AD

1	Ta Ti (Sun Ch'uan)	222	
2	Fei Ti	252	S1
3	Ching Ti	258	S1
4	Mo Ti	264–280	BS3

c *Shu-Han* 221–263 AD

1	Chao-Lieh Ti (Liu Pei; DT5 W.Han)	221	
2	Hou Ti	223–263	S1

230 **CHINA** THE SIXTEEN KINGDOMS

a *Northern Han (Earlier Chao) (Shansi)* 304–329

1	Kao Tsu (Liu Yuan; = S. Hsiung-Nu 23.)	304	
2	Lieh Tsung	310	S1
3	Liu Ts'an	318	S2
4	Liu Yao	318–329	

b *Ch'eng-Han (Szechuan)* 302–347

1	Shih Tsu (Li Te)	302	
2	Ch'in-Wen Wang	303	B1
3	T'ai Tsung	304	S1
4	Ai Ti	334	BS3
5	Yu Kung	334	S3
6	Chung Tsung	338	BS1
7	Kuei-I Hou	343–347	S6

c *Earlier Liang (Shansi)* 313–376

1	T'ai Tsu (Chang Kuei)	313	
2	Kao Tsu	314	S1
3	T'ai Tsung	320	S1
4	Shih Tsu	324	S2

5	Shih Tsu	346	S4
6	Wei Wang	354	S4
7	Ch'ung Wang	355	S5
8	Tao Kung	363–376	S4

d *Later Chao (Hopei)* 319–352

1	Kao Tsu (Shih Lo) (DT19 S. Hsiung-Nu)	319	
2	Hai-Yang Wang	333	S1
3	T'ai Tsu	334	BGS1
4	Shih Shih	349	S3
5	Shih Tsun	349	S3
6	Shih Chien	349	S3
7	Shih Chih	350	S3
8	Jan Min	350–352	

e *Earlier Yen (Hopei)* 348–370

1	Lieh Tsu (Mu-Yung Chun)	348	
2	Yu Ti	360–370	S1

f *Tai (Shansi)* 338–377

1	Kao Tsu (T'o-Pa Shih-I-Chien)	338–377	

g *Earlier Ch'in (Shensi)* 351–395

1	Kao Tsu (Fu Chien)	351	
2	Li Wang	355	S1
3	Shih Tsu	357	BS1
4	Ai-P'ing Ti	385	S3
5	T'ai Tsung	386	BGS3
6	Fu Ch'ung	394–395	S5

h *Later Ch'in (Shensi)* 384–417

1	T'ai Tsu (Yao Ch'ang)	384	
2	Kao Tsu	394	S1
3	Yao Hung	416–417	S2

i *Western Yen (Shansi)* 384–396

1	Mu-Yung Hung	384	
2	Mu-Yung Ch'ung	385	S1
3	Tuan Sui	386	
4	Mu-Yung Chi	386	
5	Mu-Yung Wang	386	S2
6	Mu-Yung Chung	386	S1
7	Mu-Yung-Yung	386–396	

j *Later Yen (Hopei)* 386–409

1	Shih Tsu (Mu-Yung Ch'ui)	386	
2	Lieh Tsung	396	S1
3	Mu-Yung Hsiang	397	
4	Mu-Yung Lin	397	
5	Chung Tsung	399	S2

6 Chao-Wen Ti	401	SI
7 Hui-I Ti	407–409	AS2

k *Western Ch'in (Kansu)* 385–431

1 Lieh Tsu (Ch'i-Fu Kuo-Jen)	385	
2 Kao Tsu	388	BI
3 T'ai Tsu	412	S2
4 Ch'i-Fu Mu-Mo	428–431	S3

l *Later Liang (Kansu)* 386–403

1 T'ai Tsu (Lu Kuang)	386	
2 Yin Wang	400	SI
3 Ling Ti	400	SI
4 Lu Lung	401–403	BSI

m *Southern Liang (Kansu)* 397–414

1 Lieh Tsu (T'u-Fa Wu-Ku)	397	
2 K'ang Wang	399	BI
3 Ching Wang	402–414	BI

n *Northern Liang (Kansu)* 397–439

1 Chien K'ang Kung	397	
2 Wu Hsuan Wang	401	
3 Ai Wang	433–439	S2

o *Southern Yen (Shantung)* 398–410

1 Shih Tsung (Mu-Yung Te; BI Earlier Yen)	398	
2 Chao-Wen Ti	405–410	BSI

p *Western Liang (Kansu)* 400–423

1 T'ai Tsu (Li Kao)	400	
2 Li Hsin	417	SI
3 Li Hsun	420	SI
4 Li Ch'ung-Erh	421–423	S2

q *Hsia (Shensi)* 407–431

1 Shih Tsu (Ho-Lien Po-Po)	407	
2 Ho-Lien Ch'ang	425	SI
3 Ho-Lien Ting	428–431	SI

r *Northern Yen (Hopei)* 409–436

1 T'ai Tsu (Feng Pa)	409	
2 Chao-Ch'eng Ti	430–436	BI

231 CHINA THE TEN KINGDOMS

a *Wu (Kiangsu)* 902–937

1 T'ai Tsu (Yang Hsing-Mi)	902	
2 Lieh Tsung	905	SI

3 Kao Tsu	908	S1
4 Jui Ti	920–937	S1

b *Wu-Yueh (Chekiang) 902–978*

1 T'ai Tsu (Ch'ien Ch'iu)	902	
2 Shih Tsung	932	S1
3 Ch'eng Tsung	941	S2
4 Chung-Hsun Wang	947	S2
5 Chung-I Wang	948–978	S2

c *Southern T'ang (Kiangsu) 937–975*

1 Lieh Tsu (Li Pien)	937	
2 Yuan Tsung	943	S1
3 Hou Chu	961–975	S2

d *Ch'u (Hunan) 927–963*

1 Wu-Mu Wang (Ma Yin)	927	
2 Heng-Yang Wang	930	S1
3 Wen-Chao Wang	932	S1
4 Ma Hsi-Kuang	947	S1
5 Ma Hsi-O	950	S1
6 Ma Hsi-Ch'ung	951	S1
7 Chou Hsing-Feng	952	
8 Chou Pao-Ch'uan	962–963	S7

e *Southern Han (Kwangtung) 917–971*

1 Kao Tsu (Liu Yen)	917	
2 Shang Ti	942	S1
3 Chung Tsung	943	S1
4 Nan Yueh Wang	958–971	S3

f *Earlier Shu (Szechuan) 901–925*

1 Kao Tsu (Wang Chien)	901	
2 Shun-Cheng Kung	918–925	S1

g *Later Shu (Szechuan) 934–965*

1 Kao Tsu (Meng Chih-Hsiang)	934	
2 Ch'u Wang	934–965	S1

h *Southern P'ing (Hupei) 925–963*

1 Wu-Hsin Wang (Kao Chi-Hsing)	925	
2 Wen-Hsien Wang	929	S1
3 Cheng-I Wang	948	S2
4 Kao Pao-Hsu	960	S2
5 Kao Chi-Ch'ung	962–963	S3

i *Min (Fukien) 909–945*

1 T'ai Tsu (Wang Shen-Chih)	909	
2 Wang Yen-Han	925	S1
3 T'ai Tsung	927	S1

4 K'ang Tsung	·935	S3
5 Ching Tsung	939–944	S1
6 Wang Yen-Cheng	943–945	S1

j *Northern Han (Shansi)* 951–979

1 Shih Tsu (Liu Ch'ung; B1 Later Han)	951	
2 Jui Tsung	955	S1
3 Liu Chi-En	968	AS2
4 Ying-Wu Ti	968–979	B3

232 **CHINA** THE NORTHERN DYNASTIES

a *Northern Wei* 386–557

1 T'ai Tu (T'o-Pa Kuei: GS1 Tai)	386	
2 T'ai Tsung	409	S1
3 Shih Tsu	423	S2
4 Nan-An Wang	452	S3
5 Kao Tsung	452	GS3
6 Hsien Tsu	465	S5
7 Kao Tsu	471	S6
8 Shih Tsung	499	S7
9 Su Tsung	515	S8
10 Ching Tsung	528	BS7
11 Tung Hai Wang	530	GG4
12 Ch'ien Fei Ti	531–532	BS7
13 Hou Fei Ti	531–532	GG6
14 Hsiao-Wu Ti	532–535	BS8
15 Hsiao-Ching Ti (Eastern Wei)	534–550	DT7
16 Wen Ti (Western Wei)	535–551	GS7
17 Fei Ti (Western Wei)	551–554	S16
18 Kung Ti (Western Wei)	554–557	S16

b *Northern Ch'i* 550–577

1 Hsien Tsu (Kao Yang)	550	
2 Fei Ti	559	S1
3 Hsiao-Chao Ti	560	B1
4 Shih Tsu	561	B1
5 Hou Chu	565	S4
6 Yu Chu	577·	S5

c *Northern Chou* 557–581

1 Hsiao Min Ti	557	
2 Shih Tsung	557	B1
3 Kao Tsu	560	B1
4 Hsuan Ti	578	S3
5 Ching Ti	580–581	S4

d *Later Liang (Hopei)* 555–587

1 Chung Tsung (Hsiao Ch'a; GS1 Southern Liang)	555	

2	Shih Tsung	562	S1
3	Chu Kung	585–587	S2

e *Liao (Khitan) 907–1125*

1	T'ai Tsu (Yeh-Lu A-Pao-Chi)	907	
2	T'ai Tsung	926	S1
3	Shih Tsung	947	BS2
4	Mu Tsung	951	S2
5	Ching Tsung	969	S3
6	Sheng Tsung	982	S5
7	Hsing Tsung	1031	S6
8	Tao Tsung	1055	S7
9	T'ien-Tsu Ti	1101–1125	GS8

f *Chin (Juchen) 1115–1234*

1	T'ai Tsu (Wan-Yen A-Ku-Ta)	1115	
2	T'ai Tsung	1123	B1
3	Hsi Tsung	1135	GS1
4	Hai-Ling Wang	1150	GS1
5	Shih Tsung	1161	GS1
6	Chang Tsung	1189	GS5
7	Wei-Shao Wang	1208	S5
8	Hsuan Tsung	1213	B6
9	Ai Tsung	1224	S8
10	Mo Ti	1234.	

g *Western Hsia (Tangut) 1032–1227*

1	Ching Tsung (Li Yuan-Hao)	1032	
2	I Tsung	1048	S1
3	Hui Tsung	1069	S2
4	Ch'ung Tsung	1086	S3
5	Jen Tsung	1139	S4
6	Huan Tsung	1193	S5
7	Hsiang Tsung	1206	GS4
8	Shen Tsung	1211	
9	Hsien Tsung	1223	S8
10	Li Hsien	1226–1227	

233 CHINA MANCHURIA

a *Kings of P'o-Hai (Parhae) 698–927*

1	Ko (Kao Wang)	698	
2	Mu (Wu Wang)	719	S1
3	Mun (Wen Wang)	737	S2
4	Wonui	794	S2
5	Song	794	GS3
6	Kang (K'ang Wang)	794	S3
7	Chong (Ch'eng Wang)	809	S6
8	Hui (Hsi Wang)	812	S6

9	Kan (Chien Wang)	817	DTBI
10	Son (Hsuan Wang)	818	S9
11	Yijin (Ta-I Chen)	830	S10
12	Konhwang (Ta Ch'ien-Huang)	857	S10
13	Kyong (Ta Hsuan-Hsi)	871	
14	Wigye (Ta Yin-Shan)	893	
15	Ae	906–927	

b *Emperor of Manchukuo 1934–1945*

| 1 | Kang Te (Ch'ing Mo Ti of China) | 1934–1945 |

234 CHINA KINGDOM OF NAN CHAO 629–1252

1	Kao Tsu (Hsi-Nu-Lo)	629	
2	Shih Tsung	674	S1
3	Wei-ch'eng Wang	712	S2
4	P'i-Lo-Ko	728	S3
5	Shun-wu Ti (Ko-Lo-Feng)	748	S4
6	Hsiao Heng Ti	778	GS5
7	Hsiao Wen Ti	808	S6
8	Yu Ti	809	S6
9	Ching Wang	819	S7
10	Chao Ch'eng Ti	824	S9
11	Ching Chuang Ti	859	
12	Hsuan Wu Ti	877	S11
13	Hsiao Ai Ti	897	S12
14	Te Heng Ti	901	
15	Su Wen Ti	910	S14
16	Kung Hui Ti	927	S15
17	Tao K'ang Ti	928	
18	Su Kung Ti	928	
19	T'ai Tsu (Tuan Ssu-P'ing)	937	
20	Wu Liao Ti	944	S19
21	Sheng Tzu Wen Ti	946	B19
22	Chih Tao Kuang Chih Ti	952	S21
23	Ying Tao Ti	969	S22
24	Chao Ming Ti	985	S23
25	Ching Ming Ti	1009	S24
26	P'ing I Ti	1022	S25
27	Sheng Te Ti	1026	BS26
28	T'ien Ming Ti	1041	GS27
29	Shih Tsung	1044	GG19
30	Shang Te Ti	1075	S29
31	Yang I-Ch'en	1080	
32	Shang Ming Ti	1080	
33	Pao Ting Ti	1082	
34	Kao Sheng T'ai	1099	
35	Chung Tsung	1105	
36	Hsien Tsung	1108	
37	Ching Tsung	1147	S36

38	Hsuan Tsung	1171	
39	Heng T'ien Ti	1200	S38
40	Shen Tsung	1205	S38
41	Hsiao I Ti	1238	S40
42	Tuan Hsing-Chih	1251–1252	S41

235 **KOREA** KINGDOMS AND DYNASTIES

a *Kings of Koguryo* 37 BC–668 AD

1	Tong-myong	37 BC	
2	Yu-ri	19	S1
3	Tae-mu-sin	18 AD	S2
4	Min-jung	44	S3
5	Mo-bon	48	S3
6	T'ae-jo	53	GS2
7	Ch'a-dae	146	B6
8	Sin-dae	165	B6
9	Ko-guk-ch'on	179	S8
10	San-sang	197	S8
11	Tong-ch'on	227	
12	Chung-ch'on	248	S11
13	So-ch'on	270	S12
14	Pong-sang	292	S13
15	Mi-ch'on	300	
16	Ko-gug-won	331	
17	So-su-rim	371	S16
18	Ko-gug-yang	384	S16
19	Kwang-gae-t'o	391	S18
20	Chang-su	413	S19
21	Mun-ja	492	GS20
22	An-jang	519	GG17
23	An-won	531	
24	Yang-won	545	
25	Pyong-won	559	
26	Yong-yang	590	
27	Yong-yu	618	S26
28	Po-jang	642–668	

b *Kings of Paekche* 18 BC–661 AD

1	On-jo	18 BC	
2	Ta-ru	28 AD	
3	Ki-ru	77	
4	Kae-ru	128	S3
5	Ch'o-go	166	S4
6	Ku-su	214	
7	Sa-ban	234	S6
8	Ko-i	234	S6
9	Ch'ae-gye	286	S8
10	Pun-su	298	S8

11	Pi-ryu	304	B6
12	Kye	344	S10
13	Kun-ch'o-go	346	S11
14	Kun-gu-su	375	S13
15	Ch'im-yu	384	S13
16	Chin-sa	385	S15
17	A-sin	392	S15
18	Chon-ji	405	S17
19	Ku-i-sin	420	S18
20	Pi-yu	427	
21	Kae-ru	455	S20
22	Mun-ju	475	S21
23	Sam-gun	477	S22
24	Tong-song	479	S21
25	Mu-ryong	501	
26	Song	523	S25
27	Ui-dok	554	
28	Hye	598	
29	Pop	599	
30	Mu	600	
31	Ui-ja	641–661	S30

Note: Dates prior to 4th century AD are solely traditional.

c *Kings of Silla 57 BC–935 AD*

1	Hyok-ko-se	57 BC	
2	Nam-hae	4 AD	
3	Yu-ri	24	
4	T'al-hae	57	
5	Pa-sa	80	
6	Chi-ma	112	
7	Il-song	134	
8	A-dal-la	154	
9	Por-hyu	184	
10	Nae-hae	196	
11	Cho-bun	230	
12	Chom-hae	247	
13	Mi-ch'u	262	
14	Yu-rye	284	
15	Ki-rim	298	S14
16	Kor-hae	310	DT10
17	Nae-mul	356	S13
18	Sil-song	402	
19	Nul-chi	417	S17
20	Cha-bi	458	
21	So-ji	479	
22	Chi-jung	500	GG17
23	Pop-hung	514	
24	Chin-hung	540	B23
25	Chin-ji	576	

26	Chin-p'yong	579	
27	Son-dok★	632	D26
28	Chin-dok★	647	GD26
29	Mu-yol	654	GS25
30	Mun-mu	661	
31	Sin-mun	681	S30
32	Hyo-so	692	
33	Song-dok	702	B32
34	Hyo-song	737	S33
35	Kyong-dok	742	S33
36	Hye-gong	765	S35
37	Son-dok	780	
38	Won-song	785	
39	So-song	799	GS38
40	Ae-jang	800	
41	Hon-dok	809	B40
42	Hung-dok	826	
43	Hui-gang	836	GS38
44	Min-ae	838	GS38
45	Sin-mu	839	GS38
46	Mun-song	839	S45
47	Hon-an	857	S45
48	Kyong-mun	861	GS43
49	Hon-gang	875	S48
50	Chong-gang	886	S49
51	Chin-song★	888	D49
52	Hyo-gong	898	S49
53	Sin-dok	913	
54	Kyong-myong	917	S53
55	Kyong-ae	924	S53
56	Kyong-sun	927–935	

Note: Dates prior to 4th century AD solely traditional.

d *Later Koguryo Dynasty 904–917*

1	Kong-wo	904–917

e *Later Paekche Dynasty 892–936*

1	Chinhwon Wang	892
2	Singom Wang	935–936

f *Wang Dynasty 918–1392*

1	T'ae-jo	918	
2	Hye-jong	944	S1
3	Chong-jong	945	S1
4	Kwang-jong	949	S1
5	Kyong-jong	975	S4
6	Song-jong	981	BS4
7	Mok-chong	997	S5

8	Hyon-jong	1009	BS4
9	Tok-chong	1031	S8
10	Chong-jong	1034	S8
11	Mun-jong	1046	S8
12	Sun-jong	1083	S11
13	Son-jong	1083	S11
14	Hon-jong	1094	S13
15	Suk-chong	1095	S11
16	Ye-jong	1105	S15
17	In-jong	1122	S16
18	Ui-jong	1146	S17
19	Myong-jong	1170	S17
20	Sin-jong	1197	S17
21	Hui-jong	1204	S20
22	Kang-jong	1211	S19
23	Ko-jong	1213	S22
24	Won-jong	1259	S23
25	Ch'ung-yol	1274	S24
26	Ch'ung-son	1308	S25
27	Ch'ung-suk (1)	1313	S26
28	Ch'ung-hye (1)	1330	S27
	Ch'ung-suk (2)	1332	
	Ch'ung-hye (2)	1339	
29	Ch'ung-mok	1344	S28
30	Ch'ung-jong	1349	S28
31	Kong-min	1351	S27
32	Wi-ju	1374	S31
33	Ch'ang	1388	S32
34	Kong-yang	1389–1392	DT20

g *Yi Dynasty* 1392–1910

1	T'ae-jo	1392	
2	Chong-jong	1398	S1
3	T'ae-jong	1400	S1
4	Se-jong	1418	S3
5	Mun-jong	1450	S4
6	Tan-jong	1452	S5
7	Se-jo	1455	S4
8	Ye-jong	1468	S7
9	Song-jong	1469	BS8
10	Yon-san	1494	S9
11	Chung-jong	1506	S9
12	In-jong	1544	S11
13	Myong-jong	1545	S11
14	Son-jo	1567	BS13
15	Kwang-hae	1608	S14
16	In-jo	1623	BS15
17	Hyo-jong	1649	S16
18	Hyon-jong	1659	S17
19	Suk-chong	1674	S18

20	Kyong-jong	1720	S19
21	Yong-jo	1724	S19
22	Chong-jo	1776	GS21
23	Sun-jo	1800	S22
24	Hon-jong	1834	GS23
25	Ch'ol-chong	1849	BGS22
26	Ko-jong	1864	DT16
27	Sun-jong	1907–1910	S26

236 **JAPAN** EMPERORS AND SHOGUNS

a *Emperors since 660/40 BC*

		Probable date	*Traditional date*	
1	Jimmu	*c.*40 BC	660 BC	
2	Suizei	*c.*10	581	S1
3	Annei	*c.*20 AD	549	S2
4	Itoku	*c.*50	510	S3
5	Kosho	*c.*80	475	S4
6	Koan	*c.*110	392	S5
7	Korei	*c.*140	290	S6
8	Kogen	*c.*170	214	S7
9	Kaika	*c.*200	157	S8
10	Sujin	*c.*230	97	S9
11	Suinin	259	29	S10
12	Keiko	291	71 AD	S11
13	Seimu	323	131	S12
14	Chuai	356	192	BS13
—	(Jingo★ regent)	363	201	W14
15	Ojin	380	270	S14
16	Nintoku	395	313	S15
17	Richu	428	400	S16
18	Hanzei	433	406	S16
19	Inkyo	438	412	S16
20	Anko	455	454	S19
21	Yuryaku	457	457	S19
22	Seinei	490	480	S21
23	Kenso	495	485	GS17
24	Ninken	498	488	B23
25	Muretsu	504	499	S24
26	Keitai	510	507	BGG17
27	Ankan		534	S26
28	Senka		536	S26
29	Kimmei		540	S26
30	Bidatsu		572	S29
31	Yomei		586	S29
32	Sujun		588	S29
33	Suiko★		593	D29
34	Jomei		629	GS30
35	Kogyoku (1)★		642	BGS33

36	Kotoku	645	B35
	Saimei (Kogyoku) (2)★	655	
37	Tenchi	662	S34
38	Kobun	672	S37
39	Temmu	673	S34
40	Jito★	686	D37
41	Mommu	697	GS39
42	Gemmyo★	708	D37
43	Gensho★	715	ST41
44	Shomu	724	S41
45	Koken (1)★	749	D44
46	Junnin	759	GS39
	Shotoku (Koken) (2)★	765	
47	Konin	770	BGS40
48	Kwammu	782	S47
49	Heijo	806	S48
50	Saga	810	S48
51	Junna	824	S48
52	Nimmyo	834	S50
53	Montoku	851	S52
54	Seiwa	859	S53
55	Yozei	877	S54
56	Koko	885	S52
57	Uda	889	S56
58	Daigo	898	S57
59	Shujaku	931	S58
60	Murakami	947	S58
61	Reizei	968	S60
62	Enyu	970	S60
63	Kazan	985	S61
64	Ichijo	987	S62
65	Sanjo	1012	S61
66	Go-Ichijo	1017	S64
67	Go-Shujaku	1037	S64
68	Go-Reizei	1047	S67
69	Go-Sanjo	1069	S68
70	Shirakawa	1073	S68
71	Horikawa	1087	S70
72	Toba	1108	S71
73	Sutoku	1124	S72
74	Konoe	1142	S72
75	Go-Shirakawa	1156	S72
76	Nijo	1159	S75
77	Rokujo	1166	S76
78	Takakura	1169	S75
79	Antoku	1181	S78
80	Go-Toba	1184	S78
81	Tsuchi-Mikado	1199	S80
82	Juntoku	1211	S80
83	Chukyo	1221	S82

84	Go-Horikawa	1222	s80
85	Shijo	1233	s84
86	Go-Saga	1243	s81
87	Go-Fukakusa	1247	s86
88	Kameyama	1260	s86
89	Go-Uda	1275	s88
90	Fushima	1288	s87
91	Go-Fushima	1299	s90
92	Go-Nijo	1302	s89
93	Hanazono	1308	s87
94	Go-Daigo (1)	1319	s89
95	Kogen	1331	s87
	Go-Daigo (2) (South only from 1336)	1333–1339	
96	Komyo (North)	1336–1349	s91
97	Go-Murakami (South)	1339–1368	s94
98	Suko (North)	1349–1352	s95
99	Go-Kogen (North)	1352–1372	s95
100	Chokei (South)	1368–1373	s97
101	Go-Enyu (North)	1372–1384	s95
102	Go-Kameyama (South)	1373–1392	s97
103	Go-Komatu (North; South 1392)	1384–1413	s101
104	Shoko	1413	s103
105	Go-Hanazono	1429	GG98
106	Go-Tsuchi-Mikado	1465	s105
107	Go-Kashiwabara	1501	s106
108	Go-Nara	1527	s107
109	Ogimachi	1558	s108
110	Go-Yozei	1587	GS109
111	Go-Mizu-no-o	1612	s110
112	Myosho★	1630	D111
113	Go-Komyo	1644	s111
114	Go-Saiin	1655	s111
115	Reigen	1663	s111
116	Higashiyama	1687	s114
117	Naka-no-Mikado	1710	s116
118	Sakuramachi	1736	s117
119	Momozono	1748	s118
120	Go-Sakuramachi★	1763	D118
121	Go-Momozono	1771	s119
122	Kokaku	1780	s121
123	Ninko	1817	s122
124	Komei	1847	s123
125	Meiji (Mutsuhito)	1867	s124
126	Taisho (Yoshihito)	1912	s125
127	Showa (Hirohito)	1926	s126

b *Minamoto Shoguns* 1192–1219

1	Yoritomo	1192	
2	Yori-ie	1199	S1
3	Sanetomo	1203–1219	S1

c *Fujiwara Shoguns* 1220–1251

1 Yoritsune	1220	
2 Yoritsugu	1244–1251	S1

d *Imperial Shoguns* 1251–1333

1 Munetaka	1251	(s86)
2 Koreyasu	1266	S1
3 Hisakira	1289	(s87)
4 Morikune	1308–1333	S3

e *Ashikaga Shoguns* 1338–1573

1 Takauji	1338	
2 Yoshiaki	1358	S1
3 Yoshimitsu	1367	S2
4 Yoshimochi	1395	S3
5 Yoshikazu	1423	S4
6 Yoshinori	1428	S3
7 Yoshikatsu	1441	s6
8 Yoshimasa	1443	s6
9 Yoshihisa	1474	s8
10 Yoshitane (1)	1490	BS8
11 Yoshizume	1493	BS8
Yoshitsane (Yoshitane) (2)	1508	
12 Yoshiharu	1521	S11
13 Yoshiteru	1545–1565	S12
14 Yoshihide	1568	GS10
15 Yoshiaki	1568–1573	S12

f *Tokugawa Shoguns* 1603–1867

1 Ieyasu	1603	
2 Hidetada	1605	S1
3 Iemitsu	1623	S2
4 Ietsuna	1651	S3
5 Tsunayoshi	1680	S3
6 Ienobu	1709	BS5
7 Ietsugu	1713	s6
8 Yoshimune	1716	DT1
9 Ieshige	1745	s8
10 Ieharu	1761	S9
11 Ienari	1787	BGS9
12 Ieyoshi	1838	S11
13 Iesada	1853	S12
14 Iemochi	1858	BS12
15 Yoshinobu	1866–1867	DT1

237 **BURMA** KINGS

a *Pagan Dynasty* 1044–1325

1 Anawrahta	1044

2	Sawlu	1077	S1
3	Kyanzittha	1084	S1
4	Alaungsithu	1112	GS3
5	Narathu	1167	S4
6	Naratheinhka	1170	S5
7	Narapatisithu	1173	S5
8	Htilominlo	1210	S7
9	Kyaswa	1234	S8
10	Uzana I	1250	S9
11	Narathihapate	1254	S10
12	Kyawswa	1287	S11
13	Sawhnit	1298–1299	S12
14	Uzana II	1325.	S13

b *Kings of Myinsaing and Pinya 1289–1364*

1	Athinhkaya	1289–?	
2	Yazathinkayan	1289–?	B1
3	Thihathu (Pinya 1312)	1289–1324	B1
4	Uzana (S12 Pagan)	1324	
5	Ngashishin	1343	
6	Kyawswange	1350	S5
7	Narathu	1359	S5
8	Uzana Pyaung	1364	S5
9	Thadominbya (K. of Ava)	1364–(1368)	DT3

c *Kings of Sagaing 1315–1364*

1	Sawyun (S3 Myinsaing)	1315	
2	Tarabyagyi	1323	
3	Shwetaungtet	1336	S2
4	Kyaswa	1340	S1
5	Nawrahtaminye	1350	S1
6	Tarabyange	1350	S1
7	Minbyauk Thihapate	1352–1364	

d *Kings of Ava 1364–1555*

1	Thadominbya (of Myinsaing)	1364	
2	Myinkyiswasawke	1368	
3	Minhkaung I	1401	S2
4	Thihathu	1422	S3
5	Kalekyetaungnyo	1426	GS2
6	Mohnyinthado	1427	
7	Minrekyawswa	1440	S6
8	Narapati	1443	S6
9	Thihathura	1469	S8
10	Minhkaung II	1481	S9
11	Shwenankyawshin	1502	S10
12	Thohanbwa	1527	
13	Hkonmaing	1543	
14	Mobye Narapati	1546	S13

15	Sithukyawhtin	1552–1555	

e *Toungoo Dynasty* 1486–1752

1	Minkyinyo	1486	
2	Tabinshwehti	1531	S1
3	Bayin Naung	1551	HD1
4	Nanda Bayin	1581–1599	S3
5	Anaukpetlun	1605	BS4
6	Minredeippa	1628	S5
7	Thalun	1629	B5
8	Pindale	1648	S7
9	Pye	1661	S7
10	Narawara	1672	S9
11	Minrekyawdin	1673	BS9
12	Sane	1698	S11
13	Taninganwe	1714	S12
14	Mahadammayaza-Dipati	1733–1752	S13

f *Alaungpaya Dynasty* 1752–1885

1	Alaungpaya	1752	
2	Naungdawgyi	1760	S1
3	Hsinbyushin	1763	S1
4	Singu Min	1776	S3
5	Maung Maung	1781	S4
6	Bodawpaya	1781	S1
7	Bagyidaw	1819	GS6
8	Tharrawaddy	1838	B7
9	Pagan Min	1846	S8
10	Mindon Min	1853	S8
11	Thibaw	1878–1885	S10

g *Kings of Pegu* 1287–1757

1	Wareru	1287	
2	Hkun Law	1306	B1
3	Saw O	1310	BS2
4	Saw Zein	1324	B3
5	Zein Pun	1331	
6	Saw E Gan Gaung	1331	BS4
7	Binnya E Law	1331	S2
8	Binnya U	1353	S7
9	Razadarit	1385	S8
10	Binnya Dammayaza	1423	S9
11	Binnya Ran I	1426	S9
12	Binnya Waru	1446	BS11
13	Binnya Kyan	1450	
14	Mawdaw	1453	
15	Shin Sawbu★	1453	D9
16	Dammazedi	1472	HD15
17	Binnya Ran II	1492	S16

18	Takayutpi	1526–1539	S17
19	Smim Sawhtut	1550	
20	Smim Htaw	1551.	S17
21	Smim Htaw Buddhaketi	1740	
22	Binnya Dala	1747–1757	

238 BURMA KINGDOM OF ARAKAN

a *Chandra Dynasty* 788–1018

1	Mahataing Chandra	788	
2	Suriyataing Chandra	810	S1
3	Mawlataing Chandra	830	S2
4	Pawlataing Chandra	849	S3
5	Kalataing Chandra	875	S4
6	Tulataing Chandra	884	S5
7	Sritaing Chandra	903	S6
8	Thinhkataing Chandra	935	S7
9	Chulataing Chandra	951	S8
10	Amyahtu	957	
11	Yehpyu	964	
12	Nga-pin-nga-ton	994–1018	S9

b *First Pyinsa Dynasty* 1018–1103

1	Hkittathin	1018	
2	Chandrathin	1028	B1
3	Minyinpyu	1039	S2
4	Nagthuriya	1040	S3
5	Thuriyaza	1052	S4
6	Ponnaka	1054	S5
7	Minpyugyi	1058	S6
8	Sithabin	1060	
9	Minnangyi	1061	S7
10	Minlade	1066	S9
11	Minkala	1072	S10
12	Minbilu	1075	S11
13	Thinhkaya	1078	
14	Minthan	1092	S13
15	Minpati	1100–1103	S14

c *Parin Dynasty* 1103–1167

1	Letya-min-man	1103	
2	Thihaba	1109	S1
3	Yazagyi	1110	S2
4	Thagiwingyi	1112	S3
5	Thagiwinnge	1115	S4
6	Kawhya	1133	S5
7	Datharaja	1153	S6

8 Ananthiri	1165–1167	S7

d *Hkrit Dynasty* 1167–1180

1 Min Onsa	1167	
2 Pyinsakawa	1174	S1
3 Keinnayok	1176	S2
4 Salinkabo	1179–1180	

e *Second Pyinsa Dynasty* 1180–1237

1 Misuthin	1180
2 Nga Yanman	1191
3 Nga Pogan	1193
4 Nga Yahkaing	1195
5 Nga Kyon	1198
6 Nga Su	1201
7 Nga Swethin	1205
8 Minhkaunggyi	1206
9 Minhkaungnge	1207
10 Kabalaunggyi	1208
11 Kabalaungnge	1209
12 Letyagyi	1210
13 Letyange	1218
14 Thanabin	1229
15 Nga Nathin	1232
16 Nga Nalon	1234–1237

f *Launggyet Dynasty* 1237–1404

1 Alawmahpyu	1237
2 Yazathugyi	1243
3 Sawlu	1246
4 Ossanagyi	1251
5 Sawmungyi	1260
6 Nankyagyi	1268
7 Min Bilu	1272
8 Sithabin I	1276
9 Min Hti	1279–?
10 Ossanange	1385
11 Thiwarit	1387
12 Thinhse	1390
13 Razathu (1)	1394
14 Sithabin II	1395
15 Myinhsainggyi	1397
Razathu (2)	1397
16 Theinhkathu	1401–1404

g *Mrohaung Dynasty* 1404–1785

1 Narameikhla	1404	
2 'Ali Khan	1434	B1
3 Kalima Shah	1459	S2

4	Dawlya	1482	S3
5	Basawnyo	1492	S2
6	Yanaung	1494	S4
7	Salingathu	1494	MB6
8	Minyaza	1501	S7
9	Kasabadi	1523	S8
10	Min Saw-o	1525	B7
11	Thatasa	1525	S4
12	Minbin	1531	S8
13	Dikha	1553	S12
14	Sawhla	1555	S13
15	Minsetya	1564	S13
16	Minpalaung	1571	S12
17	Salim Shah	1593	S16
18	Husain Shah	1612	S17
19	Thirithudamma	1622	S18
20	Minsani	1638	S19
21	Narapatigyi	1638	GG11
22	Thado	1645	
23	Sandathudamma	1652	S22
24	Thirithuriya	1684	S23
25	Waradhammaraza	1685	S23
26	Munithudhammaraza	1692	S23
27	Sandathuriyadhamma	1694	S23
28	Nawrahtazaw	1696	S27
29	Mayokpiya	1696	
30	Kalamandat	1697	
31	Naradipati I	1698	S27
32	Sandawimala I	1700	GS22
33	Sandathuriya I	1706	GS23
34	Sandawizaya I	1710	
35	Sandathuriya II	1731	HD34
36	Naradipati II	1734	S35
37	Narapawara	1735	
38	Sandawizaya II	1737	
39	Katya	1737	
40	Madarit	1737	B38
41	Nara-Apaya	1742	
42	Thirithu	1761	S41
43	Sandapayama	1761	S41
44	Apaya	1764	
45	Sandathumana	1773	
46	Sandawimala II	1777	
47	Sandathaditha	1777	
48	Thamada	1782–1785	

239 THAILAND THAI KINGDOMS

a *Kings of Sukhothai 1238–1438*

1 Sri Indraditya	1238	
2 Ban Muang	1275	S1
3 Rama Khamheng	1279	S1
4 Lo Thai	1317	S3
5 Li Thai Mahadharmaraja I	1354	S4
6 Mahadharmaraja II	1376	S5
7 Mahadharmaraja III	1406	S6
8 Mahadharmaraja IV	1419–1438	S7

b *Kings of Chiang Mai 1296–1556*

1 Meng Rai	1296	
2 Sen P'u (1)	1318	
3 Khun K'rua	1319	
4 Nam Thuom	1322	
Sen P'u (2)	1324	
5 Kham Fu	1328	
6 Pha Yu	1345	
7 Ku Na	1367	
8 Sen Muang Ma	1387	
9 Fang Ken	1401	
10 Sri Sut'am Tilok	1442	
11 P'raya Yot	1487	
12 P'raya Keo	1495	
13 P'raya Muang Ket (1)	1525	
14 Sai Kam	1538	
P'raya Muang Ket (2)	1543–1545	
15 Jai Jettha (Sett'at'irat of Lan Chang)	1547	
16 Mekut'i	1549–1556	

c *Kings of Ayuthia 1350–1767*

1 Rama T'ibodi I	1350	
2 Ramesuen I (1)	1369	S1
3 Boromoraja I	1370	
4 T'ong Lan	1388	S3
Ramesuen I (2)	1388	
5 Ram Raja	1395	S2
6 Int'araja I	1408	BS3
7 Boromoraja II	1424	S6
8 Boroma Trailokanat	1448	S7
9 Boromoraja III	1488	S8
10 Rama T'ibodi II	1491	S8
11 Boromoraja IV	1529	S10
12 Ratsada	1534	S11
13 P'rajai	1534	S10
14 Keo Fa	1546	S13
15 Khun Worawongsa	1548	

16	Maha Chakrap'at	1549	S10
17	Mahin	1569	S16
18	Maha Dharmaraja I	1569	
19	Naresuen	1590	S18
20	Ekat'otsarot	1605	S18
21	Songt'am Int'araja II	1610	S20
22	Jett'atirat	1628	S21
23	At'ityawong	1630	S21
24	Prasat T'ong	1630	
25	Chao Fa Jai	1656	S24
26	Sri Suthammaraja	1656	B24
27	Narai	1657	S24
28	P'ra P'etraja Ramesuen II	1688	
29	P'rachao Sua	1703	S28
30	T'ai Sra Pumint'araja	1709	S29
31	Boromokot Maha Dharmaraja II	1733	S29
32	Ut'ump'on	1758	S31
33	Ekat'at Boromoraja V	1758–1767	S31

d *Kings of Thailand since* 1767

1	P'ya Taksin	1767	
2	P'ra P'utt'a Yot Fa Chulalok Rama I	1782	
3	Phendin-Klang Rama II	1809	S2
4	P'ra Nang Klao Rama III	1824	S3
5	Maha Mongkut Rama IV	1851	S3
6	Chulalongkorn Rama V	1868	S5
7	Maha Vajiravudh Rama VI	1910	S6
8	Prajadhipok Rama VII	1925	S6
9	Ananda Mahidol Rama VIII	1935	BS8
10	Bhumibol Adulyadej Rama IX	1946	B9

240 LAOS LAOTIAN KINGDOMS

a *Kings of Lan Chang* 1353–1707

1	Fa Ngoun	1353	
2	Sam Sene T'ai	1373	S1
3	Lan Kham Deng	1416	S2
4	P'ommat'at	1428	S3
5	Pak Louei Luong	1429	S2
6	T'ao Sai	1430	S2
7	P'aya Khai	1430	S3
8	Chieng Sai	1433	S2
9	(Unknown)	1434	S3
10	Kam Kheut	1435	
11	Sai Tiakap'at	1438	S2
12	T'ene Kham	1479	S11
13	La Sene T'ai	1486	S11
14	Som P'ou	1496	S13
15	Visoun	1501	S11

16	P'ot'isarat I	1520	S15
17	Sett'at'irat	1548	S16
18	Sene Soulint'a (1)	1571	
19	Maha Oupahat	1575	
	Sene Soulint'a (2)	1580	
20	Nakhone Noi	1582–1583	S18
21	Nokeo Koumane	1591	S17
22	T'ammikarat	1596	
23	Oupagnouvarat	1622	S22
24	P'ot'isarat II	1623	S18
25	Mone Keo	1627	S18
26	Oupagnaovarat	?	S25
27	Tone Kham	?	S26
28	Visai	?	S26
29	Souligna Vongsa	1637	S27
30	Tian T'ala	1694	HD29
31	Nan T'arat	1700	
32	Sai Ong Hue	1700–1707	GS29

b *Kings of Vien Chang (Vientiane)* 1707–1828

1	Sai Ong Hue (of Lan Chang)	1707	
2	Ong Long	1735	S1
3	Ong Boun	1760–1778	S2
4	Chao Nan	1782	S3
5	Chao In	1792	S3
6	Chao Anou	1805–1828	S3

c *Kings of Luang Prabang (of Laos from 1947)* 1707–1975

1	King Kitsarat (s29 Lan Chang)	1707	
2	Khamone Noi	1726	
3	Int'a Som	1727	B1
4	Sotika Koumane	1776	S3
5	Tiao Vong	1781–1787	S3
6	Anourout	1791	S3
7	Mant'a T'ourat	1817	S6
8	Souka Seum	1836	S7
9	Tiantha	1851	S7
10	Oun Kham	1872–1887	S7
11	Zakarine	1894	S10
12	Sisavang Vong	1904	S11
13	Sri Savang Vatthana	1959–1975	S12

241 CAMBODIA KINGS *c.*500–1960

1	Kaundinya Jayavarman	*c.*500 AD	
2	Rudravarman	514	S1

3	Bhavavarman I	*c.*550	GS2
4	Mahendravarman	*c.*600	BS3
5	Isanavarman I	*c.*616	S4
6	Bhavavarman II	*c.*635	S5
7	Jayavarman I	657	S6
8	Jayadevi★	*c.*681–720	W7
		—	
9	Jayavarman II	802	
10	Jayavarman III	850	S9
11	Indravarman I	877	MBS10
12	Yasovarman I	889	S11
13	Harshavarman I	900	S12
14	Isanavarman II	*c.*922	S12
15	Jayavarman IV	928	STH12
16	Harshavarman II	942	S15
17	Rajendravarman	944	STS12
18	Jayavarman V	968	S17
19	Udayadityavarman I	1001	
20	Jayaviravarman	*c.*1002	
21	Suryavarman I	1002	
22	Udayadityavarman II	1050	S21
23	Harshavarman III	1066	S21
24	Jayavarman VI	1080	
25	Dharanindravarman I	1107	B24
26	Suryavarman II	1113	BGD25
27	Dharanindravarman II	1150	BGS25
28	Yasovarman II	1160	S27
29	Tribhuvanadityavarman	1166	
30	Jayavarman VII	1181	S28
31	Indravarman II	*c.*1219	S30
32	Jayavarman VIII	1243	S31
33	Indravarman III	1295	S32
34	Indrajayavarman	1308	S33
35	Jayavarmadiparamesvara	1327–*c.*1353	S34
		—	
36	Nirvanapada	*c.*1362	
37	Kalamegha	*c.*1371	
38	Kambujadhiraja	*c.*1377	
39	Dharmasokaraja	*c.*1387	
40	Paramarajadhiraja	1389	
41	Narayana Ramadhipati	1404	S40
42	Sodaiya	1429	S40
43	Dharmarajadhiraja	1444	S42
44	Srey Sukonthor	1486	S43
45	Nay Kan	1512	
46	Ang Chan I	1516	S43
47	Barom Reachea I	1566	S46
48	Chettha I	1576	S47
49	Reamea Chung Prei	1594	
50	Barom Reachea II	1596	S48

51	Barom Reachea III	1599	S47
52	Chao Ponhea Nhom	1600	S48
53	Barom Reachea IV	1603	S47
54	Chettha II	1618	S53
55	Ponhea To	1628	S54
56	Ponhea Nu	1630	S54
57	Ang Non I	1640	S53
58	Chan Rama Thupdey	1642	S54
59	Batom Reachea	1659	GS54
60	Chettha III	1672	BS59
61	Ang Chei	1673	S59
62	Obbarac Ang Non	1674	
63	Chettha IV (1)	1675	S59
64	Outey I	1695	BS63
	Chettha IV (2)	1695	
65	Ang Em (1)	1699	HD63
	Chettha IV (3)	1701	
66	Thommo Reachea (1)	1702	S63
	Chettha IV (4)	1703	
	Thommo Reachea (2)	1706	
	Ang Em (2)	1710	
67	Satha Ang Chei	1722	S65
	Thommo Reachea (3)	1738	
68	Ang Ton (1)	1747	S66
69	Chettha V	1749	GS66
	Ang Ton (2)	1755	
70	Preah Outey II	1758	GS68
71	Ang Non II	1775	S67
72	Ang Eng	1779–1796	S68
73	Ang Chan II	1806	S72
74	Ang Mey*	1834	D73
75	Ang Duong	1841	S73
76	Norodom	1860	S75
77	Sisovath	1904	S75
78	Monivong	1927	S77
79	Norodom Sihanouk	1941	S80
80	Norodom Suramarit	1955–1960	GS78

242 CHAMPA KINGS c.270–1471

1	Fan Hiong	c.270 AD
2	Fan Yi	
3	Fan Wen	336
4	Fan Fo	349
5	Bhadravarman I	c.377
6	Gangaraja	
7	Manorathavarman	
8	Wen Ti	
9	Fan Yang Mai I	c.420

10	Fan Yang Mai II	*c.*431	
11	Fan Shen Ch'eng	*c.*455	
12	Fan Tang Ken Ch'uan	*c.*484	
13	Fan Chou Nong	*c.*492	
14	Fan Wen Tsan	*c.*502	
15	Devavarman	*c.*510	
16	Vijayavarman	*c.*526	
17	Rudravarman I	*c.*529	
18	Sambuvarman	*c.*605	S17
19	Kandharpadharma	*c.*629	S18
20	Bhasadharma	*c.*640	S19
21	Bhadresvaravarman	645	STS20
22	(Unknown)★		D19
23	Prakasadharma Vikrantavarman I	653	H22
24	Vikrantavarman II	*c.*686	S22/23
25	Rudravarman II	*c.*731	S24
26	Prithivindravarman	*c.*758	
27	Satyavarman	*c.*770	S26
28	Indravarman I	*c.*787	S26
29	Harivarman I	*c.*803	HD26
30	Vikrantavarman III		S29
31	Indravarman II	*c.*854	
32	Jaya Sinhavarman I	*c.*898	STS31
33	Jaya Saktivarman		S32
34	Bhadravarman II		S33
35	Indravarman III	*c.*918	S34
36	Jaya Indravarman I	*c.*960	S35
37	Paramesvaravarman I		S36
38	Indravarman IV	982	S37
39	Liu Chi-tsung	*c.*986	
40	Harivarman II	989	
41	Yan Pu Ku Vijaya	*c.*999	S40
42	Harivarman III		S41
43	Paramesvaravarman II		S42
44	Vikrantavarman IV		S43
45	Jaya Sinhavarman II	1044	S44
46	Jaya Paramesvaravarman I	1044	
47	Bhadravarman III		S46
48	Rudravarman III	1061	S46
49	Harivarman IV	1074	
50	Jaya Indravarman II (1)	1080	S49
51	Paramabhodisatva	1081	B49
	Jaya Indravarman II (2)	1086	
52	Harivarman V	*c.*1114	BS50
53	Jaya Indravarman III	1139	
54	Rudravarman IV		
55	Jaya Harivarman I	1147	
56	Jaya Harivarman II		
57	Jaya Indravarman IV	1167	S55
58	Suryajayavarman (at Vijaya)	1190–1191	

59 Suryavarman (Panduranga; Vijaya 1192)	1190–1203	
60 Jaya Indravarman V (at Vijaya)	1191–1192	
61 Jayavarman (VII of Cambodia)	1203	
62 Jaya Paramesvaravarman II	1220	S56
63 Jaya Indravarman VI	1252	S56
64 Indravarman V	c.1265	STS63
65 Jaya Sinhavarman III	1288	S64
66 Jaya Sinhavarman IV	1307	S65
67 Che Nang	1312	S65
68 Che A-nan	1318	
69 Tra Hoa	1342	
70 Che Bong Nga	1360	
71 Ko Cheng	1390	
72 Jaya Sinhavarman V	1400	S71
73 Mahavijaya	1441	
74 Maha Kui-lai	1446	
75 Maha Kui Yu	1449	B74
76 Maha P'an-lo-yueh	1458	
77 P'an-lo T'u-ts'uan	1460–1471	B76

243 VIET-NAM DYNASTIES

a *Earlier Li Dynasty 544–602*

1 Li Nam-Viet De Bon	544	
2 Trieu Viet-Vuong Quang-Phuc	549–571	
3 Li Dao-Lang Vuong Thien Bao	549–555	
4 Li Hau-De Phat-Tu	571–602	

b *Ngo Dynasty 939–965*

1 Ngo Vuong Quyen	939	
2 Duong-Binh Vuong Tam-Kha	945	STH1
3 Ngo Nam-Tan Vuong Xuong-Van	951–965	S1
4 Ngo Thien-Sach Vuong Xuong-Ngap	951–954	S1

c *Dinh Dynasty 968–980*

| 1 Dinh Tien-Hoang De | 968 | |
| 2 Dinh De-Toan | 979–980 | S1 |

d *Earlier Le Dynasty 980–1009*

| 1 Le Dai-Hanh Hoang-De | 980 | |
| 2 Le Trung-Ton Hoang-De | 1005–1009 | S1 |

e *Later Li Dynasty 1009–1225*

1 Li Thai-To	1009	
2 Li Thai-Ton	1028	S1
3 Li Thanh-Ton	1054	S2
4 Li Nhon-Ton	1072	S3
5 Li Than-Ton	1127	AS4
6 Li Anh-Ton	1138	S5

7 Li Cao-Ton	1175	s6
8 Li Hue-Ton	1210	s7
9 Li Chieu-Hoang★	1224–1225	D8

f *Tran Dynasty* 1225–1413

1 Tran Thai-Ton (H9 Later Li)	1225	
2 Tran Thanh-Ton	1258	SI
3 Tran Nhon-Ton	1278	S2
4 Tran Anh-Ton	1293	S3
5 Tran Minh-Ton	1314	S4
6 Tran Hien-Ton	1329	s6
7 Tran Du-Ton	1341	S5
8 Duong Nhut-Le	1369	
9 Tran Nghe-Ton	1370	B7
10 Tran Due-Ton	1372	B7
11 Tran De-Hien	1377	BS7
12 Tran Thuan-Ton	1388	S9
13 Tran Thieu-De	1398–1400	SI2
	———	
14 Tran De-Qui	1407	S9
15 Tran De-Qui-Khoang	1409–1413	GS9

g *Ho Dynasty* 1400–1407

1 Ho Qui-Li	1400	
2 Ho Han-Thuong	1400–1407	SI

h *Later Le Dynasty* 1428–1788

1 Le Thai-To (Cao Hoang-De; Le Loi)	1428	
2 Le Thai-Ton (Van Hoang-De)	1433	SI
3 Le Nhon-Ton (Tuyen Hoang-De)	1442	S2
4 Le Nghe-Dan	1459	S2
5 Le Thanh-Ton (Thuan Hoang-De)	1460	S2
6 Le Hien-Ton (Due Hoang-De)	1497	S5
7 Le Tuc-Ton (Kham Hoang-De)	1504	s6
8 Le Ui-Muc De	1504	s6
9 Le Tuong-Duc De	1509	DT2
10 Le Chieu-Ton (Than Hoang-De)	1516–1526	DT5
11 Le Hoang-De-Xuan (Cung Hoang-De)	1522–1527	
	———	
12 Le Trang-Ton (Du Hoang-De)	1533	SIO
13 Le Trung-Ton (Vo Hoang-De)	1548	DTBI
14 Le Anh-Ton (Tuan Hoang-De)	1556	SI3
15 Le The-Ton (Nghi Hoang-De)	1573	
16 Nguyen Duong-Minh	1597	
17 Nguyen Minh-Tri	1597	
18 Le Kinh-Ton (Hue Hoang-De)	1599	SI5
19 Le Thanh-Ton (Uyen Hoang-De) (1)	1619	SI8
20 Le Chan-Ton (Thuan Hoang-De)	1643	SI9
Le Thanh-Ton (Uyen Hoang-De) (2)	1649	
21 Le Huyen-Ton (Muc Hoang-De)	1662	SI9

22	Le Gia-Ton (Mi Hoang-De)	1671	S19
23	Le Hi-Ton (Chuong Hoang-De)	1671	S19
24	Le Du-Ton (Hoa Hoang-De)	1705	
25	Le De Duy-Phuong	1729	S24
26	Le Thuan-Ton (Gian Hoang-De)	1732	S24
27	Le I-Ton (Huy Hoang-De)	1735	S24
28	Le Hien-Ton (Vinh Hoang-De)	1740	S26
29	Le Man Hoang-De	1786–1788	GS28

i *Mac Dynasty* 1527–1677

1	Mac Dang-Dung	1527	
2	Mac Dang-Doanh	1530	S1
3	Mac Phuc-Hai	1540	S2
4	Mac Phuc-Nguyen	1546	S3
5	Mac Mau-Hop	1562	
6	Mac Toan	1592	
7	Mac Kinh-Chi	1592	
8	Mac Kinh-Cung	1593	
9	Mac Kinh-Khoan	1623	
10	Mac Kinh-Hoan	1638–1677	

j *Trinh Dynasty (Tonkin)* 1539–1787

1	Trinh Kiem	1539	
2	Trinh Coi	1569	S1
3	Trinh Tong	1570	S1
4	Trinh Trang	1623	S3
3	Trinh Tac	1657	S4
6	Trinh Con	1682	
7	Trinh Cuong	1709	
8	Trinh Giang	1729	
9	Trinh Dinh	1740	
10	Trinh Sam	1767	
11	Trinh Can	1782	
12	Trinh Khai	1782	
13	Trinh Phung	1786–1787	

k *Tay-Son Dynasty* 1788–1802

1	Nguyen Van-Hue (Quang-Trung)	1788–1792	
2	Nguyen Quang-Toan (Cahn-Thinh)	1792–1802	S1

l *Nguyen Dynasty of Hue* 1558–1776

1	Nguyen Hoang	1558	
2	Nguyen Phuc-Nguyen	1613	S1
3	Nguyen Phuc-Lan	1635	S2
4	Nguyen Phuc-Tan	1648	S3
5	Nguyen Phuc-Tran	1687	S4
6	Nguyen Phuc-Chu	1691	S5
7	Nguyen Phuc-Chu	1725	S6
8	Nguyen Phuc-Khoat	1738	S7
9	Nguyen Phuc-Thuan	1765–1776	S8

m *Nguyen Dynasty of Annam 1788–1955*

1	Gia-Long (Nguyen Anh; BS8 Hue)	1788	
2	Minh-Mang	1820	S1
3	Thieu-Tri	1841	S2
4	Tu-Duc	1848	S3
5	Nguyen Duc-Duc	1883	BS4
6	Nguyen Hiep-Hoa	1883	S3
7	Kien-Phuc	1884	S4
8	Ham-Nghi	1885	S4
9	Dong-Khanh	1886	BS4
10	Thanh-Thai	1889	S5
11	Duy-Tan	1907	S10
12	Khai-Dinh	1916	S9
13	Bao-Dai	1925–1955	S12

244 **MALAYA** MALAY STATES

a *Sultans of Malacca c.1400–1511*

1	Megat Iskandar Shah (Paramesvara)	c.1400	
2	Muhammad Shah	1424	S1
3	Abu-Shahid Ibrahim Shah (Sri Paramesvara Deva)	1444	S2
4	Muzaffar Shah	1446	S2
5	Mansur Shah	1458	S4
6	'Ala-ud-Din Ri'ayat Shah	1477	S5
7	Mahmud Shah	1488–1511	S6

b *Rajas of Patani c.1540–1729*

1	Isma'il Shah	c.1540	
2	Muzaffar Shah	?	S1
3	Mansur Shah	1564	S1
4	Patik Siam	1572	S2
5	Bahadur Shah	1573	S3
6	Raja Ijau★	1584	D3
7	Raja Biru★	1616	D3
8	Raja Ungu★	1624	D3
9	Raja Kuning★	1635	D8
10	Raja Bakal	c.1688	
11	Raja Emas Kalantan	1690	
12	Raja Emas Jayam Baginda (1)	1704	
13	Raja Devi Phra-Cao★	1707	
14	Paduka Shah 'Alam	1716	
15	Raja Lakshmana Dajang	1720	
	Raja Emas Jayam Baginda (2)	1721	
16	Alung Yunus	1728–1729	

c *Sultans of Kedah since c.1160*

1	Muzaffar Shah I	c.1160	
2	Mu'azzam Shah	1179	S1
3	Muhammad Shah	1201	S2

4	Ma'azul Shah	1236	S3
5	Mahmud Shah I	1280	S4
6	Ibrahim Shah	1320	S5
7	Sulayman Shah I	1373	S6
8	Ata-illah Muhammad Shah I	1422	S7
9	Muhammad Jiwa Zain-ul-'Abidin	1472	S8
10	Mahmud Shah II	1506	S9
11	Muzaffar Shah II	1546	S10
12	Sulayman Shah II	1602	S11
13	Rijal-ud-Din Shah	1625	S12
14	Muhyi-ud-Din Shah	1651	S13
15	Zia-ud-Din Mukarram Shah	1661	S14
16	Ata-illah Muhammad Shah II	1687	S15
17	'Abdullah Mu'azzam Shah	1698	S16
18	Muhammad Jiwa Zain-ul-'Abidin Mu'azzam Shah	1706	S17
19	'Abdullah Mukarram Shah	1760	S18
20	Zia-ud-Din Mu'azzam Shah	1798	S18
21	Ahmad Taj-ud-Din Halim Shah (1)	1803–1821	S19
		———	
	Ahmad Taj-ud-Din Halim Shah (2)	1843	
22	Zain-ul-Rashid Mu'azzam Shah I	1843	S21
23	Ahmad Taj-ud-Din Mukarram Shah	1854	S22
24	Zain-ul-Rashid Mu'azzam Shah II	1879	S23
25	'Abdul-Hamid Halim Shah	1881	S23
26	Badlishah	1943	S25
27	'Abdul-Halim Mu'azzam Shah	1958	S26

d *Sultans of Pahang since* 1470

1	Muhammad Shah (s5 Malacca)	1470	
2	Ahmad Shah I	1475	B1
3	'Abdul-Jamal Shah I	c.1500–1512	S1
4	Mansur Shah I	c.1500–1515	S2
5	Mahmud Shah I	1515	S1
6	Muzaffar Shah	1530	S5
7	Zain-ul-'Abidin Shah	1540	S5
8	Mansur Shah II	c.1555	S7
9	'Abdul-Jamal Shah II	c.1560	S7
10	'Abdul-Qadir 'Ala-ud-Din Shah	?	S7
11	Ahmad Shah II	c.1590	S10
12	'Abdul-Ghafur Muhyi-ud-Din Shah	c.1590	S10
13	(Unknown)	1613	S12
14	'Abdul-Jalil Shah II (of Johore)	1641–(1677)	
		———	
15	'Ali (Bendahara)	1806	
16	Wan Mutahir (Bendahara)	1857	S15
17	Ahmad Mu'azzam Shah (Sultan 1884)	1863	S15
18	Mahmud Shah II	1914	S17
19	'Abdullah Muktasim Billah Shah	1917	S17
20	Abu-Bakr Ri'ayat-ud-Din Mu'azzam Shah	1932	S19
21	Ahmad Shah III al-Musta'in	1974	S20

e *Sultans of Johore since* 1511

1	Mahmud Shah (of Malacca)	1511	
2	'Ala-ud-Din Ri'ayat Shah I	1529	SI
3	Muzaffar Shah	1564	S2
4	'Abdul-Jalil Shah I	1580	STS3
5	'Abdul-Jalil Ri'ayat Shah I	1580	F4
6	'Ala-ud-Din Ri'ayat Shah II	1597	S5
7	'Abdullah Ma'ayat Shah	1613	S5
8	'Abdul-Jalil Shah II	1623	S6
9	Ibrahim Shah	1677	GS7
10	Mahmud Shah II	1685	S9
11	'Abdul-Jalil Ri'ayat Shah II	1699	
12	'Abdul-Jalil Rahmat Shah (Raja Kechil of Siak)	1717	HDII
13	Sulayman Badr-ul-'Alam Shah	1722	SII
14	'Abdul-Jalil Mu'azzam Shah	1760	SI3
15	Ahmad Ri'ayat Shah	1761	SI4
16	Mahmud Ri'ayat Shah	1761	SI4
17	'Abdul-Rahman Mu'azzam Shah	1812	SI6
18	'Abdul-Rahman (Tememggong)	1819	DTII
19	Ibrahim (Temenggong)	1825	SI8
20	Abu-Bakr (Temenggong; Sultan 1885)	1862	SI9
21	Ibrahim Shah	1895	S20
22	Isma'il Shah	1959	S21

f *Sultans of Perak since* 1529

1	Muzaffar Shah I (SI Johore)	1529	
2	Mansur Shah I	1549	SI
3	Ahmad Taj-ud-Din Shah	1577	BS2
4	Taj-ul-'Arifin Shah	?	B3
5	'Ala-ud-Din Shah	?	GS3
6	Muqadam Shah	1603	GD3
7	Mansur Shah II	1619	B5
8	Mahmud Shah I	1619	B6
9	Salah-ud-Din Shah	1630	S8
10	Muzaffar Shah II	1635	
11	Muhammad Iskandar Shah	1654	SIO
12	'Ala-ud-Din Ri'ayat Shah	c.1720	SII
13	Muzaffar Shah III	c.1728–1754	SII
14	Muhammad Shah	c.1728–1750	SII
15	Iskandar Dhu'l-Qarnain Shah	c.1754–1765	SI4
16	Mahmud Shah II	1765	SI4
17	'Ala-ud-Din Mansur Iskandar Shah	c.1773	SI4
18	Ahmadin Shah	?	SI4
19	'Abdul-Malik Mansur Shah	1806	SI8
20	'Abdullah Mu'azzam Shah	1825	SI9
21	Shihab-ud-Din Ri'ayat Shah	1831	GSI8
22	'Abdullah Muhammad Shah I	1851	GSI8
23	Ja'far Mu'azzam Shah	1857	GDI9
24	'Ali al-Kamil Ri'ayat Shah	1865	S21

25 Isma'il Mu'abidin Shah	1871	
26 'Abdullah Muhammad Shah II	1874	S23
27 Yusuf Sharif-ud-Din Mufzal Shah	1877	S22
28 Idris Murshid-ul-'Azam Shah	1887	BS23
29 'Abdul-Jalil Shah	1916	S28
30 Iskandar Shah	1918	S28
31 'Abdul-'Aziz Shah	1938	BS26
32 Yusuf 'Izz-ud-Din Shah	1948	S29
33 Idris al-Mutawakkil Shah	1963	S30

g *Sultans of Trengganu since* 1725

1 Zain-ul-'Abidin Shah I (B11 Johore)	1725	
2 Mansur Shah I	1733	S1
3 Zain-ul-'Abidin Shah II	1793	S2
4 Ahmad Shah	1808	S3
5 'Abdul-Rahman Shah	1827	S3
6 Da'ud Shah	1831	S4
7 Mansur Shah II	1831	S3
8 Muhammad Shah I	1836	S7
9 'Umar Shah	1839	S4
10 Ahmad Mu'azzam Shah	1876	BS9
11 Zain-ul-'Abidin Mu'azzam Shah	1881	S10
12 Muhammad Shah II	1918	S11
13 Sulayman Badr-ul-'Alam Shah	1920	S11
14 Isma'il Nasir-ud-Din Shah	1945	S11

h *Sultans of Selangor since* 1756

1 Salah-ud-Din Shah	1756	
2 Ibrahim Shah	1778	S1
3 Muhammad Shah	1826–1857	S1
	———	
4 'Abdul-Samad Shah	1859	BS3
5 'Ala-ud-Din Sulayman Shah	1898	GS4
6 Hisam-ud-Din 'Alam Shah (1)	1938	S5
7 Musa Ghiyath-ud-Din Ri'ayat Shah	1942	DT3
Hisam-ud-Din 'Alam Shah (2)	1945	
8 Salah-ud-Din 'Abdul-'Aziz Shah	1960	S6

i *Yang Di-Pertuan Besars of Negri Sembilan since* 1773

1 Raja Melawar	1773	
2 Raja Hitam	1795	HD1
3 Raja Lenggang	1808	HD2
4 Raja Kerjan	1824	
5 Raja Laboh	1826	
6 Raja Radin	1830	S3
7 Raja Ulin	1861–1869	S3
	———	
8 Tengku Antah	1872	S6
9 Muhammad	1888	S8
10 'Abdul-Rahman	1933	S9

11	Munawir	1960	S10
12	Ja'far	1967	S10

j *Sultans of Kelantan since c.1790*

1	Long Yunus	c.1790	
2	Muhammad Shah I	c.1800	S1
3	Muhammad Shah II	1838	BS2
4	Ahmad Shah	1886	S3
5	Muhammad Shah III	1889	S4
6	Mansur Shah	1891	S4
7	Muhammad Shah IV	1899	S5
8	Isma'il Shah	1919	S7
9	Ibrahim Shah	1946	S7
10	Yahya Petra	1960	S9
11	Isma'il Petra	1979	S10

k *Sultans of Riau-Lingga 1819–1911*

1	'Abdul-Rahman Mu'azzam Shah (of Johore)	1819	
2	Muhammad Shah	1830	S1
3	Mahmud Muzaffar Shah	1841	S2
4	Sulayman Badr-ul-'Alam Shah	1857–1883	S1
5	'Abdul-Rahman Mu'azzam Shah II	1885–1911	GS3

l *Rajas of Perlis since 1843*

1	Sayyid Husain Jamal-ul-Lail	1843	
2	Sayyid Ahmad Jamal-ul-Lail	1873	S1
3	Sayyid Safi Jamal-ul-Lail	1897	GS2
4	Sayyid Alwi Jamal-ul-Lail	1905–1943	S3
5	Sayyid Harun Putra Jamal-ul-Lail	1945	BGS4

m *Yang Di-Pertuan Agongs of Malaysia since 1957*

1	'Abdul-Rahman (of Negri Sembilan)	1957
2	Sayyid Harun Putra Jamal-ul-Lail (of Perlis)	1960
3	Isma'il Nasir-ud-Din Shah (of Trengganu)	1965
4	'Abdul-Halim Mu'azzam Shah (of Kedah)	1970
5	Yahya Petra (of Kelantan)	1975
6	Ahmad Shah al-Musta'in (of Pahang)	1979

245 SUMATRA SULTANATES

a *Sultans of Achin 1496–1903*

1	'Ali Mughayat Shah	1496	
2	Salah-ud-Din	1528	S1
3	'Ala-ud-Din al-Qahhar	1537	S1
4	Husain 'Ali Ri'ayat Shah	1568	S3
5	Sultan Muda	1575	S4
6	Sri 'Alam	1575	S3

7	Zain-ul-'Abidin	1576	GS3
8	'Ala-ud-Din Mansur Shah (B3 Perak)	1577	
9	Sultan Buyong	c.1589	
10	'Ala-ud-Din Ri'ayat Shah	1596	FBGSI
11	'Ali Ri'ayat Shah	1604	SIO
12	Iskandar Shah	1607	GDIO
13	Iskandar Thani 'Ala-ud-Din Mughayat Shah	1636	(SII Pahang)
14	Safiyat-ud-Din Taj-ul-'Alam★	1641	WI3/DI2
15	Naqiyat-ud-Din Nur-ul-'Alam★	1675	
16	Zaqiyat-ud-Din 'Inayat Shah★	1678	
17	Kamalat Shah Zinat-ud-Din★	1688	
18	Badr-ul-'Alam Sharif Hashim Jamal-ud-Din	1699	
19	Perkara 'Alam Sharif Lamtui	1702	
20	Jamal-ul-'Alam Badr-ul-Munir	1703	
21	Jawhar-ul-'Alam Amin-ud-Din	1726	
22	Shams-ul-'Alam	1726	
23	'Ala-ud-Din Ahmad Shah	1727	
24	'Ala-ud-Din Shah Jahan	1735	
25	Mahmud Shah I	1760–1781	
26	Badr-ud-Din	1764–1765	
27	Sulayman Shah	1775	
28	'Ala-ud-Din Muhammad	1781	
29	'Ala-ud-Din Jawhar-ul-'Alam (1)	1795	
30	Sharif Saif-ul-'Alam	1815	
	Jawhar-ul-'Alam (2)	1818	
31	Muhammad Shah	1824	
32	Sulayman Shah	1838	
33	Mansur Shah	1857	
34	Mahmud Shah II	1870	
35	Muhammad Da'ud Shah	1874–1903	

b *Sultans of Palembang* 1662–1823

1	'Abdul-Rahman	1662	
2	Muhammad Mansur	1682	SI
3	Qamar-ud-Din	1696	SI
4	Mahmud Badr-ud-Din I	1707	S2
5	Ahmad Najm-ud-Din I	1743	S4
6	Muhammad Baha-ud-Din	1769	S5
7	Mahmud Badr-ud-Din II	1798–1821	S6
8	Ahmad Najm-ud-Din II	1812–1818	S6
9	Ahmad Najm-ud-Din III	1821–1823	S8

c *Sultans of Siak* 1721–1890

1	'Abdul-Jalil (Raja Kechil)	1721	
2	Muhammad Shah	1746	SI
3	Ahmad 'Abdul-Jalil Shah (1)	1760	S2
4	Atlim-ud-Din Shah	1761	SI
	Ahmad 'Abdul-Jalil Shah (2)	1765	
5	Ahmad Shah	1781	S3
6	'Abdul-Jalil Saif-ud-Din 'Ali	1791	GD4

7	'Abdul-Jalil Khalil-ud-Din Ibrahim	1811	S6
8	'Abdul-Jalil Saif-ul-'Alam Isma'il	1827	S7
9	'Abdul-Jalil Saif-ud-Din Qasim	1864–1890	S7

246 JAVA KINGDOMS AND SULTANATES

a *Singosari/Majapahit Dynasty* 1222–*c.*1478

1	Rajasa	1222	
2	Anusapati	1227	
3	Tohjaya	1248	SI
4	Vishnuvardhana	1248	S2
5	Kertanagara	1268	S4
6	Jayakatwang (of Kediri)	1292	
7	Kertarajasa Jayavardhana	1293	HD5
8	Jayanagara	1309	S7
9	Tribhuvana★	1329	D7
10	Rajasanagara Hayam Wuruk	1350	S9
11	Vikramavardhana	1389	HD10
12	Suhita★	1429	D11
13	Kertavijaya Bhre Tumapel	1447	S11
14	Rajasavardhana Bhre Pamotan	1451–1453	
15	Hyang Purvavisesa	1456	
16	Bhre Pandan Salas	1466–*c.*1478	

b *Sultans of Demak c.*1500–1550

1	Raden Patah Senapati	*c.*1500	
2	Pangeran Sabrang Lor (Adipati Yunus)	1518	SI
3	Pangeran Sultan Tranggana	1521	SI
4	Pangeran Sultan Prawata	1546–*c.*1550	S3

c *Sultans of Bantam* 1526–1832

1	Sunan Gunong-Jati Nur-ud-Din Ibrahim	1526	
2	Mawlana Hasan-ud-Din	1552	SI
3	Mawlana Yusuf	1570	S2
4	Mawlana Muhammad	1580	S3
5	'Abdul-Qadir	1596	S4
6	'Abdul-Fatah Agong	1651	S5
7	'Abdul-Qahhar Hajji	1682	S6
8	Muhammad Yahya	1687	S7
9	Muhammad Zain-ul-'Abidin	1690	S7
10	Muhammad Zain-ul-'Arifin	1733	S9
11	Ratu Sharifa Fatima★	1748	W10
12	Muhammad Wasi al-Halimin	1750	S9
13	'Abdul-Nasar Muhammad 'Arif	1753	S12
14	Muhammad 'Ala-ud-Din	1777	S13
15	Muhammad Muhyi-ud-Din	1802	S13
16	'Abdul-Nasar Muhammad Ishaq	1804	S14
17	'Abdul-Mufakhir Muhammad 'Ala-ud-Din	1808	S14
18	Muhammad Saif-ud-Din (1)	1810	S15

19	Ahmad	1811	
20	Muhyi-ud-Din	1813	
	Muhammad Saif-ud-Din (2)	1816–1832	

d Sultans of Mataram 1582–1755

1	Panembahan Senapati Ingalaga	1582	
2	Mas Jolang Panembahan Krapyak	1601	S1
3	'Abdul-Rahman Agung	1613	S2
4	Prabu Amangkurat I	1645	S3
5	Amangkurat II	1677	S4
6	Amangkurat III	1703	S5
7	Pakubuwana I	1705	S3
8	Amangkurat IV	1719	S7
9	Pakubuwana II	1725	S8
10	Pakubuwana III	1749–1755	S9

e Sultans of Jogjakarta 1755–1949

1	'Abdul-Rahman Amangkubuwana I (s8 Mataram)	1755	
2	'Abdul-Rahman Amangkubuwana II	1792	S1
3	'Abdul-Rahman Amangkubuwana III	1810	S2
4	'Abdul-Rahman Amangkubuwana IV	1814	S3
5	'Abdul-Rahman Amangkubuwana V	1822	S4
6	'Abdul-Rahman Amangkubuwana VI	1855	S4
7	'Abdul-Rahman Amangkubuwana VII	1877	s6
8	'Abdul-Rahman Amangkubuwana VIII	1921	
9	'Abdul-Rahman Amangkubuwana IX	1939–1949	

f Susuhunans of Surakarta 1755–1949

1	Pakubuwana (III of Mataram)	1755	
2	Pakubuwana IV	1788	S1
3	Pakubuwana V	1820	S2
4	Pakubuwana VI	1823	S3
5	Pakubuwana VII	1830	S2
6	Pakubuwana VIII	1858	S2
7	Pakubuwana IX	1861	S4
8	Pakubuwana X	1893	
9	Pakubuwana XI	1939	
10	Pakubuwana XII	1944–1949	

247 BORNEO BRUNEI AND SARAWAK

a Sultans of Brunei since c.1405

1	Muhammad	c.1405	
2	Ahmad	c.1415	B1
3	Sharif 'Ali Bilfakih		HD2
4	Sulayman	c.1433	S3
5	Bulkiah		S4
6	'Abdul-Qahhar		S5
7	Saif-ul-Rijal	c.1578	s6

8	Shah Berunai		S7
9	Hasan		S7
10	'Abdul-Jalil Akbar		S9
11	'Abdul-Jalil Jabbar		S10
12	Muhammad 'Ali		S9
13	'Abdul-Mubin	c.1662	GD9
14	Muhyi-ud-Din		S10
15	Nasr-ud-Din		GS10
16	Kamal-ud-Din		S12
17	'Ala-ud-Din		GS14
18	'Umar 'Ali Saif-ud-Din I		S17
19	Muhammad Taj-ud-Din (1)	1780	S18
20	Muhammad Jamal-ul-'Alam I	1792	S19
	Muhammad Taj-ud-din (2)	1793	
21	Muhammad Khanz-ul-'Alam	1806	S18
22	Muhammad 'Alam	1822	S21
23	'Umar 'Ali Saif-ud-Din II Jamal-ul-'Alam	1822	S20
24	'Abdul-Mu'min	1852	HD20/DT16
25	Hashim Jalil-ul-'Alam Akam-ud-Din	1885	S23
26	Muhammad Jamal-ul-'Alam II	1906	S25
27	Ahmad Taj-ud-Din	1924	S26
28	'Umar 'Ali Saif-ud-Din III	1950	S26
29	Hasan-ul-Bulkiah Mu'izz-ud-Din	1967	S28

b *Rajas of Sarawak* 1841–1946

1	James Brooke	1841	
2	Charles Brooke	1868	STS1
3	Charles Vyner Brooke	1917–1946	S2

248 PHILIPPINES SULU AND MAGUINDANAO

a *Sultans of Sulu* c.1450–1915

1	Sharif-ul-Hashim	c.1450	
2	Kamal-ud-Din	c.1480	S1
3	'Ala-ud-Din		S1
4	Amir-ul-Umara		
5	Mu'izz-ul-Mutawadi'in		
6	Nasir-ud-Din I		
7	Muhammad al-Halim		
8	Batarah Shah Tengah	c.1596	
9	Muwallit Wasit	c.1610–1650	
10	Nasir-ud-Din II	c.1645–1648	
11	Salah-ud-Din Bakhtiyar	c.1650	S9
12	'Ali Shah	c.1680	
13	Nur-ul-'Azam Sultanah★		
14	al-Haqunu		
15	Shihab-ud-Din	c.1685	S11
16	Mustafa Shafi-ud-Din	c.1710	S11
17	Badr-ud-Din I	c.1718	S11

18	Nasr-ud-Din	1732	S15
19	'Azim-ud-Din I (1)	1735	S17
20	Mu'izz-ud-Din	1748	S17
	'Azim-ud-Din I (2)	1764	
21	Muhammad Isra'il	1774	S19
22	'Azim-ud-Din II	1778	S20
23	Sharaf-ud-Din	1791	S19
24	'Azim-ud-Din III	1808	S23
25	'Ali-ud-Din	1808	S23
26	Shakirullah	1821	S23
27	Jamal-ul-Kiram I	1823	S24
28	Muhammad Fadl	1842	S27
29	Jamal-ul-'Azam	1862	S28
30	Badr-ud-Din II	1881	S29
31	Jamal-ul-Kiram II	1884–1915	S29
32	Harun ar-Rashid	1886–1894	DT19

b *Sultans of Maguindanao c.1645–1888*

1	Qudarat Nasir-ud-Din	c.1645
2	Dundang Tidulay Saif-ud-Din	c.1671
3	'Abdul-Rahman	c.1678
4	Qahhar-ud-Din Kuda	c.1699
5	Bayan-ul-Anwar	c.1702–1745
6	Muhammad Ja'far Sadiq Manamir	c.1710–1733
7	Tahir-ud-Din	c.1736–1748
8	Muhammad Khair-ud-Din	c.1748
9	Pahar-ud-Din	c.1755
10	Kibad Sahriyal	c.1780
11	Kawasa Anwar-ud-Din	c.1805
12	Iskandar Qudratullah Muhammad	c.1830
13	Muhammad Makakwa	1854
14	Muhammad Jalal-ud-Din Pablu	1884–1888

PACIFIC ISLANDS

249 **POLYNESIA** KINGDOMS

a *Kings of Hawaii* 1810–1893

1 Kamehameha I	1810	
2 Kamehameha II	1819	S1
3 Kamehameha III	1825	S1
4 Kamehameha IV	1854	STS3
5 Kamehameha V	1863	B4
6 Lunalilo	1873	
7 Kalakaua	1874	
8 Liliuokalani★	1891–1893	ST7

b *Kings of Tahiti* 1797–1880

1 Otu Vairatoa Pomare I	1797	
2 Otu Pomare II (1)	1803–1809	S1
Otu Pomare II (2)	1815	
3 Pomare III	1824	S2
4 Aimatta Pomare IV★	1827	S2
5 Teriitaria Ariiaue Pomare V	1877–1880	S4

c *Kings of Tonga since* 1845

1 George Tubou I	1845	
2 George Tubou II	1893	GS1
3 Salote Tubou III★	1918	D2
4 Taufa'ahu Tubou IV	1965	S3

THE AMERICAS

250 **MEXICO** RULERS

a *Kings of Tenochtitlan (Aztec Kings)* 1372–1521

1	Acamapichtli	1372	
2	Huitzilihuitl	1391	S1
3	Chimalpopoca	1415	S2
4	Itzcoatl	1426	S1
5	Moctezuma I Ilhuicamina	1440	S2
6	Axayacatl	1468	GS4
7	Tizoc	1481	B6
8	Ahuitzotl	1486	B6
9	Moctezuma II Xocoyotzin	1502	S6
10	Cuitlahuac	1520	S6
11	Cuauhtemoc	1520–1521	S8

b *Kings of Texcoco c.1300–1521*

1	Quinatzin	c.1300	
2	Techotlala	c.1357	S1
3	Ixtlilxochitl	c.1409	S2
4	Tezozomoc (of Azcapotzalco)	1418	
5	Maxtla (of Azcapotzalco)	1426–1428	S4
6	Nezahualcoyotl	1431	S3
7	Nezahualpilli	1472	S6
8	Cacama	1515	S7
9	Coanacochtzin	1520–1521	S7

c *Emperors of Mexico*

1	Augustin de Iturbide	1822–1823
2	Maximilian of Habsburg (B3 Austria)	1864–1867

251 **HAITI** KINGS AND EMPERORS

1	Jacques Dessalines (Emperor)	1804–1806
2	Henri Christophe (King of Northern Haiti)	1811–1820
3	Faustin Soulouque (Emperor)	1849–1858

252 PERU INCAS c.1100–1572

1	Manco Capac	c.1100	
2	Sinchi Roca		S1
3	Lloque Yupanqui		S2
4	Mayta Capac		S3
5	Capac Yupanqui	c.1200	S4
6	Inca Roca		S5
7	Inca Yupanqui (Yahuar Huacac)		S6
8	Viracocha		S7
9	Inca Urco	1438	S8
10	Pachacuti	1438	S8
11	Tupac Yupanqui	1471	S10
12	Huayna Capac	1493	S11
13	Tupac Cusi Hualpa (Huascar)	1526–1532	S12
14	Atahualpa	1530–1533	S12
15	Tupac Hualpa	1533	S12
16	Manco Inca Yupanqui	1533	S12
17	Sayri Tupac	1545	S16
18	Titu Cusi Yupanqui	1560	S16
19	Tupac Amaru	1571–1572	S16

253 BRAZIL BRAGANZA EMPERORS 1822–1889

1	Peter I (IV of Portugal)	1822	
2	Peter II	1831–1889	S1

254 UNITED STATES OF AMERICA PRESIDENTS since 1789

1	George Washington	1789
2	John Adams	1797
3	Thomas Jefferson	1801
4	James Madison	1809
5	James Monroe	1817
6	John Quincy Adams	1825
7	Andrew Jackson	1829
8	Martin Van Buren	1837
9	William Henry Harrison	1841
10	John Tyler	1841
11	James Knox Polk	1845
12	Zachary Taylor	1849
13	Millard Fillmore	1850
14	Franklin Pierce	1853
15	James Buchanan	1857
16	Abraham Lincoln	1861
17	Andrew Johnson	1865
18	Ulysses S. Grant	1869
19	Rutherford B. Hayes	1877
20	James A. Garfield	1881
21	Chester A. Arthur	1881

22	Grover Cleveland (1)	1885
23	Benjamin Harrison	1889
	Grover Cleveland (2)	1893
24	William McKinley	1897
25	Theodore Roosevelt	1901
26	William H. Taft	1909
27	Woodrow Wilson	1913
28	Warren G. Harding	1921
29	Calvin Coolidge	1923
30	Herbert C. Hoover	1929
31	Franklin D. Roosevelt	1933
32	Harry S. Truman	1945
33	Dwight D. Eisenhower	1953
34	John F. Kennedy	1961
35	Lyndon B. Johnson	1963
36	Richard M. Nixon	1969
37	Gerald R. Ford	1974
38	James E. Carter	1977
39	Ronald W. Reagan	1981